Understanding Section 8:
Search, Seizure, and the Canadian Constitution

Understanding Section 8:
Search, Seizure, and the Canadian Constitution

Susanne Boucher & Kenneth Landa

IRWIN LAW

Understanding Section 8: Search, Seizure, and the Canadian Constitution
© Irwin Law Inc., 2005

All rights reserved. No part of this publication may be reproduced, stored in a retrieval system, or transmitted, in any form or by any means, without the prior written permission of the publisher or, in the case of photocopying or other reprographic copying, a licence from Access Copyright (Canadian Copyright Licensing Agency), 1 Yonge Street, Suite 1900, Toronto, Ontario, M5E 1E5.

Published in 2005 by

Irwin Law
347 Bay Street
Suite 501
Toronto, Ontario
M5H 2R7

www.irwinlaw.com

ISBN: 1-55221-087-1

Library and Archives Canada Cataloguing in Publication

Boucher, Susanne
  Understanding section 8 : search, seizure and the Canadian constitution / Susanne Boucher, Kenneth Landa.

Includes bibliographical references and index.

ISBN 1-55221-087-1

1. Searches and seizures--Canada. I. Landa, Kenneth II. Title.

KE9270.B69 2004   345.71'0522   C2004-905965-3
KF9630.B69 2004

The publisher acknowledges the financial support of the Government of Canada through the Book Publishing Industry Development Program (BPIDP) for its publishing activities.

Printed and bound in Canada.

1 2 3 4 5   08 07 06 05 04

Summary Table of Contents

PREFACE *xv*

CHAPTER 1: Constitutional Protections Against Unreasonable Search and Seizure *1*

CHAPTER 2: What Is a Search or a Seizure? *6*

CHAPTER 3: Reasonable Expectation of Privacy *26*

CHAPTER 4: Determining Reasonableness: The *Collins* Test and *Hunter v. Southam* *89*

CHAPTER 5: Reasonable and Probable Grounds *143*

CHAPTER 6: Privilege and Search and Seizure *161*

CHAPTER 7: Searches With a Warrant: Execution and Litigation Issues *189*

CHAPTER 8: Warrantless Searches *230*

CHAPTER 9: Remedies for Unreasonable Search and Seizure *262*

CHAPTER 10: Summary of Essential Principles *301*

APPENDICES *305*

TABLE OF CASES *399*

INDEX *415*

Detailed Table of Contents

Preface xv

Chapter 1:
CONSTITUTIONAL PROTECTIONS AGAINST UNREASONABLE SEARCH AND SEIZURE 1

Chapter 2:
WHAT IS A SEARCH OR A SEIZURE? 6

A. What Constitutes a Search? 6

B. What Constitutes a Seizure? 11

   1) Renewed Emphasis on Context in the Definition of Seizure 14
      a) *Quebec (Attorney General) v. Laroche* 14
      b) *R. v. Gettins* 17

C. Section 8 Solely Protects Against "Government" Searches or Seizures 18

   1) State Agents 18
      a) Security Guards as State Agents 20
   2) Searches in Foreign Countries 22

CHAPTER 3:
REASONABLE EXPECTATION OF PRIVACY 26

A. A Reasonable Expectation of Privacy is Necessary to Challenge a Search 26
B. Personal Privacy Interest, Not Property Interest 27
C. *R. v. Edwards*: "Totality of Circumstances" Test 28
D. Third Parties and Establishing a Breach of Section 8 30
E. Limited Waivers of Privacy 31
F. Onus for Establishing Privacy: Obligation for Evidentiary Basis 34
G. The Importance of Context to Determine the Existence and Level of Protection for Privacy 35
H. Level of Protection Afforded in Various Contexts 36
   1) The Human Body 37
      a) In General 37
      b) Body Cavity Searches 38
      c) Strip Searches 40
      d) Bedpan Vigils 43
      e) Taking Bodily Samples and Impressions 45
      f) Fingerprinting 54
      g) Privacy While in Custody 58
      h) The Human Identity and Confidential Relationships 60
   2) Private Conversations 61
   3) Surreptitious Videotaping 63
   4) The Home 64
      a) "Implied Licence" to Knock 65
      b) Investigation of Criminal Activity for the Protection of Owners or Occupants 65
      c) Implied Licence Extended by Businesses to Members of the Public 66
      d) Gathering or Securing Evidence: "Seizing and Freezing" 66
      e) Nature of Interest in the Home 66
      f) Area of the Home as Determinative of Expectation of Privacy 67
   5) When the Police Use "Advanced Technologies": FLIR, Low-flying Planes, and Trained Dogs 68
      a) FLIR 70
      b) Aerial Surveillance 73
      c) Drug-Detection Dogs 74

6) At the Border 77
7) In Luggage and Parcels in Transit 77
8) At School 78
9) In Garbage and Abandoned Property 80
10) In Motor Vehicles 83
11) Regulatory Matters 84
    a) Utility Records and Meters 85
12) Firearms 87
13) Expectation of Privacy and Section 24(2) 87

CHAPTER 4:
DETERMINING REASONABLENESS: THE *COLLINS* TEST AND *HUNTER v. SOUTHAM* 89

A. Authorized by Law 90
   1) Specific Powers of Search and Seizure 91
   2) Interpreting the Scope of Statutory Search and Seizure Powers 91
      a) The Scope of Statutory Powers: *CanadianOxy Chemicals v. Canada* 91
      b) The Scope of Common Law Powers: *R. v. Waterfield* 92
B. Is the Law Authorizing the Search Reasonable? 94
   1) How to Determine if the *Hunter v. Southam* Criteria Are Inapplicable 98
      a) Exigent Circumstances 100
      b) Application of the Exigency Exception to Specific Categories of Exigent Situations 101
      c) Pursuit of Interests Other Than Law Enforcement 113
      d) Higher Protections Against Intrusion Where Competing/ Compound Interests Are Affected by the Search 125
C. Was the Search Conducted in a Reasonable Manner? 139

CHAPTER 5:
REASONABLE AND PROBABLE GROUNDS 143

A. Definition 143
B. "Reasonable Grounds" and "Reasonable and Probable Grounds" are Synonymous 147
C. Reasonable Suspicion 148

D. Reasonable Grounds Must Exist Both Objectively and Subjectively 150
E. Who Must Have Reasonable Belief? The Officer Directing the Search 152
F. What Evidence Can Lead to a Belief on Reasonable and Probable Grounds? 152
    1) Hearsay Information Can Constitute Reasonable Grounds 153
G. "Tips" From Informants 153
    1) Reliability of a Tip: Is the Information Compelling, Credible, and Corroborated? 153
        a) What Makes a Tip Compelling and Credible? 154
        b) Corroboration of the Information 156
H. "Smell" as a Component of Reasonable Grounds 158

CHAPTER 6:
PRIVILEGE AND SEARCH AND SEIZURE 161

A. Informer Privilege 161
    1) Purpose of the Privilege 161
    2) Who is Entitled to the Privilege? 163
    3) The Scope of Informer Privilege 163
        a) Scope of Privilege for Anonymous Informants 164
    4) Maintaining Secrecy as to the Informer's Identity 165
        a) Justice System's Duty of Silence and Officer's Responsibility to Maintain Secrecy in Drafting Materials 166
        b) Publication Bans to Protect Identity 166
        c) Sealing of Documents to Protect the Informer's Identity 167
        d) Section 37 of the *Canada Evidence Act* 167
    5) Revealing the Identity of the Informer 168
        a) The "Innocence at Stake" Exception 168
        b) When Is the "Innocence at Stake Exception" Engaged? 169
        c) Summary of the Procedure for Establishing the "Innocence at Stake" Exception 171
        d) The "Innocence at Stake" Exception Inapplicable at a Preliminary Hearing 172
B. Public Interest Privilege 172
    1) Summary of the Procedure for Determining a Claim of Public Interest Privilege 173
    2) Observation Post-Privilege 174

C. Solicitor–Client Privilege 177
  1) Scope of Solicitor–Client Privilege 177
  2) Duty to Minimize Intrusions into Solicitor–Client Privilege in Conducting Searches 180
  3) Section 487 Does Not on Its Face Violate Solicitor–Client Privilege 185
  4) Solicitor–Client Privilege Beyond the Law Office 186

Chapter 7:
SEARCHES WITH A WARRANT: EXECUTION AND LITIGATION ISSUES 189

A. General Requirements for Execution of Search Warrants 189
  1) Who Can Execute and Assist in Executing the Warrant 190
    a) Who May Execute the Warrant 190
    b) Who May Assist in the Execution 191
  2) Knock and Announce 195
  3) Use of Force 196
  4) Duty to Show Warrant 198
  5) Treatment of "Found-Ins" 199
  6) Expiry Time 200

B. Special Rules for Litigating the Validity and Reasonableness of Warrants and Othe Investigative Orders 202
  1) Access to Materials Relating to an Investigative Order 202
  2) The Standard of Review of Issuance of an Investigative Order 204
    a) General Rule for Review of Investigative Orders 204
    b) Review of Special Search Warrants and Restraint Orders 205
    c) Effect of Fraud on the Standard of Review 207
    d) "Amplifying" the Information on Review 211
    e) Leave of the Court Required to Attack the Evidentiary Basis through Cross-Examination 213
    f) Leave Requirement May Apply for All Investigative Order Reviews 216
    g) Both the Trial Judge and the Preliminary Hearing Judge Can Grant Leave to Cross-Examine 217
    h) Standing to Challenge Investigative Orders 217
    i) Accused Person's Standing to Challenge Interceptions Made against Third Parties 218

Chapter 8:
WARRANTLESS SEARCHES 220

A. Consent Searches 220
  1) Informed Consent 221
  2) Third-Party Consent 227
     a) Apparent Authority 232

B. Searches Incidental to Arrest 233
  1) Nature of the Power 233
  2) Scope of the Search 237
  3) Search Incidental to Arrest and the Right to Counsel 238
  4) Timing of the Search 239
  5) More Intrusive Searches of the Body Incident to Arrest: Bodily Samples and Strip Searches 240

C. Search Incidental to Investigative Detention 241
  1) What Is an Investigative Detention? 242
  2) When Can the Police Search as an Incident to an Investigative Detention? 243
     a) When Will an Investigative Detention Meet the *Waterfield* Test? 244
  2) When Will a Search Incidental to an Investigative Detention be Justified? 246
     a) What Can Be Searched Incidentally to Detention? 250

D. The "Plain View" Doctrine 253
  1) Lawfully on the Premises 254
  2) Immediately Apparent 256
  3) Inadvertent Discovery 258
  4) "Plain View" and the *Criminal Code* 259
  5) No Exception for "Plain Smell" 260

Chapter 9:
REMEDIES FOR UNREASONABLE SEARCH AND SEIZURE 262

A. Section 24 *Charter* Remedies 262
  1) Starting the Process: Giving Notice of Motion 263

B. Court of Competent Jurisdiction 265

C. Exclusion of Evidence: Section 24(2) 270

1) Obtained in a Manner 271
   a) Common Law Power of Exclusion 273
2) Section 24(2): *Collins* Test for Exclusion of Evidence 275
   a) Trial Fairness 276
   b) Seriousness of the Breach 282
   c) Effect of Exclusion 287
3) Appellate Review of Section 24(2) Analysis 289

D. Section 24(1) Remedies 290
1) Exclusion of Evidence under Section 24(1) 291
2) Stays of Proceedings under Section 24(1) 292
3) Sentence Reduction for *Charter* Violations 293

E. Non-*Charter* Remedies: Prerogative Relief 296

CHAPTER 10:
SUMMARY OF ESSENTIAL PRINCIPLES 301

APPENDIX 1: Basic Search Powers (*Criminal Code*) 305

APPENDIX 2: Interception of Communications (Wiretaps) 313

APPENDIX 3: Offence-Specific Authorizations (*Criminal Code*) 321

APPENDIX 4: Additional *Criminal Code* Powers and Restrictions 325

APPENDIX 5: Proceeds of Crime 337

APPENDIX 6: Seizures of Bodily Substances and Impressions 352

APPENDIX 7: Related Statutes: Search and Seizure Powers 370

TABLE OF CASES 399

INDEX 415

Preface

ROADMAP FOR THIS BOOK

This book provides a framework for answering two questions: First, what constitutes an unreasonable search or seizure under section 8 of the *Charter*?[1] Second, when an unreasonable search or seizure occurs, what is the appropriate legal or evidentiary consequence?

We have attempted to provide a problem solving approach applicable to both of these questions. We begin by outlining the general rules that apply to all searches, and then identify the principal exceptions to the general rules. Understanding the rationale for those exceptions will assist the reader to indentify when a factual situation falls within an exception or when it will be appropriate to carve out new exceptions. Optimally, the book should be read as a whole (at least the first few chapters!) to best understand the types of protections afforded by section 8 and the manner in which concerns about unreasonable searches can be litigated in court.

Each chapter of the book addresses a different topic essential to understanding the protections guaranteed by section 8 and establishing a breach of those protections.

- Chapter 1 outlines the importance of constitutional protections against unreasonable state searches and seizures, and contrasts constitutional

---

[1] Part I of the *Constitution Act, 1982*, being Schedule B to the *Canada Act 1982* (U.K.), 1982, c. 11, s. 8. [*Charter*].

protections with the protections afforded to the individual at common law.
- Chapter 2 looks at the rights and interests protected by section 8, and answers the questions: What are searches and seizures? and Whose actions are subject to *Charter* scrutiny?
- Chapter 3 examines the concept of a reasonable expectation of privacy, without which there is no constitutional basis to make a claim of unreasonable search and seizure.
- Chapter 4 analyses the standard legal tests used to determine whether an intrusion into an expectation of privacy is reasonable, and outlines the accepted deviations from the general rules of reasonableness.
- Chapter 5 defines and examines reasonable and probable grounds, one of the hallmarks of a reasonable search.
- Chapter 6 addresses how issues of privilege affect the conduct of searches and the litigation of a claim of unreasonable search or seizure.
- Chapter 7 identifies special rules for the execution of search warrants.
- Chapter 8 addresses the power to conduct warrantless searches or seizures in four special circumstances: with the consent of the party; as an incident to an arrest; in furtherance of an investigative detention; and under the plain view doctrine.
- Chapter 9 deals with the most common remedies available from a court once an unreasonable search or seizure has been established.
- The appendices provide summaries of the threshold requirements for engaging statutory search and seizure powers under the *Criminal Code* and in select related statutes.

CHAPTER 1

Constitutional Protections Against Unreasonable Search and Seizure

Section 8 of the *Canadian Charter of Rights and Freedoms* guarantees:

> Everyone has the right to be secure against unreasonable search and seizure.[1]

Legal protections against unreasonable search and seizure are fundamentally important to a free and democratic society. At both common law and under our constitution, the twin goals of protecting the individual from unwarranted intrusions by the state and protecting the state and its citizens against crime require a delicate balancing of interests. This balancing has shaped the statutory, common law and constitutional framework in which police investigations and criminal proceedings are conducted. Judicial decisions often make this balancing process explicit. In *R. v. Genest*, police executing a defective search warrant on a house smashed in a door without warning.[2] Chief Justice Dickson of the Supreme Court of Canada quoted the following passage from the author Polyviou[3] summarizing the concerns and conflicting interests involved in state searches:

---

1 Part I of the *Constitution Act, 1982*, being Schedule B to the *Canada Act 1982* (U.K.), 1982, c. 11, s. 8.
2 *R. v. Genest* (1989), 45 C.C.C. (3d) 385 (S.C.C.) [*Genest*].
3 Polyvios G. Polyviou, *Search and Seizure: Constitutional and Common Law* (London: Duckworth, 1982) vii.

> The privacy of a man's home and the security and integrity of his person and property have long been recognised as basic human rights, enjoying both an impressive history and a firm footing in most constitutional documents and international instruments. *But much as these rights are valued they cannot be absolute.* All legal systems must and do allow official power in various circumstances and on satisfaction of certain conditions to encroach upon rights of privacy and security in the interests of law enforcement, either to investigate an alleged offence or to apprehend a lawbreaker or to search for and seize evidence of crime. *The interests at stake are compelling. On the one hand the security and privacy of a person's home and possessions should not be invaded except for compelling reasons. On the other hand society, represented by its organised institutions, also has an undeniable and equally powerful interest in effectively investigating crime and punishing wrongdoers.* The task of balancing these conflicting interests is a matter of great importance and of considerable difficulty; but it must be attempted, and so far as possible, for the health of civil liberty and law enforcement alike, satisfactorily performed. [emphasis added][4]

Section 8 of the *Charter* acts as a limitation on the search and seizure powers of government.[5] Although the common law and various statutory provisions purport to give the state certain powers to encroach on a person's privacy, it is important to note that section 8 does not itself authorize government conduct or create or confer search or seizure powers, but rather acts as a constraint on state action inconsistent with the *Charter*.[6]

At common law, protections against governmental search and seizure arose from property rights and were founded primarily in the ordinary law of trespass.[7] Unless the law authorized an intrusion — and such authorizations were only for limited purposes — the state was not permitted to conduct a search. The historic case of *Entick v. Carrington*,[8] framed the protection as follows:

> Our law holds the property of every man so sacred, that no man can set his foot upon his neighbour's close [that is, land] without his leave: if he does he is a trespasser though he does no damage at all; if he will tread upon his neighbour's ground, he must justify it by law.[9]

---

4   *Genest*, above note 2 at 388.
5   *Hunter et al. v. Southam Inc.* (1984), 14 C.C.C. (3d) 97 (S.C.C.) [*Hunter*] at 106.
6   Ibid.
7   Ibid. at 157 [S.C.R.].
8   *Entick v. Carrington* (1765), 19 State Tr. 1029 [*Entick*].
9   Ibid. at 1067, as cited in *Hunter*, above note 5 at 107.

At the time of *Entick v. Carrington*, the law would authorize a search only if the search were for stolen goods and if "authorized by a justice on the basis of evidence upon oath that there was 'strong cause' to believe the goods were concealed in the place sought to be searched."[10] If the proper prior legal authorization were lacking, the person under investigation would be protected from the intended search by the law of trespass.[11] The protection against unlawful intrusions was viewed as a necessary function of preserving property rights in civil society:

> The great end, for which men entered into society, was to preserve their property. That right is preserved sacred and incommunicable in all instances where it has not been taken away or abridged by some public law for the good of the whole.[12]

The present legal context is markedly different from the days when searches were limited to searches for stolen property and protection from searches was tied closely to the law of trespass. First, the purposes for which searches may be conducted are considerably wider. The modern *Criminal Code* and a number of other statutes create a wide range of powers to search, set standards for their exercise, and detail their various limitations.[13] Second, the rights guaranteed by section 8 are not tied to the protection of property or the law of trespass. Rather, section 8 acts as a general protection against "unreasonable search and seizure," if stated in the negative, or the protection of "a reasonable expectation of privacy," if stated in the positive.[14] Privacy, and not property, is the touchstone of the modern protection against unreasonable search and seizure.

In further contrast to the pre-*Charter* legal context, the protections afforded by section 8 of the *Charter* are considerably more forceful.[15] By the very nature of the Constitution as the "supreme law of Canada,"[16] the rights guaranteed in section 8 are not vulnerable to erosion by legislative enactments or common law decisions.[17]

---

10 *Hunter*, above note 5 at 158 [S.C.R.].
11 *Ibid.* at 107.
12 *Entick*, above note 8 at 1066.
13 *Criminal Code*, R.S.C. 1985, c. C-46. See Appencides 1–7.
14 *Hunter*, above note 5 at 108.
15 For an overview of the impact of the *Charter* on criminal law, see K. Roach, "The Effects of the Canadian *Charter of Rights* on Criminal Justice" (1999) 33 Isr. L. Rev. 607.
16 Section 52(1) of the *Constitution Act, 1982*, states: "The Constitution of Canada is the supreme law of Canada, and any law that is inconsistent with the provisions of the Constitution is, to the extent of the inconsistency, of no force or effect."
17 *Hunter*, above note 5 at 108.

Perhaps most important, there are meaningful remedies available for violations of the protections against unreasonable search and seizure. Before the *Charter*, there were few remedies for unreasonable searches conducted by the state. While certain limited remedies existed for the violation of pre-*Charter* protections against state search and seizure,[18] illegally obtained "real" or tangible evidence, once seized by the state, was typically not excluded at trial — even in the face of illegal or unfair police conduct — but rather was admitted as a matter of course.[19] As long as evidence was both relevant and reliable, the evidence would be admitted, regardless of the manner in which it was obtained. This fact may be particularly surprising for readers steeped in media portrayals of the American criminal justice system, where the exclusion of unlawfully obtained evidence is automatic.[20] The common law rules are perhaps best exemplified by this statement by the majority of the Supreme Court of Canada in *R. v. Wray*:[21]

> I am not aware of any judicial authority in this country or in England which supports the proposition that a trial judge has a discretion to exclude admissible evidence because, in his opinion, its admission would be calculated to bring the administration of justice into disrepute. The test of admissibility of evidence was stated by Lord Goddard in *Kuruma v. The Queen* [[1955] A.C. 197 at 203], as follows:
>
>> In their Lordships' opinion the test to be applied in considering whether evidence is admissible is whether it is relevant to the matters in issue. If it is, it is admissible and the court is not concerned with how the evidence was obtained.

Since the enactment of the *Charter*, courts are very much concerned with how evidence is obtained, and remedies are available under section 24, which reads as follows:

---

18 For example, a person targeted by an unlawful search could file a civil suit for trespass or assault. In most cases, this would have had no effect on the underlying criminal proceedings.

19 See the discussion of Zuber J.A. in *R. v. Duguay* (1985), 18 C.C.C. (3d) 289 (Ont. C.A.) at 306. See, e.g., *R. v. Wray*, [1970] 4 C.C.C. 1 (S.C.C.). However, see the recent judgment of *R. v. Buhay* 2003 SCC 30 in which Arbour J. contemplates the possible existence of common law remedies for the exclusion of evidence in citing *R. v. Rothman*, [1981] 1 S.C.R. 640 at 696, *per* Lamer J., as he then was; *R. v. Oickle*, [2000] 2 S.C.R. 3, 2000 SCC 38 at para. 69, *per* Iacobucci J.

20 For an interesting review of the history of the American automatic exclusionary rule and differences between the Canadian and American approaches to the exclusion of evidence, see J. Stribopoulos "Lessons from the Pupil: A Canadian Solution to the American Exclusionary Rule Debate" 22 B.C. Int'l & Comp. L. Rev. 77 (1999).

21 *R. v. Wray*, [1971] S.C.R. 272 at 287.

24(1) Anyone whose rights or freedoms, as guaranteed by this *Charter*, have been infringed or denied may apply to a court of competent jurisdiction to obtain such remedy as the court considers appropriate and just in the circumstances.

(2) Where, in proceedings under subsection (1), a court concludes that evidence was obtained in a manner that infringed or denied any rights or freedoms guaranteed by this *Charter*, the evidence shall be excluded if it is established that, having regard to all the circumstances, the admission of it in the proceedings would bring the administration of justice into disrepute.

Accordingly, a court with the appropriate jurisdiction may award any remedy that is appropriate and just in the circumstances for a violation of section 8 of the *Charter*. The remedy most commonly sought is the exclusion of unreasonably obtained evidence under section 24(2).[22] Other available remedies might include a stay of proceedings,[23] an award of costs or damages,[24] or a reduction in sentence under section 24(1).[25] The common law has also evolved, in light of "*Charter* values," to allow for exclusion of evidence in certain extraordinary circumstances, notwithstanding the fact that the *Charter* does not apply.[26] See chapter 9 for further discussion on these topics.

---

22 Generally, the applicant bears the burden of establishing that the evidence was obtained unlawfully and that impugned evidence ought to be excluded.
23 *R. v. Young* (1984), 13 C.C.C. (3d) 1 (Ont.C.A.); *R. v. S.F.*, [2003] O.J. No. 92 (S.C.J.); *R. v. Agostinelli*, [2002] O.J. No. 5008 (C.J.); *R. v. Lau*, [2003] B.C.J. No. 1929 (Prov. Ct.); *R. v. Pringle*, [2003] A.J. No. 118 (Prov. Ct.).
24 See *Illnicki v. MacLeod*, [2003] A.J. No. 605 (Q.B.); *Nurse v. Canada* (1997), 132 F.T.R. 131; *Blouin v. Canada* (1991), 51 F.T.R. 194.
25 See *R. v. Collins* (1999), 22 C.R. (5th) 269 (Nfld. C.A.); *R. v. MacPherson* (1995), 100 C.C.C. (3d) 216 (N.B.C.A.); *R. v. Charles* (1987), 61 Sask. R. 166, 36 C.C.C. (3d) 286. The availability of this remedy is not without question. Contra, see *R. v. Carpenter* (2002), 4 C.R. (6th) 115 (B.C.C.A.) (leave to appeal dismissed), *R. v. Glykis* (1995), 41 C.R. (4th) 310 (Ont. C.A.); *R. v. Coulter*, [2000] O.J. No. 3452 (Ont. Ct. Jus.) (appeal dismissed [2001] O.J. No. 5608 (S.C.J.)). See also A. Mewitt, "Charter Violations in Mitigation of Sentence" (1995), 41 C.R. (4th) 318.
26 This might arise when evidence is discovered in a search conducted outside of Canada by foreign officials. See *R. v. Harrer* (1995), 42 C.R. (4th) 269 (S.C.C.). See also *R. v. Buhay* (2003), 10 C.R. (6th) 205 (S.C.C.), which may open the door to a broader application of the common law exclusion remedy, and D. Tanovich's article, "Recent Trends in Remedies for Unconstitutional Searches," from the Third Symposium on Issues in Search and Seizure Law, Professional Development Program, Continuing Legal Education, Osgoode Hall Law School, York University, September 20, 2003.

CHAPTER 2

☙

What Is a Search or a Seizure?

Section 8 of the *Charter* protects against "unreasonable search and seizure." Since search and seizure are distinct concepts, it is important to determine what constitutes each of "search" and "seizure" under the *Charter*. Accordingly, this chapter will examine two questions central to establishing that something is a search or seizure for the purpose of section 8: (1) What are the kinds of activities that will constitute a search or seizure? and (2) Who are the persons whose activities are constrained by section 8 of the *Charter*?

A. WHAT CONSTITUTES A SEARCH?

The range of activities that will constitute a search is much wider than the stereotypical image of the police rummaging around in a person's home looking for evidence. A search is any invasion of a person's reasonable expectation of privacy, in whatever form, by the state.[1] In *R. v. Wise*,[2] the Supreme Court provided a simple definition of a search:

> It is clear that s. 8 of the *Charter* guarantees a broad and general right to be secure from unreasonable search where the person who is the object of

---

1 *Hunter et al. v. Southam Inc.* (1984), 14 C.C.C. (3d) 97 (S.C.C.) at 108–9; *R. v. Dyment* (1988), 45 C.C.C. (3d) 244 (S.C.C.) at 253 [*Dyment*]; *R. v. Duarte* (1990), 53 C.C.C. (3d) 1 (S.C.C.) [*Duarte*] at 10–11; *R. v. Dersch* (1993), 85 C.C.C. (3d) 1 (S.C.C.); *R. v. Wise* (1992), 70 C.C.C. (3d) 193 (S.C.C.) at 219 [*Wise*]; *R. v. Law* (2002), 160 C.C.C. (3d) 449 (S.C.C.) [*Law*] at 457–58.
2 *Wise, ibid.*

the search has a reasonable expectation of privacy. In determining whether the beeper monitoring constitutes a search, the initial question is whether there is a reasonable expectation of privacy in respect of the monitored activity. *If the police activity invades a reasonable expectation of privacy, then the activity is a search.* [emphasis added][3]

Therefore, if a person cannot establish both that he or she had a reasonable expectation of privacy and that this privacy was breached, then there is no "search" to scrutinize for the purposes of section 8. In *R. v. Hufsky*,[4] the Supreme Court held that a police officer's demand that a driver produce licence and insurance information during a random motor vehicle spotcheck was not a "search," because driving is a highly regulated activity and the motorist could not reasonably expect to keep such information private. As the Court explained:

> [T]he demand by the police officer, pursuant to the above legislative provisions, that the appellant surrender his driver's licence and insurance card for inspection did not constitute a search within the meaning of s. 8 because it did not constitute *an intrusion on a reasonable expectation of privacy.* Cf. *Hunter v. Southam Inc.*, [1984] 2 S.C.R. 145. There is no such intrusion where a person is required to produce a licence or permit or other documentary evidence of a status or compliance with some legal requirement that is a lawful condition of the exercise of a right or privilege. [emphasis added][5]

We can see, therefore, that identifying a search is not simply a matter of identifying specific police behaviour. Rather, it is an evaluation of the impact of state activity on the individual and a question of whether society is prepared to accept that intrusion as reasonable.

When analyzing whether the state's conduct constitutes a search under section 8, it is also important to ascertain the *intentions* of the officer who performs the activity in question. If the police have specifically adverted to the possibility of securing evidence through their investigative technique, then the technique may be considered a search.[6] For example, in *R. v. Evans*,[7] the Supreme Court of Canada noted that occupants of a home extend an "implied licence" to the general public to knock at the front door of their home, for the purpose of communicating with the occupants. This

---

3   *Ibid.*; see also *R. v. Evans*, [1996] 1 S.C.R. 8 [*Evans*]; and *Law*, above note 1 at para.1.
4   *R. v. Hufsky* (1988), 40 C.C.C. (3d) 398 (S.C.C.).
5   *Ibid.* at 410.
6   *Evans*, above note 3 at 33.
7   *Ibid.*

deemed invitation acts as an exception permitting what would otherwise constitute a trespass to private property. However, the implied licence to knock does not extend to permitting police to enter onto private property to conduct investigations of the occupants. As the Court explained:

> [T]here are sound policy reasons for holding that the intention of the police in approaching an individual's dwelling is relevant in determining whether or not the activity in question is a "search" within the meaning of s. 8. If . . . intention is not a relevant factor, the police would then be authorized to rely on the "implied licence to knock" for the purpose of randomly checking homes for evidence of criminal activity. The police could enter a neighbourhood with a high incidence of crime and conduct surprise "spot checks" of the private homes of unsuspecting citizens, surreptitiously relying on the implied licence to approach the door and knock. Clearly, this Orwellian vision of police authority is beyond the pale of any "implied invitation."[8]

In view of the Supreme Court's expansive definition of "search" (that is, *all* intrusions by the state into zones subject to a reasonable expectation of privacy), the protections guaranteed by section 8 cover a wide variety of state conduct. Investigative activities, such as collecting discarded facial tissues in a jail,[9] the interception or recording of any kind of private communication, regardless of whether one of the parties consents to the interception,[10] approaching someone's door to attempt to smell drugs,[11] using a dog to sniff for drugs at a bus terminal,[12] aerial surveillance,[13] and a demand for information or documents for an income tax audit[14] may all be considered searches under the *Charter*.

At what point does state activity constitute a search? The courts have determined that a person's expectation of privacy begins to be infringed at the very earliest stages of police investigation. This can encompass activities such as the questioning of a suspect that happens before any physical contact or taking of an item occurs. For example, in *R. v. Mellenthin*,[15] police stopped Mr. Mellenthin's vehicle during a random check-stop program. The officer observed an open gym bag, which contained another small bag.

---

8   Ibid.
9   *R. v. Stillman* (1997), 113 C.C.C. (3d) 321 (S.C.C.).
10 *Duarte*, above note 1.
11 *Evans*, above note 3.
12 *R. v. Lam*, [2003] A.J. 811 (C.A.).
13 *R. v. Kelly* (1999), 169 D.L.R. (4th) 720 (N.B.C.A.). Contra, see *R. v. Mercer*, [2004] A.J. 634 (Prov. Ct.).
14 *R. v. McKinlay Transport Ltd.*, [1990] 1 S.C.R. 627 [*McKinlay*].
15 *R. v. Mellenthin* (1992), 76 C.C.C. (3d) 481 (S.C.C.) [*Mellenthin*].

When the officer asked what was in the bag, Mellenthin responded by opening the bag and telling the officer it contained food. The officer saw what appeared to be glass and suspected that narcotics were inside. Mellenthin showed the officer the small bag after the officer again asked about its contents, leading the officer to discover the bag contained glass vials, strengthening his belief that the vials were drug paraphernalia. The officer searched the car and found cannabis resin.

The Supreme Court held that the activities described above, including Mellenthin's actions in presenting the bag to the officer, the officer's questioning about the gym bag, and presumably Mellenthin's answers to those questions "were all elements of a search."[16] Also notable from this decision is the fact that the opening of the bag was held to be a police search, despite the fact that Mellenthin himself opened the bag, since it was in response to a police request.[17]

Similarly, in *R. v. Simpson*,[18] the Ontario Court of Appeal held that the "search" commenced almost immediately upon the police officer's initial contact with the accused. The *Simpson* case involved the detention of the occupants of a vehicle that was seen leaving the driveway of a suspected "crack-house." Although the officer had no grounds to believe that the persons in the car were involved in criminal activity (aside from their mere presence at the particular location), the officer requested the occupants to exit their vehicle. In response to police questioning, Simpson told the officer he had previously been in trouble "for theft and a knife," but said that he did not have a knife in his possession at the time.[19] The officer then observed a bulge in Simpson's pocket, felt it, and asked what it was. After Simpson responded "nothing," the officer asked Simpson to slowly remove the bulge from his pocket. It appeared to the officer that Simpson was trying to dispose of the object, so the officer grabbed it and discovered that it was cocaine.

Among other constitutional violations (including the arbitrariness of the detention due to lack of "articulable cause"[20]), the Ontario Court of Appeal held that the police officer's interaction with Simpson violated section 8 of the *Charter*, because the officer lacked a lawful basis for the search that he conducted.[21] In finding a section 8 violation, the Court noted that the "search" was not simply the officer's patting of the pocket and taking of the cocaine:

---

16   Ibid. at 488.
17   Ibid.
18   *R. v. Simpson* (1993), 79 C.C.C. (3d) 482 (Ont. C.A.) [*Simpson*].
19   Ibid. at 483.
20   See chapter 8, "Searches Incidental to Investigative Detention."
21   *Simpson*, above note 18 at 505–6.

The appellant's reliance on s. 101 of the *Criminal Code*[22] also assumes that the search of the appellant began when Constable Wilkin felt the appellant's front pant pocket. The reasons in *Mellenthin, supra*, indicate that *the search cannot be so limited but must be taken as having commenced when the appellant was initially questioned by the police officer. The search proceeded from that point until the cocaine was recovered.* Once the questioning of the appellant is taken as part of the search, then s. 101 of the *Criminal Code* cannot provide any authority for the search. [emphasis added][23]

In *R. v. Young*,[24] the Ontario Court of Appeal held that the search in that case began with the questioning of Mr. Young. Police had initially observed Young within a block of a very recent break and entry into a store. The officer believed Young was intoxicated and noticed a bulge in his pocket. The officer asked Young where he lived and where he had been, and became suspicious because Young was not taking a direct route home. He asked Young to empty his pocket. Young complied and produced a large quantity of cash. In response to questions about how much money he was carrying, Young gave three answers ranging from $500 to $832. The officer counted the cash and determined it to be $1,151. Increasingly suspicious, the officer told Young that there had been a break-in down the street, and asked Young to accompany him to the scene, where he determined that a cash box had been tampered with. Lacking reasonable grounds to arrest Young for the break and enter, the officer then arrested Young for being intoxicated in public. Eventually, police learned that the sum of money in Young's possession approximated that stolen from the store, and they found glass particles in Young's clothing that were consistent with glass from a broken door at the premises. The Court of Appeal found a violation of section 8 because the police had no reasonable grounds or articulable cause to detain or search Mr. Young, and the Crown had not proven a valid consent to the search.[25]

Relying on the reasoning in *R. v. Mellenthin*[26] and *R. v. Simpson*[27] as to exactly when the search commenced, the Court held that the search began

---

22 The former s.101 permitted warrantless search for prohibited weapons, restricted weapons, firearms or ammunition. The Court also noted that the officer never suggested he had grounds to believe that Simpson was carrying any of the above, and therefore could not rely on s.101 as authorizing the search. Note that s.101 has been replaced by the current s.117.02. See *Simpson*, above note 18 at 505.
23 *Simpson*, above note 18 at 506.
24 *R. v. Young* (1997), 116 C.C.C. (3d) 350 (Ont. C.A.) [*Young*].
25 *Ibid.* at 357–59.
26 *Mellenthin*, above note 15.
27 *Simpson*, above note 18.

with the officer's questions and included Mr. Young's co-operation in handing over the money:

> Once it is concluded that *the search begins with the questioning* and that there was no reasonable basis for a search then, on the facts of this case, *the officer put into motion what became an illegal search by simply inviting the appellant to permit an intrusion on his person* in the form of emptying his pockets. It was the same as if the officer had reached out and physically emptied the pockets. [emphasis added][28]

B. WHAT CONSTITUTES A SEIZURE?

Early Supreme Court *Charter* jurisprudence on what constitutes a seizure focused less on the "context" of the state activity and more on the "process" involved. For example, in *R. v. Dyment*,[29] LaForest J. defined a seizure as "the taking of a thing from a person by a public authority without that person's consent."[30] In *Thomson Newspapers*,[31] Wilson J. reiterated the possessory-based definition of seizure enunciated in *Dyment*, defining a seizure as: "the taking hold by a public authority of a thing belonging to a person against that person's will."[32]

An exception to these early possessory-based definitions of seizure is found in the Supreme Court's decision in *R. v. McKinlay Transport*,[33] the companion case to *Thomson Newspapers*. The Court in *McKinlay* held that a reasonable expectation of privacy in the things taken was a condition precedent to a determination that the taking of an item constituted a seizure. Just as no search occurs for the purpose of section 8 unless the person has an expectation of privacy in the place or thing searched, the Court held that no

---

28 *Young*, above note 24 at 358, para. 16
29 *Dyment*, above note 1.
30 *Ibid*. at 257. The issue of what constitutes a valid consent is discussed in chapter 8. Although valid and informed consent may cause governmental actions to pass the scrutiny of s. 8, if the consent of the person is obtained by virtue of a legal obligation or an order of the state this may still constitute a seizure. For example, an order from a regulatory agency compelling a person to produce documents will constitute a search. See *Thomson Newspapers Ltd. v. Canada (Director of Investigation and Research, and Restrictive Trade Practices Commission)*, [1990] 1 S.C.R. 425 at 505 [*Thomson Newspapers*]. Further, if the person consents to the seizure for one purpose, and the state uses the items seized for another purpose, the consent may not be a sufficient substitute for prior judicial authorization: see *R. v. Borden* (1994), 92 C.C.C. (3d) 404 (S.C.C.); *R. v. Arp* (1998), 129 C.C.C. (3d) 321 (S.C.C.).
31 *Thomson Newspapers, ibid*.
32 *Ibid*. at 493.
33 *R. v. McKinlay Transport Ltd.*, above note 14.

seizure occurs if there is no expectation of privacy found in the materials taken by the state. As Wilson J. explained:[34]

> Undoubtedly there will be instances in which an individual will have no privacy interest or expectation in a particular document or article required by the state to be disclosed. Under such circumstances, the state-authorized inspection or the state demand for production of documents will not amount to a search or seizure within s. 8: see *R. v. Hufsky*, [1988] 1 S.C.R. 621, at p. 638.[35]

In *R. v. Colarusso*,[36] the Supreme Court continued to move away from process-oriented definitions of seizure in favour of examining the context in which the seizure occurred, to determine whether section 8 protections applied. In *Colarusso*, the police, acting without a warrant, seized blood and urine samples of a person accused of causing a fatal car accident. These samples had been originally obtained by medical staff at the hospital in connection with Mr. Colarusso's treatment following the accident, and had been taken with his consent. The coroner then legally obtained the samples from the hospital laboratory under the *Coroner's Act* in order to conduct an investigation under that Act.[37] Ultimately, the police seized the samples from the coroner. It was the police action that Mr. Colarusso challenged.

Although the Court of Appeal in *Colarusso* found that no seizure occurred because the police did not take the samples from the accused, the majority of the Supreme Court rejected this approach, finding it to be overly tied to the process of obtaining the materials. As LaForest J. explained:

> The Court of Appeal obviously did not see the present case as falling within the ambit of the principles set forth in *Dyment*. It narrowly focused on the actions of the coroner in physically taking the blood and urine samples.
>
> . . .
>
> In proceeding in this way, it seems to me, the actions of the police, the nature of the coroner's possession of the blood sample and other surrounding circumstances are completely obscured. Assuming for the moment that the seizure by the coroner . . . is constitutionally valid, such an approach is still, in my opinion, inappropriate. It is obvious from *Dyment* that all the surrounding circumstances must be assessed to determine whether there has been a search by law enforcement officers, and I

---

34   *Ibid.*
35   *Ibid.* at 540.
36   (1994), 87 C.C.C. (3d) 193 (S.C.C.) [*Colarusso*].
37   *Coroner's Act*, R.S.O. 1980, c. 93 (now R.S.O. 1990, c. C. 37).

have no doubt the same is true in assessing the reasonableness of a search . . . .[38]

Instead, the Supreme Court engaged in a broader analysis of what constitutes a seizure, finding that the context of the state's action rendered it a seizure within the meaning of section 8. At paragraphs 82 and 85 the Court said:

> It is evident, however, that the officers who transported the blood and urine samples knew of the potential incriminatory nature of the samples and intended to use the results of the analysis for their own purposes at the outset. They possessed the samples then and because of their close relationship with the coroner's office were effectively empowered and intended to deal with them for their own purposes — criminal investigation.
>
> . . .
>
> There is only one logical explanation for the strategy employed by the police: when the coroner gave possession of the blood and urine samples to the police officers for transportation to the Centre for Forensic Science, the police knew that they could use the results of the analysis as evidence against the appellant. Indeed, the police may have regarded the blood sample as the best available evidence. Not only was it obtained within an hour of the accident, but also the analysis was to be undertaken by the same analysts at the Centre for Forensic Sciences who worked for the police on a regular basis. As a result, the police saw no need to obtain further evidence of intoxication through the various means available to them. In my opinion, there can be no question that the police took possession of the samples and transferred them to the Centre of Forensic Sciences with the full knowledge that they might incriminate the appellant and with the intention of appropriating the results of the analysis for use in the criminal prosecution of the appellant. Given the effective control by the police over the samples held by another agent of the state, I would conclude that the police seized the blood sample from the appellant independently of the coroner's seizure (although the police seizure was obviously facilitated by the actions of the coroner).

Additionally, the Court found that the type of information taken by the police was relevant to determining whether their actions constituted a seizure. In this case, the accused had a high expectation of privacy in the information seized, which ultimately supported the application of section 8 to the police actions:

---

38   *Colarusso*, above note 36 at paras. 72–73.

At all events, they seized information involving the bodily integrity of the individual that could only be obtained originally with his consent or later pursuant to a statute for the limited purposes intended by the statute. This really goes to the underlying reason for the protection afforded by s. 8; one must not overemphasize the purely physical aspects of the seizure. In both *Hunter* and *Dyment*, the Court emphasized that what is protected by s. 8 is people, not places or things. The principal right protected by s. 8 is individual privacy, and the provision must be purposively applied to that end.[39]

1) Renewed Emphasis on Context in the Definition of Seizure

a) *Quebec (Attorney General) v. Laroche*

In *Quebec (Attorney General) v. Laroche*,[40] the Supreme Court further refined the definition of a seizure, emphasizing the importance of the context in which the governmental action occurs, as highlighted in *Colarusso*, rather than looking simply at the issue of transfer of physical control. The Court examined the narrow definitions of seizure applied in *Dyment* and *Thomson Newspapers*,[41] and noted that such definitions hinged on the *process* used (that is, a physical "taking" or change in possession).[42] While such a definition was appropriate to those cases, in *Laroche* the Court was faced with a state action that arguably constituted a seizure *without* a change in possession or physical taking — specifically, a court-ordered freeze on property believed to be the proceeds of crime. Justice LeBel cautioned against an overly literal interpretation of the word "seizure" as applying only in cases of a change in possession, and stated that a court must examine both the *context* and the *objective* of the government action to determine whether it constitutes a seizure and thereby engages section 8 protections.[43]

At issue in *Laroche* was the reasonableness of government actions under two *Criminal Code* provisions for the interim preservation of proceeds of crime pending a criminal trial and final forfeiture proceedings. Section 462.33 of the *Criminal Code* provides for restraint orders for real property and intangibles and section 462.32 creates special warrants of search and seizure for tangible property (other than real property). Justice LeBel found that both provisions — physical seizure pursuant to a special warrant and

---

39   *Ibid.* at para. 86.
40   *Quebec (Attorney General) v. Laroche*, 2002 SCC 72 [*Laroche*].
41   The relevant passages are quoted in the previous section.
42   *Laroche*, above note 40 at para. 52.
43   *Ibid.* at paras. 53–54.

the restraint order freezing the property — constituted seizures subject to scrutiny under section 8. Special warrants were easily identifiable as seizures under the *Dyment* formulation, because the state took physical possession of the property.[44] The more remarkable development is that restraint orders were also held to be seizures.

The Court reviewed the context in which the restraint order is made (an ongoing criminal investigation) and the objectives of the order (to facilitate the investigation and to prevent the wasting or disappearance of property, which makes it possible to punish the crimes more effectively, and to facilitate the enforcement of any eventual forfeiture order).[45] When viewed in this light, the Court concluded that the restraint order was indeed a seizure within the meaning of section 8, despite the fact that there was no physical change in possession.[46]

In summary then, it appears from the Supreme Court's decision in *Laroche* that the following factors will be relevant to the determination of whether or not a government action constitutes a seizure:

1. Did the action occur in the context of a criminal or administrative investigation?[47]
2. Was there a transfer of possession or control from the individual to the government?[48]
3. Does the action facilitate other government objectives related to investigations, punishment or other criminal (or regulatory) objectives?[49]
4. Does the action coincide with other criminal or administrative investigative procedures?[50]

Justice LeBel took pains to note that an overly broad definition of "seizure" (that is, one triggered by *any* government restriction on or alienation of property) "would eventually transform a provision intended to protect individual privacy into a constitutional guarantee of property rights, which was deliberately not included in the *Charter*."[51] He went on to quote with approval the following statement:

> One limitation ought to be put on the scope of "seizure" under the *Charter*. The "enjoyment of property," as a specific right, as protected in the

---

44 *Ibid.* at para. 54.
45 *Ibid.* at para. 55.
46 *Ibid.*
47 *Ibid.* at para. 53.
48 *Ibid.* at paras. 54–55.
49 *Ibid.*
50 *Ibid.*
51 *Ibid.* at para. 52.

Canadian Bill of Rights, is not protected in the *Charter*. The prohibition of unreasonable search and seizure is designed to promote privacy interests and not property rights. Hence, *Charter* protections against unreasonable seizure should not apply to governmental actions merely because those actions interfere with property rights. <u>Specifically, where property is taken by governmental action for reasons other than administrative or criminal investigation a "seizure" under the *Charter* has not occurred.</u> A number of cases illustrate this view of seizure. A detention of property, in itself, does not amount to a seizure for *Charter* purposes — *there must be a superadded impact upon privacy rights occurring in the context of administrative or criminal investigation* . . . [underlining in *Laroche*; italics added][52]

The ultimate effect of the *Laroche* decision is not entirely clear. Despite Justice LeBel's caution about "transforming" section 8 to protect property rights, it is not apparent from *Laroche* what elements constituted the "superadded impact upon privacy rights" necessary to establish *Charter* protection in that case. As we have stressed throughout this text, section 8 has traditionally recognized only the protection of privacy interests,[53] and the consideration of other interests, such as economic interests, proprietary interests,[54] and liberty and security interests beyond the protection of privacy are not part of the recognized protections afforded by section 8.[55] Additionally, the *Laroche* decision itself supports the contention that privacy interests are still important in determining whether actions constitute a seizure: the Court's justification for departing from the *Dyment* seizure definition and for engaging in contextual considerations was grounded in the concern that the ealier definition risked under-protecting privacy interests.[56]

---

52 *Ibid.* at para. 53 quoting from Scott C. Hutchison, James C. Morton, and Michael P. Bury, *Search and Seizure Law in Canada*, loose-leaf ed. (Toronto: Carswell, 1993; updated 2002, release 2).

53 Although in *Hunter v. Southam*, Dickson J. recognized that s. 8 might protect more than privacy interests: "I would be wary of foreclosing the possibility that the right to be secure against unreasonable search and seizure might protect interests beyond the right of privacy, but for purposes of the present appeal I am satisfied that its protections go at least that far" (at S.C.R. 159). Note, however, that the Court in *Hunter* was very clear in divorcing concepts of property interests from privacy considerations.

54 That is not to say that possession is not important to the determination of s. 8 claims. Possession has been recognized as one of several indicia that a person has a reasonable expectation of privacy in a place or item. See the discussion of the "*Edwards* test" for the reasonable expectation of privacy in chapter 3.

55 See, e.g., the discussions in *R. v. Jarvis*, 2002 SCC 73; *R. v. Mills*, [1999] 3 S.C.R. 668; *R. v. Edwards* (1996), 104 C.C.C. (3d) 136 (S.C.C.).

56 *Laroche*, above note 40 at para 53.

b) R. v. Gettins

Further support for the idea that privacy interests must be central to any definition of whether a seizure occurred can be found in the recent case of *R. v. Gettins*.[57] In *Gettins*, the Ontario Court of Appeal emphasized the importance of context in defining whether state action constituted a seizure:[58]

> The decisions in *Tessier* and *Silveira* demonstrate the importance of a contextual analysis. . . . That analysis requires us to appropriately balance the goal of law enforcement with the individual's interest in being left alone: *Hunter v. Southam Inc.*, [1984] 2 S.C.R. 145 per Dickson J. at pp. 159–160. In this regard, in *R. v. S.A.B.*, 2003 SCC 60 at para. 40 Arbour J. stated:
>
>> In weighing the reasonable privacy interests that are at stake . . . it is useful to consider the categories set out by LaForest J. in *R. v. Dyment*, [1988] 2 S.C.R. 417, at p. 428: privacy may include territorial or spatial aspects, aspects related to the person, and aspects that arise in the informational context.[59]

In *Gettins*, the police believed that Mr. Gettins caused a fatal motor vehicle accident while driving under the influence of alcohol. The police, with the permission of the hospital treating Gettins, placed Centre for Forensic Sciences (CFS) sealing labels on vials of his blood taken by the hospital, after the samples were no longer required for medical treatment. The police then obtained a search warrant authorizing the seizure of the vials of blood in order to test Gettins' blood-alcohol level. The Court of Appeal found that the police actions did not constitute a seizure, as the placing of the labels on the vials of blood did not constitute an intrusion on any protected sphere of privacy:

> By comparison, placing CFS seals on vials of the appellant's blood involves no interference with the spatial aspect of the appellant's privacy interests. There was no intimidation or interference with the appellant's dignity. The doctor and nurses in the hospital already knew that Const. Baillie was investigating the accident to see if alcohol was involved. There was no interference with the appellant's physical integrity because the blood had already been taken. The police officer's actions were brief, limited to sealing the vials of the accused's blood, and the vials remained under the control of the hospital in the event they were needed for medical purposes.
>
> In *Dyment, supra*, the Supreme Court made it clear that a person's privacy interest in his blood taken for medical purposes means that the blood

---

57 *R. v. Gettins*, [2003] O.J. No. 4758 (C.A.) [*Gettins*].
58 The *Gettins* Court did not refer to the *Laroche* decision.
59 *Gettins*, above note 57 at para. 15.

can only be used for the purpose for which it has been given and cannot be used for other purposes without the donor's consent or without a warrant. Here, there was no "use" of the appellant's blood, in the sense that any information was obtained from it, prior to a search warrant being obtained.

. . .

The sealing of the vials of blood did not amount to an unreasonable search or seizure of the appellant because it did not interfere with the appellant's spatial interests, dignity, physical integrity or his interest in controlling the release of information about himself.[60]

C. SECTION 8 SOLELY PROTECTS AGAINST "GOVERNMENT" SEARCHES OR SEIZURES

Of course, not every invasion of privacy will constitute a search or seizure under section 8. Section 32 of the *Charter* dictates that the *Charter of Rights and Freedoms* applies only to the actions of government:

> 32. (1) This *Charter* applies
>
> (a) to the Parliament and government of Canada in respect of all matters within the authority of Parliament including all matters relating to the Yukon Territory and Northwest Territories; and
>
> (b) to the legislature and government of each province in respect of all matters within the authority of the legislature of each province.

Accordingly, in order for the conduct at issue to trigger the protections of the *Charter*, the parties engaging in the search or seizure must also be categorized either as part of the legislative or executive branches of the government, as performing a specific government function,[61] or as state agents.[62]

1) State Agents

In *R. v. Broyles*,[63] the Supreme Court was faced with the issue of deciding when a person is an agent of the state in the context of an alleged violation of section 7 of the *Charter*.[64] The evidence at issue in *Broyles* was an admis-

---

60 *Gettins*, above note 57 at paras. 17, 18, and 20.
61 *Eldridge v. British Columbia (Attorney General)*, [1997] 3 S.C.R. 624.
62 *R. v. Buhay* (2003), 174 C.C.C. (3d) 97 (S.C.C.) [*Buhay*] at para. 25; *R. v. Broyles* (1991), 68 C.C.C. (3d) 308 (S.C.C.) [*Broyles*]; *R. v. M.(M.R.)* (1998), 129 C.C.C. (3d) 361 (S.C.C.) [*M.(M.R.)*].
63 *Broyles, ibid.*
64 Section 7 of the *Charter* provides: "Everyone has the right to life, liberty and security of the person and the right not to be deprived thereof except in accordance with the principles of fundamental justice."

sion recorded by Mr. Broyles's friend, who had visited him in jail and recorded their conversation at the behest of the police. In finding that the state had indeed violated Broyles's section 7 rights, the Court formulated the following test for determining whether an informer was an agent of the state:

> Only if the relationship between the informer and the state is such that the exchange between the informer and the accused is materially different from what it would have been had there been no such relationship should the informer be considered a state agent for the purposes of the exchange. I would, accordingly, adopt the following simple test: *would the exchange between the accused and the informer have taken place, in the form and manner in which it did take place, but for the intervention of the state or its agents?* [emphasis added][65]

The same basic test applies in the search and seizure context to determine whether the actions of the party conducting the search are subject to *Charter* scrutiny.[66] In *M.(M.R.)*,[67] the Supreme Court considered whether the search of a student, conducted by the school vice-principal in the presence of a police officer, violated section 8. The majority of the Supreme Court held that the essential elements of the *Broyles* test for determining police agency were applicable in *M.(M.R.)*, and formulated the following test for determining police agency in the search and seizure context:

> Applying the test to this case, it must be determined whether the search of the appellant would have taken place, in the form and in the manner in which it did, but for the involvement of the police.[68]

The majority found that the search would have taken place without police involvement in essentially the same manner, since the primary motive for the search was the enforcement of school discipline for which the vice-principal was responsible under the *Education Act*.[69] Therefore, the school officials were not acting as agents of the police in conducting the search, and there was no violation of section 8.

---

65   *Broyles*, above note 62.
66   *M.(M.R.)*, above note 62 at para. 29.
67   Ibid.
68   Ibid. at para. 19.
69   Ibid.

a) Security Guards as State Agents

Recently in *R. v. Buhay*,[70] the Court considered whether the *Charter* restricted the actions of private security guards. In *Buhay*, bus station security guards smelled marijuana coming from a rented locker in a bus depot and requested that Greyhound bus company agents open the locker. The guards found marijuana in a duffel bag, put it back in the locker, and contacted police. The police attended, smelled the marijuana, had the agents open the locker, and seized the drugs. Mr. Buhay was arrested the next day when he tried to retrieve the bag from the locker.

Although the Court ultimately found that the police search, without a warrant or other legal authority, had violated Buhay's section 8 rights, the actions of the private security guards were not subject to *Charter* restrictions. The Court held that private security guards, in the regular execution of their duties, did not fall under section 32 of the *Charter* because they are neither part of the government nor government agents. The Court reiterated the restricted application of the *Charter*:

> Volunteer participation in the detection of crime by private actors, or general encouragements by the police authorities to citizens to participate in the detection of crime, will not usually be sufficient direction by the police to trigger the application of the *Charter*. Rather, the intervention of the police must be specific to the case being investigated. . . . *In the case at bar, there is nothing in the evidence which supports the view that the police instructed the security guards to search locker 135 and therefore the security guards cannot be considered state agents.* [emphasis added][71]

The Court, however, contemplated the possibility that private security guards could be considered state agents if the security guards simply seized the marijuana on their own and turned it over to police later, rather than having the police enter the locker. Although not explicitly ruling that the *Charter* would have applied, Arbour J. opened the door for a broadened *Broyles/M.(M.R.)* test for the application of the *Charter* in a situation where security guards involved the police or created a "seizure" by transferring control of the drugs to police:

> [W]e do not have to decide whether there would have been a "search" by the police had the security guards not replaced the contents inside the locker but had held it in a corner cupboard. This is not what they did here. Had

---

70   *Buhay*, above note 62.
71   *Ibid.* at para. 30; on the issue of security guards not constituting state agents, see also *R. v. Chang*, [2003] A.J. 1281 (C.A.) [*Chang*].

they done so, we might have had to adapt the test in *Broyles, supra*, to determine if and when the security guards would have become state agents or, alternatively, if the "mere transfer of control" in that case could have been characterized as a "seizure" by the police within the meaning of s. 8.[72]

It is unclear why the Court would require a new test for determining agency or answering the question of what would constitute a seizure under section 8. One would assume that an application of the existing principles enunciated in *Broyles* and *M.(M.R.)* would determine whether or not security guards could be considered state agents in any circumstance. Further, given the Court's decision in *R. v. Laroche*,[73] the mere "transfer of control" may not be sufficient to constitute a seizure. Rather, considerations of privacy interests and the other factors articulated in *Laroche* ought to determine whether the state's taking possession of an item constitutes a seizure. Presumably, in some instances, the possession by a third party of an item or information may be the factor negating the reasonable expectation of privacy in that item or information.[74]

On a more practical level, the decision in *Buhay* is troubling because it appears to suggest that civilians who come into possession of contraband, dangerous items, or evidence of a crime may be forced to remain the custodian of the item until the police obtain a warrant. Following the reasoning in *Buhay*, the proprietors of the bus lockers would have been pressed into retaining possession and control of illegal narcotics until a warrant could be obtained. This is clearly an unsatisfactory outcome. While retention of marijuana is troubling, the situation becomes more bizarre when imagining the retention of a murder weapon, bloody clothing or sensitive items containing DNA evidence.[75] A preferable approach might be to assess whether the third party is acting as an agent of the state in gathering and transferring the evidence, so as to prevent unwitting third parties from being conscripted into being custodians of evidence and subject to the *Charter*.[76]

---

72 *Buhay*, above note 62 at para. 39.
73 *Laroche*, above note 40.
74 See, e.g., *R. v. Plant* (1993), 84 C.C.C. (3d) 203 (S.C.C.), where records in the possession of a public utility were not subject to an expectation of privacy, given that the utility allowed third parties to access the information.
75 The nature of some evidence, if inherently dangerous or prone to degradation if not collected and preserved properly, might justify the warrantless seizure under s. 487.11.
76 See the case of *Chang*, above note 71 at paras. 35–42, where the Alberta Court of Appeal found that the transfer of control of drugs seized incident to an arrest by private security guards constituted a seizure, as per the suggestion in *Buhay*, above note 62.

2) Searches in Foreign Countries

The *Charter* will only apply to searches occurring in a foreign country if a Canadian government,[77] or its agents, perform the search. Searches performed by foreign governments and their agents are not subject to the *Charter*.[78]

The courts have taken a restrictive approach to determining whether a foreign government is acting as an agent of the Canadian government. For example, co-operation with the Canadian government is not sufficient on its own to attract *Charter* protections as against the actions of a foreign government.[79] Even if a Canadian government actor requests a foreign state to conduct a search, if the foreign state conducts the search with no assistance from the Canadian government, the actions will not be subject to the *Charter*.[80]

It will be nearly impossible to establish that a foreign government is an agent of the Canadian government; the common law of agency does not apply to the relationship between states, even where the foreign state is acting at the specific request of the Canadian government. In *R. v. Terry*,[81] Canadian authorities requested California police to arrest Mr. Terry for a murder that occurred in British Columbia and to obtain a statement from him. Returned to face trial in Canada, Terry asserted that the statement taken from him was in breach of his right to counsel guaranteed by section 10(b) of the *Charter*. The Supreme Court held that the *Charter* did not apply to the U.S. authorities, as it "would run counter to the settled rule that a state is only competent to enforce its laws within its own territorial boundaries," and that to rule otherwise would violate the principles of state sovereignty and international comity.[82] Justice McLachlin (now Chief Justice) suggests that principles of state sovereignty make establishing an agency relationship between Canada and a foreign government a near impossibility, and that even if there were an agency relationship, the *Charter* would not apply:

> The personal decision of a foreign officer or agency to assist the Canadian police *cannot dilute the exclusivity of the foreign state's sovereignty within its territory, where its law alone governs the process of enforcement*. The gathering of evidence by these foreign officers or agency is subject to the rules of that country and none other. Consequently, any *cooperative investigation* involv-

---

77 Although the cases we deal with in this section involve the federal government, the same principles will apply to provincial government actors.
78 *R. v. Terry*, [1996] 2 S.C.R. 207 at 217 [*Terry*]; *Schreiber v. Canada (Attorney General)*, [1998] 1 S.C.R. 84 1at para. 32 [*Schreiber*].
79 *Schreiber*, *ibid.* at para. 29.
80 *Ibid.* at paras. 29–31.
81 *Terry*, above note 78.
82 *Ibid.* at para. 16.

ing law enforcement agencies of Canada and the United States will be governed by the laws of the jurisdiction in which the activity is undertaken: see Williams and Castel, *Canadian Criminal Law: International and Transnational Aspects* (1981), at p. 320. [emphasis added][83]

. . .

I conclude that the appellant's contention that the conduct of the Santa Rosa police amounts to a *Charter* breach must fail. The officers were bound only by the laws of California. Even if one could somehow classify them as "agents" of the Canadian police, so long as they operated in California they would be governed by California law. In view of this conclusion, it is unnecessary to determine whether the police in California were acting as agents of the Canadian police.[84]

Justice McLachlin's judgment in *Terry* was in contrast to the Court's previous decision in *Harrer* (McLachlin J. dissenting).[85] In *Harrer*, the Court had accepted the possibility that a foreign government could act as an agent of the Canadian government:[86]

Let me first say a word about the argument concerning the territorial limits of the *Charter*, which appears to have played a considerable role in the thinking of the Court of Appeal. That argument is not necessary to the disposition of the case, but *I would not wish my remarks to be interpreted as giving credence to the view that the ambit of the Charter is automatically limited to Canadian territory.*

. . .

[I]t strikes me that the automatic exclusion of *Charter* application outside Canada might unduly restrict the protection Canadians have a right to expect against the interference with their rights by our governments or their agents. Consequently, had the interrogation about a Canadian offence been made by Canadian peace officers in the United States in circumstances that would constitute a violation of the *Charter* had the interrogation taken place in Canada, an entirely different issue would arise. *A different issue would also arise if the United States policemen and immigration authorities had been acting as agents of the Canadian police in furthering a criminal prosecution in Canada.* These issues do not arise and I shall say no more about them. [emphasis added][87]

---

83 *Ibid.* at para. 19.
84 *Ibid.* at para. 29.
85 *R. v. Harrer*, [1995] 3 S.C.R. 562, 101 C.C.C. (3d) 193 [*Harrer*].
86 This is as summarized in *R. v. Cook*, below, at para. 33, from *Harrer, ibid*, at paras. 10–11.
87 *Harrer*, above note 85 at paras. 10–11.

In *R. v. Cook*,[88] the Supreme Court attempted to reconcile these conflicting positions. While recognizing that the "door was closed" with respect to the agency argument, the Court moved away from the idea that the *Charter* could never apply in any extraterritorial circumstances, and accepted that the *Charter* could apply to the actions of Canadian authorities themselves while in a foreign country, although not to foreign state actors:

> The respondent incorrectly assumes that there is no difference between applying the *Charter* to U.S. officials acting as agents of or at the request of Canadian law enforcement authorities and in applying the *Charter* to Canadian authorities themselves. In fact, there is a fundamental distinction that can be drawn between these two scenarios which illustrates that *Terry*, *supra*, is not at all determinative of the present appeal. Jurisdictional competence under international law to apply the *Charter* to the actions of Canadian law enforcement authorities gathering evidence abroad rests in this instance not on the principle of territoriality, but of nationality. Whereas in the present case the interrogation was conducted by the Vancouver police, the evidence in *Terry* was gathered by the U.S. authorities who were subject to U.S. jurisdiction on the basis of territoriality. Unlike the Vancouver police, the U.S. authorities in *Terry* could not be subjected to an extraterritorial assertion of Canadian jurisdiction on the basis of nationality.[89]

Despite the *Charter*'s non-applicability to foreign state actors, it is possible in exceptional cases that a court could grant a remedy at trial for violations occurring in a foreign country, if the manner in which the evidence was obtained would render the trial unfair in violation of sections 7 or 11(d).[90] As the British Columbia Court of Appeal explained in *R. v. Hyatt*:[91]

> In *R. v. Harrer*, [1995] 3 S.C.R. 562, and in *R. v. Terry*, [1996] 2 S.C.R. 207, the Court considered the admissibility of evidence obtained abroad in a manner that did not meet *Charter* standards. Although in neither case did the Court rule that the evidence should have been excluded, it did recognize that, apart from cases within s. 24(2), there may be cases in which the

---

88 *R. v. Cook*, [1998] 2 S.C.R. 597.
89 *Ibid.* at para. 41.
90 Section 7 of the *Charter* provides: "Everyone has the right to life, liberty and security of the person and the right not to be deprived thereof except in accordance with the principles of fundamental justice." Section 11(d) of the *Charter* provides: "Any person charged with an offence has the right . . . (d) to be presumed innocent until proven guilty according to law in a fair and public hearing by an independent and impartial tribunal."
91 *R. v. Hyatt* (2003), 171 C.C.C. (3d) 409 (B.C.C.A.).

evidence is obtained in a manner that is so abusive as to amount to a violation of the principles of fundamental justice and of the guarantee of a fair trial under ss. 7 and 11(d). [parallel citations omitted][92]

---

92   *Ibid.* at para. 54.

CHAPTER 3

Reasonable Expectation of Privacy

In chapter 2 we noted that issues of privacy are central to section 8 of the *Charter*. The purpose of section 8 is the protection of privacy, and searches are defined with reference to whether a government action intruded on a reasonable expectation of privacy. This chapter will examine the concept of a reasonable expectation of privacy by first providing definition and scope to the concept. The bulk of the chapter will be devoted to the examination of the importance of "context" in determining whether there exists a reasonable expectation of privacy. We will illustrate the importance of the contextual analysis by demonstrating the different levels of protection afforded by the courts to state intrusion in a variety of different areas that are commonly subject to state intrusion.

A. A REASONABLE EXPECTATION OF PRIVACY IS NECESSARY TO CHALLENGE A SEARCH

The fundamental objective of section 8 of the *Charter* is "to protect individuals from unjustified State intrusion upon their privacy,"[1] by ensuring them "a reasonable expectation of privacy."[2] Accordingly, an individual can only establish that a search or seizure breached his or her section 8 rights if the individual can demonstrate that he or she had a reasonable expectation of

---

1 *Hunter et al. v. Southam Inc.* (1984), 14 C.C.C. (3d) 97 (S.C.C.) [*Hunter*].
2 *R. v. Evans* (1996), 104 C.C.C. (3d) 23 at 29 (S.C.C.) [*Evans*].

privacy in the place searched, the thing seized, or both.[3] If the individual is unable to demonstrate a reasonable expectation of privacy, and that the expectation of privacy was (unjustifiably) intruded upon, then the state cannot have violated the person's rights under section 8.[4]

B. PERSONAL PRIVACY INTEREST, NOT PROPERTY INTEREST

Although the expectation of privacy attaches to a place searched or a thing seized, the guarantees in section 8 are actually a protection of the person's independent privacy interests as opposed to particular property rights over those places and things. Historically, common law privacy protections were tied to the home and the intrusions of government onto private property. In *Hunter v. Southam*,[5] Dickson J. for the Supreme Court made clear that section 8 of the *Charter* "protects people and not places," and that concepts of privacy were not necessarily tied to property rights:

> In my view, the interests protected by s. 8 are of a wider ambit than those [protected at common law]. . . . There is, further, nothing in the language of the section to restrict it to the protection of property or to associate it with the law of trespass. It guarantees a broad and general right to be secure from unreasonable search and seizure.[6]

Accordingly, the analysis of whether a person has an expectation of privacy is not limited to factors such as an individual being "legitimately on the premises"[7] or having a possessory or proprietary interest in the premises or items seized.[8] Because the purpose of section 8 is the protection of a person's privacy interests, and not the protection of property, the person's exposure to the consequences of the search and the admission of the evidence into his or her trial provides the access to and rationale for remedies under the *Charter*.[9] However, note from chapter 2 that state interference with a

---

3 *Ibid.*
4 *R. v. Edwards* (1996), 104 C.C.C. (3d) 136 (S.C.C.) [*Edwards*] at 149–50. However, see the section below on the interests of third parties and section 8, and the discussion in chapter 2, "What Constitutes a Seizure?" regarding seizures and expectation of privacy.
5 *Hunter*, above note 1.
6 *Ibid.* at 107.
7 *Jones v. United States*, 362 U.S. 257 (1960) at 267; *Edwards*, above note 4 at paras. 54, 55].
8 *R. v. Pugliese* (1992), 71 C.C.C. (3d) 295 (Ont. C.A.) [*Pugliese*] at 300–1.
9 *Ibid.*

possessory or proprietary claim in the context of a criminal or administrative investigation may, in some circumstances, be sufficient to engage section 8 protections.[10]

Because privacy is an abstract concept that can be divorced from property rights, courts have sought to define the scope of the concept, and have considered the ways in which privacy interests can be affected. In *R. v. Dyment*,[11] the Supreme Court confirmed that privacy interests are rooted in the dignity and integrity of the individual, and exist apart from property interests. Justice LaForest noted that there were three zones or realms in which an individual has a privacy interest: territorial or spatial (which are typically tied to places or things), personal (or bodily) claims to privacy, and informational privacy (information about the individual).[12]

C. *R. v. EDWARDS*: "TOTALITY OF CIRCUMSTANCES" TEST

The leading case on establishing a reasonable expectation of privacy is the Supreme Court's decision in *R. v. Edwards*.[13] The Court confirmed in *Edwards* that the determination of whether a person has an expectation of privacy requires a multifactor analysis on the "totality of circumstances" presented by the case.[14]

Justice Cory summarized the principles applicable to establishing "standing" or a privacy interest sufficient to challenge a search or seizure.[15] This portion of the judgment is worth reprinting at length, as it is a helpful review of

---

10 See chapter 2, "What Constitutes a Seizure?"
11 *R. v. Dyment* (1988), 45 C.C.C. (3d) 244 (S.C.C.) [*Dyment*].
12 *Ibid.* at 255–56.
13 *R. v. Edwards* (1996), 104 C.C.C. (3d) 136 (S.C.C.) [*Edwards*].
14 *Ibid.* at 150; *Pugliese*, above note 8 at 302.
15 In *R. v. Belnavis* (1996), 107 C.C.C. (3d) 195 (Ont. C.A.) [*Belnavis*] at 207, aff'd (1997), 188 C.C.C. (3d) 405 (S.C.C.), Doherty J.A. explained that although this initial inquiry is sometimes referred to as establishing "standing," the term is actually a misnomer:

> Since the evidence produced by the search is being tendered against an accused, that accused has standing to challenge its admissibility. However, an accused can only gain access to the exclusionary remedy in s. 24(2) of the *Charter* by showing a breach of his or her personal *Charter* rights: *R. v. Edwards*, *supra*, at p.150; *R. v. Wijesinha* (1995), 100 C.C.C. (3d) 410 at p.431, 127 D.L.R. (4th) 242, [1995] 3 S.C.R. 422. Where an accused relies on an alleged breach of s. 8 of the *Charter*, the accused must show that his or her reasonable expectation of privacy was breached by the state conduct. That inquiry goes, not to the question of standing, but to the substantive question of whether the accused person's s.8 rights were breached: *Rakas v. Illinois*, 99 S.Ct. 421 (1978) at pp. 424–25.

relevant principles and jurisprudence on the issue of standing in the context of section 8. Particular attention should be paid to point number 6 below, which lists factors to be considered when analysing whether a person has a reasonable expectation of privacy "in the totality of the circumstances":

> A review of the recent decisions of this court and those of the United States Supreme Court, which I find convincing and properly applicable to the situation presented in the case at bar, indicates that certain principles pertaining to the nature of the s. 8 right to be secure against unreasonable search or seizure can be derived. In my view, they may be summarized in the following manner:
> 1. A claim for relief under s. 24(2) can only be made by the person whose *Charter* rights have been infringed: see *R. v. Rahey* (1987), 33 C.C.C. (3d) 289 at p. 308, 39 D.L.R. (4th) 481 at p. 500, [1987] 1 S.C.R. 588.
> 2. Like all *Charter* rights, s. 8 is a personal right. It protects people and not places: see *Hunter v. Southam Inc., supra*.
> 3. The right to challenge the legality of a search depends upon the accused establishing that his personal rights to privacy have been violated: see *Pugliese, supra*.
> 4. As a general rule, two distinct inquiries must be made in relation to s. 8. First, has the accused a reasonable expectation of privacy? Second, if he has such an expectation, was the search by the police conducted reasonably?: see *Rawlings, supra*.
> 5. A reasonable expectation of privacy is to be determined on the basis of the totality of the circumstances: see *Colarusso, supra*, at pp. 215–16 C.C.C., pp. 320–21 D.L.R., and *Wong, supra*, at p. 465.
> 6. The factors to be considered in assessing the totality of the circumstances may include, but are not restricted to, the following:
>   (i) presence at the time of the search;
>   (ii) possession or control of the property or place searched;
>   (iii) ownership of the property or place;
>   (iv) historical use of the property or item;
>   (v) the ability to regulate access, including the right to admit or exclude others from the place;
>   (vi) the existence of a subjective expectation of privacy; and
>   (vii) the objective reasonableness of the expectation.
>   See *United States v. Gomez*, 16 F.3d 254 (8th Cir. 1994) at p. 256.
> 7. If an accused person establishes a reasonable expectation of privacy, the inquiry must proceed to the second stage to determine whether the search was conducted in a reasonable manner.[16]

---

16   *Edwards*, above note 13 at 150–51.

At issue in *Edwards* was whether drugs seized during a warrantless search of Mr. Edwards' girlfriend's apartment were properly admissible at Edwards' trial. Ultimately, the Supreme Court concluded that Edwards had not established a reasonable expectation of privacy in his girlfriend's apartment. Although he had a key, kept a few personal belongings there, and had been a visitor to the apartment during the course of their three-year dating relationship, he was "no more than an especially privileged guest." He did not contribute to the rent or household expenses of the apartment, and had no authority to regulate access to the apartment.[17] The Court's conclusion highlights the importance of a totality of circumstances approach.

In argument before the Supreme Court, Edwards' counsel suggested that Edwards ought to be granted standing based on a privacy interest in the drugs themselves, rather than the apartment. The Court rejected this submission on the facts in the case, but left open the possibility for such a finding where the proper evidentiary foundation exists:

> In the case at bar, one of the bases upon which the appellant asserted his right to privacy in Ms Evers' apartment was his interest in the drugs. It is possible, in certain circumstances, to establish an expectation of privacy in the goods that are seized. . . . However, this contention cannot be raised in the circumstances of this case. At trial, the appellant denied that the drugs were his and Ms Evers testified that they might have belonged to someone else. The appellant maintained in the Court of Appeal that the drugs were not his. It was only in this court that he acknowledged for the first time that the drugs were his. He should not now be permitted to change his position with regard to a fundamentally important aspect of the evidence in order to put forward a fresh argument which could not be considered in the courts below.[18]

D. THIRD PARTIES AND ESTABLISHING A BREACH OF SECTION 8

As explained above, the general rule is that an individual must have a personal expectation of privacy in the place searched or thing seized to establish an unreasonable search or seizure. There are some instances, however, where the courts have recognized that the effect of government actions on

---

17 *Edwards*, above note 13 as summarized in *Belnavis*, above note 15 at 118–19.
18 *Edwards*, ibid. at para. 44; see also *R. v. Sandhu* (1993), 82 C.C.C. (3d) 236, 22 C.R. (4th) 300, 47 W.A.C. 203 (B.C.C.A.), where the issue was raised in relation to the suitcase of a co-accused, and *R. v. Major*, [2004] O.J. No. 2651 (C.A.), where the issue is discussed in relation to a privacy interest possibly existing in drugs.

third parties may enable a person to establish that a search was unreasonable. For example, a court may find that a search was conducted in an unreasonable manner if the rights of unrelated third parties were infringed during the search.[19] This is a clear exception to the general rule. See chapter 4, "Was the Search Conducted in a Reasonable Manner?" for a further discussion on this point; see also chapter 7, "Accused Person's Standing to Challenge Interceptions Made against Third Parties," where the rules of standing appear to be slightly more flexible for cases involving the challenge of intercepted communications of third parties.

Recently, in *R. v. Jarvis*,[20] the Supreme Court considered a statutory regime that purported to authorize a regulatory agency (Canada Customs and Revenue Agency) to compel the object of an investigation, *or any third party*, to produce documents for inspection. The statutory provisions did not require the agency to obtain a warrant. The Court ruled that once the predominant purpose of the agency's inquiry shifted from a compliance audit to a penal liability investigation (as determined according to the test set out in *Jarvis*), the regulator could no longer rely on the warrantless production provisions. Interestingly, the Court did not explicitly tie the prohibition on seizure of documents from a third party to an individual establishing whether he or she had an expectation of privacy in those documents. It is conceivable, however, that given the expectation of privacy jurisprudence, reliance on audit powers might be reasonable under section 8 if a court could find that no expectation of privacy existed in the material seized from the third party.[21]

E. LIMITED WAIVERS OF PRIVACY

Since the purpose of section 8 is the protection of privacy, it follows that where a person waives the right to the protection of his or her privacy, the constitutional limits on state invasions of privacy will be removed.[22] However, consent to the reduction in privacy in one circumstance does not erode the privacy for all purposes. The waiver of privacy is limited to its original purpose and does not extend to intrusions that were not contemplated in the original waiver.

---

19 See, e.g., *R. v. Thompson* (1990), 59 C.C.C. (3d) 225 (S.C.C.).
20 *R. v. Jarvis* (2002), 169 C.C.C. (3d) 1 (S.C.C.) [*Jarvis*].
21 See, e.g., *R. v. Pheasant*, [2000] O.J. No. 4237 (Sup. Ct.).
22 For a full discussion of the legal threshold to establish a valid waiver see chapter 8, "Consent Searches."

A clear example of this principle can be found in *R. v. Smith*.[23] In that case, a woman (Ms. Oak) placed a 911 call from Mr. Smith's home. Two police officers arrived, and Smith gave them permission to enter the house to check on the woman. Additional officers arrived as "backup," opened the door and entered the home. One of the backup officers, Constable Leggatt, detected the smell of damp marijuana, apparently emanating from the basement. He suspected that there was a grow operation on the premises and proceeded into the basement to investigate. The officer's suspicions proved correct, and on the basis of his observations, he obtained a search warrant for the residence. Both the trial judge and Conrad J.A., for a unanimous Court of Appeal, rejected the defence's argument that the initial consent to enter the home was limited to permit only the *first* two officers (to whom it was directly given) to enter the home. Nevertheless, the Court of Appeal held that the consent was limited to the *purpose* for which it had been granted:

> Even if the entry onto the premises was legal, consent to entry was for a limited purpose, namely, to ensure the safety of the telephone complainant. This does not imply that a search of those premises for other purposes is allowable. No consent to enter the basement where the marijuana was found was given, yet Constable Leggatt proceeded down to the basement. In doing so he was conducting a search, and his actions went beyond what was authorized by Mr. Smith's invitation to enter the house.
>
> . . .
>
> Similarly, I conclude that the accused's invitation to the police to enter his home to check on the well-being of Ms. Oak was only an invitation to enter that portion of the house that was necessary to locate her and was not an invitation to search the remainder of the house. As Constable Rooney testified, the accused "was co-operative and stated that, you know, we were allowed to go in the house and check on her." The accused did not authorize them to enter for any other purpose. There was no authority to search the balance of the house once Ms. Oak was located.[24]

The idea that the waiver of privacy is limited to the purpose for which it is granted applies equally whether the waiver is explicit, implied by law, or implied by the conduct of the individual. In *R. v. Evans*,[25] the police suspected that there was a marijuana grow-operation in the Evans' home. The police approached the home intending to knock on the door and, if the door were answered, to "sniff" for marijuana. The Supreme Court held that, at

---

23 *R. v. Smith* (1998), 126 C.C.C. (3d) 62 (Alta. C.A.) at para 7.
24 *Ibid.* at paras. 8 and 10.
25 *Evans*, above note 2.

common law, occupants of premises are deemed to extend "an implied licence for all members of the public, including police, to approach the door of a residence and knock."[26] The majority held that the purpose of the waiver is to facilitate communication between the public and the occupier, and rejected the assertion that the waiver went so far as to permit the police to investigate the occupant:[27]

> [W]hile an individual may explicitly "invite" another to engage in private conversation, the invitation cannot be extended to authorize an activity with a different purpose, namely, the surreptitious recording of what is said. Where the person purporting to act on the "invitation to converse" exceeds the bounds of that invitation, the activity in question may constitute a "search" for constitutional purposes. Similarly, where the police, as here, purport to rely on the [implied] invitation to knock and approach a dwelling for the purpose, *inter alia*, of securing evidence against the occupant, they have exceeded the bounds of any implied invitation and are engaging in a search of the occupant's home. *Since the implied invitation is for a specific purpose, the invitee's purpose is all-important in determining whether his or her activity is authorized by the invitation.* [emphasis added][28]

Similarly, if a person has consented to the police using personal information or a sample of DNA believing that it would be used for a specific purpose, the person has not waived his or her privacy rights for all purposes. In *R. v. Borden*,[29] the Supreme Court held that a waiver of privacy in one set of circumstances does not extend to all circumstances, absent valid consent intended to apply to all purposes:

> In order for a waiver of the right to be secure against an unreasonable seizure to be effective, the person purporting to consent must be possessed of the requisite informational foundation for a true relinquishment of the right. A right to choose requires not only the volition to prefer one option over another, but also sufficient available information to make the preference meaningful. This is equally true whether the individual is choosing to forego consultation with counsel or choosing to relinquish to the police something which they otherwise have no right to take.[30]

---

26 *Ibid.* at para. 13.
27 *Ibid.* at para.14. Justice Major (L'Heureux-Dubé J. concurring) in dissent, did not recognize such a limit.
28 *Evans*, above note 2 at 32.
29 *R. v. Borden* (1994), 92 C.C.C. (3d) 404 (S.C.C.) [*Borden*].
30 *Ibid.* at 417; See also *R. v. Arp*, [1998] 3 S.C.R. 339; *R. v. Colarusso*, [1994] 1 S.C.R. 20 (S.C.C.) [*Colarusso*]; *R. v. Law* (2002), 160 C.C.C. (3d) 449 (S.C.C.) at paras. 21–22 [*Law*].

F. ONUS FOR ESTABLISHING PRIVACY: OBLIGATION FOR EVIDENTIARY BASIS

The applicant who wishes to have evidence excluded at trial has the onus to establish an expectation of privacy that was reasonable in the circumstances.[31] That means the individual must have a subjective expectation of privacy, and the expectation must be objectively reasonable in the "totality of the circumstances." To meet this onus, the applicant must make more than "bare assertions" of privacy, and has a positive obligation to provide evidence of an expectation of privacy. For example, in *R. v. Belnavis*,[32] a car was stopped for speeding. After the police officer saw garbage bags of clothing marked with price tags in the back seat, he searched the car for evidence that the property was stolen. The Court found that the driver's expectation of privacy had been breached, as she had a certain expectation of privacy by virtue of her control of the car. The passenger, however, (who on the *Edwards* analysis had no expectation of privacy in the car itself), failed to assert any interest in the bags of clothing; this was ultimately fatal to her claim of privacy in any part of the seized evidence.[33]

Similarly, in *R. v. Khuc and Pham*,[34] police executed a search warrant on a home, finding a large amount of cocaine in a bag hanging on a door in a bedroom. The appellants Khuc and Pham (and two children) were in the home at the time of the search, and some documents in their names were found. At trial, the Crown asserted that Khuc and Pham were in possession of both the cocaine and the home, based on the evidence of their presence and the documents found in proximity to the drugs. The defence asserted that his clients were simply visitors and temporary babysitters for their niece and nephew, but nonetheless argued that they had an expectation of privacy in the premises. It is interesting to note that this legal formulation places the defence in the position of arguing a connection to the premises sufficient to attract constitutional protection, but still disclaim knowledge or control over the contraband. The Crown's position is even more curious, asserting that the defendants are insufficiently connected to the premises to create a reasonable expectation of privacy, yet sufficiently connected that they would know and consent to the presence of the drugs.

---

31 *Edwards*, above note 13 at 146; *Pugliese*, above note 8 at 302.
32 *Belnavis*, above note 15.
33 *Ibid.* at 211. Note that it was not the absence of an ownership interest in the goods that defeated the claim of an expectation of privacy. Rather, it was the failure to demonstrate a link to the bag sufficient to ground a privacy claim.
34 *R. v. Khuc*, [2000] B.C.J. No. 50 (B.C.C.A.).

The trial judge in *Khuc* found that the two had no expectation of privacy, as there was no evidentiary foundation establishing their privacy interests. The judge refused the defence's application to hold a further *voir dire* after his initial ruling, as the defence informed the judge they would not call any further evidence as to ownership interests, tenancy, or babysitting arrangements that had been made for the evening. The British Columbia Court of Appeal held that the trial judge was not required to look at factors that may have supported an expectation of privacy in the absence of the accused establishing a basis for such a finding:

> Was the trial judge required to consider a privacy interest on a basis expressly repudiated by the accused? I think not. To do so would give the accused the benefit of a position they expressly, and for their own reasons, declined to adopt. They had a choice of asserting occupation and challenging the search or of risking the admission of the product of the search. They chose to distance themselves from the occupation of the premises and chose the latter. Nothing further need be said about that.[35]

G. THE IMPORTANCE OF CONTEXT TO DETERMINE THE EXISTENCE AND LEVEL OF PROTECTION FOR PRIVACY

The protections afforded by section 8 cover a wide range of privacy interests. The Supreme Court has taken a liberal approach to determining what will qualify for privacy protection, finding privacy interests in the body, the home, the office, in lockers, in vehicles, in documents, and beyond the physical into the informational realm, finding privacy interests in nearly every area a person seeks to keep confidential from the interference of others.[36]

However, the level of protection afforded to the privacy interest in a given situation will depend on the context and "can vary with the nature of the matter sought to be protected, the circumstances in which and the place where state intrusion occurs, and the purposes of the intrusion."[37] The more confidential or sensitive the information, the higher the individual's expectation of privacy will be, and the level of tolerance for state intrusion will correspondingly diminish.[38]

---

35 *Ibid.* at para. 31.
36 *Law*, above note 30; *R. v. Buhay* (2003), 174 C.C.C. (3d) 97 (S.C.C.) at para. 24 [*Buhay*].
37 *Colarusso*, above note 30 at 214.
38 *R. v. Dersch* (1993), 85 C.C.C. (3d) 1 (S.C.C.) at 13–14; *Dyment*, above note 11 at 255–56.

In *R. v. Plant*,[39] the Supreme Court of Canada was faced with determining the extent of the privacy interest in an individual's residential electricity consumption records. The police obtained the records from the Calgary Utilities Commission, a public utility, in the course of a drug investigation. Justice Sopinka held that the factors that follow "allow for a balancing of the societal interests in protecting individual dignity, integrity and autonomy with effective law enforcement" in determining the degree of privacy attaching to information:[40]

1. the nature of the information obtained by the state;
2. the nature of the relationship between the party releasing the information and the party claiming its confidentiality;
3. the place where the information was obtained;
4. the manner in which the information was obtained;
5. the seriousness of the crime being investigated.[41]

H. LEVEL OF PROTECTION AFFORDED IN VARIOUS CONTEXTS

Although the issue of whether a person has *any* reasonable expectation of privacy at all is important, equally important is the determination of the degree of privacy enjoyed in a given set of circumstances. This is because the degree of privacy enjoyed in a set of circumstances determines the degree of state intrusion that can be tolerated before a search is deemed to be unreasonable.[42] The level of privacy intruded upon also affects the determination of whether evidence ought to be excluded under section 24(2) of the *Charter*.[43] The higher the level of privacy enjoyed in a given situation, the more likely it is that the evidence will be excluded, and the *Charter* breach will be considered more serious.

In the subsections below, we will examine different types of state intrusion and the level of privacy the courts have afforded individuals in those circumstances. While the structure of this section might suggest that the courts have taken a categorical approach to the determination of expectation of privacy and section 8 rights, in fact, the activity engaged in or type of intrusion is simply a factor in a contextual approach to assessing whether privacy

---

39 *R. v. Plant* (1993), 84 C.C.C. (3d) 203 (S.C.C.).
40 *Ibid.* at 212.
41 *Ibid.*
42 *R. v. M.(M.R.)* (1998), 129 C.C.C. (3d) 361 (S.C.C.) at para. 33; *Belnavis*, above note 15 at 208; *Evans*, above note 2.
43 See chapter 9.

rights have been violated. In each case discussed below, the whole of the context was examined by the court with the ultimate issue being the balance of the state's interests and goals on the one hand, against the public's interest in being left alone. What is important to note, however, is that the higher the level of privacy expected, the less tolerance a court will have for deviations from the general hallmarks of a reasonably justified intrusion, such as reasonable grounds and prior judicial authorization.[44]

1) The Human Body

a) In General

Interference with the human body is at one extreme end of the spectrum of privacy protections. In *R. v. Stillman*,[45] Cory J. reiterated the Supreme Court's position that searches of the body require more rigorous standards for justification due to the heightened privacy interests associated with the body:

> It has often been clearly and forcefully expressed that state interference with a person's bodily integrity is a breach of a person's privacy and an affront to human dignity. The invasive nature of body searches demands higher standards of justification. In *R. v. Pohoretsky*, [1987] 1 S.C.R. 945, at p. 949, Lamer J., as he then was, noted that, "a violation of the sanctity of a person's body is much more serious than that of his office or even of his home." In addition, LaForest J. observed in *R. v. Dyment*, [1988] 2 S.C.R. 417, "the use of a person's body without his consent to obtain information about him, invades an area of personal privacy essential to the maintenance of his human dignity." [parallel citations omitted][46]

The privacy concerns related to the body are not limited to those in the physical realm, such as pain or discomfort. In *R. v. Dyment*,[47] LaForest J. explained that the violation of bodily integrity constituted an affront to a person's dignity:

> This Court has recently dealt with privacy of the person in *R. v. Pohoretsky*, [1987] 1 S.C.R. 945. The case bears some resemblance to the present one, but there the doctor had taken the blood sample from a patient, who was in an incoherent and delirious state, at the request of a police officer. In holding this action to constitute an unreasonable search and seizure, my colleague Lamer J. underlined the seriousness of a violation of the sancti-

---

44 *Hunter*, above note 1.
45 *R. v. Stillman* (1997), 113 C.C.C. (3d) 321 (S.C.C.) [*Stillman*].
46 *Ibid.* at para. 42.
47 *Dyment*, above note 11.

ty of a person's body. It constitutes a serious affront to human dignity. As the Task Force on *Privacy and Computers, supra,* put it, at p. 13:

> this sense of privacy transcends the physical and is aimed essentially at protecting the dignity of the human person. Our persons are protected not so much against the physical search (the law gives physical protection in other ways) as against the indignity of the search, its invasion of the person in a moral sense.[48]

Justice LaForest also held that both bodily substances and information about the person shared equally heightened degree of privacy:

> Finally, there is privacy in relation to information. This too is based on the notion of the dignity and integrity of the individual. As the Task Force put it (p. 13): "This notion of privacy derives from the assumption that all information about a person is in a fundamental way his own, for him to communicate or retain for himself as he sees fit." In modern society, especially, retention of information about oneself is extremely important. We may, for one reason or another, wish or be compelled to reveal such information, but situations abound where the reasonable expectations of the individual that the information shall remain confidential to the persons to whom, and restricted to the purposes for which it is divulged, must be protected.[49]

The protection of information about the person does not extend, however, to information not revealing particularly personal information. For example, the *fact* of a visit to the doctor[50] or the *fact* that blood samples were taken may not be protected. The expectation of privacy extends only to the personal or intimate information itself, such as the results of any tests taken at a doctor's visit.[51]

b) Body Cavity Searches

Searches of body cavities attract the greatest protection against state intrusion as compared to other less invasive body searches. In *R. v. Simmons*,[52] the Supreme Court discussed the kinds of searches conducted at international border crossings.[53] The Court identified three distinct "types" of border searches. First, the traveller may be subjected to routine questioning,

---

48 *Ibid.* at 429.
49 *Ibid.* at 430.
50 *R. v. Dorfer* (1996), 104 C.C.C. (3d) 528 (B.C.C.A.) [*Dorfer*].
51 *R. v. Day*, [1998] O.J. No. 4461 (C.A.).
52 *R. v. Simmons*, [1988] 2 S.C.R. 495, 45 C.C.C. (3d) 296, 55 D.L.R. (4th) 673 [*Simmons*].
53 "[T]he degree of personal privacy reasonably expected at customs is lower than in most other situations." *Simmons*, above note 52 at S.C.R. 528.

baggage searches, and pat or frisk searches of the person. No special justification needs to be made for such searches, since the reasonable international traveller must expect this kind of scrutiny and treatment. The second level of search includes "skin" or strip searches conducted in private rooms. This type of search can be justified only if the customs official has the reasonable suspicion that the target has "secreted on or about his person" items subject to the *Customs Act* or other contraband.[54]

With respect to body cavity searches, the Court explained:

> The third and most highly intrusive type of search is that sometimes referred to as the body cavity search, in which customs officers have recourse to medical doctors, to X-rays, to emetics, and to other highly invasive means. . . . Searches of the third or bodily cavity type may raise entirely different constitutional issues for it is obvious that the greater the intrusion, the greater must be the justification and the greater the degree of constitutional protection.[55]

The Court reiterated these concerns about the level of intrusiveness of body cavity searches in *R. v. Greffe*,[56] a case involving a rectal search conducted following an arrest for traffic tickets. The rectal search was performed despite the absence of reasonable grounds to believe a drug offence had been committed, and was accompanied by a violation of the right to counsel guaranteed by section 10(b) of the *Charter*:

> *[It] is the intrusive nature of the rectal search and considerations of human dignity and bodily integrity that demands the high standard of justification before such a search will be reasonable.* . . . [W]e cannot accept that police officers subject persons to rectal examinations incident to arrests for traffic warrants when they do not have reasonable and probable grounds to believe that those people are actually in possession of drugs. Indeed, in this case the absence of proof of reasonable and probable grounds, or even of "objective articulable facts" to support the officer's suspicions, makes the unreasonable search a more serious *Charter* violation.[57] [emphasis added; citations omitted]

Notwithstanding the greater protection afforded against body cavity searches, in many circumstances the "belief threshold" required to comply with section 8 may be no higher than reasonable grounds:[58]

---

54 *Customs Act*, S.C. 1986, c. 1, s. 98.
55 *Simmons*, above note 52; as quoted in *Stillman*, above note 45 at 342.
56 *R. v. Greffe* (1990), 55 C.C.C. (3d) 161 (S.C.C.).
57 *Ibid.* at 192–93.
58 See chapter 5.

In *R. v. Greffe* (1990), 55 C.C.C. (3d) 161 (S.C.C.), a case involving a rectal examination by use of a sigmoidoscope, a metal apparatus inserted eight inches into the accused's rectum, revealed a packet of heroin. This was a warrantless search and the analysis that took place was under s. 24(2) of the *Charter*. In that case the Court said that had there been reasonable and probable grounds to believe Greffe was in possession of heroin, a search would have been reasonable. In *R. v. Collins*, [1987] 1 S.C.R. 265, the Court held that a choke search enabling the peace officer to reach into the mouth would be reasonable if there were reasonable grounds to believe that the person was in possession of a narcotic. Indeed, the British Columbia Court of Appeal in *R. v. Garcia & Guiterrez* (1991), 65 C.C.C. (3d) 15 at 19–22 found a search to be reasonable in which officers took handcuffs, placed them between the suspect's lips and the edge of his teeth, forcing his mouth open in order to seize a narcotic. The Court justified this on the basis that the officers had reasonable grounds to believe that that person was committing a drug offence. These are all highly intrusive forms of search.[59]

c) Strip Searches

As noted above, strip searches are considered to be significantly intrusive of privacy interests. In *R. v. Golden*,[60] the Supreme Court described the inherently degrading nature of the procedure:[61]

> Strip searches are thus inherently humiliating and degrading for detainees regardless of the manner in which they are carried out and for this reason they cannot be carried out simply as a matter of routine policy. The adjectives used by individuals to describe their experience of being strip searched give some sense of how a strip search, even one that is carried out in a reasonable manner, can affect detainees: "humiliating," "degrading," "demeaning," "upsetting," and "devastating" . . . Some commentators have gone as far as to describe strip searches as "visual rape" . . . Women and minorities in particular may have a real fear of strip searches and may experience such a search as equivalent to a sexual assault. The psychological effects of strip searches may also be particularly traumatic for individuals who have previously been subject to abuse. . . . Routine strip searches may also be distasteful and difficult for the police officers conducting them. [citations omitted][62]

---

59 *R. v. Brighteyes*, [1997] A.J. 362 (Q.B.) at para. 40.
60 *R. v. Golden*, [2001] 3 S.C.R. 679 [*Golden*].
61 *Ibid.*
62 *Ibid.* at para. 90.

As such, strip searches may only be performed in appropriate circumstances, and may be conducted only where authorized by a statute, such as the *Customs Act*, or in limited circumstances under the common law:

> In light of the serious infringement of privacy and personal dignity that is an inevitable consequence of a strip search, such searches are only constitutionally valid at common law where they are conducted as an incident to a lawful arrest *for the purpose of discovering weapons in the detainee's possession or evidence related to the reason for the arrest. In addition, the police must establish reasonable and probable grounds justifying the strip search in addition to reasonable and probable grounds justifying the arrest.* Where these preconditions to conducting a strip search incident to arrest are met, it is also necessary that the strip search be conducted in a manner that does not infringe s. 8 of the *Charter*. [emphasis added][63]

To emphasize, when a search incident to arrest is as intrusive as a strip search, in most circumstances the police must have reasonable grounds to justify the conduct of the search.

Strip searches are conducted in a range of circumstances: "on the street" arrests, bookings into police custody, including voluntary surrenders for arrest, and in custodial circumstances, such as holding cells, jails, and prisons.[64] There is some authority for the proposition that prior to conducting a strip search in such situations, the authorities must consider the individual circumstances of the person about to be searched in order to decide whether a strip search is justifiable. In *R. v. S.F.*[65] the Court found that a strip search of two youths who had voluntarily presented themselves at the police station violated section 8. According to the police officers who testified, the strip searches were conducted pursuant to routine booking procedures for anyone being placed in the holding cells.[66] After a detailed review of the facts, Katarynych J. stated:

---

63 *Ibid.* at para. 99.
64 The authority for such searches may be common law, as in search incident to arrest, or statutory, such as under the *Corrections and Conditional Release Act*, 1992, c. 20, ss. 47–66.
65 *R. v. S.F.*, [2003] O.J. No. 92 (C.J.) [*S.F.*].
66 Several courts have expressed disapproval of strip searches being conducted as routine matter of procedure, most notably the Supreme Court in *Golden*, above note 60, noting at a "disturbing trend" (para. 72) and commenting that "routine" strip searches with "no compelling reason for performing a strip search in the circumstances of the arrest" will be unconstitutional (para. 95); see also *R. v. A.B.*, [2003] O.J. 2010 (Sup. Ct. J.) at paras. 27–32.

[T]here is no reasonable and probable ground to believe that either girl presented any safety concern at the time of their arrest, or at any time subsequent to that arrest.

None of the officers who were part of the strip search decision that day had any information, apart from the circumstances alleged against them that had prompted their arrest, upon which to ground a reasonably [sic] belief that either girl presented any safety risk at all. The officers involved with these girls at the station admitted that they had no reason to believe that either of these girls had come to the police station with their parents on November 9, 2002, with instruments on their person that could be used by them or anyone else to cause harm.

The issue, in their collective mind, was not whether the girls had anything secreted on them that could only be discovered through a strip search. For them, the issue was that they had no reason to believe that they did not. That is a spectre of danger. That is not a sufficient rationale in law for the choice that was made for these two girls.

It is precisely the sort of thinking that is prohibited by *Golden*. The court makes clear that the mere possibility that an individual may be concealing evidence or weapons upon his person is not sufficient to justify a strip search. *Golden* is also clear that strip searches cannot be carried out as a matter of routine police department policy applicable to all arrestees.[67]

While in most cases reasonable and probable grounds will be required to justify a strip search, when such searches are performed at the border, the protection afforded against the intrusion is markedly lower. In *R. v. Simmons*,[68] the Supreme Court held that, given state sovereignty and security concerns and a lowered expectation of privacy at the border,[69] a strip search could be conducted in private by an officer of the same sex on the basis of a reasonable suspicion that the individual has contraband secreted on his or her person, without the need for prior judicial authorization.

Since the custodial context and border searches present similar arguments for diminished expectations of privacy and more intrusive searches in the interests of safety and control, it may be that an approach similar to *Simmons* would be appropriate for custodial strip searches.[70] This would be

---

67 *S.F.*, above note 65 at paras. 68–71.
68 *Simmons*, above note 52.
69 See also *R. v. Monney* (1999), 133 C.C.C. (3d) 129 (S.C.C.) [*Monney*].
70 For a brief discussion of the distinction between "strip searches immediately incidental to arrest, and searches related to safety issues in a custodial setting," see *Golden*, above note 60 at paras. 96–97; the Supreme Court acknowledges the importance of keeping weapons and contraband out of prisons.

something of a departure from the view implicit in the passage above from *R. v. S.F.*, where Katarynych J.'s reasons were based in part on her finding that the officers had no "reason to believe" that the youths presented a safety risk.[71] Note further that the threshold of reasonable suspicion in *Customs Act* searches is imposed by statute, not by operation of the common law.[72]

d) Bedpan Vigils

Customs officials sometimes detain travellers in a "drug-loo" facility until the detainee passes urine or has a bowel movement that can be inspected for evidence of drug ingestion and smuggling. This procedure is referred to as a "bedpan vigil."

In *R. v. Monney*,[73] the Supreme Court considered the reasonableness of conducting a bedpan vigil pursuant to the criteria in the *Customs Act*. Section 98 authorizes searches of the persons on a threshold of reasonable suspicion that a person "has secreted on or about his person" any contraband or evidence of a violation of the *Customs Act* or any other Act related to the importation or exportation of goods:

> 98(1) An officer may search
>
> (a) any person who has arrived in Canada, within a reasonable time after his arrival in Canada,
>
> (b) any person who is about to leave Canada, at any time prior to his departure, or
>
> (c) any person who has had access to an area designated for use by persons about to leave Canada and who leaves the area but does not leave Canada, within a reasonable time after he leaves the area,
>
> if the officer suspects on reasonable grounds that the person has secreted on or about his person anything in respect of which this Act has been or might be contravened, anything that would afford evidence with respect to a contravention of this Act or any goods the importation or exportation of which is prohibited, controlled or regulated under this or any other Act of Parliament.
>
> (2) An officer who is about to search a person under this section shall, on the request of that person, forthwith take him before the senior officer at the place where the search is to take place.

---

71 *Quaere* on the facts of *R. v. S.F.* whether the circumstances would have supported a reasonable suspicion that the youths presented a safety risk that might justify a strip search.
72 See *Customs Act*, s. 98.
73 *Monney*, above note 69.

(3) A senior officer before whom a person is taken pursuant to subsection (2) shall, if he sees no reasonable grounds for the search, discharge the person or, if he believes otherwise, direct that the person be searched.

In *Monney*, the Court found that where the bedpan vigil is conducted in accordance with the criteria set out in section 98, the search is consistent with section 8 of the *Charter*.[74] The Court held that detaining a person at the border until he or she defecates (thereby confirming or dispelling the suspicion of ingestion) falls within the second of the three categories of searches described in *Simmons*[75] (i.e., less intrusive than body-cavity searches and on par with the level of invasiveness of strip searches). The Court found the level of invasiveness of bedpan vigils to be more akin to border strip searches than the collection of samples for DNA analysis for several reasons:[76] first, the traveller has a diminished expectation of privacy at the border given the compelling state interest in controlling its borders,[77] and second, the bedpan vigil for narcotics did not implicate the individual's dignity and autonomy in the same manner as, for example, a DNA sample:

> Heroin pellets contained in expelled faecal matter cannot be considered as an "outward manifestation" of the respondent's identity. An individual's privacy interest in the protection of bodily fluids does not extend to contraband which is intermingled with bodily waste and which is expelled from the body in the process of allowing nature to take its course.[78]

However, subsequent jurisprudence suggests that certain types of bedpan vigils may require a degree of constitutional protection greater than that normally afforded to the person at the border. The British Columbia Court of Appeal in *R. v. Carpenter*[79] distinguished the "passive bedpan vigil" (as in *Monney*) where officers detain the suspect and wait for nature to take its course, from other more invasive searches in which a bedpan vigil is conducted with the assistance of laxatives, X-rays, or other techniques.[80] The Court held that an "active" bedpan vigil constituted a greater interference with the person and in the circumstances of the case was an unreasonable search. It was conducted in

---

74 *Ibid.* at para. 39 *et seq.* and para. 47.
75 *Simmons*, above note 52.
76 In *Stillman*, above note 45, the Supreme Court found the collection of DNA samples from a person in custody to be highly invasive.
77 *Monney*, above note 69 at para. 42.
78 *Ibid.* at para. 45.
79 *R. v. Carpenter* (2002), 165 C.C.C. (3d) 159 (B.C.C.A.).
80 *Ibid.* at paras. 47–50.

the absence of any evidence, medical or otherwise, to indicate the need for urgency in expulsion of the heroin pellets in order to protect the appellant's life or health, and by the failure of the Customs officers to obtain the appellant's written consents when specifically called for by their own procedure manual, particularly when there are no good reasons as to why the consents were not obtained.[81]

e) Taking Bodily Samples and Impressions

The taking of bodily samples and impressions is an intrusion on the heightened privacy interest in the body. There are no common law powers authorizing the state to seize bodily substances or impressions. In *R. v. Borden*,[82] the Supreme Court declared that, in the absence of valid consent, the seizure of blood and hair samples from an accused was a violation of section 8; there was (at that time) no legal authority for such a seizure. In *R. v. Stillman*,[83] the Supreme Court confirmed the unreasonableness of seizures of bodily substances in the absence of specific legislative authority. Therefore, in order for such seizures to be lawful, the state must rely on a specific statutory provision authorizing the seizure.

i) Statutory Provisions for the Seizure of Bodily Samples (DNA)

The *Criminal Code* now has a scheme governing the seizure of bodily substances for conducting DNA analysis. The *Criminal Code* authorizes such seizures in two situations for two distinct purposes: (1) DNA warrants are available to assist in the investigation of a specific offence;[84] and (2) DNA collection orders are available for the inclusion of the offender's DNA in a federal databank following a finding of guilt for a "designated" offence.[85] Appendix 6, "Seizures of Bodily Substances and Impressions" sets out the preconditions and limitations on the use of each of these procedures. The following sections highlight the jurisprudence analysing the constitutional reasonableness of the provisions.

---

81 *Ibid.* at 225.
82 *Borden*, above note 29.
83 *Stillman*, above note 45.
84 See s. 487.05.
85 Each of ss. 487.051, 487.052, and 487.055 authorize DNA databank seizures, but the procedure differs based on when the offence was committed or the finding of guilt was entered. See Appendix 6, "Seizures of Bodily Substances and Impressions" at the end of this book. See also Appendix 7, "Related Statutes: Search and Seizure Powers" regarding the provisions of the *DNA Identification Act*.

ii) DNA Investigative Warrants: Reasonable Intrusion into Privacy

In *R. v. S.A.B.*,[86] the Supreme Court upheld the sections of the *Criminal Code* authorizing the seizure of blood, hair, and epithelial cells for investigative purposes.[87] S.A.B. challenged the DNA seizure provisions under sections 7 and 8 of the *Charter*, arguing that (1) the legislation did not minimally intrude into his constitutional rights; (2) the reasonable grounds standard was constitutionally insufficient to justify a highly intrusive seizure; and (3) the legislation allowed for only *ex parte* applications and therefore did not allow the suspect to make submissions as to whether the warrant should issue.

The Supreme Court held that the provisions authorizing seizure of DNA for investigative purposes complied with section 8 of the *Charter*. In determining the appropriate balance between the individual's privacy interests and the state's interest in law enforcement, the Court recognized that the state had a significant and legitimate interest in seeking investigative DNA warrants: the provisions allow for the use of a valuable identification tool, enabling the state to seek the truth, bring offenders to justice, and avoid wrongful convictions.[88]

The Court also found that the detailed and fairly restrictive warrant provisions minimized the intrusions into the individual's privacy interests. DNA samples can be obtained only as a result of the prior authorization of a provincial court judge (as opposed to a justice of the peace, the standard for many other search powers),[89] on an evidentiary standard of reasonable grounds. The warrants are available only for designated offences, and the judge must be satisfied that issuing the warrant is in the best interests of the administration of justice.[90] The prescribed manner of taking the samples is relatively non-intrusive and non-invasive, not constituting a "partic-

---

86 *R. v. S.A.B.*, 2003 SCC 60 [*S.A.B.*]; S.A.B. was accused of sexually assaulting and impregnating a 14-year-old girl. A DNA warrant under s. 487.05 was issued authorizing the taking of a bodily sample from S.A.B., which was forensically "matched" with the DNA of the girl's aborted fetus.
87 Several provincial courts of appeal had already found the provisions to be constitutionally reasonable, including the Ontario Court of Appeal in *F.(S.)* (2000), 141 C.C.C. (3d) 225 [*F.(S.)*], and the Alberta Court of Appeal in *B.(S.A.)* (2001), 157 C.C.C. (3d) 510 (Alta. C.A.) [*B.(S.A.)*]. The *Criminal Code* DNA databank seizure provisions were not at issue in *S.A.B.*, and have not yet been addressed by the Supreme Court.
88 *S.A.B.*, above note 86 at para. 51.
89 *Ibid*. at para. 38.
90 *Ibid*. at para. 39.

ularly serious affront to privacy or dignity";[91] the person taking the samples is under a legislative duty to do so in a manner that respects a person's privacy and is reasonable in the circumstances.[92] The seizure may also be done on such terms as the issuing judge considers advisable to ensure the reasonableness of the seizure.[93]

The Court rejected S.A.B.'s argument that a higher evidentiary standard such as the "investigative necessity" standard imposed for wiretap authorizations was required. The Court noted that unlike wiretaps, which are sweeping and intrude on the privacy rights of third parties, investigative DNA warrants are target-specific. Further, investigative DNA warrants could also potentially exonerate the innocent.[94] Finally, equally or more intrusive types of searches, such as the inherently humiliating strip search, require only a standard of reasonable grounds.[95]

The Court also rejected the argument that the constitution required notice of the application for the investigative DNA warrant. The Court held that the *ex parte* nature of the process is constitutionally appropriate for this and most investigative orders, due to the risk that the suspect would frustrate the proper execution of the warrant. In any case, a judge is not precluded from ordering notice in appropriate cases.[96]

Most importantly, the Court found the provisions to be an appropriate balance of state and individual interests because the scheme protects against undue intrusion into the individual's "informational" privacy in the body. The scheme limits the intrusion by using non-coding (or junk) DNA information for forensic DNA analysis, which does not reveal any medical, physical, or mental characteristics about the individual, and can be used only to provide identifying information that can be compared to an existing sample.[97] The scheme also limits the use of the information obtained from DNA analysis, and makes it an offence to use a bodily substance obtained

---

91   Ibid. at para. 44 (the plucking of pubic hair would be an exception to the non-intrusive/dignified manner of the procedure).
92   For example, a person would not ordinarily be required to expose a part of the body that is not ordinarily exposed to view: *ibid*. at para. 45.
93   Ibid. at para. 46.
94   Ibid. at para. 54.
95   Ibid. at para. 55.
96   Ibid. at para. 56. Note however the recent case of *R. v. Rodgers*, [2004] O.J. No. 1073 (C.A.), where the Ontario Court of Appeal held that a judge must specifically consider the issue of notice in the content of orders under s.487.055, and that notice must be given unless the Crown can demonstrate legitimate grounds based on more than speculation that the application ought to proceed *ex parte*.
97   Ibid. at para. 49.

in execution of a DNA warrant (or information derived therefrom) except in the course of an investigation of the designated offence.[98]

The Court also found that the legislation respected the principle against self-incrimination. The Court considered the test from *R. v. White*[99] for assessing the impact on self-incrimination concerns. In that case, the Court repeated the long-standing rule that coerced confessions are inherently unreliable. Such a concern obviously does not apply to reliable physical evidence such as DNA. The second foundation for the rule against coerced self-incrimination is the avoidance of state abuses of power. Although the process is highly adversarial, the Court found that the legislation provided a number of safeguards against abuses of power by the state:

> In particular, the prior judicial authorization, circumscribed by strict requirements of reasonable and probable grounds and stringent limits on the potential use of the collected DNA evidence, ensures that the power to obtain bodily samples is not abused. It is also important to acknowledge that, as previously noted, the degree of intrusion both physical and informational is limited.[100]

For further discussion of the relationship between sections 7 and 8 see chapter 4, "Higher Protections Against Intrusions Where Competing/Compound Interests Are Affected by the Search."

iii) "DNA Databank" Seizures: Reasonable Intrusion into Privacy

Although not yet considered by the Supreme Court, appellate courts have given similar constitutional approval to the DNA databank seizure-order provisions of the *Criminal Code* and *DNA Identification Act*.[101] These provisions authorize a judge to order the seizure of DNA samples from people found guilty of "primary" and "secondary" designated offences as defined under section 487.04, to permit DNA analysis on those samples. The "designated offences" encompass the more serious offences contained in the *Criminal Code*. See Appendix 6, "Seizures of Bodily Substances and Impressions," for details on the preconditions for obtaining such orders.

In *R. v. Briggs*,[102] the Ontario Court of Appeal found the threshold for issuance of an authorization to seize a DNA sample as set out in section 487.052 (seizures in relation to offences committed *prior* to June 30, 2000)

---

98 *Ibid.* at para. 50.
99 *R. v. White*, [1999] 2 S.C.R. 417.
100 *S.A.B.*, above note 86 at para. 59.
101 *DNA Identification Act*, S.C. 1998, c. 37. See Appendix 7 for the statutory provisions of the Act.
102 *R. v. Briggs* (2001), 157 C.C.C. (3d) 38 (Ont. C.A.) [*Briggs*].

to be constitutionally reasonable under section 8, and a valid intrusion on security of the person under section 7 of the *Charter*.[103] In summary, the Court found that the following factors created a reasonable balance between the individual's privacy interests and the state's interests in obtaining the DNA sample:[104]

> 1. Whether or not there is evidence at the scene of the crime of which the offender was convicted that would likely yield a DNA profile of the perpetrator is not necessarily a relevant consideration.
>
> 2. The phrase "best interests of the administration of justice" does not import as a prerequisite to making the order that there be reasonable and probable grounds to believe a further offence will be committed.
>
> 3. The state interest in obtaining a DNA profile from an offender is not simply law enforcement by making it possible to detect further crimes committed by this offender. Rather, the provisions have much broader purposes including the following:
> 1. Deter potential repeat offenders;
> 2. Promote the safety of the community;
> 3. Detect when a serial offender is at work;
> 4. Assist in the solving of "cold" crimes;
> 5. Streamline investigations; and
> 6. Most importantly, assist the innocent by early exclusion for investigative suspicion or in exonerating those who have been wrongfully convicted.
>
> 4. Provisions in the *Criminal Code* and the *DNA Identification Act* restricting the use that can be made of the DNA profile and protecting against improper use of the information offer significant protection of the offender's privacy.
>
> 5. The procedures for seizures of bodily substances authorized by the provisions are of short duration and involve no, or minimal, discomfort. There is a minimal intrusion with no unacceptable affront to human dignity.
>
> 6. A person convicted of a crime has a lesser expectation of privacy.
>
> 7. The trial judge is entitled to look at the offender's entire record, not just the crimes that may be designated offences.[105]

---

103 Note that this is not the combined approach to ss. 7 and 8 taken by the Supreme Court in its subsequent decision in *S.A.B.*
104 *R. v. Hendry* (2001), 161 C.C.C. (3d) 275 (Ont. C.A.) [*Hendry*] at para. 17.
105 All as summarized by Rosenberg J.A. in *ibid*.

Similarly in *R. v. Murrins*,[106] the Nova Scotia Court of Appeal found that section 487.052 complied with section 7.[107] The Court made the somewhat dubious finding that because the (physical) intrusions occasioned by DNA collection were trivial in nature,[108] they did not attract the protection of section 7.[109] The Court found that, even if the intrusions did attract section 7 protections, the legislation was not overly broad or arbitrary. The legislation applied only to those convicted of serious offences, the issuing of the order was discretionary, with the judge required to consider factors such as the offender's record and circumstances of the offence.[110] Further, the seizures are minimally intrusive, and any intrusion was not outweighed by the importance of the state's interest in crime solution and prevention, which interest was advanced by better and more accurate identification of offenders.[111]

See also *R. v. Ku*,[112] in which the British Columbia Court of Appeal upheld the section 487.052 seizure provisions.[113]

---

106 *R. v. Murrins* (2002), 162 C.C.C. (3d) 412 (N.S.C.A.) [*Murrins*].
107 Murrins also argued that the legislation violated his section 11(i) right, which guarantees the accused person's right to the benefit of the lesser punishment if such penalty has changed between the time of commission of the offence and the time of sentencing. The Court dismissed this argument, too, finding that a DNA seizure order is not a "punishment": see para. 107.
108 The Court compared the physical intrusion of the DNA sampling techniques to the far more significant intrusions that would occur if abortion were outlawed, thereby forcing women to carrying fetuses to term, the intrusion occasioned by the taking of bodily samples *without* statutory or common law authority, and laws prohibiting assisted suicide: see para. 41. Although this analysis is sensible as far as it goes, with respect, it neglects those fairly obvious constitutional interests that are not directly linked to the *physical* process of DNA sampling.
109 *Murrins*, above note 106 at para. 41. This finding does not accord with most s. 7 jurisprudence — any intrusion into the protected interests in s. 7 attract a degree of protection by the section, although the weight accorded to the interests are balanced against the other principles of fundamental justice, and the protections will diminish the more minimal the intrusion: see *Briggs*, above note 102 at para. 41; *Stillman*, above note 45; *B.(S.A.)*, above note 87.
110 *Murrins*, above note 106 at paras. 50, 60 & 65–67.
111 *Ibid.* at paras. 83–93.
112 *R. v. Ku* (2002), 169 C.C.C. (3d) 535 (B.C.C.A.) [*Ku*].
113 *Ibid.* at para. 21. *Note*: Although *Briggs*, *Murrins*, and *Ku* did not employ the integrated s. 7 / s. 8 analysis later developed in *S.A.B.*, it is unlikely that the outcome of these cases would have been different if they had properly considered whether self-incrimination concerns rendered the legislation unreasonable under s. 8. There is little difference in the type of s. 7 concerns raised in the DNA databank context, in terms of its compliance with the underlying rationale articulated in *White* for the principle against self-incrimination (the inherent reliability of the evidence and the safeguards within the legislation against the abuse of state power).

The reasonableness of the seizure provisions under section 487.055 (permitting the seizure of DNA samples from dangerous or repeat offenders who committed offences before the enactment of the legislation) was considered by the Ontario Court of Appeal in R. v. Rodgers.[114] The Court held that the statutorily enumerated factors the judge must consider,[115] in addition to considering whether the order is in "the best interests of the administration of justice," provided for a constitutionally sufficient balancing of state and individual interests:

> These are the same factors which must be considered in determining whether to make DNA databank orders for offenders falling under the other two categories described in the Act: Criminal Code s. 487.051(3), s. 487.052(2). These factors considered in combination with the stated purpose (s. 3) and principles (s. 4) of the Act implicitly impose a best interests of the administration of justice standard into s. 487.055. Recognizing that a best interests of the administration of justice standard is implicit in s. 487.055 also renders it consistent with the other provisions relating to DNA databank orders. Counsel for Rodgers accepts this interpretation. The best interests of the administration of justice standard was held to be constitutional in R. v. Briggs, supra, at pp. 63–64. We agree with that finding.[116]

The Court also rejected the argument that section 8 required that an order ought to issue only if there was evidence that a specific crime had been committed, and that the order would provide evidence of that crime:

> The appellants contend that s. 487.055(1) infringes s. 8 of the Charter in that it permits the seizing of bodily samples for the purpose of DNA analysis without the state first establishing that an offence was probably committed and that the sample will probably afford evidence in connection with that offence. In making this submission, counsel equate the taking of a DNA sample for databank purposes from convicted persons with the taking of a DNA sample pursuant to a DNA warrant from a suspect.
>
> Counsel acknowledge that this court rejected this argument in R. v. Briggs, supra, at pp. 53–59, where the constitutionality of s. 487.052 was

---

114 R. v. Rodgers, [2004] O.J. No. 1073 (C.A.) [Rodgers].
115 Those factors are the offender's criminal record, the nature and circumstances of the standard of the offence, and the effect of the order on the offender's privacy and security interests: see s.489.055 (3.1); the Court also recognized that a finding that an order is in "the best interests of the administration of justice" is implicitly required by the provision: see ibid. at para.27.
116 Ibid. at para. 27.

challenged. Counsel accept that the analysis in *Briggs* has equal application to s. 487.055. We see no reason to reconsider *Briggs, supra*. In our view, it was correctly decided. Indeed, counsel did not suggest that we should reconsider *Briggs*, but advanced this argument to "preserve potential further appellate rights."[117]

Notably though, the Court imposed a new evidentiary burden on the Crown in the pursuit of orders under section 487.055. The Court found that notice of the hearing must be given to the offender, unless the Crown can establish legitimate grounds to hold the hearing *ex parte*:

> A judge hearing a s. 487.055(1) application should start from the assumption that the target of the application whose liberty and security of the person will be significantly affected if the order is granted should receive notice of the application. It is open to the Crown to rebut the presumption of notice with evidence that in the particular circumstances, notice could frustrate the process contemplated by s. 487.055. Evidence showing a real risk of flight if notice was given, would clearly justify a decision to proceed *ex parte*.
>
> In holding that notice should generally be given to the subject of the application, I do not mean to suggest that a proceeding under s. 487.055(1) should take on the trappings of a criminal trial. I see no place for the strict application of the rules of evidence, the assigning of burdens of proof or the re-litigation of factual or legal issues decided in previous proceedings involving the offender who is the subject of the application. A summary form of procedure would be appropriate as long as it would allow for the effective exercise of the discretion called for under the section, and would be responsive to the particular issues that arise on the specific application. I would think that in most cases the judge can rely on transcripts from prior proceedings, pre-sentence reports, victim impact statements and criminal records unless the subject of the application, having been given an opportunity to do so, can show cause why the material should not be relied on by the judge. The manner in which the subject of the application can challenge the Crown material should depend on the nature of the challenge and the nature of the material. I do not think that cross-examination will always be necessary to afford the requisite procedural fairness. Procedural matters will have to be worked out on a case-by-case basis.[118]

---

117 *Ibid.* at paras. 23–24.
118 *Ibid.* at paras. 46–47. Further, the Court held that the judge would lose jurisdiction over the proceedings if the issue of notice is not specifically addressed, and any decision on notice must be based on more than speculation: see paras. 48–54.

There have also been trial-level decisions finding section 487.055 to be reasonable. In *R. v. Engum*,[119] Shaw J. of the British Columbia Supreme Court found these provisions constitutionally valid under sections 7 and 8 of the *Charter*.[120] In so finding, Shaw J. adopted the reasoning of provincial appellate decisions regarding the constitutionality of sections 487.05 and 487.052.[121] Justice Shaw found the provisions to be sufficiently similar to merit comparison, and any differences were insignificant given that section 487.055 dealt with offenders at the most serious end of the spectrum.[122] In assessing the balance struck by Parliament between the interests of the administration of justice and the privacy and bodily integrity of the individual, Shaw J. held:

> I have no doubt that s. 487.055 represents a reasonable and sensitive balance between the interests of the state and the rights of the individual. This balance takes into account the broad array of the state's interests in the administration of justice for the protection of our citizens, the diminished rights of privacy and bodily integrity of individuals convicted of multiple crimes, the dangerous nature of their crimes, the requirement of judicial authorization, the matters the authorizing judge must consider, the safety of the techniques used to take samples, the minimally invasive methods that are used, and the means adopted to protect individual privacy as much as possible.[123]

Justice Shaw also rejected the submission that people whose offences dated back prior to the legislation (those at whom the section 487.055 provision was explicitly aimed) presented a markedly lower risk of reoffending than those convicted of "new crimes" and subject to the other databank provisions:

> In my opinion, Mr. Engum's submission overlooks the full breadth of Parliament's purpose in enacting the DNA provisions. While the potential risk of reoffending is one reason for the provisions, the legislation also aims to aid in solving past crimes, some occurring many years ago. This process involves both the identification of offenders as well as the elimination of suspects where DNA evidence shows those individuals were not responsible.

---

119 *R. v. Engum* (2002), 163 C.C.C. (3d) 198 (B.C.S.C.) [*Engum*].
120 *Engum* involved a s. 487.055 order for the seizure of DNA from a person who was declared a dangerous offender in 1994 and sentenced to fourteen years imprisonment after convictions for twenty sexual offences and one threatening offence.
121 Including *F.(S.)*, above note 87; and *Briggs*, above note 102.
122 *Engum*, above note 119 at para. 21.
123 *Ibid.* at para. 31.

Mr. Engum's argument that the likelihood of reoffending decreases with time must be tempered by a consideration of the nature of the offenders covered by s. 487.055. They are individuals who have been declared dangerous offenders, have murdered more than once, or are repeat sexual offenders. Such offenders are at the high end of risk to reoffend, and these individuals may be responsible for unsolved crimes of the past. These factors lead me to conclude that the "old crimes" argument raised by Mr. Engum has no significant bearing upon the validity of Parliament's carefully thought out weighing of state needs and individual rights.[124]

f) Fingerprinting

The taking of fingerprints[125] by law enforcement is authorized under section 2 of the *Identification of Criminals Act*.[126] Although fingerprinting involves the taking of information about the body, the procedure is not considered to be as intrusive on privacy interests as the taking of other bodily impressions. As LaForest J. noted in *R. v. Beare*:[127]

> While some may find [fingerprinting] distasteful, it is insubstantial, of very short duration, and leaves no lasting impression. There is no penetration into the body and no substance is removed from it.[128]

So long as a person has been either convicted or charged on reasonable grounds to believe that he or she has committed a serious criminal offence, and the fingerprints are taken in accordance with the *Identification of Criminals Act*, the seizure will be reasonable under section 8.[129] The individual's heightened expectation of privacy in the body is not outweighed by the state's interests in light of the minimally intrusive procedure for taking fingerprints, and the value of the technique to law enforcement.[130] According-

---

124 *Ibid.* at paras. 33–35; Shaw J. also rejected Engum's s. 7 arguments, for the reasoning in *F.(S.)*, above note 87 and *B.(S.A.)*, above note 87, see para. 46.
125 The taking of photographs and certain physical measurements are also authorized; see s. 2 *Identification of Criminals Act*.
126 *Identification of Criminals Act*, R.S.C. 1985, c. I-1. See Appendix 6, "Seizures of Bodily Substances and Impressions," for the statutory preconditions for obtaining fingerprints.
127 *R. v. Beare* (1988), 45 C.C.C. (3d) 57 (S.C.C.) (*subnom R. v. Beare*; *R. v. Higgins*) [*Beare*].
128 *Ibid.* at 77–78.
129 *Ibid.*; *Stillman*, above note 45 at 356.
130 *Beare*, above note 127 at 67. The factors listed by the Court in *Beare* as illustrating the technique's value include: the ease of the procedure and its reputation of infallibility as an identification tool (no two persons' fingerprints are identical); its use in identifying people in a wide variety of circumstances, including the identifying of people who have touched objects at crime scenes, the exclusion of innocent persons as suspects, the identification of prisoners with suicidal tendencies, particular

ly, the traditional *Hunter v. Southam* criteria for a reasonable search power are inapplicable:

> While a search of one's premises requires a prior authorization based on reasonable and probable grounds to believe both that the offence has been committed and that evidence will be found, the custodial fingerprinting process is entirely different. It involves none of the probing into an individual's private life and effects that mark a search.[131]

i) *If the Basis for the Seizure Is Invalid, the Taking and Retention of Prints Will Be Unconstitutional*

If the underlying arrest is found to be unconstitutional or if the fingerprints were obtained other than in accordance with the *Identification of Criminals Act*, the taking of the prints may constitute a violation of section 8. In *R. v. Feeney*,[132] Sopinka J. found that, where the arrest was unlawful, the person's privacy interests in fingerprints gained heightened importance so as to render the seizure unreasonable:

> Compelling the accused to provide fingerprints in the present context was, in my view, a violation of s. 8 of the *Charter*, involving as it did a search and seizure related to the appellant's body, about which, at least in the absence of a lawful arrest, there is clearly a high expectation of privacy.[133]

Similarly in *R. v. Dore*,[134] the Ontario Court of Appeal held that the importance of a person's privacy interests in fingerprints changes once the person has been acquitted of the underlying offence. In *Dore*, the Crown argued that once a person's fingerprints were in the police databank, the expectation of privacy in the prints was lost, regardless of the outcome of their criminal charges. Justice Feldman rejected this argument, finding that a change in status from an alleged perpetrator to someone who was acquitted or had charges withdrawn renewed a person's expectation of privacy in the fingerprints:

> Linked to the inherent privacy interest one has in anything emanating from one's body, is the factor that the fingerprints are stored by the police criminal records, or a history of escape attempts so they can be segregated or monitored as may appear appropriate; and to assist a court to determine suitability for release on bail or the appropriate sentence. Outside the criminal sphere, fingerprinting is used to identify: injured or missing children, dead bodies, applicants for citizenship, and persons subject to security clearance.

131 *Ibid.* at 77–78.
132 *R. v. Feeney* (1997), 115 C.C.C. (3d) 129 (S.C.C.).
133 *Ibid.* at 162.
134 *R. v. Dore* (2002), 166 C.C.C. (3d) 225 (Ont. C.A.) [*Dore*].

because they were originally obtained under the *Identification of Criminals Act*. Therefore, the storage and use of the fingerprints is associated with the identification of the person as a criminal, when the person has not been convicted of the offence. Some U.S. courts identified this "rogues' gallery" problem in early cases on the privacy interest.[135] This concern was also identified by the Saskatchewan Court of Appeal in *Beare* and *Higgins* as a serious problem with retention (the issue not dealt with by the Supreme Court).

...

On the issue of whether a person does retain any expectation of privacy in the informational component of fingerprints, I conclude that there is no basis in the case law or otherwise, to infer that a person who was subjected to fingerprinting upon arrest will not have some reasonable expectation of maintaining or regaining his or her privacy in fingerprint information if the charge is disposed of in his or her favour. There is no reason to differentiate the expectation of privacy that an acquitted person has in such information from the expectation that a person who has never been charged with an indictable offence would have, because it is information about and from one's body not normally available without one's consent.[136]

ii) Retention of Prints after an Acquittal or Withdrawal of Charges May Not Violate Section 8

Despite the increased importance of privacy interests in fingerprints following an acquittal or withdrawal of charges, the Ontario Court of Appeal in *R. v. Dore*[137] held that the continued detention of those fingerprints following acquittal or withdrawal might still be reasonable under section 8 if the person did not act diligently to assert their renewed privacy interest.[138]

Applying the *Collins* test for reasonableness of a search, the Court held that the retention of fingerprints was "authorized by law" under the provision of the *Identification of Criminals Act* authorizing publication of prints for the use of law enforcement officers, with no temporal or other restrictions on retention.[139] In assessing the reasonableness of the retention, the

---

135 See, e.g., *Eddy v. Moore*, 5 Wash. App. 334 (1971); *U.S. v. Kalish*, 271 F. Supp. 968 (D.P.R. 1967).
136 *Dore*, above note 134 at paras. 54 and 64.
137 *Ibid.*
138 *Ibid.*
139 Section 4 of the amended *Identification of Criminals Act* now mandates the destruction of fingerprints (and photographs) that have been taken upon arrest, where the offence was one to which the *Contraventions Act*, S.C. 1992, c. 47 applies, and the Attorney General has elected under s. 50 of the *Contraventions Act* to proceed as a contravention and not pursuant to the information originally laid. This is the only

Court held that the dismissal of a charge does not *automatically* render the ongoing retention of the fingerprints unconstitutional. Rather, a court must make a case-specific determination of whether a person's privacy interests[140] override the state's interest in maintaining a large databank of fingerprints,[141] considering such factors as:

- whether new charges have arisen since the dismissal of the charges that are subject to fingerprinting;[142]
- whether the police are aware of the dismissal of the charges, and whether the person has taken the initiative to request destruction;[143] and
- whether the police tend to honour requests for destruction following dismissal of charges (so as to mitigate the effect of lack of conditions on retention in the *Identification of Criminals Act*).[144]

Applying these factors in *Dore*, the Court held that retention of fingerprints only unreasonably intrudes on a reasonable expectation of privacy if the person has requested destruction of the prints:

> In this context, where the state of retention is a static one, where the nature and degree of the privacy interest in the fingerprints is more minimal, and where the affected person is in the best position to know whether he or she does regain an expectation of privacy in the informational component of his or her fingerprints when a charge is disposed of in the person's favour, it seems to me that *a reasonable balance is struck by holding that the right to be left alone in those circumstances arises if and when the person asserts his or her privacy interest by asking for the fingerprints to be returned or destroyed. It is at that point that further retention of the fingerprints would become unconstitutional retention unless, in the particular circumstances, it could be shown that there*

---

section of the Act that addresses the issue of destruction of fingerprints and requires destruction in the limited circumstances described.

140 Following the dismissal of charges the privacy interests may be heightened given that fingerprints are information emanating from the body and given the stigma associated with being identified as a criminal in a databank. See *Dore*, above note 134 at paras. 68 and 70.

141 *Ibid.* at para. 66.

142 *Ibid.* at para. 70.

143 *Ibid.* at para. 69.

144 *Ibid.* at paras. 72–79 and 83; in *Dore* the evidence showed that the police forces involved in the matter honoured these requests with only limited exceptions — the local police force honoured 100 percent of requests, and the RCMP honoured nearly all requests, despite many investigatory and non-investigatory purposes for retaining prints. The Court held that the effect of the law that permits retention and does not define time limits for retention was effectively limited by the policy of destruction on request.

were other factors that would trump the privacy interest. If the police asserted a special case, the retention could be challenged. [emphasis added][145]

The fact that the state provided no notification to the individual that prints could be destroyed was deemed to be constitutionally irrelevant by the Court, as the individual was in the best position to assert his or her privacy interests at the relevant time.[146]

g) Privacy While in Custody

A person's expectation of privacy in the body decreases after the person comes into sustained contact with the criminal justice system. When a person is in custody following an arrest, the expectation of privacy will decrease, and will be even lower following conviction and sentence for an offence.[147] The decrease in privacy is not due to a lowered societal status from being branded a criminal, but rather is due to the lack of control over choices that the person can make about his or her body, once the person's body is in direct control of the state.[148]

Notwithstanding the generally lowered expectation of privacy while in custody, the person will receive some degree of protection in relation to the body and information about the body (as opposed to general personal belongings). This is so even if the information is in the form of garbage, such as a used facial tissue. In *R. v. Stillman*,[149] Cory J. found a breach of the right to privacy in the police's seizing of discarded tissues:

> [W]here an accused who is not in custody discards a kleenex or cigarette butt, the police may ordinarily collect and test these items without any concern for consent. A different situation is presented when an accused in custody discards items containing bodily fluids. Obviously an accused in custody cannot prevent the authorities from taking possession of these items. Whether the circumstances were such that the accused had abandoned the items and relinquished any privacy interest in them will have to be determined on the particular facts presented in each case.

---

145 *Ibid.* at para. 71.
146 *Ibid.* at paras. 84–85.
147 *Stillman*, above note 45 at 348; *R. v. Jordan* (2002), 162 C.C.C. (3d) 385 (N.S.C.A.) [*Jordan*] at para. 47; *Briggs*, above note 102; *Beare*, above note 127; *Weatherall v. Canada (Attorney General)*, [1993] 2 S.C.R. 872 at 877, 83 C.C.C. (3d) 1 (where the Supreme Court found that male inmates serving sentences had no expectation of privacy with respect to frisk searches, prisoner body counts, or "winds" through cell ranges being conducted by female prison guards); *Hendry*, above note 104 at para. 18; *R. v. Osmond*, [2000] O.J. No. 4267 (S.C.J.).
148 *Briggs*, above note 102.
149 *Stillman*, above note 45.

However, in this case, the accused had announced through his lawyers that he would not consent to the taking of any samples of his bodily fluids. The police were aware of his decision. Despite this they took possession of the tissue discarded by the appellant while he was in custody. In these circumstances the seizure was unreasonable and violated the appellant's s. 8 *Charter* rights.[150]

In *R. v. F.(D.M.)*,[151] the Alberta Court of Appeal found that an accused had no expectation of privacy in items discarded while in police custody, as the seizure occurred following the accused's departure from the police station.[152] In *F.(D.M.)*, a young person was interviewed at the police station in connection with an alleged sexual assault. During the interview, the young person refused to voluntarily provide a DNA sample. The young person was permitted to leave the interview, and left behind several cigarette butts in an ashtray, from which the police obtained a DNA sample. The Alberta Court of Appeal found that the young person had no expectation of privacy in the cigarette butts, as he was *not detained* when the butts were gathered. The Court found that even if he had been detained, the young person could have prevented police seizure by refraining from smoking initially, or taking the cigarette butts with him when he left.[153]

Where searches of the body in the custodial setting are related to *safety* issues, however, there may be a lowered standard of protection. As the Supreme Court noted in *R. v. Golden*:[154]

> It may be useful to distinguish between strip searches immediately incidental to arrest, and searches related to safety issues in a custodial setting. We acknowledge the reality that where individuals are going to be entering the prison population, there is a greater need to ensure that they are not concealing weapons or illegal drugs on their persons prior to their entry into the prison environment. However, this is not the situation in the present case. The type of searching that may be appropriate before an individual is integrated into the prison population cannot be used as a means of justifying extensive strip searches on the street or routine strip searches of individuals who are detained briefly by police, such as intoxicated individuals held overnight in police cells: *R. v. Toulouse*, [1994] O.J. No. 2746 (QL) (Prov. Div.).[155]

---

150 *Ibid.* at 348; see also *R. v. Nguyen* (2002), 161 C.C.C. (3d) 433 (Ont. C.A.) at paras. 14 and 15.
151 *R. v. F.(D.M.)* (1999), 139 C.C.C. (3d) 144 (Alta. C.A.).
152 *Ibid.*
153 *Ibid.* at paras. 68 and 141.
154 *Golden*, above note 60.
155 *Ibid.* at para. 96.

The Court also noted a distinction between strip searches performed during mere detention and those performed in situations of actual incarceration:

> The difference between the prison context and the short-term detention context is expressed well by Duncan J. in the recent case of *R. v. Coulter*, [2000] O.J. No. 3452 (QL) (C.J.), at paras 26–27, which involved a routine strip search carried out incident to an arrest and short-term detention in police cells for impaired driving. Duncan J. noted that whereas strip searching could be justified when introducing an individual into the prison population to prevent the individual from bringing contraband or weapons into prison, different considerations arise where the individual is only being held for a short time in police cells and will not be mingling with the general prison population. While we recognize that police officers have legitimate concerns that short-term detainees may conceal weapons that they could use to harm themselves or police officers, these concerns must be addressed on a case-by-case basis and cannot justify routine strip searches of all arrestees.[156]

h) The Human Identity and Confidential Relationships

The high level of protection that attaches to the human body also applies to information about a person's essential identity, including information about a person's lifestyle, intimate relations, or political or religious opinions.[157] In holding that the protections of section 8 applied to information divulged to a therapist, the Supreme Court in *R. v. Mills*[158] discussed the fundamental privacy interests attached to information about an individual's thoughts and feelings:

> This Court recognized these fundamental aspects of privacy in *R. v. Plant*, [1993] 3 S.C.R. 281, where Sopinka J., for the majority, stated, at p. 293:
>
> > In fostering the underlying values of *dignity, integrity and autonomy*, it is fitting that s. 8 of the *Charter* should seek to protect a biographical core of personal information [for example, lifestyle,

---

156 Ibid. at para. 97.
157 *R. v. Mills*, [1999] 3 S.C.R. 668 [*Mills*]; *Thomson Newspapers Ltd. v. Canada (Director of Investigation and Research, Restrictive Trade Practices Commission)*, [1990] 1 S.C.R. 425 [*Thomson Newspapers*], at 517, per LaForest J., cited with approval in *British Columbia Securities Commission v. Branch*, [1995] 2 S.C.R. 3 [*Branch*] at para. 62. Regarding religion, see *Re Church of Scientology and the Queen (No. 6)* (1987), 31 C.C.C. (3d) 449 (Ont. C.A.); *Re Walsh* (1987), 31 C.C.C. (3d) 449 (Ont. C.A.) at 534–43.
158 *Mills*, ibid. Note that *Mills* was a case in which the accused sought access to the complainant's therapy records, and did not involve police access to the accused's records.

intimate relations, political or religious opinions] which individuals in a free and democratic society would wish to maintain and control from dissemination to the state. This would include information which tends to reveal intimate details of the lifestyle and personal choices of the individual. [emphasis in *Mills*]

> That privacy is essential to maintaining relationships of trust was stressed to this Court by the eloquent submissions of many interveners in this case regarding counselling records. The therapeutic relationship is one that is characterized by trust, an element of which is confidentiality. Therefore, the protection of the complainant's reasonable expectation of privacy in her therapeutic records protects the therapeutic relationship.[159]

The protection afforded to confidential relationships receives special attention in the context of solicitor–client relationships. In order for a search power to be valid under section 8, the court must assess whether the power minimally impairs solicitor–client privilege before it can be a reasonable intrusion into the person's expectation of privacy.[160] For a more in-depth discussion of this topic, see chapter 6, "Solicitor–Client Privilege."

2) Private Conversations

Private communications[161] arguably receive more privacy protection under section 8 than the human body. Surreptitious interception of private communications will not be a constitutionally reasonable intrusion into a person's privacy interests unless the police adhere to the rigorous strictures of the *Criminal Code* sections respecting intercepting private communications. These statutory limitations include conditions that such interceptions are to be authorized only the police can establish "investigative necessity"[162] and only where it is in the best interests of the administration of justice that the authorization be granted.[163] The courts have interpreted the latter requirement to import, as a minimum requirement, the existence of reasonable and probable grounds to believe that an offence has been, or is being, com-

---

159 *Mills, ibid.* at paras. 81 and 82.
160 *Lavallee, Rackel & Heintz v. Canada (Attorney General); White, Ottenheim & Baker v. Canada (Attorney General); R. v. Fink* (2002), 167 C.C.C. (3d) 1 (S.C.C.).
161 See also chapter 7, "Standing to Challenge Investigative Orders."
162 This requirement does not apply to criminal organization or terrorism offences, or to one-party consent interceptions: *Criminal Code* ss.186(1.1) and 184.2. For a more detailed explanation, see Appendix 3, "Basic Search and Seizure Powers (*Criminal Code*)."
163 *R. v. Duarte* (1990), 53 C.C.C. (3d) 1 (S.C.C.) [*Duarte*] at 11, 19–20; see Part VI of the *Criminal Code*.

mitted and that the authorization sought will afford evidence of that offence.[164] As LaForest J. explained in *R. v. Duarte*,[165] once these requirements are fulfilled, the appropriate balance is struck in favour of law enforcement interests against the individual's interest in privacy:

> Parliament has, in my view, succeeded in striking an appropriate balance. It meets the high standard of the *Charter* which guarantees the right to be secure against unreasonable search and seizure by subjecting the power of the state to record our private communications to external restraint and requiring it to be justified by application of an objective criterion. *The reason this represents an acceptable balance is that the imposition of an external and objective criterion affords a measure of protection to any citizen whose private communications have been intercepted*. . . . [A] reasonable expectation of privacy would seem to demand that an individual may proceed on the assumption that the state may only violate this right by recording private communications on a clandestine basis when it has established to the satisfaction of a detached judicial officer that an offence has been or is being committed and that interception of private communications stands to afford evidence of the offence. [emphasis added][166]

An individual's expectation of privacy in private communications is not substantially diminished even where one party to the conversation consents to the interceptions. The Supreme Court in *Duarte*[167] rejected the "risk analysis" approach, which is based on the notion that any time a person communicates with another, the person bears the risk that the other might not keep the information confidential. The Court considered "risk analysis" to be an unsatisfactory approach to assessing whether a person who was the object of an electronic search had a reasonable expectation of privacy in the circumstances:

> The Court of Appeal was correct in stating that the expression of an idea and the assumption of the risk of disclosure are concomitant. However, it does not follow that, because in any conversation we run the risk that our interlocutor may in fact be bent on divulging our confidences, it is therefore constitutionally proper for the person to whom we speak to make a permanent electronic recording of that conversation. The *Charter*, it is accepted, proscribes the surreptitious recording by third parties of our private communications on the basis of mere suspicion alone. It would be strange

---

164 *R. v. Finlay* (1985), 23 C.C.C. (3d) 48 (Ont. C.A.) at 70; *Duarte*, above note 163 at 11.
165 *Duarte*, ibid.
166 *Ibid.* at 12–13.
167 *Ibid.*

indeed if, in the absence of a warrant requirement, instrumentalities of the state, through the medium of participant surveillance,[168] were free to conduct just such random fishing expeditions in the hope of uncovering evidence of crime, or by the same token, to satisfy any curiosity they may have as to a person's views on any matter whatsoever.[169]

Accordingly, prior judicial authorization based on reasonable grounds is required before the police can reasonably intrude on a private communication, even where the communication is recorded on consent of one party:

> To conclude, the *Charter* is not meant to protect us against a poor choice of friends. If our "friend" turns out to be an informer, and we are convicted on the strength of his testimony, that may be unfortunate for us. But the *Charter* is meant to guarantee the right to be secure against unreasonable search and seizure. A conversation with an informer does not amount to a search and seizure within the meaning of the *Charter*. Surreptitious electronic interception and recording of a private communication does.[170]

3) Surreptitious Videotaping

The privacy concerns that apply to the surreptitious interception of private communications apply equally to the surreptitious videotaping of individuals. In *R. v. Wong*,[171] police officers conducted video surveillance of a hotel room, without a warrant, in order to investigate an illegal gambling operation. The Supreme Court found the search to be an unreasonable violation of privacy of the occupant of the hotel room. Justice LaForest explained that the implications of *Duarte* were meant to embrace all existing means by which the agencies of the state can electronically intrude on the privacy of the individual, and any means which technology may place at the disposal of law enforcement authorities in the future.[172]

The Court held that the protections against unauthorized surreptitious videotaping applied equally in homes or in hotel rooms, and regardless of whether strangers were authorized to be present and whether illegal activities were engaged in, given that the Court had previously rejected "risk analysis" as an appropriate method of assessing reasonable expectation of privacy:[173]

---

168 Participant surveillance often entails the "wearing of a wire" by a party to a conversation — that party obviously consenting to its being monitored or recorded.
169 *Duarte*, above note 163 at 14–15.
170 *Ibid.* at 21.
171 *R. v. Wong* (1990), 60 C.C.C. (3d) 460 (S.C.C.) at 481.
172 *Ibid.* at 476.
173 *Ibid.* at 480–81.

Normally, the very reason we rent such rooms is to obtain a private enclave where we may conduct our activities free of uninvited scrutiny. Accordingly, I can see no conceivable reason why we should be shorn of our right to be secure from unreasonable searches in these locations which may be aptly considered to be our homes away from home.[174]

The heightened privacy interests attaching to surreptitious videotaping do not, however, extend to videotaping by hand-held cameras in areas that are not subject to a reasonable expectation of privacy, such as outside of commercial premises frequented by the general public.[175] Nor do the protections extend to non-covert videotaping during the execution of a search warrant, provided that the videotaping is a *bona fide* component of the law enforcement activity.[176] Inviting the media to the execution of a search, however, is a severe violation of a person's privacy interest in the residence.[177]

4) The Home

As noted throughout this book, the home attracts special privacy concerns. Justice Cory stated in *R. v. Silveira*:[178] "[t]here is no place on earth where persons can have a greater expectation of privacy than within their 'dwelling-house.'"[179] Almost without exception, the residents of a home enjoy heightened privacy rights, as "[a] person can expect that his home can and should be a safe castle of privacy."[180] Accordingly, a warrantless entry into a home will almost always violate a person's expectation of privacy.[181]

There are exceptions, of course, to the idea that warrantless entry by the state onto a person's residential property is a breach of privacy. The police officer's motivation for entering the property plays a central role in determining whether the person's expectation of privacy has been violated.[182] It is unlikely that the courts will find a section 8 violation when the state enters residential property with the purpose of communicating or assisting the resident or others, but privacy will be violated if the state's intent is to secure evidence against the householder. For a discussion of the former situation, see chapter 4, "Exigent Circumstances."

---

174 *Ibid.* at 481.
175 *R. v. Elzein* (1993), 82 C.C.C. (3d) 455 (Que. C.A.).
176 *R. v. Gladwin* (1997), 116 C.C.C. (3d) 471 (Ont. C.A.).
177 *R. v. West* (1997), 122 C.C.C. (3d) 218 (B.C.C.A.) at para. 22.
178 *R. v. Silveira* (1995), 97 C.C.C. (3d) 450 (S.C.C.) [*Silveira*].
179 *Ibid.* at 495.
180 *Belnavis* (S.C.C.), above note 15 at 42.
181 See, e.g., *R. v. Kokesch* (1990), 61 C.C.C. (3d) 207 (S.C.C.) [*Kokesch*] at 218–19.
182 *Evans*, above note 2 at 32–33.

a) "Implied Licence" to Knock

In *R. v. Evans*,[183] the Supreme Court recognized that, at common law, homeowners and occupants are deemed to extend an implied licence to all members of the general public who are on legitimate business, including the police, to approach the door of a residence and knock.[184] This implied licence extended to all members of the public is effectively a partial waiver of the occupant's reasonable expectation of privacy in the home.[185]

However, the Court in *Evans* held that the implied licence to knock extends no further than is required to permit convenient communication with the occupant of the dwelling,[186] and any resulting waiver of privacy from the implied licence extends no further than is required for convenient communication.[187] Thus, if the police approach the door of a residence, the implied waiver of privacy extends only to activities that are reasonably associated with the purpose of communicating with the occupant.[188] If the police are attempting to gather evidence against the occupants in approaching their door, the terms of the implied waiver have been exceeded, and the police are acting as trespassers in violation of the occupants' reasonable expectation of privacy.[189] For a broader discussion of these concepts, see chapter 4, "Exigent Circumstances."

b) Investigation of Criminal Activity for the Protection of Owners or Occupants

Similar to the implied licence to knock is the implied licence extended to police to investigate criminal activity committed against private property. In *R. v. Mulligan*,[190] the Ontario Court of Appeal held that property owners are deemed to extend an implied licence to the police to enter private property and investigate suspected criminal activity in relation to that property, provided that the activity is suspected to have been committed *against* the owner and not *by* the owner. So long as the officer has a *bona fide* suspicion that criminal activity is occurring against the premises,[191] the warrantless

---

183 *Ibid.*
184 *Ibid.* at 29–32; *Robson v. Hallett*, [1967] 2 All E.R. 407, [1967] 2 Q.B. 939 [*Robson*]; *R. v. Tricker* (1995), 96 C.C.C. (3d) 198 at 203, 8 M.V.R. (3d) 47, 21 O.R. (3d) 575 [*Tricker*].
185 *Evans*, above note 2 at 30.
186 *Ibid.*; *R. v. Bushman*, [1968] 4 C.C.C. 17, 4 C.R.N.S. 13, 63 W.W.R. 346 (B.C.C.A.).
187 *Evans*, above note 2 at 29–32; *Robson*, above note 184; *Tricker*, above note 184.
188 *Evans*, *ibid.* at 31.
189 *Ibid.*
190 *R. v. Mulligan* (2000), 142 C.C.C. (3d) 14 (Ont. C.A.) [*Mulligan*].
191 *Ibid.*

entry onto the property will likely not be an unreasonable violation of the person's expectation of privacy.[192]

c) Implied Licence Extended by Businesses to Members of the Public

The jurisprudence suggests that business owners who allow the general public into their premises are deemed to extend a general purpose licence that permits the police to enter a business to investigate. In *R. v. Fitt*,[193] the Nova Scotia Court of Appeal held:

> A business establishment that is open to the public with an implied invitation to all members of the public to enter has no reasonable expectation of privacy from having a police officer enter the area of the premises to which the public is impliedly invited: *R. v. Kouyas*, C.A.C. No. 104861, rendered December 19, 1994 N.S.C.A. (unreported) [now reported 136 N.S.R. (2d) 195, 25 W.C.B. (2d) 593].[194]

d) Gathering or Securing Evidence: "Seizing and Freezing"

As noted above, it is a violation of section 8 for the state to enter onto private property without a warrant for the purpose of gathering evidence against the resident. Accordingly, entry into a home to "freeze" the premises in order to secure and preserve evidence until a warrant can be obtained is a violation of privacy and a breach of section 8.[195] Similarly, a warrantless entry onto the perimeter of a home to gather evidence or conduct observations will violate section 8.[196]

e) Nature of Interest in the Home

The nature of a particular person's interest in the home, or area of the home, changes the scope of the expectation of privacy. For example, if the person is a minor living in the parent's home, the child may not have an expectation of privacy in his or her bedroom and belongings.[197] If a person is a trespasser on lands, or if the search occurs in an "open field," the per-

---

192 See *Mulligan*, *ibid.* at paras. 24–35, *R. v. Dreysko* (1990), 110 A.R. 317; *R. v. Hern* (1993), 149 A.R. 75. *Quaere* whether an appropriately worded sign would rescind the implied licence to enter.
193 *R. v. Fitt* (1995), 96 C.C.C. (3d) 341 (N.S.C.A.); affirmed (1996), 103 C.C.C. (3d) 224 (S.C.C.).
194 *Ibid.*
195 *Silveira*, above note 178.
196 *Kokesch*, above note 181; *R. v. Plant* (1993), 84 C.C.C. (3d) 203 (S.C.C.) [*Plant*]; *R. v. Wiley* (1993), 84 C.C.C. (3d) 161 (S.C.C.) [*Wiley*]; *R. v. Grant* (1993), 84 C.C.C. (3d) 173 (S.C.C.) [*Grant*].
197 *R. v. F.(D.M.)* (2000), 139 C.C.C. (3d) 144 (Alta. C.A.).

son will either have no expectation of privacy,[198] or at most, a reduced expectation of privacy. Even if the person is an owner of the property, if the owner is not a resident, but merely a landlord, the owner will likely not have an expectation of privacy.[199] A tenant of an apartment building will likely not have an expectation of privacy in common hallways of an apartment building,[200] unless the police use intrusive techniques (like key-hole peeping) or take unusual advantage of their presence in a common area.[201] Note, however, that the Ontario Court of Appeal found a breach of section 8 where the police conducted observations from the side yard of an apartment building without authorization, despite the fact that the tenant had no ability to control access to that area of the property.[202]

f) Area of the Home as Determinative of Expectation of Privacy

Despite the home yielding a heightened expectation of privacy for its residents, there is some support for the suggestion that not all areas of the home enjoy the same level of privacy. For example, a person might enjoy a reduced expectation of privacy in his or her backyard.[203] In *R. v. Puskas*,[204] the Ontario Court of Appeal found a reduced level of privacy in the backyard, in that case, resulting from the fact that the marijuana plants Mr. Puskas was growing in the backyard were in plain view of anyone who would venture into the backyard for legitimate reasons, such as sales or delivery people.[205] The Court also noted that these plants would have been readily observable from the air.[206]

---

198 *R. v. Lauda* (1998), 122 C.C.C. (3d) 74 (Ont. C.A.) at 88, aff'd, (1998), 129 C.C.C. (3d) 225 (S.C.C.) at 226.
199 *Pugliese*, above note 8.
200 *R. v. Laurin* (1997), 113 C.C.C. (3d) 519 (Ont. C.A.) [*Laurin*] at 354–55; *R. v. Joyal* (1995), 43 C.R. (4th) 317 (Que. C.A.).
201 *Laurin, ibid.* at 354–55; Wayne R. LaFave, *Search and Seizure: A Treatise of the Fourth Amendment*, 3d ed. (St. Paul, MN: West Publishing Co., 1996) 492–93; *R. v. Sandhu* (1993), 82 C.C.C. (3d) 236 (B.C.C.A.).
202 *Laurin, ibid.* at 532.
203 *R. v. Puskas* (1997), 120 C.C.C. (3d) 548 (Ont. C.A.).
204 *Ibid.* at 554.
205 *Ibid.* While "sales or delivery people" might seem a bit of stretch, recall that telephone and electrical power utilities generally retain easements over private property for system maintenance.
206 *Ibid.* Note, however, the case of *R. v. Kelly* (1999), 169 D.L.R. (4th) 720 (N.B.C.A.), which held that warrantless observations in air space from a low-flying plane was a violation of s. 8. See "When Police Use 'Advanced Technologies,'" later in this chapter.

The decision in *Puskas* must, however, be contrasted with the Supreme Court's decisions in *R. v. Kokesch*,[207] *R. v. Grant*,[208] *R. v. Plant*,[209] and *R. v. Wiley*,[210] each of which found violations of section 8 for warrantless observations made from the perimeter of a residential property. Accordingly, in light of the perimeter search jurisprudence, and other recent jurisprudence from the courts extending heightened privacy interests to heat emissions and air space above the home (each discussed in the following section), it is more likely than not that a court would find a breach of privacy for illegal entries onto private property, regardless of the exact location on the property.

5) When the Police Use "Advanced Technologies": FLIR, Low-flying Planes, and Trained Dogs

There appears to be a general rule that an individual has no reasonable expectation of privacy with regard to things that can be detected by the unaided senses of either a police officer or a member of the general public.[211] However, when the police wish to use "advanced technologies" or other specialized aids to investigate crime, it is necessary to engage in a more detailed analysis of whether the person's privacy will be invaded unreasonably by the use of that particular technology.

The state's ability to use advanced investigative technologies has been clarified by the Supreme Court's recent decision in *R. v. Tessling*.[212] Prior to the *Tessling* decison, the jurisprudence on whether police could use certain investigative technologies without a warrant was inconsistent. Certain decisions severely restricted the use of advanced technology without a warrant[213] (broadly interpreting "technology" and giving a wide scope to privacy interests[214]). Others took a narrower view of how far privacy interests extend, particularly if the information captured was exposed to the public at some level, and did not reveal intimate details.[215] The latter approach is the one adopted by the Supreme Court in *Tessling*. Although the *Tessling* case dealt specifical-

---

207 *Kokesch*, above note 181.
208 *Grant*, above note 196.
209 *Plant*, above note 196.
210 *Wiley*, above note 196.
211 This is something of an over-simplification. Generally speaking, the investigator must be lawfully situated when he or she detects the thing. This rule takes its clearest form in the plain view doctrine; see Chapter 8, "The Plain View Doctrine."
212 2004 SCC 67 [*Tessling* SCC], rev'g (2003), 171 C.C.C. (3d) 361 (Ont. C.A.) [*Tessling* CA].
213 *R. v. Kelly*, below note 234; *Tessling* CA, *ibid*.
214 *R. v. Lam*, [2003] A.J. 811 (C.A.) [*Lam*].
215 *R. v. Hutchings* (1996), 111 C.C.C. (3d) 215 (B.C. C.A.), leave refused [1997] S.C.C.A. No. 21 [*Hutchings*]; *R. v. Mercer*, [2004] A.J. No. 634 (Prov. Ct.).

ly with the warrantless use of Forward-Looking Infrared (FLIR) technology, we believe that the Court's approach to resolving the issue applies equally to other advanced technologies used by the state. In *Tessling*, the Court examined whether the warrantless use of FLIR technology on a home violated the occupant's reasonable expectation of privacy (see the section on FLIR, below). In determining whether Mr. Tessling had a reasonable expectation of privacy barring the warrantless use of FLIR technology over his home, the Supreme Court employed the familiar *R. v. Edwards* "totality of the circumstances" test. However, the Court incorporated into the *Edwards* analysis a tailored set of factors that it considered appropriate for determining whether privacy interests existed in the particular circumstance:

1. What was the subject matter of the FLIR image?
2. Did the respondent have a direct interest in the subject matter of the FLIR image?
3. Did the respondent have a *subjective* expectation of privacy in the subject matter of the FLIR image?
4. If so, was the expectation *objectively* reasonable? In this respect, regard must be had to:
    a. the place where the alleged "search" occurred;
    b. whether the subject matter was in public view;
    c. whether the subject matter had been abandoned;
    d. whether the information was already in the hands of third parties; If so, was it subject to an obligation of confidentiality?
    e. whether the police technique was intrusive in relation to the privacy interest;
    f. whether the use of surveillance technology was itself objectively unreasonable;
    g. whether the FLIR heat profile exposed any intimate details of the respondent's lifestyle, or information of a biographical nature.[216]

The Court's approach to the reasonableness of the use of the FLIR technology is appropriate for, and easily transferable to, questions of whether other technologies violate privacy interests. It appears from the Court's statement of the relevant issues above, that advanced technologies ought to be evaluated on their own merits and assessed for their particular, immediate impact on intimate or biographical details of an individual. In the sections below, we examine in more detail how Canadian courts have approached advanced investigative technologies in different contexts, in particular with respect to the use of FLIR, aerial surveillance, and drug-detection dogs.

---

216 *Tessling* SCC, above note 212 at para. 32.

a) FLIR

As a consequence of the Supreme Court's decision in *Tessling*,[217] individuals do not have a reasonable expectation of privacy in the heat emissions emanating from their residences, and the police will not require a warrant to use FLIR to capture and analyze residential heat emissions.[218]

Mr. Tessling was suspected of carrying on a marijuana grow operation in his home. Large-scale use of "grow-lamps" and the maintenance of a greenhouse environment to cultivate marijuana generate a large amount of heat energy, which can be detected with a FLIR device. The Supreme Court of Canada described FLIR technology as follows:

> Thermal infrared systems are often used to conduct "structure profiles." These devices are passive instruments which are sensitive to only thermal surface radiant temperature. The devices do not see into, or through structures. The FLIR system detects only energy which is radiated from the outside surface of an object. Internal heat which is transmitted to the outside surface of an object is detectable. This device ... is essentially a camera that takes photographs of heat instead of light ... The rooms of marijuana growing operations with halide lights are warmer than the average room in a residence. The walls of these rooms emanate this heat to the outside, and are therefore detectable by the FLIR. Heat in a residence is usually evenly distributed throughout the building's exterior. By comparing the pattern of heat emanating from the structure, it is possible to detect patterns of heat showing rooms or sections of a structure that may be housing the marijuana growing operation.[219]

The Ontario Court of Appeal in *Tessling*[220] held that an individual had a reasonable expectation of privacy in the heat emissions emanating from his or her residence, and it found that Mr. Tessling's privacy rights were violated. The Court of Appeal's reason stood on two basic premises: first, despite the fact that the thermal imaging takes place outside the home, FLIR technology reveals information about activities taking place within the home; second, the FLIR device reveals information that could not be otherwise observed or quantified. The court found, therefore, that the use of FLIR was a significant intrusion into the privacy of the home and should be unlawful in the absence of a warrant.[221] Indeed, the breach of privacy in the heat emis-

---

217 *Tessling* SCC, above note 212.
218 For reasons that will be discussed below, this general rule may change if the FLIR technology becomes more sophisticated.
219 *Tessling* SCC, above note 212 at para. 34.
220 *Tessling* CA, above note 212.
221 *Ibid.* at para. 65.

sions was deemed by the Court of Appeal to be so serious that it could not survive the test for exclusion of evidence under section 24(2) of the *Charter*. The court viewed the intrusion as "almost Orwellian in its theoretical capacity" and disproportionate to the seriousness of the offence of production of marijuana.[222]

The Court of Appeal's decision accorded with the United States Supreme Court's decision in *Kyollo v. United States*,[223] which held that the warrantless use of FLIR technology violated the Fourth Amendment protections against unreasonable search and seizure[224] because it was a device not in general public use, and it allowed exploration of private details of home life unknowable in the absence of the technology.

However, the Court of Appeal's decision in *Tessling* was reversed by the Supreme Court of Canada. The Supreme Court found that, although the FLIR technology implicated both the informational sphere of privacy (regarding the individual's activities) and the territorial sphere of privacy (since the activities took place at the home), the use of the technology was *not* equivalent to a search of a home:

> The distinction between informational and territorial privacy is of some assistance in drawing the "reasonableness" line in the factual situation before the Court. Whereas Abella J.A. treated the FLIR imaging as *equivalent* to a search *of* the home, and thus "worthy of the state's highest respect" (at para. 33), I think it is more accurately characterized as an external search for information *about* the home which may or may not be capable of giving rise to an inference *about* what was actually going on inside, depending on what other information is available.[225]

It is essential to note, however, that the Supreme Court based its decision on the "relative crudity" of presently available FLIR technology. The Supreme Court rejected the Court of Appeal's approach to analysing the use of investigative technology, which took into consideration the foreseeable uses of the technology and the potential for technological advances. While the Court of Appeal considered FLIR "almost Orwellian in its theoretical

---

222 *Ibid.* at paras. 77–82.
223 121 S.Ct. 2038. (2001)
224 The Fourth Amendment to the U.S. Bill of Rights provides:

> The right of the people to be secure in their persons, houses, papers, and effects, against unreasonable searches and seizures, shall not be violated, and no Warrants shall issue, but upon probable cause, supported by Oath or affirmation, and particularly describing the place to be searched, and the persons or things to be seized.

225 *Tessling* SCC, above note 212 at para. 27.

capacity"[226] to invade privacy, the Supreme Court focussed on the actual, not the theoretical, capacity of the technology:

> In my view, with respect, the reasonableness line has to be determined by looking at the information generated by *existing* FLIR technology, and then evaluating its impact on a reasonable privacy interest. If, as expected, the capability of FLIR and other technologies will improve and the nature and quality of the information hereafter changes, it will be a different case, and the courts will have to deal with its privacy implications at that time in light of the facts as they then exist.[227]

In focussing exclusively on the current capacities of technology, and the use to which it was actually put in the case under consideration, the Supreme Court moved away from the approach suggested by the cases of *R. v. Wong* and *R. v. Duarte*:

> Counsel for the respondent of course views these matters somewhat differently. He points to the observation of La Forest J. in *R. v. Wong*, [1990] 3 S.C.R. 36, a case dealing with surveillance by *video* camera, at pp. 43–44:
>
>> In *Duarte* [[1990] 1 S.C.R. 30], this Court held that unauthorized electronic *audio* surveillance violates s. 8 of the *Charter*. It would be wrong to limit the implications of that decision to that particular technology. Rather what the Court said in *Duarte* must be held to embrace all existing means by which the agencies of the state can electronically intrude on the privacy of the individual, and any means which technology places at the disposal of law enforcement authorities in the future. [Emphasis in original.]
>
> *I do not read this passage as entrenching a free-standing prohibition on electronic or other technologies without a warrant. The question is: does FLIR technology in fact intrude on the reasonable sphere of privacy of an individual?* [Italic emphasis added; underlined emphasis in original.][228]

As noted in the section above, the Supreme Court applied the "totality of the circumstances" test from *R. v. Edwards* and concluded that Mr. Tessling had no expectation of privacy in the heat emissions from his home. The Court incorporated a specially tailored set of factors (set out in the section above) into this analysis. The Court's key findings relating to the absence of a privacy interest were as follows:

---

226 *Tessling* CA, above note 212 at para. 79.
227 *Tessling* SCC, above note 212 at para. 29.
228 *Ibid.* at para 30.

- The emissions information captured by the FLIR indicated only the patterns of heat emitted different locations in the home relative to each other. The images on their own could not permit inferences about the precise activity generating the heat, nor could they be the sole grounds in support of a search warrant.[229]
- The heat emissions detected by FLIR are on the external surface of the building, and are in that sense exposed to the public (although the FLIR device is required to detect them). The technology did not allow investigators to "see" inside the home.[230]
- The information generated by FLIR imaging did not touch on "'a biographical core of personal information,'" nor does it "'ten[d] to reveal intimate details of [his] lifestyle'" and as such was not objectively unreasonable.[231]

It would appear from the foregoing discussion, then, that the police are free to use FLIR technology in its current format, and probably other versions of the technology, without a warrant, provided that the investigative technique does not reveal core biographical information about a person and so long as the technology does not permit the police to "see" inside a person's home.[232]

As noted above, prior to the Supreme Court's decision in *Tessling*, the jurisprudential trend seemed to be towards finding that a warrant would be required when the police wish to use "advanced technology" to facilitate the gathering evidence or making of observations that would be impossible otherwise.[233] However, all of the earlier jurisprudence in this area must now be relied upon with caution, in light of the contrary approach taken by the Supreme Court in *R. v. Tessling*.

b) Aerial Surveillance

In *R. v. Kelly*,[234] the New Brunswick Court of Appeal held that warantless low-level aerial surveillance of a residential lot (conducted from a helicopter at thirty feet above ground) infringed the occupant's reasonable expectation of privacy. The court found that lawful occupants of land have a reasonable expectation of privacy in all open spaces within the residential lot, which protects them against the lawful search of both terrestrial and aerial spaces.[235]

---

229 *Ibid.* at para. 36.
230 *Ibid.* at para. 47.
231 *Ibid.* at para. 62.
232 See also *Hutchings*, above note 215, where the B.C.C.A. found no expectation of privacy in heat emissions from a barn, using the same "core biographical information" approach as the Supreme Court did in *Tessling*.
233 See, for example, *Tessling* SCC, above note 212; *Lam*, above note 214.
234 (1999), 169 D.L.R. (4th) 720 (N.B.C.A.).
235 *Ibid.* at paras. 50–53; contrast the protections for residential property recognized by Canadian courts with the United States Supreme Court decision in *Dow Chemi-*

This decision may still be sound notwithstanding the Supreme Court's decision in *Tessling*. This is because investigators may be able to make aerial observations that intrude into a protected sphere of privacy. However, note that FLIR readings are often taken from the air, and that a FLIR-equipped airplane was in fact used on Mr. Tessling's home, and the Supreme Court did not disapprove of that practice in its decision. Future cases in this area may focus on the extent of the privacy interest in a person's backyard or other similarly exposed areas.[236]

c) Drug-Detection Dogs

The use of drug-detection dogs for criminal investigation has received inconsistent treatment from the courts. However, many of the cases in which courts found that the warrantless use of a drug-dog was an unreasonable intrusion into privacy were rendered before the Supreme Court's decision in *Tessling*. The *Tessling* case may have an important effect on future cases.

In *R. v. Lam*,[237] the Alberta Court of Appeal found that the warrantless use of a trained drug-detection dog to detect the smell of drugs emanating from an area in which a person had a reasonable expectation of privacy constituted an unreasonable search. In that case, officers were conducting an investigation at the Calgary Bus Terminal to locate drugs being transported on buses. The officers were aided by a trained drug-detection dog. Officers became suspicious of two bus passengers, Lam and Dinh, who were passing through Calgary on route to Toronto. The officers and the dog followed Lam and Dinh to the locker area of the station. The dog indicated that it detected the scent of drugs at the locker where Dinh had stored her luggage. The officers then searched all the bags in the suspects' possession and within the locker, and found over $16,000 in cash, nearly four kilograms of marijuana, and one gram of heroin.

The Alberta Court of Appeal upheld the trial judge's finding that the officers' use of the drug dog constituted an unreasonable violation of Dinh's privacy; the use of the dog's sense of smell was "designed to see inside the locker."[238] This finding extended the Ontario Court of Appeal's reasoning in *Tessling* that if the police (without a warrant) used technology not in common use by the general population, then the use of that technique would constitute an unreasonable search:

---

cal Co. v. United States, 476 U.S. 227 (1986), which held that there is no expectation of privacy in the aerial space over business premises.
236 See, for example, *R. v. Puskas*, above note 203.
237 *Lam*, above note 214.
238 *Lam*, ibid. at para. 22.

I agree with the position taken by the Ontario Court of Appeal in *Tessling*, *supra*, and the majority of the United States Supreme Court in *Kyllo*, *supra*. The police were intending, through the use of the police dog, to see inside Dinh's suitcase — sheltered, as it was, by the locker. If the dog indicated drugs were present, it was the further intention of the police, as the facts proved, to arrest the respondent and conduct further searches on arrest. This was not a case where the police were present for some other lawful purpose and happened upon the smell. In my view, the police cannot deny the respondent's privacy interest in either her suitcase, or her locker, by saying they were only interested in the smell that might be drifting into the public area.

Furthermore, *by using the dog-sniff to discover what was within the bag inside the locker, the police were conducting a proscribed warrantless search because they were using a technique that enabled them to see what would have remained private were they left to rely on their ordinary senses.* [Emphasis added.][239]

In the court's view, there was no difference between the use of FLIR technology and the use of a trained dog, as both techniques allowed the police to go beyond the capabilities of the ordinary human senses:

If it is improper for the police to invade a privacy interest using a technique or device that goes beyond enhancing the human senses,[240] it does not matter whether it is a sophisticated technological FLIR device or a police dog with an acute sense of smell. The effect is the same.[241]

The Alberta Court of Appeal based its decision that the warrantless use of the dog constituted a constitutionally prohibited search in part on the police's *intention* to use the dog to find evidence. In the absence of reasonable grounds, the police were not entitled to approach a bus station locker[242] for the purpose of investigating the user:

Applying these principles to the facts here, there is no question that, along with the Jetway Unit, Constable Bouey was in the bus depot with the police dog in order to search for drugs. The trial judge found that Constable

---

239 *Ibid.* at paras. 33 and 34.
240 *Quaere* whether the phrase "*beyond* enhancing the human senses" implies that, for example, binoculars are constitutionally different from FLIR or chemical swabs for explosive residue. Binoculars enhance the human sense of sight; FLIR goes beyond enhancing any human sense and allows humans to "see" heat emissions.
241 *Lam*, above note 214 at para. 35. Of course, the converse is not necessarily true. Notwithstanding the Supreme Court's *Tessling* decision, warrantless drug-dog searches may still be unlawful.
242 A bus station locker, incidentally, is located in what could be described as the paradigmatic example of a *public place* that, unlike a *home*, requires no special invitation or authorization to enter.

Bouey did not have any grounds upon which to conduct the sniff-searches with the dog, first outside, and then inside, the locker.

. . .

It follows, therefore, consistent with the logic set out by Sopinka J. in *Evans* and *Kokesch*, that the dog-sniff search of the locker was a section 8 search. The police had nothing more than suspicion when Constable Bouey approached the locker with the police dog, and the purpose of the dog-sniff was to determine what was in the bag inside the locker. In these circumstances, the police were obliged to leave her alone.[243]

By contrast, there may not be an expectation of privacy against warrantless drug-dog searches where the odours do not emanate from a private place. In *R. v. Mercer*,[244] Justice Daniel of the Alberta Provincial Court found that there was no expectation of privacy against police dogs sniffing bags left unattended in a bus terminal:

> Section 8 is a personal right, protecting people and not places. It does not protect the air in a public place over which an accused has no ownership interest or control. Written notice that luggage was subject to investigation upon demand had been given. The accused was not present when the dog sniff took place nor was he exercising any degree of proximate care, custody or control over his luggage or the area in which he had placed it. While the police had an intention to have the dog sniff the air to detect illegal drugs, the area they intended to explore was not the accused's person, his private home, an approach to his private home, his car in which he had been riding or a locker over which he exercised any degree of ownership or control. Rather, it was a very public loading area in a large urban bus station.[245]

In addition to distinguishing baggage held in a bus station locker from unattended baggage within the bus station, Justice Daniel was also of the view that the need to ensure the physical security of transportation hubs means that privacy interests are generally lower in train or bus stations, just as they are diminished in airports:

> An argument has also been advanced that there is a higher expectation of privacy at a train or bus station as opposed to an airport. Just because Canadians have not yet had the Japanese, Spanish or Israeli experiences [with terrorist attacks on transportation hubs] first hand, does not mean there should be any enhanced expectation of privacy at train or bus terminals in Canada. This is particularly so given that the security concerns are just as

---

243 *Lam*, above note 214 at paras. 48 and 49.
244 (2004), A.J. No. 634 (Prov. Ct.)
245 *Ibid.* at para. 53.

real and the Notice posted [warning, among other things that the bus company would remove baggage left unattended] signals the same search potential and safety concerns as at airports. I find this argument has no merit.[246]

It should be recalled that the reasonableness of an expectation of privacy will depend on the context. While a warrantless sniff search of unattended baggage may be reasonable in some circumstances, that may not always be the case. In *R. v. A.M.*,[247] police used a drug dog on students' bags that were left unattended in a school gymnasium. The officers had no reasonable grounds to believe that any particular student possessed drugs, or that drugs were in any particular bag. Justice Hornblower of the Ontario Court of Justice found that such a search constituted a violation of section 8. Unfortunately, the Court did not provide a detailed analysis of why the dog-sniff activity itself constituted a search, or why the students had a reasonable expectation of privacy in the unattended bags.

The reasoning in the drug-dog cases discussed above must be approached with caution; all were decided before the Supreme Court's decision in *Tessling*, and Lam in particular relied heavily upon the *Tessling* appellate decision in its finding that there was an expectation of privacy in the drug odours. On a contextual analysis, such as the one used by the Supreme Court in *Tessling*, a court may be far more likely to find that drug odours emanating from a private place into a public place are exposed to the public, and that the information gathered therefrom is not biographical or similarly important.

6) At the Border

Individuals have a lower expectation of privacy at border crossings, and they receive correspondingly lower levels of protection against searches and seizures by the government, even with respect to searches of the body.[248] See the discussion of searches of the body earlier in this chapter in relation to the conduct of strip searches and body-cavity searches. See also chapter 4, "Border Control: Security and Sovereignty Interests."

7) In Luggage and Parcels in Transit

There is some debate as to whether there is a reduced expectation of privacy for passengers on domestic flights, or goods carried on such flights. In *R. v. Truong*,[249] the British Columbia Court of Appeal held that a seizure of

---

246 *Ibid.* at para. 36.
247 [2004] O.J. No. 2716 (C.J.).
248 *Simmons*, above note 52.
249 *R. v. Truong* (2002), 168 C.C.C. (3d) 132 (B.C.C.A.) [*Truong*].

baggage from a domestic flight, on the basis of mere suspicion, was an unreasonable search. While legislative authority exists for searches and seizures on domestic flights in relation to security matters,[250] the majority of the Court found that the authority does not extend to searches for contraband that does not directly impact flight safety, such as narcotics.[251] In dissent, Newbury J.A. held that such searches do not violate section 8, as the power to search for security reasons diminishes the reasonable expectation of privacy in luggage, and because in this case, the police had reason to suspect the passenger was carrying contraband.[252]

Justice Newbury's dissenting view accords with the position of Doherty J.A. in *R. v. Lewis*,[253] as to a lowered expectation of privacy in baggage, even in the domestic context:

> I cannot agree . . . that the respondent's expectation of privacy was not affected by the fact that he was in the airport and intending to board an airplane. *The respondent had to know that his luggage could be examined and searched at random by state authorities for security purposes* before it was placed or taken on the airplane. While the security personnel would be looking for things which might affect the safety of the air travellers and the police were looking for cocaine, I do not see why the reason for the search would materially affect the respondent's privacy expectation in the circumstances of this case. [Emphasis added.][254]

8) At School

Students have a markedly reduced expectation of privacy at school.[255] In *R. v. M.(M.R.)*,[256] the Supreme Court held that although a student would at least subjectively have a high expectation of privacy in relation to a search of the person, the reasonableness of that expectation was significantly dimin-

---

250 *Aeronautics Act* R.S.C. 1985, c. A-2, s. 47 and regulations thereunder.
251 See also *R. v. Fry* (1999), 142 C.C.C. (3d) 166 (Nfld. C.A.), where the majority held that the seizure of package couriered by air, based solely on a "hunch" was unreasonable.
252 *Truong*, above note 239 at paras. 23–26; see also *R. v. Matthiesen* (1999), 133 C.C.C. (3d) 93 (Alta. C.A.) at para. 24; *R. v. Daley* (2001), 156 C.C.C. (3d) 225 (Alta. C.A.) at para. 49.
253 *R. v. Lewis* (1998), 122 C.C.C. (3d) 481 (Ont. C.A.) at para. 40.
254 *Ibid*. See also *Mercer*, above note 236.
255 This was a case involving a "public school" and the respondent conceded that the *Charter* applied. *Quaere* whether similar *Charter* protections would apply in a private school situation.
256 *R. v. M.(M.R.)* (1998), 129 C.C.C. (3d) 361 (S.C.C.).

ished because students are aware of, and must accept, school officials' responsibilities for maintaining order and safety:

> [T]he reasonable expectation of privacy, although it exists, may be diminished in some circumstances, and this will influence the analysis of s. 8 and a consideration of what constitutes an unreasonable search or seizure. For example, it has been found that individuals have a lesser expectation of privacy at border crossings, because they know they may be subject to questioning and searches to enforce customs laws. . . . Similarly, the reasonable expectation of privacy of a student in attendance at a school is certainly less than it would be in other circumstances. Students know that their teachers and other school authorities are responsible for providing a safe environment and maintaining order and discipline in the school. They must know that this may sometimes require searches of students and their personal effects and the seizure of prohibited items. It would not be reasonable for a student to expect to be free from such searches. A student's reasonable expectation of privacy in the school environment is therefore significantly diminished.[257]

Coupled with the duty of school officials to ensure student safety, this reduced expectation of privacy results in a standard of reasonableness for intrusions on privacy markedly reduced from the usual *Hunter v. Southam* criteria, provided that the school is acting in the scope of its responsibilities and not acting as an agent of the police.[258] The Court summarized the approach to the assessment of reasonableness of a search at school as follows:[259]

1. A warrant is not essential in order to conduct a search of a student by a school authority.
2. The school authority must have reasonable grounds to believe that there has been a breach of school regulations or discipline and that a search of a student would reveal evidence of that breach.
3. School authorities will be in the best position to assess information given to them and relate it to the situation existing in their school. Courts should recognize the preferred position of school authorities to determine if reasonable grounds existed for the search.
4. The following may constitute reasonable grounds in this context: information received from one student considered to be credible, information received from more than one student, a teacher's or prin-

---

257 *Ibid.* at para. 33.
258 *Ibid.* at paras. 55–56. See also the discussion of what constitutes a "search" in chapter 2.
259 *Ibid.* at paras. 44–49.

cipal's own observations, or any combination of these pieces of information which the relevant authority considers to be credible. The compelling nature of the information and the credibility of these or other sources must be assessed by the school authority in the context of the circumstances existing at the particular school.[260]

Notwithstanding the Supreme Court's sanction of the warrantless search of the person in *M.(M.R.)*, the Court left open the possibility that a student could be afforded greater protections against searches in different factual circumstances:

> In some cases a court may be required to determine with greater precision whether and to what extent a student has a reasonable expectation of privacy in the location of the search. In the case of locker searches, for example, courts have engaged in more detailed factual analyses to determine the degree of control that school authorities maintain over the lockers and the effect that this may have on the reasonable expectation of privacy and the reasonableness of the search (see, for example, *Zamora v. Pomeroy*, 639 F.2d 662 (1981); *People v. Overton*, 301 N.Y.S.2d 479 (1969); *State in Interest of T.L.O. v. Engerud*, 94 N.J. 331 (1983), affirmed 469 U.S. 325 (1985) sub nom. *New Jersey v. T.L.O.* Here [in addition to the search of the person] there was a search of the appellant's locker. However, since no evidence was found there, the lawfulness of that search is not in issue. For the purposes of these reasons the findings that the appellant did have a reasonable expectation of privacy with respect to his person, but that he would have reasonably expected a lesser degree of privacy in a school environment, will suffice. They may be taken into account in defining the standard to be applied to the search of the appellant.[261]

9) In Garbage and Abandoned Property

An individual does not generally have an expectation of privacy in abandoned property, including garbage, if left at the side of the road, or in a dumpster, or discarded by other means, including during police pursuit;[262] essentially, the person is deemed to have abandoned their privacy interest in the items contained within the trash at the time it was discarded.[263]

---

260 *Ibid.* at para. 50.
261 *Ibid.* at para. 34. See also *A.M.*, above note 235.
262 *Stillman*, above note 45 at para. 62; *R. v. Kennedy* (1996), 95 O.A.C. 321, (1996), O.J. No. 4401 at paras. 4 and 5; *R. v. Krist* (1995), 100 C.C.C. (3d) 58 (B.C.C.A.) [*Krist*] at para. 26; *R. v. Poitras*, [1998] O.J. No. 5628 (Gen. Div.); *R. v. Collins* (1999), 133 C.C.C. (3d) 8 (Nfld. C.A.).
263 *Krist, ibid.* at paras. 25–27.

The view that there can be no reasonable expectation of privacy in garbage accords with the United States Supreme Court's decision in *California v. Greenwood*,[264] which held there cannot be any objectively reasonable privacy interest in items abandoned at the roadside that are available for any member of the public to access:

> It may well be that respondents did not expect that the contents of their garbage bags would become known to the police or other members of the public. An expectation of privacy does not give rise to Fourth Amendment protection, however, unless society is prepared to accept that expectation as objectively reasonable.
>
> Here, we conclude that respondents exposed their garbage to the public sufficiently to defeat their claim to Fourth Amendment protection. It is common knowledge that plastic garbage bags left on or at the side of a public street are readily accessible to animals, children, scavengers, snoops, and other members of the public. See *Krivda*, 5 Cal 3d, at 367, 486 P2d, at 1269. Moreover, the respondents placed their refuse at the curb for the express purpose of conveying it to a third party, the trash collector, who might himself have sorted through respondents' trash or permitted others, such as the police, to do so. Accordingly, having deposited their garbage "in an area particularly suited for public inspection and, in a manner of speaking, public consumption, for the express purpose of having strangers take it," *United States v. Reicherter*, 647 F2d 397, 399 (CA3 1981), respondents could have had no reasonable expectation of privacy in the inculpatory items that they discarded.[265]

The dissenting opinion of Brennan J. in *Greenwood* accepted that a reasonable expectation of privacy exists in trash. It has been argued (unsuccessfully in *Krist*[266]) that Brennan J.'s dissent more accurately reflects the state of Canadian jurisprudence, since in *Duarte* the Supreme Court rejected the "risk analysis" approach to determining expectations of privacy. As Brennan J. explained:

> A single bag of trash testifies eloquently to the eating, reading, and recreational habits of the person who produced it. A search of trash, like a search of the bedroom, can relate intimate details about sexual practices, health, and personal hygiene. Like rifling through desk drawers or intercepting phone calls, rummaging through trash can divulge the target's financial and professional status, political affiliations and inclinations, private thoughts, personal relationships, and romantic interests. It cannot be

---

264 *California v. Greenwood*, 486 U.S. 35, 100 L.Ed.2d 30 (1988) [*Greenwood*].
265 *Ibid.* at 36–37.
266 *Krist*, above note 262.

doubted that a sealed trash bag harbors telling evidence of the "intimate activity associated with the 'sanctity of a man's home and the privacies of life,'" which the Fourth Amendment is designed to protect.[267]

The Supreme Court of Canada appears to have accepted the idea that discarding items in the trash results in a loss of privacy, provided that the person is not in custody when the items are discarded.[268] The Court could retreat from this position and become more closely aligned with Brennan J.'s dissenting opinion, especially for example if the Supreme Court upholds the Ontario Court of Appeal's decision in *R. v. Tessling* (which found an expectation of privacy in heat emanating from a home).[269]

Any finding that the person has abandoned his or her property must, of course, be supported by objectively reasonable evidence. The Supreme Court of Canada held in *R. v. Law*[270] that it was not reasonable to conclude that a person had abandoned something if it had been stolen, and recovered by police. As the Court explained, any waiver of privacy would be limited to certain necessary procedures for the investigation of the theft:

> I conclude the police's conduct in this case amounted to a search within the meaning of s. 8 of the *Charter*. While a reasonable accused would have expected a certain degree of state intrusion into his stolen safe — a fingerprint analysis, a security check, an investigation of content for the purpose of identifying the perpetrator of the theft — he would otherwise have expected the contents of the safe to remain private. Moreover, to the extent the officer was driven by another law enforcement objective (namely, investigation of GST violations), he lacked reasonable and probable grounds to suspect the appellants. Such conduct is precisely what the search warrant process is meant to prevent.[271]

A notable exception to the lack of privacy in garbage and abandoned property may be found in situations where waste is created by medical procedures. In *R. v. Dorfer*,[272] the British Columbia Court of Appeal explained

---

267 *Greenwood*, above note 264 at 43.
268 See *Stillman* above note 45 at para. 62. The Supreme Court in *Stillman* did leave open the possibility that a court could find, in appropriate circumstances, that an accused in custody had abandoned items and relinquish any privacy interest in them; however, the threshold of proving such an abandonment would likely be very high, given that the Court found that an accused in custody had little choice in the manner of disposal or any ability to prevent the seizure of such items by the state.
269 *Tessling*, above note 212.
270 *Law*, above note 30.
271 *Ibid.* at para. 28.
272 *Dorfer*, above note 50.

that a person can reasonably expect medical personnel not be acting in concert with the authorities to incriminate him or her as a result of medical procedures.[273] The provision of medical waste to the police in such circumstances may accordingly constitute a violation of section 8. Although the accused in *Dorfer* was in custody (and thus the beneficiary of heightened protections of privacy in garbage), persons who are not in custody probably also can expect a higher level of protection from state intrusion into medical waste in such circumstances, due to the lack of choice in creating the waste and the heightened privacy interest in information about the body.

As discussed above in relation to bodily samples found in discarded tissue collected by police for DNA analysis, there is a heightened expectation of privacy that may apply to garbage created in custodial contexts (a problem not shared by the general public, who may shred or burn confidential garbage if they so choose).[274] Given the difficulty faced by inmates in discarding items without having their effects scrutinized, special considerations may apply to all garbage discarded while in custody.

10) In Motor Vehicles

The courts have tended to find a very limited expectation of privacy with respect to searches occurring in motor vehicles. Individuals have *no* expectation of privacy in relation to certain aspects of their operation of a motor vehicle. For example, drivers of motor vehicles cannot reasonably expect to keep confidential any licence, registration or other documentation related to their entitlement to drive that motor vehicle.[275] This absence of privacy exists however only with respect to licensing and safety issues. Drivers can reasonably expect some level of privacy with respect to agents of the state entering their vehicle and examining its contents, for example.[276] Passengers, however, generally have a more difficult time to convince courts that they have an expectation of privacy in motor vehicle; typically, they may need to establish some greater connection to the vehicle than temporary occupancy, or perhaps an expectation of privacy in the items seized from the car.[277]

---

273   *Ibid.* at para. 34. Note, however, that police may be able to obtain a warrant for information or evidence held by medical personnel.
274   *Stillman*, above note 45 at 348.
275   *Belnavis*, above note 15 at 208 (Ont. C.A.); *R. v. Hufsky* (1988), 40 C.C.C. (3d) 398 (S.C.C.) at 410 [*Hufsky*].
276   *Ibid.*
277   See *Belnavis*, above note 15 (passenger asserted no evidentiary basis for privacy in car or goods); *R. v. Hyatt* (2003), 171 C.C.C. (3d) 409 (B.C.C.A.) (passengers had no expectation of privacy in items contained in glove box).

Even when a person can claim an expectation of privacy in a motor vehicle, it is a *reduced* expectation. In *R. v. Belnavis*,[278] Cory J. explained:

> [T]he expectation of privacy in a vehicle cannot be as high as that in a home or office:
>
>> Society . . . requires and expects protection from drunken drivers, speeding drivers and dangerous drivers. A reasonable level of surveillance of each and every motor vehicle is readily accepted, indeed demanded, by society to obtain this protection. All this is set out to emphasize that, *although there remains an expectation of privacy in automobile travel, it is markedly decreased relative to the expectation of privacy in one's home or office.* [emphasis in *Belnavis*][279]

11) Regulatory Matters

Those who are the subject of regulatory investigations, rather than criminal investigations, can also expect a lower protection of their privacy interests. The rationale for the lower standard in the regulatory context is based on a number of factors, including: (1) an expectation by the person of state regulation of certain activities;[280] (2) a lower stigma associated with wrongdoing in the regulatory sphere versus wrongdoing alleged in a criminal investigation;[281] (3) the social utility and importance of the given regulatory scheme beyond the provision of criminal-type penalties, such as the regulation of business and the market economy;[282] or the collection and audit of government revenues in the form of taxation;[283] and, (5) the difficulty of investigating regulatory compliance if standards of reasonableness were higher.[284] For

---

278 *Belnavis*, above note 15.
279 *Ibid.* at 424 (S.C.C.).
280 *Thomson Newspapers*, above note 157, *per* LaForest J. at 506–7.
281 *Ibid.*; see also *R. v. Wholesale Travel* (1991), 67 C.C.C. (3d) 193 (S.C.C.).
282 See *Branch*, above note 157; *Thomson Newspapers*, above note 157.
283 See *McKinlay Transport Ltd.* (1990), 68 D.L.R. (4th) 568 [*McKinlay*]; *Jarvis*, above note 20.
284 See, e.g., *McKinlay*, *ibid.* at 545, where Wilson J. cites the difficulty in spotting misrepresentations on the face of a tax return and the corresponding ease of making such misrepresentations in a self-reporting/self-assessment context as justification for a departure from *Hunter*; see *Thomson Newspapers*, above note 157, where both LaForest J. at 523–24 and L'Heureux Dubé J. at 591–97 note the "invisibility" of infractions of the *Combines Investigation Act*, citing hidden offences occurring in the boardrooms of corporations and the existence of little outside evidence to show that an offence had been committed as a justification for departure from the strictures of *Hunter*.

further discussion of the standard of reasonableness and levels of *Charter* protection in the regulatory context, see chapter 4, "Regulatory or Administrative Interests."

a) Utility Records and Meters

The courts have found that a person has no expectation of privacy in records in the hands of a public utility. In *R. v. Plant*,[285] Sopinka J. explained that hydro-electric consumption records do not contain the type of information that is protected by the *Charter*:

> In fostering the underlying values of dignity, integrity and autonomy, it is fitting that s. 8 of the *Charter* should seek to protect a biographical core of personal information which individuals in a free and democratic society would wish to maintain and control from dissemination to the state. This would include information which tends to reveal intimate details of the lifestyle and personal choices of the individual. The computer records investigated in the case at bar while revealing the pattern of electricity consumption in the residence cannot reasonably be said to reveal intimate details of the appellant's life since electricity consumption reveals very little about the personal lifestyle or private decisions of the occupant of the residence.[286]

Additionally, the Court found no privacy interest in the records due to the commercial nature of the relationship between the utility and the accused, who did not contract for confidentiality, and which was characterized by the utility's practice of sharing the information with members of the general public.[287]

The courts have also found there is no expectation of privacy preventing a public utility from entering onto private property to verify metered information, provided that the utility's enabling legislation permits the entry, and regardless of whether the utility is facilitating the investigation of theft of electricity.[288] The reasoning for the absence of privacy in this regard

---

285 *Plant*, above note 196.
286 *Ibid*.
287 *Ibid*. However, now see the *Personal Information Protection and Electronic Documents Act*, S.C. 2000, C.5, which appears to create, by statute, an expectation of privacy in all "personal information" in the possession of an organization, and prohibits disclosure of that information unless specifically authorized by law.
288 *R. v. Benham* (2003), 175 C.C.C. (3d) 231 (B.C.C.A.) [*Benham*]; *R. v. Bourque* (2001), 50 W.C.B. (2d) 344, 2001 BCSC 621, [2001] B.C.J. No. 1298 [*Bourque*]; *R. v. Breckner* (September 10, 1993), Parksville Registry No. 292599 (S.C.); *R. v. Aukton and Koszulap* (June 29, 1994), Vancouver Registry No. CC921461 (S.C.) and *R. v. Brass* (June 29, 1994), Vancouver Registry No. CC921461 (S.C.); *Hutchings*, above note 215.

is set out in the following passage from Neilson J. in *R. v. Bourque*,[289] as adopted by the British Columbia Court of Appeal in *R. v. Benham*:[290]

> In my view, there is an ample basis to support a similar conclusion on the constitutional issue before me. I find that B.C. Hydro employees entering the private property of B.C. Hydro customers to investigate electrical theft are not operating in a pure law enforcement context. Their role and activities stem primarily from the regulatory scheme and objectives of B.C. Hydro, in particular, its mandate to provide electricity to its customers in an "adequate, safe, efficient, just and reasonable" manner. I find that there are significant and appropriate limitations to their right of access which are in accord with those objectives. Their entry is limited to investigating equipment which belongs to B.C. Hydro, and matters relevant to the commodity which it sells. Their activities on the property, and the information they obtain, are minimally intrusive in terms of privacy concerns of the residents. The customers have imputed knowledge of this right of entry, and of B.C. Hydro's right to investigate whether its customers are paying for electricity and using its equipment properly. Finally, B.C. Hydro acknowledges it does not have general powers of law enforcement. While the theft of electricity is a criminal offence, it is intimately bound to the activities of B.C. Hydro. I find that the limited ability to carry out preliminary investigations into that offence is insufficient to raise the expectation of privacy in what is otherwise clearly a regulatory context.
>
> Accordingly, I find that there is a low expectation of privacy with respect to the entry of B.C. Hydro employees on customer property, even if they are there to investigate the criminal offence of theft of electricity. The failure of the access provision of the Tariff to meet the strict standards set by *Hunter v. Southam* does not render that provision unconstitutional.[291]

---

289 *Bourque*, above note 288.
290 *Benham*, above note 288.
291 *Bourque*, above note 288 at paras. 89–90; as adopted by the British Columbia Court of Appeal in *Benham*, above note 278 at paras. 25–26. However, now see the *Personal Information Protection and Electronic Documents Act*, S.C. 2000, C.5, which appears to create, by statute, an expectation of privacy in all "personal information" in the possession of an organization, and prohibits disclosure of that information unless specifically authorized by law. Personal information includes almost every kind of information, including name, address, credit card information, birth dates, but does not include information such as would be found on a business card (name, business title, business phone numbers, and so on).

12) Firearms

It appears that Parliament has determined that firearms holders have no expectation of privacy in documentation relating to the authorized possession of firearms. Section 177.03(1) of the *Criminal Code* empowers police to demand proof of authorization and to seize[292] firearms and prohibited weapons, without a warrant, if a person fails to produce proof of authorized possession.[293]

It would appear that the rationale for such a power is based in the highly regulated nature of firearms possession in Canada. Much like the requirement to carry and produce a driver's licence when operating a motor vehicle, the ability to verify, on the spot, that a person has the proper authorization to possess a firearm ensures the proper functioning of the regulatory system attached to firearms possession and overall public safety, as opposed to any direct criminal law interests. In fact, section 117.03 carries no penalty for non-compliance (other than the seizure of the firearm and perhaps a charge of obstruction of police). There is likely no expectation of privacy in the documentation itself, just as there is no expectation of privacy in vehicular licence and insurance information.[294]

No doubt this section will be subject to challenge from firearms owners, many of whom protest the current firearms registration scheme. Any such challenge is likely to be based on the lack of any grounds for the initial demand, and the lack of prior authorization for a seizure. For the reasons highlighted above (including the criminal law and public safety interests that influence the regulatory scheme) such a challenge is not likely to be successful.

13) Expectation of Privacy and Section 24(2)

Once a person establishes that his or her reasonable expectation of privacy has been unreasonably intruded upon, the degree of privacy the person expects will affect the court's decision whether to exclude from proceeding the evidence in question under section 24(2).[295] One of the three categories

---

292 The provision is a power of seizure only, and not a search power. See *R. v. Lind*, [2000] S.J. No. 757 (Prov. Ct.).
293 See *Criminal Code*, s. 117.03(1)(a) and (b). This power does not apply if the person is under the direct supervision of another person who may lawfully possess the firearm.
294 *Hufsky*, above note 275.
295 For a discussion of the exclusion of unconstitutionally obtained evidence, see chapter 9.

of factors to examine in assessment of whether evidence will be excluded is the seriousness of the section 8 violation. The seriousness of the breach varies proportionately to the degree of the privacy intrusion: If the person has an increased expectation of privacy, the breach will be deemed more serious; if the person's interest is decreased, the breach will be considered less serious.[296] For instance, a court is more likely to exclude evidence at trial if the person's expectation of privacy in the body[297] or the home has been violated,[298] and accordingly less likely to exercise its discretion where the privacy interest is low, such as in the regulatory or motor vehicle context.[299] Of course, the extent of the privacy interest is but one factor to consider in the overall assessment of whether evidence should be excluded, and will not on its own be determinative.[300] For a more complete discussion of the exclusion of evidence under section 24(2), see chapter 9.

---

296 *Belnavis*, above note 15 at 424 (S.C.C.).
297 See, e.g., *Stillman*, above note 45 and *Dyment*, above note 11.
298 See *Kokesch*, above note 181.
299 See, e.g., *Belnavis*, above note 15.
300 See, e.g., *Silveira*, above note 178, where evidence obtained following the warrantless search of a dwelling was not excluded; see also *Buhay*, above note 36, where evidence stored in a bus locker was excluded despite a low expectation of privacy.

CHAPTER 4

೦ಽ

Determining Reasonableness: The *Collins* Test and *Hunter v. Southam*

Determining whether a search is reasonable involves a balancing of competing interests — the court must decide if the state's interest (for example, advancing the goals of law enforcement, national security, or public administration) outweighs an individual's interest in being left alone by the government (that is, privacy interests).[1] The cases of *Hunter v. Southam*[2] and *R. v. Collins*[3] set out the primary legal tests for striking this balance.

In *R. v. Collins*,[4] a case involving the warrantless search of a person, the Supreme Court stated a simple framework for assessing the reasonableness of a search. Very generally, a search will be considered reasonable under section 8 of the *Charter* if:

1. the search is authorized by law;
2. the law that authorizes the search is itself reasonable; and,
3. the manner in which the search is conducted is reasonable.[5]

The following subsections will address each component of the *Collins* test and illustrate how the courts determine whether a search meets the cri-

---

1 *Hunter et al. v. Southam Inc.* (1984), 14 C.C.C. (3d) 97 [*Hunter*] at 109; *R. v. Araujo*, [2000] 2 S.C.R. 992, 2000 SCC 65, 149 C.C.C. (3d) 449, 193 D.L.R. (4th) 440; *R. v. Golden* (2001), 159 C.C.C. (3d) 449 (S.C.C.) [*Golden*] at 473.
2 *Hunter*, above note 1.
3 *R. v. Collins* (1987), 33 C.C.C. (3d) 1 (S.C.C.) [*Collins*].
4 *Ibid.*
5 *Ibid.* at 14.

89

teria identified in it. (*Hunter* will be addressed in the section "Is the Law Authorizing The Search Reasonable?")

A. AUTHORIZED BY LAW

As at common law,[6] section 8 of the *Charter* requires that the state have specific legal authorization, derived either from a statute or the common law, to conduct a search or seizure. The court must ensure that all the statutory or common law prerequisites to the exercise of a search power were fulfilled before the search can be considered reasonable and "authorized by law."[7] If there is no legal authorization for the search, or if the statutory or common law requirements for the search were not fully met, then the search will be deemed to be unreasonable.[8]

For example, the seizure by police of a blood sample in the absence of specific authority was held to be unlawful in *R. v. Colarusso*,[9] even though the sample was originally seized (lawfully) by the coroner. Although the *Coroner's Act*[10] authorized the seizure of the blood sample by the coroner, the police required prior authorization relating to the criminal investigative purpose for which they seized the sample. Similarly, in *R. v. Dyment*,[11] the collection of free-flowing blood from an unconscious victim by a doctor for medical purposes did not enable the police to seize the blood from the doctor, without a warrant, for a non-medical (criminal investigation) purpose. The consent deemed to have been given by the victim for medical treatment was considered by the court to be "restricted to the use of the sample for medical purposes."[12]

---

6 *Entick v. Carrington* (1765), 19 State Tr. 1029 at 1066–67.
7 For example, in *R. v. Garofoli* (1990), 60 C.C.C. (3d) 161 (S.C.C.) at 187, Sopinka J. held that the application of s. 8 of the *Charter* required the trial judge to ensure statutory compliance with the preconditions for issuing an authorization for a wiretap interception; previously, by virtue of *R. v. Wilson* (1983), 9 C.C.C. (3d) 97 (S.C.C.), reviewing courts were precluded from assessing the authorizing judge's decision that the statutory preconditions for a wiretap authorization were satisfied.
8 *Collins*, above note 3 at 14; *R. v. Law* (2002), 160 C.C.C. (3d) 449 (S.C.C.); *R. v. Inco Ltd.* (2001) 155 C.C.C. (3d) 383 (Ont. C.A.) at 397.
9 *R. v. Colarusso*, [1994] 1 S.C.R. 20.
10 R.S.O. 1980, C. 93 (now R.S.O. 1990. c. C. 37).
11 *R. v. Dyment* (1988), 45 C.C.C. (3d) 244 (S.C.C.) [*Dyment*].
12 *Ibid.* at 431.

1) Specific Powers of Search and Seizure

The charts in the appendices to this book outline the statutory search and seizure powers set out in the *Criminal Code* and select related statutes, and the various requirements necessary in order to validly resort to those powers. Note that certain authorizations are fairly broad in scope while others are narrowly tailored to apply in specific circumstances for limited purposes.

2) Interpreting the Scope of Statutory Search and Seizure Powers

a) The Scope of Statutory Powers: *CanadianOxy Chemicals v. Canada*

In *CanadianOxy Chemicals v. Canada*,[13] the Supreme Court provided guidance on interpreting whether statutory provisions authorize a particular search or seizure in the criminal context. The Court was tasked with determining the scope of section 487(1)(b) of the *Criminal Code*, which permits a justice to authorize the seizure of evidence of the commission of an offence. At issue was whether the section also permitted officers to seize evidence related to a possible "due diligence" defence to a charge of dumping pollutants in a waterway.

The Court held that it was necessary to examine the *purpose* of the statute itself (the *Criminal Code*), in order to gauge the scope of its provisions. The *Criminal Code*, as with other penal statutes, was found to have the promotion of "a safe, peaceful and honest society" as its purpose, which is achieved in part through the "prompt and comprehensive investigation of potential offences."[14] Given the statute's purpose, the Court held that its search and seizure provisions should be broadly interpreted to allow investigators to unearth as much evidence as possible, without imposing undue restrictions on their capability to gather relevant evidence:

> The purpose of s. 487(1) is to allow the investigators to unearth and preserve as much relevant evidence as possible. To ensure that the authorities are able to perform their appointed functions properly they should be able to locate, examine and preserve all the evidence relevant to events which may have given rise to criminal liability. It is not the role of the police to investigate and decide whether the essential elements of an offence are made out — that decision is the role of the courts. The function of the police, and other peace officers, is to investigate incidents which might be

---

13   *CanadianOxy Chemicals Ltd. v. Canada* (1998), 133 C.C.C. (3d) 426 (S.C.C.) [*CanadianOxy*].
14   *Ibid.* at para. 20.

criminal, make a conscientious and informed decision as to whether charges should be laid, and then present the full and unadulterated facts to the prosecutorial authorities. To that end an unnecessary and restrictive interpretation of s. 487(1) defeats its purpose. See *Re Church of Scientology and the Queen (No. 6)* (1987), 31 C.C.C. (3d) 449, p. 475:

> Police work should not be frustrated by the meticulous examination of facts and law that is appropriate to a trial process. . . . There may be serious questions of law as to whether what is asserted amounts to a criminal offence. . . . However, these issues can hardly be determined before the Crown has marshalled its evidence and is in a position to proceed with the prosecution.[15]

Presumably, the same reasoning ought to apply to all statutorily authorized powers of search and seizure within a penal statute (or potentially a regulatory statute with search provisions and penal liability). The courts should not restrictively interpret the enabling power of a search function; rather, any limitations to search powers ought to come from a separate determination that section 8 requires the limitation of the powers provided for under statute.[16]

b) The Scope of Common Law Powers: *R. v. Waterfield*

The common law provides police officers with a range of powers and duties, including powers to conduct searches or seizures in appropriate circumstances. The test enunciated in *R. v. Waterfield*[17] is used to determine whether police activity falls within those common law powers.[18]

In *Waterfield*, the English Court of Appeal identified two factors essential to assessing whether the police were authorized by the common law to undertake certain action:

> (a) First, does the conduct fall within the general scope of any duty imposed by statute or recognised at common law; and

---

15 *Ibid.* at para. 22.
16 See also S. Hutchinson and S. Gray, "The Swiss-Army Knife of Criminal Investigations: General Warrants and Assistance Orders," printed in the materials for the Third Symposium on Issues in Search and Seizure Law in Canada, September 2003, at 8, where the authors endorse a similarly expansive interpretation of the search and seizure powers under s. 487.01 ("General Warrants").
17 *R. v. Waterfield*, [1963] 3 All E.R. 659, [1964] 1 Q.B. 164 (C.C.A.) [*Waterfield*].
18 *R. v. Stenning*, [1970] 3 C.C.C. 145 (S.C.C.); *Knowlton v. The Queen* (1973), 10 C.C.C. (2d) 377 (S.C.C.); *R. v. Dedman* (1985), 20 C.C.C. (3d) 97 (S.C.C.) [*Dedman*]; *R. v. Godoy* (1998), 131 C.C.C. (3d) 129 (S.C.C.) [*Godoy*]; *R. v. Ferris* (1998), 126 C.C.C. (3d) 298 (B.C.C.A.); *R. v. Simpson* (1993), 79 C.C.C. (3d) 482 (Ont. C.A.) [*Simpson*]; *R. v. Mann* (2002), 169 C.C.C. (3d) 272 (Man. C.A.).

(b) Second, does the conduct, albeit within the general scope of such a duty, involve an unjustifiable use of powers associated with the duty.

The first branch of *Waterfield* requires the identification of a specific duty imposed on police officers either by the operation of the common law or a statute. In *R. v. Dedman*,[19] the Supreme Court recognized that, at common law, police officers' duties included:

> the preservation of the peace, the prevention of crime, and the protection of life and property, from which is derived the duty to control traffic on the public roads: see *Rice v. Connolly*, [1966] 2 Q.B. 414 at p. 419; *Johnson v. Phillips*, [1975] 3 All E.R. 682 at p. 685; Halsbury's Laws of England, 3rd ed. vol. 30, p. 129, para. 206.[20]

The second branch of *Waterfield* requires an assessment of the reasonableness and necessity of the action taken in fulfillment of the duty identified in the first branch. In *R. v. Dedman*,[21] Le Dain J. held that the second branch of *Waterfield* ought to be determined as follows:

> The interference with liberty must be necessary for the carrying out of the particular police duty and it must be reasonable, having regard to the nature of the liberty interfered with and the importance of the public purpose served by the interference.[22]

In *R. v. Simpson*,[23] Doherty J.A. expanded on Le Dain J.'s formulation of the second branch of *Waterfield* for determining the justifiability of the police power:

> The reasons of Le Dain J. in *Dedman*, *supra*, at pp. 121–2, indicate that the justifiability of an officer's conduct depends on a number of factors including the duty being performed, the extent to which some interference with individual liberty is necessitated in order to perform that duty, the importance of the performance of that duty to the public good, the liberty interfered with, and the nature and extent of the interference. This "totality of the circumstances" approach is similar to that found in the American jurisprudence referable to the constitutionality of investigative stops.[24]

---

19 *Dedman*, above note 18.
20 *Ibid.* at 119.
21 *Ibid.*
22 *Ibid.* at 35.
23 *Simpson*, above note 18.
24 *Ibid.* at 499; see also *United States v. Cortez*, 449 U.S. 411 at 417–8, 101 S. Ct. 690 (1981); *Alabama v. White*, 110 S. Ct. 2412 at 2416 (1990), and *R. v. Garofoli* (1990), 60 C.C.C. (3d) 161 at 189–90 (S.C.C.).

In the same vein, the police officer's general duty to prevent and investigate crime will not permit the police to engage in otherwise illegal and unreasonable conduct.[25] As Dickson C.J.C. explained (in dissent) in the *Wiretap Reference*:[26]

> The fact that police officers could be described as acting within the general scope of their duties to investigate crime cannot empower them to violate the law whenever such conduct could be justified by the public interest in law enforcement. Any such principle would be nothing short of a fiat for illegality on the part of the police whenever the benefit of police action appeared to outweigh the infringement of an individual's rights. For the *Waterfield* principle to apply, the police must be engaged in lawful execution of their duty at the time of the conduct in question.[27]

The exigent circumstances section that follows sets out examples in Canadian law where the *Waterfield* test has been used to identify common law police powers to search and seize. See also chapter 8, "Searches Incidental to Arrest."

B. IS THE LAW AUTHORIZING THE SEARCH REASONABLE?

If the constitutional validity of legislation or a common law power authorizing a search is challenged, the first issue to examine is the purpose of the law. If the law's purpose is invalid, then the law is invalid, and there is no need to examine the effect of the law in its operation. As the Supreme Court held in *R. v. Big M Drug Mart Ltd.*:[28]

> [T]he legislation's purpose is the initial test of constitutional validity and its effects are to be considered when the law under review has passed or, at least, has purportedly passed the purpose test. If the legislation fails the purpose test, there is no need to consider further its effects, since it has already been demonstrated to be invalid. Thus, if a law with a valid purpose interferes by its impact, with rights or freedoms, a litigant could still argue the effects of the legislation as a means to defeat its applicability and possibly its validity. In short, the effects test will only be necessary to defeat

---

25 *Waterfield*, above note 17 at 170–71.
26 *Reference re an Application for an Authorization* (1984), 15 C.C.C. (3d) 466 (S.C.C.) (sub nom. *Wiretap Reference*).
27 *Ibid.* at 483.
28 *R. v. Big M Drug Mart Ltd.*, [1985] 1 S.C.R. 295, 18 C.C.C. (3d) 385.

legislation with a valid purpose; effects can never be relied upon to save legislation with an invalid purpose.[29]

If, however, the law is found to have a valid purpose, then reasonableness of the effect of the law can be assessed.

As stated at the outset of this chapter, the primary issue in determining the reasonableness of a search power is a balancing of interests — whether the state's interest in conducting the search or seizure outweighs a person's privacy interests. The default test for determining that balance of competing interests was established by the Supreme Court in *Hunter v. Southam*.[30] The Court set three minimum requirements for what constitutes a constitutionally reasonable search power:[31]

1. **Prior authorization:** The search power must require (where feasible) that the investigators obtain prior authorization, usually in the form of a valid warrant. A warrantless search is *prima facie* unreasonable[32] and the Crown bears the onus of rebutting this presumption.[33] The Court in *Hunter* held that a *post facto* approval of a search (that is, a retroactive process) would fail to achieve the purpose of section 8 because it would not prevent unreasonable searches before they happen; however, the Court recognized that not all situations could reasonably be dealt with by prior authorization. The prior authorization requirement also confirmed the common law principle that a warrant is generally required for intrusions onto private property.[34]

2. **Impartial judicial officer:** If there is prior authorization, the person authorizing the search must be *an impartial judicial officer*. The officer does not have to be an actual "judge," but rather an official capable of acting judicially (to be independent, neutral, and impartial).[35] In *Hunter v. Southam*, the office responsible for granting authorizations under the

---

29 *Ibid.* at 334.
30 *Hunter*, above note 1.
31 In *Thomson Newspapers Ltd. v. Canada (Director of Investigation and Research, Restrictive Trade Practices Commission)*, [1990] 1 S.C.R. 425 [*Thomson Newpapers*] at 470, the Court recognized that *Hunter* also provided a fourth criteria "that only documents strictly relevant to the inquiry be seized."
32 *Hunter*, above note 1 at 109–10.
33 *Ibid.* at 109. However, the Crown does not bear the onus to establish that a warrantless search is reasonable if the search is conducted as an incident to a lawful arrest: *Golden*, above note 1. See chapter 8, "Searches Incidental to Arrest."
34 *R. v. Grant* (1993), 84 C.C.C. (3d) 173 (S.C.C.) [*Grant*] at 187, citing *Eccles v. Bourque* (1974), 19 C.C.C. (2d) 129 (S.C.C.) and *Colet v. The Queen* (1981), 57 C.C.C. (2d) 105 (S.C.C.).
35 *Hunter*, above note 1 at 110.

relevant legislative scheme (the Director of Investigation and Research of the Combines Investigation Branch) was primarily dedicated to an investigative function, and the decision to conduct a search was guided equally by considerations of expediency and public policy.[36] Accordingly, the Director was not well placed to be an independent arbiter capable of balancing individual and state interests.[37]

3. **Reasonable and probable grounds:**[38] Reasonable and probable grounds[39] to believe that an offence has been committed and that there is evidence to be found at the place of the search,[40] is the minimum standard for authorizing search and seizure in most cases involving law enforcement interests. If the interests engaged involve issues other than law enforcement (such as state security), then a lower standard than reasonable grounds may apply; similarly, a higher standard may apply where bodily integrity issues are engaged.[41] In *Hunter*, Dickson J. set the threshold for what constitutes reasonable and probable grounds: "The State's interest in detecting and preventing crime begins to prevail over the individual's interest in being left alone at the point *where credibly-based probability replaces suspicion.*"[42]

The courts have also interpreted *Hunter v. Southam* as requiring a fourth factor: that the only documents [or items] which are authorized to be seized are those which are strictly relevant to the offence under investigation.[43]

Finally, in *Baron v. Canada*,[44] the Court held that discretion over whether to issue the warrant was a constitutional requirement for a reasonable power of search and seizure,[45] to allow the justice to balance the competing interests identified in *Hunter*. Essentially, the justice empowered to issue a search warrant must have a discretionary power to decline to issue the warrant, even if all the statutory preconditions have been met; if the leg-

---

36   *Ibid.* at 111–12.
37   *Ibid.* at 112.
38   For a more detailed examination of the concept of reasonable and probable grounds see chapter 5.
39   Established on oath, before the impartial judicial officer, where the search requires prior authorization.
40   Regarding "in a place" see also *R. v. Hurrell* (2002), 166 C.C.C. (3d) 343 (Ont. C.A.) striking down 117.04(1) *Criminal Code* for not requiring reasonable grounds to believe that a weapon would be found on the person or in the place sought to be searched.
41   *Hunter*, above note 1 at 114–15.
42   *Ibid.*
43   *Thomson Newspapers*, above note 31 at 470, per Wilson J.
44   *Baron v. Canada* (1993), 78 C.C.C. (3d) 510 (S.C.C.) [*Baron*].
45   *Ibid.* at 526–27.

islation requires the issuance of a warrant, then it will be deemed unreasonable.[46] In *Baron*[47] the Supreme Court held section 231.3(3) of the *Income Tax Act* to be in violation of section 8 bacause it provided that a judge *shall* issue a search and seizure warrant where satisfied that all the grounds required for the warrant were established:

> The circumstances in which these conflicting interests must be balanced will vary greatly. The strength of the interests will be affected by matters such as the nature of the offence alleged, the nature of the intrusion sought including the place to be searched, the time of the search and the person or persons who are the subjects of the search. The variability of the factors affecting the decision of the authorizing judge was stressed by Lamer J. (as he then was) in *Descôteaux v. Mierzwinski* [(1982), 70 C.C.C. (2d) 385 (S.C.C.)]. This was a pre-*Charter* case in which this court held that s. 443 (now s. 487) provided for a discretion when a warrant is sought before a justice under the *Criminal Code*, R.S.C. 1970, c. C-34. At pp. 410–11 C.C.C., pp. 615–16 D.L.R., Lamer J. said:
>
>> I come down on the side of the discretion, as it allows more effective judicial control of the police. Searches are an exception to the oldest and most fundamental principles of the common law, and as such the power to search should be strictly controlled. It goes without saying that the justice may sometimes be in a poor position to assess the need for the search in advance. After all, searches, while constituting a means of gathering evidence, are also an investigative tool. It will often be difficult to determine definitively the probative value of a particular thing before the police investigation has been completed. Be that as it may, there are places for which authorization to search should generally be granted only with reticence and, where necessary, with more conditions attached than for other places. One does not enter a church in the same way as a lion's den, or a warehouse in the same way as a lawyer's office. One does not search the premises of a third party who is not alleged to have participated in the commission of a crime in the same way as those of someone who is the subject of such an allegation.
>
> *In order to take account of the various factors affecting the balancing of the two interests, the authorizing judge must be empowered to consider all the circum-*

---

46 *Baron*, above note 44.
47 *Ibid*.

stances. No set of criteria will always be determinative or sufficient to override the right of the individual to privacy. It is imperative, therefore, that a sufficient degree of flexibility be accorded to the authorizing officer in order that justice be done to the respective interests involved. [emphasis added]

It is critical to note, however, that the *Hunter v. Southam* criteria for a reasonable power of search are not absolute, and do not apply in all circumstances. In *Hunter*, Dickson J. acknowledged that these criteria could be modified in appropriate cases, such as in circumstances where it would be otherwise impracticable to obtain a warrant, or where interests other than simple law enforcement are being pursued, such as the protection of state security interests.[48]

1) How to Determine if the *Hunter v. Southam* Criteria Are Inapplicable

In cases following *Hunter*, the Supreme Court has confirmed that certain search powers will be reasonable despite their non-conformance with the *Hunter v. Southam* criteria, despite also emphasizing that reasonable departures from those standards will be "exceedingly rare."[49] Twenty years after the *Hunter* decision, a significant array of search powers have been declared reasonable, despite failing to meet the standards declared by Dickson J.[50] Those supposedly exceedingly rare circumstances where a law establishing a search power may still be reasonable, even if the law does not comply with the *Hunter v. Southam* criteria, include:[51]

---

48 *Hunter*, above note 1.
49 *R. v. Simmons* (1988), 45 C.C.C. (3d) 296 (S.C.C.) [*Simmons*] at 319; *Thomson Newspapers*, above note 31. The claim that such circumstances will be rare is best read as a conceptual statement that the *types* of search powers will be limited. Empirically, it is clear that search powers that do not meet the *Hunter v. Southam* criteria are among the most frequently *used* police search powers, for example, search incident to arrest.
50 The propensity of Canadian courts to diverge from the rigorous requirements of *Hunter v. Southam* inspired has inspired spirited criticism. See D. Stuart, "The Unfortunate Dilution of Section 8 Protection: Some Teeth Remain" (1999) 25 Queen's L. J. 65.
51 See the brief summary in *Grant*, above note 34 at 188. Also note: many police activities will be reasonable despite apparent departures from *Hunter* so long as the activities do not actually trigger s. 8 concerns, *e.g.*, where the person has no expectation of privacy in the place or thing searched or seized. See chapters 2 and 3 for discussions of how to determine when police activity constitutes a search or seizure and when a person has no expectation of privacy in the thing or place.

1. where exigent circumstances render obtaining a warrant impracticable;[52]
2. where the person searched enjoys a significantly lower expectation of privacy;[53]
3. where interests other than law enforcement are protected in conducting the search (such as national security interest,[54] regulatory or administrative interests[55] or other public interests including exculpating innocent suspects[56]);
4. where the type of search or seizure is minimally intrusive (such as an order compelling production of tax documents as opposed to a wide-scale search of a residence or business), or is necessary for the proper administration of criminal justice (as in searches incident to arrest to ensure officer safety);[57]
5. certain situations require a more restrictive approach to the assessment of reasonableness than outlined in *Hunter*. For example, where other *Charter* rights, such as section 2(b) freedom of expression,[58] or fundamen-

---

52 *Hunter*, above note 1 at 109–10; *Grant*, above note 34 at 188; see also chapter 8, "Searches Incidental to Arrest" and chapter 4, "Exigent Circumstances."
53 This could occur at a border crossing (see *Simmons*, above note 49), or in a regulatory or administrative law context (see *Thomson Newspapers*, above note 31 and *British Columbia Securities Commission v. Branch* (1995), 97 C.C.C. (3d) 505 (S.C.C.) [*Branch*] at 531–32. See also sections 492.1 and 492.2 of the *Criminal Code*, which empowers a justice to authorize the implantation of tracking devices in vehicles and the obtaining of "dial-number recorder" information based solely on a standard of reasonable suspicion, presumably on the justification that those types of information implicate a less significant privacy interest.
54 *Simmons*, above note 49.
55 *Thomson Newspapers*, above note 31; *Branch*, above note 53 at 527; *R. v. McKinlay Transport Ltd.* (1990), 68 D.L.R. (4th) 568 [*McKinlay*] at 580–81; 55 C.C.C. (3d) 530 at 542–43.
56 *R. v. Briggs* (2001), 157 C.C.C. (3d) 38 (Ont. C.A.).
57 *Thomson Newspapers*, above note 31; *Branch*, above note 53 at 527; *Baron*, above note 44 at 529; *McKinlay*, above note 55 at 542–43; *Grant*, above note 34 at 187; *Cloutier v. Langlois* (1990), 53 C.C.C. (3d) 257 (S.C.C.) at 277–78. Though s. 8 of the *Charter* was not pleaded in *Cloutier*, L'Heureux Dubé J. provides an analysis of the constitutionality of the common law power to search incident to arrest: such searches are necessary and are to be conducted in the least intrusive way to ensure the proper administration of criminal justice; see also the discussions in *R. v. F.(S.)* (2000), 141 C.C.C. (3d) 225 (Ont. C.A.) [*F.(S.)*] and *B.(S.A.)*, (2001), 157 C.C.C. (3d) 510 (Alta. C.A.), where the minimally intrusive nature of taking the DNA sample helped justify the absence of a "reasonable grounds" requirement.
58 *Attorney-General of Quebec v. Canadian Broadcasting Corp.* (1991), 67 C.C.C. (3d) 517 (S.C.C.) [*CBC*]; *National Post v. Canada*, [2004] 178 O.J. (Sup. Ct.) [*Post*].

tal principles such as solicitor client privilege,[59] are involved in a search or seizure, a higher standard of justification for the search will be required.

Each of the above-noted factors will be covered in greater detail elsewhere in this book. Below, we examine reasonableness in the context of exigent circumstances, non-criminal law situations, and where competing interests are at stake.

a) Exigent Circumstances

Exigent circumstances in and of themselves generally do not operate to justify a search. Exigent circumstances will usually instead be the precondition to the exercise of a statutory or common law power to conduct a search without a warrant. Second, the presence of exigent circumstances may mitigate the seriousness of a breach of section 8 on a motion to exclude evidence under section 24(2) of the *Charter*.[60]

The following are categories of recognized warrantless search powers applicable in exigent circumstances. Each operates without the requirement for prior authorization, and some require an evidentiary threshold lower than reasonable grounds:

1. where there is a need to secure and preserve evidence, and it is impracticable to obtain a warrant, provided that the search falls under *Controlled Drugs and Substances Act*[61] section 11(7) or *Criminal Code* section 487.11, or a recognized common law exception;[62]
2. where there is a risk to the safety of the public or peace officers;[63]
3. where the police officers have a duty to protect life;[64]
4. The courts have also recognized an exigency-type exception for warrantless entry into dwelling while in "hot pursuit" of a suspect[65] (with the consequence that any search incidental to such an entry may be justifiable under section 8).

---

59 *Lavallee, Rackel & Heintz v. Canada (Attorney General)* [*Lavallee*]; *White, Ottenheim & Baker v. Canada (Attorney General)* [*White*]; *R. v. Fink* (2002), 167 C.C.C. (3d) 1 (S.C.C.) [*Fink*].
60 *R. v. Silveira* (1995), 97 C.C.C. (3d) 450 (S.C.C.) [*Silveira*] at 465.
61 *Controlled Drugs and Substances Act*, 1996, C. 19 [*CDSA*].
62 *R. v. McCormack* (2000), 143 C.C.C. (3d) 260 (B.C.C.A.); *Grant*, above note 35; *R. v. Duong* (2002), 162 C.C.C. (3d) 242 (B.C.C.A.), leave refused [2002] S.C.C.A. No. 112 [*Duong*].
63 See reference in *R. v. Feeney*, (1997) 115 C.C.C. (3d) 129 [*Feeney*]; *R. v. Golub* (1997), 117 C.C.C. (3d) 193 (Ont. C.A.) [*Golub*] at 213.
64 *Godoy*, above note 18.
65 *R. v. Macooh* (1993), 82 C.C.C. (3d) 481 [*Macooh*] at 494; *Feeney*, above note 63 at 156; *R. v. Haglof* (2000), 149 C.C.C. (3d) 248 (B.C.C.A.) [*Haglof*].

b) **Application of the Exigency Exception to Specific Categories of Exigent Situations**

i) *Preservation of Evidence: Prior to the Enactment of* CDSA *section 11(7) and* Criminal Code *section 487.11*

In *R. v. Grant*,[66] the Supreme Court held that only the impracticability of obtaining a warrant in exigent circumstances could justify conducting a warrantless search for the preservation of evidence,[67] even where a statutory provision contemplated a warrantless search. In *Grant*, the Court read-down section 10 of the *Narcotic Control Act*,[68] which purported to authorize the warrantless search of places (other than dwelling-houses), and limited its operation to the conduct of searches in exigent circumstances.[69] Justice Sopinka held that exigent circumstances sufficient for section 10 would exist where there was an *imminent danger of loss, removal, destruction or disappearance of the evidence sought* if the search or seizure were delayed to obtain a warrant.[70]

In *R. v. Silveira*,[71] the Supreme Court discussed the implications of exigent circumstances on search powers involving a home. The Court noted that in view of the high expectation of privacy one has in the home, absent "clear statutory language authorizing" the warrantless search of a dwelling-house, a law that purported to authorize warrantless searches could not extend to searches of a home:

> The principle that a search of a dwelling-house without a warrant is unjustifiable is firmly entrenched in the common law. . . . No exception to this principle has since been made to permit a search in exigent circumstances or otherwise. The principle has in recent years been restated in *Colet v. The Queen* (1981), 57 C.C.C. (2d) 105, where this court unanimously held that police who enter and search a dwelling-house without a warrant are trespassers, and that specific statutory authority is required to alter this rule. Moreover, Ritchie J. made it clear that any such provision would be narrowly interpreted, concluding, at p. 112 C.C.C., that "any provision authorizing police officers to search and enter private property *must* be phrased in express terms" (emphasis added). The terms of ss. 10 and 12 of the *Narcotic Control Act* are clear. They authorize entry into a dwelling-house only

---

66 *Grant*, above note 34.
67 *Ibid*. at 188–89.
68 *Narcotic Control Act*, R.S.C. 1985, c. N-1 (repealed and replaced by the *CDSA*, above note 61).
69 *Grant*, above note 34.
70 *Ibid*.
71 *Silveira*, above note 60.

under the authority of a warrant. No exception is made for exigent circumstances; there is thus no "specific statutory authority" to use the words of Ritchie J. There is no mention of exigent circumstances as a ground for an unwarranted police entry to search a dwelling-house. The common law since *Entick v. Carrington* has created no such justification, and it would require a marked departure from the law as set forth in *Colet v. The Queen* to do so, one that would involve a consideration of whether this conformed to s. 8 of the *Charter*. [parallel citations omitted][72]

In *Feeney*,[73] the Court reiterated the point that specific authority (namely, a warrant) for entry into a dwelling house to affect an arrest was required before any such arrest or incidental search could be considered reasonable. The Court recognized an exception to this principle for cases of hot pursuit, but did not definitively rule on whether other exigent circumstances could displace the *Hunter* requirement for prior authorization.[74]

There is some authority recognizing a common law power to conduct a warrantless search of a vehicle to preserve evidence, in exigent circumstances, in certain prescribed circumstances. In *R. v. D.(I.D.)*,[75] the Saskatchewan Court of Appeal held that, in exigent circumstances, a warrantless search of a vehicle may be lawfully conducted[76] provided the following preconditions are met:

(1) that the vehicle be stopped or the occupants be detained lawfully.

(2) that the officer conducting the search have reasonable and probable grounds to believe that an offence has been, is being, or is about to be committed and that a search will disclose evidence relevant to that offence.

(3) that exigent circumstances, such as imminent loss, removal, or destruction of the evidence, make it not feasible to obtain a warrant.

(4) that the scope of the search itself bear a reasonable relationship to the offence suspected and the evidence sought.[77]

The fact that vehicles and other conveyances can move away quickly does not, in and of itself, create exigent circumstances to justify a warrantless search. As the Supreme Court explained in *R. v. Grant*:[78]

---

72 *Ibid.* at paras. 49 and 50.
73 *Feeney*, above note 63.
74 *Ibid.* at paras. 49–50.
75 *R. v. D.(I.D.)* (1987) 38 C.C.C. (3d) 289 at 296–97.
76 The onus will still be on the Crown to justify the reasonableness of such a search, however: *ibid.* at 297.
77 *Ibid.*
78 *Grant*, above note 34.

> Exigent circumstances will often be created by the presence of narcotics on a moving conveyance such as a motor vehicle, a water vessel or aircraft. However, I do not favour a blanket exception for this species of private property. Such an exception does exist under the American Constitution. In *Rao, supra*, Martin J.A. pointed out the justification for the American exception was that vehicles, vessels and aircraft may move away quickly and frustrate an investigation. While I accept this fact, I must also be mindful of the fact that this court has recognized the existence of an expectation of privacy in respect of motor vehicles, albeit on a lower scale than that which exists in relation to a dwelling or a private office. In *Wise, supra*, the installation of a tracking device in a motor vehicle was held to be an unreasonable search in circumstances in which it would have been practicable for the police to have obtained a search warrant. The capability of these conveyances to move rapidly away will not in all circumstances create a situation in which it is impracticable to obtain a warrant and in which the criteria I have set out above will be present.[79]

See also the Ontario Court of Appeal's decision in *R. v. Belnavis*,[80] in which the Court accepts the existence of the common law power to conduct a search of a vehicle in exigent circumstances, without a warrant, provided the preconditions stated above are met.[81]

ii) *Preservation of Evidence: Post-Enactment of* CDSA *section 11(7) and* Criminal Code *section 487.11*

Following *Silveira* and *Feeney*, Parliament enacted legislation permitting the execution of searches (including searches of dwelling houses) without warrants in exigent circumstances. Section 487.11 of the *Criminal Code* and section 11(7) of the *CDSA* permit the warrantless execution of a search under sections 487 of the *Code* or section 11 of the *CDSA*, respectively, provided that all the preconditions for the issuance of the warrant are present but exigent circumstances make obtaining a warrant impracticable. *Criminal Code* section 529.3 also permits the warrantless entry into a home to affect an arrest where the officer has reasonable grounds to suspect entry will prevent imminent bodily harm or death, or prevent the imminent loss or destruction of evidence.

In *R. v. McCormack*,[82] the British Columbia Court of Appeal considered whether the circumstances were sufficiently exigent to justify a warrantless

---

79 Ibid.
80 R. v. Belnavis (1996), 107 C.C.C (3d) 195 (Ont. C.A.).
81 Ibid. at 213.
82 R. v. McCormack (2000), 143 C.C.C. (3d) 260 (B.C.C.A.).

"seizing" of a home pursuant to section 11(7) of the *CDSA* to prevent the destruction of evidence in the home. The police had seen an unidentified woman entering the house and the police had reason to believe that McCormack's girlfriend might be inclined to tamper with the evidence in the home. The Court found the following circumstances supported the finding that exigent circumstances existed to justify the warrantless seizure:

> The existence of exigent circumstances involves the subjective belief of the police, and the objective basis for the belief. Factors which favour a conclusion that there were exigent circumstances include:
> [1] an hour before the appellant's arrest the police intercepted a telephone call from the appellant's girlfriend in which she said she would meet him at his apartment in one hour;
> [2] the police had learned from earlier wiretap interceptions between the appellant and his girlfriend that she was supportive of the appellant's involvement in the drug trade;
> [3] the police had learned from earlier wiretap interceptions that the girlfriend had looked after the appellant's apartment while he was on a trip to Mexico and therefore was likely to have a key to his apartment;
> [4] as the police were arresting the appellant, a woman fitting the girlfriend's description drove by and made eye contact with the appellant;
> [5] at the time of the arrest the police were wearing police vests and thus were easily identifiable as police constables;
> [6] the woman believed to be the girlfriend was seen leaving the parking lot heading in the direction of the appellant's apartment building;
> [7] also present in the parking lot was another vehicle which was similar to a vehicle the police had seen an associate of the appellant drive the evening before.[83]

In *R. v. Duong*,[84] the British Columbia Court of Appeal approved a warrantless search in exigent circumstances (again under section 11(7) of the *CDSA*), for the purpose of preserving evidence. In *Duong*, officers smelled fresh and burning marijuana as they attended a residence to canvass about a neighbourhood home invasion, and as a result believed they had found a marijuana grow-operation. Police arrested Duong at the door and entered to arrest Tran, observing evidence in the process. One officer remained in the residence while the other went to obtain a warrant to search the premises, based in part on the observations made during the arrest. The court found the initial search to be reasonable under section 8, agreeing with the trial

---

83   *Ibid.*
84   *Duong*, above note 62.

judge that the observations inside the apartment were made incident to a lawful arrest under section 529.3 of the *Criminal Code*:

> Here, the trial judge accepted Constable Picard's testimony that he was concerned that, if he should leave Mr. Duong in order to obtain a search warrant, Mr. Duong could escape and he would subsequently be unable to identify him; that Mr. Duong and the female occupant and anyone else who might be inside could destroy evidence; that he would have difficulty obtaining supporting officers to watch the house until his return because of a police personnel shortage that evening; and that he believed that he was dealing with the scene of an active crime rather than with something that could be addressed later. He concluded that exigent circumstances existed because of the likelihood that evidence in relation to the grow operation could be destroyed by someone inside the residence during the time it would have taken Constable Picard to obtain a search warrant, which he found would have been about one hour. Therefore, relying on *R. v. McCormack* (2000), 143 C.C.C. (3d) 260 (B.C.C.A.), he found that the warrantless search was lawful.[85]

The Court of Appeal found that the circumstances were sufficiently exigent to satisfy the requirements of section 11(7) of the *CDSA* and that the officers were justified in conducting the warrantless search, since the officers were uncertain whether others had access to the premises and there was the potential for evidence to be destroyed without their immediate intervention:

> [I]mportant pieces of evidence could have been destroyed during the hour it would have taken for Constable Picard to return with a search warrant. Many other incriminating pieces of evidence were found that might have similarly been made unavailable to the police had the appellants been left inside the premises for that hour.
>
> Thus, there was in this case important evidence that could have been destroyed if an opportunity to destroy it had existed. In my opinion, the conclusion that there were exigent circumstances justifying the entry of the house to effect the arrests and justifying the warrantless initial search is supported by the evidence and I see no basis upon which we could interfere.[86]

iii) *Officer Safety and Public Safety*
In cases where officer safety or public safety would be put at risk by delaying a search, the need to ensure the safety of law enforcement officers can

---

85   Ibid. at para. 24.
86   Ibid. at paras. 30–31.

also create exigent circumstances sufficient to justify exceptions to the *Hunter v. Southam* requirements. In *R. v. Golub*,[87] police received information from a third party that Golub had shown him an Uzi submachine gun, had made threats to another person, and was distraught. Police attended Golub's apartment building to arrest him. The building was evacuated; officers found Golub right outside his apartment, and took him into custody. The officers then entered the apartment and conducted a search, finding a loaded rifle under the mattress.

Justice Doherty found no violation of section 8, as the search was lawfully conducted incidental to the arrest.[88] Searches of the home as an incident to arrest were not to be treated as routine events, however; as Doherty J.A. noted:

> In my opinion, searches of a home as an incident of an arrest, like entries of a home to effect an arrest, are now generally prohibited subject to exceptional circumstances where the law enforcement interest is so compelling that it overrides the individual's right to privacy within the home.[89]

In *Golub*, the exceptional circumstances permitting a search of dwelling-house incident to arrest were grounded in officer and public safety: the officers believed Golub to still be in possession of a dangerous weapon, they were concerned that another person might still be in the apartment, and the judgment call to conduct the search was made in the heat of the moment out of safety concerns.[90] Justice Doherty held that the preservation of the legitimate safety of those present at the scene of the arrest could justify a warrantless search incident to arrest, even of a dwelling-house:[91]

> I would hold that where immediate action is required to secure the safety of those at the scene of an arrest, a search conducted in a manner which is consistent with the preservation of the safety of those at the scene is justified. If, in order to secure the safety of those at the scene, entry into and search of a residence is necessary, I would hold that the risk of physical harm to those at the scene of the arrest constitutes exceptional circumstances justifying the warrantless entry and search of the residence. The search must be conducted for the purpose of protecting those at the scene

---

87   *Golub*, above note 63.
88   For a discussion of the common law power of search incidental to arrest see chapter 8.
89   *Golub*, above note 63 at para. 41.
90   *Ibid.* at para. 47.
91   *Ibid.* at para. 43.

and must be conducted in a reasonable manner which is consistent with that purpose.[92]

. . .

I conclude that the police had legitimate concerns about their safety and the safety of other when they arrested the respondent right outside the door to his apartment. The police were entitled to take reasonable steps to ensure their safety and the safety of others. In these circumstances, those steps included entry into the residence and a search of the residence for other persons. The search by members of the [Emergency Task Force] was conducted for that purpose and in a reasonable manner which was consistent with that purpose. The search was a lawful incident of the arrest of the respondent and a reasonable search. There was no violation of s. 8 of the *Charter*.[93]

Notably, Doherty J.A. also referred to the competing privacy interests of the neighbours who had been forced from their apartments during the arrest as weighing in favour of the state's interest to search the apartment — a quick resolution to the siege through a warrantless search would assist the neighbours in preserving their privacy interests.[94]

iv) *911 Calls: Duty to Protect Life*

Emergency calls to police, or "911" calls, also provide an exigent circumstances–based exception to the prior authorization requirement for a search. In *R. v. Godoy*,[95] the 911-dispatcher received an "unknown trouble call": a call that is disconnected before the caller speaks.[96] The dispatcher traced the address of the call, and sent officers to the address. Godoy came to the door, but only partially opened the door, and stated that nothing was wrong. The police prevented Godoy from closing the door and entered the apartment, where they heard a woman crying. The police then located the crying woman, who was curled in the fetal position, with swelling around her eye. The officers arrested Godoy for assaulting the woman, and also charged him with assaulting the police officers that arrested him.

In deciding that the police had lawful authority for their warrantless entry into the residence, the Court applied the test from *R. v. Waterfield*[97] for

---

92   *Ibid.* at para. 46.
93   *Ibid.* at paras. 46 and 54.
94   *Ibid.* at para. 52; see also *R. v. Hurrell* (2002), 166 C.C.C. (3d) 343 (Ont. C.A.), (leave granted February 20, 2003), at para. 43.
95   *Godoy*, above note 18.
96   *Ibid.* at para. 2.
97   *Waterfield*, above note 17.

evaluating the powers and duties of police: "first, does the conduct fall within the general scope of any duty imposed by statute or recognized at common law; and second, does the conduct, albeit within the general scope of such a duty, involve an unjustifiable use of powers associated with the duty."[98]

The Supreme Court recognized that the common law duties of police include the "preservation of the peace, the prevention of crime, and the protection of life and property," and that the duty to protect life is a "general duty" that is engaged whenever a 911 call is made:

> A 911 call is a distress call — a cry for help. It may indeed be precipitated by criminal events, but criminal activity is not a prerequisite for assistance. The duties specifically enumerated in s. 42(1) of the [*Police Services*] *Act* may or may not be engaged. The point of the 911 emergency response system is to provide whatever assistance is required under the circumstances of the call. In the context of a disconnected 911 call, the nature of the distress is unknown. However, in my view, it is reasonable, indeed imperative, that the police assume that the caller is in some distress and requires immediate assistance. To act otherwise would seriously impair the effectiveness of the system and undermine its very purpose. The police duty to protect life is therefore engaged whenever it can be inferred that the 911 caller is or may be in some distress, including cases where the call is disconnected before the nature of the emergency can be determined.[99]

The Court found that it was necessary and reasonable for the police to forcibly enter a residence without a warrant to respond to such calls, given that there was no other way to verify whether the potential victim's interests were preserved. Were it otherwise, a burglar could answer through the door that everything was all right inside, or an unconscious heart attack victim would never be rescued.[100] Accordingly, any such intrusion into a person's home would be reasonable:

> In summary, emergency response systems are established by municipalities to provide effective and immediate assistance to citizens in need. The 911 system is promoted as a system available to handle all manner of crises, including situations which have no criminal involvement whatsoever. When the police are dispatched to aid a 911 caller, they are carrying out their duty to protect life and prevent serious injury. This is especially true where the call is disconnected and the nature of the emergency unknown.

---

98 *Godoy*, above note 18 at para. 12.
99 *Ibid.* at para. 16.
100 *Ibid.* at para. 20.

When a caller uses a 911 system, he or she has requested direct and immediate intervention and has the right to expect emergency services will arrive and locate the caller. The public interest in maintaining this system may result in a limited intrusion in one's privacy interests while at home. *This interference is authorized at common law as it falls within the scope of the police duty to protect life and safety and does not involve an unjustifiable use of the powers associated with this duty.* [emphasis added][101]

Since *Godoy*, other appellate courts have considered the applicability of the 911 public safety exception for warrantless entries. In *R. v. Nicholls*,[102] the Ontario Court of Appeal held a warrantless entry to be reasonable following a 911 call regarding a psychiatric patient who was believed to be a danger to himself and others.

In *R. v. Jamieson*,[103] the British Columbia Court of Appeal found reasonable a warrantless search conducted following a 911 call from neighbours alerting police to someone who had emerged from the address suffering from acid burns. The search was considered reasonable as the police had reason to believe that the house contained a dangerous chemical lab, and that additional persons could still be in the residence.

In *R. v. Brown*,[104] the British Columbia Court of Appeal found that a 911 call from a hotel regarding an armed assault was sufficient justification for warrantless entry into and search of a hotel room in order for police to ascertain whether any assailants or victims remained in the room.

In *R. v. Bedard*[105] the Ontario Court of Appeal held a warrantless search of a residence to be reasonable following a 911 call from a victim's wife regarding injuries her husband received during a "pistol-whipping" assault that had some connection to drug activity. While investigating the victim's complaint, the police also retrieved a spent shell casing on the scene. The court found that the circumstances justified the police search of the suspect's residence for the additional attacker and for the weapon believed to have been used in the assault. The evidence of weapons and ammunition found in the process of that search was accordingly admissible.

In *R. v. Sanderson*,[106] the police responded to a 911 call in the middle of the night from a distraught woman who alleged that her boyfriend had assaulted her and threatened her dog and her property. The police accompa-

---

101 *Ibid.* at 28.
102 *R. v. Nicholls* (1999), 139 C.C.C. (3d) 253 (Ont. C.A.).
103 *R. v. Jamieson* (2002), 166 C.C.C. (3d) 501 (B.C.C.A.).
104 *R. v. Brown*, [2003] B.C.J. No.506 (C.A.).
105 *R. v. Bedard* (1998), 125 C.C.C. (3d) 348 (Ont. C.A.).
106 *R. v. Sanderson*, [2003] O.J. No. 1481 (C.A.).

nied her back to her boyfriend's home, where she had been living, so that she could safely obtain some belongings. The boyfriend resisted her efforts to obtain the belongings and would not allow the police access to assist. He was arrested and a scuffle ensued. The Ontario Court of Appeal held the warrantless entry to the home was authorized because the officers had common law and statutory duties to preserve the peace and protect property. As MacPherson J.A. explained:[107]

> In my view, the police officers' entry into the respondent's residence complied with the general *Waterfield* test and with the overlay of factors for applying it in the Canadian context as articulated in *Dedman* and *Simpson*. The officers were faced with a distraught woman in the middle of the night. She, and an independent witness, reported that she had been assaulted by the respondent. She had left the residence in only her pyjamas and without footwear — on March 29. The altercation continued, and another assault took place, when the complainant returned to the house with Farrell to retrieve her dog and personal belongings. After she left a second time, the respondent followed her to Menzies' and Farrell's apartment where, in a heated exchange, he threatened to burn her personal belongings.
>
> Hearing all of this when they arrived, the police were fully justified, in my view, in deciding to go to the respondent's house and, accompanied by the complainant who told them that she lived there and had a key, to enter it. They were investigating several potential criminal offences and they had reason to believe that the respondent would destroy the complainant's personal property. Moreover, they wanted to assist the complainant with retrieving her clothing and personal belongings, and getting away from the respondent, so that she could proceed to her parents' home in Belleville.[108]
>
> . . .
>
> I described the police entry into the respondent's residence as logical, laudable and lawful. The same words apply to their conduct inside the dwelling.[109]

v)   Hot Pursuit

There will be no violation of section 8 if officers discover or seize evidence after a warrantless entry into a dwelling while in "hot pursuit of a suspect."[110]

---

107   *Ibid.* at para. 25.
108   *Ibid.* at paras. 33–34.
109   *Ibid.* at para. 51.
110   The "hot pursuit" exception to the strict application of the *Hunter* criteria is conceptually different from situations where the police enter private property to investigate criminal activity committed against the owners of the property. While the

In *R. v. Macooh*,[111] the Supreme Court held that police officers had the power to enter a residence without prior judicial authorization in order to arrest a suspect without a warrant, provided the police were in hot pursuit of the individual, and provided that the offence was one for which the *Code* authorized warrantless arrests.[112] The Court defined "hot pursuit" as

> continuous pursuit conducted with reasonable diligence, so that pursuit and capture along with the commission of the offence may be considered as forming part of a single transaction.[113]

The Court explained the rationale for this exception:

> [I]t would be unacceptable for police officers who were about to make a completely lawful arrest to be prevented from doing so merely because the offender had taken refuge in his home or that of a third party. . . . These concerns are nowhere as relevant as in the case of hot pursuit. The offender is then not being bothered by the police unexpectedly while in domestic tranquility. He has gone to his home while fleeing solely to escape arrest. In such circumstances, the police could not be obliged to end the pursuit on the offender's doorstep, without making his residence a real sanctuary, contrary to the principles stated by this court in *Eccles*. The flight of the offender, an act contrary to public order, also should not be thus rewarded.
>
> As LaForest J. pointed out in *Landry*, in a case of hot pursuit the police officer may have personal knowledge of the facts justifying the arrest, which greatly reduces the risk of error. Flight also usually indicates some awareness of guilt on the part of the offender. Then too, it may often be difficult, even if that was not the case here, to identify the offender without arresting him on the spot.[114]

---

powers may appear similar, they have quite different theoretical bases — one set of activities constitutes a search, and one does not. The police activities in conducting a *hot pursuit* (and any subsequent search) will constitute a search under s. 8, but the exigent circumstances make prior authorization impracticable and therefore constitutionally unnecessary. By contrast, when police are *investigating criminal activity* on private property (not committed by the property owners themselves), they are *not* conducting a search *vis-à-vis* the property owner. Owners of private property are deemed to extend an implied licence for police to enter and investigate crimes committed against their property, and as such, waive their expectation of privacy against police entry for those purposes. The concept of implied licences is discussed in chapter 3.

111 *Macooh*, above note 65.
112 *Ibid.* at 494.
113 *Ibid.* at 491, taking its definition from R.E. Salhany, *Canadian Criminal Procedure*, 5th ed. (1989), 44; *Feeney*, above note 63.
114 *Macooh*, above note 65 at 490–91, as quoted in *Haglof*, above note 65 at para. 26.

In *R. v. Feeney*,[115] the Supreme Court preserved the "hot pursuit exception" despite holding all other warrantless entries into dwelling houses violate section 8,[116] noting that "in cases of hot pursuit, society's interest in effective law enforcement takes precedence over the privacy interest":[117]

> [I]n general, the following requirements must be met before an arrest for an indictable offence in a private dwelling is legal: a warrant must be obtained on the basis of reasonable and probable grounds to arrest and to believe the person sought is within the premises in question; and proper announcement must be made before entering. An exception to this rule occurs where there is a case for hot pursuit. Whether or not there is an exception for exigent circumstances generally has not been fully addressed by this Court, nor does it need to be decided in the present case.[118]

In *R. v. Haglof*,[119] the "hot pursuit" exception justified a warrantless entry into a dwelling house in a case involving a hit and run accident that had occurred 35 minutes prior to the arrest, which the officers had not personally witnessed. Upon entering the home, the officers discovered a marijuana grow-operation. The Court found that the officers had the requisite reasonable grounds to justify an arrest and that the investigation into the incident and the subsequent pursuit formed a single transaction:

> [T]he case at bar represents a situation of hot pursuit notwithstanding that the officers did not in fact see the accident occur or the appellant enter the house. The time between the accident and the arrest was only some 35 minutes. Within approximately fifteen minutes of the accident, Constable King arrived at the Ethel Residence. This represented the length of time it took to locate the suspect. The remaining 20 minutes were spent at the premises of the appellant attempting to and finally succeeding in effecting an arrest. In my view, these events are sufficiently proximate to be considered as forming part of a single transaction.[120]

Hagolf was charged with drug offences, and the evidence of the marijuana grow-operation discovered as a result of the warrantless entry was

---

115 *Feeney*, above note 63.
116 *Ibid.* at 154.
117 *Ibid.* at 156.
118 *Ibid.* at 158; note that *Feeney* was decided prior to the enactment of legislation specifically authorizing warrantless searches in certain circumstances, see s. 487.11. Parliament also authorized a warrantless power of arrest in s. 529.3.
119 *Haglof*, above note 65.
120 *Ibid.* at para. 38.

admissible at trial, since the discovery of the evidence was incident to the initial hot pursuit entry that was authorized by law.

In *R. v. Caissie*,[121] the New Brunswick Court of Appeal rejected the applicability of the hot pursuit exception where no true hot pursuit had been in progress (that is, there was no attempted flight) prior to police entry onto private property:

> [I]t is clear that the trial judge's assessment of the evidence and the findings of fact which he drew from it would not have permitted him to find hot pursuit. On the contrary, he found that the police officer never signaled to Mr. Caissie to stop nor even turned on his patrol car's flashing lights, but that after seeing him on the highway, he had decided to follow Mr. Caissie onto his property and to where he stopped close to his residence. The judge's conclusions are not contradicted, are supported by the evidence and are not unreasonable having regard to the evidence in the record.
>
> In light of the trial judge's conclusions, it seems obvious that Mr. Caissie did not attempt to flee at any time and that there was no pursuit by the police officer within the meaning of the definition of this concept in the *Macooh* decision, *supra*.[122]

c) Pursuit of Interests Other Than Law Enforcement

i) Border Control: Security and Sovereignty Interests

The Supreme Court has recognized that the *Hunter v. Southam* criteria for determining the reasonableness of a search will be more flexible in circumstances where national security and sovereignty interests are at stake. In *Simmons*,[123] the Court considered the constitutionality of sections of the *Customs Act* that authorized a warrantless search of the person "if the officer or person so searching has reasonable cause to suppose that the person searched has goods subject to entry at the customs, or prohibited goods, secreted about his person."[124] This sets a threshold of suspicion rather than reasonable belief. In addition to requiring a lowered evidentiary threshold, the provisions also did not require prior authorization for the search.

Without explicitly adopting a formal test for determining when the *Hunter v. Southam* criteria were inapplicable, the Court in *Simmons* accepted that a contextual analysis is necessary for an accurate appraisal of the reason-

---

121 *R. v. Caissie* (1999), 138 C.C.C. (3d) 205 (N.B.C.A.).
122 *Ibid.* at paras. 14–15.
123 *Simmons*, above note 49.
124 *Customs Act*, R.S.C. 1970, c. C-40, s. 143 (repealed and replaced with *Customs Act*, S.C. 1986, c. 1, s. 98).

ableness of a search that might involve a departure from *Hunter*. The key contextual factors identified by the Court in considering the border search were the lower level of privacy enjoyed in the circumstances, and the state sovereignty and security interests engaged at the border.[125] As the Court explained:

> [T]he degree of personal privacy reasonably expected at customs is lower than in most other situations. People do not expect to be able to cross international borders free from scrutiny. It is commonly accepted that sovereign states have the right to control both who and what enters their boundaries. For the general welfare of the nation the state is expected to perform this role.[126]

The Court noted that sovereign states have a strong national interest "in preventing the entry of undesirable persons and prohibited goods, and in protecting tariff revenue."[127] In light of the interests at stake and the lowered expectation of privacy, the Act provided for constitutionally reasonable standards of intrusion on privacy interests at the border:[128]

> In light of the existing problems in controlling illicit narcotics trafficking and the important government interest in enforcing our customs laws, and in light of the lower expectation of privacy one has at any border crossing, I am of the opinion that ss. 143 and 144 of the *Customs Act* are not inconsistent with s. 8 of the *Charter*.[129]

The Court held that a variety of searches, including body pat-down searches and strip searches, would be considered constitutionally reasonable if conducted under the criteria set out in the *Customs Act*, despite the absence of reasonable grounds and judicial authorization:

> [R]outine questioning by customs officers, searches of luggage, frisk or pat searches, and the requirement to remove in private such articles of clothing as will permit investigation of suspicious bodily bulges permitted by the framers of ss. 143 and 144 of the *Customs Act*, are not unreasonable within the meaning of s. 8. Under the *Customs Act* searches of the person are not routine but are performed only after customs officers have formed reasonable grounds for supposing that a person has contraband secreted about his or her body. The decision to search is subject to review at the request of the

---

125 *Simmons*, above note 49 at 318–21.
126 *Ibid.* at 528.
127 *Ibid.*
128 *Ibid.* at 320–21.
129 *Ibid.* at 321. Those sections have been replaced with s. 98 of the *Customs Act*, and provide essentially the same powers and threshold for use of those powers.

person to be searched. Though in some senses personal searches may be embarrassing, they are conducted in private search rooms by officers of the same sex. In these conditions, requiring a person to remove pieces of clothing until such time as the presence or absence of concealed goods can be ascertained is not so highly invasive of an individual's bodily integrity to be considered unreasonable under s. 8 of the *Charter*.

I also emphasize that, according to the sections in question: (i) before any person can be searched the officer or person so searching must have reasonable cause to suppose that the person searched has goods subject to entry at the customs, or prohibited goods, secreted about his or her person, and (ii) before any person can be searched, the person may require the officer to take him or her before a police magistrate or justice of the peace or before the collector or chief officer at the port or place who shall, if he or she sees no reasonable cause for search, discharge the person.[130]

The Court did not, however, endorse the conduct of all types of customs searches under these criteria. Certain types of invasive searches, such as the highly intrusive body cavity search, might require greater degrees of constitutional protection than what was afforded under sections 143 and 144 of the *Customs Act*.[131]

See also the discussion of reduced standards of protection against state intrusion at the border in chapter 3, "The Human Body," and the case of *R. v. Monney*[132] (dealing with "bedpan vigils" conducted on grounds of "reasonable suspicion").

ii) *Regulatory or Administrative Interests*

In *B.C. Securities Commission v. Branch*,[133] the majority of the Supreme Court recognized a general exception to the *Hunter* criteria for searches in the administrative or regulatory (as opposed to the criminal law) context. The Court summarized the exceptions to the *Hunter* criteria previously accepted in the regulatory sphere and concluded that the standard for determining reasonableness in the circumstances would move higher or lower on a sliding scale depending on the nature of the interests at stake and the extent of the expectation of privacy. As the Court explained, the greater the departure from the sphere of criminal law, the more flexible the application of the *Hunter v. Southam* criteria:

---

130 *Simmons*, above note 49 at 320–21.
131 *Ibid.* at 310.
132 *R. v. Monney*, [1999] 1 S.C.R. 652 at para. 42.
133 *Branch*, above note 53.

It is important to note, however, that [the *Hunter v. Southam* criteria] were articulated in the context of an appeal concerning the validity of a section which was, in essence, criminal or quasi-criminal. It is clear that the context within which the alleged violation takes place must be considered, for it is the context which determines the expectation of privacy that is legitimately expected. The following comments of Wilson J. in *R. v. McKinlay Transport Ltd.* [citation omitted]:

> Since individuals have different expectations of privacy in different contexts and with regard to different kinds of information and documents, it follows that the standard of review of what is "reasonable" in a given context must be flexible if it is to be realistic and meaningful.

Therefore, it is clear that the standard of reasonableness which prevails in the case of a search and seizure made in the course of enforcement in the criminal context will not usually be the appropriate standard for a determination made in an administrative or regulatory context: per LaForest J. in *Thomson Newspapers*. *The greater the departure from the realm of criminal law, the more flexible will be the approach to the standard of reasonableness. The application of a less strenuous approach to regulatory or administrative searches and seizures is consistent with a purposive approach to the elaboration of s. 8: Thomson Newspapers.* [emphasis added][134]

The rationale for adopting a more flexible standard in the regulatory context is based on a number of factors, including:

1. an expectation that the state will regulate certain activities;[135]
2. a lower stigma associated with wrongdoing in the regulatory sphere versus wrongdoing alleged in a criminal investigation;[136]
3. the social utility and importance of the given regulatory scheme (beyond the provision of criminal-type penalties), such as the regulation of business and the market economy,[137] or the collection and audit of government revenues in the form of taxation;[138] and,

---

134 *Ibid.* at 526–27; see also *McKinlay*, above note 55 at 541–42.
135 *Thomson Newspapers*, above note 31, *per* LaForest J. at 506–7.
136 *Ibid. per* La Forest J. at 506–7; see also *R. v. Wholesale Travel* (1991), 67 C.C.C. (3d) 193 (S.C.C.).
137 See *Branch*, above note 53; *Thomson Newspapers*, above note 31.
138 See *McKinlay*, above note 55; *R. v. Jarvis* (2002), 169 C.C.C. (3d) 1 (S.C.C.) [*Jarvis*].

4. the difficulty of investigating compliance if standards of reasonableness were higher.[139]

The relevance of the lower stigma associated with regulatory offence to search powers was articulated by LaForest J. in *Thomson Newspapers*:

> The situation is, of course, quite different when the state seeks information, not in the course of regulating a lawful social or business activity, but in the course of investigating a criminal offence. For reasons that go to the very core of our legal tradition, it is generally accepted that the citizen has a very high expectation of privacy in respect of such investigations. *The suspicion cast on persons who are made the subject of a criminal investigation can seriously, and perhaps permanently, lower their standing in the community.* This alone would entitle the citizen to expect that his or her privacy would be invaded only when the state has shown that it has serious grounds to suspect guilt. This expectation is strengthened by virtue of the central position of the presumption of innocence in our criminal law. *The stigma inherent in a criminal investigation requires that those who are innocent of wrongdoing be protected against overzealous or reckless use of the powers of search and seizure* by those responsible for the enforcement of the criminal law. The requirement of a warrant, based on a showing of reasonable and probable grounds to believe that an offence has been committed and evidence relevant to its investigation will be obtained, is designed to provide this protection. [emphasis added][140]

Justice LaForest in *Thomson Newspapers* also noted that the "stakes" were somewhat lower in non-criminal contexts:

> [T]he relevance of the regulatory character of the offences defined in the Act is that conviction for their violation does not really entail, and is not intended to entail, the kind of moral reprimand and stigma that undoubtedly accompanies conviction for the traditional "real" or "true" crimes. It follows that investigation for purposes of the Act does not cast the kind of

---

139 See, e.g., *McKinlay*, above note 55 at 545, where Wilson J. cites the difficulty in spotting misrepresentations on the face of a tax return and the corresponding ease of making such misrepresentations in a self-reporting/self-assessement context as justification for a departure from *Hunter*; see *Thomson Newspapers*, above note 31, where both LaForest J. at 490 and L'Heureux Dubé J. at 542–46 note the "invisibility" of infractions of the *Combines Investigation Act*, citing offences occurring in the hidden boardrooms of corporations and the existence of little outside evidence to show that an offence had been committed as a justification for departure from the strictures of *Hunter*.

140 *Thomson Newspapers*, above note 31 at 507–8.

suspicion that can affect one's standing in the community and that, as was explained above, entitles the citizen to a relatively high degree of respect for his or her privacy on the part of investigating authorities. . . . [T]he degree of privacy that can reasonably be expected within the investigative scope of the Act is akin to that which can be expected by those subject to other administrative and regulatory legislation, rather than to that which can legitimately be expected by those subject to police investigation for what I have called "real" or "true" crimes.[141]

As noted above, the fact that people must expect to be audited and regulated while engaging in certain activities, and the overall importance of ongoing regulation are also key to the lower standards of reasonableness associated with the regulatory search.[142]

The rationale for exemption from *Hunter* based on a clear expectation of being regulated and audited by the state is especially true of *documents* that must be produced to comply with regulations:[143]

Generally, an individual has a diminished expectation of privacy in respect of records and documents that he or she produces during the ordinary course of regulated activities: In the particular context of the self-assessment and self-reporting income tax regime, a taxpayer's privacy interest in records that may be relevant to the filing of his or her tax return is relatively low. [citations omitted][144]

A search of premises in the regulatory context will require greater privacy protections than simple document seizures,[145] but such searches may not be subject to the full *Hunter* criteria. As Cardiff J. of the British Columbia Supreme Court explained in *R. v. Mitton*[146] in relation to the search provisions under section 143(3) of the B.C. *Securities Act*, the extent of the protection afforded will depend on the overall context:

Although something less than the full *Hunter* standard applies, the nature of the search that may be authorized under s. 143(3) — that being, the entry

---

141 *Ibid.* at 516–17.
142 *Ibid.* at 507; see also *Branch*, above note 53 at 529–30.
143 *Jarvis*, above note 138; *Thomson Newspapers*, above note 31 at 507, per LaForest J.; *143471 Canada Inc. v. Quebec (Attorney General)*, [1994] 2 S.C.R. 339 at 378, per Cory J. [*143471 Canada*]; *Comité paritaire de l'industrie de la chemise v. Potash*, [1994] 2 S.C.R. 406 at 420–21 [*Potash*]; *R. v. Fitzpatrick*, [1995] 4 S.C.R. 154 at para. 49 [*Fitzpatrick*].
144 *Jarvis*, above note 138 at para. 72; see also *Fitzpatrick, ibid.* at para. 49.
145 *Baron*, above note 44 at 529; *Thomson Newspapers*, above note 31; *Hunter*, above note 1.
146 *Mitton v. British Columbia (Securities Commission)*, [2001] B.C.J. 665 (S.C.) [*Mitton*].

onto private business premises to search and seize material — must be kept in mind. Section 143(3) does not permit searches of private residences. While business premises have a lower expectation of privacy than residential premises for the purposes of s. 8 of the *Charter*, there still remains a reasonable expectation of privacy surrounding business premises even in the securities regulatory context.[147]

Unfortunately, the courts have not been clear as to what the alternate standard of reasonableness will be in the regulatory context. Justices Sopinka and Iacobucci explained in *Branch*[148] that although the standard of reasonableness in a regulatory context was not well-defined, the standard would, at least, be flexible and vary with the context:

> While the expectation of privacy with respect to criminal matters seems certain, the standard of reasonableness to be applied in the regulatory and administrative realm is less well-defined. Wilson J. found in *McKinlay Transport*, at p. 581 D.L.R., p. 543 C.C.C., that the point was aptly made by Alan D. Reid and Alison Harvison Young in "Administrative Search and Seizure Under the *Charter*" (1985), 10 Queen's L.J. 392 at pp. 398–9:
>
>> There are facets of state authority, generically associated with search or seizure, that are so intertwined with the regulated activity as to raise virtually no expectation of privacy whatsoever. . . . Other activities are regulated so routinely that there is virtually no expectation of privacy from state intrusion. Annual filing requirements for banks, corporations, trust companies, loan companies, and the like are inextricably associated with carrying on business under state licence.
>>
>> There are other situations in which government intrusion cannot be as confidently predicted, yet the range of discretion extended to state officials is so wide as to create in the regulatee an expectation that he may be inspected or requested to provide information at some point in the future. This may arise in the form of an inspection carried out either on a "spot check" basis, or on the strength of suspected non-compliance. The search may be in the form of a request for information that is not prescribed as an annual filing requirement, but is required to be produced on a demand basis. For the most part, there is no requirement that these powers be exercised on belief or suspicion of non-com-

---

147 *Ibid.* at paras. 43–44.
148 *Branch*, above note 53.

pliance. Rather, they are based on the common sense assumption that the threat of unannounced inspection may be the most effective way to induce compliance. They are based on a view that inspection may be the only means of detecting non-compliance, and that its detection serves an important public purpose.[149]

The purpose of the state's search in the regulatory context will determine the extent of the protections afforded to the individual's expectation of privacy. The *Charter* can afford different level of protection even within the same regulatory statute, depending on the values at stake in the circumstances:[150]

> [T]he *ITA* is a regulatory statute, but non-compliance with its mandatory provisions can in some cases lead to criminal charges being laid. In prosecution thereof, the state is pitted against the individual in an attempt to establish culpability. Stiff jail terms can result from a conviction. To conduct an appropriately contextual *Charter* analysis in these cases, the various regulatory and penal considerations must all exert some influence.[151]

As Catliff J. explained in *Mitton v. B.C. Securities Commission*,[152] in relation to the section 143(3) *B.C. Securities Act* search provisions:

> [T]he purpose of the search [in *Baron*, where the full *Hunter* criteria were found to apply] was to gather evidence to be used in the prosecution of offences under the *Income Tax Act*. That is not the purpose of s. 143(3) [of the *Securities Act*]. The Act is regulatory legislation with strong public welfare goals. The Act is not criminal or quasi-criminal legislation. The purpose of s. 143(3) is the gathering of information to advance an investigation that has been commenced under s. 142 to determine if there has been non-compliance with the Act and whether a hearing is required.[153]

Regulatory search powers that have been entitled to a more flexible standard of reasonableness than the *Hunter* criteria include:

1) The compelled production of business documents or documents made in course of regulated activity.[154]

---

149 *Ibid.* at 527–28, para. 53.
150 *Jarvis*, above note 138 at paras. 60–61.
151 *Ibid.* at para. 62.
152 *Mitton*, above note 146.
153 *Ibid.* at paras. 42–44.
154 *Thomson Newspapers*, above note 31 at 507, per LaForest J.; *143471 Canada*, above note 143 at 378, per Cory J.; *Potash*, above note 143 at 420–21; *Fitzpatrick*, above note 143 at para. 49; *McKinlay*, above note 55 at 649–50. In some instances, these types of documents may have no expectation of privacy such as in *McKinlay*, above

2) Spot inspections at business premises to demand production of records and make copies of documents.[155]
3) Compelled production of documents and answering of questions related to taxation, in the course of an audit.[156]

Search powers that have not been entitled to a more flexible standard, despite occurring in the regulatory context, include:

1) Compelled production of personal documents (as opposed to business documents).[157]
2) Searches of premises (as opposed to simple production order seizures), as there is a greater potential for incidental intrusions into other private matters and to affect persons present during the search.[158] This is especially true if the premises is a home.[159]
3) Where the state is pursuing penal liability rather than regulatory enforcement.[160]

iii) Pursuit of Penal Liability and the Predominant Purpose Test: R. v. Jarvis
The flexibility generally afforded to regulatory investigations will cease to apply once the predominant purpose of the state's interaction with the individual has become adversarial and has shifted to the pursuit of penal consequences.[161] In *R. v. Jarvis*,[162] the Canada Customs and Revenue Agency (CCRA) audited a farmer for compliance with the *Income Tax Act* (*ITA*) on suspicion that he had not reported the full extent of the income derived from the sale of his late wife's art. The Supreme Court held that the compliance audit (a non-penal proceeding designed to ensure compliance with the statute rather than punishment) had become an investigation once the auditor completed her review of the entire file, and passed the file on to the investigation department. The transformation from a general compliance audit to a criminal investigation meant that the CCRA was, after that point,

---

note 55; *Fitzpatrick*, above note 143; and *R. v. Hufsky* (1988), 40 C.C.C. (3d) 398 (S.C.C.). See also *Smith v. Canada*, [2001] 3 S.C.R. 902, which found no expectation of privacy in the information in a Customs declaration form.
155 *Thomson Newspapers*, above note 31, per LaForest J. at 476; *Potash*, above note 154 at 347–48.
156 *McKinlay*, above note 55 at 649–50; *Jarvis*, above note 137 at para. 72.
157 *Thomson Newspapers*, above note 31 at 483 and 490; *McKinlay*, above note 55.
158 *Hunter*, above note 1. See also *Thomson Newspapers*, above note 31; *McKinlay*, above note 55.
159 *McKinlay*, above note 55.
159 *Jarvis*, above note 138.
161 *Ibid*.
162 *Ibid*.

unable to resort to sections 231.1 and 231.2 *ITA* (which allowed the agency to compel information and statements without a warrant) for the purpose of advancing the criminal investigation.[163] The Court was clear to point out, however, that the regulator was not barred from pursuing an audit or from using the powers of the statute for the audit alone; what was prohibited was the collection of the information for criminal investigation.[164] Since the *Hunter v. Southam* level of protections would instead apply, the criminal investigators would be obliged to obtain such information by way of search warrant or other independent means.[165]

To determine when the relationship between the state and the individual has become sufficiently adversarial as to require full (or closer) adherence to the *Hunter* criteria, the Supreme Court directed that the "totality of the circumstances" must be assessed, with no one factor being necessarily determinative of the state's intentions.[166] Once it can be shown that the state has "crossed the Rubicon" from regulatory to criminal investigation, the full panoply of *Charter* protections apply, and the state can no longer use the provisions to compel documents in the absence of a warrant, either from the accused or any third party.[167] However, merely demonstrating that investigators suspected criminal activity is insufficient to demonstrate that the predominant purpose of the investigation is the pursuit of penal liability.[168]

The Court held that consideration of all the following listed factors, with no one factor being determinative, would assist in ascertaining whether the

---

163 *Ibid.* at para. 92.
164 *Ibid.* at para. 97.
165 *Ibid.*
166 *Ibid.* at para. 93.
167 *Ibid.* at para. 96.
168 *Ibid.*; see also *R. v. Dial Drugs* (2003), 63 O.R. (3d) 529 (Sup. Ct.) at 556–58, where Reilly J. held that, in light of *Jarvis*, the trial judge erred in finding that the purpose of CCRA's contact with the individuals was to determine penal liability at the moment the investigators had reasonable suspicion of misrepresentations to CCRA. Justice Reilly found that even if the auditors reasonably suspected misreporting at the outset of the audit, the contact with the persons did not become a criminal investigation until the file was turned over to Special Investigations and the foundation for a criminal investigation was complete. In *Dial Drugs*, although the auditor suspected wrongdoing, three outcomes were possible from the compliance audit interview: (1) that CCRA would have found that income in question was properly reported; (2) that there was an innocent explanation for non-reporting which would be followed by a civil demand by CCRA for payment; or (3) that the auditor would compile sufficient grounds to commence a penal investigation. The fact that other outcomes (aside from penal liability) were possible, and the lack of reasonable grounds, contributed to the Court's finding that CCRA's actions were an audit rather than investigation until the file was presented to Special Investigations.

predominant purpose of an inquiry is the pursuit of penal liability — noting that a context other than a CCRA investigation may require the application of additional factors to suit the context:[169]

    a.   Did the authorities have reasonable grounds to lay charges?[170] Does it appear from the record that a decision to proceed with a criminal investigation could have been made?

    b.   Was the general conduct of the authorities such that it was consistent with the pursuit of a criminal investigation?

    c.   Had the auditor transferred his or her files and materials to the investigators?

    d.   Was the conduct of the auditor such that he or she was effectively acting as an agent for the investigators?

    e.   Does it appear that the investigators intended to use the auditor as their agent in the collection of evidence?

    f.   Is the evidence sought relevant to taxpayer liability generally? Or, as is the case with evidence as to the taxpayer's *mens rea*, is the evidence relevant only to the taxpayer's penal liability?

    g.   Are there any other circumstances or factors that can lead the trial judge to the conclusion that the compliance audit had in reality become a criminal investigation?[171]

Interestingly, the Supreme Court found that even after the focus of the inquiry has shifted, the state is free to use the evidence gathered during the audit or non-penal stage to further its criminal case:[172]

> The predominant purpose test does not thereby prevent the CCRA from conducting parallel criminal investigations and administrative audits. The fact that the CCRA is investigating a taxpayer's penal liability, does not preclude the possibility of a simultaneous investigation, the predominant purpose of which is a determination of the same taxpayer's tax liability. *However, if an investigation into penal liability is subsequently commenced, the*

---

169 *Jarvis*, above note 138 at para. 88.
170 The Court in *Jarvis* specifically noted that the presence of reasonable grounds was not on its own determinative of whether an audit has become an investigation. In *Jarvis*, it appeared that reasonable grounds were present long before the Court determined that the focus of the investigation had shifted. However, the Court also noted that in most cases, if all ingredients of an offence are reasonably thought to have occurred, it is likely that the investigation function is triggered. See *Jarvis*, above note 138 at para. 89.
171 *Ibid.* at 41–42, para. 94.
172 *Ibid.* at para. 97.

investigators can avail themselves of that information obtained pursuant to the audit powers prior to the commencement of the criminal investigation, but not with respect to information obtained pursuant to such powers subsequent to the commencement of the investigation into penal liability. This is no less true where the investigations into penal liability and tax liability are in respect of the same tax period. So long as the predominant purpose of the parallel investigation actually is the determination of tax liability, the auditors may continue to resort to ss. 231.1(1) and 231.2(1). It may well be that there will be circumstances in which the CCRA officials conducting the tax liability inquiry will desire to inform the taxpayer that a criminal investigation also is under way and that the taxpayer is not obliged to comply with the requirement powers of ss. 231.1(1) and 231.2(1) for the purposes of the criminal investigation. On the other hand, the authorities may wish to avail themselves of the search warrant procedures under ss. 231.3 of the *ITA* or 487 of the *Criminal Code* to access the documents necessary to advance the criminal investigation. Put another way, the requirement powers of ss. 231.1(1) and 231.2(1) cannot be used to compel oral statements or written production for the purpose of advancing the criminal investigation. [emphasis added][173]

The ability to use the compelled fruits of a regulatory audit would appear to be a departure from the concept of "use immunity" introduced by the Supreme Court in cases such as *B.C. Securities Commission v. Branch*[174] and *R. v. S.(R.J.)*,[175] to protect an individual against the use in a subsequent criminal proceeding of evidence gathered in a non-criminal penalty context. However, the approach is consistent with cases such as *Laroche* that approved of information sharing between regulators and the police, so long as warrants are obtained for the actual seizure of evidence once a criminal investigation begins.[176]

Presumably, the ability to conduct parallel audits and investigations would be limited to regulatory agencies that have separate audit and investigation arms; it would be an impossible task to keep separate the work product from two related streams of inquiry that each required different levels of *Charter* protections. For agencies with no such division of responsibilities, it is likely that the predominant purpose test would be satisfied once the agents had reasonable grounds to believe that an offence has been com-

---

173   *Ibid.* at para. 97.
174   *Branch*, above note 53.
175   *R. v. S.(R.J.)* (1995), 96 C.C.C. (3d) 1 (S.C.C.).
176   *Quebec (Attorney General) v. Laroche*, [2002] 3 S.C.R. 708 [*Laroche*].

mitted and the agents began to turn their minds to penal aspects of their statutes.

d) Higher Protections Against Intrusion Where Competing/Compound Interests Are Affected by the Search

Although section 8 is principally concerned with protecting privacy interests, certain searches (and search powers) may also intrude on other important and constitutionally relevant interests, such as the freedom of the press, solicitor–client privilege, the right to life, liberty and security of the person or the privacy rights of third parties. The determination of whether a search power is reasonable in such circumstances, accordingly, must take into account these other compound or competing interests implicated by the search power, in addition to the usual *Hunter v. Southam* criteria for assessing reasonableness. The sections below will examine the courts' attempts to resolve these interests in the context of a claim of unreasonable search and seizure.[177]

i) Section 7

The Supreme Court's recent decision in *R. v. S.A.B.*[178] illustrates how a court ought to resolve the question of whether a search or seizure power that has an incidental effect on interests protected by section 7 of the *Charter*[179] is reasonable under section 8. In *S.A.B.*, the Supreme Court examined the reasonableness of the provisions of the *Criminal Code* authorizing the seizure of bodily samples for DNA analysis during a criminal investigation.[180] These provisions authorizing the taking of such samples *prima facie* implicate both the principle against forced self-incrimination[181] and privacy interests.[182]

The Supreme Court parted company from the Alberta Court of Appeal, and from the approaches taken by other provincial courts of appeal,[183] in its

---

177 See also the discussion in this chapter on "Was the Search Conducted in a Reasonable Manner" on the effect of a violation of section 10(b) on a determination of reasonableness.
178 *R. v. S.A.B.*, 2003 SCC 60 [*S.A.B.*].
179 Section 7 of the *Charter* guarantees to everyone "the right to life, liberty and security of the person and the right not to be deprived thereof except in accordance with the principles of fundamental justice."
180 See *Criminal Code*, ss. 490.04 to 490.09.
181 In *S.A.B.*, above note 178, Arbour J. explained, at para. 33: "The principle against self-incrimination imposes limits on the extent to which an accused person can be used as a source of information about his or her own criminal conduct."
182 *S.A.B.*, above note 175; see also *R. v. Stillman* (1997), 113 C.C.C. (3d) 321 (S.C.C.) [*Stillman*] at paras. 83–86.
183 See, e.g., the approaches taken by the Ontario Court of Appeal in *F.(S.)*, above note 57, and the British Columbia Court of Appeal in *Feeney*, above note 63.

approach to the evaluation of self-incrimination concerns. The Alberta Court held that it was necessary to conduct a separate section 7 analysis to assess the legislation's impact on the principle against self-incrimination, as a section 8 analysis could only properly consider privacy interests. Other courts of appeal had held that since the legislation complied with section 8, it necessarily complied with section 7 — if samples were taken under a "reasonable search and seizure," and a reasonable search and seizure was a principle of fundamental justice, any deprivation of security was necessarily in accordance with those principles.[184]

The Supreme Court, by contrast, considered it proper to incorporate section 7 self-incrimination concerns into its analysis of whether the legislation was reasonable under section 8 of the *Charter*. Finding that the cases of *R. v. Mills*[185] and *Hunter v. Southam*[186] allowed courts to consider broader interests than simple privacy interests in appropriate cases, Arbour J. declined to conduct a separate section 7 analysis. Instead, Arbour J. opted for a blended approach that incorporated considerations of the legislation's impact on the principle against self-incrimination into the analysis of the legislation's impact on the accused's section 8 rights :

> In light of *Stillman, supra*, searches and seizures pursuant to a DNA warrant engage the principle against self-incrimination. However, the principles of fundamental justice that are alleged to be implicated by a DNA search and seizure, including the principle against self-incrimination, are more appropriately considered under a s. 8 analysis. Indeed in *Hunter v. Southam* Inc., [1984] 2 S.C.R. 145, at p. 159, Dickson J. (as he then was) noted that he would "be wary of foreclosing the possibility that the right to be secure against unreasonable search and seizure might protect interests beyond the right of privacy". In *R. v. Mills*, [1999] 3 S.C.R. 668, at para. 88, a majority of this Court held that it was appropriate to consider an accused's right to full answer and defence in determining whether a search and seizure of a complainant's therapeutic counselling records was reason-

---

184 See, e.g., *F.(S.)*, above note 57; *Feeney*, above note 63.
185 *R. v. Mills*, [1999] 3 S.C.R. 668 [*Mills*]. It is interesting that the Court used *R. v. Mills* in support of the proposition that s. 8 could include the protection of rights broader than privacy rights. In *Mills*, the Court explained that if legislation authorizing the seizure of confidential medical records complied with s. 8 of the *Charter*, that is, by authorizing a *reasonable search and seizure*, then the legislation would necessarily comply with s. 7. In *S.A.B.*, the Court appears to have come to the opposite conclusion: in order for legislation to comply with s. 8, it had to also comply with s. 7 principles.
186 *Hunter*, above note 1.

able. Similarly, in my view, it is proper to consider an accused's right not to incriminate him or herself in determining whether a DNA warrant complies with s. 8 of the *Charter*.[187]

Justice Arbour further rejected the idea that if the legislation was reasonable under section 8, then it would necessarily comply with section 7 as any deprivation would be in accordance with the right to privacy, a "principle of fundamental justice." In her view, an analysis of privacy interests alone could not completely satisfy concerns about the principle against self-incrimination:

> Determining the particular requirements of, and limits on the principle against self-incrimination requires a consideration of the principle's underlying rationales. This Court has identified two such rationales — (i) to protect against unreliable confessions (or in this case, evidence), and (ii) to protect against the abuse of power by the state. As this Court recognized in *White, supra*, these rationales are linked to the importance of privacy in Canadian society. However, considerations of privacy (which generally form the core of the s. 8 analysis) cannot exhaust the analysis where the principle against self-incrimination is at issue. It is true that where a person is forced to provide evidence contrary to the principle against self-incrimination, he or she is revealing information, thus engaging privacy interests. However, more fundamentally, that evidence is given so that it may be *used in a case against him or her*. Thus, as this Court recognized in *S.(R.J.), supra*, the principle against self-incrimination rests on the fundamental notion that the Crown has the burden of establishing a "case to meet" and must do so without the compelled participation of the accused.[188]

The Court ultimately found that the legislation did not infringe the principle against self-incrimination, and was accordingly reasonable under section 8. See chapter 3 and Appendix 6 for further discussion of the Court's reasons for finding that the statute complied with the principles of section 7.

In our view, the Court rejected an analytical framework that could permit a law to be declared reasonable under section 8 and yet simultaneously infringe another *Charter* right. As Arbour J. highlighted in her analysis, there appears to be room in the section 8 analysis for consideration of these broader concerns. Specifically, the assessment of whether the law authorizing the search itself is reasonable[189] ought to properly include considera-

---

187   S.A.B., above note 178 at para. 35.
188   *Ibid.* at para. 57.
189   That is, the second *Collins* factor for assessing reasonableness of a search (was the search reasonable?).

tions of the impact of the law on other *Charter* rights, as it would be an affront to *Charter* values to declare a search power reasonable if it somehow improperly infringed on other rights.

The Supreme Court's approach to the blending of the section 7 and section 8 analysis is an important development in search and seizure law. Primarily, it confirms the availability of an analysis broader than an assessment of simple privacy concerns to determine reasonableness under section 8. While privacy interests may always act as the trigger to engage a section 8 analysis, subsequent assessments of legislation ought to incorporate an analysis of the effect of search provisions on broader constitutional rights and protections beyond privacy concerns in appropriate cases where competing rights are engaged.

ii) Privacy Rights of Third Parties

The privacy interests of third parties are in many circumstances proper considerations within a section 8 analysis of the reasonableness of a search, either for evaluating the manner the search was conducted, or for assessing the legality of the proposed or conducted search itself. The latter will be an issue when common law or statutory rules govern the issuance of third-party rights in a search and seizure.

The case of R. v. *Mills*[190] provides a framework for incorporating the competing constitutional claims of third parties into an analysis of whether legislation or state actions generally comply with the *Charter*. In *Mills*, the accused argued that the *Criminal Code* provisions governing the method of and threshold for production of witnesses' therapeutic records in sexual offence proceedings infringed the accused's right to full answer and defence and the right to a fair trial. The Supreme Court found that these provisions were constitutionally sound, and complied with the *Charter*'s protections of the right to full answer and defence and the right to a fair trial, as well as the complainant's right to privacy and to equality.

In determining the constitutionality of the provisions, the Court held that a constitutional analysis must be contextual.[191] In the *Mills* case, the relevant context was the potential for a production order to intrude on a witness's or complainant's right to privacy and equality. The Court reasoned that no constitutional right could trump another;[192] specifically, the right to fairness and fundamental justice were not absolute or immutable, and were influenced by the relevant context.[193] Since there were competing constitu-

---

190 *Mills*, above note 185.
191 *Ibid.* at para. 63.
192 *Ibid.* at para. 65.
193 *Ibid.* at para. 73.

tional interests at stake in this case, the right to full answer and defence and a fair trial had to be defined in light of the competing rights of the witnesses. Additionally, what would be considered a reasonable search and seizure as against the witnesses or complainants had to be defined with reference both to the accused's right to full answer and defence and the witness or complainant's right to privacy and equality.[194] The following passage summarizes the Court's findings on the influence of a complainant's privacy rights on a competing constitutional claim:

> The right of the accused to make full answer and defence is a core principle of fundamental justice, but it does not automatically entitle the accused to gain access to information contained in the private records of complainants and witnesses. Rather, the scope of the right to make full answer and defence must be determined in light of privacy and equality rights of complainants and witnesses. It is clear that the right to full answer and defence is not engaged where the accused seeks information that will only serve to distort the truth-seeking purpose of a trial, and in such a situation, privacy and equality rights are paramount. On the other hand, where the information contained in a record directly bears on the right to make full answer and defence, privacy rights must yield to the need to avoid convicting the innocent. Most cases, however, will not be so clear, and in assessing applications for production, courts must determine the weight to be granted to the interests protected by privacy and full answer and defence in the particular circumstances of each case. Full answer and defence will be more centrally implicated where the information contained in a record is part of the case to meet or where its potential probative value is high. A complainant's privacy interest is very high where the confidential information contained in a record concerns the complainant's personal identity or where the confidentiality of the record is vital to protect a therapeutic relationship.[195]

See also the media search cases discussed later in this chapter; *R. v. Shearing*,[196] which involved the introduction of a complainant's diary into evidence at trial; and *R. v. Serendip*,[197] which involved a warrant for health records. Related issues are raised in the earlier discussion regarding the incorporation of section 7 concerns into determinations of reasonableness under section 8, and the case of R. v. S.A.B.[198]

---

194 *Ibid.* at paras. 88 and 90.
195 *Ibid.* at para. 94.
196 *R. v. Shearing* (2002), 165 C.C.C. (3d) 225 (S.C.C.).
197 *R. v. Serendip Physiotherapy Clinic* (2003), 175 C.C.C. (3d) 474 (Ont. Sup. Ct.), rev'd [2004] O.J. No. 4653 (C.A.) [*Serendip*].
198 *S.A.B.*, above note 178.

iii) Solicitor–Client Privilege

Chapter 6 discusses the special requirements that must be attached to searches of law offices, where the competing interest of solicitor–client privilege must be given precedence over the state interest in obtaining evidence.

iv) Media Searches

Another example of a competing interest deserving more protection than those afforded by the *Hunter* criteria is searches involving the media. The courts have expressed concern that the "vital role" of the media in a democratic society not be unduly inhibited by law enforcement. In *Attorney-General of Quebec v. C.B.C.*[199] and *Attorney-General of New Brunswick v. C.B.C.*,[200] videotapes of protests and resulting arson damage were seized from the Canadian Broadcasting Corporation pursuant to search warrants. The sworn information to obtain the warrants failed to disclose that police officers had been present during the protest incidents and did not set out whether alternative sources of the information were available. In those decisions, the Court summarized the additional factors that must be taken into account in the balancing process in determining whether a search warrant should be issued for a media establishment:

(1) It is essential that all the requirements set out in s. 487(1)(b) of the *Criminal Code* for the issuance of a search warrant be met. [This, of course, is true for the issuance of all investigative orders].

(2) Once the statutory conditions have been met, the justice of the peace should consider all of the circumstances in determining whether to exercise his or her discretion to issue a warrant.

(3) The justice of the peace should ensure that a balance is struck between the competing interests of the state in the investigation and prosecution of crimes and the right to privacy of the media in the course of their news gathering and news dissemination. It must be borne in mind that the media play a vital role in the functioning of a democratic society. Generally speaking, the news media will not be implicated in the crime under investigation. They are truly an innocent third party. This is a particularly important factor to be considered in attempting to strike an appropriate balance, including the consideration of imposing conditions on that warrant.

---

199 *CBC*, above note 58.
200 *Canadian Broadcasting Corp. v. Attorney-General for New Brunswick* (1991), 67 C.C.C. (3d) 544 (S.C.C.).

(4) The affidavit in support of the application must contain sufficient detail to enable the justice of the peace to properly exercise his or her discretion as to the issuance of a search warrant.

(5) Although it is not a constitutional requirement, the affidavit material should ordinarily disclose whether there are alternative sources from which the information may reasonably be obtained and, if there is an alternative source, that it has been investigated and all reasonable efforts to obtain the information have been exhausted.

(6) If the information sought has been disseminated by the media in whole or in part, this will be a factor which will favour the issuing of the search warrant.

(7) If a justice of the peace determines that a warrant should be issued for the search of media premises, consideration should then be given to the imposition of some conditions on its implementation, so that the media organization will not be unduly impeded in the publishing or dissemination of the news.

(8) If, subsequent to the issuing of a search warrant, it comes to light the authorities failed to disclose pertinent information that could well have affected the decision to issue the warrant, this may result in a finding that the warrant was invalid.

(9) Similarly, if the search itself is unreasonably conducted, this may render the search invalid.[201]

Ultimately, though, the Supreme Court held the searches that occurred in the particular circumstances of these cases were reasonable, despite the existence of deficiencies in the warrant application, largely because a chilling effect on the media's source of news had not occurred. In *Attorney-General of Quebec v. C.B.C.*[202] the Court explained:

> The failure to set out the lack of alternative sources was simply another factor to be taken into account in assessing the reasonableness of the search. Here, the actual search was conducted reasonably and properly. There was no interference with the operation of the news media, nor was the freedom of the press threatened. The media had already completed their basic function of news gathering and news dissemination; thus, in my view, the seizure of the tapes at this stage could not be said to have a chilling effect

---

201 *CBC*, above note 58 at 533–35.
202 *Ibid*.

on the media's sources of news. It was therefore appropriate for the justice of the peace to issue the search warrant in this case.[203]

Recently, in *National Post v. Canada*,[204] Benotto J. of the Ontario Superior Court issued a judgment that significantly broadens the protections against search and seizure afforded to the media. In that case, the *National Post* was subject to a general warrant under section 487.01 and an assistance under section 487.02 of the *Criminal Code* requiring the newspaper to produce to the RCMP a document, allegedly forged, that had been obtained by a *Post* reporter from a confidential source. The document purported to be an internal Business Development Bank of Canada loan authorization, which in its footnotes appeared to reveal a debt to a holding company related to the prime minister of Canada. After disclosing the document to the reporter, the confidential source expressed safety concerns and sought to have the document destroyed; the reporter instead secured the document and promised confidentiality. The RCMP notified the *Post* that it would be seeking a search warrant for the document; the *Post* repeatedly asked for prior notice of the application for the warrant so that it could make submissions as to the propriety of its issuance. No such notice was given to the *Post*, and the warrant issued on an *ex parte* basis.

Justice Benotto found that although there was sufficient evidence of forgery to ground the warrant, the issuing justice did not adequately consider the impact the search would have on the *Charter* right of freedom of expression under section 2(b) and potential issues of privilege. Justice Benotto expressly declined to develop guidelines for the production of journalistic information, preferring instead a case-by-case approach to the problem.[205]

In conducting the case-specific analysis, Benotto J. first affirmed that special protections should be given to the media against searches due to the importance of section 2(b) in a democratic society:

> Section 2(b) also encompasses the receipt of information by members of the public. Listeners and readers have a right to information pertaining to public institutions. It is only through the press that most individuals can learn of what is transpiring in government and come to their own assessment of the institution and its actions. By protecting the freedom of expression of the press, s. 2(b) thereby guarantees the further freedom of members of the public to develop, put forward and act upon informed opinions about government and other matters of public interest.

---

203 *Ibid.* at 533–35.
204 *Post*, above note 58.
205 *Ibid.* at para. 82.

It is because of the fundamental importance of a free press in a democratic society that special considerations arise in applications to search media premises or to seize material from journalists, pursuant to powers granted to the police under the *Criminal Code*. The effect of the search and seizure on the ability of the press to fulfill its function must be considered by the justice of the peace before issuing the order. Moreover, the overall reasonableness of the search is protected by s. 8 of the *Charter*. In this regard, the damaging effect of the search on the freedom and functioning of the press is highly relevant to the assessment of the reasonableness of the search. It is essential that flexibility in the balancing process be preserved so that all the factors relevant to the individual case may be taken into consideration and properly weighed.[206]

Justice Benotto next examined the effect of a media search on issues of confidentiality of sources. Recognizing that confidential sources were essential to a journalist's ability to uncover controversial or sensitive material of public interest, Benotto J. found that a justice must carefully consider issues of confidentiality before issuing a search warrant on the media:

> To compel a journalist to break a promise of confidentiality would do serious harm to the constitutionally entrenched right of the media to gather and disseminate information. The reasonableness of the search will be considered in the context of these *Charter* values. A Justice of the Peace considering a search warrant application must undertake a careful weighing of the privacy interests of individuals in a democratic society against the interest of the state investigating and prosecuting crimes. This weighing and balancing will vary with each case. The media are entitled to this "special consideration because of the importance of its role in a democratic society."[207]

In addition to her *Charter* holdings, Justice Benotto found that the documents sought by the police were protected by common law privilege. The documents met the first three "Wigmore" criteria for determining new cases of privilege: the documents originated in a confidence that the communication would not be disclosed, confidentiality was necessary to the maintenance of the relationship, and the relationship is one that the community has an interest in fostering.[208] In assessing the fourth criteria, whether "the interests served by protecting the communications from disclosure outweigh the interest of pursuing the truth and disposing correctly of the litigation," the judge held that confidentiality prevailed:

---

206 *Ibid.* at paras. 44–45.
207 *Ibid.* at para. 52.
208 *Ibid.* 59 at paras. 55–78.

The balancing of these competing interests leads me to confirm the privilege. Here, the document is required as part of an investigation, not the defence of an accused. There is evidence that the document was probably extensively handled. There is only a remote and speculative possibility that the fingerprints were those of the alleged forgerer [sic]. Disclosure of the document will minimally, if at all, advance the investigation while at the same time damage freedom of expression.

There are unique factors here, including, the confidential relationship between X and Mr. McIntosh: the fact that he/she was promised confidentiality; the politically charged nature of the information obtained; the importance of informing Canadians with respect to the most powerful political figure in the country; and the vast body of evidence and jurisprudence produced which show the importance of confidentiality in the news gathering role of the press. All these factors outweigh the benefits of disclosure in the context of this investigation.

Insofar as the documents may reveal the confidential identity of a source, they are privileged.[209]

Accordingly, Benotto J. quashed the warrants on the basis that the issuing judge did not adequately consider the *Charter* issues involved, and could not have done so on an *ex parte* basis:[210]

> The issuing justice was required to ensure that there was a sufficient evidentiary basis before him upon which he could exercise his discretion. The issuing justice failed to give adequate consideration to the pertinent issue of confidentiality because adequate information was not before him. This had to affect the decision to issue the warrant and results in a finding that the warrant is invalid and should not have been issued.[211]

The effect of this judgment is to require a justice to have an *inter partes* hearing on notice to the affected parties in all instances where the police seek the production of a document delivered to a media outlet by a confidential source. On a case-by-case basis, the justice would have to determine whether the interest in disclosure would outweigh the importance of the privilege. Such a showing might be possible in cases where the evidence was in better condition for testing: in *National Post*, the document had been overly handled, and would therefore have limited evidentiary value for fingerprint or DNA testing. The arguments in favour of production will of course be correspondingly higher in a case where such evidence could exonerate an accused person.

---

209   *Ibid.* at paras. 79–81.
210   *Ibid.* at paras. 84 and 87.
211   *Ibid.* at para. 83.

Justice Benotto's recognition of a media privilege will no doubt continue to raise interesting issues in subsequent cases. One implication of the decision is that items perfectly subject to seizure, and afforded no privilege, are suddenly protected by media privilege once handed to a journalist. Not even solicitor–client privilege could protect tangible evidence in such circumstances.

Interesting problems may also be created the definition of "media." In the Internet age, anyone can be a journalist. While the *inter partes* model might be appropriate for a national newspaper, will courts pay the same deference to smaller — even one person — media outlets? It is not clear why a self-publisher of a website with a readership in the hundreds should be entitled to fewer constitutional protections than a media conglomerate. However, one of the rationales for *ex parte* warrant applications is to prevent the hiding or destruction of evidence. It remains to be seen whether courts will afford media privilege protections to such persons, and trust them to preserve evidence subject to an *inter partes* application, and turn it over if so ordered.

v) Search and Seizure of Health Records
Where a search or seizure interferes with the confidentiality of health records, the courts may, in appropriate circumstances, demand protections greater than those afforded by the *Hunter v. Southam* criteria. The case of *R. v. Serendip*,[212] a recent decision by the Ontario Court of Appeal, gives some guidance as to the nature and scope of the additional protections that must be provided. As will be discussed below, the same degree of privacy protections will not be appropriate in all cases. The greater the sensitivity of the records, the greater protections the courts must provide. Note that even where additional protection of privacy is required, in most cases the additional protections may amount to only a requirement for the issuing justice to impose a sealing order for seized health records. However, cases involving the seizure of psychiatric records,[213] or cases which could potentially "chill" the doctor-patient relationship will likely be subject to more restrictive terms.

In *R. v. Serendip*, the police obtained a search warrant for a physiotherapy clinic believed to be submitting insurance claims in relation to bogus injuries and for physiotherapy services that were over-inflated or never provided.[214] The warrant authorized the seizure of documents, including clinical records and health histories of patients, which related in any way to Mr. Devendra, a phys-

---

212 *Serendip* (C.A.), above note 197.
213 For reasons alluded to briefly below, the Ontario Court of Appeal has suggested that psychiatric records may be afforded more privacy protection than other forms of medical records.
214 *Serendip*, above note 197 at para.4 (Sup. Ct.).

iotherapist practising at the clinic.[215] Nothing in the warrant addressed the issue of protecting patients' privacy in the records. Justice Ferguson of the Ontario Superior Court granted an order in the nature of *certiorari*, quashing the search warrant. He found that any search warrant purporting to authorize the search for and seizure of health records must incorporate terms to protect the privacy interests associated with the health records of patients. *Certiorari* was granted because, in the application judge's view, the justice of the peace exceeded his or her jurisdiction by issuing the warrant without including conditions to protect the privacy of the medical records. The application judge then devised a set of criteria to be followed by the police and the issuing justice in all such cases[216] and suggested a detailed list of guidelines for the issuance of any warrant for health records. The guidelines were primarily concerned with a procedure for sealing and unsealing any seized health records.[217]

The *certiorari* decision in *Serendip* was reversed on appeal.[218] The court found that, in the absence of a direct challenge to section 487,[219] the search warrant issuance scheme struck a sufficient balance between the interests of patients and the state.[220] The court essentially held that a case-by-case approach to the protection of patients' privacy was reasonable; the issuing justice has the discretion to impose conditions on the warrant, including a condition to seal any seized document to protect patients' rights. And, in certain unique circumstances where a justice perceives that the doctor-patient relationship may be chilled, the justice may require police to demonstrate a compelling state interest that justifies the seizure of the records.[221]

The Court of Appeal distinguished all the authorities relied upon by the application judge to support his more restrictive approach to the seizure of health records. In the Court of Appeal's view, the rules applying to searches of lawyers' offices[222] were not applicable to the healthcare field. The restrictions on law office searches are premised on unique evidentiary and sub-

---

215 *Ibid.* at para 8 (Sup. Ct.).
216 The court found that not all seizure of health records would actually implicate patient privacy interests: e.g., in circumstances where the records sought are of an undercover officer posing as a patient, or the records of a patient who has consented to the seizure of the records.
217 *Serendip*, above note 197 at para. 68 (Sup. Ct).
218 *Ibid.*
219 Because of the procedural history, the Court of Appeal did not proceed as if s. 487 itself had been challenged, but rather on the narrower basis of the alleged jurisdictional error.
220 *Serendip*, above note 197 at paras. 34–35 (Ont. C.A.).
221 *Ibid.* at paras. 38–41 (Ont. C.A.).
222 See Chapter 8.

stantive legal protections against the use of solicitor-client communications;[223] there is no comparable concern that applies to records arising from the physiotherapist-patient relationship.[224]

The Court of Appeal also found the health record cases relied upon by the application judge to be distinguishable. While agreeing that *R. v. O'Connor*[225] required enhanced privacy protections for healthcare records, the Court recognized that the context was different; *O'Connor* involved a subpoena compelling production of such records in the absence of statutory or constitutional protections.[226] The Court of Appeal noted, moreover, that Supreme Court *dicta* required a reasonable system of pre-authorization for the production of records, but it did not suggest that section 487 was an inadequate check on the process where the state (as opposed to an accused person) seeks the information.[227] Similarly, the court distinguished *R. v. J.O.*,[228] a case that imposed restrictions on the seizure of psychiatric records,[229] as the records specifically targeted in that case belonged to innocent parties, there was legislation governing the release of psychiatric records which provided substantive protections against seizing such records, and, unlike regular medical records, psychiatric records may be subject to privilege.[230]

Subject to any future direct constitutional challenge to section 487 of the *Code*, the Court of Appeal unanimously expressed the view that section 487 adequately balanced the right to patient privacy against the state's interests. The court reasoned that since section 487 could reasonably permit seizures of even very personal information and could even authorize invasions into the privacy of the home, without detailed requirements for sealing such information after its seizure, there was no compelling justification to draw more distinctions for health records.[231] Further, the court noted that even where a

---

223 See Chapter 6, Privilege in Search and Seizure.
224 *Ibid.* at paras. 17–18 (Ont. C.A.).
225 (1995), 103 C.C.C. (3d) 1 (S.C.C.).
226 The test for the issuance of a subpoena turns on relevance to a court proceeding, and it does not allow for the sort of balancing approach possible on a warrant application.
227 *Serendip*, above note 197 at paras. 19–23 (Ont. C.A.) This point relies on the discretion of the justice hearing the application to impose appropriate conditions, or to deny the investigative order in the interests of justice, even when the statutory preconditions for the order are satisfied.
228 [1996] O.J. No. 4799 (Gen. Div.) [*J.O.*].
229 The criteria that were imposed by Ferguson J. in *Serendip* were modelled on the restrictions developed in *J.O.*
230 *Serendip*, above note 197 at 25–29 (Ont. C.A.).
231 *Ibid.* at para. 35. The court noted that psychiatric records might be entitled to higher protections than other kinds of information for reasons that would not apply to other kinds of medical records.

search warrant involves the news media and could potentially interfere with section 2(b) rights to freedom of expression, rather than mandate conditions for the issuance of all such warrants, they were capable of being dealt with on a case-by-case basis where the particular circumstances required.[232]

For these reasons, the court held the issuing justice *may* impose discretionary conditions to protect patients' privacy interests in appropriate cases, such as special sealing requirements for the records following a seizure.[233] Further, the court held that a justice could refuse to issue a warrant in an appropriate case, where the minimum requirements would offer inadequate protection and no "compelling state interest" is demonstrated. This is analogous to justice's discretion to refuse the issuance of a warrant where the media's functioning would be impeded without compelling cause:

> In *Canadian Broadcasting Corp. v. New Brunswick (Attorney General)* at p. 556, Cory J. held that if a search would impede the functioning of the media and the impediments could not be reasonably controlled by the imposition of conditions, a warrant should only be issued "where a compelling state interest is demonstrated." This suggests that while no particular factors, such as the *Pacific Press* alternative source conditions, may be constitutionally mandated, a search pursuant to a warrant that otherwise complies with s. 487 might nevertheless be found to violate the protection against unreasonable search and seizure because of the failure to demonstrate a compelling state interest in the particular circumstances of the case. As Cory J. went on to hold at p. 558, "it is the over-all reasonableness of a search which is protected by s. 8 of the *Charter*."[234]

The court also found that under this case-by-case approach, in unique circumstances, such as where a warrant is issued for the search and seizure of psychiatric records in the absence of sufficient protections imposed by the issuing justice, a search and seizure of medical records could be rendered unreasonable:

> Similarly, it may be that in a particular case, the search and seizure of medical records failed to meet constitutional standards because of circumstances unique to that case. The seizure of the psychiatric records in the *R. v. J.O.* case may well be an example. But, the violation of s. 8 in such a case will not be the result of failure to meet a set of rigid conditions like those set out by the application judge in this case.[235]

---

232 *Ibid.* at para. 36.
233 *Ibid.* at para. 38.
234 *Ibid.* at para. 40.
235 *Ibid.* at para. 41.

In light of the Court of Appeal's decision in *Serendip*, any search or seizure that might involve health records should be approached with caution, and consideration should be given to whether a warrant ought to contain conditions protecting the privacy of the person under investigation or third-parties. Further, if there is potential for the violation of third-party patients' rights for a chilling effect on doctor-patient relationships, or if psychiatric records are involved, the grounds for the warrant should demonstrate a "compelling state interest" justifying the issuance of the warrant. In the specific case of psychiatric records, whic according to the court's comments may be privileged, any searches for such records should be carried out with the strictest of conditions.

C. WAS THE SEARCH CONDUCTED IN A REASONABLE MANNER?

If a search or seizure is conducted in an unreasonable manner, the search or seizure will violate section 8, even if the search was conducted pursuant to the proper legal authority.[236] The question of whether a search or seizure is conducted in a reasonable manner involves an assessment of the conduct of the officials involved in executing the search or seizure — the "physical way in which the search was carried out"[237] to determine whether it meets a reasonableness standard.

The reasonableness of the search will be affected by factors such as risk to the health or safety of the individual being searched, or unnecessary discomfort or embarrassment to the individual.[238] The use of excessive force or lack of prior announcement before entering a private residence can render a search unreasonable, unless the police officers proffer some evidence to support the reasonableness of their actions specifically tied to the circumstances of the individual case.[239] Blanket policies (such as one for "no-knock" searches on drug raids) will not satisfy this requirement.

The potential for violations of the rights of third parties may also lead to a finding that the search was conducted in an unreasonable manner. For example, in a case where the police recorded conversations at a public pay phone but made no effort to avoid the interception of conversations of inno-

---

236 *Collins*, above note 3; *Hunter*, above note 1.
237 *R. v. Debot* (1989), 52 C.C.C. (3d) 193 at 200 (S.C.C.) [*Debot*].
238 *Golden*, above note 1 at 499–500.
239 *R. v. Genest* (1989), 45 C.C.C. (3d) 385 (S.C.C.) at 409; *Feeney*, above note 63; *R. v. McAllister*, [2000] B.C.J. 963 (S.C.); *R. v. Lau* (2003), 175 C.C.C. (3d) 273 (B.C.C.A.) at 283–84; *R. v. Schedel* (2003), 175 C.C.C. (3d) 193 (B.C.C.A.).

cent third parties unrelated to the investigation, the Supreme Court found the search was executed in an unreasonable manner.[240]

The violation of other *Charter* rights, such as the right to counsel under section 10(b), may affect the determination of whether a search was conducted in a reasonable manner, although the cases have been somewhat inconsistent in determining when the breach of other *Charter* rights will affect the reasonableness of a search. The impact of the violation of another *Charter* right on the reasonableness of the search will likely depend on the type of *Charter* violation alleged in the particular case.[241]

When a violation of section 7 is alleged to have occurred during the conduct of a search, the Supreme Court's approach to the intersection of section 7 and section 8 claims as articulated in *R. v. S.A.B.*,[242] should be followed. In that case, the Court held that a determination of reasonableness under section 8 must incorporate considerations of whether the search violated rights under section 7. The essence of the *S.A.B.* decision is that a reasonable search cannot violate another constitutional right. The intersection of section 7 and section 8 rights and its impact on determinations of reasonableness is discussed in greater detail in the discussion of "Section 7," earlier in this chapter.

While a violation of section 7 might render a search unreasonable, a violation of section 10(b) might not. Violations of section 10(b) (the section guaranteeing the right to counsel) may not *always* be subsumed into the analysis of whether a search was reasonably executed. As will be discussed in greater detail below, a blended approach may not be appropriate when the alleged violations are of a "stand-alone" nature (that is, the 10(b) violation had no effect on the conduct of the search); this will be the case for most section 10(b) violations. However, the blended approach from *S.A.B.* may be applicable to certain violations of section 10(b), such as where the proper provision of the right to counsel could have affected the conduct of the search.

An example of a situation where the violation of 10(b) rights is not "stand-alone" and will affect the reasonableness of the search is found in *R. v. Simmons*.[243] In *Simmons*, the Supreme Court found that a customs search was executed in an unreasonable manner in violation of section 8 because Ms Simmons was denied her rights under section 10(b) of the *Charter*. The violations of Ms Simmons' section 10(b) rights had a direct impact on her treatment in relation to the search. First, the Court observed that counsel could have

---

240 *R. v. Thompson* (1990), 59 C.C.C. (3d) 225 (S.C.C.) *per* Sopinka J. at 274.
241 For further discussion on this topic, see "Higher Protections against Intrusion Where Competing/Compound Interests Are Affected by the Search" earlier in this chapter.
242 *S.A.B.*, above note 178.
243 *Simmons*, above note 49.

explained the *Customs Act* provisions that authorized the search and that she had the right to have a senior officer review whether she should be searched, and could have assured Simpson that the officers had the right to insist removal of her clothing. Further, counsel could have ensured that the statutory prerequisites and grounds for the search were met.[244] In the end, Dickson J. held that the denial of the right to counsel rendered the search unreasonable:

> It is clear from the foregoing that the right to counsel *has an important impact on the execution of the search*. Had the appellant been informed of her right to counsel at the point she was detained, and she availed herself of that right, the appellant would have had the benefit of legal advice. . . . In my view, the denial of the appellant's right to counsel cannot avoid having an impact on the reasonableness of the subsequent search of the appellant.
>
> Although the court has not been asked to decide the point, I am of the view that the denial of the right to counsel in this case in conjunction with the absence of any explanation to the appellant of her rights under the *Customs Act* rendered the search unreasonable. The violation of the right to counsel deprived the appellant of her ability to exercise a legal right provided in the *Customs Act*. A search that might not have been conducted had the appellant had the benefit of legal advice was performed in circumstances in which the appellant was ignorant of her legal position. In my view, the violation of the right to counsel combined with the statutory right of prior authorization rendered the performance of the search unreasonable. [emphasis added][245]

An example of a "stand-alone" 10(b) violation that would not affect a determination of the reasonableness of the search, even in light of *S.A.B.*, can be found in *R. v. Debot*.[246] In *Debot*, Lamer J. rejected the view that the breach of another *Charter* right in the context of a search could affect the "manner" in which the search was conducted:

> [I]n the present case, Wilson J. has stated that the denial of the right to counsel affects the "manner" in which the search is conducted. With respect, I cannot agree. The "manner" in which the search is conducted relates to the physical way in which it is carried out and should not, in my view, be inclusive of restrictions of other rights that already receive the benefit of protection from the *Charter*.[247]

---

244 *Ibid.* at 321–22.
245 *Ibid.*
246 *Debot*, above note 237 at 200.
247 *Ibid.*

Justice Lamer did not completely exclude the possibility that a breach of another *Charter* right could constitute a breach of section 8, provided that the breach itself rendered the search *unlawful*. In his view, such a result would be possible only in *exceptional circumstances*:

> It is my view that it will only be in exceptional circumstances that the denial of the right to counsel will trigger a violation of s. 8. Such would be the case when the lawfulness of the search is dependent upon the consent of the person detained. If a detained person's consent to a search of his house, which, under the circumstances of the case and the applicable law, requires a warrant, was given while that person's s. 10(b) rights were being violated (either because he has not been informed of his right to counsel or because the police have obtained his consent to search his house before he has been given a reasonable opportunity to exercise his right to counsel), then the search is unlawful and, as such, unreasonable. Apart from a situation such as this or other situations analogous to those dealt with in *R. v. Simmons, supra*, where the s. 10(b) violation goes to the very lawfulness of the search, I have not been able to imagine situations where the right to counsel will be relevant to a determination of the reasonableness of a search.[248]

At first glance, the blended approach to competing or compound *Charter* claims taken by the Supreme Court in the recent case of *S.A.B.* might appear equally applicable searches impacting on all *Charter* rights, including section 10(b). However, Lamer J.'s comments in *Debot* highlight an important difference between potential violations of section 7 and violations of section 10(b) that are separate from the conduct of the search itself. In most cases, the right to counsel will have no effect on the way in which the search progresses or the treatment of the subject during the search;[249] more precisely, the failure to caution can be conceptually isolated from the search itself. On the other hand, within the context of a search, the section 7 rights of life, liberty, and security of the person will be inextricably linked to the "physical way in which [the search] is carried out"[250] or have "an important impact on the execution of the search."[251] Accordingly, it would seem that in most cases section 10(b) violations should be considered separately from any section 8 analysis, unless the violation is linked closely to the conduct of the search.

---

248 *Ibid.* at 199.
249 In saying "most cases" we specifically exclude the kinds of situations contemplated by Lamer J. in *Debot*: cases such as *Simmons*.
250 *Debot*, above note 237 at 200.
251 *Simmons*, above note 49 at 322.

CHAPTER 5

☙

Reasonable and Probable Grounds

The Supreme Court of Canada in *Hunter v. Southam*[1] set reasonable and probable grounds as the minimum standard of belief required for a reasonable power of search and seizure, for most cases.[2] There are, of course, exceptions to this rule, but where the person's expectation of privacy is undiminished, where the interests pursued are strictly "law enforcement vis-à-vis an individual,"[3] and in the absence of exigent circumstances, the state typically must have reasonable and probable grounds to believe that (1) an offence has been committed, and (2) that evidence of that offence exists in the place to be searched, in order for a search to be reasonable.

A. DEFINITION

The standard of reasonable and probable grounds is a fairly amorphous concept, lacking a rigid mathematical formula for its determination. In *Hunter v. Southam*, Dickson J. provided a useful working definition of the standard:

> The State's interest in detecting and preventing crime begins to prevail over the individual's interest in being left alone at the point *where credibly-*

---

1 *Hunter v. Southam Inc.* (1984), 14 C.C.C. (3d) 97 (S.C.C.) [*Hunter*].
2 *Ibid.* at 108, 114–15.
3 As opposed to other public safety interests, or national or border security interests: see, e.g., *R. v. Briggs* (2001), 157 C.C.C. (3d) 38 (Ont. C.A.) at para. 32; *R. v. Monney* (1999), 133 C.C.C. (3d) 129 (S.C.C.) [*Monney*] at 146–47.

143

based probability replaces suspicion. History has confirmed the appropriateness of this requirement as the threshold for subordinating the expectation of privacy to the ends of law enforcement.[4]

In *R. v. Debot*,[5] Wilson J. provided a further refinement of the standard of proof required to meet the threshold of reasonable grounds for a search:

> To establish reasonable grounds ... the appropriate standard is one of "reasonable probability" rather than "proof beyond a reasonable doubt" or "*prima facie* case." The phrase "reasonable belief" also approximates the requisite standard."[6]

As is evident from the excerpts above, the reasonable grounds standard is one of probability rather than certainty. The threshold is not "proof beyond a reasonable doubt" and is not even as high as "a *prima facie* case," which is a standard requiring proof of reliable evidence of guilt for all elements of the offence.[7] As the Supreme Court explained in *R. v. Storrey*:[8]

> [T]he police need not establish more than reasonable and probable grounds for an arrest. The vital importance of the requirement that the police have reasonable and probable grounds for making an arrest and the need to limit its scope was well expressed in *Dumbell v. Roberts*, [1944] 1 All E.R. 326 (C.A.), wherein Scott L.J. stated at p. 329:
>
>> That [reasonable grounds] requirement is very limited. The police are not called on before acting to have anything like a *prima facie* case for conviction; but the duty of making such inquiry as the circumstances of the case ought to indicate to a sensible man is, without difficulty, presently practicable, does rest on them; for to shut your eyes to the obvious is not to act reasonably.
>
> ...

---

4 *Hunter*, above note 1 at 114.
5 *R. v. Debot* (1989), 52 C.C.C. (3d) 193 (S.C.C.) [*Debot*]. See also *R. v. Saunders* (2003), 181 C.C.C. (3d) 268 (Nfld. C.A.) [*Saunders*] and *R. v. Law* 2002 BCCA 594 at paras. 11–12.
6 *Ibid.* at 213.
7 See *R. v. Storrey*, [1990] 1 S.C.R. 241 [*Storrey*] at 250–51; *R. v. Stillman* (1997), 113 C.C.C. (3d) 321 (S.C.C.) at 241 S.C.R. The "*prima facie* case" standard is one that would provide sufficient reliable evidence of guilt for all elements of the offence if unchallenged by the accused: see *United States of America v. Sheppard* (1976), 30 C.C.C. (2d) 424 (S.C.C.); *Mezzo v. The Queen* (1986), 27 C.C.C. (3d) 97 (S.C.C.); *Monteleone v. The Queen* (1987), 35 C.C.C. (3d) 193 (S.C.C.).
8 *Storrey, ibid.*

Specifically [the police] are not required to establish a *prima facie* case for conviction before making the arrest.[9]

What constitutes reasonable grounds will vary with the context. In *R. v. Jacques*,[10] the Supreme Court noted the importance of context to an assessment of reasonableness, quoting from the concurring opinion of L'Heureux-Dubé J. in *R. v. Bernshaw*[11] addressing the contextual approach to assessing reasonable grounds:[12]

> Contextual analysis of *Charter* rights and freedoms is well established in this Court. As L'Heureux-Dubé J. observed, concurring, in *R. v. Bernshaw*, [1995] 1 S.C.R. 254, at pp. 304–6, in which the appellant challenged the admissibility of breathalyser evidence under s. 8 of the *Charter*:
>
>> Even under the *Charter*, "reasonable and probable grounds" can mean different things in different contexts. This Court has previously referred to the standard of "reasonable and probable grounds" as one of "credibly-based probability": *Hunter v. Southam Inc.*, [1984] 2 S.C.R. 145, at p. 167; *Baron v. Canada*, [1993] 1 S.C.R. 416, at p. 446, and, on another occasion, of "reasonable probability" or "reasonable belief": *R. v. Debot*, [1989] 2 S.C.R. 1140, at p. 1166 (per Wilson J.). These different formulations are, themselves, unhelpful for the purpose of deciding what "reasonable and probable grounds" mean in the case at bar. What is more important is an examination of the context in which that phrase, and the values underlying that phrase, arise.
>>
>> Notably, this Court has recognized on numerous occasions that what constitutes "reasonableness" and what constitutes a "reasonable expectation of privacy" may vary from one context to the other, depending upon the competing considerations at the heart of the issue: *Hunter v. Southam Inc.*, supra, at p. 155; *R. v. Simmons*, [1988] 2 S.C.R. 495, at pp. 526–28. "[T]he standard of review of what is 'reasonable' in a given context must be flexible if it is to be realistic and meaningful": *McKinlay Transport Ltd.*, supra, at p. 645 (*per* Wilson J.). [emphasis added][13]

Accordingly, officers making decisions in the field, in the heat of the moment, will not be held to the same standard as a justice assessing reason-

---

9   Ibid. at 250–51.
10 *R. v. Jacques*, [1996] 3 S.C.R. 312 [*Jacques*].
11 *R. v. Bernshaw*, [1995] 1 S.C.R. 254.
12 *Jacques*, above note 10.
13 Ibid. at para. 20.

able grounds for a search warrant with lesser time constraints.[14] Police officers must take into account all information available to them in deciding whether they have reasonable grounds to arrest, and may disregard only what they have good reason to believe is unreliable in the assessment.[15]

In *R. v. Golub*,[16] a witness reported to police that Golub had shown him an "uzi submachine gun" concealed under his coat, and heard Golub threaten to get even with the staff of a bar for refusing to serve him alcohol. The witness also reported that Golub had struck him. Police treated the information seriously as a high priority "gun call" and immediately attempted to find Golub. They went to his apartment building, and learned from the witness that Golub was distraught over his wife leaving him the previous day, and had been drinking and possibly using cocaine. The apartment building was evacuated and police phoned Golub and asked him to exit the premises. Eventually, he did so and was taken into custody. The officer in charge was concerned that another suspect or person might be in the apartment and might therefore have access to dangerous weapons. The officer therefore ordered the apartment be searched. One of the officers found a loaded .22 calibre sawed-off semi-automatic rifle under a mattress and several boxes of ammunition.

On appeal, Golub's counsel argued that the officers did not have reasonable and probable grounds to arrest Golub because the information from the witness was uncorroborated by police. Counsel argued that, just as information from an untested informant requires corroboration before a search warrant may issue, so too must police corroborate the information of a witness of unknown reliability.

In rejecting this assertion, Doherty J.A. emphasized that the nature of the power exercised and the context for its exercise must be considered in determining whether the standard of reasonable grounds was met. The standard for an officer in the field is lower than for a justice reviewing a warrant, and requires only the inquiries or corroboration reasonably permitted by the circumstances:

> [Defence counsel's] reliance on the search warrant cases is misplaced. Both a justice and an arresting officer must assess the reasonableness of the information available to them before acting. It does not follow, however, that information which would not meet the reasonableness standard on an

---

14   *R. v. Golub* (1997), 117 C.C.C. (3d) 193 (Ont. C.A.), (leave ref'd May 4, 1998, [1997] S.C.C.A. No. 571) [*Golub*].
15   *Chartier v. The Attorney-General of Quebec* (1979), 48 C.C.C. (2d) 34 (S.C.C.) at 56; *Golub*, ibid.
16   Ibid.

application for a search warrant will also fail to meet that standard in the context of an arrest. In determining whether the reasonableness standard is met, the nature of the power exercised and the context within which it is exercised must be considered. The dynamics at play in an arrest situation are very different than those which operate on an application for a search warrant. Often, the officer's decision to arrest must be made quickly in volatile and rapidly changing situations. Judicial reflection is not a luxury the officer can afford. The officer must make his or her decision based on available information which is often less than exact or complete. *The law does not expect the same kind of inquiry of a police officer deciding whether to make an arrest that it demands of a justice faced with an application for a search warrant.*

. . .

In deciding whether reasonable grounds exist, the officer must conduct the inquiry which the circumstances reasonably permit. The officer must take into account all information available to him and is entitled to disregard only information which he has good reason to believe is unreliable. [citations omitted, emphasis added][17]

Although *Golub* dealt with grounds for an arrest as opposed to a search, there is reason to believe a court would extend the same rationale for a less-exacting reasonable grounds standard to officers acting in the field. An officer making a decision to search in the heat of the moment, presumably because he or she believes an offence has been committed and evidence is available on the spot, ought only to be held to the same standard as an officer effecting an arrest — there is little reason to differentiate between the standards for effecting arrests and searches, given that the underlying rationale for the lower standard is the difficulty of assessing the situation, the potential for loss, or destruction of evidence, or potential harm to the officer and others. Moreover, an arrest carries with it a power to search incident to that arrest.[18]

B. "REASONABLE GROUNDS" AND "REASONABLE AND PROBABLE GROUNDS" ARE SYNONYMOUS

The terms *reasonable grounds* and *reasonable and probable grounds* are synonymous. In *Baron v. Canada*,[19] Sopinka J. explained that "probability" is merely an element of "reasonableness" — accordingly, a statute stipulating

---

17 *Ibid.* at 202–3.
18 See chapter 8, "Searches Incidental to Arrest."
19 *Baron v. Canada* (1993), 78 C.C.C. (3d) 510 (S.C.C.).

a standard of reasonable grounds will be interpreted as also requiring probability to meet the threshold of reasonableness:

> In my view nothing turns on the omission of the word "probable" from s. 231.3(3).
>
> ...
>
> To my mind, *Hunter, supra,* does not give rise to legitimate controversy on this point. That decision required reasonable "and probable" grounds and simultaneously established that the two words import the same standard. "Reasonableness" comprehends a requirement of probability. As Wilson J. said in *R. v. Debot* (1989), 52 C.C.C. (3d) 193 at p. 213, affirming 30 C.C.C. (3d) 207 at p. 219 (Ont. C.A.), the standard to be met in order to establish reasonable grounds for a search is "reasonable probability." It appears that the normal statutory phrase in Canada is "reasonable grounds," and that some of the remaining exceptions requiring "reasonable and probable grounds" have been amended in recent years, one imagines for the sake of uniformity, by deleting "and probable": see Locke J.A.'s reasons in *Kourtessis, supra,* at pp. 223–24. This use of "reasonable grounds" as the basis for the issuance of search warrants is not constitutionally fatal. Rather, it meets the requirements of s. 8. [parallel citations omitted][20]

C. REASONABLE SUSPICION

By contrast, *reasonable suspicion* is a lower threshold than *reasonable grounds,* and is a constitutionally acceptable standard of proof to justify only certain types of searches. Typically, this standard will be sufficient to justify searches conducted in situations where the individual has a lowered expectation of privacy, such as searches conducted in a jail setting,[21] or where the movements of an automobile or the numbers dialled on a telephone are tracked by an electronic device,[22] or where interests apart from criminal law enforcement are engaged by the search. Examples of the latter include customs searches conducted to maintain border integrity,[23] and searches of the per-

---

20   *Ibid.* at 531–32.
21   See, e.g., the *Corrections and Conditional Release Act,* ss. 47–54; *R. v. Conway* (1993), 83 C.C.C. (3d) 1 (S.C.C.).
22   See s. 492.1, *Criminal Code.*
23   See *R. v. Simmons* (1988), 45 C.C.C. (3d) 296 (S.C.C.); *Monney,* above note 3; *Jacques,* above note 10 at para. 15; *Customs Act* ss. 91–92.

son that are conducted incident to an "investigative detention" for the purpose of preserving officer and public safety.[24]

Several decisions have defined the level of proof that constitutes a reasonable suspicion.[25] In *R. v. Jacques*,[26] the Supreme Court explained that while the reasonable suspicion standard was not as stringent as the reasonable grounds threshold, it was also not "illusory." In *Jacques*, Gonthier J. approved of the definition of "articulable cause" set out by Doherty J.A. in *R. v. Simpson*[27] as an appropriate threshold for the standard of reasonable suspicion:

> A sound approach to the assessment of evidence was canvassed by Doherty J.A. of the Ontario Court of Appeal in *R. v. Simpson* (1993), 12 O.R. (3d) 182, albeit in a different context, one in which the officer lacked statutory authority unlike in the present case. In determining whether or not a police officer's detention of a vehicle and its driver and passenger could be authorized by common law in the absence of statutory authority, Doherty J.A. reviewed U.S. jurisprudence on the doctrine of articulable cause and stated (at p. 202): "These cases require a constellation of objectively discernible facts which give the detaining officer reasonable cause to suspect that the detainee is criminally implicated in the activity under investigation."[28]

Further, the Court in *Jacques* accepted that the reasonableness of the suspicion was to be assessed in the totality of the circumstances, rather than assessing the value of each indicator of suspicion on its own:[29]

> Viewing the facts and circumstances as a whole, rather than isolating each in turn, is an approach which commends itself beyond the fact situation in *Simpson*. As Belleghem J. observed in *R. v. Marin*, [1994] O.J. No. 1280 (Gen. Div.), with respect to the facts (or "indicators") warranting a detention and search for narcotics under the *Customs Act* (at para. 16):

24 See *R. v. Simpson* (1993), 12 O.R. (3d) 182 (C.A.) [*Simpson*]; *R. v. Ferris* (1998), 126 C.C.C. (3d) 298 (B.C.C.A.) [*Ferris*]; *R. v. Mann* (2002), 169 C.C.C. (3d) 272 (Man. C.A.), leave granted [2002] S.C.C.A. No. 484; *R. v. Wills* (1992), 70 C.C.C. (3d) 529 (Ont. C.A.). In the "investigative detention" context, the relevant evidentiary standard for conducting the search is "articulable cause"; however, the Supreme Court in *Jacques*, above note 10, has effectively equated these two standards. See the discussion later in this chapter. See also chapter 8, "Search Incidental to Investigative Detention," for further discussion of this topic.
25 See *Simpson*, ibid.; *Jacques*, above note 10; *R. v. Marin*, [1994] O.J. No. 1280 (Gen. Div.); *Ferris*, ibid.
26 *Jacques*, above note 10.
27 *Simpson*, above note 24.
28 *Jacques*, above note 10 at paras. 17 and 24.
29 See also *Monney*, above note 3 at para. 50, regarding the application of a totality of circumstances test, rather than isolating individual factors.

The "indicators" are to be seen as a constellation, or cluster, leading or tending to a general conclusion. Looked at individually no single one is likely sufficient to warrant the grounds for the detention and seizure. The whole is greater than the sum of the individual parts viewed individually.[30]

D. REASONABLE GROUNDS MUST EXIST BOTH OBJECTIVELY AND SUBJECTIVELY

The police officer's grounds to conduct the search must be reasonable on both a subjective and an objective level of evaluation. That is to say, the officer must *believe* that he or she has reasonable and probable grounds, and the authorizing or reviewing court must find that belief to be *objectively reasonable*.

The Supreme Court first recognized that the reasonableness of an officer's grounds must be objectively supportable in *R. v. Storrey*,[31] a case dealing with the constitutional validity of a warrantless arrest. The Court required that the officer's grounds be measured against an objective standard of reasonableness to protect against the potential for arbitrary arrests:

> [T]he *Criminal Code* requires that an arresting officer must subjectively have reasonable and probable grounds on which to base the arrest. Those grounds must, in addition, be justifiable from an objective point of view. That is to say, a reasonable person placed in the position of the officer must be able to conclude that there were indeed reasonable and probable grounds for the arrest. On the other hand, the police need not demonstrate anything more than reasonable and probable grounds. Specifically they are not required to establish a *prima facie* case for conviction before making the arrest.[32]

This requirement that the reasonableness of grounds be both subjectively and objectively supportable has also been recognized in the search and seizure context.[33]

The party defending the search must show both an objectively and subjectively reasonable basis for the belief, or risk a finding that no proper foundation existed for the exercise of a power of search or seizure. For example, in *R. v. Feeney*,[34] Sopinka J. held that the officers' lack of subjective belief that

---

30   *Jacques*, above note 10 at para. 25.
31   *Storrey*, above note 7.
32   *Ibid.* at 324.
33   See, e.g., *R. v. Belvanis* (1997), 118 C.C.C. (3d) 405 (S.C.C.) at 420–22.
34   *R. v. Feeney* (1997), 115 C.C.C. (3d) 129 (S.C.C.) [*Feeney*].

he had reasonable grounds rendered the arrest and subsequent search unreasonable:

> In considering the legality of the arrest in the case at bar under pre-*Charter* law, the trial judge did not consider adequately the lack of subjective belief in the reasonableness of the grounds to arrest. Leggatt J. set out the reasonableness test as an objective one: so long as there were, objectively speaking, reasonable and probable grounds, the standard is satisfied.
>
> . . .
>
> Whether or not the trial judge was correct in concluding that the objective standard was met, a conclusion with which I disagree below, the trial judge erred by relying exclusively on an objective standard. According to the plain wording of s. 495, the peace officer may arrest someone only if, on reasonable grounds, he or she believes the person to have committed an indictable offence. An objective standard was added in *Storrey, supra*, but this did not displace the subjective requirement: see *Storrey, supra*, at p. 250. Indeed, it would be inconsistent with the spirit of the *Charter* to permit a police officer to make an arrest without a warrant even though she or he does not believe reasonable grounds for the arrest exist. The absence of subjective belief, therefore, rendered the arrest in the present case unlawful irrespective of the existence of objective grounds for the arrest and the effect of the *Charter* on powers of police officers to enter a dwelling-house without a warrant in order to effect an arrest.[35]

The Supreme Court again stressed the importance of the subjective component of the officer's belief in *R. v. Caslake*.[36] In *Caslake*, the Court held that officers must consider whether the constitutional elements of a search power exist prior to conducting the search. The Court's discussion illustrates the importance of demonstrating the existence of the prerequisites to the search at both objective and subjective levels of review:

> Naturally, the police cannot rely on the fact that, objectively, a legitimate purpose for the search existed when that is not the purpose for which they searched. The *Charter* requires that agents of the state act in accordance with the Rule of Law. This means that *they must not only objectively search within the permissible scope, but that they must turn their mind to this scope before searching*. The subjective part of the test forces the police officer to satisfy him or herself that there is a valid purpose for the search incident to arrest before the search is carried out. This accords with the ultimate

---

35 Ibid. at para. 29.
36 R. v. Caslake (1998), 121 C.C.C. (3d) 97 (S.C.C.) [*Caslake*].

purpose of s. 8, which, as Dickson J. stated in *Hunter, supra*, is to prevent unreasonable searches before they occur. [emphasis added][37]

There is no magic incantation that an officer must recite while giving evidence as to his or her grounds for conducting a search, and it is not strictly necessary for the officer to specifically articulate that he or she had reasonable grounds. Appropriate inferences may be drawn from the facts and circumstances of the case if necessary for the court to conclude that the officer had a subjective belief in reasonable grounds.[38]

E. WHO MUST HAVE REASONABLE BELIEF? THE OFFICER DIRECTING THE SEARCH

An officer conducting a search is entitled to rely on the subjective belief of the officer who orders the search, and need not necessarily have his or her own independent belief. As Wilson J. explained in *R. v. Debot*:[39]

> The police officer who must have reasonable and probable grounds for believing a suspect is in possession of a controlled drug is the one who decides that the suspect should be searched. That officer may or may not perform the actual search. If another officer conducts the search, he or she is entitled to assume that the officer who ordered the search had reasonable and probable grounds for doing so. Of course, this does not prove that reasonable grounds actually existed.[40]

This is a pragmatic response to the fact that multiple officers may be involved in a given investigation, and each will not be privy to all relevant information. Accordingly, it is the reasonableness of the directing officer's grounds for belief that will be subject to *Charter* scrutiny.

F. WHAT EVIDENCE CAN LEAD TO A BELIEF ON REASONABLE AND PROBABLE GROUNDS?

The types of information that can legitimately be considered in forming reasonable and probable grounds are wide-ranging. Reasonable grounds may be based on any lawfully obtained information, and can include information

---

37   *Ibid.* at 110–11, para. 27.
38   *R. v. Cochrane* 2003 PESCTD 47 at paras. 10–16; relying upon *Feeney*, above note 34 at para. 124 *per* L'Heureux-Dubé J., dissenting; *R. v. Hall* (1995), 22 O.R. (3d) 289 (C.A.); *R. v. Clarke*, [2003] O.J. 3884 (Sup. Ct.).
39   *Debot*, above note 5.
40   *Ibid.* at 214.

that may not ordinarily be introduced at trial as evidence of guilt, such as hearsay information, tips from police informants, the reputations of the suspects, and the criminal records of suspects.[41]

1) Hearsay Information Can Constitute Reasonable Grounds

The grounds for a police officer's search may be based on hearsay information. As discussed above, the officer is entitled to rely on the information of another officer in forming a basis for belief. The written information in support of the application for an investigative order may also be based on hearsay information. It is important to note, however, LeBel J.'s recommendation in *R v. Araujo*,[42] that officers should consider submitting affidavits from all police officers with the best first-hand knowledge of the supporting facts.[43] The Court suggested that if the principal affiant obtained first-hand affidavits from the officer with relevant information as opposed to relying on hearsay, this would render the information much more reliable on any subsequent review of the investigative order.

G. "TIPS" FROM INFORMANTS

Tips from police informants can form either part or the whole of the basis for believing that reasonable grounds exist to justify a search, depending on the quality of the information.[44] The tips given by informants must be carefully scrutinized to ensure the information is sufficiently reliable to form part of the grounds for a search.

1) Reliability of a Tip: Is the Information Compelling, Credible, and Corroborated?

In *R. v. Debot*,[45] Wilson J. set out the test for assessing the reliability of an informant's tip:

> [T]here are at least three concerns to be addressed in weighing evidence relied on by the police to justify a warrantless search. First, was the infor-

---

41 *Debot*, ibid.
42 *R. v. Araujo* (2000), 149 C.C.C. (3d) 449 (S.C.C.).
43 *Ibid.* at 470–71.
44 In *R. v. Garofoli* (1990), 60 C.C.C. (3d) 161 (S.C.C.) [*Garofoli*], Sopinka J. wrote at 148: "[E]vidence of a tip, by itself, is insufficient to establish reasonable and probable grounds." In view of the context (and in light of *Debot*, above note 5), this comment is best understood as meaning the *mere fact* of the tip cannot provide reasonable grounds, but that a tip of sufficient quality may in certain circumstances do so.
45 *Debot*, above note 5.

mation predicting the commission of a criminal offence compelling? Secondly, where that information was based on a "tip" originating from a source outside the police, was that source credible? Finally, was the information corroborated by police investigation prior to making the decision to conduct the search? I do not suggest that each of these factors forms a separate test. Rather . . . the "totality of the circumstances" must meet the standard of reasonableness. Weaknesses in one area may, to some extent, be compensated by strengths in the other two.[46]

Although *Debot*[47] dealt specifically with a warrantless search by police, the principles regarding the assessment of informants' tips apply equally to the assessment of such information in warranted searches.[48]

The three-part *Debot* totality of circumstances test is not a rigid formula. Weaknesses in one area (such as credibility of the informant) can be compensated or offset by strengths in other areas (such as corroboration). Further, factors that indicate reliability apart from whether the information is compelling, credible, corroborated, may be considered by the court in determining the tip's overall value.[49]

a) What Makes a Tip Compelling and Credible?

The reliability of a tip cannot be buttressed *ex post facto*. That is, the reliability of a tip cannot be established by the fact that investigation based on that tip bears fruit. Rather, there must be an inquiry into the source and reliability of the tip based on information available prior to conducting or authorizing the search in order to determine whether the information was sufficient to satisfy the requirement of reasonable and probable grounds.[50]

Certain factors make an informant's tip more compelling and credible. The following factors can be distilled from the jurisprudence as helpful in evaluating whether the tip is reliable in the totality of circumstances:

1. The degree of detail of the "tip":[51] Specific information, rather than bald, conclusory statements, is obviously more compelling.[52] The following types of information can make a tip more compelling:

---

46 *Ibid.* at 215.
47 *Debot*, above note 5.
48 *Garofoli*, above note 44 at 191.
49 *Debot*, above note 5; *Garofoli, ibid.*
50 *Debot, ibid.*; *R. v. Greffe* (1990), 55 C.C.C. (3d) 161 (S.C.C.) at 177.
51 *Garofoli*, above note 44 at 191.
52 *Debot*, above note 5 at 215.

a) Names of the participants in the offence;[53]
   b) The location of the event.[54] In *R. v. Plant*,[55] the statement of a location of marijuana cultivation alone, from an anonymous informant, was (when coupled with police corroboration of increased hydro bills for the address) sufficient information to make the tip reliable and constitute reasonable grounds;[56]
   c) The time of day when the event was to take place.[57]
   d) A description of the particular means by which the crime would be committed.[58]
   e) The source of the information:[59] Did the informer's knowledge come from first-hand observations or was it to mere "rumour or gossip"?[60] Further, the officer (or the court) is not entitled to assume that the information was gained from first-hand observations; the source of knowledge ought to be specifically stated by the informant to be compelling and credible.[61]

2. The suspect's past record and reputation.[62] The suspect's reputation can form part of the reasonable grounds, provided that the reputation is related to the reasons for the search (that is, a record for offences in the same general class as the one being investigated). Further, the information about the suspect's reputation should be verifiable, such as through police records, or through other reliable sources.[63]
3. The informant's history with police as a reliable source of information. Have the police used this person as an informant in the past? Were the prior tips corroborated? Did the information result in successful searches?[64]
4. The informant's criminal record. Does it contain entries for offences of dishonesty?
5. Anonymity: the information from unknown tipsters can form *part* of the reasonable grounds, provided it is sufficiently reliable and corrobo-

---

53   *Ibid.*
54   *Ibid.*
55   *R. v. Plant* (1993), 84 C.C.C. (3d) 203 (S.C.C.) [*Plant*].
56   *Ibid.* at 216–17.
57   *Debot*, above note 5 at 215.
58   *R. v. Lewis* (1997), 122 C.C.C. (3d) 481 at 489.
59   *Garofoli*, above note 44 at 191.
60   *Debot*, above note 5 at 215.
61   *R. v. Day*, [1998] O.J. No. 4461 (C.A.) at para. 2.
62   *Debot*, above note 5, at 215–16.
63   *Ibid.* at 216.
64   *Ibid.* at 217; *Garofoli*, above note 44 at 191.

rated (as in *R. v. Plant*, above).[65] However, "the quality of the information and corroborative evidence may have to be such as to compensate for the inability to assess the credibility of the source."[66]

b) Corroboration of the Information

In *R. v. Debot*,[67] Wilson J. stressed that not every detail of the tip needs to be corroborated:

> [I]t should not be necessary for the police to confirm each detail in an informant's tip so long as the sequence of events actually observed conforms sufficiently to the anticipated pattern to remove the possibility of innocent coincidence.[68]

The amount and kind of corroboration required will depend on the quality of the tip, with the extent of the corroboration required varying with the credibility of the informant. As Wilson J. further explained:

> [T]he level of verification required may be higher where the police rely on an informant whose credibility cannot be assessed or where few details are provided and the risk of innocent coincidence is far greater."[69]

When the informant is of unknown reliability (or is an anonymous informant), the police must corroborate more than "innocuous details." Rather, information relating to the heart of the tip must be corroborated.[70] In *R. v. Lewis*,[71] an unproven, anonymous tipster provided information that a heavy-set black man named Kevin Lewis and a two-year-old boy would be passengers the following day on a Canada 3000 flight to Edmonton, and that Lewis would be carrying cocaine sealed in a wine or Appleton Rum bottle. The police confirmed that a Mr. D. Lewis was scheduled to fly on Canada 3000 to Edmonton the following day. One of the officers was aware of two prior occasions when cocaine had been found concealed in Appleton Rum bottles. The next day, the officers saw a man matching the description provided by the informer attend at the Canada 3000 ticket counter with a small boy. The officers took Lewis aside and informed him of the drug investigation. Lewis allowed the police to search his carry-on bag, wherein the officers found an Appleton Rum bottle containing cocaine.

---

65 *Plant*, above note 55.
66 *Debot*, above note 5 at 217.
67 *Ibid.*
68 *Ibid.* at 218.
69 *Ibid.*
70 See *R. v. Zammit* (1994), 81 C.C.C. (3d) 112 (Ont. C.A.) at 121.
71 *R. v. Lewis* (1998), 122 C.C.C. (3d) 481 (Ont. C.A.).

In holding that police had no reasonable grounds to conduct the search, Doherty J.A. explained that more than innocent details had to be confirmed from an anonymous tip before providing the requisite grounds to search:

> The Crown's position comes down to this. If a person shows up at the airport and acts exactly as one would expect a normal traveller to act, that person is subject to arrest if an anonymous, unproven tipster has predicted that the person would attend at the airport in possession of cocaine and act like a normal traveller. I cannot accept that contention. *Absent confirmation of details other than details which describe innocent and commonplace conduct, information supplied by an untested, anonymous informant cannot, standing alone, provide reasonable grounds for an arrest or search.* [emphasis added][72]

Although the police must corroborate more than innocent details from an anonymous tip, Doherty J.A. held that it is not necessary for police to corroborate the *criminality* of the information:

> In concluding that the totality of the circumstances did not provide reasonable grounds for an arrest, I do not suggest that there must be confirmation of the very criminality of the information given by the tipster. The totality of the circumstances approach is inconsistent with elevating one circumstance to an essential prerequisite to the existence of reasonable grounds.[73]

While it may not be necessary to corroborate the criminal aspects of the tip, the absence of such corroboration may, in the totality of circumstances, be a factor indicating that the information from the tipster does not meet the threshold for issuance of a warrant. In *R. v. Puskas*,[74] police relied on a detailed and specific tip from an anonymous Crime Stoppers informer in obtaining a warrant that resulted in the seizure of 500 marijuana plants from Mr. Puskas's backyard. The police corroborated a number of aspects of the tip, however, none of the criminal aspects of the tip were verified. The trial judge held that in the totality of circumstances, reasonable grounds had not been established because of the absence of confirmation of the criminal aspects of the tip. The Court of Appeal declined to interfere with the judge's determination that reasonable grounds did not exist, as the judge applied the correct "totality of circumstances" test in determining there were no grounds. The Court did, however, note that the trial judge's finding was not

---

72 *Ibid.* at 490.
73 *Ibid.* at 491.
74 *R. v. Puskas* (1997), 120 C.C.C. (3d) 548 (Ont. C.A.).

"entirely free from doubt" and that if the information did not establish reasonable grounds "it missed the mark by very little."[75]

H. "SMELL" AS A COMPONENT OF REASONABLE GROUNDS

Canadian courts have accepted that the smell of illegal substances can form all or part of the grounds for conducting a search.[76] The reliance on smell to justify a search is sometimes termed the "plain smell doctrine"; however, this term should be avoided, because it tends to imply a false analogy to the "plain view doctrine."[77]

The odour of illegal substances may constitute or contribute to reasonable grounds, provided the officer has the requisite training or experience to accurately identify *present* possession of contraband based on odour (as opposed to the lingering smell of substances no longer present).[78] In *R. v. Polashek*,[79] a police officer stopped a motorist for a traffic violation in an area where drugs were prevalent and noticed a strong odour of marijuana emanating from the vehicle. The motorist was arrested for possession of marijuana and was searched incident to the arrest. The search revealed a quantity of cannabis resin. The Ontario Court of Appeal held that, as the odour was not the sole basis for the arrest, the search was reasonable in the circumstances.[80] However, the Court left open the possibility that the odour of narcotics could form the sole basis for reasonable grounds, in the right circumstances:

---

75 *Ibid.* at 553.
76 See, e.g., *R. v. Smith* (1998), 126 C.C.C. (3d) 62 (Alta. C.A.) at para. 30. In a recent decision, Allen J. doubted that *Smith* stood for the proposition that smell alone could be sufficient grounds for an arrest: *R. v. Krall*, [2003] A.J. No. 1161 (Prov. Ct.) at para. 65 *et seq.* With respect, Allen J.'s reasoning on this point is neither clear nor convincing. Reliance on smell alone is not, however, without its difficulties. In the passage from *R. v. Polashek* quoted below, Rosenberg J.A., for a unanimous Court of Appeal, cautions that over-reliance on a transitory factor like smell might create an "unreviewable discretion" in the hands of police: *R. v. Polashek*, below note 79 at 194.
77 For an explanation of the important difference between smell and the "plain view" doctrine, see chapter 8, "No Exception for Plain Smell."
78 There is some authority that the smell of burnt marijuana may contribute to the belief that a suspect possesses additional marijuana. In *R. v. Prussic*, [2000] O.J. No. 3224 (S.C.J.), the court accepted the officer's evidence that "in his experience on investigating narcotics matters, in nine cases out of ten the person who had recently finished smoking a cannabis cigarette would be found with more cannabis in his/her possession."
79 *R. v. Polashek* (1999), 134 C.C.C. (3d) 187 (Ont. C.A.).
80 *Ibid.* at para. 15.

Had Constable Ross based his arrest of the appellant solely on the presence of the odour I would have held that there were not reasonable and probable grounds to make the arrest. Given Constable Ross' admission that he could not from the odour alone determine whether the marijuana had been smoked recently or even if he was detecting the smell of smoked marijuana, the presence of odour alone did not provide reasonable grounds to believe that the occupant was committing an offence. The sense of smell is highly subjective and to authorize an arrest solely on that basis puts an unreviewable discretion in the hands of the officer. By their nature, smells are transitory and thus largely incapable of objective verification. A smell will often leave no trace. As Doherty J.A. observed in *R. v. Simpson* at p. 202 "subjectively based assessments can too easily mask discriminatory conduct based on such irrelevant factors as the detainee's sex, colour, age, ethnic origin or sexual orientation."

On the other hand, I would not go so far as was urged by the appellant that the presence of the smell of marijuana can never provide the requisite reasonable and probable grounds for an arrest. The circumstances under which the olfactory observation was made will determine the matter. It may be that some officers through experience or training can convince the trial judge that they possess sufficient expertise that their opinion of present possession can be relied upon.[81]

In *R. v. Omelusik*,[82] the British Columbia Court of Appeal affirmed that a contextual approach was necessary to assess whether the smell of marijuana could constitute reasonable grounds. In that case, the smell of marijuana was held to be sufficient to justify the detention of the accused. The search was justified to ensure the officer's safety during the detention:

> One of the principal arguments advanced by the appellant is that the smell of marihuana alone in this case could not provide sufficient grounds for a detention and therefore the search incidental to that detention was unlawful and, in the result, the evidence should have been excluded.
>
> . . .
>
> Whether the smell of marihuana is enough for a lawful arrest, or in this case detention, depends on the circumstances. . . . In the present case, the trial judge accepted Constable Kodak's evidence that the odour was of cut marihuana, not marihuana smoke, and that, together with the other circumstances, was sufficient, in my view, to justify detention. It followed that, for the officer's safety, he needed to search the appellant for weapons

---

81   *Ibid.* at 194–95, paras. 13–14.
82   *R. v. Omelusik*, [2003] B.C.J. 1237 (C.A.).

and, in the course of that, he came upon the drugs in the pouch which gave ample grounds for his arrest. [citations omitted][83]

See also:

- R. v. Richardson:[84] the majority of the British Columbia Court of Appeal found that the odour of drugs did not constitute reasonable grounds in the circumstances; Hall J.A. in dissent found the grounds to be sufficient.
- R. v. Brownridge:[85] the trial judge found the officer's belief in the smell of marijuana not to be objectively supportable;
- R. v. P.K.:[86] the trial judge found that the smell of smoked marijuana and other evidence of prior use (that is, glassy eyes and slurred speech) were insufficient to support reasonable ground for an arrest for possession.
- R. v. Duong:[87] the British Columbia Court of Appeal accepted the trial judge's assessment that the smell of marijuana could constitute reasonable grounds in the circumstances of that case.
- R. v. Wong:[88] the smell of marijuana was not considered sufficient grounds for a search, but the evidence was admitted under s.24(2).

---

83   Ibid. at paras. 19–20.
84   R. v. Richardson (2001), 153 C.C.C. (3d) 449 (B.C.C.A.) at para. 9.
85   R. v. Brownridge, [2000] B.C.J. 1549 (S.C.).
86   R. v. P.K., [1999] O.J. No. 2447 (Ont. C.J.).
87   R. v. Duong (2002), 162 C.C.C. (3d) 242 (B.C.C.A.) at paras. 32 and 38; leave ref'd [2002] S.C.C.A. No. 112.
88   R. v. Wong, 2003 BCCA 188.

CHAPTER 6

Privilege and Search and Seizure

This chapter will address three areas where issues of legal or evidentiary privilege affect the litigants' ability to establish violations of section 8 of the *Charter* or the Crown's ability to obtain a search warrant: informer privilege, public interest privilege, and solicitor–client privilege. Recent jurisprudence has also found a privilege attaching to journalists' confidential-source information; this fourth category of privilege is addressed in chapter 4, "Media Searches."

A. INFORMER PRIVILEGE

1) Purpose of the Privilege

Investigations frequently begin with information provided by a member of the public who alerts the police to the possibility that someone is engaging in criminal activity. If the person providing information to the police is considered an "informer," that person's identity will be sheltered by "informer privilege" and will be concealed from the public, including from the accused person, to protect the safety of the informer, even if the person's identity would have some bearing on the assessment of the credibility of the tip.

The concept of informer privilege is an ancient and hallowed protection premised on the duty of all citizens to aid in law enforcement.[1] The common law recognizes that a citizen's assistance in providing information to police

---

1 *R. v. Leipert* (1997), 112 C.C.C. (3d) 325 (S.C.C.) [*Leipert*] at 390.

carries the risk of retribution from those involved in criminal activity.[2] Consequently, the rule of informer privilege was developed to protect those who provide information, and to encourage all citizens to assist the police by passing on information about criminal activity.[3] As the Supreme Court of Canada noted in *Bisaillon v. Keable*,[4] the rule of informer privilege was afforded not simply for the protection of individuals, but also because it is necessary to ensure the proper functioning of the criminal justice system:

> The rule gives a peace officer the power to promise his informers secrecy expressly or by implication, with a guarantee sanctioned by the law that this promise will be kept even in court, and to receive in exchange for this promise information without which it would be extremely difficult for him to carry out his duties and ensure that the criminal law is obeyed.
>
> The common law did not give a peace officer this right simply because it would be useful to him, but because it concluded empirically that the right was necessary. It is certainly not possible to go so far as to say that, without this right, a peace officer would be entirely powerless and the criminal laws would be totally ineffective. However, the inability of the one to act and ineffectiveness of the other would reach a point where they could no longer be tolerable.[5]

Certain kinds of informers face greater jeopardy of retribution than others. In *R. v. Scott*,[6] Cory J. examined the particularly precarious position of an informer in a drug investigation, and the corresponding importance of the rule of informer privilege:

> The role of informers in drug-related cases is particularly important and dangerous. Informers often provide the only means for the police to gain some knowledge of the workings of drug trafficking operations and networks. It has been estimated that in the United States some 95% of all federal narcotics cases involve the work of informers. . . . The investigation often will be based upon a relationship of trust between the police officer and the informer, something that may take a long time to establish. The safety, indeed the lives not only of the informers but also of the undercover police officers, will depend on that relationship of trust.
>
> Trafficking in narcotics is a lucrative enterprise. The retribution wreaked on informers and undercover officers who attempt to gather evi-

---

2   *Ibid.* at 390.
3   *Ibid.*; *R. v. Hunter* (1987), 34 C.C.C. (3d) 14 (Ont. C.A.).
4   *Bisaillon v. Keable* (1983), 7 C.C.C. (3d) 385 (S.C.C.) [*Bisaillon*].
5   *Ibid.* at 421.
6   *R. v. Scott* (1990), 61 C.C.C. (3d) 300 (S.C.C.) [*Scott*].

dence is often obscenely cruel. Little assistance can be expected from informers if their identity is not protected. There can be no relationship of trust established by the police with informers without that protection. If the investigation of drug-related crime is to continue then, to the extent it is possible, the identity of informers must be protected.[7]

2) Who is Entitled to the Privilege?

An expectation of confidentiality either expressly communicated by the informer or necessarily understood from the circumstances (for example, if the person is not coming forward as a "witness" who would testify in court), is generally a hallmark of identifying who is entitled to informer privilege.[8]

However, it is unclear whether the police must also promise confidentiality to the informer in order for the privilege to apply; certain cases have held that a promise of confidentiality must be made,[9] while other courts have found that a promise of confidentiality is unnecessary.[10] The authors suggest that the informant's subjective perception of confidentiality (determined objectively) is a more appropriate governing factor. Such an approach protects true informers who are inadvertently or unwittingly not promised confidentiality by the police (although the circumstances in which the information was given suggest such an assurance was due), and gives appropriate consideration to the person's status and motivation for providing information.[11]

3) The Scope of Informer Privilege

The scope of informer privilege is broad. It applies to all undisclosed informers who assist police by providing information.[12] The privilege applies to prevent disclosure of the informer's identity in both civil and

---

7   Ibid. at 313–14.
8   R. v. Brown, [1999] O.J. No. 4870 (Sup. Ct.) [Brown] at paras. 2, 4 & 6.
9   Ibid.; R. v. Mason (2000), 112 A. Crim. R. 266 (CCC, SA) at 271–72.
10 R. v. Thomas (1998), 124 C.C.C. (3d) 178 (Ont. Ct. Gen. Div.) at 196; R. v. 4-12 Electronics Corporation (1996), 47 C.R. (4th) 20 (Man. Q.B.) at 26–27.
11 See Brown, above note 8 at para. 6: "Accordingly, in determining the existence of the privilege all of the circumstances of the delivery of the information must be considered. The perception of the informant who is giving information to the police is a significant factor. The status and motivation of the person at the material time as a complainant, suspect, arrestee, accomplice or otherwise are also relevant. See Tipene v. Apperley, [1978] 1 N.Z.L.R. 761 at 768 (C.A.). Regard must also be had for the conduct of the officer receiving the information and the history of their relationship with one another, if any."
12 Leipert, above note 1 at 393.

criminal court proceedings.[13] It applies to witnesses giving evidence, who cannot be compelled to reveal the identity of informants,[14] or to reveal whether he or she is an informer.[15] The protection also extends beyond the courtroom, and into outside conversations and actions of police officers.[16] Further, the privilege applies whether or not the identity of the informant is "known" by the defence; inadvertent disclosure of the informer's identity does not have the effect of waiving the privilege and does not officially confirm the informer's identity.[17]

All information that could potentially, either explicitly or implicitly, identify an informer is covered by the privilege. Consequently, a wide range of information is covered by the privilege, given that the smallest details might be sufficient to reveal the informer's identity.[18] If the identity of the informer is known to police (as opposed to an anonymous tipster), the task of determining which information could potentially reveal the informer's identity if released is made easier because it may be possible to contact the informer directly to assess the extent of the information that is capable of being disclosed to the accused.[19]

Although informer privilege technically belongs to the Crown, the Crown is not entitled to waive the privilege, either expressly or impliedly (for example, by failing to assert the privilege) without the consent of the informer.[20] In that sense, the privilege also belongs to the informer.[21]

a) Scope of Privilege for Anonymous Informants

Even when the tipster remains anonymous and the informant's identity is unknown to the police, the informant is still afforded the protection of informer privilege. Indeed, the information given by anonymous informers must be treated with even more caution than the information from known informants. This is because the courts have recognized the precarious situation of anonymous informants: the informer and his or her circumstances are unknown to police or the Crown, and therefore it is often difficult to predict what information might identify the informer. As McLachlin J. noted in

---

13 *Bisaillon*, above note 4 at 412.
14 *Marks v. Beyfus* (1890), 25 Q.B.D. 494 at 498–99; *Bisaillon, ibid.* at 409–10.
15 *Bisaillon, ibid.* at 412.
16 *Ibid.* at 413–14.
17 *R. v. Pangman*, [2000] M.J. No. 222 (Man. Q.B.) at para. 20; *Bisaillon,ibid.* at 413.
18 *Leipert*, above note 1 at 393.
19 *R. v. Garofoli* (1990), 60 C.C.C. (3d) 161 (S.C.C.) at 192–95 [*Garofoli*].
20 *Bisaillon*, above note 4 at 412–13; *Leipert*, above note 1 at 392.
21 *Leipert, ibid.*

R. v. Leipert,[22] a detail as seemingly innocuous as the time of the telephone call may be sufficient to permit persons to deduce the identity of the informer.[23] Accordingly, the courts must exercise great care not to unwittingly deprive anonymous informers of the protection of informer privilege.[24]

In practice, the Crown or police edit information concerning tips and informers from any materials that will be disclosed to the accused. Although such editing may be sufficient to protect the identity of known informants, editing procedures might be insufficient to address the concerns in dealing with information from anonymous tipsters.[25] Information from anonymous tipsters is therefore distinguishable from other types of confidential information that can be judicially edited because it is impossible to determine which details of the information would tend to disclose the informer's identity.[26]

Accordingly, the scope of privilege for anonymous informants must be sufficiently broad so that the Crown may appropriately claim informer privilege over the entirety of the information provided by an anonymous informer, since it may be impossible to determine whether any part of the information could reveal the informer's identity.[27] It is an error of law for a court to prevent the Crown from editing references to information regarding anonymous tips from the information supporting a search warrant.[28] There are consequences to protecting the confidentiality of informants, however. If the Crown does exercise the privilege and removes references to the anonymous tip, the Crown will have correspondingly less information upon which to defend the reasonableness of the issuance of the warrant (unless a "judicial summary" of the deleted information can be provided that conveys enough information to both permit full answer and defence and protect informer privilege).[29]

4) Maintaining Secrecy as to the Informer's Identity

There are several mechanisms built into the law to preserve informer privilege and to keep the informer's identity shielded. The following is a summary of the methods for maintaining secrecy as to the identity of the informer.

---

22 Ibid.
23 Ibid. at 393.
24 Ibid.
25 Ibid. at 397.
26 Ibid. at 397–98.
27 Ibid. at 394.
28 Ibid. at 399.
29 Ibid.

a) Justice System's Duty of Silence and Officer's Responsibility to Maintain Secrecy in Drafting Materials

The court and the Crown have a common law duty to maintain the secrecy of the informer's identity;[30] the only exception recognized to this principle is where the accused's "innocence is at stake." (The procedure for revealing the informer's identity in such circumstances is discussed more fully later in this chapter.)

The police officer also has a duty to remain silent as to the identity of the informer both in the course of, and outside, court proceedings.[31] Accordingly, the officer with knowledge of the informer's identity ought to omit references to the person's identity (and other facts that may identify the informer) in conversations, in the drafting of the information to obtain a search warrant, and in the composition of notes and other documents that will be or may become available to the accused or to the public.

The jurisprudence has generally only required that the information to obtain a search warrant refer to the informer as a "confidential and reliable informer" and to indicate whether the informer has previously provided accurate information leading to arrests or seizures.[32] There is some debate as to whether the court requires details such as the informer's record, details of compensation, or motivations for assistance,[33] but given that officers are required to provide "full, frank, and fair disclosure" of all material facts in the application for a warrant, it is likely that a court will require details of the informer's record. It is preferable that confidential material within the affidavit be segregated into a separate appendix, for easy identification and editing when disclosure of the documents becomes necessary.

b) Publication Bans to Protect Identity

If the informer decides to come forward and testify in a trial, publication bans may be available from the court to shield the identity of an informer. For instance, a publication ban might be available if the person's safety could be endangered through broader publication of the person's identity.[34]

---

30   *Ibid.* at 393.
31   *Bisaillon*, above note 4 at 413–14.
32   *R. v. Walker*, [1999] O.J. No. 653 (Gen. Div.) [*Walker*].
33   *Ibid.* at para. 43 (against disclosure); *R. v. Eagle*, [1996] O.J. No. 2867 (Gen. Div.) at para. 19 (in favour of disclosure).
34   *Re Ontario (Commission on Proceedings involving Guy Paul Morin)* (1997), 113 C.C.C. (3d) 31 at 371; *CBC v. Dagenais*, [1994] 3 S.C.R. 835; *R. v. Mentuck*, [2001] 3 S.C.R. 442; see also *Re Vancouver Sun (Air India)*, [2003] B.C.J. 1992 (Sup. Ct); leave granted Oct 6, 2003, S.C.C.

c) Sealing of Documents to Protect the Informer's Identity

The courts possess common law jurisdiction to seal search warrants to protect the identity of an informer.[35] Section 487.3 of the *Criminal Code* also empowers a justice to seal the information to obtain the search warrant at the time of the issuance of the warrant. So long as the rationale for sealing outweighs the interest in disclosing the information, section 487.3 allows the justice to seal any information relating a warrant if the ends of justice would be subverted by disclosure of information that would compromise the informant's identity, an ongoing investigation, the safety of person involved in an investigation, future investigations, or "any other sufficient reason." The accused may later apply to a court to have the information unsealed, subject of course to editing by the Crown or the court to protect the identity of the informer.[36]

d) Section 37 of the *Canada Evidence Act*

Section 37 of the *Cananada Evidence Act* (*CEA*) allows the Crown to object to the disclosure of information during court proceedings on grounds of a "specified public interest," and governs the court's response to a Crown objection: the court has the discretion to authorize disclosure (subject to appropriate terms and conditions) of all, part, or a summary of the information unless the court concludes that the information would in fact "encroach on a specified public interest."[37] In criminal court proceedings, only a superior court of criminal jurisdiction may make a binding determination as to whether the public interest in disclosure outweighs the importance of the privilege, and lower courts must respect the Crown's section 37 objection, in the interim, until the superior court decides the matter.

It is unclear whether section 37 should apply to a Crown assertion of informer privilege.[38] Informer privilege is near absolute, permitting exceptions only when an accused person's innocence is at stake.[39] Section 37 sets up a straight-forward balancing test on a case-by-case basis, and may therefore be ill-suited to deal with informer privilege, just as it would be inappropriate to apply section 37 to a claim of solicitor–client privilege. In our view, to the extent that section 37 applies to informer privilege, the importance of

---

35 *R. v. Hunter* (1987), 34 C.C.C. (3d) 14 (Ont. C.A.) at 27; *Leipert*, above note 1; *Bisaillon*, above note 4; *Walker*, above note 32 at para 42.
36 *Garofoli*, above note 19.
37 *Canada Evidence Act*, s. 37(4.1).
38 For cases that have used s. 37 in the informer privilege context, see *R. v. Babes* (2000), 146 C.C.C. (3d) 465 (Ont. C.A.) [*Babes*]; *R. v. Trang* (2001) 46 C.R. (5th) 274 (Alta. Q.B.); *R. v. Lam* (2000), 148 C.C.C. (3d) 379 (B.C.C.A.) [*Lam*].
39 The "innocence at stake" test is examined in the next section.

the privilege should weigh in the balance to ensure that informer privilege is set aside only in the clearest of cases, where disclosure is necessary to establish the innocence of an accused person.

5) Revealing the Identity of the Informer

Although an accused generally has the right to full disclosure of all information in the Crown's possession that is relevant to his or her case,[40] that right does not extend to information that is privileged.[41] The only exception to disclosure of material protected by informer privilege is where the accused's innocence is at stake.

a) The "Innocence at Stake" Exception

The courts have held that the identity of the informer is generally irrelevant to criminal proceedings.[42] Even where the identity is relevant, the rule against disclosure of the informer's identity is still subject to only one exception: where the information is needed to demonstrate the innocence of accused.[43] The rationale for the "innocence at stake" exception to the protection of informer privilege is set out in the following excerpt from Lord Esher, M.R.'s judgment in *Marks v. Beyfus*:[44]

> [I]f upon the trial of a prisoner the judge should be of the opinion that the disclosure of the name of the informant is necessary or right in order to shew the prisoner's innocence, then one public policy is in conflict with another public policy, and that which says that an innocent man is not be condemned when his innocence can be proved is the policy that must prevail.[45]

In *R. v. Scott*,[46] Cory J. also stressed the primacy of the innocence of the accused over other fundamental principles:

> In our system the right of an individual accused to establish his or her innocence by raising a reasonable doubt as to guilt has always remained paramount.[47]

---

40 *R. v. Stinchcombe* (1991), 68 C.C.C. (3d) 1 (S.C.C.); *R. v. O'Connor* (1995), 103 C.C.C. (3d) 1 (S.C.C.).
41 *Leipert*, above note 1 at 395–96.
42 *Garofoli*, above note 19 at 193; *Re Rideout and The Queen* (1986), 31 C.C.C. (3d) 211 at 220, 61 Nfld. & P.E.I.R. 160 (S.C.).
43 *Bisaillon*, above note 4 at 411–12; *Garofoli*, above note 19 at 193; *Leipert*, above note 1 at 193.
44 *Marks v. Beyfus* (1890), 25 Q.B.D. 494 (C.A.).
45 *Ibid.* at 498, as cited by McLaughlin J. in *Leipert*, above note 1 at 394.
46 *Scott*, above note 6.
47 *Ibid.* at 315–16.

The "innocence at stake" exception presents a high threshold for the accused to meet to obtain disclosure of the informant's identity. The accused must first establish a foundation for asserting the exception, by showing there is an evidentiary basis for concluding that disclosure of the informant's identity is necessary to demonstrate the accused person's innocence.[48] Mere speculation that the information might assist the defence is insufficient as an evidentiary basis and must encompass something more concrete.[49]

b) When Is the "Innocence at Stake Exception" Engaged?

In *R. v. McClure*,[50] the Supreme Court formulated a two-stage test for determining when the "innocence at stake" exception is engaged. *McClure* was a case involving solicitor–client privilege, rather than informer privilege; however, the approach taken by the Court in *McClure* for determining when an accused person's innocence is at stake will likely be the same, or at the very least instructive in developing the test that will be applied in an informer privilege scenario. One would assume that informer privilege is due at least the level of protection afforded to solicitor–client privileged material, if not substantially more, given the need to protect the physical safety of the informer and the administration of justice issues identified in the preceding discussion. Additionally, the Court in *McClure* looked to the informer privilege context in formulating its test, expanding and giving texture to the approach to be employed in making the determination.

According to *McClure*, the test for determining when the exception applies is stringent and will only be satisfied in rare circumstances involving core issues relevant to the accused's guilt and genuine risk of a wrongful conviction.[51] In *R. v. Brown*,[52] the Supreme Court provided the following summary of the *McClure* test, which involves two preconditions to embarking on an analysis of whether the exception applies, followed by a two-part test of whether the exception is justified in the circumstances:

> The *McClure* test comprises a threshold question and a two-stage "innocence at stake" test, which proceed as follows.
>
> To satisfy the threshold test, the accused must establish that:

---

48 *Leipert*, above note 1 at 394; *R. v. Chiarantano*, [1990] O.J. No. 2603 (QL) (C.A.), per Brooke J.A. affirmed [1991] 1 S.C.R. 906.
49 *Leipert*, ibid. at 394–95.
50 *R. v. McClure* (2001), 151 C.C.C. (3d) 321 (S.C.C.) [*McClure*].
51 *R. v. Brown* (2002), 162 C.C.C. (3d) 257 (S.C.C.) at 271 [*Brown*].
52 Ibid.

- the information he seeks ... is not available from any other source; and
- he is otherwise unable to raise a reasonable doubt.

If the threshold has been satisfied, the judge should proceed to the innocence at stake test, which has two stages.
- Stage #1: The accused seeking production of the solicitor–client communication has to demonstrate an evidentiary basis to conclude that a communication exists that could raise a reasonable doubt as to his guilt.
- Stage #2: If such an evidentiary basis exists, the trial judge should examine the communication to determine whether, in fact, it is likely to raise a reasonable doubt as to the guilt of the accused.

It is important to distinguish that the burden in the second stage of the innocence at stake test (likely to raise a reasonable doubt) is stricter than that in the first stage (could raise a reasonable doubt).[53]

Previously, the Courts have held that the "innocence at stake" exception threshold will be met if the informer was a witness to material facts.[54] In *R. v. Leipert*,[55] McLachlin J. held that the exception must prevail if the informer was a material witness to the crime or acted as an *agent provocateur*.[56] *Quaere* whether the cases of *Brown* and *McClure* on the definition of what constitutes "innocence at stake" will alter the courts' approach to exceptions to informer privilege cases. It is most likely that informer privilege will be restricted to circumstances where the informer is a witness to events supporting "factual innocence," as opposed to more technical constitutional claims of effective innocence (such as, where the accused might have evidence excluded under section 24(2) of the *Charter*) where it is not otherwise possible to establish innocence.

---

53 *Ibid.* at 265.
54 *R. v. Chambers* (1985), 20 C.C.C. (3d) 440 (Ont. C.A.) at 451; *Garofoli*, above note 19 at 193; *Leipert*, above note 1 at 395.
55 *Leipert*, above note 1.
56 *Ibid.* at 395; *Scott*, above note 6; the *agent provocateur* is not entitled to the benefit of informer privilege: see *R. v. Davies* (1982), 1 C.C.C. (3d) 299 (Ont. C.A.) at 303; *Babes*, above note 38. However, an agent does not lose informer privilege in unrelated fields, even though she or he has acted as an agent in one field: *Babes*, above note 38 at paras. 17–23. An informer who chooses to give evidence in one matter equally cannot be asked to provide evidence about his or her informant activities at large: *R. v. Starr* (1998), 123 C.C.C. (3d) 145 (Man. C.A.) at 160–62.

In *R. v. Scott*,[57] Cory J. held that the informer's identity might be revealed in circumstances where the accused seeks to establish that a search warrant was not supported by reasonable grounds, "in circumstances where it is absolutely essential."[58] In *Leipert*,[59] McLachlin J. explained that "essential circumstances" would exist only where the accused's innocence was at stake.[60] Such a circumstance might include where there is evidence to suggest that the goods seized in the execution of the search warrant were planted, either by the informer or by another where the informer has information as to how the goods came to be planted.[61] Recall, however, that a difficult burden rests on the accused to demonstrate the proper evidentiary foundation for such an allegation, if the test as stated in *Brown* and *McClure* is adopted for cases involving informer privilege.

c) **Summary of the Procedure for Establishing the "Innocence at Stake" Exception**

The following summarizes the basic procedure the court should follow in considering whether the accused may have access to information that may tend to identify a police informer:[62]

1. The accused must show a basis to conclude that without the disclosure sought his or her innocence is at stake.
   (Note: we suggest that this step will mirror the test in *McClure* and *Brown* set out above.)
2. If such a basis is shown, the court may then review the information to determine whether, in fact, the information is necessary to prove the accused's innocence.
3. If the court then concludes that disclosure is necessary, the court should only reveal as much information as is essential to allow proof of innocence.
4. The application should be heard at the end of the Crown's case to allow the court to better appreciate whether the accused's innocence is at stake, in the context of the evidence heard at trial.[63]
5. Before disclosing the information to the accused, the Crown should be given the option of staying the proceedings.

---

57 *Scott*, above note 6.
58 *Ibid.*
59 *Leipert*, above note 1.
60 *Ibid.* at 396.
61 *Ibid.*
62 As stated in *Leipert*, above note 1 at 398 (with exception of #4 from *Brown*, above note 51).
63 *Brown*, above note 51 at 278–79.

6. If the Crown chooses to proceed, disclosure of the information essential to establish innocence may be provided to the accused.

d) The "Innocence at Stake" Exception Inapplicable at a Preliminary Hearing

The accused may not obtain access to information protected by informer privilege at the preliminary inquiry. While the accused may apply to the preliminary hearing judge for a ruling as to whether the privilege applies to the information sought, if the Crown establishes that the privilege applies, the claim of privilege is not subject to the "innocence at stake" exception at the preliminary hearing stage. In *R. v. Richards*,[64] the Ontario Court of Appeal held that:

> An accused cannot claim that his or her innocence is at stake during a preliminary inquiry. Whatever the result of that proceeding, it will not be determinative of the guilt or innocence of an accused. Since the ultimate determination of guilt is not an issue at a preliminary inquiry, the sole exception compelling disclosure cannot operate at that stage of the proceedings. Thus, while a judge conducting a preliminary inquiry has jurisdiction to determine a claim of police informant privilege since it is an evidentiary ruling, the nature of the only exception to the prohibition against disclosure requires that the preliminary inquiry judge give effect to the claim if the Crown establishes that disclosure of the information may directly or indirectly identify a police informant.[65]

B. PUBLIC INTEREST PRIVILEGE

Claims of public interest privilege arise generally in the search and seizure context when the Crown seeks to protect the confidentiality of investigative techniques and the secrecy of locations known as observation posts. The common law privilege operates to prevent disclosure of such items, even if they form part of the grounds for the issuance of a search warrant or the conduct of a warrantless search. In *Michaud v. Quebec (Attorney General)*,[66] the Supreme Court explained the rationale for retaining a privilege to protect investigative techniques:

---

64 *R. v. Richards* (1997), 115 C.C.C. (3d) 377 (Ont. C.A.) [*Richards*].
65 *Ibid.* at 380–81; see also *Babes*, above note 38, where the preliminary hearing judge ruled that informer privilege did not apply because the informer was actually an *agent provocateur* and ordered the witness to answer questions about the informer's identity.
66 *Michaud v. Quebec (Attorney-General)* (1996), 109 C.C.C. (3d) 289 (S.C.C.).

[T]he state's interest in protecting the confidentiality of its investigative methods . . . remains compelling. The reality of modern law enforcement is that police authorities must frequently act under the cloak of secrecy to effectively counteract the activities of sophisticated criminal enterprises. In that endeavour, electronic surveillance represents one of the most vital and important arrows in the state's quiver of investigative techniques, particularly in the prosecution of drug offences.

. . .

The effectiveness of such surveillance would be dramatically undermined if the state was routinely required to disclose the application and affidavits filed in support of a surveillance authorization to every non-accused surveillance target. The wiretap application will often provide a crucial insight into the modus operandi of electronic surveillance, and regular disclosure would permit criminal organizations to adjust their activities accordingly. [emphasis added][67]

Section 37 of the *CEA* provides a procedure for the determination of whether public interest privilege applies to evidence. The threshold for disclosure is far lower than for solicitor–client privilege or informer privilege claims. Under section 37, it will generally be sufficient that the accused's interest in making full answer and defence outweighs the public interest in keeping the information confidential.

1) Summary of the Procedure for Determining a Claim of Public Interest Privilege

The procedure for determining a claim of public interest privilege can be summarized as follows:

1. Section 37 of the *CEA* vests the superior court with jurisdiction to decide claims of public interest privilege.[68]
2. If the claim of privilege arises at the preliminary hearing, the Crown should attempt to obtain an evidentiary ruling on the applicability of the privilege from the preliminary hearing judge first, before engaging the procedure in section 37. If the preliminary hearing judge agrees that the privilege applies, resort to section 37 is unnecessary.[69]
3. If the preliminary hearing judge orders disclosure, then the Crown can commence a section 37 application objecting to the disclosure. Once

---

67 *Ibid.* at 320, paras. 51–52.
68 *R. v. Meuckon* (1990), 57 C.C.C. (3d) 193 (B.C.C.A.) at 199.
69 *Richards*, above note 64 at 380.

the Crown invokes section 37, only a superior court can settle the claim of privilege.[70]
4. On the application to determine whether the privilege applies, the judge must first determine whether the information sought is relevant to an issue in the proceedings.[71]
5. If relevant, evidence of investigative techniques will not be disclosed if the public interest in effective police investigation and the protection of those involved in, or who assist in such investigation, outweighs the legitimate interests of the accused in disclosure of the techniques.[72]
6. If the claim is made at trial, the accused's interests in obtaining the disclosure are encompassed by the right to make full answer and defence, as protected by section 7 of the *Charter*.[73]
7. If the claim is made at the preliminary inquiry, the accused cannot rely directly on the right to full answer and defence, since the accused is not at risk of conviction at a preliminary hearing. The accused can rely on the interest in obtaining a discharge under section 548 of the *Code* and the interest in obtaining timely disclosure that might ultimately assist the accused in making full answer and defence at trial, to attempt to outweigh the public interest in secrecy at the preliminary hearing.[74]

2) Observation Post-Privilege

The policy reasons for maintaining the confidentiality of an observation post-privilege can be summarized as follows:

1. Disclosure could threaten the safety of persons who gave permission to the police to use the location.
2. Without a guarantee of safety, persons might not be willing to co-operate with the police.
3. Disclosure could destroy the future value of the location.
4. Disclosure could threaten the safety of officers using the location in the future.[75]

Two lines of cases have emerged regarding the threshold at which the public interest in disclosure outweighs those policy concerns for protecting

---

70 *Ibid.* at 379–80.
71 *Ibid.* at 381.
72 *Ibid.*
73 *Ibid.*
74 *Ibid.*
75 As summarized in *Lam*, above note 38 at para. 20.

the privilege. The more conservative line of cases, represented by the case of *R. v. Thomas*,[76] treats the privilege as similar to informer privilege, in that the identity of a person at risk for assisting police must be protected unless the accused's innocence is put at stake through non-disclosure.[77] Finding support primarily in English cases for the proposition that people who offer observation posts should be treated as informers,[78] Molloy J. extended the application of informer privilege to the identity of those offering observation posts:

> [P]ersons who assist the police by providing them with a location from which to conduct surveillance of suspected criminal activity are *entitled to the same protections as persons who assist police by providing information. I can see no rational basis for distinguishing one from the other.* Under existing law, if a person makes observations of criminal activity through his kitchen window and gives this information to the police, his identity would be protected from disclosure by informer privilege. Why should he be in a different position if he allows the police to have access to his kitchen and the police observe criminal activity from there? All of the policy reasons which gave rise to the informer privilege are equally true for persons who assist the police by permitting surveillance to be conducted from their homes or businesses.
>
> . . .
>
> Those who provide assistance to the police in this manner are performing a valuable community service. They are every bit as vital to effective law enforcement as are police informers, and every bit as deserving of protection. Indeed, some would say, more so. [emphasis added][79]

The more liberal line of cases, illustrated by the British Columbia Court of Appeal's decision in *R. v. Lam*,[80] views observation post-privilege as importantly different from informer privilege and accords the privilege less-stringent protections. The location of an observation post is unlike a tip from an informer, which solely functions to provide reasonable grounds to a police officer and enable further investigation, whereas the observations

---

76 *R. v. Thomas* (1998), 124 C.C.C. (3d) 178 (Ont. Gen. Div.) [*Thomas*].
77 *Ibid.* at 195–96 and 199–201.
78 Cases cited in *Thomas* include *R. v. Rankine*, [1986] 2 All E.R. 566 (C.A.) at 568, 570; *R. v. Hewitt and Davis* (1992), 95 Cr. App. R. 81 (C.A.) at 87; and *R. v. Kenneth Johnson* (1989), 88 Cr. App. R. 131 (C.A.).
79 *Thomas*, above note 76 at 195–96.
80 *Lam*, above note 38.

made from the post will form part of the evidence against the accused in proving guilt.[81]

In *R. v. Lam*,[82] the Crown tendered the evidence of the officer's observations from the "privileged" post as the sole evidence of guilt on the charge of trafficking drugs. The Court held that the appropriate test to determine whether the post should be disclosed is whether the interest in protecting the post overrides the accused's right to make full answer and defence to the charges.[83] As Esson J.A. explained in *R. v. Lam*:[84]

> While it is clear that the policy considerations which support the informer's privilege are essentially the same as those which support the observation post privilege, there is a significant distinction between the two situations. That distinction was concisely stated in one of the most fully considered of the many American authorities to which we were referred:
>
>> An informer's participation usually ends with the communication of the "tip" to the police. Most often, the informer has no further involvement in the activities that lead to a defendant's arrest. However, a police officer seeking to assert a surveillance-location privilege may often be the crucial, and perhaps the only, witness to the criminal transaction. [*State v. Garcia*, 618 A.2d 326 (N.J. 1993), *per* Clifford J. for the court at p. 331.]
>
> That is the situation which arose in this case. The only witness who could give evidence of trafficking was the officer who manned the observation post and who asserted the privilege.[85]

While the observation post was not protected in *Lam*, the Court did not foreclose the possibility that the privilege could prevail in other circumstances, even in cases where the observations afforded the sole evidence of guilt. The fact that the observations afforded the sole evidence was to be treated as a compelling, rather than determinative, factor in the analysis.[86]

---

81 *Ibid.*
82 *Ibid.*
83 *Ibid.* at paras. 41–44; see also *State v. Garcia*, 618 A.2d 326 (N.J. 1993), *per* Clifford J.; *State v. Zenquis*, 618 A.2d 335 (N.J. 1993).
84 *Lam*, above note 38.
85 *Ibid.* at 382–83, paras. 5–6.
86 *Ibid.* at para. 44.

C. SOLICITOR–CLIENT PRIVILEGE

As with informer privilege, solicitor–client privilege is one of the few "class privileges" recognized at common law; that is, the privilege applies to the "class" of communications between lawyers and clients for the purpose of obtaining legal advice, and it is not necessary to establish the privilege on a case-by-case basis.[87] It is a privilege that belongs to the client, and not the solicitor. The privilege may be waived only with the "informed consent" of the client.[88] The courts' power to suspend solicitor–client privilege is constrained to situations where accused person's innocence is at stake, and can be established only by ordering disclosure of the privileged information.[89]

The rule of solicitor–client privilege becomes relevant to search and seizure law primarily when a law office is the location of a search; the target might be either the lawyer or a client. As the Supreme Court noted in *Lavallee, Rackel & Heintz v. Canada (Attorney General)*,[90] there has been a recent observable trend towards more aggressive investigations that include the issuing of investigative orders for law offices to obtain evidence of criminal activities.[91]

1) Scope of Solicitor–Client Privilege

The scope of what is covered by solicitor–client privilege is broad, covering all communications made with a view to obtaining legal advice:

> [A] lawyer's client is entitled to have all communications made with a view to obtaining legal advice kept confidential. Whether communications are made to the lawyer himself or to employees, and whether they deal with matters of an administrative nature such as financial means or with the

---

87 *Maranda v. Richer*, 2003 SCC 67 [*Maranda*] at paras. 11–12.
88 *Solosky v. The Queen*, [1980] 1 S.C.R. 821 [*Solosky*].
89 *McClure*, above note 50; *Brown*, above note 51. For further discussion of the judicial suspension and client waiver of solicitor–client privilege, see "Informer Privilege" above.
90 *Lavallee, Rackel & Heintz v. Canada (Attorney General)* [*Lavallee*]; *White, Ottenheim & Baker v. Canada (Attorney General)* [*White*]; *R. v. Fink* (2002), 167 C.C.C. (3d) 1 (S.C.C.) [*Fink*].
91 *Lavallee*, ibid.; *White*, ibid.; *Fink*, ibid. at para. 10. Some authors have related the trend in searching law offices to the Watergate scandal in the U.S. and the resulting decrease in public confidence and trust in the legal profession. See L.H. Bloom Jr., "The Law Office Search: An Emerging Problem and Some Suggested Solutions" (1980), 69 Geo. L. J. at 7; J.E. Davis, "Law Office Searches: The Assault on Confidentiality and the Adversary System" (1996), 33 Am. Crim. L. Rev. 1251.

actual nature of the legal problem, all information which a person must provide in order to obtain legal advice and which is given in confidence for that purpose enjoys the privileges attached to confidentiality. This confidentiality attaches to all communications made within a framework of the solicitor–client relationship, which arises as soon as the potential client takes the first steps, and consequently even before the formal retainer is established.[92]

There are limited exceptions to the broad scope of the privilege. For example, the privilege does not apply unless the purpose of the communication is to obtain legal advice from a lawyer acting in a professional capacity.[93] Where the communications between the client and the lawyer are aimed at facilitating the commission of a crime, the privilege does not apply.[94]

In certain cases, courts have distinguished between "facts" from "communications" in assessing what was covered by the scope of the privilege.[95] Facts (such as the *fact* of solicitor–client communication occurring or the *fact of an act*, such as the execution of a deed) have been considered exempt from the protections of solicitor–client privilege, as they convey only neutral information not related to advice sought or provided. As Linden J.A. explained in *Stevens v. Canada*:[96]

> Perhaps the most important distinction that needs to be highlighted is that it is only communications that are protected by the privilege. Acts of counsel or mere statements of fact are not protected. In *Susan Hosiery Ltd. v. Minister of National Revenue* . . . Jackett P., after reviewing the rules relating to solicitor–client privilege stated:
>
>> What is important to note about both of these rules [i.e., the rule protecting the confidentiality of solicitor-client communications and the rule protecting the confidentiality of the "lawyer's brief" or work product] is that they do not afford a privilege against the discovery of facts that are or may be relevant to the determination

---

92 *Descôteaux v. Mierzwinski*, [1982] 1 S.C.R. 860 [*Descôteaux*]; *Maranda*, above note 87 at para. 22.
93 Communications between a lawyer and a client may not be privileged if they occur in a social context, in the presence of a third-party, or where the communications are not intended to be kept confidential.
94 See discussion in *Solosky*, above note 88; see also *Maranda*, above note 87.
95 *Canada v. Stevens v. Canada (Prime Minister)*, [1998] 4 F.C. 89 (F.C.A.) [*Stevens*]; *Reiger v. Burgess*, [1989] S.J. No. 240 (Q.B.); *R. v. Joubert* (1992), 69 C.C.C. (3d) 553 (B.C.C.A.); *Kruger Inc. v. Kruco Inc.*, [1988] R.J.Q. 2323 (C.A.).
96 *Stevens*, ibid.

of the facts in issue. What is privileged is the communications or working papers that came into existence by reason of the desire to obtain a legal opinion or legal assistance in the one case and the materials created for the lawyer's brief in the other case. The facts or documents that happen to be reflected in such communications or materials are not privileged from discovery if, otherwise, the party would be bound to give discovery of them.[97]

> The general rationale for not protecting matters of fact or acts done is the detrimental effect it would have on litigation. For example, a person cannot avail himself or herself of the privilege by simply communicating a fact to a lawyer or allowing the lawyer to perform an act in his or her place. [parenthetical remark added][98]

However, this distinction between facts and communications may not apply when assessing solicitor–client privilege in criminal law matters. In *Maranda v. Richer*,[99] LeBel J. held that the importance of the accused's right to silence in a criminal proceeding and the protection against self-incrimination in criminal law matters may require broader definition for the scope of the privilege:

> The problem here must be solved in a way that is consistent with the general approach adopted in the case law to defining the content of solicitor–client privilege and to the need to protect that privilege. In the context of criminal investigations and prosecutions, that solution must respect the fundamental principles of criminal procedure, and in particular the accused's right to silence and the constitutional protection against self-incrimination.
>
> Because this Court is dealing here with a criminal case, we must not overestimate the authority of . . . judgments that may have been rendered in civil or commercial cases. . . . An application by the Crown for information concerning defence counsel's fees in connection with a criminal prosecution involves the fundamental values and institutions of criminal law and procedure. *The rule* [for determining the scope of the privilege] *that is adopted and applied must ensure that those values and institutions are preserved.* [emphasis added][100]

Consequently, the Court in *Maranda* held that, in the criminal law context, the scope of solicitor–client privilege may also extend to protect infor-

---

97 *Ibid.* at para. 25.
98 *Ibid.*
99 *Maranda*, above note 87.
100 *Ibid.* at paras. 28–29.

mation such as a lawyer's billings, as billings are both an element of the solicitor–client relationship and evidence of what transpired within the relationship.[101] However, despite this "general rule" of privilege over billings, if the Crown establishes that the search would not violate any element of confidentiality, privilege will not apply:

> Accordingly, when the Crown believes that disclosure of the information would not violate the confidentiality of the relationship, it will be up to the Crown to make that allegation adequately in its application for the issuance of a warrant for search and seizure. The judge will have to satisfy himself or herself of this, by a careful examination of the application, subject to any review of his or her decision. In addition, certain information will be available from other sources, such as the client's bank where it retains the cheques or documents showing payment of the bills of account. As a general rule, however, a lawyer cannot be compelled to provide that information, in an investigation or in evidence against his or her client.[102]

As indicated above, a search warrant may not issue for items protected by solicitor–client privilege unless the Crown can establish (under these high thresholds) that the privilege does not apply to the items sought. In *Descôteaux v. Mierzwinski*,[103] the Supreme Court held that since privileged documents are inadmissible in evidence, a justice does not have the jurisdiction to issue a search warrant for privileged documents. When a justice is faced with an application for a warrant that might involve privileged documents (as will obviously be the case when the place to be searched is a law office but may occur in other situations), the issuing justice ought to raise the issue of solicitor–client privilege to ensure that he or she has jurisdiction to authorize the search.[104]

2) Duty to Minimize Intrusions into Solicitor–Client Privilege in Conducting Searches

Solicitor–client privilege is more than a rule of evidence or procedure, but rather, has been recognized as a principle of substantive law[105] and as a "fun-

---

101 *Ibid.* at para. 32.
102 *Ibid.* at para. 34.
103 *Descôteaux*, above note 92.
104 *Ibid.* at 887.
105 An evidentiary privilege rule prevents privileged information from being introduced into evidence; a substantive rule prevents the state from obtaining the evidence or otherwise interfering with the confidentiality of the communications.

damental civil and legal right."[106] Given the societal importance of the privilege, it is a constitutional imperative that intrusions into that privilege be minimized as much as possible. In *Descôteaux v. Mierzwinski*,[107] Lamer J. set out the general principles for minimizing such intrusions:

1. The confidentiality of communications between solicitor and client may be raised in any circumstances where such communications are likely to be disclosed without the client's consent.
2. Unless the law provides otherwise, when and to the extent that the legitimate exercise of a right would interfere with another person's right to have his communications with his lawyer kept confidential, the resulting conflict should be resolved in favour of protecting the confidentiality.
3. When the law gives someone the authority to do something which, in the circumstances of the case, might interfere with that confidentiality, the decision to do so and the choice of means of exercising that authority should be determined with a view to not interfering with it except to the extent absolutely necessary in order to achieve the ends sought by the enabling legislation.[108]
4. Acts providing otherwise in situations under paragraph 2 and enabling legislation referred to in paragraph 3 must be interpreted restrictively.[109]

There are two aspects to this duty to minimize intrusions into solicitor–client privilege: (1) it requires that a search not be judicially authorized unless there is no other reasonable solution; and (2) if an authorization is appropriate, it must be granted on such terms to limit, to the extent possible, the impairment of solicitor–client privilege.[110]

Parliament's initial response to the court-imposed duty to minimize intrusions into areas protected by solicitor–client was the enactment of section 488.1 of the *Criminal Code*.[111] This response was later deemed to be

---

106 *Descôteaux*, above note 92 at 875; Justice Lamer attributed the transformation from an evidentiary to a substantive rule to the Supreme Court's decision in *Solosky*, above note 88 at 839, a case involving a challenge to the practice of prison officials censoring correspondence between solicitor and client, a situation outside of litigation.
107 *Ibid.*
108 *Ibid.* at 875.
109 *Ibid.* at 875.
110 *Maranda*, above note 87 at para. 15; *Descôteaux*, above note 92 at 893.
111 The provision contained procedures for searches involving documents in the possession of a lawyer but provided no special rules for the issuance of warrants where privilege is an issue.

insufficient by the Supreme Court in *Lavallee, Rackel & Heintz v. Canada (Attorney General)*,[112] where the Court determined that section 488.1 violated section 8 of the *Charter* because it did not place restrictions on searches sufficient to protect solicitor–client privilege. The Court identified the following constitutional deficiencies in the section:

1. Absence or Inaction of Solicitor: 488.1(2) provides for a sealing procedure of potentially privileged documents which only becomes engaged if a lawyer specifically claims privilege over the documents on behalf of his or her clients at the time of the search or at a reasonable time following the search. Accordingly, if the solicitor makes no claim either for any reason including incompetence, sickness, or nervousness, the privilege can be lost.[113]
2. Naming of clients: 488.1(2) required that the lawyer name the client on whose behalf the privilege was claimed, despite the fact that the identity of a client could itself be a privileged matter.[114]
3. No notice given to client: Section 488.1 provided no requirement for the potential privilege-holder to be notified of the seizure.[115]
4. Strict time limits: The section provided for only 14 days (which was really 10–11 days if the notice provisions were included) in which to resolve claims of privilege, which could not be extended without the consent of the Crown. The lower courts had held the limit to be unreasonably strict and unworkable.[116]

---

112 *Lavallee*, above note 90; *White*, above note 90; *Fink*, above note 90.
113 *Lavallee*, ibid. at para. 27. See also *Lavallee, Rackel & Heintz v. Canada (Attorney General)* (2000), 143 C.C.C. (3d) 187, at paras. 28 and 37 [*Lavallee*, Alta. C.A.]; *R. v. Fink* (2000), 149 C.C.C. (3d) 321, (Ont. C.A.) [*Fink*, Ont. C.A.] at para. 34; and *Festing v. Canada (Attorney General)* (2001), 206 D.L.R. (4th) 98, aff'g (2000), 31 C.R. (5th) 203, at para. 17 [*Festing*, B.C.C.A.].
114 *Lavallee*, above note 90 at para. 28. See also *Lavallee*, Alta. C.A., above note 113 at para. 50; *White, Ottenheimer & Baker v. Canada (Attorney General)* (2000), 146 C.C.C. (3d) 28 (N.F.C.A.) [*White*, N.F.C.A.]; *Fink*, Ont. C.A., above note 113 at para. 39; *Festing*, B.C.C.A., above note 113 at para. 17; and *Canada (Attorney General) v. Several Clients and Several Solicitors* (2000), 189 N.S.R. (2d) 313 at para. 38. [*Several Clients*].
115 *Lavallee*, above note 90 at para 29; *Lavallee*, Alta. C.A., above note 113 at paras. 28–39; *White*, N.F.C.A., above note 114 at para. 21; *Fink*, Ont. C.A., above note 113 at para. 42; *Festing*, B.C.C.A., above note 113 at para. 17, and *Several Clients*, above note 114 at para. 38.
116 *Lavallee*, above note 90 at para. 30; *Lavallee*, Alta. C.A., above note 113 at para. 41; *White*, N.F.C.A., above note 114 at para. 21; *Fink*, Ont. C.A., above note 112 at para. 34; *Festing*, B.C.C.A., above note 113 at para. 17, and *Several Clients*, above note 114 at para. 38.

5. Absence of discretion: The section provides no discretion to relieve the privilege-holder from default in any of the provisions, even where privilege is initially claimed on the documents.[117]
6. Access of the Attorney General prior to judicial determination: The A.G. was permitted to inspect the documents prior to a judge determining whether the documents were subject to privilege.[118]

The Court considered the potential for the breach of solicitor–client privilege without the client's knowledge or consent to be the principal problem with section 488.1. Essentially, the Court reiterated that that the privilege belongs to the client, and ruled that the client should not have to depend on his or her lawyer (or former lawyer) to ensure that the privilege is protected:

> In my view, the failings of s. 488.1 . . . all share one principal, fatal feature, namely, the potential breach of solicitor–client privilege without the client's knowledge, let alone consent. The fact that competent counsel will attempt to ascertain the whereabouts of their clients and will likely assert blanket privilege at the outset does not obviate the state's duty to ensure sufficient protection of the rights of the privilege holder. Privilege does not come into being by an assertion of a privilege claim; it exists independently. By the operation of s. 488.1, however, this constitutionally protected right can be violated by the mere failure of counsel to act, without instruction from or indeed communication with the client. Thus, s. 488.1 allows the solicitor–client confidentiality to be destroyed without the client's express and informed authorization, and even without the client's having an opportunity to be heard.[119]

The Court in *Lavallee* articulated a list of ten general principles to govern the conduct of searches of law offices, and to minimize intrusions into solicitor–client privilege. These principles will govern such searches until Parliament enacts replacement legislation, and of course will act as a guide to the constitutional considerations that Parliament must address in any replacement law. The Court explained that the factors were not intended to require Parliament to adopt any particular procedure for protecting solici-

---

117 *Lavallee*, above note 90 at para 31; *Lavallee*, Alta. C.A., above note 113 at para. 28; *White*, N.F.C.A., above note 114 at para. 21; *Fink*, Ont. C.A., above note 113 at para. 35; *Festing*, B.C.C.A., above note 113; *Several Clients*, above note 114.
118 *Lavallee*, above note 90 at para. 32; *Fink*, Ont. C.A., above note 113 at para. 34; *Festing*, B.C.C.A. above note 113 at para. 19 and 82; *Several Clients*, above note 114 at para. 41.
119 *Lavallee*, above note 90 at para. 39.

tor–client privilege, but rather were a recognition that justices are obliged by the Constitution to protect solicitor–client privilege through application of the following principles, which will continue to apply even after new legislation is enacted. The factors articulated by the Court are as follows:[120]

1. No search warrant can be issued with regards to documents that are known to be protected by solicitor–client privilege.
2. Before searching a law office, the investigative authorities must satisfy the issuing justice that there exists no other reasonable alternative to the search.
3. When allowing a law office to be searched, the issuing justice must be rigorously demanding so to afford maximum protection of solicitor-client confidentiality.
4. Except when the warrant specifically authorizes the immediate examination, copying and seizure of an identified document, all documents in possession of a lawyer must be sealed before being examined or removed from the lawyer's possession.
5. Every effort must be made to contact the lawyer and the client at the time of the execution of the search warrant. Where the lawyer or the client cannot be contacted, a representative of the Bar should be allowed to oversee the sealing and seizure of documents.[121]
6. The investigative officer executing the warrant should report to the Justice of the Peace the efforts made to contact all potential privilege holders, who should then be given a reasonable opportunity to assert a claim of privilege and, if that claim is contested, to have the issue judicially decided.
7. If notification of potential privilege holders is not possible, the lawyer who had custody of the documents seized, or another lawyer appointed either by the Law Society or by the court, should examine the documents to determine whether a claim of privilege should be asserted, and should be given a reasonable opportunity to do so.

---

120 *Lavallee*, above note 90 at para. 49.
121 In *Maranda*, the Supreme Court reiterated that contacting the lawyer and client was the required course of action, and noted that contacting the law society was an appropriate substitute only where necessary. To that end, a means of contacting the lawyer and client(s) should be reflected in the warrant application materials and the warrant itself. However, where alerting the lawyer may jeopardize the investigation, the judge must require appropriate measures to limit breaches of privilege, which may include arranging for a law society representative to be present for the search in order to preserve privilege. *Maranda*, above note 87 at para. 20.

8. The Attorney General may make submissions on the issue of privilege, but should not be permitted to inspect the documents beforehand. The prosecuting authority can only inspect the documents if and when it is determined by a judge that the documents are not privileged.
9. Where sealed documents are found not to be privileged, they may be used in the normal course of the investigation.
10. Where documents are found to be privileged, they are to be returned immediately to the holder of the privilege, or to a person designated by the court.[122]

The duty to minimize intrusions into solicitor–client privilege falls upon both the issuing justice and the investigators, and as such must be reflected not only in the warrant itself, but also in the wording of an application for an authorization to search, and in the affidavits supporting the authorization. In *Maranda v. Richer*,[123] the Supreme Court held that deficiencies in demonstrating in the supporting materials the necessity for the intrusion and the proposed mechanisms for minimizing the intrusion could render a search unreasonable:

> [T]he principle of *minimization must be reflected in the way that the application for authorization is worded*, and in particular in the wording of the affidavits presented in support. The affidavit must contain allegations that are sufficiently precise and complete that the authorizing judge is able to exercise his or her jurisdiction with full knowledge of the facts. . . . It is then up to the judge to exercise his or her jurisdiction carefully, to ensure that the application for authorization properly establishes that *there are no reasonable alternatives, and to define a procedure to be followed in executing the search that will preserve solicitor-client privilege to the greatest possible extent.* [emphasis added][124]

3) Section 487 Does Not on Its Face Violate Solicitor–Client Privilege

Prior to *Lavallee*, the BCCA in *Festing*[125] considered the constitutionality of certain *Criminal Code* search provisions *vis-à-vis* solicitor–client privilege. In addition to finding section 488.1 unconstitutional, the Court held section 487 of the *Criminal Code* (the "conventional warrant" section) to be consti-

---

122 *Lavallee*, above note 90 at para. 49.
123 *Maranda*, above note 87.
124 *Ibid.* at para. 17.
125 *Festing*, B.C.C.A., above note 113.

tutionally invalid, except to the extent that the words "except a law office" could be read into the introduction of section 487 as follows:

> 487(1) A justice who is satisfied by information on oath in Form 1 that there are reasonable grounds to believe that there is in a building, receptacle, or place, *other than a law office* . . .[126]

The BCCA suspended the operation of its judgment in *Festing* pending the Supreme Court hearing of *Lavallee*. Both rulings in *Festing* were appealed to the Supreme Court, and the Supreme Court remitted the appeals to the BCCA for reconsideration in light of its decision in *Lavallee*.[127]

The BCCA upheld its original ruling with respect to the constitutional invalidity of section 488.1, but set aside its ruling on section 487. The Court of Appeal noted that the Supreme Court had provided procedural guidelines that would apply to the issuance and execution of *any* warrant for the search of a law office, and that those guidelines could act as an "overlay" of additional requirements for a section 487 search warrant.[128] The Court's earlier exclusion of law offices from the ambit of section 487 was no longer necessary, since the additional considerations for the issuance of a warrant imposed by *Lavallee* were sufficient to address the issue of solicitor–client privilege.

4) Solicitor–Client Privilege Beyond the Law Office

The Supreme Court's decision in *Lavallee* dealt only with searches of traditional "law offices." Given the importance of the privilege, expansion of the kinds of places covered by the *Lavallee* guidelines is inevitable.[129] Indeed, shortly following *Lavallee*, in the reconsideration of *Festing v. Canada (Attorney General)*,[130] the BCCA interpreted the definition of "law office" as considered by the Court in *Lavallee* to include "any place where privileged

---

126 *Ibid.*
127 *Lavallee*, above note 90.
128 *Festing v. Canada (Attorney General)* (2003), 172 C.C.C. (3d) 321 (B.C.C.A.) [*Festing*, 2003].
129 Note that the wiretap provisions in s. 186(2) place restrictions on interceptions of communications "at the office or residence of a solicitor, or any other place ordinarily used by a solicitor and by other solicitors for the purpose of consultations with clients." This provision might require expansion to include any place *being used* by a solicitor. Note particularly that the requirement that the place be used by more than one solicitor (i.e., "a solicitor *and other solicitors*") would likely not survive constitutional scrutiny.
130 *Festing* 2003, above note 128.

documents may reasonably be expected to be located."[131] In the BCCA's view, such a definition would include such places as, but not limited to "a lawyer's home, a lawyer's office in multidisciplinary business premises; the office of in-house counsel for a business, and storage facilities where lawyers store their files."[132] The Court however declined to make pronouncements on the applicability of the guidelines beyond the expanded definition of a law office:

> [I]t is not appropriate at this time to attempt to further expand the circumstances in which the *Lavallee* guidelines may apply beyond expanding the definition of "law office." Our conclusion in that regard relates, in part, to the fact that the notices of constitutional question did not ask this Court to do so. More importantly, however, the *Lavallee* decision contemplates that Parliament may take steps to draft legislation to replace s. 488.1. Further, it is our understanding that law societies across the country have a continued interest in pursuing legislation, or local guidelines, for the purpose of ensuring that the intent of the *Lavallee* decision is carried into effect. In our view, it is appropriate to permit those bodies to do their work unencumbered by *obiter* comments from this Court, which does not have the benefit of the full consultation process available to those bodies.[133]

Although not inclined to rule on an expanded application of *Lavallee*, the Court advised the exercise of due caution in any situation where solicitor-client privilege could become an issue, regardless of the location:

> [T]he legal protection afforded solicitor–client privilege does not begin and end at the door of a law office. Rather, those applying for, issuing and executing search warrants should be alive to ensuring solicitor–client privilege is protected, to the greatest extent possible, whenever the circumstances so warrant. For example, if there is no reasonable basis to expect that documents protected by solicitor–client privilege may be found at a particular location at the time a search warrant is granted, but it becomes apparent to those executing the warrant that documents that may be protected by solicitor–client privilege are contained in those premises, steps should be taken at that time to ensure that the continuing search and seizure accords as closely as possible with the *Lavallee* guidelines. There may be exigent circumstances which make this impossible, but, short of such circumstances, appropriate protective measures in line with those set out in *Lavallee* should be taken.[134]

---

131 Ibid. at para. 24.
132 Ibid. at para. 24.
133 Ibid. at para. 26.
134 Ibid. at para. 27.

The Court in *Festing* also declined to expand the *Lavallee* guidelines to protect things beyond "documents." The Court instead adopted the broad definition of document in section 321 of the *Code* (which Parliament had previously incorporated in the now-defunct section 488.1), which provides that

> "document" means any paper, parchment or other material on which is recorded or marked anything that is capable of being read or understood by a person, computer system or other device, and includes a credit card, but does not include trade marks on articles of commerce or inscriptions on stone or metal or other like material.[135]

---

135   *Ibid.* at para. 25.

CHAPTER 7

ೂ

Searches With a Warrant: Execution and Litigation Issues

This chapter deals with two topics pertinent to pre-authorized search and seizure. First, we address the common law requirements for the execution of search warrants. (For a summary of the statutory and certain common law requirements for a wide range of investigative orders, see the charts in the appendices.) Second, we examine litigation issues regarding the review of investigative orders, and address the standard of review, the effect of fraud and misleading information on the standard of review, and the requirement to obtain leave to cross-examine the person who provided grounds in support of the investigative order.

A. GENERAL REQUIREMENTS FOR EXECUTION OF SEARCH WARRANTS

Officer compliance with the various common law and statutory procedural requirements in the execution of searches is an important component of determining whether the search was authorized by law, and in some cases, whether the search was executed in a reasonable manner. There are limits as to what investigative techniques each kind of investigative order may authorize, and the officer is, of course, limited by the terms of the order, the kind of warrant or other investigative order, and by common law and constitutional considerations.

Despite the importance of prior judicial authorization to a regime of reasonable search and seizures in Canada,[1] there is reason to believe that a

---
1   *Hunter v. Southam Inc.* (1984), 14 C.C.C. (3d) 97 (S.C.C.).

sizable proportion of investigative orders are issued on insufficient bases, or are themselves deficient in their scope or drafting. A 1999 study conducted in Toronto found numerous procedural and substantive errors in a random sample of application-warrant pairs.[2] The study serves as a reminder to scrutinize carefully any investigative order to ensure the lawfulness of any search or seizure purporting to be conducted under its authority.

1) Who Can Execute and Assist in Executing the Warrant

a) Who May Execute the Warrant

With few exceptions, each specific statutory provision authorizing the issuance of a search warrant indicates who may be authorized to execute the warrant.[3] The majority of *Criminal Code* warrant provisions contemplate authorizing a "peace officer"[4] to execute the warrant, and do not require that any specific peace officer be identified in the warrant;[5] many provisions may authorize a "public officer"[6] whose duties include the enforcement of a federal Act to execute a search,[7] usually subject to a condition that the public officer is named in the warrant; still others simply require a "person" who is named in the warrant.[8]

Of course, there are situations where persons other than peace or public officers may execute a search power. For example, warrants that require specialized skills for their execution may authorize only a person with the requisite training or experience to execute the warrant. For example, the taking of bodily samples for DNA analysis may be done only by a peace officer or by another person under the direction of a peace officer, in either case

---

2   C. Hill, S. Hutchison, and L. Pringle, "Search Warrants: Illusion or Protection" (1999), 28 C.R. (5th) 89.
3   Neither s. 164 (Obscenity) nor s. 320 (Hate Propaganda) of the *Criminal Code* appears to give the issuing judge any guidance on who may be authorized to execute warrants under those sections. However, since each type of warrant will normally require entry upon private property for execution, it seems reasonable to presume that only a peace officer may be authorized to do so.
4   "Peace officer" is defined in s. 2 of the *Criminal Code*.
5   The former requirement for the naming of a specific police officer to be authorized to execute the warrant, as discussed in cases such as *R. v. Genest* (1989), 45 C.C.C. (3d) 385 (S.C.C.) [*Genest*], has been removed from the *Criminal Code*.
6   "Public officer" is defined in s. 2 of the *Criminal Code*.
7   See, e.g., *Criminal Code* s. 487 (Conventional Warrant), where the warrant may authorize a peace officer or "a public officer who has been appointed or designated to administer or enforce a federal or provincial law and whose duties include the enforcement of this Act or any other Act of Parliament and who is named in the warrant."
8   See, e.g., *Criminal Code* s. 83.13 (Terrorism).

who "by virtue of training or experience" is qualified to take such samples.[9] Under section 256(3) (Impaired Driving), the technically rigorous procedure of taking "breathalyzer" samples must be done by a "qualified technician,"[10] and the more invasive and potentially hazardous procedure of taking blood samples for blood-alcohol analysis may only be taken "by or under the direction of a qualified medical practitioner."

Additionally, several electronic surveillance provisions permit the execution of the search by persons other than peace officers. An authorization for the interception of private communications under *Criminal Code* section 186 or section 188 must be executed by *a person* (not necessarily a peace officer) who has been specially designated by the attorney general or solicitor general (as the case may be) to intercept private communications.[11] An "agent of the state"[12] may lawfully intercept private communications under section 184.1 for the purpose of preventing bodily harm, provided the limitations under the sections are complied with.[13]

b) Who May Assist in the Execution

Persons executing a search may wish (or need) to be accompanied or assisted by other peace officers, photographers, forensic specialists, computer experts, locksmiths, or electricians, in order to effectively conduct the search.[14] Although the *Criminal Code* does not explicitly authorize such assistance, there is persuasive authority that a common law power to enlist such necessary assistance exists to fill this gap in the *Criminal Code*[15] and

---

9   See *Criminal Code* s. 487.05(2)(b).
10 Note, however, that a peace officer may administer the less technical "approved screening device" test (also referred to as the ALERT test in certain cases) under s. 254(2).
11 See *Criminal Code* s. 186(5).
12 Under s. 184.1(4) "agent of the state" is defined, for the purpose of s. 184.1, as "(a) a peace officer; and (b) a person acting under the authority of, or *in cooperation with*, a peace officer" [emphasis added].
13 Section 184.1 essentially authorizes the police to have undercover officers and civilian agents "wear a wire," to monitor the conversation to ensure the safety of undercover officers and civilian agents, and to intervene in the event of violence or threats. Additional information on this *Criminal Code* provision, including strict limits on the use of any intercepted communications, can be found in Appendix 2.
14 This power should not be confused with "assistance orders." Section 487.02 allows a justice or judge to *compel* a person to assist in the execution of a warrant or authorization where that person's assistance may be necessary. For example, an Internet service provided may be ordered to assist in the interception of a client's private communications, or a search of his or her email account.
15 *R. v. B.(J.E.)* (1989), 52 C.C.C. (3d) 224 (N.S.C.A.) [*B.(J.E.)*] (child welfare worker).

other similarly constructed statutes.[16] As outlined in the sections below, the courts have considered situations where peace officers enlist the assistance of other peace officers, and where peace officers receive assistance from non-peace officers.

Reliance on common law powers to obtain assistance in conducting a search is not necessary for drug searches: the *Controlled Drugs and Substances Act* (*CDSA*) explicitly authorizes the officer to enlist whatever assistance is required to execute the search warrant.[17]

i) Assistance of Other Peace Officers

Peace officers responsible for executing a search are permitted to enlist the assistance of other peace officers. In *R. v. Strachan*,[18] the Supreme Court considered the reasonableness of a search conducted under section 10(2) of the former *Narcotic Control Act* (*NCA*) (which required that a specific officer be authorized under the warrant to execute the search). The search in *Strachan* was executed by both "named" and "unnamed" officers. The Supreme Court noted that the *NCA*'s requirement to name a specific peace officer was intended to ensure that "[t]here must be some person responsible for the way the search is carried out." The Court held that it was nevertheless permissible for peace officers that were not named in the warrant to assist in its execution:

> This requirement is met when the officer or officers named in the warrant execute it personally and are responsible for the control and conduct of the search. The use of unnamed assistants in the search does not violate the requirement of s. 10(2) so long as they are closely supervised by the named officer or officers. It is the named officers who must set out the general course of the search and direct the conduct of any assistants. If the named officers are truly in control, participate in the search, and are present throughout, then the use of assistants does not invalidate the search or the warrant.[19]

---

16 In relation to s. 12(1) of the *Mutual Legal Assistance Act*, see *R. v. Rutherford Ltd. et al.* (1995), 101 C.C.C. (3d) 260 (B.C.S.C.) at 270–71 (foreign police officers). Under s. 37 of the *Food and Drugs Act*, R.S.C. 1970, c. F-27, see *R. v. Heikel and MacKay* (1984), 57 A.R. 221 (Alta. C.A.). Under s. 10(2) of the former *Narcotics Control Act*, which required that the executing officer be named in the warrant, see *R. v. Strachan* (1988) 46 C.C.C. (3d) 479 (S.C.C.) [*Strachan*]; and *R. v. Fekete* (1985), 17 C.C.C. (3d) 188 (Ont. C.A.) [*Fekete*] at 191–92 (assistance of officers in addition to the named officer held to be reasonable as a matter of common sense).

17 See *CDSA* s. 12(a).

18 *Strachan*, above note 16.

19 *Ibid.* at paras. 28–29; see also above note 16.

ii) Voluntary Assistance of Non-Peace Officers

In *R. v. B.(J.E.)*,[20] the Nova Scotia Court of Appeal (NSCA) considered whether peace officers may be assisted by *non-peace officers* in the execution of a *Criminal Code* search warrant. In *B.(J.E.)*, a family services worker was enlisted to assist with the execution of the warrant. The NSCA concluded that it was constitutionally permissible to have persons who are neither peace officers nor other persons named in the warrant to be present for and to assist in the execution of the warrant, provided that the officer(s) actually authorized to execute the search remains "in control of" and "responsible and accountable for" its execution.[21] As the Court noted, the authorized person may not "assign or delegate [the] power" to search and seize.[22]

The common law power to enlist the assistance of non-peace officers appears to be limited to enlisting persons who could reasonably assist or facilitate the search. The power to enlist assistance would clearly not permit members of the media or curious onlookers to be invited to the search; inviting the media to the execution of a search is a serious violation of a person's privacy.[23] Moreover, the assistance anticipated from the person must relate to a purpose within the scope of the original authorization. In *R. v. Nguyen*,[24] officers obtained a *CDSA* search warrant in relation to a marijuana grow-operation. Two BC Hydro workers, who were not mentioned in the warrant materials, attended at the premises and participated in the search. Justice Kitchen of the British Columbia Provincial Court held that a *CDSA* warrant authorizes searches only in relation to offences against that Act. The presence of the BC Hydro workers — and the expansion of the search into theft of electricity — rendered the search unreasonable. In Kitchen J.'s reasoning, the hydro workers could not reasonably be expected to assist in the drug investigation because the warrant did not and could not authorize a search in relation to theft of electricity, and there was no evidence that the hydro workers' presence would ensure officer safety.

Most dramatically, in *R. v. Peet and Ward*,[25] Spence J. of the British Columbia Provincial Court interpreted the Supreme Court's approval of the presence of "unnamed assistants" in *R. v. Strachan*[26] as being limited only to peace officers, since the provision could authorize only peace officers to

---

20 *B.(J.E.)*, above note 15.
21 *Ibid.* at 235.
22 *B.(J.E.)*, above note 15; *Fekete*, above note 16 at 191.
23 See *R. v. West* (1997), 122 C.C.C. (3d) 218 (B.C.C.A.) at para. 22; *R. v. Peet*; *R. v. Ward*, [1990] B.C.J. No. 607 (B.C.P.C.) [*Peet and Ward*].
24 *R. v. Nguyen*, [2001] B.C.J. No. 2002 (B.C.P.C.).
25 *Peet and Ward*, above note 23.
26 *Strachan*, above note 16.

conduct a search.[27] The Court held that "execution of search warrant represent[s] the delegation of *judicial* authority and does not carry with it the power to sub-delegate to a person who is not a peace officer."[28] This interpretation of *Strachan*, however, is rather extreme, and appears to be an unreasonable restriction on the common law power to obtain assistance in the execution of a search, a limit that is not demanded by the reasoning in *Strachan*. As the Supreme Court noted in *Strachan*, the purpose of the *Narcotic Control Act* naming requirement was merely to ensure that a peace officer is "responsible for the way the search is carried out."[29] Provided that the authorized person "set[s] out the general course of the search and direct[s] the conduct of any assistants" and remains "truly in control, participate[s] in the search, and [is] present throughout,"[30] then the peace officer has not delegated any powers, but rather is being assisted in exercising them. In our view, if a statute does not exclude assistance from others (peace officers or otherwise), then such assistance is and ought to be permitted.

Indeed, the ability to obtain assistance where required is an eminently sensible common law power. Technical searches require special skills to gather, document and analyze evidence; without such skills, those searches would be protracted and unreliable. Other searches may require specialists to ensure the safety of the officers and the public (for example, electricians or hazardous materials experts). Still others may require the presence of specialists to deal with the people present at the time of search, for example a child welfare worker or a person trained in psychiatric intervention. To limit the reliance on such assistance would overly restrict useful, and perhaps necessary aid; aid that could in some circumstances *reduce* intrusions into a person's privacy, ensure safety, and ensure that a warrant is executed more quickly.

iii) Compelled Assistance

Section 487.02 of the *Criminal Code* empowers the issuing justice to order any person to provide assistance where the person's assistance may reasonably be considered to be required to give effect an authorization, warrant, or order. The order that issues is commonly called an assistance order and is is directed to third parties who would not, or could not, normally voluntarily assist police in the execution of a warrant.[31]

---

27 *Peet and Ward*, above note 23.
28 *Ibid.*
29 *Strachan*, above note 16 at 28.
30 *Ibid.* at 28–29.
31 See, e.g., *Canada Post Corp. v. Canada (Attorney General)* (1995), 95 C.C.C. (3d) 568 (Ont. C.A.), where an assistance order was validly directed to Canada Post employees to copy mail and keep secret the existence of the order.

2) Knock and Announce

Warrants and common law powers can give police the authority to enter private property without permission. Even where police have such authority, they must still identify themselves and request permission to enter. This is known as the "knock and announce" requirement.

The common law requires that, in all but exigent circumstances, police notify the occupants of private premises of their presence, lawful authority, and purpose by

1. knocking or ringing the doorbell;
2. identifying themselves as law enforcement police officers;
3. stating a lawful reason for entry; and
4. requesting permission to enter and only then (if permission is denied) enter without permission.[32]

As explained by the Supreme Court in *Eccles v. Bourque*,[33] these common law procedural requirements: (1) protect the safety interests of both occupants and police, by avoiding potential violence that unannounced entry might provoke; and (2) respect the privacy interest of the individual.

The prior announcement requirements have been imported as constitutional requirements for a reasonable search under section 8 of the *Charter*. In *R. v. Feeney*,[34] Sopinka J. explained that prior announcement was an important mechanism for minimizing the intrusion into an individual's privacy interest in the home:

> I would add that the protection of privacy does not end with a warrant. . . . Specifically, before forcibly entering a dwelling house to make an arrest with a warrant for an indictable offence, proper announcement must be made. As Dickson C.J.C. stated in *Landry* at p. 161, these additional requirements "minimize the invasiveness of arrest in a dwelling and permit the offender to maintain his dignity and privacy by walking to the doorway and surrendering himself."[35]

Accordingly, failing to adhere to these requirements, except in exigent circumstances, may render a search unreasonable.[36]

---

32 *Eccles v. Bourque* (1974), 19 C.C.C. (2d) 129 (S.C.C.) [*Eccles*] at 133–34; see also *R. v. Feeney* (1997), 115 C.C.C. (3d) 129 (S.C.C.) [*Feeney*] at para. 50.
33 *Eccles*, ibid.
34 *Feeney*, above note 32.
35 Ibid. at para. 50;. See also *R. v. McAllister*, [2000] B.C.J. 963 (S.C.) [*McAllister*] at para. 62.
36 *McAllister, ibid.*; *Feeney*, above note 32 at para. 50; *Genest*, above note 5; see also *Richards. v. Wisconsin*, 520 U.S. 385; *U.S. v. Banks*, 124 S.Ct. 521 (2003).

Exigent circumstances that could justify a departure from the prior notice requirements might include "fear of [sic] safety for persons within the premises, and concern for the destruction of evidence, as well as, at times, concern for the officer's own safety."[37] However, these concerns must be specifically tied to the circumstances of the individual case; simply relying on a blanket policy or practice of no-knock entries without regard to the specific facts of the case, or the lack of evidence to support a reasonable belief in such exigent circumstances, will render a search unreasonable.[38]

For a discussion of exigent circumstances generally, see chapter 4. See also *Criminal Code* section 529.4, which provides an exemption from the "knock and announce" requirements when executing arrest warrants in exigent circumstances.

3) Use of Force

Police officers may use a reasonable amount of force in the execution of a search warrant, if the circumstances require it. Certain statutory provisions authorize the use of force,[39] and the courts have also recognized that the police have the power at common law to use force in the execution of a search warrant when it is required to ensure officer safety, so long as the use of force was both subjectively and objectively reasonable.[40] There will be, however, an evidentiary onus on the police to justify the use of force in the circumstances of the case, and to establish that the extent of the force was reasonable in the circumstances.[41]

The case of *R. v. Genest*[42] demonstrates the importance of the officers' subjective belief in the necessity for using force, in addition to the requirement that the use of force be objectively reasonable. In *Genest*, police executed a defective *Narcotic Control Act* search warrant on a home by smashing in the front door without prior warning, and seized several weapons during the search. The home was a known Hells Angels hangout and several potentially dangerous dogs were known to be present. At trial, however, the officers downplayed the importance of these facts, and the Crown called no other evidence explaining the motivations for the use of force. The Court found that, although there may have been obvious *post-hoc* and objective jus-

---

37 McAllister, above note 35 at para. 84.
38 See *Genest*, above note 5; *R. v. Lau* (2003), 175 C.C.C. (3d) 273 (B.C.C.A.) [*Lau*]; *R. v. Schedel* (2003), 175 C.C.C. (3d) 193 (B.C.C.A.) [*Schedel*].
39 See, e.g., *CDSA* s. 1, and *Criminal Code* s. 25.
40 See, e.g., *Genest*, above note 5; *Lau*, above note 38.
41 *Genest*, above note 5 at 408–9; *Lau*, above note 38; *Schedel*, above note 38.
42 *Genest*, above note 5.

tifications for the use of force (such as the presence of weapons and dangerous dogs, and the Hells Angels connection), the use of force was not reasonable because the officers did not themselves provide a justification for their conduct:

> On the issue of the amount of force used in the search, the police witnesses at no point gave any explanation for the reason they thought it necessary to use force, or why they broke into the house without giving the normal warnings the common law requires. No mention was made to why the TACTIC squadron of the Sûreté de Québec [sic] was called to assist in breaking open the door. *There is an onus on the police, in these circumstances, to explain why they have thought it necessary to depart from the common law restrictions on searches.*
>
> I agree with LeBel J.A. that fears for the safety of the searchers and the possibility of violence are reasons for the use of force in the execution of a search warrant, *but no attempt was made by the police at trial to lay the factual foundation to support this approach.*[43]

Similarly, in the case of *R. v. Lau*,[44] the British Columbia Court of Appeal considered a case in which a "no-knock" entry and forcible search occurred, in the absence of any basis to believe that the premises being searched presented a danger. In *Lau*, the police relied upon a blanket policy to conduct no-knock entries for all drug-related search warrants (unless the police had reason to believe that children or elderly people were present). The Court found this policy to be unreasonable in the absence of evidence to support the belief that using force and omitting prior announcement was necessary:[45]

> [I]t is not enough to rely on general experience alone. The general experience must be weighed with the situation prevailing at the time of the search. In the case at bar there was no evidence from the police that they had made any inquiries about the premises they searched which led them to believe that there could have been danger if they had announced their presence.[46]

---

43 *Ibid.* at 408–9.
44 *Lau*, above note 38.
45 *Ibid.* at paras. 34 and 39.
46 *Ibid.* at para. 34; see also the British Columbia Court of Appeal's decision in *Schedel*, above note 38, in which the Court made findings similar to those in *Lau* regarding lack of prior announcement and use of force.

4) Duty to Show Warrant

The *Criminal Code* places a duty upon anyone who executes a warrant to have the warrant with him or her, and to show the warrant upon request during its execution:

> 29 (1) It is the duty of every one who executes a process or a warrant to have it with him, where it is feasible to do so, and to produce it when requested to do so.
>
> . . .
>
> (3) Failure to comply with subsection (1) . . . does not of itself deprive a person who executes a process or warrant . . . or those who assist them, of protection from criminal responsibility.

Note that section 29(1) of the *Criminal Code* creates an infeasibility exception to the duty to "have" the warrant during its execution. However, there is no explicit analogous "feasibility exception" to the duty to produce the warrant; the *Criminal Code* simply requires that it be produced on request. Nevertheless, failure to *produce* in exigent circumstances would presumably not render a search unreasonable.[47]

In *R. v. Bohn*,[48] the British Columbia Court of Appeal explained that the *Criminal Code* requirement to produce the search warrant was based on the common law requirement to produce an *arrest* warrant on request. At common law, failure to produce a warrant was generally fatal to the validity of the arrest.[49] The rationale for the production requirement is related to the common law "knock and announce":

> The authors of *Search & Seizure Law in Canada* say this about the purpose of s. 29(1), at pp. 17–25:
>
>> The reason for the requirement that an officer executing the warrant have it available for production, is to allow the occupant of the searched premises to know: (1) why the search is being carried out, so as to enable the occupant to properly assess his or her legal position; and (2) that there is, at least, a colour of authority for the search and that forcible resistance is improper. This last

---

47 See *R. v. Bohn* (2000), 145 C.C.C. (3d) 320 (B.C.C.A.) [*Bohn*] at para. 28; *Feeney*, above note 32.
48 *Bohn*, ibid.
49 Ibid. at para. 26; see *Gallaird v. Laxton* (1862), 2 B. & S. 363, 31 L.J. M.C. 123, 9 Cox C.C. 127, 121 E.R. 1109; *Codd v. Cabe* (1876), 1 Ex. D. 352, 45 L.J. M.C. 101, applied in *R. v. Linder*, [1924] 2 W.W.R. 646, 42 C.C.C. 289 (Alta. C.A.).

rationale also plays a role in the second procedural requirement for a valid search, that the peace officers announce themselves before entering the premises to be searched.[50]

It has been suggested that only exigent circumstances will justify a failure to produce the warrant, given the section 29(1) duty's conceptual link to the "knock and announce" requirements.[51] However, other courts have suggested that if the failure to have the warrant was inadvertent and was remedied as soon as possible, the search may nevertheless be reasonable.[52]

See also section 471.1(7) of the *Criminal Code*, which requires that on execution of a telewarrant, the peace officer must, before entering the place to be searched, or as soon as practicable thereafter, give a facsimile to any person present and apparently in control of the place.[53] Even if the place appears to be unoccupied, section 471.1(8) requires that the peace officer must, on entering the place or as soon as practicable thereafter, cause a facsimile of the warrant to be suitably affixed in a prominent place within the place.[54]

5) Treatment of "Found-Ins"

The *Criminal Code* does not generally provide authority to detain or search a person found in the premises being searched, unless that person is being arrested for committing an offence.[55] The *CDSA* provides that found-ins may be searched provided the officer has reasonable grounds to believe that the person has on their person "any controlled substance, precursor, property or thing set out in the warrant."[56]

In addition to these fairly narrow statutory provisions, police may conduct searches of persons found in a premises during the execution of a search warrant:

1. as an incident to a lawful arrest;[57]

---

50 *Bohn*, above note 47 at para. 31.
51 *Ibid.* at para. 28; *Feeney*, above note 32.
52 See *B.(J.E.)*, above note 15.
53 For obvious reasons, s. 471.1(7) does not apply to s. 256 telewarrants for the taking of blood from incapacitated drivers.
54 It is curious that no parallel requirement exists for warrants obtained in person and executed on an empty premises.
55 There is authorization to detain and search "found-ins" in situations involving s. 199 (searches of bawdy-houses and gaming-houses).
56 See *CDSA* s. 11(5).
57 *Cloutier v. Langlois* (1990), 53 C.C.C. (3d) 257 (S.C.C.); see chapter 8, "Searches Incidental to Arrest."

2. if reasonable grounds exist to believe the person is in possession of evidence related to the warrant;[58] and
3. for officer safety (pat-down and frisk searches).[59]

As with any search, a search of a found-in must be conducted in a reasonable manner. Handcuffing and ordering a found-in to lie face down on the floor, in the absence of any basis for safety concerns or grounds to suspect possession of evidence will be unreasonable.[60] Equally, a police procedure of systematically arresting and searching all people found in the premises will result in a determination of the search being executed in an unreasonable manner.[61]

6) Expiry Time

Typically, search warrants provide time parameters for the execution of the warrant. A section 487 warrant in Form 5 will provide the following restriction:

> This is, therefore, to authorize and require you between the hours of (*as the justice may direct*) to enter into the said premises and to search for the said things and to bring them before me or some other justice.

There is conflicting authority as to the effect of the time requirements listed in a typical search warrant. British Columbia courts have taken a limiting approach to the interpretation of the wording, requiring that the execution of the search be completed within the hours of authorized entry, while in Ontario, courts have taken a more liberal interpretation of the requirement, holding only that the officers enter and commence the search within the specified time.

In *Pars Oriental Rug (c.o.b. Oriental Rug Bazaar) v. Canada (Attorney General)*,[62] Wood J. of the B.C. Supreme Court considered the effect of the time restrictions in the warrant. In *Pars*, officers executed a search warrant on a business premises under section 111 of the *Customs Act*. The officers entered the business within the time range set out in the warrant and continued to search after the time period elapsed. The warrant provided:

---

58   *R. v. Le*, 2001 BCCA 658.
59   *R. v. MacIsaac*, [2001] O.J. No. 2966 (Sup. Ct.) [*MacIsaac*] at para. 72; in *R. v. Cantin* (2001), 82 C.R.R. (2d) 161 (Ont. Ct. Jus.) [*Cantin*], Edmondson J. declined to take judicial notice of the fact that drug searches were inherently dangerous for police.
60   *Cantin, ibid.*
61   See *MacIsaac*, above note 59; *R. v. Thompson*, [1990] 2 S.C.R. 1111.
62   *Pars Oriental Rug (c.o.b. Oriental Rug Bazaar) v. Canada (Attorney General)*, [1988] B.C.J. 3055 (S.C.) [*Pars*].

THIS IS, therefore, to authorize and require you between the hours of 9:30 am. July 29th, 1988 to 6:00 p.m. July 29th, 1988 to enter into the said premises and to search for the said things and to seize same, if found.

The Crown argued that the time restriction only applied to the time of entry, and not the time for completion. Justice Wood found the language in the warrant to be ambiguous, supporting the interpretation that the whole of the search was to completed within the hours specified in the warrant, and the alternate interpretation that the search must merely be commenced within that period:

> The starting point of this inquiry must necessarily be the language of the warrant itself. Mr. Justice Paris found that language ambiguous. I agree. If as suggested, the time period described therein was intended only to set the limits within which entry into the premises may be effected and the search begun, it would have been reasonable, not to mention grammatically preferable, to place the phrase "between the hours of 9:30 a.m. July 29th, 1988 to 6:00 pm. July 29th, 1988" immediately after the word "premises." Worded the way it is, that clause of the warrant clearly lends itself to the construction that not only the time of entry but also the authorized search and resulting seizures if any, are restricted to the time frame described.[63]

Faced with an ambiguous warrant, Wood J. found himself bound "to give the citizen the benefit of that construction which least interferes with his personal rights."[64] Accordingly, the warrant was of no force or effect after the time specified therein, and any search had to be completed or abandoned prior to its expiry.

In *R. v. Woodall*,[65] Dubin C.J.O. upheld the trial judge's ruling that officers were not required to complete the search within the time range specified in the warrant.[66] It is important to note that the warrant at issue in the *Woodall* case was not reprinted in either the trial judgment or the appellate endorsement; it is therefore not certain that the warrant was plagued by precisely the same linguistic ambiguity as the warrant in *Pars*. Although the trial

---

63   *Ibid.* at paras. 6–7. The final sentence in that passage is itself ambiguous, but in light of the judge's repeated description of the impugned warrant as "ambiguous," Wood J. could not have meant that the warrant "clearly lends itself" *only* to that construction.
64   *Ibid.* at para 12.
65   *R. v. Woodall*, [1993] O.J. No. 4001 (C.A.) [*Woodall*, C.A.], upholding *R. v. Woodall*, [1991] O.J. 3558 (Gen. Div.) [*Woodall*, Gen. Div.].
66   See *Woodall*, Gen. Div. at paras. 6–8.

judge in *Woodall* considered the *Pars* case,[67] he declined to apply the rule articulated in *Pars*. On appeal, the Ontario Court of Appeal gave a brief endorsement, agreeing that the time range in the warrant applied to entry and not to the completion of the search. The Court of Appeal held in part that:

> The police were required by the terms of the warrant to enter the premises before 9:00 P.M. They did so. The warrant did not require that the search be completed before 9:00 P.M. In our view, the failure to complete the search by 9:00 P.M. does not invalidate the warrant.[68]

Notwithstanding the Ontario Court's approach, it would be preferable if the standard warrant forms were amended to remove the ambiguity and clearly indicate that the time restrictions apply to limit entry, and not to the completion of the search. This approach would lend the appropriate amount of flexibility to situations that require extra time for the completion of the search (such as in technically difficult searches, or searches for evidence dangerous to the public). This approach would not lead to abusive or unnecessarily protracted searches because the court could rule that such searches were conducted in an unreasonable manner and therefore in violation of section 8 of the *Charter*.

B. SPECIAL RULES FOR LITIGATING THE VALIDITY AND REASONABLENESS OF WARRANTS AND OTHER INVESTIGATIVE ORDERS

Special legal and procedural rules apply when a court is called on to assess whether an investigative order such as a search warrant or wiretap authorization was valid or "authorized by law." This section will examine some of these special rules that apply to challenging a judicially authorized search. We will first address the standard of review that a court will apply in assessing whether an investigative order was authorized by law, and will examine the special rules for challenging the evidentiary basis for the order, specifically, the requirement to obtain leave of the court to cross-examine the person who supplied the reasonable grounds relied on by the issuing justice.

1) Access to Materials Relating to an Investigative Order

In order to challenge an investigative order, the defence will require copies of the order and the materials filed with the court in support of that application. However, the materials filed in support of an application to obtain an

---

67 *Woodall*, C.A., above note 65 at para 7.
68 *Ibid.* at para. 2.

investigative order may not be automatically available for disclosure to the defence.

In the case of a wiretap authorization, section 187 of the *Criminal Code* requires that the judge who authorizes an application to intercept private communications order that all documents relating to the application (including the authorization itself) be sealed in a packet. The packet cannot be opened except for the purpose of a further application for an interception by the state,[69] or where a judge permits the opening of the packet for the purpose of copying and examining the documents,[70] or where the defence requires the documents for trial and makes an application to a judge of the court where the trial will be heard (and who has jurisdiction in the province where the authorization was granted) to unseal the packet.[71] An order to open the packet may be made only if notice was given to the attorney general or solicitor general on whose authority the application for the order was made, and if the attorney general or solicitor general has an opportunity to be heard.[72]

Even once an order to unseal the packet under section 187 is granted, the accused may not receive disclosure until the prosecution has an opportunity to edit the materials to protect informants, ongoing investigations, investigative techniques, and the interests of innocent persons.[73] The accused will receive an edited copy of the materials, but may apply to the trial court for disclosure of the edited portions. The court may order disclosure of the edited material if it is required to make full answer and defence, and if the provision of a "judicial summary" of the edited material is insufficient to make full answer and defence.[74] Of course, if the information ordered disclosed is legitimately protected by informer privilege, the Crown is not required to disclose it — with the consequence that the Crown will be prevented from relying on it to justify the issuance of the investigative order under attack.

For warrants obtained under section 487 of the *Criminal Code*, section 487.3 provides a procedure for sealing of the materials filed in support of the warrant. The common law also empowers the court to seal materials that would compromise a privilege.[75]

---

69   *Criminal Code* s. 187 (1.2).
70   *Ibid.*, s. 187 (1.3).
71   *Ibid.*, s. 187 (1.4).
72   *Ibid.*, s. 187 (2) and (3).
73   *Ibid.*, s. 187 (4) (a)–(d).
74   *Ibid.*, ss. 187 (6) and (7); of course, the Crown is not obligated to release information.
75   See, e.g., *R. v. Yanover* (1982), 68 C.C.C. (2d) 151 (Ont. Prov. Ct.).

2) The Standard of Review of Issuance of an Investigative Order

a) General Rule for Review of Investigative Orders

When assessing whether an investigative order was "authorized by law," the reviewing court does not conduct a *de novo* review of the evidentiary basis for the order, as if it were standing in the same place and exercising the same function as the authorizing judge.[76] Rather, as Sopinka J. held in *Garofoli*,[77] the reviewing judge must assess whether the record that was before the issuing judge, as amplified on review,[78] *could* have supported the issuance of the order:[79]

> The reviewing judge does not substitute his or her view for that of the authorizing judge. If, based on the record which was before the authorizing judge as amplified on the review, the reviewing judge concludes that the authorizing judge *could* have granted the authorization, then he or she should not interfere. [emphasis added][80]

Accordingly, the standard of review for an order on a *Charter* application is similar to the test for sufficiency of evidence on an application for *certiorari*.[81] The task of the reviewing judge in this regard is explained in the following passage cited by LeBel J.A. (as he then was) in *R. v. Sauvé*:[82]

> In essence, the task of the reviewing judge is to examine the record before the authorizing judge, as amplified on the review, thereby to determine whether there remains any evidence upon the basis of which the authorizing judge could have given the order. In this context [the review of a section 186 wiretap authorization] any evidence means any evidence capable of satisfying the criteria of s. 186 (1) of the *Code*, whose twin standards are

---

76 *R. v. Garofoli* (1990), 60 C.C.C. (3d) 161 (S.C.C.) [*Garofoli*] at 187–88; *R. v. Araujo* (2000), 149 C.C.C. (3d) 449 (S.C.C.) *Araujo* at 472.
77 *Garofoli*, above note 76.
78 See discussion in the following section on amplification of the information.
79 *Garofoli*, above note 76 at 188; although *Garofoli* involved the review of an interception of communications, the test from *Garofoli* applies more broadly; subsequent cases have held that the standard applies more broadly to all investigative orders, including search warrants. See *R. v. Grant* (1993), 84 C.C.C. (3d) 173 (S.C.C.) [*Grant*] at 195; *R. v. Budd* (2000), 150 C.C.C. (3d) 108 (Ont. C.A.) [*Budd*] at paras. 14–16.
80 *Garofoli*, above note 76 at 188.
81 The Honourable Mr. Justice David J. Watt, "Interception of Private Communications," *Current Issues in Criminal Law* (Canadian Bar Association, Ontario: Institute of Continuing Legal Education, 19 January 1991) at 28.
82 *R. v. Hiscock; R. v. Sauvé* (1992), 72 C.C.C. (3d) 303 (Que. C.A.) [*Sauvé*].

probable cause and investigative necessity. Where there is no evidence which is so capable, the reviewing (trial) judge should interfere. Where there is some evidence which is so capable, the reviewing (trial) judge should not interfere. The standard does not appear to differ materially from that which is applied upon an application for certiorari (motion to quash), as for example, in the case of a search warrant. See for example, *Re Church of Scientology v. The Queen (No. 6)*, (1987), 31 C.C.C. (3d) 449 (Ont. C.A.). [emphasis added][83]

A court will find that an order *could* have issued if the reviewing court finds that "sufficient reliable information" was before the issuing justice to justify the granting of the order.[84] Information will be considered "sufficient," for the purpose of a review application, if "there was *at least some evidence that might reasonably be believed* on the basis of which the [order] *could* have issued"[85] (and not whether the authorization should have been granted in the opinion of the reviewing court). Accordingly, as LeBel J. explained in *Laroche*[86] the reviewing judge need only find a single piece of evidence to support the application:

> If the reviewing judge determines that at least one such piece of evidence existed and could reasonably have been believed, to justify the application for the warrant, the judge's examination should stop there.[87]

b) Review of Special Search Warrants and Restraint Orders

If the order being challenged is a special search warrant pursuant to *Criminal Code* section 462.32 or a section 462.33 restraint order, and the applicant pursues review of the orders under section 462.34 of the *Code*, the *Garofoli* standard of review is not applicable; the *Code* provides for a less deferential standard of review. In *R. v. Laroche*,[88] the Supreme Court interpreted section 462.34 as requiring review of the appropriateness of the order on a standard of *correctness*, without deference to the findings of the issuing justice, given that the section mandates review of whether the order *should* have issued:

> 462.34(6) [Conditions to be satisfied] An order under paragraph (4)(b) in respect of property may be made by a judge if the judge is satisfied
> (a)   where the application is made by

---

83   *Sauvé*, above note 82.
84   *R. v. Bisson* (1994), 94 C.C.C. (3d) 94 (S.C.C.) [*Bisson*] at 96.
85   *Araujo*, above note 76 at 473 [emphasis added].
86   *Quebec (Attorney General) v. Laroche* (2002), 169 C.C.C. (3d) 97 (S.C.C.) [*Laroche*].
87   *Laroche*, ibid. at para. 64; *Araujo*, above note 76 at para. 51.
88   *Laroche*, ibid.

(i) a person charged with an enterprise crime offence or a designated substance offence, or

(ii) any person who acquired title to or a right of possession of that property from a person referred to in subparagraph (i) under circumstances that give rise to a reasonable inference that the title or right was transferred from that person for the purpose of avoiding the forfeiture of the property, *that a warrant should not have been issued pursuant to section 462.32 or a restraint order under subsection 462.33(3) should not have been made in respect of that property. . .* [emphasis added][89]

In considering this statutory regime in *R. v. Laroche*,[90] the Supreme Court held that:

> this wording calls for the use of an analytical framework which differs substantially from the framework by which a judge who must review a wiretap authorization is governed. The judge must decide whether he or she would have made the same decision as the authorizing judge, having regard to all of the evidence in the judge's possession following the hearing of the application for review. If the reviewing judge does not share the opinion of his or her colleague, the authorizing judge, the reviewing judge must correct the previous judge's error. The reviewing judge cannot simply identify sufficient basis for belief on reasonable and probable grounds, as could be done in wiretap cases.[91]

The Supreme Court recognized that, aside from the lower standard of review, the type of review hearing under section 462.34 would be similar to that contemplated in *Garofoli* for reviewing wiretap authorizations, with the same obligations on public officers to submit full, frank and fair disclosure and that misleading information could form the basis for a challenge to the order. Additionally, the applicant will be permitted to call rebuttal evidence challenging the Crown's allegations in support of the order. The Court explained the process as follows:

> [T]he applicant may also present evidence to rebut or undermine the justifications offered for authorization. In that case, the Crown may also offer rebuttal evidence. While we need not examine this question here, we might be somewhat sceptical as to the possibility of remedying, by amplification, the defects of an authorization for which the argument or evi-

---

89   *Ibid.* at para. 2.
90   *Ibid.*
91   *Ibid.* at paras. 65–66.

dence presented to the reviewing judge has been shown to be fundamentally flawed (see the comments on amplification in *Araujo*, at para. 59). Subject to that *caveat*, the reviewing judge will assess the whole of the evidence submitted to him or her and to the authorizing judge, and will then decide whether the authorization should have been given. The reviewing judge will begin the analysis by recalling that the law regards the authorization as facially valid, and that it is the task of the applicant, on review, to demolish that appearance of validity. If that attempt fails, the authorization will be upheld.[92]

c) Effect of Fraud on the Standard of Review

There is some debate about the proper approach to the review of an investigative order that was based on fraudulent or misleading information. Police misdeeds introduce difficult tensions into the analysis of whether an order is supportable on review. On the one hand, the court treats the review of an investigative order like a *certiorari* application, and is supposed to afford deference to orders unless there is no evidence to support them. The fact that part of the information was fraudulent does not detract from the fact that the non-fraudulent information still exits. On the other hand, an officer who applies for an investigative order is under a duty to provide full, fair and frank disclosure of all material facts to the issuing justice,[93] in order to allow the issuing justice to properly assess whether there exists sufficient reliable information to support an order permitting a search.[94] Courts may be understandably uncomfortable sanctioning improper conduct or deferring to orders that were issued based on fraudulent information.

As will be seen in the review of cases that follows, the balance between these conflicting concerns seems to have been resolved as follows: if the fraudulent and misleading information can be excised from the warrant, the court should assess whether there are sufficient grounds for issuance in the absence of the unreliable information.[95] However, where the fraud is too pervasive and impossible to separate from the remaining grounds,[96] or if no reliable information remains after excising the unreliable information, then

---

92   Ibid. at para. 68.
93   *Dalglish v. Jarvie* (1850), 2 Mac. & G. 231, 42 E.R. 89; *R. v. Kensington Income Tax Commissioners*, [1917] 1 K.B. 486 (C.A.); *Re Church of Scientology and the Queen (No. 6)* (1987), 31 C.C.C. (3d) 449 (Ont. C.A.) [*Scientology No. 6*] at 528; *U.S.A. v. Friedland*, [1996] O.J. No. 4399 (Gen. Div.) at paras. 26–29; all as cited in *Araujo*, above note 76 at 469.
94   *Araujo*, above note 76 at 470.
95   *Garofoli*, above note 76; *Bisson*, above note 84; *Araujo*, above note 76.
96   *R. v. Branton* (2001), 154 C.C.C. (3d) 139 (Ont. C.A.); *R. v. Hosie* (1996), 107 C.C.C. (3d) 385 (Ont. C.A.).

the order should be invalidated.[97] Additionally, there is some support for the proposition that if the extent of the fraud is such that it strikes at the core of the administration of justice, then the warrant may be invalidated, even if it is possible to excise the misleading information.[98]

Prior to *Garofoli*, cases such as *R. v. Sismey*[99] held that if a warrant was significantly based on deliberately misleading information, the warrant must be quashed to protect the integrity of the justice system.[100] However, in *R. v. Garofoli*,[101] Sopinka J. held that the presence of fraud, non-disclosure, or misleading evidence in the affidavit was relevant solely to determining whether there continued to be a basis for the issuance of the order if those facts were excised from consideration of the grounds.[102] In *R. v. Bisson*,[103] the Supreme Court held that it was an error for the reviewing judge to vitiate the entire warrant on the basis of misleading information and non-disclosure in the affidavit. Instead, the Court directed that the reviewing judge must simply excise the offending portion from the material, and then determine, based on the remaining information, whether *sufficient reliable information* still existed to support the issuance of the authorization:

> The trial judge found that the affidavit material presented to the authorizing judge contained an error of non-disclosure relating to the retraction of Eric Lortie, a failure to state his age, and an error in including him as a target and accomplice. Having found such errors, the trial judge proceeded to vitiate the wire-tap authorization, finding that the police officer deliberately misled the authorizing judge. In so doing the trial judge fell into error.
>
> As stated in *R. v. Garofoli* [citation omitted] errors in the information presented to the authorizing judge, whether advertent or even fraudulent, are only factors to be considered in deciding to set aside the authorization and do not by themselves lead to automatic vitiation of the wire-tap authorization as was done by the trial judge. *The trial judge should have examined the information in the affidavit which was independent of the [unreliable] evidence concerning Eric Lortie, in order to determine whether, in light of his finding, there was sufficient reliable information to support an authorization.* [emphasis added][104]

---

97 *Garofoli*, above note 76; *Bisson*, above note 84.
98 *R. v. Morris* (1998), 134 C.C.C. (3d) 539 (N.S.C.A.) [*Morris*]; *R. v. Colbourne* (2001), 157 C.C.C. (3d) 273 (Ont. C.A.) [*Colbourne*].
99 *R. v. Sismey* (1990), 55 C.C.C. (3d) 281 [*Sismey*].
100 *Ibid.* at 285; *R. v. Dellapenna*, [1995] B.C.J. No. 1526 (C.A.) [*Dellapenna*] at para. 46.
101 *Garofoli*, above note 76.
102 *Ibid.* at 188.
103 *Bisson*, above note 84.
104 *Ibid.* at 95–96.

Following *Bisson*, the debate continued in the lower courts as to the effect of fraud and misleading information in the supporting materials for a warrant. Despite Supreme Court *dicta*, some courts appeared to be reluctant to indirectly place a stamp of approval on bad police behaviour by upholding warrants on a deferential standard of review. In *R. v. Dellapenna*,[105] Southin J.A. of the British Columbia Court of Appeal held that *R. v. Sismey*[106] was still valid law, and found that the impugned information supporting the warrant was so inaccurate and misleading that the warrant ought to have been quashed on review.[107] In *R. v. Kesselring*,[108] the Ontario Court of Appeal also recognized a power to invalidate a warrant for reasons of non-disclosure, notwithstanding reasonable and probable grounds that remained after the excision of the unreliable material.[109] Similarly, in *R. v. Morris*,[110] the Nova Scotia Court of Appeal held that, while errors in the information in support of the warrant did not *automatically* invalidate a warrant, in appropriate circumstances, the reviewing court could conclude that, in the totality of circumstances, "the conduct of police in seeking prior authorization was so subversive of that process that the resulting warrant must be set aside to protect the process and the preventive function it serves."[111]

Other courts held that that fraud and errors require the application of a non-deferential standard of review of the warrant. *R. v. Allain*[112] and *R. v. Shalala*[113] from the New Brunswick Court of Appeal were two such cases advocating the use of a *de novo* standard of review (which argument was ultimately rejected in *R. v. Araujo*[114]). This approach would require the Crown to satisfy the reviewing judge that a warrant *would have* issued on the remaining evidence.[115] The New Brunswick Court of Appeal concluded that a *de novo* assessment was required because the record on review, with all its deletion and excisions, would be materially different than what was presented to the issuing court — and to defer to the decision of the issuing judge (made on a materially different record) was accordingly illogical.[116] The

---

105 *Dellapenna*, above note 100.
106 *Sismey*, above note 99.
107 *Ibid.* at 285
108 *R. v. Kesselring* (2000), 145 C.C.C. (3d) 119 (Ont. C.A.).
109 *Ibid.* at 127.
110 *Morris*, above note 98.
111 *Ibid.* at 553; cited in *Araujo*, above note 76 at 472–73.
112 *R. v. Allain* (1998), 205 N.B.R. (2d) 201 (C.A.) [*Allain*].
113 *R. v. Shalalah*, [2000] N.B.J. No. 14 (C.A.) [*Shalalah*].
114 *Araujo*, above note 76; the argument was also rejected by the Ontario Court of Appeal in *Budd*, above note 79.
115 *Allain*, above note 112 at paras. 18 and 19.
116 *Shalalah*, above note 113 at para. 90.

Court found support for the *de novo* assessment of the grounds for issuance in the following passage from Sopinka J.'s judgment in *R. v. Grant*,[117] which used "would have issued" as the standard for review, rather than the phrase "could have issued" as used in *Garofoli*:

> [I]t is necessary for reviewing courts to consider whether the warrant *would* have been issued had the improperly obtained facts been excised from the information sworn to obtain the warrant. [emphasis added][118]

In *R. v. Araujo*,[119] the Supreme Court rejected the view that the above-noted passage from *R. v. Grant*[120] (using the word *would* rather than *could*) set a different standard of review for cases involving excision of erroneous or fraudulent information. The Court affirmed the *Garofoli* and *Bisson* line of cases, which mandated a deferential standard of review. In a somewhat opaque passage, Justice LeBel held that Sopinka J.'s use of the word *would* in *Grant* was not an alteration of the deferential *Garofoli* standard of review, but rather a suggestion of "the sincerity of the inquiry that a reviewing judge should undertake."[121] The Court was clear, however, in holding that, on review "the test is whether there was reliable evidence that might reasonably be believed on the basis of which [evidence] the authorization could have issued, not whether in the opinion of the reviewing judge, the application should have been granted at all by the authorizing judge."[122]

Although confirming that a deferential standard was generally appropriate, the Supreme Court in *Araujo*[123] neither rejected nor fully endorsed the idea that a reviewing judge has a residual discretion to invalidate a warrant to preserve the integrity of the process in the face of fraud. Justice LeBel discussed with some approval the contextual analysis adopted by the Nova Scotia Court of Appeal in *R. v. Morris*,[124] preserving the residual discretion to invalidate, explaining that such an approach "based on looking for sufficient reliable information in the totality of the circumstances appropriately bal-

---

117 *Grant*, above note 79.
118 *Ibid.* at 195.
119 *Araujo*, above note 76.
120 *Grant*, above note 79.
121 *Araujo*, above note 76 at 472. In applying the *Garofoli* standard to situations where deletions were made to material on review, the court affirmed the approaches in the following cases: *Mitton v. B.C.S.C.* (1999), 123 B.C.A.C. 263 [*Mitton*]; *Allain*, above note 112 at 217; *R. v. Krist* (1998), 113 B.C.A.C. 176 at 179.
122 *Araujo*, above note 76 at 473; see also *Budd*, above note 79.
123 *Araujo*, above note 76.
124 *Morris*, above note 98.

ances the need for judicial finality and the need to protect prior authorization systems."[125]

Justice LeBel's approval of the "contextual approach" and lack of disapproval of the residual discretion to invalidate a warrant certainly leaves open the possibility that such a discretion to invalidate a warrant for fraud still exists. However, given the Court's repeated emphasis that the correct standard of review is deferential, and the Court's approval of cases such as *Mitton v. British Columbia (Securities Commission)*,[126] it is still open to assert that fraud does not provide a reviewing judge with the discretion to invalidate an entire warrant without regard to the sufficiency of the remaining material, unless the fraud is so pervasive as to taint the whole process.

Appellate courts have continued, post-*Araujo*, to hold that residual discretion to quash a warrant may exist.[127] Notably, the Ontario Court of Appeal in *R. v. Colbourne*,[128] appears to have accepted the idea that the reviewing court retains a residual discretion to invalidate a warrant as a result of material non-disclosure that was fuelled by improper motives or an intention to mislead.[129] Additionally, Arbour J.'s *obiter* comments in the Supreme Court's decision in *R. v. Buhay*[130] regarding the possibility of a "common law" remedy for exclusion of evidence may provide further support for the existence of a residual discretion in the courts to invalidate a warrant or exclude evidence obtained from a warrant containing pervasive fraud.

d) "Amplifying" the Information on Review

When the reviewing court assesses whether the investigative order was "authorized by law," the court may consider not only what was before the issuing court, but also may consider certain technical "amplifications" of the information on review.[131]

The concept of amplifying the record on review, as opposed to considering only the exact information that was before the issuing court, was introduced by Sopinka J. in the following passage from *R. v. Garofoli*:[132]

> The reviewing judge does not substitute his or her view for that of the authorizing judge. If, based on the record which was before the authorizing judge *as amplified on the review*, the reviewing judge concludes that the

---

125 *Araujo*, above note 76 at 472–73.
126 *Mitton*, above note 121.
127 See *R. v. Neubert*, [2001] B.C.J. No. 393 (C.A.).
128 *Colbourne*, above note 98.
129 *Ibid.* at paras. 39–41.
130 *R. v. Buhay*, 2003 S.C.C. 30.
131 *Garofoli*, above note 76; *Araujo*, above note 76.
132 *Garofoli*, ibid.

authorizing judge could have granted the authorization, then he or she should not interfere. [emphasis added][133]

Unfortunately, the *Garofoli* case provided no particular guidance as to the meaning of *as amplified on review*. Following *Garofoli*, the courts had diverging views of the meaning and purpose of amplification. When introducing amplified information into the original record, tensions arise between prior authorization (that is, preserving the issuing justice's role in reviewing the grounds for a search *before* a person's privacy is invaded, which requires that all important information must be before that court), and the reviewing court's entitlement to have a full picture of the actual knowledge of the officers at the time of the application for the warrant.[134]

In *R. v. Araujo*,[135] the Supreme Court of Canada acknowledged these tensions present on review of a warrant, and set the parameters for the type of amplification permitted on review. In essence, a court may amplify the information on review to correct good faith errors in the affidavit.[136]

> *The danger inherent in amplification is that it might become a means of circumventing a prior authorization requirement.* Since a prior authorization is fundamental to the protection of everyone's privacy interests (*Hunter v. Southam Inc., supra*, at p. 160), *amplification cannot go so far as to remove the requirement that the police make their case to the issuing judge, thereby turning the authorizing procedure into a sham. On the other hand, to refuse amplification entirely would put form above substance in situations where the police had the requisite reasonable and probable grounds* and had demonstrated investigative necessity[137] but had, in good faith, made some minor, technical error in the drafting of their affidavit material. Courts must recognize (along with investigative necessity) the two principles of prior authorization and probable grounds, the verification of which may require a close examination of the information available to the police at the time of the application for a wiretap, in considering the jurisprudence on amplification. [emphasis and footnote added][138]

Examples of correctable errors (when made in good faith) have included attributing information in the affidavit to the wrong informant or

---

133   *Ibid.* at 188.
134   *Morris*, above note 98.
135   *Araujo*, above note 76.
136   *Ibid.* at 474.
137   "Investigative necessity" is a statutory precondition for most wiretap authorizations, see Appendix 2.
138   *Araujo*, above note 76 at 474–75.

source,[139] noting in the affidavit that the informer had provided a specific address or name, when informer really only provided a description enabling police to find the correct address or name.[140]

Essentially, in order for the reviewing court to use new evidence adduced on review to further support the authorization, the reviewing judge must find that the police did not deliberately or recklessly mislead the authorizing judge in the first place. Only good faith technical or drafting errors will likely be corrected.[141]

These restrictions on amplification do not apply to the defence efforts to amplify the record, however. The reviewing court must consider all information heard on review that detracts from the basis for the issuance of the order.

e) Leave of the Court Required to Attack the Evidentiary Basis through Cross-Examination

On a motion to challenge the legal basis for the issuance of a warrant, the applicant does not have free rein to present or challenge whatever evidence he or she wishes without the approval of the reviewing court. For example, if the applicant wishes to cross-examine the person(s) who provided the grounds in support of the issuance of the order, the applicant first must obtain leave of the court to conduct the cross-examination.[142]

The requirement to obtain leave can be traced to the presumption of validity of investigative orders and to concerns about preserving the privilege associated with informers and investigative techniques.[143] Prior to the Supreme Court's decision in *R. v. Garofoli*,[144] the threshold for obtaining leave from the reviewing court was strongly influenced by the standard set by the United States Supreme Court case of *Franks v. Delaware*.[145] In *R v. Parmar*,[146] Watt J. explained the *Franks v. Delaware* based-test for leave to cross-examine as follows:

---

139 Ibid. at 475–76; Morris, above note 98 at 568–69.
140 *R. v. Plant* (1993), 84 C.C.C. (3d) 203 (S.C.C.) at 216–17; Morris, above note 98 at 569.
141 Araujo, above note 76.
142 *Re Church of Scientology and the Queen (No. 6)* (1985), 17 C.C.C. (3d) 499 (Ont. H.C.J.) [*Scientology No. 4*] at 509; *Re Church of Scientology and the Queen (No. 6)* (2987) 31 C.C.C. (3d) 449 (Ont. C.A.) [*Scientology No. 5*] at 518–19.
143 *Scientology No. 4, ibid* at 509.
144 Garofoli, above note 76.
145 *Franks v. Delaware*, 438 U.S. 154 (1978); see, e.g., *Scientology No. 4* and *Scientology No. 5*, above note 142.
146 *R. v. Parmar* (1987), 37 C.C.C. (3d) 300 (Ont. H.C.J.).

i) there must be specific allegations of deliberate falsehood or reckless disregard for the truth in respect of specific aspects of the supportive affidavit;
ii) there must be *prima facie* proof by the applicant in admissible form, of the substance of what is alleged to controvert the specific contents of the affidavit; and
iii) it must be made to appear that, if the materials impugned as false or in reckless regard to the truth is set aside, that which remains is insufficient to sustain the issuance of the impugned order under s. 178.13(1) or 178.13(4) as the case may be.[147]

The *Franks v. Delaware* standard puts the applicant in a difficult position, requiring *prima facie* proof of exactly those things that would be explored in cross-examination. Indeed, in *R. v. Garofoli*,[148] Sopinka J. held that the *Franks v. Delaware* standard placed the accused in an *impossible* position: the accused "cannot cross-examine unless he provides proof of deliberate falsehood or reckless disregard for the truth, and he cannot establish deliberate falsehood or reckless disregard for the truth unless he can cross-examine."[149] In his decision, Sopinka J. also questioned the utility of the standard: if the accused had *prima facie* proof of deliberate falsehood, then cross-examination would be superfluous to the application.[150] The Court established a new standard for seeking leave to cross-examine the affiant on an investigative order: leave to cross-examine the affiant should be granted when cross-examination is necessary for the accused to make full answer and defence.[151]

Although the Court loosened the restrictive *Franks v. Delaware* standard, the "necessary for full answer and defence" threshold is not without its own restrictions. The following list summarizes the restrictions placed by the Court in *Garofoli* on the cross-examination of the affiant:

1. Leave to cross-examine must first be obtained from court.[152]
2. The decision to grant leave is in the discretion of the trial judge.[153]
3. Leave to cross-examine is not the general rule.[154] Rather, leave is to be granted only where cross-examination is necessary for the accused to make full answer and defence.

---

147 *Ibid.* at 344.
148 *Garofoli*, above note 76.
149 *Ibid.* at 196–97.
150 *Ibid.* at 197.
151 *Ibid.* at 198.
152 *Ibid.*
153 *Ibid.*
154 *Ibid.*; *R. v. Walker*, [1999] O.J. No. 653 (Gen. Div.) at para. 57.

4. Cross-examination will be necessary for full answer and defence if the accused can show *a basis for the view* that the cross-examination will elicit testimony tending to discredit the existence of one of the preconditions to the authorization, such as the existence of reasonable and probable grounds.[155] Justice Sopinka held that an example of a basis to discredit is problems with the reliability of the informer.[156] The courts will, of course, expect that the basis for obtaining leave be supported by more than speculation or a mere assertion.[157] On the other hand, the standard for obtaining leave is not a high threshold, but rather, requires only the showing of *some basis*.[158]
5. The trial judge should limit cross-examination to questions directed to establishing there was no basis upon which the authorizations could have been granted.[159]
6. The discretion of the trial judge to grant leave should not be interfered with on appeal, absent a finding that the discretion was not judicially exercised.[160]

The accused may also apply for leave to cross-examine the so-called sub-affiants, people (generally other police officers) who have provided grounds for the application to the actual affiant,[161] if the subaffiants are the best sources of material for cross-examination challenging the basis for the issuance of an order.[162] However, a court may deny leave to cross-examine if the sworn affiant is a person who has played a senior role in the investiga-

---

155 *Garofoli*, above note 76 at 198.
156 *Garofoli*, above note 76; *R. v. Dawson* (1998), 123 C.C.C. (3d) 385 (Ont. C.A.) [*Dawson*]. Note, however, that simply identifying a reliability problem will not always ensure success in obtaining leave to cross-examine. For example, in *R. v. Multani*, [1999] O.J. No. 3487 (Gen. Div.) [*Multani*], Wein J. held that the applicant had not established a basis to obtain leave where reliability problems with the informant were identified, as the police were aware of the reliability problems, and had taken steps to corroborate the information with a reliable witness before seeking the order.
157 *Multani, ibid.*
158 See, e.g., *R. v. Williams (a.k.a. Buckshot)* (2003), 180 O.A.C. 171 (C.A.), where the Court held that on an application challenging a s.186 interception, a showing that the police had some success with alternate investigatory techniques was sufficient to raise some "basis" that the police had not met the investigative necessity threshold required for non-consensual interceptions of private communications.
159 *Garofoli*, above note 76 at 198; *R. v. Silvini* (1997), 96 O.A.C. 310 at 313.
160 *Garofoli*, above note 76 at 156.
161 The term *sub-affiant* does not imply that the information was given to the affiant under oath.
162 See *R. v. Pasaluko* (1992), 77 C.C.C. (3d) 190 (B.C.S.C.).

tion, and has "the experience to evaluate material gathered in the course of the investigation and to take the responsibility for putting it forward under oath."[163]

f) Leave Requirement May Apply for All Investigative Order Reviews

The Supreme Court in *Garofoli*[164] did not specifically address whether the requirement to obtain leave to cross-examine the affiant of a wiretap authorization, and the restrictions placed on that cross-examination, also applied to the review of other warrants and orders. However, there are sound policy arguments in favour of applying the leave requirement to the review of all investigative orders. The rationale for restricting the applicant's ability to probe the basis for a wiretap authorization appears to apply equally to other investigative orders: the protection of informers' identities and police investigative techniques.[165] In considering the constitutionality of the requirement for leave to cross-examine the affiant for a section 187 interception, the Ontario Court of Appeal in *R. v. Dawson*[166] interpreted Sopinka J.'s decision in *Garofoli* as follows:

> Looking at this issue broadly, and without regard to whether it is cross-examination at trial or a preliminary hearing, it is my view that Sopinka J. in *Garofoli* was simply laying down guidelines for cross-examinations on a subject-matter which warrants advance limitations on the extent of disclosure. *Policy reasons associated with the protection of the police investigative procedures and informers demand that proper bounds of cross-examination be preset to avoid ruling being made after the damage is done.* The judge must be satisfied cross-examination is necessary to enable the accused to make full answer and defence. Relevance, materiality and prolixity will be the guiding factors and if beyond their limits, given the context of the proposed defence, then the questions will not meet the *Garofoli* test. [emphasis added][167]

If the Supreme Court's goal in *Garofoli* was to set out guidelines for handling cross-examinations in areas where police investigative techniques and informers could be jeopardized, then surely the same sort of restrictions would apply in cases of regular search warrants where the policy considerations are largely identical, given that informers and investigative techniques would be equally exposed during cross-examination. Further,

---

163 *R. v. Durette* (1992), 72 C.C.C. (3d) 421 (Ont. C.A.) at 453–54; aff'd 88 C.C.C. (3d) 1 (S.C.C.), without direct reference to this point.
164 *Garofoli*, above note 76.
165 *Dawson*, above note 156 at 391.
166 *Dawson*, above note 156.
167 *Ibid.* at 391.

the weight of authorities in other lower-court cases also suggests that a leave requirement is necessary (although recall that the threshold for obtaining leave of the court appears to be fairly low).[168]

g) **Both the Trial Judge and the Preliminary Hearing Judge Can Grant Leave to Cross-Examine**

Although the preliminary hearing court is not in a position to rule on *Charter* motions, the Ontario Court of Appeal held in *R. v. Dawson*[169] that a preliminary hearing judge has the jurisdiction to grant leave to cross-examine an affiant on a wiretap authorization as recognized in *Garofoli*.[170] The Court ruled that there was no reason, given the amendments to section 187 of the *Code* (which allowed provincial court judges to unseal wiretap packets) to delay legitimate discovery regarding the authorization until trial. The Court held that the preliminary hearing judge could grant leave to cross-examine the affiant, provided that the terms of such leave respected policy concerns (so that the cross-examination would not address irrelevant matters, be unduly prolix, or impinge on issues of privilege).[171]

h) **Standing to Challenge Investigative Orders**

The topic of an accused person's "standing" to challenge the reasonableness of a search is discussed in chapter 3. From that discussion, we learned that if a person's expectation of privacy was intruded upon by an investigative order, for example a wiretap interception, then that person has standing to challenge the basis for the issuance of the authorization under section 8 in arguing that the search was unreasonable.

---

168 In *Dawson*, the Appellants relied upon the cases of *R. v. Cover* (1988), 44 C.C.C. (3d) 34 (Ont. H.C.J.), and *R. v. George* (1991), 69 C.C.C. (3d) 148 (Ont. C.A.), to argue that imposing a requirement to obtain leave to cross-examine would constitute a denial of the right to full answer and defence. The cases held that while incidental questions could be curtailed, a blanket refusal to permit cross-examination would violate the right to full answer and defence. Justice Carthy noted that these cases were search warrant cases, and not wiretap cases like *Garofoli*, and that the courts had not considered whether a leave requirement was necessary. Other cases since *Dawson* have adopted the requirement for leave to cross-examine in search warrant cases. See *R. v. Walker*, [1999] O.J. No. 653 (Gen. Div.), and *R. v. Agensys International Inc.*, [1999] O.J. No. 781 (Gen. Div.), which required the granting of leave to cross-examine in the case of a search warrant. See *National Post v. Canada*, [2002] O.J. No. 4752 (Sup. Ct.) at para. 9, which required the granting of leave in the case of a motion to quash a general search warrant and assistance order.
169 *Dawson*, above note 156.
170 *Garofoli*, above note 76.
171 *Dawson*, above note 156 at 392.

i) Accused Person's Standing to Challenge Interceptions Made against Third Parties

The issue of standing is somewhat more complicated in the context of interceptions of communications when the person does not have an expectation of privacy in the intercepted calls (for example, if he or she was not a participant in the communication). Prior to *Edwards*,[172] the case of *R. v. Montoute*[173] effectively held that all persons alleged to be co-actors in an offence had standing to challenge a wiretap authorization if any one of the co-actors had standing to do so; to find otherwise would bring the administration of justice into disrepute by the introduction into evidence against one party of the unlawfully obtained statements from another party.[174]

In *R. v. Cheung*,[175] the British Columbia Court of Appeal held that *Montoute* was inconsistent with the Supreme Court's decision in *Edwards*, which required that a person's own privacy rights be violated before *Charter* protection could be claimed.[176] Accordingly, the Court held that a co-conspirator did not achieve standing simply by virtue of being a party to a conspiracy, and that the conspirator's own privacy interests must have been infringed to obtain standing.[177] The Quebec Court of Appeal in *R. v. Rendon*[178] essentially agreed that *Montoute* was no longer good law, and that standing could not be achieved by simple party status in a conspiracy. The Court in *Rendon* however qualified the effect of *Cheung*, and adopted the Ontario Court of Appeal's decision in *R. v. Shayesteh*,[179] which granted standing to an accused to challenge a wiretap authorization, alleging that the interception violated a different party's rights. In *Shayesteh*, intercepted communications to which Shayesteh was not a party served as supporting evidence in an application to intercept Shayesteh's communications. Shayesteh challenged the legality of the prior interceptions as a way of collaterally attacking the basis for the authorization of his communications.[180]

Most recently, in *R. v. Chang*,[181] the Ontario Court of Appeal revisited the issues raised in *Shayesteh* and returned to a position more consistent with *Edwards*. In *Chang*, a wiretap authorization targeting the accused was

---

172 *R. v. Edwards* (1996), 104 C.C.C. (3d) 136 (S.C.C.).
173 *R. v. Montoute* (1991), 62 C.C.C (3d) 481 (Alta. C.A.).
174 *Ibid.* at 506.
175 *R. v. Cheung* (1997), 119 C.C.C. (3d) 507 (B.C.C.A.) [*Cheung*].
176 *Ibid.* at para. 65.
177 *Ibid.* at paras. 68–69.
178 *R. v. Rendon* (1999), 140 C.C.C (3d) 12 (Que. C.A.).
179 *R. v. Shayesteh* (1996), 111 C.C.C. (3d) 225 (Ont. C.A.).
180 *Ibid.* at 238–39.
181 *R. v. Chang* (2003), 173 C.C.C. (3d) 397 (Ont. C.A.).

obtained based on a prior wiretap authorization from Quebec. The accused were not targets of the Quebec authorization and their communications had not been intercepted under it. The court held that the privacy interests of the accused themselves must have been engaged by the particular interception before the court could review the evidence in support of that authorization.

> The appellants argued at trial that the concern expressed by the trial judge did not arise because they sought to limit the inquiry to only one level back. However, we agree with the trial judge that there needs to be a principled reason for taking the inquiry back even one level and a logical basis for stopping there. In our view, the trial judge articulated a principled and practical approach to the review of another province's wiretap authorizations. *In the present circumstances, where there is no evidence of a direct breach of a party's Charter rights under the [prior Quebec] Authorization, the Ontario court should not review the sufficiency of the evidence giving rise to that authorization. We are also of the view that for an Ontario superior court judge in these circumstances to review the sufficiency of the evidence underlying the authorization of another province's superior court would offend the general rule that a court order is immune from collateral attack.* . . .
>
> It may well be that if conversations of either Chang or Kullman had been intercepted by wiretaps executed pursuant to the [prior Quebec] Authorization, the trial judge would have been obliged to review the sufficiency of the evidence underlying the Quebec judge's order. However, that is not the case before us. [emphasis added][182]

The Ontario Court of Appeal also held that the reviewing court was entitled to assess the *facial* validity of the prior interception (whether the issuing judge had the jurisdiction to make the order as opposed to reviewing the sufficiency of the evidentiary basis) as against third parties in reviewing the sufficiency of the evidence in support of the wiretap authorization.[183]

Accordingly, the current state of the law in Ontario appears to allow the accused to challenge the use of the intercepted communications of third parties: (1) where the accused person was a named target of the authorization; (2) where the accused person was intercepted in the course of the third-party interception; or (3) where the authorization of the prior interceptions was itself facially invalid.

---

182 *Ibid.* at paras. 41–42.
183 *Ibid.* at para. 40.

CHAPTER 8

☙

Warrantless Searches

Most warrantless searches and seizures are *prima facie* unreasonable; that is, once the applicant for *Charter* relief has demonstrated that the state conducted a search or seizure without a warrant, the Crown has the burden of showing that the search was, in fact, reasonable,[1] unless the search power is a recognized exception to the presumption of unreasonableness.[2]

This chapter examines four of the warrantless search and seizure powers the police are authorized to use at common law: searches on consent, searches conducted incidental to arrest, searches conducted incidental to investigative detentions, and seizures authorized under the plain view doctrine. The chapter will address the threshold tests to meet in determining whether the search or seizure was authorized by the relevant common law powers and the constitutional implications of the use of those powers.

A. CONSENT SEARCHES

The essence of a search or seizure is the non-consensual inference with privacy rights by the government.[3] Therefore, if a person consents, there is no

---

[1] *Hunter v. Southam Inc.* (1984), 14 C.C.C. (3d) 97 (S.C.C.).
[2] There are exceptions to the general presumption of unreasonableness of warrantless searches: e.g., a search conducted incident to arrest is not presumed to be unreasonable: see *R. v. Golden*, [2001] 3 S.C.R. 679 [*Golden*] at para. 84; also, searches conducted by school officials without warrant are not *prima facie* unreasonable: see *R. v. M.(M.R.)* (1998), 129 C.C.C. (3d) 361 (S.C.C.) at para. 50.
[3] *R. v. Dyment* (1988), 45 C.C.C. (3d) 244 (S.C.C.) at 257.

search or seizure to be scrutinized under section 8 of the *Charter*.[4] The recognition that individuals can, in appropriate circumstances, consent to waive their *Charter* rights reinforces the principle of individual autonomy that underlies the rights guaranteed by the *Charter*.[5] At common law, consensual searches were tolerated by the courts as a "non-actionable intrusion" and as an aspect of the doctrine of *volenti fit injuria*: "One who has invited or assented to an act being done towards him cannot, when he suffers from it, complain of it as a wrong."[6]

1) Informed Consent

Although consent can provide the legal authority for conducting (what would otherwise be termed) a search or seizure, it is important to ensure that consent was genuine. As Doherty J.A. explained in *R. v. Wills*:[7]

> The danger to constitutionally protected rights implicit in the equating of consent with acquiescence or compliance is self-evident and does not require detailed elaboration. When the police rely on the consent of an individual as their authority for taking something, *care must be taken to ensure that the consent was real*. Otherwise, consent becomes a euphemism for failure to object or resist, and an inducement to the police to circumvent established limitation on their investigative powers by reliance on uninformed and sometimes situationally compelled acquiescence in or compliance with police requests. . . ." [emphasis added][8]

In order to establish a valid consent, the Crown bears the onus of demonstrating that the person waived his or her rights with "full knowledge of the existence of the right and an appreciation of the consequence of waiving that right."[9] In simple terms, the consent must be "informed." As Iacobucci J. explained in *R. v. Borden*:[10]

> In order for a waiver of the right to be secure against an unreasonable seizure to be effective, the person purporting to consent must be possessed of the requisite informational foundation for a true relinquishment of the

---

4   *R. v. Wills* (1992), 70 C.C.C. (3d) 529 (Ont. C.A.) [*Wills*] at 540; *Illinois v. Rodriguez*, 110 S. Ct. 2793 (1990) [*Rodriguez*] per Marshall J. in dissent at 2804–7.
5   *Wills*, above note 4 at 541; *R. v. Turpin* (1989), 48 C.C.C. (3d) 8 (S.C.C.) at 23.
6   The Law Reform Commission of Canada, "Police Powers — Search and Seizure in Criminal Law Enforcement," Working Paper 30 (1983) 126 at 52.
7   *Wills*, above note 4.
8   *Ibid.* at 541.
9   *Ibid.*; *R. v. Neilsen* (1988), 43 C.C.C. (3d) 548 (Sask. C.A.).
10 *R. v. Borden* (1994), 92 C.C.C. (3d) 404 (S.C.C.) [*Borden*].

right. A right to choose requires not only the volition to prefer one option over another, but also sufficient available information to make the preference meaningful. This is equally true whether the individual is choosing to forego consultation with counsel or choosing to relinquish to the police something which they otherwise have no right to take.[11]

In *R. v. Wills*,[12] Doherty J.A. set out the specific criteria that must be established in order to demonstrate a valid consent:

i. there was a consent, express or implied;
ii. the giver of the consent had the authority to give the consent in question;
iii. the consent was voluntary in the sense that that word is used in *Goldman, supra*, and was not the product of police oppression, coercion or other external conduct which negated the freedom to choose whether or not to allow the police to pursue the course of conduct requested;
iv. the giver of the consent was aware of the nature of police conduct to which he or she was being asked to consent;
v. the giver of the consent was aware of his or her right to refuse to permit the police to engage in the conduct requested,[13] and
vi. the giver of the consent was aware of the potential consequences of giving the consent. [footnotes added][14]

In order to show that the accused's consent was involuntary, and therefore fails to satisfy the third criterion in the preceding list, it is necessary to demonstrate coercion or oppression of the nature and magnitude identified by the Supreme Court in *R. v. Goldman*.[15] As Bayda J.A. held in *R. v. Sewell*:[16]

[T]he *Wills* requirement (iii) contemplates an oppression or coercion of a magnitude and kind different from that inherent in every arbitrary deten-

---

11 *Ibid.* at 417.
12 *Wills*, above note 4.
13 See also *R. v. Tang*, 2001 BCCA 165 (13 February 2001) where the failure of a police officer to inform a detainee that he could refuse to be searched, even though the officer advised him charges could result if contraband was found, rendered the consent to search invalid. The Ontario Court of Appeal in *R. v. Lewis* (1998), 122 C.C.C. (3d) 481 at para. 12, however, pointed out that the failure of the police to inform a person of the option to refuse consent to search would not on its own render a search invalid — rather, failure to inform a person of the ability to refuse to consent could render the consent invalid. If the consent was the legal basis upon which the officers sought to justify their search and if a consent were invalid for reasons of the detainee not being informed of the ability to refuse, the legal justification for the search (the consent) would accordingly be absent.
14 *Wills*, above note 4 at 546.
15 *R. v. Goldman* (1979), 51 C.C.C. (2d) 1 (S.C.C.).
16 *R. v. Sewell* (2003), 175 C.C.C. (3d) 242 (Sask. C.A.) [*Sewell*].

tion. It contemplates a magnitude and kind described in *Goldman* in these excerpts from the judgment of McIntyre J., speaking for an eight-judge majority, at pp. 1005–6:

> The consent given under s. 178.11(2)(a) [a *Criminal Code* provision permitting the interception of private communications with the consent of one of the parties to the communication] must be voluntary in the sense that it is free from coercion. It must be made knowingly in that the consentor must be aware of what he is doing and aware of the significance of his act and the use which the police may be able to make of the consent. . . . A consent under s. 178.11(2)(a) is a valid and effective consent if it is the conscious act of the consentor doing what he intends to do for reasons which he considers sufficient. If the consent he gives is the one he intended to give and if he gives it as a result of his own decision and not under external coercion the fact that his motives for so doing are selfish and even reprehensible by certain standards will not vitiate it.
>
> The word *coercion* requires some definition in this context. The consent must not be procured by intimidating conduct or by force or threats of force by the police, but coercion in the sense in which the word applies here does not arise merely because the consent is given because of promised or expected leniency or immunity from prosecution.

It is true that in *Goldman*, the Court had before it a consent under s. 178.11(2)(a) of the *Criminal Code*, R.S.C. 1970, c. C-34, and not a consent to waive a s. 8 *Charter* right. There is, however, in my view, no reason in logic or policy for any distinction of consequence between the two kinds of consent from the standpoint of the appropriate test to apply for determining the validity of the consent.[17]

Accordingly, even a person subjected to an arbitrary detention within the meaning of section 9 of the *Charter* may validly consent to a police search. As Bayda J.A. explained in *R. v. Sewell*:[18]

> In my view, it is not necessary to decide whether that detention was arbitrary and thus unlawful (unless saved by s. 1 of the *Charter*) for it is not the existence of "arbitrariness" that ultimately determines whether the consent was voluntary and thus valid. The fact that it is possible to give a valid con-

---

17 *Ibid.* at paras. 25 and 26.
18 *Sewell*, above note 16.

sent in the context of an "arbitrary" detention was made clear by Cory J., speaking for the Supreme Court of Canada, in R. v. Mellenthin, [1992] 3 S.C.R. 615 at 624, 76 C.C.C. (3d) 481:

> It has been seen that as a result of the check stop the appellant was detained. The *arbitrary* detention was imposed as soon as he was pulled over. As a result of that detention, it can reasonably be inferred that the appellant felt compelled to respond to questions put to him by the police officer. In those circumstances it is incumbent upon the Crown to adduce evidence that the person detained had indeed made an informed consent to the search based upon an awareness of his rights to refuse to respond to the questions or to consent to the search. [emphasis in *R. v. Sewell*][19]

The amount of information and degree of awareness of the consequences of waiver will vary with the circumstances.[20] It is, of course, not be necessary for the accused to have a detailed comprehension of every possible outcome of the waiver before the consent is valid.[21] However, a suspect should either be informed of the predominant purposes of the investigation or, at a minimum, be given a general warning that the evidence gathered could be used to investigate other offences in addition to the specific offences that the person is aware are being investigated.[22]

For example, in *R. v. Borden*,[23] the accused was being investigated in relation to two sexual assaults: one that occurred recently at a motel, and one that had occurred several months earlier involving an elderly victim. Borden was arrested for the sexual assault that occurred at the motel. He provided an exculpatory statement and validly consented to the taking of a hair sample in relation to that offence.[24] Later, the police obtained Borden's written consent to take a blood sample — the form Borden signed indicated the sample would be used in relation to police "investigations."[25] Though the consent form was broadly worded, the police did not inform Borden that the main purpose for taking the blood sample was the investigation into the earlier sexual assault on the elderly woman.[26] As Borden was not aware that his blood sample would be used in relation to another investigation, his con-

---

19 Ibid. at para. 24.
20 Borden, above note 10 at 418.
21 Ibid.
22 Ibid. at 418–19.
23 Borden, above note 10.
24 Ibid. at 416.
25 Ibid. at 413.
26 Ibid. at 413 and 418.

sent was not valid.[27] Justice Iacobucci held that, at a minimum, it was incumbent on the police to inform Borden they were treating his consent as blanket-consent to the use of the sample in relation to other offences in which he might be a suspect.[28]

In *R. v. Wills*,[29] an apparent consent was held to be invalid because the accused had been misled as to several aspects of the police investigation. Wills was involved in a motor vehicle accident in which one of his passengers died and another was seriously injured and later died. Wills phoned the police to report the accident; one of the officers who arrived to investigate was a friend of Wills' father. The police learned that Wills had been drinking and had him perform an ALERT test, which registered a "warn" reading.[30] In the meantime, Wills' parents arrived at the scene and the officer asked the parents to encourage Wills to take a breathalyser test to definitively determine his level of blood alcohol. Wills was told that the results might be helpful at a civil trial, and that he would not be charged with a criminal offence unless his readings were in excess of 0.1 milligrams of alcohol per one litre of blood. Wills was also advised that such a test result was unlikely because he only rated a "warn" on the ALERT (which was, unbeknown to all, improperly calibrated at the time of the test). Wills performed the breathalyser test, which demonstrated a reading of 0.128. On that evidence, he was charged with impaired driving causing death.

Prior to his consent to the breathalyser test, Wills was not advised of the fate of his passengers (which is relevant to the seriousness of the charges he might face), nor was he informed that the investigating officers had not actually ruled out alcohol-related driving charges. Justice Doherty held that, although the first five criteria for establishing valid consent were met, the non-disclosure of the injuries and the malfunction in the ALERT machine removed the possibility that Wills could understand the actual jeopardy he was facing.[31] Despite being given a general warning of the possibility of

---

27   *Ibid.* at 418.
28   *Ibid.*
29   *Wills*, above note 4.
30   A roadside breath test, such as an ALERT, can be used solely as a tool to provide reasonable grounds to believe that a person has more than 80 milligrams of alcohol in one litre of blood. The results are not admissible in court as proof of the suspect's blood-alcohol content. For that purpose, a breathalyser test administered by a qualified technician is necessary for definitive blood-alcohol content readings that are admissible to prove the amount consumed. The roadside ALERT provides one of three readings: a pass, which indicates that machine registered no significant quantity of blood alcohol; a warn, which indicates a substantial level of blood alcohol; and a fail, which indicates that the person has a significant quantity of blood alcohol.
31   *Wills*, above note 4 at 547.

charges in the event of "failing" the breathalyser, Wills did not appreciate the potential consequences of taking the test because of the specific (incorrect) information he had been given about his blood-alcohol level.[32] In the circumstances, Wills' consent was invalid.

Despite the invalid consent, the evidence in Wills' case was not excluded under section 24(2) of the *Charter*. Justice Doherty held that the trial would not be rendered unfair, because the police could have obtained the evidence by statutory compulsion if the ALERT machine had been properly calibrated. While the breach of Wills' rights was serious, the police acted in good faith and out of a desire to help Mr. Wills. The administration of justice would have been more adversely affected by the exclusion of the evidence, as in the eyes of the public, it would look as though Wills had gotten away with a crime largely due to the malfunction of the ALERT machine.[33]

The collection of evidence based on a consent given for one purpose does not always mean that the police will be precluded from using that evidence solely in pursuit of another purpose. This is especially true where the police could not have reasonably anticipated that the person would subsequently be investigated in another matter.[34]

For example, in *R. v. Arp*,[35] the accused was tried for two separate murders. Arp first consented to provide hair samples "to be used in court" in connection with a murder charge in 1990. The samples proved not to be useful for the first investigation, and the accused was discharged following a preliminary inquiry. Arp was then investigated on a second murder charge two and a half years later. Pursuant to a search warrant, the police obtained the samples, which had been retained by the laboratory that conducted the tests in relation to the first investigation. The original samples were found to match evidence collected in the course of the second investigation, and Arp was charged with the second murder and re-charged with the 1990 murder. The Supreme Court held that Arp ceased to have any expectation of privacy in the hair samples once the samples were taken by the police with his unconditional and reasonably informed consent.[36] Although the nature of the police request — or the consent actually given by the suspect — limits the uses to which the sample can be put, it is valid for police to retain the evidence and use it in connection with a later investigation not anticipated

---

32   *Ibid.* at 547–48.
33   *Ibid.* at 552–54.
34   *R. v. Arp* (1998), 129 C.C.C. (3d) 321 (S.C.C.).
35   *Ibid.*
36   *Ibid.* at 360.

by the police at the time the consent was given.[37] However, it should be noted that this rule no longer applies to bodily samples collected for DNA analysis; *Criminal Code* sections 487.04 to 487.09 have supplanted this common law rule in respect of such samples.

Just as explicit consent can be given for a limited purpose, deemed or implied waivers may also be limited in their scope or purpose. In *R. v. Evans*,[38] the Supreme Court recognized that while the residents of a home are deemed to extend a licence to the general public to approach their residence for the purpose of communicating with the residents, that waiver does not extend so far as to permit the police to conduct an investigation against the owner on the property. Similarly, members of the public extend only a limited waiver of their privacy to police to conduct investigations about criminal acts committed against them. In *R. v. Law*,[39] the police discovered incriminating evidence about the lawful owners of stolen property by examining stolen documents that had been abandoned by the thief. Justice Bastarache, for the Supreme Court, held that any waiver of privacy given by the lawful owner of stolen property would be limited to certain necessary procedures for the investigation of the theft:

> I conclude the police's conduct in this case amounted to a search within the meaning of s. 8 of the *Charter*. While a reasonable accused would have expected a certain degree of state intrusion into his stolen safe — a fingerprint analysis, a security check, an investigation of content for the purpose of identifying the perpetrator of the theft — he would otherwise have expected the contents of the safe to remain private. Moreover, to the extent the officer was driven by another law enforcement objective (namely, investigation of GST violations), he lacked reasonable and probable grounds to suspect the appellants. Such conduct is precisely what the search warrant process is meant to prevent.[40]

For more discussion of implied waivers, see chapter 3, "Limited Waivers of Privacy" and "'Implied Licence' to Knock."

2) Third-Party Consent

Consent to search must be given by someone with the *authority* to consent. While accused persons themselves generally have the authority to consent

---

37   Ibid.
38   *R. v. Evans* (1996), 104 C.C.C. (3d) 23 (S.C.C.) [*Evans*].
39   *R. v. Law* (2002), 160 C.C.C. (3d) 449 (S.C.C.), 2002 BCCA 594 [*Law*].
40   Ibid. at para. 28.

to the waiver of their *Charter* rights,[41] there is some debate as to the scope of third parties ability to validly consent to a search.

The Canadian jurisprudence with respect to the capacity of third parties to consent to searches is not yet fully developed. The courts have dealt with only a handful of cases involving third-party consent and the scope of such consent is yet to be established in all contexts.

There is some support for the proposition that a search of property will be reasonable if authorized by a third party who has common authority over the property. The United States Supreme Court has found that a joint occupant of a residence can validly consent to a warrantless search of the home.[42] In *United States v. Matlock*,[43] the Court recognized the principle that the prosecution could justify a warrantless search by proof of consent by a "third party who possessed common authority over or other sufficient relationship to the premises or effects sought to be inspected."[44] In *Matlock*, the Court also noted the idea of "common authority" was not strictly tied to a simple property interest, but rather to shared use and enjoyment of property:

> Common authority is, of course, not to be implied from the mere property interest a third party has in the property. The authority which justifies the third-party consent does not rest upon the law of property, with its attendant historical and legal refinements . . . , but rests rather on mutual use of the property by persons generally having joint access or control for most purposes, so that it is reasonable to recognize that *any of the co-inhabitants has the right to permit the inspection in his own right and that the others have assumed the risk that one of their number might permit the common area to be searched.*" [citations omitted; emphasis added][45]

The Ontario Court of Appeal's endorsement in *R. v. Gregson*[46] supports the proposition that the consent of a person with common authority over property will render a search reasonable:

> The officers who entered the shack had the permission to enter from the persons who were on authorized arrangements.
>
> In our opinion, the evidence did not support a finding that there had been a breach of the respondent's *Charter* rights.[47]

---

41 *Wills*, above note 4 at 541; *R. v. Turpin* (1989), 48 C.C.C. (3d) 8 (S.C.C.) at 23.
42 *United States v. Matlock*, 94 S. Ct. 988 (1974) at 993 (n 7) [*Matlock*].
43 *Ibid.*
44 *Ibid.* at 993.
45 *Ibid.* at note 7.
46 *R. v. Gregson*, [1985] O.J. No. 1474 (C.A.).
47 *Ibid.* as cited in *R. v. Sanelli, Fasciano* (1987), 61 O.R. (2d) 385 (C.A.).

R. v. Meyers,[48] a 1987 decision of the Alberta Court of Queen's Bench, lends further support to the third-party consent rule. Mr. Meyers was being investigated for stealing property from his employer, a public hospital. As part of the investigation, police went to Meyers' home to request his permission to search his home and vehicles. While one officer was with Mr. Meyers, searching the vehicles with his consent, another officer asked Mrs. Meyers for permission to search the home, and stated that he would obtain a warrant if she refused. Mrs. Meyers did not respond, which the officer understood as silent consent or acquiescence, and the officer searched the home. Mr. Meyers later assisted the officer in completing the search of the home, and he raised no objection to the search at the time. Justice O'Leary formulated the following test to determine the validity of a person's consent to search (including third-party consent):

> In my view a search of residential premises alleged to have been made with consent must satisfy the following criteria with respect to the nature of the consent in order to escape the purview of s. 8:
>
> 1. The consent relied upon must have been granted by someone in apparent occupation of the premises, that is by an individual with the ostensible or apparent authority to give consent.
> 2. The consent must be an informed consent. The individual seeking consent must identify himself to the occupant and must inform the occupant of the purpose of the intended search. The occupant must also be informed of his right to withhold consent and insist on the production of a warrant.
> 3. The consent must have been consciously, freely and voluntarily given. It may be given by words or by conduct. It must not have been obtained by direct or indirect inducement, threat, intimidation or manipulation.
>
> The burden is on the Crown to prove on a balance of probabilities that an apparent consent was, in all the circumstances, a genuine consent.[49]

Justice O'Leary ultimately found that the consent was genuine because the wife's silence implied consent in the circumstances, there were no threats or coercion, the purpose of the search was clear, and no one made efforts to stop the search.

The case of *R. v. Mercer*[50] also provides some support for the idea that a third party can provide a valid consent, in the right circumstances. In *Mercer*,

---

48   R. v. Meyers (1987), 52 Alta. L.R. (2d) 156 (C.A.), [1987] A.J. No. 328 [*Meyers*].
49   Ibid. at 8–9.
50   R. v. Mercer; R. v. Kenny (1992), 70 C.C.C. (3d) 180 (Ont. C.A.) [*Mercer*].

hotel management authorized the police to search a hotel room based on the mere suspicion of criminal activity and the search resulted in the seizure of drugs and money. The Ontario Court of Appeal held that, rather than examining whether a third-party consent search complied with the "law of consent" generally, it would be more useful to determine whether the consent was a sufficient substitute for prior authorization. In the Court's view, the hotel management did not have a strong enough claim in the property to override the expectation of privacy of the occupant. This accords with the U.S. case law.[51] In the absence of a valid consent, the Court found the search to be unreasonable in the circumstances: there was no urgency requiring a warrantless search, the police did not have reasonable grounds for the search, and Mercer enjoyed an expectation of privacy in the room.

R. v. Mercer was decided prior to R. v. Wills[52] and R. v. Borden,[53] and accordingly contains little guidance on how to determine whether a consented, third-party or otherwise, will be an acceptable substitute for the absence of prior judicial authorization. However, the case may stand for the principle that having only shared control of a premises may not vitiate the expectation of privacy of an individual, and that the totality of the circumstances of the intrusion must be examined before a third party's consent will stand in place of a warrant. The degree of authority the consenter has over the premises will be relevant to this issue.

Further, the cases seem to indicate that the consent of the third party must be *informed*. The judge in R. v. Meyers[54] employed the same type of reasoning later embraced in Wills[55] and Borden[56] — that any valid consent must be informed. However, each of these cases was decided prior to the Supreme Court's seminal decision in R. v. Edwards,[57] in which the Court tied section 8 rights to having a reasonable expectation of privacy, and found that the Charter did not apply to a search where the accused's girlfriend provided an essentially *uninformed* consent to the search of her apartment. The validity of the girlfriend's consent was irrelevant because the accused had no expectation of privacy in the apartment.

A more recent case on a related issue is R. v. Adams.[58] The Ontario Court of Appeal held in Adams that a third party's consent must be

---

51 Matlock, above note 42 at 993, Note 7.
52 Wills, above note 4.
53 Borden, above note 10.
54 Meyers, above note 48.
55 Wills, above note 4.
56 Borden, above note 10.
57 R. v. Edwards (1996), 104 C.C.C. (3d) 136 (S.C.C.).
58 R. v. Adams, [2001] O.J. 3240 (C.A.) [Adams].

informed before it will substitute for a warrant to enter a home to effect an arrest, provided that the person challenging the search has a privacy right in some aspect of the search conducted. In *Adams*, the accused person's landlord allowed the police into the laundry area of a multi-unit residence to arrest Adams. The police did not have a warrant under the *Criminal Code* to allow them to enter the residence to effect the arrest. The Court held that the consent of the third-party landlord had to be an informed one before it could substitute for the *R. v. Feeney*[59] warrant requirement. The Court further held that it was irrelevant whether the accused had an expectation of privacy in the residence entered, as he had an expectation of privacy in the subsequent search of his person that occurred following the entry. As the Court explained:

> Also, in our view, the evidence is clear, and it is not seriously contested by the Crown, that the consent [obtained by lying to the superintendent] in this case was not valid. . . .
>
> Crown counsel, however, argues that the appellant has no standing to question the validity of the superintendent's consent in the absence of a reasonable expectation of privacy in the premises in question. The appellant submits that since he shared the laundry room with his superintendent, he had a reasonable expectation of privacy with respect to the area where he was arrested, and therefore has standing. Alternatively, he submits that he has standing to raise this issue based on his right to contest the validity of his arrest.
>
> It is not necessary for us to determine the reasonable expectation of privacy issue with respect to standing. In our view, the appellant has standing to contest the validity of his arrest by virtue of the fact that his own *Charter* right was involved. This is not a case where an accused seeks to exclude evidence obtained as a result of a violation of a third party's s. 8 *Charter* right. It is the appellant's own s. 8 right which was engaged when the police effected the search of his person incidental to his arrest. In the circumstances of this case, absent a valid consent, the arrest was unlawful. Consequently, the appellant's s. 8 right was violated and, as agreed, the evidence should have been excluded.[60]

---

59 *R. v. Feeney* (1997), 115 C.C.C. (3d) 129 (S.C.C.). In that case, the Supreme Court held that the police may not enter a person's home to effect an arrest without a warrant specifically permitting them to enter a dwelling-house. At the time *Feeney* was decided, the *Criminal Code* provided for no such warrant. Soon after, Parliament enacted s. 529.1.

60 *Adams*, above note 58 at paras. 7–9; see also *R. v. Mellenthin* (1992), 76 C.C.C. (3d) 481 at 487 (S.C.C.); *R. v. Borden* (1994), 92 C.C.C. (3d) 404 at 417 (S.C.C.); *Wills*,

It is not clear whether the *Adams* case is authority for the proposition that third-party consents must be "informed." *Adams* may be distinguishable from other third-party consent cases because it dealt more directly with the technical constitutional requirements for a valid entry for arrest, rather than entry for the purposes of a search. Moreover, the decision hinged on Adams's expectation of privacy in his body *vis-à-vis* the search incident to arrest. Nevertheless, it is possible that the courts may adopt a strict "informed" third-party consent rule to protect the expectation of privacy in the home — even a shared one.

There remains ample room for development of the case law in the area of third-party consents. The question of whether or not a third party can waive an accused's "reasonable expectation of privacy" in property is not yet fully answered.[61] The Court of Appeal touched on the issue in the *Mercer* case in refusing to allow a guest's expectation of privacy to be waived by hotel management, but the analysis in that case is not such that it could be extended to circumstances beyond the hotel management/occupant relationship.

The cases dealing with third-party consent have also not considered whether the Supreme Court's decision in *R. v. Duarte*,[62] has implications beyond warrantless interceptions of communications. In that case, the Court held that third-party consent is not a sufficient substitute for prior judicial authorization. However, it may be that the reasoning in *Duarte* cannot be extended to other search and seizure situations. The extremely intrusive nature of surreptitious wiretap surveillance weighed heavily in the Supreme Court's analysis — the Court held that it is among the most invasive types of searches, and has Orwellian overtones.[63]

a) Apparent Authority

There is also some support in Canada for the doctrine known in the United States as "apparent authority"[64] — that a search will be reasonable if a police officer reasonably believed that a third party had authority to consent to the search, even if the person has no actual authority. However, in Canada, the doctrine of apparent authority has not been recognized as a complete justification for a search under section 8, but has been instead recognized as a mitigating factor under section 24(2).

---

above note 4 at 543–46 (Ont. C.A.); *R. v. Lewis* (1998), 122 C.C.C. (3d) 481 (Ont. C.A.) at para. 12.

61 See also *R. v. Young* (1997), 116 C.C.C. (3d) 350 (Ont. C.A.); *R. v. Milanovic*, [2002] O.J. No. 3786 (C.A.): an endorsement of the Ontario Court of Appeal upholding the admission of evidence under s. 24(2).

62 *R. v. Duarte* (1990), 53 C.C.C. (3d) 1 (S.C.C.).

63 *Ibid.* at 10–11.

64 *Rodriguez*, above note 4.

In *R. v. Mercer*,[65] the hotel search case discussed above, the Court considered the doctrine of "apparent authority" as a justification for a warrantless search. Justice Arbour (later of the Supreme Court) held that the doctrine of apparent authority could apply to situations where the police made "a reasonable mistake of fact with respect to the identity of the person giving the consent," as a person having authority to consent to a search.[66] It is unclear from the judgment, however, whether such a reasonable mistake of fact would render the search reasonable under section 8 (as in the American rule), or would simply be a factor demonstrating good faith in the section 24(2) analysis of whether evidence ought to be excluded.

In light of the fundamental notion that a lawful search must be authorized by law,[67] the better view appears to be that even a reasonable mistake of fact could not provide a complete justification for the search. In the absence of statutory or common law authority, an officer conducting a search must have *actual* valid consent in order for the search to be "authorized by law" and comply with section 8. The officer's mistaken belief that valid consent was obtained does not make a deficient consent any more valid and accordingly, ought not to provide its own legal authorization to conduct a search. Nevertheless, a reasonable mistake of fact will no doubt mitigate the seriousness of the breach in the section 24(2) analysis.

B. SEARCHES INCIDENTAL TO ARREST

The common law power to conduct a warrantless search incidental to the arrest of a person permits police to "to search a lawfully arrested person and to seize anything in his or her possession or immediate surroundings to guarantee the safety of the police and the accused, prevent the prisoner's escape or provide evidence against him."[68]

1) Nature of the Power

The power to search incidental to arrest is a recognized exception to the principles laid down in *Hunter v. Southam*.[69] First, searches incidental to arrest do not require prior judicial authorization. Second, such searches are an exception to the general rule that warrantless searches are presumed to be unreasonable.[70] Accordingly, when a search incidental to arrest is chal-

---

65 *Mercer*, above note 50.
66 *Ibid.* at 189.
67 *R. v. Collins* (1987), 33 C.C.C. (3d) 1 (S.C.C.); *R. v. Buhay*, 2003 SCC 30 [*Buhay*].
68 *Cloutier v. Langlois* (1990), 53 C.C.C. (3d) 257 (S.C.C.) at 180–81 [*Cloutier*].
69 *Hunter*, above note 1.
70 *Golden*, above note 2 at para. 84.

lenged on constitutional grounds, the defence bears the burden of establishing that the search was unreasonable. As the Supreme Court explained in *R. v. Golden*:[71]

> The law is clear in Canada that warrantless searches are *prima facie* unreasonable under s. 8 of the *Charter* (*Hunter, supra*). Where a search is carried out without prior authorization in the form of a warrant, the burden is on the party seeking to justify the warrantless search to prove that it was not unreasonable (*Hunter*, at pp. 160–61). *Searches of the person incident to arrest are an established exception to the general rule that warrantless searches are* prima facie *unreasonable*. In considering the constitutionality of strip searches carried out as an incident to arrest, it is still important to bear in mind that warrantless searches are the exception and not the norm in Canadian law. *While characterized as an exception to the normal rule that a search warrant is required for a lawful search, however, warrantless personal searches incident to arrest are an exception whose importance should not be underestimated.* The practical reality is that warrantless searches of persons incident to arrest constitute the majority of searches conducted by police.[72]

Although the power to conduct a search incidental to arrest does not conform to the standard *Hunter v. Southam* criteria for a reasonable power of search and seizure, the power is nevertheless constitutionally reasonable. In *Cloutier v. Langlois*,[73] the Supreme Court held that the power to conduct a search incident to arrest was reasonable,[74] having weighed the competing interests of the state and of the individual. The interference with liberty occasioned by a search incidental to arrest was considered both necessary to the functioning of the criminal justice system and reasonable, having regard to the liberty interfered with and the importance of the public purpose served by the interference:

> The ultimate purpose of criminal proceedings is to convict those found guilty beyond a reasonable doubt. . . . First, the process of arrest must be capable of ensuring that those arrested will come before the court. . . . In

---

71　*Ibid.*
72　*Ibid.* at para. 84.
73　*Cloutier v. Langlois*, [1990] 1 S.C.R. 158.
74　This case arose after the enactment of the *Charter* but was not argued on *Charter* grounds. On the day of his arrest, the motorist had the officers charged with assault. The officers' defence was that their frisk search could not constitute the offence of assault because it was authorized by the common law and was conducted reasonably, mirroring the *Collins* requirements. In considering the case, the Court was guided by *Charter* principles.

light of this consideration, a search of the accused for weapons or other dangerous articles is necessary as an elementary precaution to preclude the possibility of their use against the police, the nearby public or the accused himself. . . . Further, the process of arrest must ensure that evidence found on the accused and in his immediate surroundings is preserved. The effectiveness of the system depends in part on the ability of peace officers to collect evidence that can be used in establishing the guilt of a suspect beyond a reasonable doubt.[75]

Three conditions must be satisfied in order for a search to be valid under the common law power of search incident to arrest:

1. the arrest must be lawful;
2. the search must have been conducted as an incident to the lawful arrest; and
3. the manner in which the search is carried out must be reasonable.[76]

To be considered an "incident to the lawful arrest" (step 2 in the preceding list), the search must have been carried out in furtherance of "a valid objective in pursuit of the ends of criminal justice."[77] In *Cloutier*, the Supreme Court identified two valid objectives for conducting a search incident to arrest: (1) to ensure that those arrested will be brought to court; and (2) to collect evidence that can be used in establishing the guilt of a suspect beyond a reasonable doubt.[78] Accordingly, officers are permitted to conduct searches incidental to arrest in order to discover "an object that may be a threat to the safety of the police, the accused or the public, or that may facilitate escape or act as evidence against the accused."[79]

Moreover, the basis for the search must be related to the reason for the arrest: "searches which derive their legal authority from the fact of arrest must be truly incidental to the arrest in question":[80]

> Requiring that the search be truly incidental to the arrest means that if the justification for the search is to find evidence, there must be some reasonable prospect of securing evidence of the offence for which the accused is being arrested. For example, when the arrest is for traffic violations, once

---

75 *Cloutier*, above note 68 at 182.
76 *R. v. Stillman* (1997), 113 C.C.C. (3d) 321 (S.C.C.) [*Stillman*] at para. 27.
77 *Cloutier*, above note 68 at 186.
78 *Ibid.* at 182.
79 *Ibid.* at 186.
80 *R. v. Caslake* (1998), 121 C.C.C. (3d) 97 (S.C.C.) [*Caslake*] at para. 17.

the police have ensured their own safety, there is nothing that could properly justify searching any further . . .[81]

The officers need not have reasonable and probable grounds to believe that an arrestee is in possession of weapons or tools of escape, or that a search will reveal evidence of the offence, before conducting a search incident to arrest. Rather, there must be "some reasonable basis for doing what the police officer did."[82] This reasonable basis has both a subjective and an objective component, meaning that the officer must consider whether there is a valid purpose for the search, and that the officer's purpose must be objectively reasonable.[83]

Even if it is established that the common law power of search incident to arrest applies in a given situation, the conduct of the police in the course of the search must be reasonable:[84]

> The search must not be conducted in an abusive fashion and in particular, the use of physical or psychological constraint should be proportionate to the objectives sought and the other circumstances of the situation.[85]

Finally, the power to conduct a search incident to arrest does not create a duty to do so. The police may decide not to conduct such searches in appropriate circumstances:

> The police have some discretion in conducting the search. Where they are satisfied that the law can be effectively and safely applied without a search, the police may see fit not to conduct a search. They must be in a position to assess the circumstances of each case so as to determine whether a search meets the underlying objectives.[86]

---

81 *Ibid.* at para 22. See, e.g., *R. v. Belnavis* (1996), 107 C.C.C. (3d) 195 (Ont. C.A.) at 213 where Doherty J.A. held that an arrest for outstanding traffic fines did not authorize the search of the trunk of a vehicle, stating "[t]he authority to search as an incident of the arrest does not extend to searches undertaken for purposes which have no connection to the reason for the arrest."
82 *Caslake*, above note 80 at para. 20.
83 *Ibid.* at para. 27.
84 A search, otherwise incidental to an arrest, which was carried out for an improper purpose or in an unreasonable manner would be characterized as unreasonable and unjustified, and pursuant to *Collins*, would constitute a violation of s. 8 of the *Charter*.
85 *Cloutier*, above note 68 at 186.
86 *Ibid.* This passage is curious, since it appears to give the police the power to conduct a search incident to arrest even when they are satisfied that the law can be safely and effectively applied without such a search.

2) Scope of the Search

The common law power of search incident to arrest authorizes the search of the suspect and his or her "immediate surroundings."[87] This may include vehicles in which the suspect is travelling, and the contents of the vehicle as well.[88]

However, the limits of what constitute "immediate surroundings" have not been clearly defined. There has been little appellate court jurisprudence on the scope of the power. An example of a broadened concept of immediate surroundings is found in *R. v. Anderson*.[89] In *Anderson*, the accused was arrested in his friend's house trailer. The arresting officer took keys that Anderson had identified as his own, and searched Anderson's car, which was parked outside the trailer, and seized certain items. The Nova Scotia Court of Appeal characterized the search of the car as a lawful search incident to arrest without further comment.

Despite the high expectation of privacy in the home, the power to search incident to arrest may apply to a dwelling-house, even if neither the police nor the accused are in the house at the time of the arrest. In *R. v. Bedard*,[90] the Ontario Court of Appeal upheld the warrantless search of the accused's residence after he surrendered to police on his front lawn.[91] Bedard was suspected of a serious violent crime with a firearm, and police had reason to believe that he had an accomplice. Immediately following his arrest, the police searched his farmhouse for the second alleged perpetrator. Within fifteen minutes, the police confirmed that no accomplice was in the house; in the course of the search, police saw drugs and weapons. Nothing was seized, but their observations formed the basis for the issuance of a warrant to search the house. The Ontario Court of Appeal held that the warrantless search was justified, but relied in part on the exigency of the particular circumstances[92] in reaching that conclusion:

---

87   *Ibid.* at 180.
88   See, e.g., *Caslake*, above note 80; and *Sewell*, above note 16 at para. 33.
89   *R. v. Anderson* (1999), 175 N.S.R. (2d) 362 (C.A.).
90   *R. v. Bedard* (1998), 125 C.C.C. (3d) 348 (Ont. C.A.) [*Bedard*].
91   See also *Rotman v. Commissioner of Police for the Metropolis*, [2002] 2 A.C. 692 (H.L.) [*Rotman*], where the accused was arrested outside his house but on his property. Lord Hutton said for the majority: "[T]he house and the grounds surrounding it comprised the premises of the respondent and I think that it would be artificial to draw a distinction between a house and its grounds in relation to the power to search following an arrest of a suspect on his premises."
92   See, however, *ibid.*, where exigent circumstances were not in issue, and the House of Lords held that the common law power of search incident to arrest included the power to search his residence.

The circumstances of the arrest ... gave rise to a legitimate cause for concern on the part of the police with respect to the safety of those at the scene, and reasonable steps were taken to allay that concern. The police reasonably apprehended a real and serious risk to their safety and the public's safety. Alternative measures to the warrantless search did not appear to be available. In light of the circumstances, the police officers on the scene had to make their assessment on the spot with no time for careful reflection. *The police believed, and in my opinion this belief was reasonable in circumstances, that they needed to immediately search the house to see if the second suspect who was potentially armed was there and to secure the arrest scene. The search was truly incidental to the arrest.* According, [sic] I am of the opinion that the officers were acting lawfully and were authorized to search the premises. [emphasis added][93]

3) Search Incidental to Arrest and the Right to Counsel

A person being searched as an incident of his or her arrest is necessarily detained within the meaning of section 10 of the *Charter*, and the detainee has the right to be *informed* of his or her right to retain and instruct counsel immediately.[94] There may be situations in which the police, for safety reasons, "may be excused for not pausing to advise the suspect of his rights," such as when a suspect is violent or obstructive, or the police have reason to believe he or she might have a weapon.[95] However, outside such circumstances, the police must advise the detainee of the right to counsel before embarking on a search of the person.

The police are not obligated to suspend the search of the person until after the detainee has had the opportunity to retain counsel.[96] However, where the lawfulness of the search depends on the detainee's consent[97] or where a statute gives a person the right to seek review of the decision to search,[98] if the suspect invokes his or her right to counsel the police must refrain from or suspend the search until after the suspect has been given reasonable opportunity to consult counsel.[99] A failure to delay or suspend the search in such circumstances may result in a violation of section 8 in addition to the section 10(b) violation.[100]

---

93 *Bedard*, above note 90 at para 18.
94 *R. v. Debot* (1989), 52 C.C.C. (3d) 193 (S.C.C.) [*Debot*].
95 *Ibid.* at 198–200 and 211–12.
96 *Ibid.*
97 See *R. v. Ross*, [1989] 1 S.C.R. 3.
98 See *R. v. Simmons*, [1988] 2 S.C.R. 495.
99 *Debot*, above note 94 at 199.
100 *Ibid.*

4) Timing of the Search

A search incident to arrest need not be conducted contemporaneously with the arrest. In *R v. Caslake*,[101] the Court considered the reasonableness of a search of the accused's car conducted six hours after he was arrested for possession of marijuana for the purpose of trafficking. The search revealed a substantial amount of cash and two packages of cocaine. The officer who searched the car testified that the sole reason he conducted the search was an RCMP policy requiring that "inventory searches" be conducted to determine the general condition of all impounded vehicles, and to "safeguard" any valuable possessions of the owner. The majority in *Caslake* ruled that the search was unreasonable, not because of the time that had elapsed, but because of the purpose for which it was conducted:[102]

> Had Constable Boyle searched the car, even hours later, for the purpose of finding evidence which could be used at the appellant's trial on the charge of possessing marijuana for purpose of trafficking, this would have been well within the scope of the search incident to arrest power, as there was clearly sufficient circumstantial evidence to justify a search of the vehicle. However, by his own testimony, this is not why he searched. Rather, the sole reason for the search was to comply with an RCMP policy requiring that the contents of an impounded car be inventoried. This is not within the bounds of the legitimate purposes of search incident to arrest.[103]

In *R. v. Debot*,[104] Martin J.A. of the Ontario Court of Appeal suggested that a search incident to arrest could actually *precede* the arrest provided that the officer had all the prerequisiste grounds for the arrest prior to the search.[105] While the Supreme Court in its review of the decision did not explicitly deal with that

---

101 *Caslake*, above note 80.
102 But see *R. v. Nicolosi* (1998), 127 C.C.C. (3d) 176 (Ont. C.A.). In that case, there was statutory authority for an inventory search. Note also para. 21, where Doherty J. for a unanimous Ontario Court of Appeal doubts that a person has a reasonable expectation of privacy in a lawfully impounded car or any contents visible upon entry: "In my opinion, no one in the position of the appellant could reasonably expect that the police or their authorized agents would not enter the vehicle on one or more occasions while the vehicle was in 'the custody of the law.' . . . Absent a reasonable expectation that the police or their agents would not enter the vehicle while it was in their custody, I do not see how the appellant can establish a reasonable expectation of privacy with respect to any of the contents of the vehicle which were plainly visible upon entering the vehicle."
103 *Caslake*, above note 80 at para. 26.
104 *R. v. Debot* (1986), 30 C.C.C. (3d) 207 (Ont. C.A.).
105 *Ibid.*

proposition, its ruling casts some doubt on the usefulness of that approach at least as regards searches of the *person*. Since the commencement of the search will trigger the suspect's section 10 rights (which are identical in the case of arrest or detention), the suspect must be informed of the reason for his or her detention. The better view appears to be that prior to a search incident to arrest, the suspect has the right to know that he or she is being arrested.[106] See "Search Incidental to Arrest and the Right to Counsel" earlier in the chapter.

5) More Intrusive Searches of the Body Incident to Arrest: Bodily Samples and Strip Searches

Bodily samples cannot be lawfully taken as an incident to an arrest. In *R. v. Stillman*,[107] the Supreme Court held that such searches were unreasonable, given the level of intrusiveness of the search, and the reality that there is no practical danger of the evidence disappearing.[108]

The same blanket prohibition does not apply to strip searches, however. In *R. v. Golden*,[109] the Supreme Court held that strip searches[110] may legitimately be performed as an incident to arrest, provided certain criteria are met. Rather than simply having a reasonable basis to conduct the search (the low threshold for a frisk search), the police must have reasonable and probable grounds for concluding that a strip search is "necessary in the particular circumstances of the arrest."[111] Additionally, the Court held that police must conform to the following criteria:

---

106 This conclusion is supported by the Supreme Court recent decision in *R. v. Mann* 2004 SCC 52 [*Mann*], rev'g *R. v. Mann* (2002), 169 C.C.C. (3d) 272 (Man. C.A.) [*Mann* (C.A.)]. There, in a discussion of the power to conduct a search incident to an investigative detention, the majority held that s. 10(a) of the *Charter* required that "[a]t a minimum, individuals who are detained for investigative purposes must therefore be advised, in clear and simple language, of the reasons for the detention" (*Mann* at para. 21).
107 *Stillman*, above note 76.
108 *Ibid.* at para. 49.
109 *Golden*, above note 2.
110 The majority adopted the following definition of "strip search": "the removal or rearrangement of some or all of the clothing of a person so as to permit a visual inspection of a person's private areas, namely genitals, buttocks, breasts (in the case of a female), or undergarments. . . . This definition distinguishes strip searches from less intrusive "frisk" or "pat-down" searches, which do not involve the removal of clothing, and from more intrusive body cavity searches, which involve a physical inspection of the detainee's genital or anal regions. While the mouth is a body cavity, it is not encompassed by the term "body cavity search" (para. 47).
111 *Golden*, above note 2 at para. 98. Strip searches of travelers at border crossings are an exception to the rule requiring reasonable and probable grounds for the search.

Strip searches should generally only be conducted at the police station except where there are exigent circumstances requiring that the detainee be searched prior to being transported to the police station. Such exigent circumstances will only be established where the police have reasonable and probable grounds to believe that it is necessary to conduct the search in the field rather than at the police station. Strip searches conducted in the field could only be justified where there is a demonstrated necessity and urgency to search for weapons or objects that could be used to threaten the safety of the accused, the arresting officers or other individuals. The police would also have to show why it would have been unsafe to wait and conduct the strip search at the police station rather than in the field. Strip searches conducted in the field represent a much greater invasion of privacy and pose a greater threat to the detainee's bodily integrity and, for this reason, field strip searches can only be justified in exigent circumstances.[112]

The majority was careful to point out that their reasons in *Golden* applied to strip searches, and that greater justification will be required for (and greater scrutiny will be placed upon) more intrusive searches, such as body cavity searches.[113] Additionally, "where the circumstances of a search require the seizure of material located in or near a body cavity, the individual being searched should be given the opportunity to remove the material himself or the advice and assistance of a trained medical professional should be sought to ensure that the material can be safely removed."[114]

C. SEARCH INCIDENTAL TO INVESTIGATIVE DETENTION

Police officers have the power to conduct limited searches incidental to a lawful "investigative detention."[115] As will be discussed in the following pages, the police will have the power to conduct a search incidental to an investigative detention where: 1) there are reasonable grounds to suspect that the individual is connected to a particular crime and that the detention is objectively necessary to the investigation; and 2) the search is reasonably necessary, having reference to factors such as the duty being performed, the

---

See *R. v. Simmons*, [1988] 2 S.C.R. 495 and *R. v. Monney*, [1999] 1 S.C.R. 652, in which the Supreme Court concluded that strip searches of travellers carried out under the customs legislation did not violate s. 8.
112 *Golden*, above note 2 at paras. 101–2.
113 *Ibid.*
114 *Ibid.* at para. 114.
115 See *Mann*, above note 106.

extent to which the search is necessary to perform that duty, the importance of the duty to the public good, the nature of the liberty interest being interfered with, and the nature and extent of the interference with that liberty interest.[116] As we will see, several of the cases that have considered the power to search incidental to investigative detention have stated that such a search is permissible only to ensure the safety of the officer or others, and not for the purpose of gathering evidence.[117]

1) What Is an Investigative Detention?

An investigative detention is just that — a detention by the police for the purpose of conducting an investigation, where the person detained is not under arrest. This type of detention is also sometimes called a "stop and frisk" or a "*Terry* stop."[118] Investigative detentions also tend to be associated with unplanned police interaction with suspects of crimes, rather than planned investigations. As Ryan J.A. explained in *R. v. Ferris*:[119]

> [Investigative detention] arises in connection with the type of police activity of which Chief Justice McEachern (dissenting) spoke in *R. v. Klimchuk* (1991), 67 C.C.C. (3d) 385 (B.C.C.A) at pp. 390–91:
>
>> [S]ituations commonly occur in the ordinary work of police officers, often on the street at night, where they are confronted with an endless variety of circumstances which arise spontaneously. Where there are high levels of objectively based suspicion, or where ordinary prudence requires some police response, common sense may dictate that a search causing minimal interference with privacy, which may mean no more than looking into a vehicle, should probably be reasonable without a warrant. It is unnecessary to construct bizarre scenarios but occasions will undoubtedly arise where it would be absurd for a police officer not to respond to a particular situation which cries out for him or her to look into a vehicle.[120]

---

116 *Ibid.*, at paras. 39 and 45.
117 There is, however, some support for the proposition that a search incidental to an investigative detention may be conducted for other reasons. See "Scope of the Search Incidental to Investigative Detention," below.
118 So-called because the United States Supreme Court case of *Terry v. Ohio*, 392 U.S. 1 (1968) [*Terry*] approved of the practice.
119 *R. v. Ferris* (1998), 126 C.C.C. (3d) 298 (B.C.C.A.) [*Ferris*].
120 *Ibid.* at para. 5.

While an investigative detention will trigger certain *Charter* protections, obviously not every interaction with the police will trigger these protections. In *R. v. Mann*,[121] the Supreme Court explained that while the concept of a "detention" includes a broad range of encounters between police or other state agents and members of the public, not every type of encounter will constitute a "detention" for *Charter* purposes:

> [T]he police cannot be said to "detain," within the meaning of ss. 9 and 10 of the *Charter*, every suspect they stop for purposes of identification, or even interview. The person who is stopped will in all cases be "detained" in the sense of "delayed," or "kept waiting." But the constitutional rights recognized by ss. 9 and 10 of the *Charter* are not engaged by delays that involve no significant physical or psychological restraint.[122]

Consequently, detentions without a component of "significant physical or psychological restraint" will neither infringe the detainee's rights under section 9 nor trigger the rights and protections under section 10.[123] Unfortunately, the courts have as yet provided little guidance on which kinds of detentions will be constitutionally relevant.[124]

2) When Can the Police Search as an Incident to an Investigative Detention?

As discussed in chapter 4, in order for a search to be reasonable: 1) it must be authorized by law; 2) the law must be reasonable; and 3) the search must be executed in a reasonable manner. There is no statutory authority for searches incident to investigative detention (or for investigative detention, itself, for that matter). Accordingly, it is necessary to determine whether the common law authorizes such searches. The cases have focused on the "ancillary powers doctrine" from *R. v. Waterfield*,[125] in determining whether such searches are authorized by law.[126] The *Waterfield* test must be applied

---

121 *Mann*, above note 106.
122 *Ibid.*, at para. 19.
123 *Ibid.*
124 It is worthy of note that the above passage from *Mann* contemplates police stops for purposes of interview, which do not trigger *Charter* protections. This is an interesting contrast with the cases that have held that police questioning is a component of a "search" for section 8 purposes. See chapter 2, "What is a Search."
125 *R. v. Waterfield*, [1963] 3 All E.R. 659, [1964] 1 Q.B. 164 (C.C.A.) [*Waterfield*]. See chapter 4, "The Scope of Common Law Powers to Search: *R. v. Waterfield*."
126 See *Mann*, above note 106; *R. v. Simpson* (1993), 79 C.C.C. (3d) 482 (Ont. C.A.) [*Simpson*].

to the facts of the particular case, and is generally expressed as follows: 1) Did the police conduct fall within the general scope of any duty imposed by statute or recognized at common law? and 2) Did the conduct, albeit within the general scope of such a duty, involve an unjustifiable use of powers associated with the duty?[127]

In considering searches conducted as an incident to investigative detention, the courts have generally applied the *Waterfield* test in two stages: first, the court will consider whether the detention itself was justified under *Waterfield*; and second, the court will consider whether the search, as an incident of that detention, was justified under *Waterfield*.[128]

a) When Will an Investigative Detention Meet the *Waterfield* Test?

As noted in the preceding discussion, the first step to determining whether a search incidental to an investigative detention was reasonable involves assessing whether the underlying detention was a justifiable use of police powers.

In *R. v. Mann*,[129] the Supreme Court held, in reviewing the prior jurisprudence, that the police would be permitted to detain a person for investigative purposes if, on the totality of circumstances, 1) there are reasonable grounds to suspect that the person is connected to a particular crime, and 2) that the detention is objectively necessary.[130] As Iacobucci J. explained for the majority:

> [I]nvestigative detentions [must] be premised upon reasonable grounds. The detention must be viewed as reasonably necessary on an objective view of the totality of the circumstances, informing the officer's suspicion that there is a clear nexus between the individual to be detained and a recent or on-going criminal offence. Reasonable grounds figures at the front-end of such an assessment, underlying the officer's reasonable suspicion that the particular individual is implicated in the criminal activity under investigation. The overall reasonableness of the decision to detain, however, must further be assessed against all of the circumstances, most notably the extent to which the interference with individual liberty is necessary to perform the officer's duty, the liberty interfered with, and the nature and extent of that interference, in order to meet the second prong of the *Waterfield* test.[131]

---

127 *Waterfield*, above note 125; *Mann*, above note 106; *Simpson*, ibid.
128 See, e.g., the approach followed in *Mann*, above note 106 and *R. v. Hewlin* (2001), 190 N.S.R. (2d) 283 (C.A.) [*Hewlin*].
129 *Mann*, above note 106.
130 *Ibid.* at para. 34 and 45.
131 *Mann*, above note 106 at para. 34.

Prior to the Supreme Court's consideration of investigative detention in *Mann*, several cases, notably *R. v. Simpson*[132] from the Ontario Court of Appeal, described the evidentiary threshold required for a lawful investigative detention as "articulable cause" for the detention[133] (rather than "reasonable grounds to suspect," the term used by the Supreme Court in *Mann*). The Court in *Simpson* defined articulable cause as

> a constellation of objectively discernible facts which give the detaining officer reasonable cause to suspect that the detainee is criminally implicated in the activity under investigation. The requirement that the facts must meet an objectively discernible standard is recognized in connection with the arrest power (*R. v. Storrey* (1990), 53 C.C.C. (3d) 316 at p. 324), and serves to avoid indiscriminate and discriminatory exercises of the police power. A "hunch" based entirely on intuition gained by experience cannot suffice, no matter how accurate that "hunch" might prove to be.[134]

Although he expressed no concern with the substantive concept of articulable cause, Iacobucci J, for the majority of the Supreme Court in *Mann*, held that the term "reasonable grounds to detain" was preferable to "articulable cause" to detain, since it was it a term already used in analagous contexts.[135]

---

132 *Simpson*, above note 126.

133 The concept of "articulable cause" originated in the American jurisprudence, notably in the United States Supreme Court cases of *Terry v. Ohio*, above note 117, and *United States v. Cortez*, 449 U.S. 411 (1981). Although it has received "widespread approval in Canada," Twaddle J.A. of the Manitoba Court of Appeal questioned the necessity of "articulable cause" for an investigative detention and suggested that *Waterfield* could be applied "directly" without resort to a special formulation involving articulable cause. See *Mann* (C.A.), above note 106 at paras. 27–29.

134 *Simpson*, above note 126 at 501 [parallel citations omitted]; see also the following cases that have adopted a similar approach to the Ontario Court of Appeal on the resolution of whether an investigative detention is justifiable: *R. v. Chabot* (1993), 86 C.C.C. (3d) 309 (N.S.C.A.); *R. v. Pigeon* (1993), 59 Q.A.C. 103 (Que. C.A.); *R. v. Dupuis* (1994), 162 A.R. 197 (C.A.); *R. v. G.(C.M.)* (1996), 113 Man. R. (2d) 76, (C.A.); *R. v. Lake* (1997), 113 C.C.C. (3d) 208 (Sask. C.A.); *R. v. Burke* (1997), 118 C.C.C. (3d) 59 (Nfld. C.A.); *R. v. McAuley* (1998), 126 Man. R. (2d) 202 (C.A.) [*McAuley*]; and *Ferris*, above note 119; *R. v. Wilson*, [1990] 1 S.C.R. 1291 at 1297, per Cory J. In *R. v. Jacques*, [1996] 3 S.C.R. 312 at paras. 14 and 24, the Court held that the articulable cause standard was the functional equivalent of the "reasonable suspicion" or "reasonable cause to suspect."

135 *Mann*, above note 106, at para. 33. See also para. 30, where the Court acknowledged that the terms may be essentially synonymous, citing Major J.'s dissent in *Jacques*, *ibid.* at para. 52, where he recognized that "reasonable grounds to suspect" was equivalent to the articulable cause standard. In her dissent, Deschamps J. (Bastarache J. concurring) noted that the term "articulable cause" was both familiar and properly applied by the courts. Moreover, she argued that the use of "artic-

As noted above, the police must be investigating a specific "recent or on-going criminal offence" before they can lawfully detain people for the purpose of an investigation.[136] Prior to *Mann*, the Manitoba Court of Appeal held in *R. v. Willis*,[137] that the police have a duty to prevent crime and preserve the peace, and therefore may use investigative detention (with the accompanying incidental search power) proactively to prevent crime.[138] In light of the Supreme Court's decision in *Mann*, it is clear that the police may not use investigative detention as a proactive or preventive measure.

Despite the fact that investigative detention involves an interference with the rights of the individual, there is authority for the proposition that the availability of other, less intrusive, investigative techniques will not necessarily render an investigative detention unreasonable. In *R. v. Ferris*,[139] Ryan J.A. speaking for the majority of the British Columbia Court of Appeal said:

> We are dealing here with on-the-street observations by police officers who must act quickly. In this regard I prefer the views of the Supreme Court of the United States in *U.S. v. Sokolow*, 490 U.S. 1, 109 S. Ct. 1581, 104 L. Ed. 2d 1 (1989) at p. 12 (L. Ed.), which held that the reasonableness of the officer's decision to stop a person whom the officer suspects is committing or has just committed a crime does not turn on the availability of less intrusive investigatory techniques. Such a rule would unduly hamper the ability of the police to make swift, on-the-spot decisions.[140]

2) When Will a Search Incidental to an Investigative Detention be Justified?

Once it is determined that the detention itself was justified under the *Waterfield* criteria, the court can assess the appropriateness of conducting a search incident to that detention.[141]

---

   ulable cause" for investigative detention would help keep the criterion conceptually distinct from the reasonable grounds threshold required for an arrest. (*Mann* at paras. 34–35).
136 *Mann, ibid.* at para. 34.
137 *R. v. Willis* (2003), 174 C.C.C. (3d) 406 (Man. C.A.), application for leave to appeal pending, [2003] S.C.C.A. No. 281 [*Willis*].
138 *Ibid.* at para. 29. In *Brown v. Durham Regional Police Force* (1998), 43 O.R. (3d) 223 (C.A.), at part VII, Doherty J. for a unanimous Court concluded that the common law power of investigative detention could not be used as a proactive measure.
139 *Ferris*, above note 119.
140 *Ibid.* at para. 39. Justice Ryan was largely agreeing with Doherty J.A.'s formulation of investigative detention in *Simpson*, above note 125, but adding a "caution."
141 *Mann*, above note 106.

In *Mann*, the Supreme Court applied the *Waterfield* ancillary powers doctrine and held the police have the common law power to conduct a search incidental to an investigative detention *provided that the search is reasonably necessary in the circumstances*.[142] The Court explained that the power to search during an investigative detention is derived from the police duty to protect life and property, and the necessity of conducting the search would depend on

> the [police] duty being performed, the extent to which some inference with individual liberty is necessary in the performance of that duty, the importance of the performance of the duty to the public, the nature of the liberty being interfered with, and the nature and extent of the interference: *Dedman, supra*, at pp. 35–36.[143]

What kinds of situations will permit the police to conduct searches incidental to investigative detentions? The Court in *Mann* held that the police duty to protect life may justify the conduct of a "pat-down" search incidental to an investigative detention, provided that the officer believed on reasonable grounds that his or her own safety, or the safety of others is at risk. The Court was careful to explain that this power could only be exercised where the officer had a reasonable belief that safety was at risk, based on the totality of circumstances, and not on vague concerns or intuition, in order to be considered a reasonable search under section 8 of the *Charter*.[144]

Because of *Mann*'s focus on safety concerns, it is not yet possible to say definitively whether police officers may conduct investigative detention searches for reasons other than safety. In *Mann*, the police cited safety concerns as the reason for having conducted the search. While the Court did not specifically reject the idea that the police may have the power to conduct such searches for other reasons, the thrust of the majority opinion suggests that safety may be the only justifiable use of that power.[145]

Several appellate decisions prior to *Mann* support the view that searches incidental to investigative detentions are permissible only to address safety concerns. For example, in *R. v. Ferris*,[146] the British Columbia Court of Appeal reviewed the jurisprudence[147] and determined that police had the

---

142 *Ibid* at paras. 38–39.
143 *Ibid.* at para. 39.
144 *Ibid.* at para. 44.
145 See, for example, *ibid* at para. 45. See, *contra*, Deschamps J. (Bastarache J concurring) in dissent, *ibid.* at paras. 65–68.
146 *Ferris*, above note 119.
147 The Court considered a number of cases, including the decision of the United States Supreme Court in *Terry*, above note 118; the Supreme Court of Canada's

power to conduct searches for weapons, provided that the officers are "justified in believing" that the person possesses one:

> If the police have the duty to determine whether a person is engaged in crime or is about to be engaged in crime they should not be obliged to risk bodily harm to do so. It is my view that the police are entitled, if they are justified in believing that the person stopped is carrying a weapon, to search for weapons as an incident to detention. The question for the court must be whether the search was reasonably related in scope to the circumstances which justified the interference in the first place.[148]

The Court in *Ferris* found that the assessment of whether the officer was "justified in believing" that the person searched was carrying a weapon and that the search was necessary would depend on the circumstances of the particular case:

> The seriousness of the circumstances which led to the stop will govern the decision whether to search at all, and if so, the scope of the search that is undertaken. As Chief Justice Warren put it in *Terry* (at p. 905), the search must be "reasonably related in scope to the circumstances which justified the interference in the first place." Questioning an elderly shopper about a suspected shoplifting would not ordinarily require a search for weapons; questioning someone after a bank robbery might require a search of the detainee and his or her immediate surroundings. In other words, such a search can meet the reasonable necessity test depending on the circumstances.[149]

The ability to conduct a search for anything but the preservation of officer safety was specifically rejected by the British Columbia Court of Appeal in *R. v. Johnson*.[150] Further, in *R. v. Willis*,[151] the Manitoba Court of Appeal held that any expansion of the power to search a suspect for evidence incidental to an investigative detention would require careful study and a proper evidentiary record:

> Equating a search incidental to detention with one incidental to arrest does not adequately recognize the fact that detention may occur when there is only reasonable suspicion, while arrest requires reasonable and probable

---

judgment in *R. v. Mellenthin*, [1992] 3 S.C.R. 615, the Manitoba Court of Appeal decision in *McAuley*, above note 134. The Court's decision was, like *Mann*, based on the *Waterfield* test and the ancillary powers doctrine.
148 *Ferris*, above note 119 at paras. 53–54
149 *Ibid.* at para. 55; see also *Willis*, above note 137 at para. 31.
150 *R. v. Johnson* (2000), 32 C.R. (5th) 236, 2000 BCCA 204.
151 *Willis*, above note 137.

grounds. . . . Given its exceptional nature, a search incidental to an investigatory detention has generally been strictly circumscribed. We must be mindful of the expansion of police power as it affects individual freedom. Acceptance of the Crown's argument on this point would require an expansion of the law in this area that must include careful study of the possible ramifications, one that will not be attempted in this case. I am satisfied on the evidence that this search incidental to this detention was objectively necessary for the purposes of officer safety.[152]

Despite both this body of cases and the impression left by the majority opinion in *Mann*, there is some persuasive authority to suggest that investigative detention searches may be justifiable for reasons other than the protection of safety. For example, the dissenting opinion in *Mann*, which would allow searches for reasons other than safety, is worthy of note. Justice Deschamps (Bastarache J. concurring) endorsed the approach taken by the Quebec Court of Appeal in *R. v. Murray*:[153]

> A good example of a lawful search incidental to detention which was not motivated by safety concerns is provided by the decision of the Quebec Court of Appeal in *R. v. Murray* (1999), 136 C.C.C. (3d) 197. In that case, a robbery had been committed by three individuals. The police had set up a road block on a bridge which would have been a likely avenue of flight from the scene of the crime, and were stopping all vehicles which could hide three people. One of the individuals stopped and questioned was the respondent, who was driving a pickup truck. A taut piece of canvass blocked the view of the vehicle's cargo area. Thinking that the suspects in the robbery could be hiding beneath the canvass, a police officer removed it and discovered smuggled cigarettes. Fish J.A. (as he then was), applied the *Waterfield* test, and concluded that the search was a valid exercise of the common law power of search incidental to detention. He wrote (at p. 212):
>
>> A search incident to detention is a valid exercise of police powers at common law only if the detention is itself lawful. . .
>>
>> The search must be for a valid purpose that is rationally connected to the purposes of the initial detention. It must also be reasonably necessary: (1) to secure non-conscriptive evidence of a crime; (2) to protect the police or any member of the public from imminent danger; or (3) to discover and secure anything that

---

152 *Ibid.* at para. 42.
153 *R. v. Murray* (1999), 136 C.C.C. (3d) 197 (Que. C.A.) [*Murray*], written by Fish J.A., as he then was, for a unanimous court.

could endanger the police, the person detained or any member of the public, or facilitate escape.

I agree with these statements. In my view, any search incidental to detention would have to be both rationally connected to the purpose of the initial detention and reasonably necessary to ensure the security of police officers or the public, to preserve evidence or to prevent the escape of an offender. I do not rule out the possibility that other goals might be permissible, under appropriate circumstances.[154]

Justice Deschamps was careful to note that the power to search incidentally to investigative detention is less extensive than the power to search as an incident of an arrest.[155] She therefore highlighted two important restrictions on searches incident to investigative detentions. First, while justifiable for the *preservation* of evidence, the search could not be conducted for the purpose of *discovering* evidence.[156] Second, while searches incidental to arrest need only be "rationally connected" to the purpose for the arrest, in the context of investigative detention, the search must be "reasonably necessary" to the investigation.[157]

a) What Can Be Searched Incidentally to Detention?

The scope of a search incidental to an investigative detention will depend on the particular circumstances of the case.[158] As held by the Supreme Court in *Mann*, the police will generally be permitted to conduct a "protective pat-down" search, if it is justifiable for the police to be concerned about safety.[159] Although the Supreme Court did not delineate the parameters of a pat-down search in *Mann*, at the appellate-level the Manitoba Court of Appeal adopted the following description of a "frisk" search from *Cloutier v. Langlois*:[160]

> In this regard a "frisk" search is a relatively non-intrusive procedure: outside clothing is patted down to determine whether there is anything on the person of the arrested individual. Pockets may be examined but the clothing is not removed and no physical force is applied. The duration of the search is only a few seconds.[161]

---

154 *Mann*, above note 106 at para. 66–67.
155 *Ibid* at para. 68.
156 *Ibid*.
157 *Ibid*.
158 *Mann*, above note 106 at para. 39; See also Ryan J.A.'s comments in *Ferris*, above note 119 at para. 55, quoted above.
159 *Ibid.*; *McAuley*, above note 134.
160 *Cloutier*, above note 68.
161 *Mann* (C.A.), above note 106, at 185.

There is authority to suggest that the power to search incidentally to an investigative detention may also extend to searches of packages or other items held by the person being detained. In *R. v. Ferris*,[162] the British Columbia Court of Appeal sanctioned the police search of a "fanny-pack" carried by the passenger of a car suspected of being stolen, even though the fanny-pack was under police control and was being returned to the passenger following the completion of the investigation. As Ryan J.A. explained:

> [O]ne must examine the search from the point of view of the police officer at the time he made the search. . . . In these circumstances the police were entitled to briefly detain the respondent for investigation and to safeguard themselves while they did so. In my view this would include a search of the waist pack worn by the respondent. The respondent argued that the pack could have been removed and kept in a safe place while the investigation continued. I do not believe that this was required. The police were conducting a spontaneous as opposed to a planned investigation. Given those circumstances it would be unreasonable to require them to determine with precision the least intrusive manner of securing their safety in the initial stages of their investigation. *As well, at some point soon the detention would come to an end and the pack would be returned. The officers were entitled to ensure that when this was done they would not be placing themselves in danger by handing the respondent a concealed weapon.* [emphasis added][163]

In *Long v. Michigan*,[164] the United States Supreme Court upheld the lawfulness of the search of a vehicle and its trunk incidental to an investigative detention, once again, on the basis of officer safety. The Court employed reasoning similar to that of Ryan J.A. in *Ferris*:

> at might have been located in the automobile. This reasoning is mistaken in several respects. During any investigative detention, the suspect is "in the control" of the officers in the sense that he "may be briefly detained against his will. . . ." Just as a *Terry* suspect on the street may, despite being under the brief control of a police officer, reach into his clothing and retrieve a weapon, so might a *Terry* suspect in Long's position break away from police control and retrieve a weapon from his automobile. In addition, if the suspect is not placed under arrest, he will be permitted to reenter his automobile, and he will then have access to any weapons inside. Or, as here, the suspect may be permitted to reenter the vehicle before the *Terry* investigation is over, and again, may have access to weapons. In any

---

162 *Ferris*, above note 119.
163 *Ibid.* at para. 58.
164 *Long v. Michigan*, 463 U.S. 1032, 103 S. Ct. 3469, 77 L. Ed. 2d 1201 (1983).

event, we stress that a *Terry* investigation, such as the one that occurred here, involves a police investigation "at close range," when the officer remains particularly vulnerable in part because a full custodial arrest has not been effected, and the officer must make a "quick decision as to how to protect himself and others from possible danger." In such circumstances, we have not required that officers adopt alternative means to ensure their safety in order to avoid the intrusion involved in a *Terry* encounter. [citations omitted][165]

See also *R. v. Hewlin*,[166] where the Nova Scotia Court of approved of the search of a vehicle. The search was incidental to an investigative detention, and the Court accepted that the search was validly conducted in pursuit of officer safety.

Before leaving the topic of searches incident to investigative detention, it is important to note that the doctrine is not without controversy. The logical train justifying such searches requires a marked departure from the standards set in *Hunter v. Southam*. While the search incidental to investigative detention may be limited to a safety frisk, the search can quickly escalate into a more intrusive search. The objective of officer safety is no doubt of major importance, but it is not without costs; this valid concern for the safety of law enforcement officers has lead to a significant erosion of privacy. Placing so much weight on this issue forces the courts to defer to field judgments about exactly what is necessary to ensure safety. James Stribopolous, commenting on the appellate level decision in *R. v. Mann*, writes:

> Under this deferential approach, a police officer's plausible safety concerns are a sufficient basis for justifying a more probing search than a "pat-down." As a practical matter, given that "anything hard in the accused's pocket could be a weapon, and anything soft could be covering something hard,"[167] the decision, if it ultimately stands, would serve to make intrusive personal searches a routine part of most investigative stops. [footnote in original][168]

While the appellate level decision in *Mann* did not stand, the power to search as an incident of investigative detention remains. Any police interaction with a suspect involves some element of risk, which must be evaluated by the officer on a case-by-case basis. Only a very small percentage of incidents will ultimately be reviewed by a court. An important and frequently exercised police

---

165 *Ibid.* at 1221–22.
166 *Hewlin*, above note 125.
167 S. Coughlan, "R. v. Mann: Annotation" (2003) 5 C.R. (6th) 306 at 307.
168 J. Stribopolous, "A Failed Experiment? Investigative Detention: Ten Years Later" (2003) 41 Alta. L. Rev. 335 at 367.

power is therefore largely unsupervised and without detailed guidelines. For this reason among others, Stribopolous argues that the common law power of investigative detention ought to be replaced with a statutory framework, or at least ought to be considerably restricted by the courts. Indeed, the Supreme Court in *Mann* recognized the complexity of the issue of investigative detention, and appeared to suggest that legislative guidance would be welcome.[169]

D. THE "PLAIN VIEW" DOCTRINE

The common law allows for the warrantless seizure of evidence under the doctrine of "plain view." Very generally, the "plain view" doctrine permits the seizure[170] of evidence that an officer finds while conducting an activity that is otherwise authorized by law:

> "Plain view" occurs when evidence falls into the view of an officer who has a right to be in the position he is in to have the view he has had; such items have been held to be subject to seizure.[171]

Unfortunately, the Canadian jurisprudence has been somewhat inconsistent in articulating the exact preconditions for relying on the "plain view" doctrine to justify seizures, and the limitations on that power.[172] Quite often, including in the Supreme Court's recent decision in *R. v. Law*,[173] Canadian courts have recited the following criteria[174] as constituting the preconditions to relying on the doctrine:

i) the police must have gained entry or be in the premises lawfully;
ii) the nature of the evidence must be "immediately apparent" as constituting a criminal offence; and
iii) the evidence must have been discovered inadvertently.[175]

Each of these criteria will be discussed more fully in the sections that follow.

---

169 *Mann*, above note 106 at paras. 15–17.
170 Although sometimes termed *plain view searches* (e.g., see *Law*, above note 39 at para. 27), the plain view doctrine actually permits *seizures* as opposed to searches, although the seized goods may themselves be subject to examination (or searches) by the officers. See *R. v. Spindloe* (2001), 154 C.C.C. (3d) 8 at 29 (Sask. C.A.) at para. 37 [*Spindloe*]; *R. v. Smith* (1998), 126 C.C.C. (3d) 62 (Alta. C.A.) [*Smith*] at paras. 14–22.
171 J.A. Fontana, *The Law of Search and Seizure in Canada*, 3d ed. (Toronto: Butterworths, 2002), 602. See, e.g., *Spindloe*, ibid. and *R. v. Fawthrop* (2002), 166 C.C.C. (3d) 97 (O.C.A.) [*Fawthrop*].
172 *Fawthrop*, ibid. at para 22.
173 *Law*, above note 39.
174 Based on American jurisprudence, such as articulated in *Texas v. Brown*, 75 L. Ed. 2d 502 (1983).
175 *R. v. Belliveau and Losier* (1986), 54 C.R. (3d) 144 (N.B.C.A.).

It is important to note, however, that although courts often repeat these three preconditions as the thresholds for reliance on the plain view doctrine, other cases have expressed doubts about both the requirement that the incriminating nature of the evidence be "immediately apparent" and the "inadvertence requirement." For the reasons discussed below, we believe that the ruling in R. v. Law can and should be read in a manner consistent with the cases moving away from strict interpretations of the latter two requirements.

1) Lawfully on the Premises

There is no debate that the police must have the lawful authority to enter the premises where they find the evidence for the "plain view" doctrine to apply. In R. v. Askov,[176] Borins D.C.J (as he then was) found this criterion to be of primary importance:

> What is central to the application of the "plain view" doctrine is that the police officer had a prior justification for the intrusion into the place where the "plain view" seizure occurred.

As the Supreme Court explained in R. v. Buhay,[177] being lawfully on the premises (or lawfully permitted to engage in the underlying activity) is the first step to putting an officer in a lawful position to see the evidence that is ultimately seized:

> The Crown also contends that the seizure was justified under the "plain view" doctrine, because the actions of the security guards put the contraband in plain view of the police. This argument must fail. It is not sufficient to argue that the evidence was in plain view at the time of the seizure. Indeed, it will nearly always be the case that police see the object when they seize it (see *Coolidge v. New Hampshire*, 403 U.S. 443 (1971); *R. v. Spindloe* (2001), 154 C.C.C. (3d) 8 (Sask. C.A.), at para. 36). It stretches the meaning of "plain view" to argue that an item placed in a duffel bag inside a locked locker is somehow in plain view of the police. The "plain view" doctrine requires, perhaps as a central feature, that the police officers have a prior justification for the intrusion into the place where the "plain view" seizure occurred. [citations omitted][178]

A valid search warrant for a location will always provide the police with the lawful authority to be on the premises mentioned within the warrant. If

---

176 *R. v. Askov* (1987), 60 C.R. (3d) 261 (Ont. Dist. Ct.) [*Askov*].
177 *Buhay*, above note 67.
178 *Ibid.* at para 37.

the whole of the warrant is invalid, then the police cannot be said to be lawfully on the premises. However, a court may, in certain circumstances, find that a warrant is not *completely* invalid; a court may find a search warrant to be partially valid and partially invalid. In such circumstances, police may be considered "lawfully on the premises" provided that they are engaged in executing the *valid* portion of the warrant *when the evidence is discovered*.[179] If, however, the police are executing the unlawful portion of the warrant when they discover the impugned evidence, the plain view doctrine will not authorize the seizure.[180]

Police will also be lawfully on the premises if they can legitimately rely on an implied licence to be on a premises; for example, when they attend at a place of business that is open to the public.

> A business establishment that is open to the public with an implied invitation to all members of the public to enter has no reasonable expectation of privacy from having a police officer enter *the area of the premises to which the public is impliedly invited*. [emphasis added][181]

However, the entry by police into "private" areas of the business to which the public is not invited, for example, private offices or filing cabinets,[175] will not, in the absence of specific prior authorization, meet the "lawfully on the premises" requirement.

Note that this approach diverges somewhat from the Supreme Court's treatment of the issue of implied licences in *R. v. Evans*.[182] That case involved the scope of the "implied licence" that residents extend to the general public to approach the front door of their home and knock for the purpose of communicating with the occupants of the home. The Court noted that this implied licence was limited in its purpose, and did not extend to permitting the police to gather evidence against the occupants.[183] Presumably, if given the choice, the business proprietor would similarly limit the implied licence to enter the premises to those wishing to engage in commerce, and would prefer to exclude police attempting to gather incriminating evidence. However, the very public nature of a business establishment may sufficiently distinguish it from a dwelling house to justify the extension of an implied licence for a range of purposes, including those antagonistic to the proprietor.

---

179 *Fawthrop*, above note 171 para 32.
180 *Ibid*.
181 *R. v. Fitt* (1995), 96 C.C.C. (3d) 341 (N.S.C.A.) at para. 12, aff'd 103 C.C.C. (3d) 224 (S.C.C.) [*Fitt*].
182 *R. v. Rao* (1984), 12 C.C.C. (3d) 97.
183 *Evans*, above note 38.

2) Immediately Apparent

Courts often restate the requirement that it must be "immediately apparent" to the police that the items they observe may be evidence of a crime, contraband, or otherwise subject to seizure.

For example, in *R. v. Law*,[184] the Supreme Court relied on this factor in determining that the seizure was not authorized under the plain view doctrine. In *Law*, a safe containing business records had been stolen from a Chinese restaurant; the safe and the business records (written in Chinese) were found in a field. An officer, Corporal Desroches, who was unconnected with investigation of the theft of the safe, had previously suspected that the restaurateurs were evading taxes. Based on his unsubstantiated "gut feeling," Desroches took advantage of the fact that the restaurant's records were in police custody, and asked permission of the officers investigating the theft to see the contents of the safe. Desroches photocopied the business records and provided them to a Revenue Canada official.

Justice Bastarache for a unanimous Supreme Court held that the seizure of the incriminating evidence in the records was not justified by the plain view doctrine:

> [T]he incriminating evidence was neither *immediately obvious to Corporal Desroches nor discovered inadvertently*. On the contrary, it came to light only after he examined, translated and photocopied several documents. Corporal Desroches admitted there was nothing facially wrong with the documents. He testified they contained a series of numbers and Chinese characters, and that he lacked both accounting expertise and proficiency in Chinese. Not having detected anything incriminating through the unaided use of his senses, Corporal Desroches cannot rely on the plain view doctrine either to establish reasonable and probable grounds to search, or to avoid the requirement of reasonable and probable grounds entirely. [citations omitted; emphasis added][185]

Prior to the Supreme Court's ruling in *Law*, the Saskatchewan Court of Appeal took a fresh look at the Canadian plain view jurisprudence in *R. v. Spindloe*.[186] In her comprehensive survey of the doctrine, Jackson J.A. noted

---

184 *Law*, above note 39.
185 *Ibid.* at para. 27.
186 *Spindloe*, above note 170. In *R. v. Fawthrop*, Borins J.A. of the Ontario Court of Appeal (Catzman J.A. concurring) described Jackson J.A.'s reasons in *R. v. Spindloe* as "thoughtful and careful" (*Fawthrop*, above note 171 at para. 28).

that the "immediately apparent" rule had not been "rigidly applied" in the jurisprudence.[187] Indeed, Jackson J.A. noted that even in *Texas v. Brown*, the American case from which the plain view criteria were developed, there was resistance to the phrase *immediately apparent*, as it did not adequately describe the rule:

> Indeed Rehnquist J., again speaking in *Texas v. Brown*, criticizes the choice of the words *"immediately apparent"* since they can be taken to imply that an "unduly high degree of certainty as to the incriminatory character of evidence is necessary for an application of the plain view doctrine" (see p. 513). In so far as the Court in *Texas v. Brown* upheld this requirement, the substance admitted into evidence in that case was contained in a balloon, was not visible until the balloon was opened and was not known conclusively to be heroin until examined by an expert. *Words like "reasonable grounds to believe that the discovered item constitutes evidence of a crime" better express the need to provide direction to the police with respect to the application of the doctrine.* [emphasis added][188]

The Saskatchewan Court of Appeal's reformulation of the "immediately apparent" criterion to "reasonable grounds to believe that the discovered item constitutes evidence of a crime" is compelling. The "incriminating nature" of a baggie of white powder must be ascertained by an expert before it can be relied on in court; so too with a viscous red substance on a knife. Accordingly, if the plain view doctrine is to have any practical use, it ought to authorize the seizure of a baggie of drugs or a bloody knife on reasonable grounds — the same threshold required to justify an arrest — rather than a vague and elevated standard such as "immediately apparent as evidence of crime."

Such a reformulation is not necessarily inconsistent with the Supreme Court's decision in *R. v. Law*,[189] despite the fact that the Court restated and applied the immediately apparent requirement. The Supreme Court's statement went further than necessary to reach the result, since impugned seizure did not meet either standard: not only was the incriminating nature of the evidence not immediately apparent, the information did not rise to the level of reasonable grounds. Even after Corporal Desroches had the documents from the safe in his hands, he did not have reasonable grounds to believe that the documents contained incriminating evidence. If at that point Desroches *had* such grounds, the reformulated test would have been

---

187 *Spindloe*, above note 170 at para. 39.
188 *Ibid.* at para. 40.
189 *Law*, above note 39.

satisfied,[190] justifying the seizure. Consistent with this view, the Supreme Court noted that where "evidence of illegal activity appears on the face of a document" (*not* the case in *R. v. Law*), the "plain view" doctrine might authorize examining, photocopying, or translating the document.[191]

3) Inadvertent Discovery

Certain cases have also cast doubt on the necessity of the "inadvertence" requirement to relying on the "plain view" doctrine.[192] In *R. v. Neilson*,[193] Bayda C.J.S. agreed with the Ontario cases stating that the "lawfully on the premises" requirement was the central to the plain view doctrine. In *R. v. Spindloe*,[194] Jackson J.A. developed this idea further and downplayed the importance of the inadvertence requirement, noting:

> [T]he foundation for a lawful seizure on the basis of the "plain view" doctrine is lawful presence in the premises where the property is found in "plain view." As a requirement for the plain view doctrine, *the inadvertence requirement becomes less important when the police have a right of access to the premises in the first place.* [citation omitted; emphasis added][195]

Indeed, the Court in *Spindloe* found that the "plain view" doctrine operated to justify a seizure even where the discovery of the items was not inadvertent. In *Spindloe*, the police executed a warrant to search the accused's record shop for "instruments of illicit drug use" being offered for sale, contrary to section 462.2 of the *Criminal Code*, and seized a variety of items displayed openly for sale or as samples, in addition to items that were in closed drawers or behind the sales counter out of sight. Although the search warrant was later ruled to be defective in its entirety, the Court held that the plain view doctrine operated to justify the seizures of the items that were on display in the part of the store open to the public. The Court found that

---

190 This assumes for the purposes of argument that it was lawful for Desroches to obtain the documents in the first place. The Supreme Court expressed disapproval of Desroches' actions in acquiring the items (see *Law*, above note 39 at para 23). This is in some sense analogous to the "lawfully on the premises" requirement.
191 *Ibid.* at para 26.
192 See, e.g., *Fitt*, above note 181, where police seized slot machines from premises open to the public. The police "did not stumble on them, as they knew the machines were there prior to attending at the premises" (at 346).
193 *R. v. Neilson* (1988), 43 C.C.C. (3d) 548 (Sask. C.A.).
194 *Spindloe*, above note 170.
195 *Ibid.*, quoting with approval from Borins D.C.J. (as he then was) in *Askov*, above note 175.

because businesspeople extend a licence to the public to be present in public areas of the store, there could be no expectation of privacy violated when the police observed evidence of a crime while in those public areas.[196] The Court found that the doctrine applied even to items locked in a glass case:

> As to the items found behind glass, those too must be considered to be in plain view. Just as in *Texas v. Brown* there was no legitimate expectation of privacy shielding the interior of an automobile from scrutiny by a member of the public, including the police, similarly, *there is no legitimate expectation of privacy shielding the interior of a display counter in the store. The reason why the glass is there is to permit the public to see into the interior of the counter.* The fact that a clerk's assistance is required to get at the items does not remove them from the category of plain view. [emphasis added][197]

Of course, this ruling did not apply to the items that were boxed, in closed drawers, or in non-public areas of the store.

4) "Plain View" and the *Criminal Code*

Section 489 of the *Criminal Code* authorizes warrantless seizures in circumstances similar to those authorized by the plain view doctrine.[198] The section authorizes officers who are executing a warrant to seize items beyond those listed in the warrant,[199] and permits seizure of evidence provided that the officer "is lawfully present in a place pursuant to a warrant or otherwise in the execution of duties."[200] Items that may be seized are those "used in," "obtained by," or that "will afford evidence" of a federal offence.

There have been few cases on the interpretation of section 489. Despite the similarities between section 489 and the common law "plain view" doctrine, there is little support for the view that the two are co-extensive.[201] In *R. v. Fawthrop*,[202] Borins J.A. expressed the opinion that section 489 was not

---

196 See the discussion "Lawfully on the Premises" earlier in the chapter.
197 *Spindloe*, above note 170 at para. 47.
198 For a similar statutory plain view authorization for drug offences, see the *Controlled Drugs and Substances Act*, ss. 11(6) and (8).
199 *Criminal Code* s. 489(1).
200 *Ibid.* s. 489(2).
201 However, see *R. v. Grenier* (1991), 65 C.C.C. (3d) 76 (Que. C.A.), which suggests that s. 489 is a codification of the common law doctrine of "plain view" (see *Grenier* p. 84). Note that the issue in *Grenier* was not decided on the basis of s. 489, because the Court found that it had no application in that case, but found that the common law test was met. This actually supports the contrary view that s. 489 is *not* a codification of the "plain view" doctrine.
202 *Fawthrop*, above note 171.

necessarily tied to the "plain view" doctrine, although resolution of the issue was not necessary in that appeal:

> Although I have serious doubt that the trial judge was correct in stating that s. 489 is a codification of the common law plain view doctrine, and although the authorities may not be clear in describing the requirements of the plain view doctrine, in the view that I hold of this appeal I find it unnecessary to resolve these questions. This is because the evidence before the trial judge was insufficient to render lawful the seizure of the pedophile collection either under s. 489 of the *Criminal Code* or the plain view doctrine.[203]

In *Fawthrop*, a case involving the execution of a warrant, Borins J.A. held that section 489 authorized the seizure of items provided that: (1) the officers located the items while lawfully present executing a search warrant;[204] and (2) that reasonable grounds to believe that the things seized met the preconditions listed in either sections 489(1) or (2). The officers in *Fawthrop* had no reasonable grounds to believe that the items had been obtained by, used in, or would afford evidence of, a criminal offence, and accordingly could not rely on section 489. Justice Borins recognized and considered plain view as an authorization for seizure separate from the powers granted in section 489.[205] On the facts of *Fawthrop*, neither the plain view doctrine nor section 489 operated to justify the seizure of the items.

5) No Exception for "Plain Smell"

Chapter 5 discussed how smells, often the smell of marijuana, have contributed to reasonable grounds in support of a warrant or arrest.[206] In such cases, counsel and courts have occasionally referred to a "plain smell" doctrine, and drawn parallels to plain view seizures. Such parallels must be approached with care.[207] When the plain view doctrine is properly understood, it is clear that that cases of a lawful "plain smell seizure" will be rare,

---

203 *Ibid.* at para. 22.
204 Clearly, not all s. 489 seizures will require that the officers have a warrant; the section also permits seizures if an officer is at a place *while in the execution of duties*.
205 See also *R. v. Middleton* (2000), 150 C.C.C. (3d) 556 (B.C.C.A.). The B.C. Court of Appeal did not bind the applicability of s. 489 to the common law doctrine of plain view, but rather simply referred to the requirement for the officers to have been originally acting under the jurisdiction of a valid warrant (i.e., lawfully on the premises).
206 See chapter 5, "Smell as a Component of Reasonable Grounds."
207 *Smith*, above note 170 at para. 24.

if they occur at all. The doctrine of plain view permits warrantless seizures, and not searches,[208] and only items visible by an officer lawfully situated at his or her vantage-point are subject to seizure. The underlying concept of the plain view doctrine is that items of an apparently incriminating nature may be seized, provided that the officer does not unlawfully intrude into a protected zone of privacy in doing so. Therefore, while smell will sometimes support the belief that a visible item, such a marijuana joint, is contraband, smell alone cannot justify an intrusion into a zone of privacy to render a hidden item visible or to effect a seizure.[209]

The cases dealing with "plain smell" are best understood as situations where the smell of marijuana was sufficiently distinct to support a reasonable belief that the suspect was in current possession of marijuana,[210] leading to the arrest of the suspect, which, in turn, authorized the search of the suspect and his or her immediate surroundings as an incident of that arrest. If the smell leads an officer to form the reasonable belief that an illegal substance is present, but is insufficient to support an arrest,[211] then the officer must obtain a warrant before conducting a search.

---

208 See the foregoing discussion of the plain view doctrine.
209 A situation in which an officer sees a suspect smoking, detects a smell of marijuana, and seizes the joint on the basis of the smell might properly be characterized as a "plain smell seizure." Note, however, that the joint was also in plain view, and except for the seizure itself, no search has occurred.
210 See chapter 5, "Smell as a Component of Reasonable Grounds," for further discussion.
211 For example, this might occur if an officer smelled fresh marijuana emanating from an unattended vehicle. The officer would not necessarily know *whom* to arrest and might wish to continue investigating without waiting for a driver to return.

CHAPTER 9

☙

Remedies for Unreasonable Search and Seizure

This chapter will address the most common remedies for breaches of the right against unreasonable search and seizure. The chapter begins with a discussion of *Charter* remedies, in particular the exclusion of evidence from trial proceedings under section 24(2) of the *Charter*, and finishes with a discussion of the availability of the non-*Charter* prerogative remedies, such as *certiorari*, to quash an investigative order.

A. SECTION 24 *CHARTER* REMEDIES

Section 24 of the *Charter* grants the court the power to provide remedies, or "*Charter* relief," for violations of its protections. Accordingly, it is this section that gives the *Charter* its teeth and gives life to the protections afforded by the *Charter*'s guarantees. The section reads as follows:

> 24(1) Anyone whose rights or freedoms, as guaranteed by this *Charter*, have been infringed or denied may apply to a court of competent jurisdiction to obtain such remedy as the court considers appropriate and just in the circumstances.
>
> (2) Where, in proceedings under subsection (1), a court concludes that evidence was obtained in a manner that infringed or denied any rights or freedoms guaranteed by this *Charter*, the evidence shall be excluded if it is established that, having regard to all the circumstances, the admission of it in the proceedings would bring the administration of justice into disrepute.

1) Starting the Process: Giving Notice of Motion

Charter relief under section 24 is typically obtained from the court by way of a pretrial motion.[1] Evidence in support of the motion is received outside the presence of the jury (or outside the trial proper), during a *voir dire*.[2]

The accused generally commences the process by objecting to the admissibility of the evidence in question, optimally before the Crown proffers the evidence.[3] Prior objection is preferable, especially in the case of a jury trial; if the accused waited to object until the jury heard the evidence, mistrials could result. This objection can be made by filing an application in writing that specifies which *Charter* right has allegedly been breached.[4] If the accused is challenging an authorization to intercept private communication, the jurisprudence requires specific notice; in *R. v. Parmar*,[5] Watt J. held that an application to set aside an authorization ought to be commenced by filing, on reasonable notice to the prosecutor and other accused persons, a notice of application that contains, *inter alia*, the following information:

(i) the date and place of hearing;
(ii) the nature of order requested;
(iii) the specific ground upon which the application is founded; and
(iv) the documentary and other evidence to be relied upon by the applicant.

The notice of application should not only identify the orders to be impeached but equally should record, in precise terms, the nature of relief requested, including any ancillary orders such as production of the deponent for the purposes of cross-examination upon his supportive affidavit on the return of the application. The grounds upon which the application is founded should be articulated in the notice of application with specificity. Conclusory statements such as:

(i) the affidavit of the affiant fails to fully, frankly and fairly disclose the basis for the application for the Part IV.1 authorization to intercept private communications, or

---

1   *R. v. Mills*, [1986] 1 S.C.R. 863, 26 C.C.C. (3d) 481 (S.C.C.) [*Mills*] at 494–95; *R. v. Clauson* (1986), 31 C.C.C. (3d) 286 (Alta. C.A.) [*Clauson*] at 287.
2   *Clauson*, ibid. at 288.
3   *R. v. Kutynec* (1992), 70 C.C.C. (3d) 289 (Ont. C.A.) [*Kutynec*] at 296.
4   *Clauson*, above note 1 at 288. The rules of criminal procedure of the particular court or the common law jurisprudence of the province may require notice in writing or may set out a specific notice period, or notice may simply be given orally: *Kutynec*, ibid.
5   *R. v. Parmar* (1987), 37 C.C.C. (3d) 301 (Ont. Gen. Div.).

(ii) the authorization is constitutionally deficient, as being violative of the applicant's rights to be secure against unreasonable search and seizure as guaranteed by the *Charter*

are not only unhelpful but, in my view, wholly inadequate to the task.[6]

If the accused does not give timely notice of an intention to contest the admissibility of evidence obtained pursuant to a search or seizure, then the trial judge (having taken into account all relevant circumstances) may refuse to entertain the application.[7] The Ontario Court of Appeal in *R. v. Loveman*[8] held that the following factors are relevant in deciding whether to refuse to hear an application for *Charter* relief because of untimely notice:

> In deciding how to proceed when faced with the Crown's objection, the trial judge had to balance various interests. He had to bear in mind an accused's right to raise constitutional objections to the admissibility of evidence and the Crown's right to have an adequate opportunity to meet *Charter* arguments made on behalf of an accused. In addition, the trial judge had to be concerned with the effective use of court resources and the expeditious determination of criminal matters. This latter factor was of particular concern in this case because there had already been some considerable delay (attributable to the [accused]) in bringing the matter to trial.
>
> In balancing those interests in this case, the trial judge should have considered the absence of any statutory rule or practice direction requiring notice, the notice that was given to the Crown, the point during the trial proceedings when the [accused's] counsel first indicated he intended to seek exclusion under s. 24(2) of the *Charter*, and the extent to which the Crown was prejudiced by the absence of any specific reference to a *Charter*-based argument in the notice given to the Crown. The trial judge also should have considered the specific nature of the *Charter* argument which counsel proposed to advance and the impact the application could have on the course of the trial.[9]

The judge has the discretion to require the accused to state the basis upon which the evidence is being challenged in advance of the *voir dire*, so that the judge can determine whether there is a sufficient evidentiary foundation to suggest that evidence could be excluded following a full hearing.[10] If such a basis is not revealed, the judge may decline to hear the application.

---

6   *Ibid.* at 342–43.
7   *Kutynec*, above note 3 at 296.
8   *R. v. Loveman* (1992), 71 C.C.C. (3d) 123 (Ont. C.A.).
9   *Ibid.* at 126–27.
10 *Kutynec*, above note 3 at 298–99 and 300–1.

B. COURT OF COMPETENT JURISDICTION

Who is considered to be a "court of competent jurisdiction" under section 24 of the *Charter* to provide relief for infringements? In *R. v. Mills*,[11] Lamer J. held that to be a "court of competent jurisdiction" the court must have:

(1) jurisdiction over the person;
(2) jurisdiction over the subject matter; and
(3) jurisdiction to grant the remedy.[12]

Having jurisdiction to grant the remedy sought involves an examination of whether the court possesses the remedial authority necessary to engage in the awarding of *Charter* remedies. As McLachlin J. explained in *Weber v. Ontario Hydro*:[13]

> It is thus Parliament or the legislature that determines if a court is a court of competent jurisdiction; as McIntyre J. puts it [in *Mills*], the jurisdiction of the various courts of Canada is fixed by Parliament and the legislatures, not by judges. Nor is there magic in labels; it is not the name of the tribunal that determines the matter, but its powers. (It may be noted that the French version of s. 24(1) uses "tribunal" rather than "cour.") The practical import of fitting *Charter* remedies into the existing system of tribunals, as McIntyre J. notes, is that litigants have "direct" access to *Charter* remedies in the tribunal charged with deciding their case.
>
> It follows from *Mills* that statutory tribunals created by Parliament or the legislatures may be courts of competent jurisdiction to grant *Charter* remedies, provided they have jurisdiction over the parties and the subject-matter of the dispute and are empowered to make the orders sought.[14]

In assessing the third *Mills* factor, whether the court has jurisdiction to grant *Charter* remedies, a court must apply a "structural and functional" approach.[15] Discerning the intent of the legislature in providing a court with

---

11 *Mills*, above note 1.
12 *Ibid.* at 515; *R. v. Hynes* (2001), 159 C.C.C. (3d) 359 (S.C.C.) [*Hynes*] at 373; *Mooring v. National Parole Board*, [1996] 1 S.C.R. 75 [*Mooring*] at 108; *Cuddy Chicks Ltd. v. Ontario (Labour Relations Board)* (1991), 81 D.L.R. (4th) 121, [1991] 2 S.C.R. 5, 50 Admin. L.R. 44; and *Tétreault-Gadoury v. Canada (Employment and Immigration Commission)* (1991), 81 D.L.R. (4th) 358, [1991] 2 S.C.R. 22, 50 Admin. L.R. 1; *Weber v. Ontario Hydro* (1995), 125 D.L.R. (4th) 583 (S.C.C.) at 606, [1995] 2 S.C.R. 929, 30 Admin. L.R. (2d) 1 [*Weber*].
13 *Weber*, above note 12.
14 *Ibid.* at paras. 65–66 (as excerpted by Sopinka J. in *Mooring*, above note 12 at 108).
15 *Mooring*, above note 12 at para. 24; *R. v. 974649 Ontario Inc.*, 2001 SCC 81 [*974649*]; *Hynes*, above note 12 at paras. 23–25.

its jurisdiction is key to determining its power to grant *Charter* remedies. As McLachlin J. explained in *Hynes*:[16]

> The question in all cases is whether Parliament or the legislature intended to empower the court or tribunal to make rulings on *Charter* violations that arise incidentally to their proceedings, and to grant the remedy sought as a remedy for such violations.[17]

As a result, unless the court or tribunal's governing legislation expressly refers to the ability to grant *Charter* remedies, the assessment of the court's jurisdiction must be made with reference to "the function performed by the court or tribunal and the structure, powers and processes conferred on it by Parliament or the legislature."[18] The court or tribunal must be equipped with processes and procedures that will allow it to fairly resolve *Charter* issues; simply put, the court or tribunal must be "suited to grant the remedy sought under s. 24 in light of its function and structure."[19]

Determining whether a court or tribunal is suitable to award *Charter* remedies under a structural and functional approach will include considerations of:

- whether the court performs "trial-like" (or judicial or quasi-judicial) functions or something more specialized;
- whether traditional rules and proof of evidence apply;
- whether the court has any other remedial authority;
- whether the court is a suitable forum to address the full implications of assessing a *Charter* breach, including the extent of evidence it is able to assess and receive; and
- whether the court has expertise in fashioning remedial awards.[20]

The preceding rules apply to situations where a court or tribunal is asked to provide remedies under section 24 of the *Charter*, such as the exclusion of evidence, the awarding of costs, or the granting of a stay of proceedings. If, however, the remedy sought is a declaration that a law itself is unconstitutional, there is a slightly different approach to the determination of the court's competence. In *Nova Scotia (Worker's Compensation Board) v. Martin*,[21] the Supreme Court of Canada held that if a tribunal has the jurisdiction to decide questions of law under the impugned provision, then it

---

16 *Hynes*, above note 12 at para. 27.
17 *Ibid.* at para. 26.
18 *Ibid.* at para. 27.
19 *Ibid.*
20 *Hynes*, above note 12; *Mooring*, above note 12; *Mills*, above note 1.
21 *Nova Scotia (Worker's Compensation Board) v. Martin*, 2003 SCC 54.

will, unless there was evidence demonstrating the contrary,[22] have the jurisdiction to determine constitutional validity of those provisions. As stated by Justice Gonthier:

> The current, restated approach to the jurisdiction of administrative tribunals to subject legislative provisions to *Charter* scrutiny can be summarized as follows:
>
> (1) The first question is whether the administrative tribunal has jurisdiction, explicit *or* implied, to decide questions of law arising under the challenged provision.
>
> (2) (a) Explicit jurisdiction must be found in the terms of the statutory grant of authority. (b) Implied jurisdiction must be discerned by looking at the statute as a whole. Relevant factors will include the statutory mandate of the tribunal in issue and whether deciding questions of law is necessary to fulfilling this mandate effectively; the interaction of the tribunal in question with other elements of the administrative system; whether the tribunal is adjudicative in nature; and practical considerations, including the tribunal's capacity to consider questions of law. Practical considerations, however, cannot override a clear implication from the statute itself.
>
> (3) If the tribunal is found to have jurisdiction to decide questions of law arising under a legislative provision, this power will be presumed to include jurisdiction to determine the constitutional validity of that provision under the *Charter*.
>
> (4) The party alleging that the tribunal lacks jurisdiction to apply the *Charter* may rebut the presumption by (a) pointing to an explicit withdrawal of authority to consider the *Charter*; or (b) convincing the court that an examination of the statutory scheme clearly leads to the conclusion that the legislature intended to exclude the *Charter* (or a category of questions that would include the *Charter*, such as constitutional questions generally) from the scope of the questions of law to be addressed by the tribunal. Such an implication should generally arise from the statute itself, rather than from external considerations.[23]

The trial court is always a court of competent jurisdiction to provide constitutional remedies.[24] The trial court has the jurisdiction to make final dispositions regarding the accused, and will always have the best evidentiary

---

22 *Ibid.* at para. 42.
23 *Ibid.* at para. 48.
24 *Hynes*, above note 12; *Mills*, above note 1; *R. v. Rahey* (1987), 33 C.C.C. (3d) 289 (S.C.C.) [*Rahey*].

record upon which to make findings on constitutional reasonableness, thus making it the most appropriate forum to obtain relief. Prior to *R. v. Garofoli*,[25] only the issuing court could entertain attacks contesting the basis for issuance of an investigative order.[26] In *Garofoli*, however, the Supreme Court confirmed that such restrictions were incompatible with the type of review necessary under section 8,[27] and empowered the trial court to receive all applications related to the validity of the authorization.[28]

The power to grant *Charter* remedies is, of course, not limited to the trial court; a provincial superior court of criminal jurisdiction also has jurisdiction to grant remedies under section 24, even where it is not acting as the trial court.[29] However, the superior court will normally defer the exercise of its jurisdiction to the trial court, unless it is in the interests of justice to do otherwise,[30] given "the risk of delay, the fragmentation of the trial process and the multiplicity of proceedings,"[31] associated with interlocutory decisions on *Charter* applications. As McIntyre J. explained in *R. v. Mills*,[32] the trial court is generally best suited to awarding *Charter* relief, and the granting of interlocutory relief should be exceptional:

> It must be remembered that everyone who claims *Charter* relief will not necessarily get what he seeks. There will be successful claims and unsuccessful claims, and in respect of each claim the question of breach of the right and entitlement to relief will have to be dealt with. This is true of all rights, *Charter* and non-*Charter*. If we recognize some priority arising out of an allegation of a breach of a *Charter* right so that it is somehow lifted from the ordinary flow of cases and given a special right of immediate interlocutory appeal, I fear that the confusion which would result would far outweigh any benefit which successful individuals would achieve. Furthermore, there is no guarantee that an interlocutory appeal will accelerate the

---

25 *R. v. Garofoli* (1990), 60 C.C.C. (3d) 161 (S.C.C.) [*Garofoli*].
26 See *R. v. Wilson*, [1990] 1 S.C.R. 1291.
27 *Garofoli*, above note 25 at 185.
28 The only issue where another court is the more appropriate forum is when the wiretap "packet" must be unsealed. See *Garofoli*, above note 25 at 186. The *Criminal Code* in s. 187 designates specific courts, in specific circumstances, as the forum for unsealing materials related to an application for authorization to intercept private communications.
29 *Mills*, above note 1 at 494.
30 *Rahey*, above note 24; *Mills*, above note 1 at 494–95 and 500–1.
31 *R v. Eton Construction Co.* (1996), 106 C.C.C. (3d) 21 at 24 [*Eton*]; *Mills*, above note 1 at 499–500. See also *Re Zevallos and the Queen* (1987), 37 C.C.C. (3d) 79 at 86 [*Zevallos*].
32 *Mills*, above note 1 at 499–501.

process. Rather, experience has shown that the interlocutory motion or appeal has all too frequently been the instrument of delay. In my view, it does not follow that interlocutory appeals will hasten the process. They are far more likely to delay the disposition of cases and would themselves tend to prolong the proceedings involved in the determination of *Charter* infringement. The history of this case affords an example.[33]

A judge sitting at a preliminary hearing is not a court of competent jurisdiction to grant *Charter* relief.[34] In *R. v. Hynes*,[35] the Supreme Court (in a 5–4 decision) affirmed its own *obiter* from *Mills* and *Seaboyer*, that Parliament neither expressly, nor by implication, gave the preliminary hearing judge (whose jurisdiction is completely governed by the *Criminal Code*) the jurisdiction to grant *Charter* relief.[36] While empowered to make evidentiary rulings (in the context of determining the sufficiency of evidence) and to allow discovery of the Crown's case (including evidence that might form the basis for a future *Charter* application),[37] the preliminary hearing judge has no power to grant *remedies*, such as ordering the production of disclosure, the production of third-party records, or granting relief against informer privilege, which all involve assessments of the effect on rights and administration of justice.[38] The majority held that trial courts are simply better suited to determine these potentially wide-ranging and complex concerns that are engaged in a section 24(2) application for the exclusion of evidence, since the trial court will enjoy the fullest appreciation of all the relevant circumstances.[39]

A parole board is not a court of competent jurisdiction for the purpose of awarding remedies under section 24 of the *Charter*. In *Mooring v. National Parole Board*,[40] the Supreme Court held that the Board was not suited to the awarding of remedies under section 24: the Board did not act in a judicial capacity and is quite different from a court; the traditional rules of proof and evidence do not apply to proceedings before the Board; and the Board

---

33 *Ibid.*
34 Such as in *Mills*, above note 1 at 954–55 (McIntyre J. for the majority) and 970–71 (LaForest J. in a separate, concurring opinion); 26 C.C.C. (3d) 481 (S.C.C.); *R. v. Seaboyer* (1991), 66 C.C.C. (3d) 321 (S.C.C.); *Hynes*, above note 12 at 375.
35 *Hynes*, above note 12.
36 *Ibid.* at 380; *R. v. Patterson*, [1970] S.C.R. 409 at 412.
37 *R. v. Dawson* (1998), 123 C.C.C. (3d) 385 (Ont. C.A.) at 392; *R. v. George* (1991), 5 O.R. (3d) 144 at 148.
38 *Hynes*, above note 12 at 378–79 and 384.
39 *Ibid.* at 381–82.
40 *Mooring*, above note 12.

lacks the ability to exclude from consideration any evidence as its function is primarily concerned with public safety.[41]

Similarly, it may be that a court considering whether an offender has breached a term of a conditional sentence order under section 742.6 of the *Criminal Code* is not a court of competent jurisdiction. In *R. v. Casey*,[42] Osbourne J.A. held that a court acting under that provision of the *Code* performed functions analogous to those of the National Parole Board in finding that the standard of proof under section 742.6 did not violate section 7 of the *Charter*.[43] If it is the case that a court acting under section 742.6 performs only a sentence management function, with its primary concern being the safety of the public,[44] it is reasonable then, of course, to conclude that the court is not one of competent jurisdiction.

In *R. v. Francis*,[45] Festeryga J. adopted the Ontario Court of Appeal's *obiter* comments in *Casey* and held that a court acting under 742.6 was not a court of competent jurisprudence. Note, however, the cases of *R. v. Kanak*[46] and *R. v. N.D.K.*,[47] which excluded evidence from a conditional sentence breach hearing; these cases did not consider the issue of whether they were, in fact, of competent jurisdiction to award *Charter* remedies. Also see the detailed reasons in *R. v. Palmer*,[48] where Durno J. held that a court acting under section 742.6 was a court of competent jurisdiction, citing, among other factors, the following points in support of a finding of competence: although the rules of proof and evidence were relaxed in breach hearings, it was not an inquisitorial proceeding (such as before the National Parole Board), and the decisions in such hearings are made by legally trained judges; additionally, not having the jurisdiction to exclude evidence of conditional sentence breach hearings might invite the commission of breaches by the police.[49]

C. EXCLUSION OF EVIDENCE: SECTION 24(2)

The most commonly sought remedy for a breach of the right against unreasonable search and seizure is the exclusion of evidence from trial. While

---

41   *Ibid.* at paras. 25–30.
42   *R. v. Casey* (2000), 141 C.C.C. (3d) 506 (Ont. C.A.).
43   *Ibid.* at para. 38.
44   *R. v. Wismayer* (1997), 115 C.C.C. (3d) 18 (Ont. C.A.) at 32.
45   *R. v. Francis* (unreported judgment of Festeryga J., Ont. Sup. Ct., 3 October 2003).
46   *R. v. Kanak*, [2003] A.J. 886 (Prov. Ct.).
47   *R. v. N.D.K.*, [2001] B.C.J. 1831 (Prov. Ct.).
48   *R. v. Palmer* (unreported decision of Durno. J., Ont. Sup. Ct., 13 November 2003).
49   *Ibid.* at paras. 33–44.

section 24(1) grants a broad power to give *Charter* relief, the exclusion of evidence at trial is governed by section 24(2):

> 24(2) Where, in proceedings under subsection (1), a court concludes that evidence was obtained in a manner that infringed or denied any rights or freedoms guaranteed by this Charter, the evidence shall be excluded if it is established that, having regard to all the circumstances, the admission of it in the proceedings would bring the administration of justice into disrepute.

1) Obtained in a Manner

As set out in the preceding excerpt, the wording of section 24(2) allows for exclusion of evidence if it was "obtained in a manner" that infringed the *Charter*. The meaning of evidence being obtained in a manner that infringed the *Charter* has been analysed and refined in several Supreme Court cases.[50] It is still a fairly fluid concept, with the courts using a "case-by-case" approach for its determination.[51] Essentially, the Supreme Court has rejected the necessity of finding a causal (or "but for") connection between the *Charter* violation and obtaining the evidence, as a precondition to triggering the application of section 24(2).[52] Instead, the Court has interpreted "obtained in a manner" more broadly, in some cases finding a "nexus" sufficient to justify exclusion if the violation preceded or occurred in the course of obtaining the evidence.[53] In determining whether a sufficient nexus exists, the entire chain of events must be examined to assess the strength of the nexus.[54]

A temporal link between the violation and the evidence will often suffice to trigger the application of section 24(2), especially where the *Charter* violation and the discovery of evidence occur in the course of a single transaction.[55] However, a temporal connection alone is not determinative.[56] In certain situations, even through evidence was obtained after the *Charter* breach, the collection of the evidence will not be sufficiently connected to the violation to taint the evidence and ground finding that it was obtained in a manner that infringed the *Charter*.[57]

---

50   Most notably in *R. v. Strachan* (1988), 46 C.C.C. (3d) 479 (S.C.C.) [*Strachan*] at 498; *R. v. Therens* (1985), 18 C.C.C. (3d) 481 (S.C.C.) [*Therens*]; and *R. v. Goldhardt* (1996), 107 C.C.C. (3d) 481 (S.C.C.) [*Goldhardt*].
51   *Goldhardt*, ibid. at 493.
52   *Strachan*, above note 50 at 498; *Therens*, above note 50 at 509–10 (Le Dain J.); *Goldhardt*, ibid. at 493.
53   *Strachan*, ibid. at 498–99; *Therens*, ibid. at 509–10.
54   *Strachan*, ibid. at 498–99; *Goldhardt*, above note 50 at 494–96.
55   *Strachan*, ibid. at 498.
56   Ibid. at 498–99.
57   Ibid. at 499.

Remoteness in both time and causality from the collection of the evidence may make establishing a nexus more difficult. On the one hand, if both the temporal connection and the causal connection are tenuous, the court may very well conclude that the evidence was not obtained in a manner that infringes a right or freedom under the *Charter*.[58] On the other hand, even where there is no causal connection, the temporal connection may be so strong that the *Charter* breach is an integral part of a single transaction.[59]

In *R. v. Plant*,[60] two searches occurred: an illegal search of the perimeter of a home and a subsequent search of the home on the authority of a warrant. Information gathered in the perimeter search was included in the warrant application, and the execution of that warrant ultimately led to the seizure of marijuana from the home. The Court found that the search of the residence itself was not unreasonable (despite the breach of section 8 in conducting the illegal perimeter search) because there were sufficient grounds to justify the search even after the results of the perimeter search were excised on review.[61] Nevertheless, the Court found that the perimeter search was an integral component in a series of investigative tactics leading to the uncovering of the evidence, and was sufficiently connected to the search of the home to allow consideration of excluding the evidenced uncovered in the (otherwise legal) search of the premises.[62] The Court found both a temporal and a *tactical* connection between the *Charter* violation and the discovery of evidence, which tainted the otherwise legitimate components of the search.[63]

The type of evidence in issue may have a bearing on a court's determination of whether that evidence was "obtained in a manner" that infringed the *Charter*. *R. v. Goldhardt*[64] involved the testimonial evidence of a witness obtained in connection with an unreasonable search of an old schoolhouse that housed a marijuana grow-operation. Despite the unlawfulness of the search, one of the occupants arrested during the search plead guilty and agreed to testify against the other accused. The accused sought to have the witness's evidence excluded because the witness was discovered as a result of an illegal search. The Court held that the connection between the illegal search and the witness's decision to testify was too remote to warrant exclu-

---

58 *Goldhardt*, above note 50 at 495.
59 *Strachan*, above note 50 at 499; *R. v. Kokesch* (1990), 61 C.C.C. (3d) 207 (S.C.C.) at 220.
60 *R. v. Plant* (1993), 84 C.C.C. (3d) 203 (S.C.C.) [*Plant*].
61 *Ibid.* at 197.
62 *Ibid.* at 198.
63 *Ibid.*
64 *Goldhardt*, above note 50.

sion of the evidence. Unlike inanimate objects, such as guns or drugs, witnesses can and do come forward of their own volition. Since the witness's decision to testify was a voluntary choice, spurred on by a recent religious conversion, any temporal or causal connection was extremely tenuous and did not meet the threshold required for exclusion.[65]

a) Common Law Power of Exclusion

Even in situations where evidence was not obtained in a manner that violated the *Charter*, there may be, in exceptional circumstances, a common law power to exclude evidence. In *R. v. Harrer*,[66] the Supreme Court held that evidence obtained in technical compliance with the *Charter* (in that case, because it was obtained by American investigators not subject to the *Charter*'s application) could nonetheless be excluded under the court's common law obligation to protect trial fairness. As LaForest J. explained:

> I should add that, had the circumstances been such that the admission of the evidence would lead to an unfair trial, I would have had no difficulty rejecting the evidence by virtue of the *Charter*. I would not take this step under s. 24(2), which is addressed to the rejection of evidence that has been wrongfully obtained. Nor would I rely on s. 24(1), under which a judge of competent jurisdiction has the power to grant such remedy to a person who has suffered a *Charter* breach as the court considers just and appropriate. Rather, I would reject the evidence on the basis of the trial judge's duty, now constitutionalized by the enshrinement of a fair trial in the *Charter*, to exercise properly his or her judicial discretion to exclude evidence that would result in an unfair trial.
>
> . . .
>
> The law of evidence has developed many specific rules to prevent the admission of evidence that would cause a trial to be unfair, but the general principle that an accused is entitled to a fair trial cannot be entirely reduced to specific rules. In *R. v. Corbett*, [1988] 1 S.C.R. 670, a majority of this Court made it clear that a judge has a discretion to exclude evidence that would, if admitted, undermine a fair trial; see also *R. v. Potvin*, [1989] 1 S.C.R. 525. Similarly, Sopinka, Lederman and Bryant, *The Law of Evidence in Canada* (1992), at p. 401, conclude that "if the admission of certain evidence would adversely affect the fairness of an accused's trial, the evidence *ought* to be excluded" (emphasis added). In *Thomson Newspapers, supra*, I attempted to explain that this approach is a necessary adjunct to a fair trial as guaranteed by s. 11(d) of the *Charter* in the following passage, at p. 559:

---

65 *Ibid.* at 496–97; see also *R. v. Hyatt* (2003), 171 C.C.C. (3d) 409 (B.C.C.A.) [*Hyatt*].
66 *R. v. Harrer*, [1995] 3 S.C.R. 562, 101 C.C.C. (3d) 193 [*Harrer*].

> ... there can really be no breach of the *Charter* until unfair evidence is admitted. Until that happens, there is no violation of the principles of fundamental justice and no denial of a fair trial. Since the proper admission or rejection of derivative evidence does not admit of a general rule, a flexible mechanism must be found to deal with the issue contextually. That can only be done by the trial judge.

I went on to further explain, as I had in *Corbett, supra*, that the common law principle had now been constitutionalized by the *Charter*'s guarantee of a fair trial under s. 11(d) of the *Charter*. At page 560, I continued:

> The fact that this discretion to exclude evidence is grounded in the right to a fair trial has obvious constitutional implications. The right of an accused to a fair hearing is constitutionalized by s. 11(d), a right that would in any event be protected under s. 7 as an aspect of the principles of fundamental justice (see *R. v. Corbett, per* Beetz J., at p. 699, and my reasons, at pp. 744–46; Dickson C.J. does not really comment on this issue).

> The effect of s. 11(d), then, is to transform this high duty of the judge at common law to a constitutional imperative. As I noted in *Thomson Newspapers*, at p. 563, judges must, as guardians of the Constitution, exercise this discretion where necessary to give effect to the *Charter*'s guarantee of a fair trial. In a word, there is no need to resort to s. 24(2), or s. 24(1) for that matter. In such circumstances, the evidence is excluded to conform to the constitutional mandate guaranteeing a fair trial, i.e., to prevent a trial from being unfair at the outset.[67]

In *R. v. Buhay*,[68] Arbour J. further discussed a court's ability to award common law exclusion of evidence remedies, although in a case that did not involve trial fairness concerns:

> Second, and more importantly, I wish to stress that even if the reasoning of the Court of Appeal were sound and that there had been no search and seizure triggering s. 8 of the *Charter*, remedies other than under the *Charter* might be available in such a case to an accused seeking exclusion of the impugned evidence. Indeed, even in the absence of a *Charter* breach, judges have a discretion at common law to exclude evidence obtained in circumstances such that it would result in unfairness if the evidence was

---

67 Ibid. at paras. 21–24.
68 *R. v. Buhay*, 2003 SCC 30 [*Buhay*].

admitted at trial, *or if the prejudicial effect of admitting the evidence outweighs its probative value.* [emphasis added][69]

To date, it would seem that such common law remedies for rights-related issues have only been awarded in cases involving trial fairness concerns.[70] It is expected that there will be litigation of whether a common law exclusion of evidence remedy is available in circumstances other than where an unfair trial could result from the admission of evidence. Justice Arbour's *obiter* discussion of the availability of such a remedy (especially the clause italicized above) may support the expansion of the common law power of exclusion because trial fairness was not an issue in *Buhay* and the *Harrer* formulation was clearly inapplicable.

2) Section 24(2): *Collins* Test for Exclusion of Evidence

Evidence that was obtained in a manner that violated the *Charter* will only be excluded at trial[71] "if it is established that . . . the admission of it in the proceedings would bring the administration of justice into disrepute."[72] In *R. v. Collins*,[73] the Supreme Court articulated three categories of factors the court must balance in making that determination in a section 24(2) application for exclusion:

1. the effect of admission of the evidence on the fairness of the trial;
2. the seriousness of the *Charter* violation; and
3. the possibility that *excluding* the evidence would bring the administration of justice into greater disrepute than admitting it.[74]

---

69 *Ibid.* at para. 40; in the context of confessions, see: *R. v. Rothman*, [1981] 1 S.C.R. 640, at 696, *per* Lamer J., as he then was [*Rothman*]; *R. v. Oickle*, [2000] 2 S.C.R. 3, 2000 SCC 38, at para. 69, *per* Iacobucci J. [*Oickle*]; see also J. Sopinka, S.N. Lederman and A.W. Bryant, *The Law of Evidence in Canada*, 2d ed., (Markham, ON: Butterworths, 1999) at 339–40; see also, in other contexts, *R. v. Harrer*, [1995] 3 S.C.R. 562, *per* LaForest J.; Sopinka, Lederman and Bryant, at 30–33; see also *Hyatt*, above note 65 at para. 54.
70 *Rothman, ibid.* at 696, *per* Lamer J., as he then was; *Oickle, ibid.* at para. 69, *per* Iacobucci J.
71 For a discussion of jurisprudential trends in the exclusion of evidence under s. 24(2) as a remedy for violations of s. 8, see D. Stuart, "Eight Plus Twenty-Four Two Equals Zero" (1998), 13 C.R. (5th) 50 at 59, and N. Gorham, "Eight Plus Twenty-Four Two Equals Zero-Point-Five" (2003), 6 C.R. (6th) 257.
72 *Charter* s. 24(2).
73 *R. v. Collins* (1987), 33 C.C.C. (3d) 1 (S.C.C.) [*Collins*].
74 *Ibid.*; *R. v. Stillman* (1997), 113 C.C.C. (3d) 321 (S.C.C.) [*Stillman*] at 349; *R. v. Jacoy*, [1988] 2 S.C.R. 548 at 560, 45 C.C.C. (3d) 296 [*Jacoy*] at 54.

a) Trial Fairness

Trial fairness has a fairly narrow meaning and refers only to the use of evidence that would impermissibly force the accused to implicate himself or herself in a crime.[75] If the admission of evidence would render the trial unfair by "conscripting" the accused against his or her will, the evidence generally will be excluded without consideration of the other *Collins* factors. As Cory J. held in *R. v. Stillman*:[76]

> If after careful consideration it is determined that the admission of evidence obtained in violation of a *Charter* right would render a trial unfair then the evidence must be excluded without consideration of the other *Collins* factors. A fair trial for those accused of a criminal offence is a cornerstone of our Canadian democratic society. A conviction resulting from an unfair trial is contrary to our concept of justice. To uphold such a conviction would be unthinkable. It would indeed be a travesty of justice. The concept of trial fairness must then be carefully considered for the benefit of society as well as for an accused.[77]

However, it is important to note that simply because evidence will usually be excluded for infringing principles of trial fairness, evidence will not mechanically be excluded for that reason. In *R. v. Richfield*,[78] the Ontario Court of Appeal held that there was no automatic exclusionary rule for evidence affecting the fairness of a trial. Although exclusion may be the general rule, certain types of *minimally intrusive* breaches that nonetheless affect trial fairness because of the conscriptive nature of the evidence[79] may result in exceptions to the general exclusionary rule:

> The general rule that conscripted evidence obtained in violation of an accused's s. 10(b) *Charter* rights should automatically be excluded because it impacts on trial fairness has the advantage of predictability. This general rule may, however, provide a disproportionate remedy when the resulting *Charter* violation is minimal. See D.M. Paciocco, "*Stillman*, Disproportion

---

75 Not all forced self-incrimination is unconstitutional. See the discussion in *R. v. S.A.B.*, 2003 SCC 60 at para 57.
76 *Stillman*, above note 74.
77 *Ibid.* at 350–51; however, see *R. v. Richfield*, [2003] O.J. No. 3230 (C.A.) [*Richfield*], where the Ontario Court of Appeal stressed that a finding that the admission of evidence could affect the fairness of a trial would not result in automatic exclusion of the evidence, in all circumstances.
78 *Ibid.*
79 In *Stillman*, above note 74 at 356, Cory J. noted that examples of the admission of evidence that would result in only minimal breaches of the right to a fair trial might include fingerprinting and breath samples.

and the Fair Trial Dichotomy under Section 24(2)" (1997) 2 *Can. Crim. L.R.* 163. In *Stillman*, Cory J. also commented, at p. 351, that although the admission of conscriptive evidence would generally render a trial unfair, "[t]hat general rule, like all rules, may be subject to rare exceptions." Other *obiter* comments by the Supreme Court, in *R. v. Fliss* (2002), 161 C.C.C. (3d) 225 at 247–8 and *R. v. Law* (2002), 160 C.C.C. (3d) 449 at 469, suggest that the Supreme Court may be prepared to modify its approach to the automatic exclusion of conscriptive evidence obtained through a minor breach of *Charter* rights.[80]

i) Conscriptive vs. Non-Conscriptive Evidence

Since only unconstitutionally obtained "conscriptive" evidence could affect the fairness of trial, it necessary to first classify the evidence as conscriptive or non-conscriptive.[81] This classification will depend on the manner in which the evidence was obtained.[82]

ii) Conscriptive Evidence Defined

Evidence will be classified as conscriptive "when an accused, *in violation of his* Charter *rights, is compelled to incriminate him or herself at the behest of the state* by means of a statement, the use of the body, or the production of bodily samples."[83] Examples of conscriptive evidence include a statement by the accused following a violation of his or her right to counsel, or the compelled provision by the accused of a bodily substance in violation of a *Charter* right.[84] Of course, if self-incriminatory evidence is obtained without the violation of a *Charter* right, the fairness of the trial will not be affected by the admission of that evidence.

"Real" or tangible evidence that is not normally thought of as being "self-incriminatory" may also constitute conscriptive evidence if the evidence was discovered as a result of other conscriptive evidence.[85] The Supreme Court has termed this type of evidence "derivative" conscriptive

---

80 *Richfield*, above note 77 at para. 18; see also *Buhay*, above note 68 and *R. v. Burlingham* (1995) 97 C.C.C. (3d) 385 (S.C.C.) [*Burlingham*] on the idea that the rule is not one of automatic exclusion for conscriptive evidence obtained in breach of the *Charter*. See also D. Stuart, "Buhay: No Automatic Inclusionary Rule Under Section 24(2) When Evidence is Non-Conscripted and Essential to the Crown's Case" (2003), 10 C.R. (6th) 233 at 234.
81 *Stillman*, above note 74 at 351.
82 *Ibid.* at 363.
83 *Ibid.* at 353 [emphasis added].
84 *Ibid.*
85 *Ibid.* at 359.

evidence. The case of *R. v. Burlingham*,[86] provides an example of derivative conscriptive evidence. In *Burlingham*, the police obtained a statement from the accused in violation of his right to counsel. This conscriptive statement led to the discovery of a gun at the bottom of a frozen river. Though the gun was "real" evidence, it was treated as derivative or conscriptive evidence, because it was only discovered as the result of a conscripted statement.[87] The location of the gun was "derived" from the conscriptive evidence (hence the term "derivative" evidence).[88]

In order to classify "derivative" evidence as conscriptive, the relationship between the derivative piece of evidence and the conscriptive evidence must be closely examined. Evidence will only be considered derivative of conscriptive evidence if it would not have been obtained but for the evidence conscripted from the accused by the state.[89] For this inquiry, it is irrelevant whether the other means that would have revealed the evidence are constitutionally valid, as the test is only to determine whether the evidence by its nature is connected to the accused's self-incrimination.[90]

The admission of conscriptive or derivative evidence will, as a general rule, render a trial unfair,[91] unless it can be shown on a balance of probabilities that the evidence *would* have been (not *could* have been) discovered by an alternative non-conscriptive means.[92] There are two ways to demonstrate that evidence would have been discovered[93] — the Crown can establish either that the evidence would have been obtained, even absent the conscription of the accused, from an independent source;[94] or, alternatively that the evidence would inevitably have been discovered though normal, constitutionally valid, investigative procedures.[95] Additionally, the alternate means of discovery must be constitutionally valid in order to show that the admission of the conscriptive or derivative evidence would not violate principles of trial fairness.[96]

If the conscriptive or derivative evidence was not otherwise discoverable by constitutionally valid means without the conscription of the accused,

---

86 *Burlingham*, above note 80.
87 *Stillman*, above note 74 at 359.
88 See also *R. v. Feeney* (1997), 115 C.C.C. (3d) 129 (S.C.C.) [*Feeney*] at para. 67.
89 *Ibid.* at paras. 69–70.
90 *Ibid.*
91 *Stillman*, above note 74 at 359.
92 *Ibid.* at 365.
93 *Ibid.* at 364.
94 *R. v. Colarusso* (1994), 87 C.C.C. (3d) 193 (S.C.C.).
95 *R. v. Black* (1989), 50 C.C.C. (3d) 1 (S.C.C.).
96 *Feeney*, above note 88 at paras. 69–70.

then the admission of the evidence would affect the fairness of the trial, and must ordinarily be excluded, making it unnecessary to consider of the seriousness of the violation or the effect of the exclusion of the evidence.[97]

iii) Non-Conscriptive Evidence Defined

Evidence will be classified as non-conscriptive "if the accused was not *compelled to participate in the creation or discovery of the evidence* (that is, the evidence existed independently of the *Charter* breach in a form useable by the state)."[98] Many early cases focused on determining whether the evidence was "real" — meaning physical evidence in a tangible form, as opposed to intangible evidence such as a statement, for example. However the "real evidence" classification is no longer particularly relevant or helpful.[99] Rather, the distinguishing feature and determinative issue is whether the evidence exists independently of the accused being compelled (in breach of a *Charter* right) to provide it.[100]

The admission of non-conscriptive evidence will rarely render a trial unfair.[101] Once the judge has concluded that the evidence is non-conscriptive, the court should move to consider the two remaining *Collins* factors, the seriousness of the violation and the effect of exclusion of the evidence.[102]

Examples of what can be considered non-conscriptive evidence are found in the case of *R. v. Feeney*.[103] At issue in *Feeney* was the admissibility of several pieces of evidence, including statements, cigarettes, stolen money, clothing, and shoes, all of which were obtained following various constitutional violations.

Initially, the police entered Feeney's home, without either a warrant or his consent, in order to question him. The officers roused Feeney from bed and had him step into the light, where they discovered his clothes were spattered with blood. Feeney was provided with a constitutionally deficient caution under section 10(b) of the *Charter*, and was asked how he got blood on his clothes. Feeney explained that he had been hit with a baseball bat the day before. The police then seized Feeney's shirt and brought him to the detachment for questioning, where he made several incriminating statements, including information in relation to evidence concealed within his residence, such as cigarettes and money that he had stolen from the victim and

---

97 *Stillman*, above note 74 at 365.
98 *Ibid.* at 352 [emphasis added].
99 *Ibid.*
100 *Ibid.*
101 *Ibid.* at 351–52.
102 *Ibid.* at 352.
103 *Feeney*, above note 88.

concealed under his mattress. A search warrant was obtained for the residence, resulting in the seizure of a package of cigarettes, Feeney's shoes, and the money stolen from the victim. The Court found that the police who had made the initial warrantless entry violated section 8 of the *Charter* and that the deficient caution violated section 10(b).

In determining whether the tangible pieces of evidence should be excluded under section 24(2), the Court set out first to classify the evidence as conscriptive or non-conscriptive, in order to determine whether its admission would affect trial fairness. The Court classified the seized shoes and cigarettes as non-conscriptive evidence. While Feeney had made statements about the cigarettes, the Court found that the statements were not a "necessary cause of" the seizure:

> A characterization of such evidence as conscriptive, "derivative evidence" is appropriate where the initial conscriptive evidence is a necessary cause of the obtention of the derivative evidence. In the present case, the statements given to the police at Williams Lake did not indicate the location of the cigarettes; thus the statements could not even have been a sufficient cause for obtaining the cigarettes. While the statements might, if admissible, have added evidentiary significance to the cigarettes, the statements were not related to the discovery and seizure of the evidence; thus the cigarettes are not conscriptive, derivative evidence. Their admission would not affect trial fairness.[104]

Similarly, the Court classified the stolen money as non-conscriptive evidence. Although Feeney's self-incriminatory statements made following a breach of his right to counsel identified the location of the money, Sopinka J., for the majority, did not consider the statements to have directly *caused* the discovery of the evidence:

> [I]n making a conscriptive statement at Williams Lake, the appellant told police that he had stolen cash and had hidden it under his mattress. In the second unconstitutional search of the trailer, the police seized the cash. Like the cigarettes and the shoes, the cash is facially non-conscriptive evidence. Unlike the statement about the cigarettes, however, the conscriptive statement at Williams Lake about the cash was a sufficient cause for obtaining the cash, stating as it did the location of the cash. *However, in my view, the statement was not a necessary cause of the taking of the cash. The police clearly intended to search the trailer again and I am satisfied would have done so even in the absence of the statement as to the location of the money.* In con-

---

104 *Ibid.* at para. 67.

ducting a second search, in my view they would have located the cash under the mattress. Given that the conscriptive statement was not a necessary cause of the taking of the money, the money was not conscriptive, derivative evidence. In this respect, this situation is similar to *R. v. Black*, [1989] 2 S.C.R. 138, 50 C.C.C. (3d) 1.[105]

Determining whether something is "conscriptive derivative evidence" does not involve an inquiry as to whether the alternate means of discovery are constitutionally permissible. Rather, when classifying evidence as conscriptive or non-conscriptive, the Court is solely concerned with determining whether the evidence can be considered as emanating in some way from the accused's mind or body. As Sopinka J. explained:

> It is important to note the distinction between the test for characterizing evidence as conscriptive, derivative evidence and the test for determining whether conscriptive evidence is discoverable. Discoverability is concerned with whether a *Charter* breach was necessary to the discovery of and obtaining conscriptive evidence. If the conscriptive evidence would have been obtained even if the *Charter* had not been breached, the evidence is discoverable and its admission, despite the conscription of the accused, would not affect trial fairness. In determining discoverability, therefore, the alternative means to obtain the evidence must comply with the *Charter*.
>
> The derivative evidence inquiry, on the other hand, is directed at determining whether a piece of evidence should be viewed as having a conscriptive nature because of its intimate relationship with other conscriptive evidence. Evidence is derivative evidence if it would not have been obtained but for the conscriptive evidence. In analyzing this question, it is not relevant whether the means by which the evidence would have been discovered in the absence of the conscription were constitutional. The inquiry is directed at whether evidence should be treated as a product of the accused's mind or body for the purposes of s. 24(2), which treatment does not depend on the constitutionality of the alternative means of discovery. Thus, in the present case, to conclude that the cash is not derivative evidence, it is sufficient to conclude that the police would have discovered the cash even if the conscripted statement at Williams Lake had not been made. It is irrelevant for the purpose of the derivative evidence inquiry that the police would have found the evidence by unconstitutional means such as the second search. Given the probable, although unconstitutional, discovery of the cash even if the conscripted statement had not been made, the cash was not conceptually a product of the appellant's mind or body.

---

105 *Ibid.* at para. 68.

The cash, therefore, should be treated not as derivative evidence, but as non-conscriptive evidence; its admission would not affect trial fairness. I note, of course, that the unconstitutionality of the second search is a factor to be considered under other branches of the *Collins* test.[106]

Issues as to the constitutionality of the alternate means of discovery for "non-conscriptive" evidence are relevant only to the serious of the breach, and not to issues regarding the fairness of the trial.

b) Seriousness of the Breach

Determining the seriousness of a *Charter* breach involves assessing the nature and extent of the violation, and the motivations behind the unconstitutional act. Justice Sopinka explained the purpose of the assessment of the seriousness of the violation in *R. v. Kokesch*:[107]

> The purpose of considering factors relating to the seriousness of the *Charter* violation is to assess the disrepute that the administration of justice would suffer as a consequence of judicial acceptance of evidence obtained through a serious *Charter* breach. The court must refuse to condone, and must dissociate itself from, egregious police conduct.[108]

In assessing seriousness, the court must take into consideration the totality of the circumstances.[109] Generally, the court will consider the following factors in determining the gravity of the breach:

- was the violation inadvertent or committed in good faith or was it wilful, deliberate and flagrant;
- was the violation serious or merely of a technical nature;
- was the violation motivated by a situation of urgency or necessity;
- were there other investigative means available to the police which would not infringe the *Charter of Rights*.[110]

i) Good Faith/Flagrance

In assessing the seriousness of the breach, a court will consider the manner in which the police conducted themselves in obtaining the evidence, and their motivations for committing the breach.[111] As noted above, if the breach was committed in good faith, or by inadvertence, or was only technical in

---

106 *Ibid.* at paras. 69–70.
107 *R. v. Kokesch* (1990), 61 C.C.C. (3d) 207 (S.C.C.) [*Kokesch*].
108 *Ibid.*; see also *Buhay*, above note 68 at para. 70.
109 *R. v. Belnavis* (1996), 107 C.C.C. (3d) 195 at 424 [*Belnavis*].
110 *R. v. Silveira* (1995), 97 C.C.C. (3d) 450 (S.C.C.) [*Silveira*] at 498; see *Collins*, above note 73; *Strachan*, above note 50.
111 *Kokesch*, above note 107 at 228.

nature, the breach will be rendered less serious.[112] If not committed in good faith, the court will assess whether the breach was instead deliberate, wilful or flagrant, thereby rendering the violation more serious.[113] The seriousness of the breach will be exacerbated if the police demonstrated an ongoing disregard for the accused's *Charter* rights.[114]

Good faith can be demonstrated if police acted pursuant to express statutory authority. Even if that authority is later held to be unconstitutional, so long as the investigators could not reasonably have been aware of the constitutional deficiency, they may be considered as acting in good faith.[115] Although there is an obligation on police to educate themselves as to the state of the law, the police are not expected to immediately be aware of changes to or pronouncements on the law. They will, however, be deemed to be aware of those changes and pronouncements within a reasonable amount of time.[116]

The claim that police officers were acting in good faith must be objectively reasonable. The courts will be less ready to recognize that police actions were conducted in good faith if there are obvious defects in the search warrant,[117] or if they knew or ought to have known that the conduct they engaged in was illegal.[118] For example, in *R. v. Lau*,[119] the British Columbia Court of Appeal declined to find that the officers acted in good faith in enforcing a blanket policy of "no-knock" entries when executing search warrants at marijuana grow houses:

> [G]ood motives do not permit the police to formulate policies which are contrary to legislative requirements. The difficulty in this case is that s. 12 of the *Controlled Drugs and Substances Act* does not permit the formulation of a blanket policy for searches under s. 11 of the Act. By s. 12 Parliament has required that the use of force be as is necessary in the circumstances. Therefore, each case must be considered independently. The officers in this case did not advert to this requirement. Rather, they based their decision to enter the premises in the manner that they did on a policy which, contrary to the Act, requires surprise entries with respect to every marijua-

---

112 *Therens*, above note 50 at 512.
113 *Ibid.* at 512.
114 *Belnavis*, above note 109 at 425; *R. v. Simmons*, [1988] 2 S.C.R. 495, 45 C.C.C. (3d) 296; *Jacoy*, above note 74.
115 *Kokesch*, above note 107; *Plant*, above note 60.
116 *Kokesch, ibid.* at 230–31.
117 *R. v. Genest* (1989), 45 C.C.C. (3d) 385 (S.C.C.) [*Genest*] at 406–9.
118 *Kokesch*, above note 107 at 230–31; *R. v. Laurin* (1997), 113 C.C.C. (3d) 519 (Ont. C.A.) [*Laurin*] at 537.
119 *R. v. Lau* (2003), 175 C.C.C. (3d) 273 (B.C.C.A.).

na grow operation (unless the police know children or old people are present) without regard to the circumstances which prevail in the situation at hand. Good faith cannot be founded on a policy which is made contrary to the dictates of the legislation.[120]

If the police have acted in a casual manner toward the preservation of constitutional rights, this will tend to aggravate the seriousness of the breach, and will tend to show blatant disregard for the accused's rights.[121] Similarly, a pattern of sloppiness or negligence in the investigation will aggravate the seriousness of a breach of section 8.[122] As Arbour J. noted in *R. v. Buhay*:[123]

> I share Aquila J.'s view that the fact that obtaining a warrant did not even cross the mind of one officer demonstrates a certain casual attitude toward the appellant's *Charter* rights. Moreover, the admission of Constable Riddell that he did consider obtaining a warrant but that he thought that he lacked sufficient grounds to get one also suggests blatant disregard for the appellant's rights. In *Kokesch, supra*, at p. 29, Sopinka J. stressed the significance of the admission by the police that they were aware they did not have reasonable and probable grounds sufficient to obtain a search warrant:
>
>> Where the police have nothing but suspicion and no legal way to obtain other evidence, it follows that they must leave the suspect alone, not charge ahead and obtain evidence illegally and unconstitutionally. *Where they take this latter course, the* Charter *violation is plainly more serious than it would be otherwise,* not less. Any other conclusion leads to an indirect but substantial erosion of the *Hunter* standards. The Crown would happily concede s. 8 violations if they could routinely achieve admission under s. 24(2) with the claim that the police did not obtain a warrant *because* they did not have reasonable and probable grounds. The irony of this result is self-evident. [first emphasis added by Arbour J.; second emphasis in original *Kokesch* decision][124]

Additionally, if the breach of the *Charter* right was motivated by a factor such as racial bias, the breach will obviously be considered extremely serious. David Tanovich, in his paper "Recent Trends in Remedies for Uncon-

---

120 *Ibid.* at para. 39
121 *Buhay*, above note 68.
122 *Ibid.* at para. 57; *R. v. Hosie* (1997), 107 C.C.C. (3d) 385 (Ont. C.A.).
123 *Buhay*, above note 68.
124 *Ibid.* at para. 60.

stitutional Searches,"[125] advocates an automatic exclusionary rule for evidence obtained as a result of a detention motivated by racial profiling (in breach of section 9 of the *Charter*), given recent statements in the law, such as by Trafford J. in *R. v. Peck*:[126]

> Stopping people merely on the basis of a "hunch" is a serious departure from the standards we demand of, and expect from, our police officers. Stereotypical assumptions, including those concerning young black men and narcotics, have no proper place in a properly conducted investigation. The inherent worth and dignity of all people regardless of their race or ethnic origin must be respected by the police at all times during the investigation of even the most heinous crimes.[127]

ii) Serious or Technical?

Did the police have reasonable grounds for the search, thereby mitigating the seriousness of the breach?[128] Were the police acting on what appeared to be a validly issued warrant in conducting the search? If so, the seriousness of the breach is mitigated.[129]

The level of the person's expectation of privacy when the violation was committed is an important factor in determining the seriousness of the breach.[130] An unreasonable search of a person's body is among the most serious types of breaches of section 8, as are unlawful wiretap recordings.[131] Illegal intrusions onto a person's private property are also extremely serious. Prior to the enactment of the *Charter*, the common law required the state to refrain from intruding on a person's environs unless the conditions for specified legal authority to be present on the property were met.[132] A per-

---

125 D. Tanovich, "Recent Trends in Remedies for Unconstitutional Searches," paper presented at the Third Symposium on Issues in Search and Seizure Law in Canada, Professional Development Program – Continuing Legal Education, Osgoode Hall Law School, York University, September 2003.
126 *R. v. Peck*, [2001] O.J. 4581 (S.C.J.).
127 *Ibid.* at para. 21.
128 *Belnavis*, above note 109 at 425 (S.C.C.); *R. v. Harris and Lighthouse Video Centres Ltd.* (1987), 35 C.C.C. (3d) 1 (Ont. C.A.); *Collins*, above note 73; *R. v. Sieben*, [1987] 1 S.C.R. 295 at 299, 32 C.C.C. (3d) 574; *Jacoy*, above note 74; *R. v. Duarte*, [1990] 1 S.C.R. 30 at 60, 53 C.C.C. (3d) 1 [*Duarte*].
129 *Plant*, above note 60; *Laurin*, above note 118 at 537.
130 See chapter 3 for a complete discussion of this concept.
131 *R. v. Dyment* (1988), 45 C.C.C. (3d) 244 (S.C.C.) [*Dyment*]; *Stillman*, above note 74; *Duarte*, above note 128.
132 *Kokesch*, above note 107 at 228; *Silveira*, above note 110 at 498–99; *Eccles v. Bourque* (1974), 19 C.C.C. (2d) 129, 50 D.L.R. (3d) 753, [1975] 2 S.C.R. 739; *Semayne's Case* (1604), 5 Co. Rep. 91 a, 77 E.R. 194 (K.B.).

son's home will be a "safe castle of privacy"[133] and a person will enjoy a high level of privacy in the home, and will possibly extend to attached components of the home such as the garage[134] (but curiously, not necessarily the backyard[135]). This level of privacy afforded to the home is not lowered by the fact that criminal business is being conducted in there.[136] In contrast, a person enjoys a more limited expectation of privacy in a motor vehicle,[137] in regulated activities,[138] at the border,[139] and at school.[140]

iii) Exigency/Necessity
If the breach was motivated by urgency or necessity to prevent the loss or destruction of evidence, the admission of evidence in such circumstances may not be considered as serious.[141] Certainly, a breach motivated by safety concerns will be less serious. Conversely, in the absence of exigent circumstances, a search or seizure in violation of section 8 may result in a finding that the breach is serious.[142]

iv) Availability of Other Investigative Techniques
Were other investigative techniques available? Could the evidence have been obtained without the *Charter* violation? These factors tend to render the breach more serious. Failure to observe proper procedures tends to indicate a blatant disregard for the *Charter*, and supports the exclusion of evidence.[143]

Even if other investigatory techniques were not available to obtain the evidence, this will not render the actions of the state less serious. In fact, pursuing evidence in the absence of constitutionally permissible techniques will render the violation more serious.[144] In *Kokesch*,[145] Sopinka J. held that

---

133   *Belnavis*, above note 109 at 424.
134   *Ibid*.
135   *R. v. Puskas* (1997), 120 C.C.C. (3d) 548 (Ont. C.A.) [*Puskas*].
136   *Silveira*, above note 110; *R. v. McCormack*, 2000 B.C.C.A. 57 at para 11.
137   *Belnavis*, above note 109 at 424.
138   *Thomson Newspapers Ltd. v. Canada (Director of Investigation and Research, Restrictive Trade Practices Commission)* (1990), 54 C.C.C. (3d) 417; *R. v. Potash* (1994), 91 C.C.C. (3d) 315.
139   *R. v. Simmons* (1988), 45 C.C.C. (3d) 296 (S.C.C.) at 319–20; *Canada (Director of Investigation & Research, Combined Investigation Branch) v. Southam Inc.*, [1984] 2 S.C.R. 145.
140   *R. v. M.(M.R.)*, [1998] 3 S.C.R. 393 [*M.(M.R.)*].
141   *Therens*, above note 50 at 512; *Silveira*, above note 110. See also chapter 4, "Exigent Circumstances."
142   See *Buhay*, above note 68 at para. 62.
143   *Collins*, above note 73 at 20; *Feeney*, above note 88 at para. 76; *Dyment*, above note 131 at 440; *Buhay*, above note 68 at para. 63.
144   *Kokesch*, above note 107 at 227.
145   *Ibid*.

the admission of evidence in these circumstances would lead to a substantial erosion of the *Hunter v. Southam* standard of not permitting *ex post facto* justifications of searches by their result.[146]

c) Effect of Exclusion

The third factor the Court must consider in deciding whether to exclude evidence under section 24(2) deals with the effect of the exclusion of the evidence on the administration of justice: Would the exclusion of the evidence bring the administration of justice into greater disrepute than would its admission? If exclusion would occasion greater disrepute than admission, then the impugned evidence ought to be admitted.[147] Note that this factor is something of a reversal of the literal phrasing of section 24(2) ("the *admission* of [the evidence] . . . would bring the administration of justice into disrepute") and serves a balancing function in the overall evaluation. This third *Collins* factor is generally only relevant in deciding if non-conscriptive (and non-derivative) evidence will be admissible at trial (since conscriptive evidence tends to be excluded if it will render a trial unfair).

The reputation of the overall administration of justice is the key concern in considering the effect exclusion of the evidence. In *R. v. Burlingham*,[148] Iacobucci J. explained:

> [W]e should never lose sight of the fact that even a person accused of the most heinous crimes, and no matter the likelihood that he or she actually committed those crimes, is entitled to the full protection of the *Charter*. *Short-cutting or short-circuiting those rights affects not only the accused but also the entire reputation of the criminal justice system*. It must be emphasized that the goals of preserving the integrity of the criminal justice system as well as promoting the decency of investigatory techniques are of fundamental importance in applying s. 24(2). [emphasis added][149]

Generally, this factor relates to the seriousness of the criminal offence and the importance of the evidence to the Crown's case, and embodies concepts relating to the public's concern about offenders "getting off on a technicality," especially in cases of serious crime. The more serious the offence, the greater is the likelihood that the administration of justice would be brought into disrepute by the exclusion of relevant evidence.[150] Similarly, the

---

146 *Ibid.* at 227.
147 *Collins*, above note 73 at 20–21.
148 *Burlingham*, above note 80.
149 *Ibid.* at 408.
150 *Collins*, above note 73 at 21.

more minimal the *Charter* breach, the greater the harm done to the repute of the administration of justice by the exclusion of evidence.[151] If the evidence is essential to prove the accused's guilt, the argument for admission is strengthened, especially where the breach of the *Charter* right is trivial, and the evidence is reliable.[152] Even if the evidence is not *essential* to the prosecution, and is only *valuable* to the Crown's case, a court may be persuaded not to exclude the evidence under the third branch of *Collins*. As Doherty J.A. explained in *R. v. Kitaitchik*:[153]

> The appellant was charged with murder, the most serious offence known to our criminal law. The evidence which the appellant sought to exclude was reliable. It was also important to the Crown's case. If accepted by the jury, it could provide valuable confirmation of the evidence of Shemtov, a clearly unsavoury witness. Convictions which rely heavily on the unconfirmed evidence of a witness like Shemtov are troubling. Surely, the reliability of such verdicts is greatly enhanced when the jury is permitted to hear evidence that is independent of, and confirmatory of, the evidence offered by a person like Shemtov. I see no error in the trial judge's conclusion that the exclusion of this evidence would tend to bring the administration of justice into disrepute.[154]

On the other hand, a court will be more likely to find that admitting unconstitutionally obtained evidence would bring the administration of justice into disrepute if the evidence was obtained through a serious breach that was flagrant in its disregard for constitutional procedures. A court will likely want to dissociate itself from the conduct of the police and exclude the evidence in such cases.[155] As Arbour J. explained in *R. v. Buhay*,[156] although section 24(2) is not to be used to *punish* police, it is possible that the administration of justice could be brought into disrepute through the *condonation* of improper police conduct:

> Lamer J. stressed at p. 281 in *Collins* that s. 24(2) is not a remedy for police misconduct. However, he also stressed that the purpose of s. 24(2) "is to prevent having the administration of justice brought into *further disrepute*

---

151 *Belnavis*, above note 109 at 426 (S.C.C.).
152 *Collins*, above note 73 at 20; *R. v. Grant* (1993), 84 C.C.C. (3d) 173 (S.C.C.) [*Grant*]; *Belnavis*, above note 109 at 426 (S.C.C.); *Puskas*, above note 135 at 556.
153 *R. v. Kitaitchik* (2002), 166 C.C.C. (3d) 14 (Ont. C.A.).
154 *Ibid.* at para. 48
155 *Collins*, above note 73 at 22–23; *Kokesch*, above note 107 at 232; *Genest*, above note 117 at 410.
156 *Buhay*, above note 68.

by the admission of the evidence in the proceedings. This further disrepute will result from the admission of evidence that would deprive the accused of a fair hearing, or *from judicial condonation of unacceptable conduct by the investigatory and prosecutorial agencies*" [first emphasis in original; second emphasis added]. Iacobucci J. also recalled in R. v. Burlingham, [1995] 2 S.C.R. 206, at para. 25, that the purpose of the *Collins* test is "to oblige law enforcement authorities to respect the exigencies of the *Charter* . . . ". The expressed concern of the trial judge that admitting the evidence in these circumstances may encourage similar police conduct in the future is in line with this purpose of the *Collins* test. More importantly, provincial court judges handle these kinds of issues on a daily basis. They have a much better understanding than we do about the likely effects of their decisions on their communities and on those who enforce the law in those communities. A concern such as the one expressed by Aquila J. should not, in my view, be dismissed lightly. The administration of justice does not have to be brought into disrepute on a national scale before courts may interfere to protect the integrity of the process within which they operate.[157]

3) Appellate Review of Section 24(2) Analysis

A trial judge's findings with respect to the impact on the administration of justice of unconstitutionally obtained evidence should be deferred to on appeal provided the judge has applied the correct test. The trial judge should only be reversed on a section 24(2) ruling if there was an error in the application of the relevant principles or an unreasonable finding.[158] As the Supreme Court held in *R. v. Greffe*:[159]

> I note that it is not the proper function of this court, absent some apparent error as to the applicable principles or rules of law, or absent a finding that is unreasonable, to review findings of courts below in respect of s. 24(2) of the *Charter* and substitute its opinion for that arrived at by the Court of Appeal: see *R. v. Duguay* (1989), 46 C.C.C. (3d) 1 at pp. 5–6, 56 D.L.R. (4th) 46, [1989] 1 S.C.R. 93.[160]

---

157 *Ibid.* at para. 70.
158 *R. v. Duguay* (1989), 46 C.C.C. (3d) 1 at 5–6, 56 D.L.R. (4th) 46 at 50, [1989] 1 S.C.R. 93; *R. v. Greffe* (1990), 55 C.C.C. (3d) 161 at 182–83, [1990] 1 S.C.R. 755, 75 C.R. (3d) 257 [*Greffe*]; *Grant*, above note 152; and *R. v. Borden* (1994), 92 C.C.C. (3d) 404 at 421, 119 D.L.R. (4th) 74, [1994] 3 S.C.R. 145. *Silveira*, above note 110 at 497; *Belnavis*, above note 109 at 217; *R. v. Law* (2002), 48 C.R. (5th) 199 at 215, 160 C.C.C. (3d) 449 (S.C.C.).
159 *Greffe, ibid.*
160 *Ibid.* at 182.

In *R. v. Buhay*,[161] the Supreme Court explained the rationale for affording deference to the findings of a trial judge in a section 24(2) analysis:

> On the s. 24(2) issue as on all others, the trial judge hears evidence and is thus better placed to weigh the credibility of witnesses and gauge the effect of their testimony. Iacobucci J., dissenting in part in *Belnavis, supra*, at para. 76, explained cogently the rationale for deference to the findings of trial judges:
>
>> The reasons for this principle of deference are apparent and compelling. Trial judges hear witnesses directly. They observe their demeanour on the witness stand and hear the tone of their responses. They therefore acquire a great deal of information which is not necessarily evident from a written transcript, no matter how complete. Even if it were logistically possible for appellate courts to re-hear witnesses on a regular basis in order to get at this information, they would not do so; the sifting and weighing of this kind of evidence is the particular expertise of the trial court. The further up the appellate chain one goes, the more of this institutional expertise is lost and the greater the risk of a decision which does not reflect the realities of the situation.
>
> The findings of the trial judge which are based on an appreciation of the testimony of witnesses will therefore be shown considerable deference. In s. 24(2) findings, this will be especially true with respect to the assessment of the seriousness of the breach, which depends on factors generally established through testimony, such as good faith and the existence of a situation of necessity or urgency (*Law, supra*, at paras. 38–41).[162]

D. SECTION 24(1) REMEDIES

In the search and seizure context, remedies other than the exclusion of evidence under section 24(2) of the *Charter* are less often awarded. There are, however, examples of various other remedies that may be awarded in appropriate cases under section 24(1) of the *Charter*.[163] Section 24(1) of the *Charter* provides as follows:

---

161 *Buhay*, above note 68.
162 *Ibid.* at paras. 46–47.
163 Courts may award stays of proceedings, reductions in sentences, and even the exclusion of evidence under s. 24(1): see discussions on these topics later in this chapter. Courts have also awarded damages (although in the context of a civil application for relief) in *Illnicki v. MacLeod*, [2003] A.J. No. 605 (Q.B.), *Nurse v.*

24(1) Anyone whose rights or freedoms, as guaranteed by this *Charter*, have been infringed or denied may apply to a court of competent jurisdiction to obtain such remedy as the court considers appropriate and just in the circumstances.

1) Exclusion of Evidence under Section 24(1)

In addition to being a remedy available under section 24(2), exclusion of evidence is a remedy available under section 24(1) in certain cases. Remember from the discussion above, that in order for evidence to qualify for the remedy of exclusion under section 24(2) specifically, the evidence had to have been obtained in a manner that violated the *Charter*. Section 24(1) of the *Charter* provides no such stipulations — rather, the section simply permits a court of competent jurisdiction to grant a remedy for violations of the *Charter*.

In *R. v. White*,[164] the Supreme Court clarified its position with respect to the availability of the exclusionary remedy under section 24(1). In prior cases, such as *R. v. Therens*,[165] *R. v. Collins*,[166] and *R. v. Strachan*,[167] members of the Court seemed to adopt the position that exclusion of evidence could only be awarded as a remedy under the jurisdiction of section 24(2). In *White*, however, the Court distinguished the approach taken in the prior jurisprudence, finding that *Therens* factually dealt with a situation where evidence *had* been obtained in violation of the *Charter*.[168] The Court preferred instead the approach taken by McLachlin J. in *R. v. Harrer*[169] and Lamer J. in *R. v. Schreiber*[170] (both being concurring reasons), which found that section 24(1) would enable a court to exclude evidence that if admitted at trial would infringe the *Charter* regardless of the manner in which it was obtained. Accordingly, the Court in *White* held that evidence obtained in conformity with the *Charter*, but that would nonetheless violate the *Charter* by its admission into evidence, could be excluded under section 24(1) (as opposed to section 24(2)). As Iacobucci J. explained:

Canada (1997), 132 F.T.R. 131 (F.C.T.D.), and *Blouin v. Canada* (1991), 51 F.T.R. 194 (F.C.T.D.), and ordered the quashing of a Canada Customs and Revenue Agency request for taxpayer's information in *Kligman v. Canada*, [2003] F.C.J. No. 70 (T.D.), for violations of s. 8.

164 *R. v. White*, [1999] 2 S.C.R. 417 [*White*].
165 *Therens*, above note 50.
166 *Collins*, above note 73 at 13, *per* Lamer J.
167 *Strachan*, above note 50 at 494–95, *per* Dickson C.J.
168 *White*, above note 164 at para. 85.
169 *Harrer*, above note 66.
170 *Schreiber v. Canada (Attorney General)*, [1998] 1 S.C.R. 841.

Thus it may be seen that this Court has never affirmatively decided that s. 24(1) of the *Charter* may serve as the mechanism for the exclusion of evidence whose admission at trial would violate the *Charter*. In the present appeal, the parties and the courts below appear to have proceeded on the basis that s. 24(1) is the appropriate mechanism for exclusion of evidence whose admission would contravene the principle against self-incrimination under s. 7. None of the argument before this Court was directed to this specific issue.

Although I agree with the majority position in *Harrer*, *supra*, that it may not be *necessary* to use s. 24(1) in order to exclude evidence whose admission would render the trial unfair, I agree also with McLachlin J.'s finding in that case that s. 24(1) may appropriately be employed as a discrete source of a court's power to exclude such evidence. In the present case, involving an accused who is entitled under s. 7 to use immunity in relation to certain compelled statements in subsequent criminal proceedings, exclusion of the evidence is required. Although the trial judge could have excluded the evidence pursuant to his common law duty to exclude evidence whose admission would render the trial unfair, he chose instead to exclude the evidence pursuant to s. 24(1) of the *Charter*. I agree that he was entitled to do so.[171]

2) Stays of Proceedings under Section 24(1)

In certain contexts, a stay of proceedings may be available under section 24(1), following a breach of section 8.[172] However, a stay of proceedings is appropriate only "in the clearest of cases," where the prejudice to the accused's right to make full answer and defence cannot be remedied or where irreparable prejudice would be caused to the integrity of the judicial system if the prosecution were continued.[173] As Finlayson J.A. noted in *R. v. Flintoff*[174] (a case involving an unlawful strip-search that resulted in the exclusion of breathalyser evidence from trial) if the evidence tainted by the breach is severable from the rest of the trial process or other the charges before the court, a stay of proceedings is not appropriate:

---

171   *White*, above note 164 at paras. 88–89; see also the foregoing discussion of Arbour J.'s comments in *Buhay*, above note 68, regarding the availability of a common law exclusionary power.

172   See, e.g., the provincial court level cases of *R. v. F.(S.)*, [2000] O.J. No. 60 (Ct. Jus.); *R. v. Lau*, 2003 BCCA 337; *quaere* whether these cases meet the threshold articulated by the Supreme Court of "clearest of cases."

173   *R. v. O'Connor* (1995), 103 C.C.C. (3d) 1 (S.C.C.); *R. v. Young* (1984), 13 C.C.C. (3d) 1 (Ont. C.A.).

174   *R. v. Flintoff* (1998), 126 C.C.C. (3d) 321 (Ont. C.A.) [*Flintoff*].

Since it is conceded that the breathalyzer test results are the only evidence to support the charge under s. 253(b) of the *Code*, that charge cannot be sustained. However, I would not stay the charge of driving while impaired under s. 253(a) of the *Code*. The conduct of the investigating officer at the scene of the accident cannot be criticized. The evidence to support that charge is entirely severable from what took place at the police station. The Crown cannot, of course, rely upon the breathalyzer reading in support of this charge.

L'Heureux-Dubé J. for the majority of the Supreme Court of Canada in *R. v. O'Connor* . . . stated that [at p. 43]:

> [i]t must always be remembered that a stay of proceedings is only appropriate "in the clearest of cases," where the prejudice to the accused's right to make full answer and defence cannot be remedied or where irreparable prejudice would be caused to the integrity of the judicial system if the prosecution were continued.

I do not think this is the clearest of cases, particularly when a proper result can be obtained by a more surgical use of s. 24(2) of the *Charter*. The two charges arise out of a motor vehicle accident, the seriousness of which is not apparent on this record. There is no reason why the offence for which there can be no due process complaint should not proceed on other evidence available to the Crown.[175]

3) Sentence Reduction for *Charter* Violations

One of the more controversial alternate remedies sometimes awarded for a breach of a *Charter* right is the reduction of an offender's sentence. Most courts have recognized that section 24(1) permits such an award: see, for example, *R. v. Glykis*,[176] *R. v. Collins*, *R. v. Charles*,[177] *R. v. Chabot*,[178] *R. v. Dennison*,[179] and *R. v. MacPherson*.[180]

However, several provincial courts of appeal have expressed reservations about the appropriateness of sentence reduction as a remedy, unless certain extenuating circumstances are present. For example, the Ontario Court of Appeal in *R. v. Glykis*[181] held that the reduction of an offender's sen-

---

175 *Ibid.* at paras. 40–42.
176 *R. v. Glykis* (1995), 100 C.C.C. (3d) 97 (Ont. C.A.) [*Glykis*].
177 *R. v. Charles* (1987), 36 C.C.C. (3d) 286 (Sask. C.A.).
178 *R. v. Chabot* (1992), 77 C.C.C. 371 (Que. C.A.).
179 *R. v. Dennison* (1990), 60 C.C.C. (3d) 342 (N.B.C.A.).
180 *R. v. MacPherson* (1995), 100 C.C.C. (3d) 216 (N.B.C.A.).
181 *Glykis*, above note 176.

tence as a remedy for a violation of section 10(b) of the *Charter* was not generally an appropriate award. Chief Justice Dubin, for the Court, explained that the sentencing proceeding should not be to punish police where a higher disposition would be otherwise warranted:

> The breach of s. 10(b) of the *Charter* did not in any way mitigate the seriousness of the offence, nor constitute in itself a form of punishment. The actions of the police in this case were entirely divorced from the commission of the offence, and ultimately unrelated to the evidence gathering process and to the guilt or innocence of the respondents.
>
> In my respectful opinion, it is inappropriate to view sentencing proceedings as an avenue for sending a message to the law enforcement agencies.[182]

The Court left open the possibility, however, for the award of a reduction in sentence where the *Charter* violation itself acted as a form of punishment in place of the additional penalty that the accused would have suffered, recognizing that other courts had awarded sentence reduction as a remedy in such circumstances:

> I recognize that there have been cases where the courts, by reason of a *Charter* violation, have apparently imposed a lesser sentence than that which would normally have been imposed. However, in most of those cases the breach has resulted in some form of punishment or added hardship.
>
> In *R. v. Charles* (1987), 36 C.C.C. (3d) 286, 59 C.R. (3d) 94, 31 C.R.R. 362 (Sask. C.A.), the accused had been arbitrarily detained for a period of some 12 hours. The Saskatchewan Court of Appeal held that the arbitrary detention was a factor to be considered in imposing sentence: see also *R. v. Chabot* (1992), 77 C.C.C. (3d) 371, 11 C.R.R. (2d) 281, 47 M.V.R. (2d) 70, sub nom. *Quebec (Attorney-General) v. Chabot* (Que. C.A.).
>
> In *Mills, supra*, LaForest J., in a dissenting judgment, opined, at pp. 567–8, that as an alterative to a stay in a case where an accused has been denied the right to a trial within a reasonable time, "if the accused were ultimately convicted, delay might be taken into account in sentencing, even in situations not otherwise considered in imposing sentence."
>
> Similarly, in *R. v. Bosley* (1992), 18 C.R. (4th) 347 at p. 358, 59 O.A.C. 161, 18 W.C.B. (2d) 179, Doherty J.A., for this court, stated:
>
> . . .
>
> I would add that excessive delay which causes prolonged uncertainty for the appellant but does not reach constitutional limits can be taken into consideration as a factor in mitigation of sentence.[183]

---

182   *Ibid.* at 102.
183   *Ibid.*

The Court also recognized that a remedy of sentence reduction could be appropriate in cases where the *Charter* violation mitigated the seriousness of the offence or effectively served as a substitute punishment:

> In cases where the police had been implicated in either creating or encouraging the commission of offences, and prior to *R. v. Mack* (1988), 44 C.C.C. (3d) 513, [1988] 2 S.C.R. 903, 67 C.R. (3d) 1, which provided a remedy disentitling the state to a conviction because of entrapment, police wrongdoing was considered a factor in determining the appropriate sentence: see *R. v. Kirzner* (1977), 32 C.C.C. (2d) 76, 74 D.L.R. (3d) 351, 14 O.R. (2d) 665 (C.A.); *R. v. Ormerod*, [1969] 4 C.C.C. 3, 6 C.R.N.S. 37, [1969] 2 O.R. 230 (C.A.).
>
> In this case, the conduct of the police was not a relevant factor for consideration in the sentencing process as it neither mitigated the seriousness of the offence, nor imposed any undue hardship on the offenders and ought not to have been considered as mandating a remedy under s. 24(1) of the *Charter* by way of mitigation of sentence.[184]

The British Columbia Court of Appeal in *R. v. Carpenter*[185] took a similarly guarded approach to sentence reduction as a remedy for *Charter* breaches. While recognizing that section 24(1) was broad enough to provide jurisdiction for the granting of such a remedy, the Court found that a reduction in sentence for a *Charter* breach would be contrary to the principles of sentencing codified in the *Criminal Code*:

> [T]he use of sentence reductions ... also carries the potential for mixed messages in the real world in which courts must operate. In 1995, Parliament enacted s. 718 of the *Code* to clarify the fundamental purposes and principles of sentencing. These principles include the provision of reparations for "harm done to victims or to the community" and the denunciation of unlawful conduct — presumably on the part of offenders. No mention is made of providing a remedy for illegal or tortious conduct by law enforcement authorities or providing reparations for *Charter* breaches. ... It is difficult to determine how a court could grant a reduction in sentence to "signify" its disapproval of, for example, police conduct occurring after the commission of the offence, and at the same time remain faithful to these principles.
>
> ...
>
> Overall, I find myself in agreement with Professor K. Roach, who in an article entitled "Section 24(1) of the *Charter*: Strategy and Structure" in (1986–87), 29 C.L.Q. 222 writes:

---

184 *Ibid.* at 103.
185 *R. v. Carpenter* (2002), 165 C.C.C. (3d) 159 (B.C.C.A.) [*Carpenter*].

Within the rights protection model it is best that the provision of remedies is not blurred with the subjective and open-ended factors that enter into the sentencing disposition. It is too much to expect judges, at the same time, to sentence a guilty offender to the punishment and treatment most appropriate to his or her character, and also to reduce the sentence because the accused, as an abstractly considered rights bearer, has suffered a *Charter* violation. [At p. 262.][186]

In *R. v. Collins*,[187] the Newfoundland Court of Appeal demonstrated a similar reluctance to entertain the reduction of sentence as an appropriate remedy. While recognizing that section 24(1) could empower a court to award the remedy, the Court held that it would generally not be available:

> This opinion, therefore, adopts the position that there is no hard and fast absolute answer to the question of the use of *Charter* violations in mitigation or reduction of sentences. *It is proposed, however, as a matter of principle that reductions should generally not be entertained where there has been an antecedent ruling that the breach does not warrant exclusion of evidence garnered as a result of it under the powers invested in courts to do so under s-s. 24(2).* Where the breach has not triggered consideration under s-s. 24(2), however, the wide latitude of s-s. 24(1) comes into play and has sway. Under it, a sentencing judge would appear to have a discretion to consider sentence reduction for *Charter* breaches if "appropriate and just in the circumstances" to do so. [emphasis added][188]

For further discussion of section 24(1) remedies, see David Tanovich's paper, "Recent Trends in Remedies for Unconstitutonal Searches."[189]

E. NON-*CHARTER* REMEDIES: PREROGATIVE RELIEF

The accused may also resort to non-*Charter* prerogative remedies to obtain relief against governmental searches and seizures. The prerogative remedy of *certiorari* is available to quash a search warrant, provided that the appli-

---

186 *Ibid.* at paras. 26–27.
187 [1999] N.J. No. 44 (C.A.).
188 *Ibid.* at para. 133.
189 D. Tanovich, "Recent Trends in Remedies for Unconstitutional Searches," paper presented at the Third Symposium on Issues in Search and Seizure Law in Canada, Professional Development Program – Continuing Legal Education, Osgoode Hall Law School, York University, 20 September 2003.

cant can establish that the justice committed a jurisdictional error in issuing of the warrant.[190]

Superior courts of criminal jurisdiction are charged at common law with the responsibility to supervise the decisions of lower courts. Lower courts, such as a justice of the peace or provincial courts, do not have inherent jurisdiction at common law, and obtain all their powers to act from statutes. Accordingly, where the lower courts do not act in accordance with the powers granted to them by statutes, the superior courts may step in to remedy any errors related to the exercise of jurisdiction.

In the search and seizure context, a justice only has jurisdiction to issue a search warrant where all the statutory prerequisites for issuing a search warrant are demonstrated; accordingly, if one of the statutory prerequisites to issuance is missing (for example, the absence of any evidence of reasonable grounds),[191] this will constitute jurisdictional error sufficient for the granting of a prerogative remedy. In *R. v. Branton*,[192] the Ontario Court of Appeal found that the minimum statutory requirements for issuing a warrant were absent in a case where the affiant did not provide full, fair, and frank disclosure of all relevant circumstances; this was because the justice would have been deprived of the ability to assess all the circumstances in determining where the warrant should have issued. Although incomplete disclosure would not normally be a sufficient basis to justify the quashing of a warrant, in *Branton*, the remaining useable information failed to satisfy the statutory grounds for issuance of a warrant.[193] The Court in *Branton* also found that the issuing justice committed a jurisdictional error by issuing a section 487 warrant in respect of a "suspected or intended offence" rather than for an offence actually committed.[194]

Even if an applicant to the superior court can establish jurisdictional error, there is no guarantee that a court will grant the remedy. Prerogative remedies are discretionary remedies, to be given by a court only where it is in the interests of justice to do so.[195] If there is another forum more appro-

---

190 *Mills*, above note 1 at 963.
191 *Re Church of Scientology and the Queen (No. 6)* (1987), 31 C.C.C. (3d) 449 (Ont. C.A.) at 494; *R. v. Pratas*, [2000] O.J. No. 2286 (C.A.) at paras. 3–4.
192 *R. v. Branton* (2001), 154 C.C.C. (3d) 139 (Ont. C.A.).
193 *Ibid.* at 155.
194 *Ibid.* at 156. A "General Warrant" may issue under s. 487.01 in advance of the commission of an offence; see appendices.
195 *R. v. Janda*, [2003] O.J. 326 (Sup. Ct.) at para. 22; *R. v. Currie* (1871), 31 U.C.Q.B. 582 per Wilson J. at 584: "It is said that the granting of a *certiorari* is not of right, but is grantable in the exercise of a sound legal discretion: *Re Mayo County*, 14 Ir. C.L. Rep 392; *Re Andre Corbeil & The Queen* (1986), 27 C.C.C. (3d) 245, *per* Lacourciere J.A. at

priate for the determination of the issues raised on the application for prerogative relief, the superior court will likely not exercise its discretion in favour of granting prerogative relief.[196]

Generally speaking, the trial court is a more appropriate forum for obtaining relief than the prerogative remedy court.[197] Often, the jurisdictional errors raised on prerogative review are identical to the issues that would be litigated at trial on a *Charter* application to determine a violation of section 8. Deferring the determination of these issues until trial avoids "the risk of delay, the fragmentation of the trial process and the multiplicity of proceedings" that can occur with interlocutory motions in criminal proceedings.[198]

The case for deferring the issues to the trial court is especially strong where the main relief sought is the exclusion of evidence; the prerogative remedy court cannot *finally* determine whether the evidence is admissible at trial, as the trial court retains jurisdiction over whether to exclude evidence under section 24(2) of the *Charter*.[199] It is also appropriate for a court to refuse to give a prerogative remedy where a decision on the *certiorari* application would not likely be rendered before the commencement of trial.[200]

However, an application for prerogative relief at the beginning of a lengthy process where no dates for preliminary hearing and no disclosure has been received is more likely to be entertained by the supervisory court.[201] Prerogative remedies may also be appropriate in situations where an application to quash is brought for reasons other than the admissibility of evidence at trial, such as to prevent the execution of search warrant, or to obtain the return of goods seized pursuant to a warrant (especially where the Crown's case is not dependent on retaining the goods seized).[202] Additionally, prerogative remedies may be available in instances where the overall interests of justice favour the granting of relief prior to trial.[203]

251: "[E]ven in a case where there might be a lack of jurisdiction, the prerogative remedies are discretionary and are not to be exercised as of right."
196 *Re Forsythe and The Queen* (1980), 53 C.C.C (2d) 225 (S.C.C.) at 228. *Dubois v. The Queen* (1986), 25 C.C.C. (3d) 221 (S.C.C.) at 232–33.
197 *Zevallos*, above note 31 at 81 and 84.
198 *Eton*, above note 31 at 24; *Mills*, above note 1 at 499–500. See also *Zevallos*, above note 31 at 86.
199 *Zevallos*, above note 31.
200 *Prime Realty Ltd. v. British Columbia (Superintendent of Real Estate)*, [1994] B.C.J. No. 561 (C.A.).
201 *R. v. Branton* (2001), 154 C.C.C. (3d) 139 (Ont. C.A.) at 146–47 [*Branton*].
202 *Zevallos*, above note 31 at 86–87; also *Branton, ibid.* at 147.
203 *Zevallos*, above note 31 at 87; *Branton*, above note 201 at 147.

There may be an expanded right of *certiorari* beyond the traditional formulation of "jurisdictional error" for cases involving competing *Charter* rights. For example, in *Dagenais*,[204] the lower court imposed a ban on publication of the details of the accused's criminal proceedings. This ban was contested by the media, who argued that it unduly infringed their right to freedom of expression under the *Charter*. The Supreme Court held that if a lower court erred in the application of a common law rule, and that the error infringed upon a person's *Charter* rights, the lower court's decision may be subject to review on *certiorari*. The Court held that such an error would constitute "an error of law on the face of the record," and thus is subject to *certiorari*:

> Provincial superior courts have jurisdiction to hear applications for the extraordinary remedy of *certiorari* against provincial court judges for excesses of jurisdiction and for errors of law on the face of the record. As I will explain in Part C of these reasons, the common law rule governing the issuance of orders banning publication must be consistent with the principles of the *Charter*. Since the common law rule does not authorize publication bans that limit *Charter* rights in an unjustifiable manner, an order implementing such a publication ban is an error of law on the face of the record. Therefore, if a publication ban order is made by a provincial court judge, the media can apply to the superior court for *certiorari* and argue that the ban is not authorized by the common law rule. If this is the case, the ban will then constitute an error of law on the face of the record. By virtue of s. 784(1) of the *Criminal Code*, an appeal lies to the Court of Appeal from a decision granting or refusing the relief sought in proceedings by way of *certiorari*.[205]

---

204 *Re Dagenais et al. v. C.B.C. et al.*, [1994] 3 S.C.R. 835.
205 *Ibid.* at 864–65; see also *R. v. C.B.C. et al.* (2001), 52 O.R. (3d) 757 (C.A.), *per* Moldaver J. at 52–55.

CHAPTER 10

☙

Summary of Essential Principles

Like many areas of law, the jurisprudence in the area of search and seizure seems to be subject to constant change. However, despite this fluidity, a core set of basic principles underlies the case law. We have attempted to illuminate these principles throughout this book. The following is a brief summary of the Canadian courts' general approach to determining the constitutional validity of a search or seizure:

1. The overarching issue to be resolved in an allegation of an unreasonable search is a balancing of interests: the "reasonableness" of a government intrusion is determined by balancing an individual's privacy interests against the state's particular goal in intruding on privacy, and the manner in which the intrusion is conducted.[1]
2. Generally speaking, the applicant seeking to have evidence excluded bears the burden of proving that the evidence should be inadmissible. If the search was not authorized in advance by way of an investigative order, the burden will shift to the prosecution to prove that the evidence ought to be admitted.[2]

---

[1] *Hunter et al. v. Southam Inc.* (1984), 14 C.C.C. (3d) 97 (S.C.C.) [*Hunter*] at 108.
[2] Although that is the general rule, it does not apply when the warrantless search is a type recognized as *prima facie* reasonable by the common law, such as a search incident to arrest or a search conducted at a school. In such cases, the burden remains on the Applicant to justify exclusion. See *R. v. Golden*, [2001] 3 S.C.R. 679 and *R. v. M.(M.R.)*, [1998] 3 S.C.R. 393.

3. The fundamental purpose of section 8 is the protection of privacy interests.[3] In order to establish that a search was unreasonable, the applicant must demonstrate that he or she had a reasonable expectation of privacy in the location searched or in the things seized. If the applicant cannot show a reasonable expectation of privacy, generally speaking, section 8 will provide no protection.
4. In order for a search to comply with section 8, three conditions must be satisfied: there must be specific statutory or common law authorization for the search, the law authorizing the search must be reasonable, and the manner in which the search is conducted must be reasonable.[4]
5. The reasonableness of a statutory or common law power of search or seizure is generally assessed according to the *Hunter v. Southam* standard. The basic requirements are that the search must be authorized in advance by an independent judicial officer and the authorization must be based on sworn evidence showing reasonable grounds to believe that an offence has been committed and that evidence will be found in the place to be searched.[5] There are, however, many exceptions to the *Hunter* standard, with some searches requiring higher standards of justification (where other competing constitutional rights or privileges are at stake), and others providing lower standards of protection to the individual (for example, where interests such as safety or national security or public administration are engaged).[6] In some cases, a power of search or seizure must comply with other *Charter* rights, such as the principle against self-incrimination, before it can be considered reasonable under section 8.[7]
6. The presence of reasonable grounds is a necessary element of reasonableness in most types of searches.[8] Reasonable grounds exist "where credibly based probability replaces suspicion."[9] It is not a standard of exactitude, but something closer to probability. The standard of what constitutes reasonable grounds is a sliding scale depending on who is making the assessment of the evidence, and in what context (for exam-

---

3 *Hunter*, above note 1; *R. v. Edwards* (1996), 104 C.C.C. (3d) 136 (S.C.C.).
4 *R. v. Collins* (1999), 22 C.R. (5th) 269 (Nfld. C.A.); *R. v. S.A.B.*, 2003 SCC 60 [*S.A.B.*].
5 *Hunter*, above note 1.
6 *R. v. Mills*, [1999] 3 S.C.R. 668; *Attorney-General of Quebec v. Canadian Broadcasting Corp.* (1991), 67 C.C.C. (3d) 517 (S.C.C.); *Lavallee, Rackel & Heintz v. Canada (Attorney General)*; *White, Ottenheim & Baker v. Canada (Attorney General)*; *R. v. Fink* (2002), 167 C.C.C. (3d) 1 (S.C.C.).
7 *S.A.B.*, above note 4.
8 *Hunter*, above note 1.
9 *Ibid.*

ple, an officer making an evaluation in the field may be held to a lower standard than a justice of the peace considering a warrant application in chambers).[10]

7. If an investigative order is being challenged under section 8, special rules apply to the challenge, and generally, the reviewing court will defer to the issuing justice and the order will stand if it *could* have issued on the evidence presented to the issuing court.[11]

While every fact situation will require a slightly different solution, the ideas presented in this book represent the core concepts in the section 8 jurisprudence. The approach outlined above should assist the reader in fashioning an appropriate argument to either formulate or counter a claim of unreasonable search and seizure.

---

10 *R. v. Godoy* (1998), 131 C.C.C. (3d) 129 (S.C.C.).
11 *R. v. Garofoli* (1990), 60 C.C.C. (3d) 161 (S.C.C.); *R. v. Araujo*, [2000] 2 S.C.R. 992, 2000 SCC 65, 149 C.C.C. (3d) 449, 193 D.L.R. (4th) 440.

APPENDIX 1: Basic Search Powers (*Criminal Code*)

Statutory Power	Judicial Officer	Person to be Authorized	Scope	Special Requirements
Conventional warrant s. 487	Justice of the Peace[1]	Peace officer; or Public officer appointed or designated to administer or enforce any federal or provincial law and whose duties include enforcement of any federal law, *provided* that the public officer is named in the warrant	Applies to items (i.e., "anything") Authorizes the search of a "building, receptacle or place" for anything listed in the warrant, and the seizure of those items (includes computer systems and data)	• Requires RPG,[2] on oath, in Form 1, to believe that there is in the building, place or receptacle to be searched: i) anything on or in respect of which a federal offence is *suspected* to have been committed; ii) anything that there are *reasonable grounds* to believe will afford evidence with respect to the commission of a federal offence; iii) anything that there are *reasonable grounds* to believe will reveal the whereabouts of a person who is believed to have committed a federal offence; iv) anything that there are *reasonable grounds* to believe is intended to be used for the purpose of an offence against the person for which the offender may be arrested without a warrant; or v) any offence-related property.[3] • Must be executed by day, unless otherwise ordered (s. 488).[4] • May be obtained by telewarrant (s. 487.1).. • Issuing justice has the authority to attach "execution procedures" in special circumstances[5] — note the restrictions on warrants for searches of law offices and members of the media outlined in chapter 6.

1 *Justices of the Peace Act*, R.S.O. 1990 c. J-4 s. 5 provides that every judge of the Supreme Court of Canada, the Federal Court of Canada, the Court of Appeal, the Superior Court of Justice, and every provincial court is a justice of the peace.
2 For a discussion of the reasonable grounds standard, see chapter 5.
3 "Offence-related property" means any property, within or outside Canada,
  a) by means or in respect of which an indictable offence under this Act is committed,
  b) that is used in any manner in connection with the commission of an indictable offence under this Act, or
  c) that is intended for use for the purpose of committing an indictable offence under this Act (*Criminal Code* s. 2).
4 For a discussion of the justification required for a night search, see, e.g., *R. v. Sutherland* (2000), 150 C.C.C. (3d) 231 (Ont. C.A.) at para. 15 *et seq*.
5 See, for example, *Descôteaux v. Mierzwinski*, [1982] 1 S.C.R. 860 at 899.

Statutory Power	Judicial Officer	Scope	Person to be Authorized	Special Requirements
				• Where the building, receptacle or place to be searched is in another territorial division, the justice may issue the warrant in like form modified according to the circumstances, and the warrant may be executed in that territorial division after it has been endorsed by a justice having jurisdiction in that territorial division (s. 487(2)). • An extra-territorial execution endorsement is sufficient authority to the peace officers or public officers to whom it was originally directed, and to all peace officers within the jurisdiction of the justice by whom it was endorsed, to execute the warrant and deal with the things seized in accordance with s. 489.1 or as otherwise provided by law (s. 487(4)). • Search warrants must specifically state on face of warrant the offence alleged to have been committed or else the warrant will be facially invalid: see Fontana p. 36 (*R. v. Solloway Mills and Company* (1930), 53 C.C.C. 261 (Alta. C.A.); *Rex v. La Vesque* (1918), 30 Can. C.C. 190, 42 D.L.R. 120, 45 N.B.R. 522 (N.B.S.C.A.D.). However, the authority for this requirement is strictly the common law, interpreting that the Form set out in the *Code* imposes legal requirements. *Quarae* whether these decisions still stand in the *Charter* era, given that the *Code* does not require such a recitation in the warrant; only Form 5 suggests the statement of an offence. • Section 487 and other warrants: Place to be searched should be fully described. The authorization to search will be limited to place it describes. A warrant authorizing the search of a house will not necessarily authorize the search of a detached garage[6] or a vehicle (unless parked in an attached garage or driveway).[7] • Section 487(1)(b) authorizes seizure of goods that the officer reasonably believes "will afford evidence" with respect to the commission of an offence. In *CanadianOxy Chemicals Ltd. v. Canada*,[8] the Supreme Court held that s. 487(1)(b) must be interpreted as having the widest possible scope, and permits the seizure of all relevant information and evidence, without the need for police officers to decide what is required for a prosecution. Search and seizure of evidence related to due diligence offence is also permitted under s. 487(1)(b): See *CanadianOxy Chemicals*, above. • See also the broader disclosure requirements listed under s. 186 Wiretap (such as the requirement to make full, fair and frank disclosure of all material facts, and the requirement to disclose the existence of all informants).

6   *R. v. LaPlante* (1987), 40 C.C.C. (3d) 63 (Sask. C.A.).
7   *R. v. Haley* (1986), 27 C.C.C. (3d) 454 (Ont. C.A.).
8   *CanadianOxy Chemicals Ltd. v. Canada (Attorney General)* (1999), 133 C.C.C. (3d) 426 (S.C.C.).

Appendix 1: Basic Search Powers (Criminal Code) • 307

Statutory Power	Judicial Officer	Scope	Person to be Authorized	Special Requirements
Search/seizure in exigent circumstances s. 487.11	N/A	Same as s. 487	Same as s. 487 (without a naming requirement for a public officer)	• Requires that the conditions for obtaining a s. 487 warrant exist, but permits a search or seizure where by reason of exigent circumstances it is impracticable to obtain one.[9]
Telewarrant *Criminal Code* s. 487.1	Justice of the Peace designated for the purpose by the chief judge of the provincial court having jurisdiction over the matter	Same as s. 487 or s. 256 (as the case may be)	Peace officer	Provides for application for and issuance of s. 487 and s. 256 warrants via telephone or other means of telecommunication (including fax). Several other warrant provisions adopt and incorporate the s. 487.1 telewarrant procedure.[10] Requires RPG to believe that: i) an indictable offence has been committed; ii) it would be impracticable to appear personally before a justice to make application for a warrant under ss. 487 or 256. The peace officer may submit an information on oath by telephone or other means of telecommunication to the designated justice. If the means of submission does not "produce a writing" (e.g., telephone), the information must be on oath (which may itself be administered by telecom), and the justice must record the information verbatim and file a record of it (certified as to date, time and contents) with the clerk of the court for the appropriate territorial jurisdiction as soon as is practical.

9 For a discussion of the definition of exigent circumstances, see chapter 4.
10 A s. 487 or s. 256-type telewarrant issues under the authority of s. 487.1, and is a s. 487.1 warrant. For sections that incorporate s. 487.1 procedures, the warrant issues under the underlying section, but remains a warrant under that section (e.g. note the wording of s. 487.092(4): "a warrant may be issued *under this section* on an information submitted by telephone ... and, for that purpose, s. 487.1 applies" [emphasis added]. Such warrants are not limited by requirements specific to s. 487.1, such as the limitation to indictable offences.

Statutory Power	Judicial Officer	Scope	Person to be Authorized	Special Requirements
				If the means of submission "produces a writing" (e.g., fax), the justice must file the writing (certified as to date and time) with the clerk of the court for the appropriate territorial jurisdiction as soon as is practical. A statement in writing that all matters contained in the information true to the peace officer's knowledge and belief satisfies the requirement that the information be under oath.
				The information (however submitted) must include a statement of: i) the circumstances that make it impracticable for the peace officer to appear personally before a justice; ii) the indictable offence alleged, the place or premises to be searched and the items alleged to be liable to seizure; iii) the peace officer's grounds for believing that items liable to seizure in respect of the offence alleged will be found in the place or premises to be searched; and iv) a statement as to any prior application for any other search warrant in respect of the same matter of which the peace officer has knowledge.
				Requires the justice to be satisfied that that the information: i) is in respect of an indictable offence and conforms to the requirements for such an information; ii) discloses reasonable grounds to dispense with an information presented personally and in writing; and iii) discloses reasonable grounds in accordance with s. 256(1) or s. 487(1)(a), (b) or (c), as the case may be, for the issuance of a warrant.
				The justice may issue a warrant under 487.1 conferring the same authority respecting search and seizure as would have been conferred has the peace officer appeared personally pursuant to ss. 487 or 256, as the case may be.
				The justice may require that the warrant be executed within a certain time period.
				Where a justice issues a telewarrant by a means that does not produce a writing: i) the justice must complete and sign the warrant, noting on its face the date, time and place of issuance; ii) the peace officer (on the direction of the justice) must complete, in duplicate, a facsimile[11] of the warrant, noting on its face name of the issuing justice and the date, time and place of issuance; and

11   For the purposes of this section, "facsimile" means a "reasonable copy" (taking into account the fact that two documents are being prepared in two locations by two people) without significant or misleading errors capable of prejudicing the accused (*R. v. Skin* (1988), 13 M.V.R. (2d) 130 (B.C. Co. Ct.)).

Statutory Power	Judicial Officer	Scope	Person to be Authorized	Special Requirements
				iii) the justice must cause the warrant to be filed with the clerk of the court for the appropriate territorial jurisdiction as soon as is practical.
				Where a justice issues a telewarrant by a means that produces a writing:
				i) the justice must complete and sign the warrant, noting on its face the date, time and place of issuance;
				ii) the justice must transmit the warrant to the peace officer (by the means of telecommunication);
				iii) the peace officer must procure another facsimile of the warrant; and
				iv) the justice must cause the warrant to be filed with the clerk of the court for the appropriate territorial jurisdiction as soon as is practical.
				The peace officer must, prior to entering the place to be searched or as soon as practicable thereafter, give a facsimile of the warrant to a person present and ostensibly in control of the place. If the place is unoccupied, the peace officer must on entering the place or as soon as practicable thereafter, cause a facsimile of the warrant to be suitably affixed in a prominent place within the place.
				Following issue of the warrant, the peace officer must, as soon as practicable but no more than 7 days after execution, file a written report with the clerk of the court for the appropriate territorial jurisdiction, which report must include:
				i) a statement of the date and time the warrant was executed, or if the warrant was not executed a statement of the reasons why it was not;
				ii) a statement of the things, if any, that were seized pursuant to the warrant and the location where they are being held; and
				iii) a statement of the things, if any, that were seized in addition to the things mentioned in the warrant and the location where they are being held, together with a statement of the peace officer's grounds for believing that those additional things had been obtained by, or used in, the commission of an offence.[12]

12 It is important to note that the officer would have authorization to seize items not mentioned in the warrant that were neither "obtained by" nor "used in" the commission of an offence, pursuant to several other statutory provisions (e.g., s. 489(1)(c) — "will afford evidence in respect of a [federal] offence"; and s. 492(1) — explosive substances, etc., suspected to be intended for an unlawful purpose). Note further that s. 492.1 specifically refers to the execution of a s. 487.1 warrant. Presumably, in such cases, a statement of the officer's grounds for believing he or she had authority to seize the item would satisfy the requirement.

Statutory Power	Judicial Officer	Scope	Person to be Authorized	Special Requirements
				The clerk of the court must take the peace officer's report together with the information and the warrant before a justice to be dealt with in the same manner as if the things were seized pursuant to a warrant obtained in person. On any challenge of a telewarrant search, the absence of the information or warrant (each signed and certified by the justice as required) (or a duplicate or facsimile of either of them) is, *prima facie* proof that the search or seizure was not authorized.

General warrant s. 487.01	Provincial Court, Superior Court, or s. 552 Judge	Permits the use of a "device, investigative technique or procedure" and the doing of "any thing", which, absent prior authorization, would contravene s. 8 of the *Charter*
		
		Applies to "information" (therefore potentially very broad scope)
			Peace officer	• Requires RPG to believe that:
				  i) a federal offence has been or *will be* committed; and
				  ii) "information" concerning the offence will be obtained through the authorized technique, etc.
				• Must establish:
				  i) that it is in the best interests of administration of justice to issue the warrant; and
				  ii) that no other provision of the *Criminal Code* or of any other federal Act would allow the investigative method.
				• Can authorize search or seizure in advance of the commission of an offence.
				• Can be issued authorize search for or seizure in advance of the commission of an offence.
				• Can issue for seizure of items that a peace officer believes *will be* in a place[13]
				• Cannot authorize interferences with bodily integrity.
				• Warrant shall contain such terms and conditions required to ensure that any search or seizure is reasonable in the circumstances.

13   *R. v. Noseworthy*, 166 C.C.C. (3d) 376 (Ont. C.A.). Both this power and the power to authorize searches in advance of the commission of an offence have sometimes been referred to as "anticipatory warrants" because the application is based on the peace officer's anticipation of a future state of affairs.

Appendix 1: Basic Search Powers (Criminal Code) • 311

Statutory Power	Judicial Officer	Scope	Person to be Authorized	Special Requirements
				• Video surveillance warrants where targets have a reasonable expectation of privacy are subject to the Part VI limits and authorization procedures for interceptions of communications (s. 487.01(5)). • Where a warrant authorizes the covert entry and search of a place, the warrant must specify a time (after execution) at which notice of such entry and search must be given.[14] • May be obtained by s. 487.1 telewarrant (s. 487.01(7)). • Extra-territorial execution governed by s. 487(2) and (4).

Tracking device s. 492.1[15]	Justice of the Peace	Tracking device	Peace officer; or
			
			Public officer appointed or designated to administer or enforce any federal or provincial law and whose duties include enforcement of any federal law, *provided* that the public officer is named in the warrant
				• Requires reasonable suspicion that
				  i) any federal offence has been or will be committed; and
				  ii) information relevant to the commission of the offence (including the whereabouts of any person) can be obtained through the use of a tracking device.
				• Can authorize tracking in advance of commission of offence.
				• Includes the authority to install, maintain and remove a tracking device "in or on anything," including anything "carried, used or worn" by a person, and to monitor the device.
				• The warrant may be valid for no longer than sixty days; however subsequent warrants may be issued.
				• On *ex parte* application in writing, the justice *may* authorize the covert removal of the tracking device after the expiration of the warrant under any terms or conditions considered advisable in the public interest, during any specified period of no more than sixty days.

Tracking device in exigent circumstances s. 487.11	N/A	Same as s. 492.1	Same as s. 492.1 (without a naming requirement for a public officer)	• Requires that the conditions for obtaining a s. 492.1 warrant exist, but by reason of exigent circumstances it is impracticable to obtain one.

14 The original period may be as long as the judge considers "reasonable in the circumstances" (with no statutory limit); the period may be extended on application, but no extension may exceed three years (s. 487.01(5.1) and (5.2)).

15 The warrantless use of a tracking device is unconstitutional: see *R. v. Wise* (1992), 70 C.C.C. (3d) 193 (S.C.C.).

Statutory Power	Judicial Officer	Scope	Person to be Authorized	Special Requirements
Dial number recorder and telephone records s. 492.2	Justice of the Peace	Dialled numbers (as opposed to the contents of communications) Telephone records	Peace officer; or Public officer appointed or designated to administer or enforce any federal or provincial law and whose duties include enforcement of any federal law, *provided* that the public officer is named in the warrant	• Requires reasonable suspicion, in writing, on oath, that: i) any federal offence has been or will be committed; and ii) information that would assist in the investigation of the offence could be obtained through the use of a dialled "number recorder" (DNR). • Includes the authority to install, maintain and remove the DNR in relation to any telephone or telephone line, and to monitor the device.[16] • The warrant may be valid for no longer than sixty days; however subsequent warrants may be issued. • May also obtain order that a person or body in lawful possession of telephone records (e.g., the phone company) supply the records (s. 492.2(2)), on same grounds as above. • Valid for up to 60 days, with further extensions available (ss. 492.2(3), 492.1 (2)(3)).

See also general warrant s. 487.01

---

16 Although the wiretap provisions in Part VI differentiate between "private communications" and "radio-based communications" (see, e.g., s. 184.5), there appears to be no reason why the s. 492.2 reference to telephone should not include both conventional and cellular telephones, at least with respect to 492.2(2).

APPENDIX 2: Interception of Communications (Wiretaps)

Statutory Power	Judicial Officer	Scope	Person to be Authorized	Special Requirements
General s. 186	Superior Court Judge or s. 552 Judge	Private communications[1]	Person designated by the Attorney General or Solicitor General, as the case may be (s. 186(5))	Available for certain listed offences only (see s. 183) Must establish: i) that it is in the best interests of justice to order the interception (at a minimum, this includes RPG to believe (a) that a specified offence has been or is being committed, and (b) that the interception would provide evidence of that offence[2]); and ii) the "investigative necessity"[3] of using an intercept. Application must be made *ex parte*, in writing and signed by the Attorney General of the province, the Solicitor General of Canada, or a specially designated agent (depending on the offence). Application to be accompanied by an affidavit of a peace officer or public officer containing (s. 185): i) the facts relied upon to justify the interception and the particulars of the offence;[4] ii) the type of private communication to be intercepted; iii) the names, addresses and occupations (each if known)[5] of all persons, the interception of

---

1 The provisions regarding interception of private communications apply *mutatis mutandis* to "radio-based telephone communications" (i.e., cellular phones), which do not fall within the definition of private communications (see s. 184.5(2)). Application may be made "at the same time" for the interception of private communications and radio-based cellular communications (s. 184.6).

2 *R. v. Garofoli* (1990), 60 C.C.C. (3d) 161 at 182 and 187; *R. v. Finlay and Grellette* (1985), 23 C.C.C. (3d) 48 (Ont. C.A.).

3 "Investigative necessity" is a convenient shorthand for the requirements of s. 186(1)(b). Although the wiretap need not be the absolute last resort, "[t]here must be, practically speaking, *no other reasonable alternative method of investigation*, in the circumstances of the particular criminal inquiry" [emphasis in original] (*R. v. Araujo*, [2000] 2 S.C.R. 992 at para. 29).

4 Full, fair and frank disclosure of all material facts is the guideline for officers to follow in deciding what information must be placed in the affidavit: see *Dalglish v. Jarvie* (1850), 2 Mac. & G. 231, 42 E.R. 89; *R. v. Kensington Income Tax Commissioners*, [1917] 1 K.B. 486 (C.A.); *Re Church of Scientology and the Queen (No.6)* (1987), 31 C.C.C. (3d) 449 (Ont. C.A.) at 528; *U.S.A. v. Friedland*, [1996] O.J. No. 4399 (Gen. Div) at paras. 26–29; all as cited in *R. v. Araujo* (2000), 149 C.C.C. (3d) 449 (S.C.C.) at 469.

5 See *R. v. Chesson* (1988), 43 C.C.C. (3d) 353 (S.C.C.) on definition of "known": someone whose existence is known and whose communications the officers believe on reasonable grounds may assist in the investigation. The name of the person is not necessary; a description is sufficient.

313

Interception of Communications (Wiretaps)

Statutory Power	Judicial Officer	Scope	Person to be Authorized	Special Requirements
				whose private communications there are RPG to believe may assist in the investigation of the offence;[6] iv) a general description of the nature and location of the place (if known) where the communications are to be intercepted;[7] v) a general description of the manner of interception proposed; vi) the history of prior applications (including denied and withdrawn applications); vii) the period for which the authorization is requested; and viii) whether other investigative techniques have been tried and failed, why it appears that such techniques would be unlikely to succeed, or what urgent circumstances make it impractical to investigate by other means. • Strict limits on authorizations for solicitor's office, residence or place ordinarily used for solicitor-client consultation (s. 186(2) and (3)). • Includes the authority to "install, maintain or remove the device covertly" (s. 186(5.1)).[8] • Requirements for the contents of the authorization listed at s. 186(4). • May be renewed on application subject to the requirements in s. 186(6) and (7).[9]

6   A "basket" clause may be inserted in the order allowing for the interception of "unknown persons" (unknown at the time of the application) if it is believed on reasonable grounds that they are acting in concert with the targets of the investigation to commit an offence. See *R. v. Thompson* (1990), 59 C.C.C. (3d) 225 (S.C.C.) [*Thompson*].

7   The order for interception may also include "resort to" clauses, allowing for the interception of communications at locations other than the known places, if resorted to by the targets of the investigation. See *ibid.* at 257–67; see also *R. v. Grabowski* (1985), 22 C.C.C. (3d) 449 (S.C.C.) [*Grabowski*], where such a clause failed by reason of being overly broad.

8   It would appear that the authority confirmed by this provision is intended to apply to all authorizations under the various interception provisions in Part VI; Authorization to surreptitiously enter private premises to install and remove method to intercept the communications is permissible, with appropriate conditions if necessary: see *Reference re an application for an Authorization* (1985), 15 C.C.C. (3d) 466 at 279 (S.C.C.).

9   Renewals are available if the only thing changing in the application is the timeline of the proposed interception; if anything more has changed, such as becoming aware of new targets or locations, new authorizations must be obtained. See *R. v. Pleich* (1980), 55 C.C.C. (2d) 13 (Ont. C.A.); *Thompson*, above note 6; *R. v. Moore*; *R. v. Bogdanich* (1993), 81 C.C.C. (3d) 161 (B.C.C.A.).

Interception of Communications (Wiretaps)

Statutory Power	Judicial Officer	Scope	Person to be Authorized	Special Requirements

				• No authorization (or renewal) may exceed sixty days.[10]
				• On *ex parte* application in writing, the judge *may* authorize the covert removal of the device after the expiration of the warrant under any terms or conditions considered advisable in the public interest, during any specified period of no more than sixty days.
				• May be executed anywhere in Canada, provided that if execution outside the province of issue will
				  i) require entry into private property in the other province, or
				  ii) an assistance order under s. 487.02 in respect of a person in the other province is required, then the officer must apply to a judge in the other province, who may confirm the authorization (s. 188.1).
				• Order must have minimization conditions with respect to whose communications are intercepted, especially with regard to the privacy interests of third parties (see *R. v. Thompson*[11]).
				
				Naming all known targets of the investigation: A person is known if there are reasonable grounds to believe his or her communications will assist the investigation (see section 185(1)(e): *R. v. Garofoli*). It is not necessary that a person's name be known before they are considered known targets — a physical or general description of the person will suffice. If a known person is not named in the authorization, that person's communications may be inadmissible at trial; in *R. v. Vanweenan and Chesson*,[12] the Supreme Court held that the intercepted communications of known target who was not named in the authorization were inadmissible under the former (now repealed) s. 178.16(1) which created an automatic exclusionary rule for intercepted private communication that were not lawfully made.[13] Although intercepting the communications of a known but unnamed target will no longer result in automatic exclusion of the evidence, doing so will likely result in a breach of s. 8 (as it would not be authorized by law), and may be subject to exclusion under s. 24(2).
				
				• Unknown targets and places: It is permissible to include clauses allowing for interception of unknown targets if reasonable grounds to believe the unknown person acting in concert with the known targets, and that their

10 With the exception, however, of criminal organization related and terrorism offences, for which offences the limit is extended to one year (s. 186.1).
11 *Thompson*, above note 6.
12 *R. v. Vanweenan and Chesson* (1988), 43 C.C.C. (3d) 353 (S.C.C.).
13 *Ibid.* at 368–69.

Interception of Communications (Wiretaps)

Statutory Power	Judicial Officer	Scope	Person to be Authorized	Special Requirements
				• conversations will assist investigation (see *R. v. Thompson*;[14] *R. v. Grabowski*[15]). • Section 187 only authorizes the interception of communications and not the interception of the number phoned (police must apply for a separate order for the number recorder information under s. 492.2: see *R. v. Fegan* (1990), 80 C.C.C. (3d) 356 (Ont. C.A.)) • The affiant must specifically pledge his or her belief in the truth of the information set out in the affidavit accompanying the application (see *R. v. Pastro* (1988), 42 C.C.C. (3d) 485 (Sask. C.A.); *R. v. Field* (unreported, April 12, 1995, Ont. Gen. Div.); *contra*, see *R. v. Yorke* (1992), 77 C.C.C. (3d) 529 (N.S.C.A.)). • The existence of all informants must be disclosed (see *R. v. Brunelle* (1990), 55 C.C.C. (3d) 347 (B.C.S.C.).
Criminal organizations s. 186(1.1)	Superior Court Judge or s. 552 Judge	Private communications	Person designated by the Attorney General or Solicitor General, as the case may be (s. 186(5))	• Available only for criminal organization related offences or terrorism offences (s. 186(1.1)). • Prerequisites and procedures are generally the same as for the general s. 186 authorization, however, no need to show investigative necessity (ss. 186(1.1) and 185(1.1)).[16] • No authorization (or renewal) may exceed one year (s. 186.1).
Exigent circumstances (with authorization) s. 188	Specially designated Superior Court or s. 552 Judge	Private communications	Person designated by the Attorney General or Solicitor General, as the case may be (s. 186(5))	• Urgent circumstances where authorization under s. 186 could not be obtained with reasonable diligence. • Application to be made by a peace officer specially designated for the purposes of s. 188[17] • Duration of the authorization may not exceed 36 hours. • May be executed anywhere in Canada, provided that if execution outside the province

14   *Thompson*, above note 6.
15   *Grabowski*, above note 7.
16   "Investigative necessity" is not a constitutional requirement, and the absence of such a requirement for a s. 186(1.1) authorization does not violate s. 8 of the *Charter* (*R. v. Pangman*, [2000] 8 W.W.R. 536 (Man. Q.B.)).
17   Must be oath if possible. See *R. v. Galbraith* (1989), 49 C.C.C. (3d) 178 (Alta. C.A.); see *R. v. Laudicina* (199), 53 C.C.C. (3d) 281 (Ont. H.C.).

Interception of Communications (Wiretaps)

Statutory Power	Judicial Officer	Scope	Person to be Authorized	Special Requirements
				of issue will: i) require entry into private property in the other province, or ii) an assistance order under s. 487.02 in respect of a person in the other province is required, then the officer must apply to a judge in the other province, who may confirm the authorization (s. 188.1). • Trial judge has the discretion to exclude any evidence obtained through a s. 188 authorization where a prior application was based on the same facts and in relation to the same person(s) or offence (s. 188(5)).
One-party consent s. 184.2[18]	Provincial Court Judge, Superior Court Judge or s. 552 Judge	Private communications where one party consents	Peace officer, or Public officer appointed or designated to administer or enforce any federal or provincial law and whose duties include enforcement of any federal law	Application is to be made *ex parte* in writing, accompanied by a sworn affidavit containing: i) RPG to believe that a federal offence has been or _will_ be committed; ii) the particulars of the offence; iii) the name of the person who consented to the interception; iv) the period for which the authorization is requested; and v) if a previous authorization has been granted under this s. or s. 186, the particulars of the prior authorization. Requires (these items should be explained in the affidavit as well): i) RPG to believe that a federal offence has been or _will_ be committed; ii) the consent of a party to the communication to the interception;[19] iii) RPG to believe that information concerning the offence will be obtained through the interception.

---

18 In *R. v. Duarte*, [1990] 1 S.C.R. 30 at 60, 53 C.C.C. (3d) 1, the Supreme Court held that the warrantless interception of private communications, even where one party consents, is a violation of s. 8. Prior authorization is required.

19 Therefore it is not subject to the restrictions in s. 193.

Interception of Communications (Wiretaps)

Statutory Power	Judicial Officer	Scope	Person to be Authorized	Special Requirements
				The order must specify (these facts should also be in the affidavit): i) the offence in respect of which the communications may be intercepted ii) the type of private communication to be intercepted iii) the identity of the persons, if known, whose communications will be intercepted iv) the place where the communications may be intercepted, if known v) the manner of intercept on that may be used vi) the terms and conditions advisable in the public interest vii) the period of validity of the order (not to exceed 60 days). • Available for any federal offence. • No need to show investigative necessity.[20] • Authorization may not exceed sixty days, except for criminal organization related or terrorism offences, for which the limit is extended to one year (s. 186.1). • May be obtained by telecom (s. 184.3). • May be executed anywhere in Canada, provided that if execution outside the province of issue will (i) require entry into private property in the other province, or (ii) an assistance order under s. 487.02 in respect of a person in the other province is required, then the officer must apply to a judge in the other province, who may confirm the authorization (s. 188.1).
To prevent bodily harm s. 184.1	N/A	Private communications (interception for the purpose of	An "agent of the state"[21]	• Consent of one of the parties to the communication.[22] • Reasonable grounds to believe that there is a risk of bodily harm to the consenting party.

---

20 The absence of the "investigative necessity" requirement for a one-party consent authorization does not violate s. 8 of the *Charter* (*R. v. Bordage* (2000), 146 C.C.C. (3d) 549 (Que. C.A.)).
21 Defined in s. 184.1(4) as "a peace officer; and (b) a person acting under the authority of, or in cooperation with, a peace officer."
22 Therefore it is not subject to the restrictions in s. 193.

Appendix 2: Interception of Communications (Wiretap) • 319

Interception of Communications (Wiretaps)

Statutory Power	Judicial Officer	Scope	Person to be Authorized	Special Requirements
		preventing bodily harm to the consenting person)		• Recordings, transcripts and notes must be destroyed as soon as is practicable if nothing in the interception indicates that bodily harm has occurred or is likely to occur. • Evidentiary use of the intercepted communication is limited to proceedings in which actual, attempted or threatened bodily harm is alleged (including proceedings in respect of an application for an authorization under Part VI, or in respect of a search warrant or warrant for the arrest of any person).
Exigent circumstances (warrantless) s. 184.4	N/A	Private Communications	Peace Officer	• Reasonable grounds to believe that in urgent circumstances authorization could not be obtained with reasonable diligence. • Reasonable grounds to believe that the interception is necessary to prevent an unlawful act that would cause serious harm to any person or to property. • One of the parties to the communication is the person who would perform the unlawful act or is the intended victim of the harm.

See also general warrant (includes video surveillance) s. 487.01

See also dial number recorder s. 492.2

Additional Provisions

Wiretaps: sealing of the "packet" *Criminal Code* s. 187	Provides that "all documents relating to an application made pursuant to any provision of [Part VI] are confidential." All such documents (with the exception of the authorization itself[23]) are to be placed in a packet and sealed by the judge to whom the application is made, immediately upon determination of the application, and the packet is to be kept in the custody of the court to be dealt with only in accordance with s. 187(1.2)–(1.5).[24]

23 Where the authorization is granted by telecom (pursuant to s. 184.3), the original authorization is to be sealed in the packet, and the facsimile is to be retained by the applicant (s. 187(1.1)).

24 For procedure re editing and disclosure of information see *R. v. Garofoli* (1990), 60 C.C.C. (3d) 161 (S.C.C.); full disclosure is the general rule regarding disclosure of the information in support of an authorization, subject to the need to maintain privilege: see *R. v. Durette* (1994), 72 C.C.C. (3d) 421 (Ont. C.A.).

	Additional Provisions
Wiretaps: disclosure of communications *Criminal Code* s. 193	Prohibits the wilful use or disclosure of (a) any of the contents or meaning of intercepted private communications, or (b) the existence of an intercepted private communication, without the express consent of the originator or intended recipient, *except*: i) for the purpose of giving evidence under oath in a legal proceeding; ii) in the course of a criminal investigation, provided that the interception was lawful; iii) as may be required by ss. 189 (notice of intention to produce evidence) or 190 (further particulars); iv) as a necessary incident of operating a telephone, telegraph or other public communication service or Government of Canada radio frequency spectrum management; v) to a peace officer or prosecutor in Canada or to an official foreign investigator or prosecutor, provided that the disclosure is intended to be in the interests of the administration of justice in Canada or elsewhere; or vi) to the Canadian Security Intelligence Service (CSIS) for the purpose of enabling CSIS to perform its functions. The above restrictions cease to apply once the information has been lawfully disclosed for the purpose of giving evidence in a legal proceeding. By its terms, it does not apply to ss. 184.1 (one-party consent — bodily harm) or 184.2 (one-party consent), but applies, with necessary modification, to "radio-based telephone communication" (i.e., cellular phone) interceptions (s. 193.1(2)).
Wiretaps: written notification to object *Criminal Code* s. 196	The Attorney General of the province in which the s. 185(1) interception application was made (or the Solicitor General of Canada, where applicable) must: i) within 90 days after the end of the period (or renewal period) for which an interception was authorized; or ii) within such other period as was fixed pursuant to s. 185(3) (extension at initial application), s. 196(3) (extension: ongoing investigation(s)), or s. 196(5) (extension: criminal organization and terrorism);[25] notify in writing the person who was the object of the interception (in the manner prescribed by regulation) and certify to the authorizing court that the person has been so notified.

25 Although s. 196(1) does not refer to extensions under s. 196(5) (and therefore would preclude them), this appears to be a drafting error, because s. 196(5) is clearly intended to authorize such extensions.

APPENDIX 3: Offence-Specific Authorizations (*Criminal Code*)

Statutory Power	Judicial Officer	Scope	Person to be Authorized	Special Requirements
Gaming-, betting- or bawdy-house s. 199(1) (See also ss. 487 and 487.01)	Justice of the Peace	Any evidence of the listed gaming-, betting–or bawdy-house offences[1]	Peace officer	• Available for listed gaming-, betting- and bawdy-house offences. • Requires RPG, set out in writing, on oath, to believe that a listed offence is being committed. • May be executed by night. • Authorizes taking "found-ins" into custody. • Triggers *in rem* forfeiture proceedings for seized items.
Gaming-house (*warrantless*) s. 199(2) (See also, s. 489(2))	N/A	Any evidence of a common gaming-house[2]	Peace officer	• Available only for common gaming-house (not for betting- or bawdy-house). • Appears to be a seizure power rather than a search power. • Authorizes taking "found-ins" into custody. • Triggers *in rem* forfeiture proceedings for seized items.

Obscenity s. 164 (See also ss. 487 and 487.01)	Judge of a "court" as defined in s. 164(8)	Obscene publications, crime comics or child pornography	*Criminal Code* is silent — presumably a peace officer, given the nature of the warrant	• Requires RPG on oath to believe that:
				  i) an obscene publication or crime comic is kept in the premises for sale or distribution; or
				  ii) child pornography is kept in the premises.
				• Triggers *in rem* forfeiture proceedings for seized items.

Hate Propaganda s. 320 (See also ss. 487 and 487.01)	Judge of a "court" as defined in s. 320(8)	Hate propaganda	*Criminal Code* is silent — presumably a peace officer, given the nature of the warrant	• Requires RPG on oath to believe that a hate propaganda publication is kept in the premises for sale or distribution. • Proceedings require the consent of the Attorney General. • Triggers *in rem* forfeiture proceedings. • Appeals of forfeiture orders governed by s. 320(6)

1 Note the restrictions on seizure of telecommunications equipment owned by a provider of telecom services to the public as evidence of certain "vice" offences, unless the equipment has the capacity to record a communication (*Criminal Code* s. 199(6), (7)).
2 See note [note to 199(1) scope].

Offence-Specific Authorizations (Criminal Code)

Statutory Power	Judicial Officer	Scope	Person to be Authorized	Special Requirements

Hate propaganda (Internet) s. 320.1	Judge of a "court" as defined in s. 320(8)	Hate propaganda on publicly accessible computer systems	N/A — court order	• Used to "shut down" offending websites.
				• Requires RPG on oath to believe that there is hate propaganda (or data that makes hate propaganda available) stored on and made available to the public on a computer system.
				• Proceedings require the consent of the Attorney General.
				• Judge may order the "custodian" of the computer to:
				  i) give an electronic copy of the material to the Court;
				  ii) ensure that the material is no longer stored on and available through the computer; and
				  iii) provide information to identify and locate the person who posted the material.
				• Court must cause notice of the proceedings to be given to the poster of the material, who may then show cause why the material should not be deleted.[3]
				• Appeals of deletion orders governed by s. 320(6).
				• Note s. 320(9) delaying the effect of deletion/return orders until final appeals exhausted

Lumber — unlawfully held Criminal Code s. 339(3)	N/A	Lumber (defined in s. 339(6)) Not a seizure power; search power only	Peace officer	Requires reasonable suspicion that lumber (a) owned by any person and (b) bearing the registered timber mark of that person is kept or detained in or on any place without the knowledge or consent of the owner. Authorizes the entry into or on that place to ascertain whether or not lumber is detained there without the knowledge or consent of the owner.[4]

---

3 If the poster of the material does not respond to the notice, the proceedings may continue *ex parte*. Regardless of whether the poster responds, it appears that the "custodian of the computer," assuming he or she is not the poster of the material, does not have standing to show cause why the material should not be deleted.

4 Presumably this provision could not apply to dwelling-houses: see *R. v. Silveira* (1995) 97 C.C.C. (3d) 450 (S.C.C.); *R. v. Feeney*, [1997] 2 S.C.R. 13; *R. v. Grant* (1993), 84 C.C.C. (3d) 173 (S.C.C.).

Appendix 3: Offence-Specific Authorizations (Criminal Code) • 323

Offence-Specific Authorizations (Criminal Code)

Statutory Power	Judicial Officer	Scope	Person to be Authorized	Special Requirements
Valuable minerals — unlawful possession Criminal Code s. 395	Justice of the Peace	Valuable minerals (defined in s. 2 — essentially a mineral, including precious metals and gemstones, the value of which exceeds $100 per kilogram)	Peace officer; or Public officer appointed or designated to administer or enforce any federal or provincial law and whose duties include enforcement of any federal law, *provided* that the public officer is named in the warrant	Requires RPG set out in writing, on oath, to believe that, contrary to any federal Act, any valuable mineral is deposited in a place or held by a person. Requires information in writing, under oath. Justice may issue a warrant authorizing the search of any of the places or persons[5] mentioned in the information. Anything seized pursuant to this warrant must be brought before the justice who must order: i) that it be detained for the purposes of an inquiry or a trial; or ii) if it is not to be so detained, (a) that it be restored to the owner, or (b) if the owner cannot be ascertained, that it be forfeited to Her Majesty in right of the province in which the proceedings take place.
Keeping cockpit Criminal Code s. 447	N/A	Cocks (undefined in Code, type of bird not specified) Seizure power only; not a search power	Peace Officer	Seizure power only. Authorizes seizure of cocks found in a cockpit or on premises where a cockpit is located. The peace officer must take the seized cocks before a justice who must order them destroyed.
Counterfeit money and counterfeiting tools Criminal Code s. 462(2)	N/A	Counterfeit money, counterfeit tokens of value and tools, etc., for the making thereof	Peace officer	Seizure power only. All items subject to this section "belong to Her Majesty." Anything seized shall be sent to the Minister of Finance, but any item required as evidence in any proceedings may be retained until no longer required.

5   Note that this provision is unusual, in that it permits a search of the person. Few other *Criminal Code* investigative orders do so: s. 256 (blood sample — impaired driving causing injury or death), the various DNA provisions and s. 487.092 (bodily impressions).

Offence-Specific Authorizations (*Criminal Code*)

Statutory Power	Judicial Officer	Scope	Person to be Authorized	Special Requirements
Terrorism *Criminal Code* s. 83.13 (see also ss. 487 and 487.01)	Federal Court Judge	Terrorist property: seizure, restraint, and management orders	Peace officer, or a person named in the warrant	Requires RPG that property that is i) owned or controlled by (or on behalf of) a terrorist group, or ii) that has been or will be used to carry out or facilitate terrorist activity (s. 83.14), is in the building, place or receptacle to be searched. Application must be made *ex parte* in writing by the Attorney General and reviewed by the judge in private. For property situated in Canada, authorizes the issuance of a warrant for a search of the place and seizure of the listed property, and of any other property the officer reasonably believes would be subject to forfeiture under s. 83.14; triggers *in rem* forfeiture proceedings. For property situated outside of Canada, authorizes a restraint order prohibiting anyone from dealing with any interest in the property (except as may be permitted in the order). Authorizes the issuance of management orders to maintain or destroy property. Property of little or no value may be ordered destroyed.

APPENDIX 4: Additional *Criminal Code* Powers and Restrictions

Telewarrant *Criminal Code* s. 487.1	Provides for application for and issuance of s. 487 and s. 256 warrants via telephone or other means of telecommunication (including fax).[1] Several other warrant provisions adopt and incorporate the s. 487.1 telewarrant procedure.[1] For a description of the requirements for s. 487.1, see Appendix 1.
Extraterritorial execution: "backing" *Criminal Code* s. 487(2), (4)	Several warrant provisions adopt and incorporate the s. 487(2) and (4) extraterritorial "backing" provisions, allowing for the execution of warrants outside the territorial jurisdiction of the issuing justice. See s. 487, Appendix 1.
Extension of powers outside Canada: special jurisdiction *Criminal Code* s. 477.3	Extends all of the powers of arrest, entry, search or seizure or other powers that could be exercised in Canada to situations covered by s. 477.1 in relation to a violation of federal law committed outside of Canada, i) within the "exclusive economic zone" of Canada, if the offence is committed by (a) a person who is in the exclusive economic zone of Canada in connection with the natural resources of the exclusive economic zone of Canada, or (b) a person who is a Canadian citizen or permanent resident of Canada; ii) committed in a place in or above the continental shelf of Canada and that is an offence in that place by virtue of s. 20 of the *Oceans Act*; iii) that is committed outside Canada on board or by means of a ship registered or licensed, or for which an identification number has been issued, pursuant to any Act of Parliament; iv) that is committed outside Canada in the course of hot pursuit; or v) that is committed outside the territory of any state by a Canadian citizen.
Duty to carry/produce warrant *Criminal Code* s. 29(1)	Section 29(1) places a duty on any person executing a warrant to have that warrant with him or her (where it is feasible to do so), and to produce it if so requested. See chapter 7 for a detailed explanation of the requirement to produce the warrant.

---

[1] A s. 487 or s. 256-type telewarrant issues under the authority of s. 487.1, and *is* a s. 487.1 warrant. For sections that incorporate s. 487.1 procedures, the warrant issues under the underlying section, and remains a warrant under that section (e.g., note the wording of s. 487.092(4): "a warrant may be issued *under this section* on an information submitted by telephone ... and, for that purpose, s. 487.1 applies" [emphasis added]). Such warrants are not limited by requirements specific to s. 487.1, such as the limitation to indictable offences.

Additional *Criminal Code* Powers and Restrictions

Duty to carry/produce warrant *Criminal Code* s. 471.1(7), (8)	Section 471.1(7) requires that on execution of a warrant issued by telephone or other means of telecommunication (other than a s. 256 warrant), the peace officer must, before entering the place to be searched, or as soon as practicable thereafter, give a facsimile to any person present and ostensibly in control of the place. Pursuant to s. 471.1(8), if the place is unoccupied, the peace officer must on entering the place or as soon as practicable thereafter, cause a facsimile of the warrant to be suitably affixed in a prominent place within the place.
Knock/announce requirement	See chapter 7 for a discussion of the requirement that officers executing a search of a dwelling house knock and identify themselves prior to entry. See also section 529.4, which permits the omission of the prior announcement in certain arrest situations.
Use of force *Criminal Code* s. 25	Section 25(1) permits everyone who is required or authorized by law to do anything in the administration or the enforcement of the law is justified in using as much force as is necessary if acting on reasonable grounds in doing what he is required or authorized to do. Section 25(2) protects persons acting in good faith while executing a process that is later discovered to be defective if they use force in effecting the process. Section 25(3) permits the use of force likely to cause grievous bodily harm or death unless necessary for self-preservation or the preservation of someone under the person's protection from death or grievous bodily harm. Sections 25(4) and (5) deal with the use of force in situations of arrest or escaping prisoners. See also chapter 7.
Law-office search (with s. 487 warrant)[2]	Warrant should not issue for documents known to be privileged, or if other *reasonable alternatives* to search exist. Any documents seized under the warrant *must be sealed* before being examined. The lawyer, client, or representative of the Bar should be contacted and oversee sealing of documents. Documents may not be examined until privilege claim determined. See *Lavallee, Rackel & Heintz v. Canada (Attorney General)*. Also note the restrictions on wiretapping where solicitor-client communications may be involved (s. 186(2)). See also chapter 6 for a detailed list of common law requirements for law office searches.

2   Note that s. 488.1, dealing with examination and seizure of documents in the possession of a lawyer, was ruled unconstitutional, leaving s. 487 (subject to additional judicial restrictions) as the principal statutory authority for law office searches. See *Lavallee, Rackel & Heintz v. Canada (Attorney General)*; *White, Ottenheimer & Baker v. Canada (Attorney General)*; *R. v. Fink* (2002), 167 C.C.C. (3d) 1 (S.C.C.).

Additional *Criminal Code* Powers and Restrictions

Media search (with s. 487 warrant)[3]	The justice of the peace must strike a balance between the state's interest in the investigation and the media's right to privacy in the course of newsgathering and news dissemination, with a view to the role that the media play in society. Alternative means of obtaining the material should ordinarily be considered. If the information has already been published, this will weigh in favour of authorizing the search. The justice should consider imposing conditions to avoid undue interference with the media. See also chapter 4, "Media Searches" for a more detailed list of requirements.
Seizure at financial institution: books and records *Canada Evidence Act* s. 29(7)	Warrants authorizing the search or seizure of items from a "financial institution" authorize (with respect to the "books or records of the institution") only the inspection and or copying of such documents *unless* the warrant specifically indicates that the restrictions in s. 29(7) of the *Canada Evidence Act* are not to limit the search authorized therein. (There is no restriction on the seizure of items that are not "books or records of the institution."). *Criminal Code* s. 490 (Detention of Seized Items) does not apply to any such copies taken.
Assistance orders *Criminal Code* s. 487.02	The judge or justice who: i) gives an authorization under ss. 184.2 (Interception with Consent), 184.3 (Interception with Consent: Telewarrant), 186 (Interception: General, Criminal Org. or Terrorism) or 188 (Interception: Exigent Circumstances); ii) grants a *Criminal Code* warrant; or iii) makes an order under s. 492.2(2) (Dial Number Recorder) *may* order any person to provide assistance where the person's assistance may reasonably be required to give effect to the authorization, warrant or order. See also chapter 7, "Who Can Execute and Assist in Executing the Warrant."

3 The Supreme Court of Canada placed constitutional limits on searches of media outlets in *Attorney-General of Quebec v. Canadian Broadcasting Corp.* (1991), 67 C.C.C. (3d) 428 (S.C.C.).
4 *Ibid.* at 533–35.

Additional *Criminal Code* Powers and Restrictions

Assistance in execution of warrant	A person authorized to execute a s. 487 warrant may be assisted in executing the warrant by persons who are not named in the warrant or peace officers, provided that the authorized person remains "in control of" and "responsible and accountable" for the execution.[5] Similar rulings have been made with regard to comparable warrant, order and authorization provisions.[6] See also chapter 7, "Who Can Execute and Assist in Executing the Warrant."
Seizure of items not listed in the warrant *Criminal Code* s. 489(1) Seizure of items in course of duties s. 489 (2)	During the execution of a warrant,[7] or while otherwise acting in the course a peace officer or public officer's duties, s. 489(1) authorizes the seizure of anything[8] the person reasonably believes: i) has been obtained by commission of any federal offence; ii) has been used in the commission of any federal offence; or iii) will afford evidence in respect of a federal offence. See also chapter 8, "The Plain View Doctrine."
Seizure of explosives *Criminal Code* s. 492(1)	During the execution of a warrant under ss. 487 or 487.1, it authorizes the seizure of any "explosive substance"[9] the person suspects is intended to be used for an unlawful purpose. Requires the removal of the explosive substance to a place of safety, and its detention until a Superior Court judge orders a disposition.

5   *R. v. B. (J.E.)* (1989) 52 C.C.C. (3d) 224 (N.S.C.A.).
6   See *ibid.* at 232 *et seq.* for examples. Presumably, this analysis would extend to all comparable warrants and authorizations, subject to the requirements of the specific statutory provision.
7   This power may not be limited to the execution of *Criminal Code* warrants. Compare s. 489(1) (i.e., "every person who executes a warrant may …") to the wording of other sections (e.g., s. 489.1(1): "a warrant *issued under this Act*" [emphasis added]).
8   Restricted in relation to telecommunications equipment by *Criminal Code* s. 199(6).
9   Defined in s. 2.

Appendix 4: Additional Criminal Code Powers and Restrictions • 329

Additional *Criminal Code* Powers and Restrictions

Detention of seized goods *Criminal Code* s. 490	Provides a procedure for the detention of goods seized pursuant to a *Criminal Code* warrant or under ss. 489 or 487.11.
	1) First, an officer must file a Report to Justice under s. 489.1 following the seizure of property under a *Criminal Code* warrant or under s. 489 or s. 487.11 of the *Code* (s. 487.1) (unless there is not issue as to ownership, and goods are being returned to the owner).
	2) Then, a justice must issue a detention order in relation to those items if the prosecutor or peace officer satisfies the justice that the items are required for the purpose of any investigation or criminal proceeding, or else return the goods to the lawful owner (if known) (s. 490 (1)(a)(b)).
	3) An order of detention under s. 490(1) remains in effect for only 3 months, unless proceedings are instituted in which the thing detained may be required, or having regard to the nature of the investigation, the justice makes a further order for further detention for a specified period (on notice to the person from whom the thing was seized) (s. 490(2)(a)(b)), or if the person from whom the thing was seized consents in writing to its detention for a specified period (s. 490(3.1)).
	4) The cumulative periods of detention on applications for further detention cannot exceed one year unless proceedings are instituted, or a judge of the Superior Court decides (on notice to the person from whom the thing was seized) having regard to the complex nature of the investigation that further detention is warranted for a specified period. (s. 490(3)).
	5) If the court retains the items ordered detained, once the accused is commit to stand trial, the items shall be forwarded to the superior court (s. 490(4)).
	6) If the period of detention has not expired, but the prosecution or police determines that detention of the goods is no longer necessary, the prosecutor or police must apply to a justice or judge of the Superior Court (if that court made the order under (3)) for an order under s. 490(9) returning the goods to the lawful owner, if known, or forfeiting the items to the Crown if possession by person from whom it was seized is unlawful or they were not seized from a person and the lawful owner is unknown (s. 490(9)).
	7) If the periods of detention have expired, and no proceedings have been instituted, the prosecutor or police must apply for an order either returning the goods to the lawful owner or for an order of forfeiture or for an order of further detention under s. 490(9.1) if the items are required for the investigation or future proceedings (s. 490(6)).
	8) A person from whom a thing was seized may apply to a justice or judge for the return of his or her property under s. 490(9) if the period of detention has expired, on notice to the Crown (s. 490(7)), or prior to the expiration of a detention period if hardship would result (s. 490(8)).
	9) The lawful owner of the property may apply under s. 490(10) for return of goods seized or payment if goods forfeited (s. 490(10(d)) at any time (on notice to the Crown), if the property was seized from another person, if the periods of detention

	Additional *Criminal Code* Powers and Restrictions
	have expired and proceedings have not instituted or if the items are not required for further investigation or potential proceedings if the periods of detention have not expired. (490(11)).
	10) Nothing can be returned or forfeited until 30 days after an order of forfeiture or return, or until the expiry of any appeal undertaken or application made with respect to those things.
	11) The crown, police or custodian of a document seized may copy any documents before they are brought to court for detention, or forfeited, or returned, and any true copy of the document has the same effect in evidence as the original of the document (s. 490(13)(14)).
	12) A person with an interest in any item ordered detained under s. 490 can apply to a justice examine the items (on notice to the Attorney General) (s. 490(15)). This order may include the right to make copies of any documents, see *R. v. Sutherland* (1977). 38 C.C.C. (2d) 252 (Ont. Co. Ct.); but see contra *R. v. Labrador Tool Supply Ltd.* (1982), 3 C.C.C. (3d) 269 (Nfld. S.C.T.D.). An order to examine can be on such terms as a justice deems necessary or desirable to safeguard and preserve the items (s. 490(16)).
	13) Appeal rights lie from orders under ss. 490 (8) (9) (9.1) or (11) to the court of appeal for summary conviction matters (as defined in s. 812) (s. 490(17)).
	14) Any period of notice can be waived by the opposite side (s. 490(18)).
Detention of perishable things *Criminal Code* s. 490.01	If perishable items are seized under the *Code*, the items may be (a) returned to the lawful owner or possessor; (b) on *ex parte* order of a justice, dispose of it and give the proceeds to the lawful owner if not a party to an offence in relation to the thing, or keep the proceeds if the lawful owner cannot be ascertained; or (c) on *ex parte* order of a justice, destroy the thing.
Forfeiture of offence-related property *Criminal Code* s. 490.1	1) Person must be convicted of an indictable offence under the *Criminal Code*.
	2) Notice must be given under s. 490.4(1–2) to any person with an interest in the property; if the property is a dwelling-house, notice must also be given to any residents of the house who are immediate family members of the person charged or convicted (s. 490.4(1–2)).
	3) Court to be satisfied that property is "offence-related property": property either inside or outside Canada, by means of or in respect of which an indictable offence under the *Code* is committed, used in connection with the commission of an indictable offence under the *Code*, or intended for use in committing an indictable offence under the *Code* (s. 2).
	4) Court must be satisfied that offence was committed in relation to that property.

Additional Criminal Code Powers and Restrictions

	5) Property shall be forfeited to either to Attorney General of the province that prosecuted the offence for disposal by Solicitor General of that province, or to the Attorney General of Canada if offence not prosecuted by a province, for disposal by appropriate designated person, unless forfeiture would be disproportionate to the nature, gravity, and circumstances of the offence, the accused's criminal record (s. 490.41(3)).
	6) If the court is not satisfied that the indictable offence was committed in relation to that property, property may still be forfeited if court believes beyond a reasonable doubt that property is offence related property. (s. 490.1(2)).
	7) If the property is a dwelling-house, before ordering forfeiture the court must consider the impact of forfeiture on any members of the immediate family of the accused residing in that home at the time the charge was laid, and whether those members were innocent of collusion or complicity in the offence (s. 490.41(4)).
	8) Right of appeal is to the court of appeal in form of a sentence appeal (s. 490.1 (3)).
Forfeiture of property where accused dead or absconded *Criminal Code* s. 490.2	1) Information has been laid for indictable *Criminal Code* offence (s. 490.2(1)).
	2) Judge of the superior court of justice is satisfied beyond a reasonable doubt that items are offence-related property (s. 490.2(2)(a)).
	3) Proceedings had commenced (s. 490.2(2)(b)).
	4) Accused is dead or has absconded (s. 490.2(2)(c)).
	5) Absconded means an information has been laid charging the accused with an offence, an arrest warrant for the accused has been issued in relation to that charge, and that the state has, unsuccessfully, made reasonable attempts to arrest the accused on the warrant for six months from the date of the issuance of the warrant (s. 490(3)(a–c)).
	6) Notice must be given under s. 490.4(1–2) to any person with an interest in the property; if the property is a dwelling-house, notice must also be given to any residents of the house who are immediate family members of the person charged or convicted.
	7) If 1–6 are true, then the property shall be forfeited to the Attorney General of the province if commenced by that entity or otherwise to the Attorney General of Canada. (s. 490.2(4)(a–b)), unless forfeiture would be disproportionate to the nature, gravity, and circumstances of the offence, the accused's criminal record. (s. 490.41(3)).
	8) If the property is a dwelling-house, before ordering forfeiture the court must consider the impact of forfeiture on any members of the immediate family of the accused residing in that home at the time the charge was laid, and whether those members were innocent of collusion or complicity in the offence. (s. 490.41(4)).
	9) Appeal rights for any person aggrieved by an order under this section lie to the court of appeal of the province, as a conviction or verdict of acquittal appeal. (s. 490.6).

Additional *Criminal Code* Powers and Restrictions

Voidable transfers for s. 490.1 or 490.2 *Criminal Code* s. 490.4	Before making an order of forfeiture under ss. 490.1 or 490.2, a court may set aside any transfer of offence-related property that occurred after the seizure of the property or the making a restraint order in relation to the property, if the transfer was not for valuable consideration to a a person acting in good faith.
Restoration of offence-related property to lawful owner *Criminal Code* s. 490.4(3)	Offence-related property that would otherwise be forfeited under ss. 490.1 or 490.2 may be ordered by a court to returned to the lawful owner of the property if the person was not charged with a *Criminal Code* indictable offence, was not transferred the property to avoid forfeiture, and appears to be innocent of collusion or complicity in an indictable offence.
Order declaring interest of certain persons not affected by forfeiture order *Criminal Code* s. 490.5	The Superior Court may order a person's interest in offence-related property not affected by an order of forfeiture, and declare the nature and extent of the value of the interest, if: 1) There is an order of forfeiture under ss. 490.1 or 490.2. 2) The Applicant for relief is neither the person convicted of an indictable offence and subject to an order of forfeiture under s. 490.1 nor the person charged with an offence and subject to an order of forfeiture under s. 490.2, nor a person who acquired an interest for the purpose of avoiding an order of forfeiture (s. 490.5(1)). 3) The Applicant has applied within 30 days of the order of forfeiture for relief. (s. 490.5(1)); the judge must also fix the hearing date for a day within 30 days of the filing of the application. (s. 490.5(2)). 4) The Applicant has served the Attorney General at least 15 days before the hearing date. (s. 490.5(3)). 5) The Applicant is not a person described under point #2 and appears to be innocent of complicity or collusion in any indictable offence relating to the forfeiture of the property (s. 490.5(4)(a)). 6) The Applicant exercised all reasonable care to be satisfied that the property was not likely used in the commission of an unlawful act by the person who had possession of the property or from whom the applicant obtained possession or by the mortgagor or lien-giver. (s. 490.5 (4)). Appeal rights from an order under s. 490.4 lie to the court of appeal for indictable offences (s. 490.5(5)). Once the appeal periods have expired, and no appeal are outstanding, the person who has received an order under s. 490.5(4) may apply to the Attorney General. The Attorney General must then direct that the property, or part of the property subject to the applicant's interest, be returned to the applicant or that the applicant be paid an amount equal to the value of the interest as described in the order (s. 490.5(6)).

Appendix 4: Additional Criminal Code Powers and Restrictions • 333

Additional Criminal Code Powers and Restrictions

Orders suspended pending an appeal *Criminal Code* s. 490.7	Orders under s. 490.1, 490.2, 490.5 are suspended pending any applications in respect of the property under the *Criminal Code* or other act of Parliament providing from restoration or forfeiture of the property.
Restraint orders pending forfeiture *Criminal Code* s. 490.8	A restraint order[10] prohibits a person from disposing or dealing with offence-related property specified in restraint order, otherwise than as provided for in the restraint order. (490.8(3))
	Section 490.8 provides for the issuance of restraint orders in the following circumstances:
	1) On *ex parte* application of the Attorney General, in writing, to a judge the superior court of justice; (490.8(1)(2)(5).
	2) If the application is in respect of offence-related property, and the judge is satisfied on reasonable grounds that the property is offence-related property; and (490.8(2)).
	3) If there is a supporting affidavit attesting to the following facts: the indictable offence to which the property is related; the person believed to be in possession of the offence-related property; a description of the property. (490.8(2)).
	The restraint order may be subject to any reasonable conditions the judge thinks fit. (490.8(4)).
	A copy of the order must be served on the person to whom the order is directed, either in the manner directed by the judge or with the rules of the court (490.8(6)); failure to comply with the order is an offence on summary conviction of by indictment (490.8(9).
	A copy of the order must be registered against property in accordance with the laws of the province where the property is situated. (490.8(7)).
	Sections 489.1 and 490 apply to this section, subject to ss. 490.1 and 490.7, and any other modifications considered to be necessary in the circumstances (490.0).
	If a judge orders under s. 490(9) the return of the property subject to a s. 490.8 restraint order, the judge may require the applicant to enter into a recognizance with or without sureties, in any amount or conditions directed, and if appropriate to deposit money or valuable security.
	Expiry: the order remains in effect until a further order under s. 490(9), (11), 490.4(3), or s. 490.41(3), or an order of forfeiture under s. 490.1(1) or s. 490.2(2).

10 See *R. v. Laroche* (2002), 169 C.C.C. (3d) 97 (S.C.C.) [*Laroche*] regarding the constitutional issues related to restraint orders.

	Additional *Criminal Code* Powers and Restrictions
Management order *Criminal Code* s. 490.81	• Allows a judge of the Superior Court to appoint a person to control, manage or otherwise deal with offence-related property in accordance with the judge's directions, and to require a person in possession of the property to give the property to the person so appointed (s. 490.81(1)). If the Attorney General requests, the judge must direct the Minister of Public Works and Government to be the person appointed (s. 490.81(2)). • Available for offence-related property, other than controlled substances under the *CDSA* seized under ss. 487 or 490.8. • May be granted by a judge (for property seized under s. 490.8) or a judge or justice (for property seized under s. 487) if the judge or justice is of the opinion that a management order for that property is required. • The Attorney General or a person with the written consent of the Attorney General (s. 490.81) must apply in writing. • The power to manage or deal with property includes the ability to make an interlocutory sale of the property, if perishable (490.81(3)(a)). • A Court may approve an application by a person appointed to manage to destroy the property, if it is of little of no financial or other value, and notice has been given to person with a valid interest in the property (on such terms and duration that the court or court rules specify) (ss. 490.81(3)(b), (4), (5), (6), (7)). • The order ceases to be in effect when the property is retuned to an applicant in accordance with the law, or forfeited (s. 487.81(8)). • The Attorney General may apply at any time to vary or cancel and condition of the order, but not the appointment itself (s. 490.81(9)).
Automatic forfeiture of weapons and ammunition *Criminal Code* s. 491	• Automatically forfeits to the Crown any "weapon, imitation firearm, prohibited device, ammunition, prohibited ammunition, or explosive substance" if a court determines that it was *used in the commission of an offence*, and that the thing has been seized or detained (s. 491(1)); or • Automatically forfeits to the Crown any "firearm, cross-bow, prohibited weapon, restricted weapon, prohibited device, ammunition, prohibited ammunition, or explosive substance" that is determined by a court to be involved in an offence or the is the subject matter of an offence (s. 491(2)). • However, if the lawful owner of the above-noted items was not a party to the offence and did not have reasonable grounds to believe that the item would be used in an offence, the items shall be returned to the lawful owner, or the owner shall be given the proceeds of any sale of the items or be given its equivalent monetary value if it was destroyed rather than sold (ss. 491(2) and (3)). • Proceeds of any sale shall be paid to the Attorney General unless (2) applies (s. 491(3)).

Additional *Criminal Code* Powers and Restrictions

Forfeiture or return of property obtained by crime following a verdict of guilty at trial *Criminal Code* s. 491.1	This section applies: • Once a court determines that an offence has been committed at a trial, whether or not a conviction or discharge has been registered (either following a formal registration of a conviction or discharge, or simply post-verdict of guilty) (s. 491.1(1)). • If property obtained by crime is before the court or has been detained, and can immediately be dealt with (s. 491.1(1)(a)). • If the property is no longer required as evidence in any other proceedings (s. 491.1(1)(b)). If the above conditions are met, the court must do the following: 1) The court must order *return* of the property to the lawful owner, if the owner is known, and is entitled to possess the property (491.1(2)(a)). 2) The court must order *forfeiture* to the Crown of the property if the lawful owner is unknown (491.1 (2)(b)). 3) The court must not order forfeiture or return of property, in the case of proceedings against "a trustee, banker, merchant, attorney, factor, broker or other agent entrusted with possession of goods or documents of title to goods" for offences under ss. 330, 331, 332, or 336 (theft by people in positions of trust). 4) The court must not order forfeiture with respect to property essentially obtained by a purchaser without notice in good faith: property obtained by a purchaser acting in good faith without notice and who has lawful title, or valuable security paid or discharged in good faith, or a negotiable instrument taken or received for valuable consideration in good faith if the person had no reasonable cause to suspect the commission of an offence, or property in respect of which there is a dispute as to ownership by claimants other than the accused (s. 491.1(3)). An order under this section must be executed at the direction of the court by peace officers normally charged with executing court process (s. 491.1(4)).
Photographic evidence *Criminal Code* s. 491.2	Authorizes the taking of photographs of any property that would be required as evidence in proceedings in respect of offences under ss. 334, 344, 348, 354, 362 or 480 (i.e., certain theft and fraud property offences) before such property is returned, forfeited or otherwise dealt with under s. 489.1). (Also provides for the admission of such photographs into evidence in lieu of the property.)
Report to justice following seizure: peace officer *Criminal Code* s. 489.1(1)	Subject to any exceptions in the *Criminal Code* or other federal legislation, where the officer has seized anything under a *Criminal Code* warrant, without a warrant pursuant to ss. 487.11 or 489, or in the execution of duties under any federal Act," the following rules apply.

11 *Quaere* whether and in what circumstances these restrictions apply to things seized under common law powers.

Additional *Criminal Code* Powers and Restrictions

	Where the officer is satisfied that: i) there is no dispute as to lawful possession of the thing seized, and ii) the continued detention of the item is no longer necessary for investigative, preliminary inquiry, trial or other purpose, the officer must: a) return the item to the lawful possessor (upon being granted a receipt therefor), *and* b) report to a justice of the territorial division in which the warrant was issued (or to a justice having jurisdiction in respect of the matter if the seizure was warrantless) reporting the return of the item. Where the officer is *not* so satisfied, the officer must: a) bring the item before a justice of the territorial division in which the warrant was issued (or to a justice having jurisdiction in respect of the matter if the seizure was warrantless), *or* b) report the seizure and detention of the item to a such a justice, to be dealt with by that justice according to s. 490.
Report to justice following seizure: non-peace officer *Criminal Code* s. 489.1(2)	Subject to any exceptions in the *Criminal Code* or other federal legislation, where the person has seized anything under a *Criminal Code* warrant, without a warrant pursuant to ss. 487.11 or 489, or in the execution of duties under any federal Act,[12] the following rules apply. The person must: a) bring the item before a justice in the territorial division in which the warrant was issued (or to a justice having jurisdiction in respect of the matter if the seizure was warrantless), *or* b) report the seizure and detention of the item to such a justice, to be dealt with by that justice according to s. 490.

12   See note to s. 489.1(1), *supra*.

APPENDIX 5: Proceeds of Crime

Statutory Power	Judicial Officer	Scope	Person to be Authorized	Special Requirements
Special search warrants for proceeds of crime *Criminal Code* s. 462.32[1]	Superior Court or s. 552 Judge (with jurisdiction in the province in which a "designated offence" is reasonably believed to have been committed)	Property that may be subject to forfeiture under ss. 462.37(1) or 463.38(2), essentially, property that may be considered "proceeds of crime." Under s. 462.3 "proceeds of crime" means any property, benefit or advantage, within or outside Canada, obtained or derived directly or indirectly as a result of a) the commission in Canada of a designated offence, or b) an act or omission anywhere that, if it had occurred in Canada, would have constituted a designated offence.	Peace officer, or a person named in the warrant	- Requires RPG that there is, in the building, place or receptacle to be searched, property that may be subject to forfeiture under ss. 462.37(1) or 462.38(2), property in respect of which a "designated offence" has been committed in the province in which the judge has jurisdiction.
- Designated offence means any indictable offence under any Act of Parliament, other than one prescribed by regulations, or conspiracy to commit any indictable offence (see definitions, s. 462.3).
- Authorizes the seizure of listed property any other property that the person reasonably believes is subject to forfeiture.
- Application must be made by the Attorney General in writing, on oath, and must include a statement as to whether any previous applications have been made in respect of the property
- May be executed anywhere in Canada, provided that if is to be executed outside the province of issue and execution would require entry into private property in the other province, then the person must apply to a superior court or s. 552 judge in the other province, who may confirm the warrant.
- Must be executed by day, unless otherwise ordered (s. 488).
- Sections 487(2)–(4) apply, with necessary modifications.
- Before issuing the warrant, the judge shall require the Attorney General to give such undertakings as are considered appropriate in the circumstances with respect to payment of damages or costs, or both, in relation to the warrant.

1   See *R. v. Laroche* (2002), 169 C.C.C. (3d) 97 (S.C.C.) re: constitutional issues regarding special search warrants and restraint orders. See also Appendix 4, s. 490.

Statutory Power	Judicial Officer	Scope	Person to be Authorized	Special Requirements

				• Before issuing the warrant, the judge may require notice be given to and may hear any person who, in the opinion of the judge, appears to have a valid interest in the property *unless* the judge is of the opinion that giving such notice would result in the disappearance, dissipation or reduction in value of the property or otherwise prevent the seizure.
				• The person who executes the warrant must
				  i) detain the property seized, taking reasonable care to preserve the property so that it may be dealt with according to law;
				  ii) as soon as practicable after execution, but within seven days prepare a report identifying the property seized and the location where it is being detained and file the report with the clerk of the court; and
				  iii) on request, provide a copy of the report to the person from whom the property was seized, and any other person who, in the opinion of the judge, appears to have a valid interest in the property.
				• Subject to the requirements of the *Criminal Code* and any other federal Act, a *peace officer* who has seized anything under such a warrant may, with the written consent of the Attorney General, on being issued a receipt for it, return the thing seized to the personal lawfully entitled to possession of it if
				  i) the peace officer is satisfied that there is no dispute as to who is lawfully entitled to possession of the thing seized;
				  ii) the peace officer is satisfied that the continued detention of the thing seized is not required for the purpose of forfeiture; and
				  iii) the thing seized is returned before the required report is filed with the clerk of the court.
				• Any person who has an interest in property seized may, at any time, apply to a superior court or s. 552 judge under s. 462.34 for an order restoring the property or revoking or varying the warrant, or allowing the person to examine the property.
				• **Time limit:** Property may not be detained uncer this section for a period exceeding 6 months unless proceedings instituted or if a further application of the Attorney General is granted if property is required for forfeiture proceedings or as evidence in other proceedings or for an investigation) or the property is ordered forfeited under any provision of an Act of Parliament (s. 462.33(10)).

Appendix 5: Proceeds of Crime • 339

Statutory Power	Judicial Officer	Scope	Person to be Authorized	Special Requirements
Restraint orders for property or proceeds of crime *Criminal Code* s. 462.33[2]	Superior Court or s. 552 Judge (with jurisdiction in the province in which a "designated offence" is reasonably believed to have been committed)	Restraint of property that may be subject to forfeiture under ss. 462.37(1) or 462.38(2), essentially, property that is considered "proceeds of crime." "Proceeds of crime" means any property, benefit or advantage, within or outside Canada, obtained or derived directly or indirectly as a result of a) the commission in Canada of a designated offence, or b) an act or omission anywhere that, if it had occurred in Canada, would have constituted a designated offence.	Service of the Order as the Court directs s. 462.33 (8)	• Application may be made *ex parte*, in writing, by the Attorney General (s. 426.33(1)(2)(6)). • Application must include an affidavit on information and belief deposing to: a) the offence or matter under investigation b) the person believed to be in possession of the property c) the grounds for belief that an order of forfeiture may be made under ss. 462.37(1) or 462.38(2) for the property d) a description of the property e) any previous application have been made under s. 462.333 regarding the property . • Notice must be given before an order can issue, unless notice would result in the disappearance, dissipation, or reduction in value of property, or affect the property so that all or part could not be subject to forfeiture under ss. 462.37 or 462.38 (s. 462.33(5)). • Order may issue if the judge believes on reasonable grounds that property that may be subject to an order of forfeiture under ss. 462.37 or 462.38 and that it is located in Canada (s. 462.33(3)), or outside of Canada (s. 462.33(3.1)). • Order may be on such reasonable conditions as the judge thinks fit (s. 462.33(4)), including requiring the Attorney General to provide undertakings with respect to payment of damages and/or costs for the making or execution of an order (s. 462.33(7)). • Order must be served on the person to whom it is addressed (s. 462.33(8)), and registered on the property according to the laws of the province where the property is situated (s. 462.33(9)).

2   See *ibid*. re: constitutional issues regarding special search warrants and restraint orders.

Statutory Power	Judicial Officer	Scope	Person to be Authorized	Special Requirements
				• Order is valid until revoked or varied under ss. 462.34(4) or 462.43(a), ceases to be in force under 462.35 (6 month time limit on order unless proceedings instituted or if a further application of the Attorney General is granted if property is required for forfeiture proceedings or as evidence in other proceedings or for an investigation), or the property is ordered forfeited under any provision of an Act of Parliament (s. 462.33(10)). • *Consequences of non-compliance with order*: offence on summary conviction or indictment (s. 462.33(11)). • Subject to review by the court on the application of an interested person pursuant to s. 462.34.
Management orders for property and proceeds of crime *Criminal Code* s. 462.331	Superior Court or s. 552 Judge	Order for management of property seized under s. 462.32 or restrained under s. 462.33	Any person appointed by the court, or if the Attorney General requests, the Minister of Public Works and Government Services s. 462.331(1) and (2)	• Available following an application by the Attorney General or a person with the written consent of the Attorney General. • If circumstances require, a judge may: a) Appoint a person to take control of and manage or otherwise deal with all or part of the property in accordance with the judge's directions; (s. 462.331(1)(a)(b) and, b) Require any person with possession of the property to give it to the person appointed to manage or deal with the property (s.462.331(b)). • The power to manage or deal with the property includes the ability to sell perishable property. • The person appointed to manage the property may also apply to a court, on notice to the person with a valid interest in the property, for an order to destroy property with little or no value (s. 462.331(3)(4)(5)(6)(7)). • The order ceases to have effect once the property is lawfully returned to an applicant or forfeited. (s. 462.331(8)) • The Attorney General may apply at any time to vary or cancel any condition of the order, except for the appointment under (2) (s.462.331(9)).

Statutory Power	Judicial Officer	Scope	Person to be Authorized	Special Requirements
Restoration of property subject to special search warrants Revocation and variation of restraint orders *Criminal Code* s. 462.34	Superior Court or s. 552 Judge	Property seized under s. 462.32 or restrained under s. 462.33(3) Sections 462.34(2) and (4)(c), (5)(5.1) and (5.2) also apply to money or bank notes seized under the *Criminal Code* or *CDSA* if proceedings are taken under ss. 462.37(1) or 462.38(2), for a person with an interest in that property		To apply for relief under this section (except with respect to simply viewing the property), the person must: • have an interest in property seized under s. 462.32 or restrained under s. 462.33(3) • provide 2 clear days notice of hearing to the Attorney General, unless the Attorney General consents to shorter notice period, and to give notice to anyone else with an interest the court requires that notice be given (s. 462.33(2)). Relief available through: *return of property to the applicant, revoking a restraint order, or varying the restraint order.* 1) If the applicant enters into a recognizance before the judge, with or without sureties, with or without deposits of money or valuable security, in such amounts and on such terms as the judge directs (s. 462.34) (4)(a) — such a recognizance may be in Form 32 (s. 462.34 (8); or 2) If a judge is satisfied that a warrant under s. 462.32 or s. 462.33 restraint order *should not have issued* or been made with respect to the property in issue, in cases where the applicant is a person charged with a designated offence, or who acquired title not in good faith (s. 462.34 (4)(b) and (6)); or 3) *If the property is no longer required for any investigation or as evidence in proceedings*, in cases where the applicant is the sole lawful owner or person entitled to possess the property and appears innocent of collusion or complicity in a designated offence (s. 462.34 (4)(b) and (6)(b)); or 4) If the applicant needs relief to *meet the reasonable living, business, or legal expenses of the person in possession of the property when the warrant was executed*, or to allow the person to enter into a recognizance under condition #1 above, if the judge is satisfied: i) that the applicant has *no other assets or means* to satisfy the need set out, and ii) that no other person is the lawful owner or lawfully entitled to possess the property (s. 462.34(c)).

Statutory Power	Judicial Officer	Scope	Person to be Authorized	Special Requirements
				• A hearing with respect to determining legal reasonable expenses under #4 above must be held in camera, in the absence of the Attorney General, taking into account the provincial legal aid tariff. The Attorney General, may however, make submissions before or after the *in camera* hearing as to what would constitute reasonable legal expenses (ss. 462.34(5) and (5.1)(b)). • The Attorney General may make representations at the hearing regarding the reasonableness of all other expenses other than legal expenses (462.34(5.1)(a)). • The reasonableness of legal fees may be taxed on application of the Attorney General (s. 462.34(5.2)). • A judge may also award relief by ordering that the applicant be permitted to view the property on terms necessary or desirable to preserve and safeguard the property (s. 462.34(3)). • Taking possession of any property seized under s. 462.32 or restrained under s.462.33, pursuant to an order under this section, does not constitute an offence under s. 354. • If an order is made under s. 462.34, the Attorney General may copy any documents before complying with the order, and use the documents in evidence with the same probative force as the original of the document if certified as true copies (s. 462.46). • 30 day waiting period and suspension pending other proceedings: the operation of an order under this section is suspended pending any applications under any Act of Parliament for the forfeiture or restoration of the property, any appeals from forfeiture or restraint, or any other proceeding questioning the seizure of the property, and no property shall be disposed of for 30 days after an order of forfeiture (s. 462.45).
Priority of other forfeiture provisions and restitution to victims of crime *Criminal Code* s. 462.49		Statutory prioritization of forfeiture provisions		1) Part XII.2 Proceeds of Crime Forfeiture provisions do not affect the other forfeiture provisions of the *Criminal Code* or any other Act of Parliament 2) Property of an offender is subject first to satisfy the operation of any other provision in any Act of Parliament respecting restitution or compensation to persons affected by the commission of criminal offences, before it may be used to satisfy any other provisions.

Appendix 5: Proceeds of Crime • 343

Statutory Power	Judicial Officer	Scope	Person to be Authorized	Special Requirements
Forfeiture of proceeds of crime following a conviction or discharge *Criminal Code* s. 462.37	The court sentencing an offender for a designated offence following a conviction or discharge under s. 730 of the *Code*.	Proceeds of crime as defined under s. 462.3 (property derived from an indictable offence)		A court *must* order forfeiture if: • The offender is *convicted or discharged* under s.730 of a designated offence (an indictable offence under any Act of Parliament or conspiracy to commit, being an accessory after the fact, or counselling to commit an indictable offence) and is before a court for sentencing. (462.37(1); and • The court is satisfied, *on a balance of probabilities*, i) that any property is the proceeds of crime as defined in 462.3 (essentially, property derived directly or indirectly from the commission of a designated offence in Canada, or an offence committed outside of Canada that would have constituted a designated offence within Canada); and ii) that the designated offence before the court was committed in relation to that property; (462.37(1)) or iii) if the court is not satisfied that the designated offence was committed in relation to that property, but is satisfied *beyond a reasonable doubt* that the property is the proceeds of crime more generally (i.e. obtained as a result of another designated offence), the court *may* (not mandatory) order forfeiture. (462.37(2)) • Unless the property: a) on the exercise of due diligence, cannot be located b) has been transferred to a third party c) is located outside of Canada d) has been substantially diminished in value or rendered worthless e) has been commingled with other property that cannot be divided without difficult • in which case, a *fine may* issue (discretionary, not mandatory) rather than forfeiture, provided that a forfeiture order could otherwise properly issue (s. 462.37(3))

Statutory Power	Judicial Officer	Scope	Person to be Authorized	Special Requirements
				• in imposing a fine, the court shall include impose a term of imprisonment in default of fine payment according to s. 462.37(4)(a)(i–ii), to be served consecutively to any other term of imprisonment imposed on the offender or being currently served (s. 462.37(4)(b)). • a fine imposed under this section is not subject to the fine option section in s. 736. Mandatory Notice to Persons with a Valid Interest in the Property • Before ordering forfeiture, the court must require notice be given to any person with a valid interest in the property, in the manner and duration directed be the court or according the rules of the court, and setting out the designated offence charged and a description of the property (s. 462.41(1)(2)). • At the hearing, the court *may order that the property be returned to any person*, other than a person charged or convicted of a designated offence or who has acquired title for the purpose of avoiding forfeiture, if: 1) the person is the lawful owner or lawfully entitled to possession of the property or any part thereof; and 2) the person is innocent of complicity or collusion in a designated offence (s. 462.41(3)). Proving that Property is the Proceeds of Crime (s. 462.39) • the court may infer that property was obtained or derived by the commission of a designated offence if: – the evidence established that the value of *all the property of the person* alleged to have committed the offence (the person's net worth) following the commission of the designated offence exceeds the value of the person's property prior to the commission of that offence (previous net worth); and – the court is satisfied that the person's *income* from sources *unrelated to designated offences* cannot account for the increase in value. Voidable Transfers • The court may also set aside any conveyance or transfer that occurred *after* the seizure of property or service of a s. 462.33 restraint order, unless conveyed for valuable consideration to a good faith purchaser (s. 462.4). An Order under this Section: • may be executed anywhere in Canada s.(462.371(2)), but must not be executed in a province other than where the order was made until notice is given under s. 462.41(2) to everyone with a valid interest in the property (s. 462.371(7)).

Appendix 5: Proceeds of Crime • 345

Statutory Power	Judicial Officer	Scope	Person to be Authorized	Special Requirements
				• has the effect of being ordered by a court of the province where the property is situated, if a certified copy of the order is filed with that court by the Attorney General of the province where the property is situated or the Attorney General of Canada (s. 462.371(3), (4), (5)) • may be subject to an application for relief by an interest person under s. 462.42; the applicant may only make one such application, regardless of the location of the initial application (s. 462.371(8)). • is subject to any determinations under s. 462.42 made by a court in relation to whether a person's interest is affected by forfeiture and the interest is binding on any court where the order is entered as a judgment (s. 462.371(9)). • Before complying with the order, the Attorney General may copy any documents of forfeiture or return, and use the documents in evidence with the same probative force as the original of the document if certified as true copies (s. 462.46)
Forfeiture of proceeds of crime where accused dead or absconded *Criminal Code* s. 462.38	Superior Court or s. 552 Judge	Proceeds of crime as defined under s. 462.3 (property derived from an indictable offence)		Forfeiture under this section is mandatory if: • The Attorney General applies to a judge (s. 462.38(1)). • An information is laid in respect of a designated offence (s. 462.38(1)). • The accused on that information has died or absconded[3] (s. 462.38(2)(c) and (3)). • The designated offence has been committed in relation to the property in issue (s. 462.38(2)(b)). • Proceedings have commenced (s. 462.38(2)(b)). • The judge is satisfied beyond a reasonable doubt that the property is the proceeds of crime (s. 462.38(2)(a)).

---

3   Absconded means that an arrest warrant or summons (for corporations) has been issued in relation to an offence on an information, and reasonable attempts have been made to arrest the accused or serve the summons for six months from the date of the issuance of the warrant or summons, or, for a person outside of Canada, that the person cannot be brought before the court within 6 months to the jurisdiction that issued the warrant or summons.

Statutory Power	Judicial Officer	Scope	Person to be Authorized	Special Requirements
				Proving that property is the proceeds of crime (s. 462.39) • the court may infer that property was obtained or derived by the commission of a designated offence if: – the evidence established that the value of *all the property of the person* alleged to have committed the offence (the person's net worth) following the commission of the designated offence exceeds the value of the person's property prior to the commission of that offence (previous net worth); and – the court is satisfied that the person's *income* from sources *unrelated to designated offences* cannot account for the increase in value. Voidable Transfers • The court may also set aside any conveyance or transfer that occurred after the seizure of property or service of a 462.33 restraint order, unless conveyed for valuable consideration to a good faith purchaser. (462.4) Mandatory Notice to Persons with a Valid interest in the Property • Before ordering forfeiture, the court must require notice be given to any person with a valid interest in the property, in the manner and duration directed be the court or according the rules of the court, and setting out the designated offence charged and a description of the property (s. 462.41(1)(2)) • At the hearing, the court *may order that the property be returned to any person*, other than a person charged or convicted of a designated offence or who has acquired lawful title for the purpose of avoiding forfeiture, if: 1) the person is the lawful owner or lawfully entitled to possession of the property or any part thereof, and 2) the person is innocent of complicity or collusion in a designated offence. (462.41(3)) • Before complying with the order of forfeiture or return, the Attorney General may copy any documents before complying with the order, and use the documents in evidence with the same probative force as the original of the document if certified as true copies(462.46) Execution of Order in another Province: • may be executed anywhere in Canada (s. 462.371(2)), but must not be executed in a province other than where the order was made until notice is given under s. 462.41(2) to everyone with a valid interest in the property (s.462.371(7)). • An order can be made in relation to property outside of Canada, subject to any necessary modifications (s. 462.38(2.1)).

Appendix 5: Proceeds of Crime • 347

Statutory Power	Judicial Officer	Scope	Person to be Authorized	Special Requirements
				• Appeals: Any aggrieved person may appeal from an order forfeiting under this section or returning property under s. 462.41 as if the order was a conviction or acquittal on an indictable offence (s. 462.44). • 30 day waiting period and suspension pending other proceedings: the operation of an order under this section is suspended pending any applications under any Act of Parliament for the forfeiture or restoration of the property, any appeals from forfeiture or restraint, or any other proceeding questioning the seizure of the property, and no property shall be disposed of for 30 days after an order of forfeiture (s. 462.45).
Relief from forfeiture after order made *Criminal Code* s. 462.42	Superior Court or s. 552 Judge	Property forfeited under s. 462.37(1) (forfeiture of proceeds of crime following conviction) or s. 462.38(2) (forfeiture of proceeds of crime following accused's death or absconding)		Available to any person with an interest in property other than: a) a person charged with or convicted of a designated offence in relation to the forfeited property, or b) a person who acquired title to or right to possession of the forfeited property in circumstances where the reasonable inference is that transfer of the property occurred to avoid forfeiture (s. 462.42 (1)). If: • property has been forfeited under ss. 462.37(1) or 462.38(2) • the person applies by notice *in writing* within 30 days of forfeiture (462.42(1)) • [the judge must correspondingly set a hearing date within 30 days of the filing of the application s. 462.42(2)] • the person serves the Attorney General with the notice of the application and hearing within 15 days of the hearing (462.42(3)) • the judge is satisfied that the applicant is not a person excluded from applying under (1), and appears to be innocent of any collusion or complicity in a designated offence that resulted in the forfeiture (s. 462.42(4)). Then: • the judge may make an order declaring that the person's interest is not affected

Statutory Power	Judicial Officer	Scope	Person to be Authorized	Special Requirements
				by forfeiture, and declaring the nature and extent of the value of the interest. (s. 462.42 (4)). • the Attorney General shall, on receiving an application from a person who received an order, after the appeal periods have expired and any appeals determined, direct that the property or part thereof be returned to the applicant, or an amount equal to the value of the interest be paid to the applicant. (s. 462.42 (6)). • Appeals: available to both the Attorney General and an appeal for any order under (4), as an indictable appeal to the provincial court of appeal (462.42(5)).
Disposal of property subject to restraint orders or special search warrants when no longer required *Criminal Code* s. 462.43	Superior Court or s. 552 Judge	Property seized under s. 462.32 or restrained under s. 462.33 that is no longer required by the state		Proceedings under this section may start: • on application of the Attorney General; • on application of any person having an interest in property; • on the judge's own motion • if notice has been given to the Attorney General and any person with an interest in property (s. 462.43(1)). If the judge is satisfied that: • the property is no longer required for any forfeiture provisions under any Act of Parliament (s. 462.43(1)), or any investigation, or as evidence in any proceeding. Then the judge shall: • revoke the restraint order; (s. 462.43(1)(a)) or • cancel the recognizance, if outstanding (s. 462.43(1)(b)) • order the property returned to the person from whom it was taken if he or she can lawfully possess it (s. 462.43(1)(c)(i)) • order the property returned to the other lawful owner who is entitled to possession (s. 462.43(1)(c)(ii)) • forfeit the property to Her Majesty if there is no lawful owner known and if possession by the person from whom it was seized is unlawful (s. 462.43(1)(c)(iii)).

Statutory Power	Judicial Officer	Scope	Person to be Authorized	Special Requirements
				• An order can be made for property outside of Canada, modified to suit the circumstances (462.43(2))
				• Appeals from orders under this section are available to anyone aggrieved, as if the order was a conviction or acquittal on an indictable offence (462.44)
				• 30 day waiting period and suspension pending other proceedings: the operation of an order under this section is suspended pending any applications under any Act of Parliament for the forfeiture or restoration of the property, any appeals from forfeiture or restraint, or any other proceeding questioning the seizure of the property, and no property shall be disposed of for 30 days after an order of forfeiture. (462.45)
Order for disclosure of Information by Canada Revenue Agency (CRA) in relation to proceeds of crime investigation *Criminal Code* s. 462.48	Superior Court or s. 552 Judge	Tax-related documents and information in the possession of CRA	Police Officer (s. 462.48(3) and (17)) (defined as an officer, constable or other person employed for the preservation and maintenance of the public peace)	The Attorney General may apply to access information from CRA if: 1) there is an investigation relating to: a) a "designated drug offence" (defined in s. 462.48 as an offence under Part I of the *CDSA* other than simple possession of drugs under s. 4(1) or conspiracy to commit such an offence); b) an offence against s. 354 (possession of property obtained by crime) or s. 462.31 (laundering the proceeds of crime), if the property or proceeds is related to a designated drug offence committed in Canada or an act or omission that was occurring outside Canada that would have constituted a designated drug offence if committed Canada; c) an offence against ss. 467.11, 467.12, or 467.18 (criminal organization offences), or any conspiracy to commit such an offence; or d) a terrorism offence (s. 462.48 (1.1)). 2) the Attorney General submits an *ex parte* application in writing detailing: a) the offence or matter under investigation; b) the identity of the person about whom the information or documents are sought;

Statutory Power	Judicial Officer	Scope	Person to be Authorized	Special Requirements
				c) the type of information, book, record, writing, return, or other document obtained by or on behalf of the Minister of National Revenue (M.N.R.) in relation to the *Income Tax Act* that is sought or proposed to be examined; d) the facts supporting the belief on reasonable grounds: i) that the person has committed the offences in question; and ii) that the information or documents sought are likely to be of *substantial value* (not mere relevance), alone or together with other material, to the investigation (s. 462.48(2))
				The Judge may order the Commissioner of Customs and Revenue (or other designate in writing of the Commissioner): a) if satisfied of 2(d) above, and b) is satisfied on reasonable grounds that it advisable in the public interest to order disclosure; c) to allow a police officer (an officer, constable or other person employed for the preservation and maintenance of the public peace — s. 462.48(17) named in the order to access *all such information documents* and examine them, or d) to produce all such information and documents to the police officer and allow the officer to remove them, if necessary in the circumstances. (s. 462.48(3)).
				The order may be in Form 47 (s. 462.48(16)).
				Service of the order is to be done according to the judge's directions or the rule of the court (s. 462.48(4)).
				The judge may grant extensions for compliance with the order if applied for by the M.N.R. (s. 462.48(5)).
				Copies may be made of documents subject to a disclosure or access order, and copies purporting to be certified by an authorized person have the same probative effect in evidence as the originals (s. 462.48(14)).
				Further Disclosure of the documents or information received under this section is prohibited except for the purposes of the investigation in relation to which the order was made (s. 462.48(15)).
				Objection by the M.N.R. to Disclosure • The M.N.R. (or special designate in writing) may object to the disclosure ordered by certifying *orally or in writing* that disclosure is not or should not be made on the ground that: a) A bilateral or international treaty, convention or agreement respecting taxation prohibits it (if Canada is a signatory);

Statutory Power	Judicial Officer	Scope	Person to be Authorized	Special Requirements
				b) The documents or information are subject to privilege; c) The documents or information are in a sealed package pursuant to the law or an order of a court; or d) Disclosure is not in the public interest (s. 462.48(6)). • The objection may be determined on an application to the Chief Justice of the Federal Court, or other judge of that Court designated by the Chief Justice to hear the application (s. 462.48(7)). • The application to determine the objection must be made within 10 days after the objection, or otherwise as permitted by the Chief Justice of the Federal Court to determine such applications (s. 462.48(9)). • The judge determining the objection may examine the information or documents if necessary to determine the objection (s. 462.38(8)). • The judge determining the objection shall grant the objection if satisfied of the grounds for the objection above (s. 462.48(8)). • Appeals from a determination of an objection lie to the Federal Court of Appeal (s. 462.48(10)), and must be brought within 10 days of the determination or as the appeal court allows (s. 462.48(11)) • All hearings and appeals regarding objections are to be heard *in camera*, in the National Capital Region if requested by the person objecting, and with an opportunity for the person objecting to make *ex parte* representations (s. 462.48(12)(13)).-

APPENDIX 6: Seizures of Bodily Substances and Impressions*

Statutory Power	Judicial Officer Person to be Authorized	Criteria for Issuance	Limitations/Incidental Powers
Fingerprinting s. 2 *Identification of Criminals Act*	N/A Not specified	The following people may be fingerprinted: a) A person *in lawful custody charged or convicted of*:[1] 　i) *an indictable offence*, other than one designated under the *Contraventions Act* if the Attorney General has made an election under that Act;[2] or 　ii) an offence under the *Security of Information Act*;[3] b) any person who has been *apprehended* under the *Extradition Act*;[4] c) any person *alleged to have committed an indictable offence* who is required to appear by an appearance notice, promise to appear, recognizance or summons (other than for an offence designated under the *Contraventions Act* if the Attorney General has made an election under that Act);[5] or d) any person who is in lawful custody in relation to terrorist activity pursuant to section 83.3 of the *Criminal Code*.[6]	Force may be used to take prints or measurements, providing that "[s]uch force may be used as is necessary to the effectual carrying out and application of the measurements, processes and operations described."[7] The Act permits "publication" of the results of the prints or measuring "for the purpose of affording information to officers and others engaged in the execution or administration of the law."[8]

* See also Appendix 7, "*DNA Identification Act*."
1 *Identification of Criminals Act*, s. 2(1)(a).
2 *Ibid.*, s. 2(1)(a)(i).
3 *Ibid.*, s. 2(1)(a)(ii).
4 *Ibid.*, s. 2(1)(b).
5 *Ibid.*, s. 2(1)(c).
6 *Ibid.*, s. 2(1)(d).

Appendix 6: Seizures of Bodily Substances and Impressions • 353

Statutory Power	Judicial Officer Person to be Authorized	Criteria for Issuance	Limitations/Incidental Powers
Prints/impressions of any part of the body including handprints, fingerprints, footprint, foot impression and teeth impression s. 487.092	Justice of the Peace Peace officer or person under the direction of a peace officer	Requires reasonable and probable grounds on oath, in writing, to believe that a federal offence has been committed, and that information concerning that offence will be obtained by the print or impression Must establish that it is in the best interests of administration of justice to issue the warrant. May be obtained by s. 487.1 telewarrant (s. 487.092(4)) Extraterritorial execution governed by s. 487(2) and (4)	
Demand for roadside breath sample (Impaired Driving) s. 254(2)	N/A Peace officer	Allows for seizure of breath sample (analysis of the concentration of alcohol in the blood) — by means of an approved screening device. Requires: i) target to be operating or have care or control of a motor vehicle, vessel, etc.;[9] and ii) reasonable suspicion that the target has alcohol in his or her body. Sample is to be given "forthwith" or at least as soon as practicable.[10] The demand for the sample is to be made forthwith, or within a reasonable time.[11] Person may have to accompany the officer to give a sample.	

7 *Identification of Criminals Act*, s. 2(2).
8 *Identification of Criminals Act*, s. 2(3).
9 Courts have interpreted this subs. (i.e., "who is operating") to include a person who "has been" operating.
10 In *R. v. Grant* (1991), 67 C.C.C. (3d) 268 (S.C.C.), 30 minutes was not considered to be "forthwith." In *R. v. Cote* (1992), 70 C.C.C. (3d) 280 (Ont. C.A.), a sample taken 14 minutes after the demand was not considered to be forthwith. The taking of a sample can be delayed, however, if necessary to ensure accuracy of the results: *R. v. Dewald* (1994), 92 C.C.C. (3d) 280 (Ont. C.A.).
11 *R. v. Quist* (1981), 61 C.C.C. (2d) 207 (Sask. C.A.); *R. v. MacGillivray* (1971), 4 C.C.C. (2d) 244 (Ont. C.A.).

354 • Understanding Section 8: Search, Seizure, and the Canadian Constitution

Statutory Power	Judicial Officer Person to be Authorized	Criteria for Issuance	Limitations/Incidental Powers
Seizure of breath sample or blood sample (Impaired Driving) s. 254(3)	N/A	Permits seizure of breath sample or, if necessary, blood sample (analysis of the concentration of alcohol in the blood) into an approved instrument.[12]	
	Peace officer or person under the direction of a peace officer	Requires reasonable and probable grounds to believe that the target is committing, or has committed within the preceding 3 hours, an offence under s. 253 involving alcohol.[13]	
		Where the officer has RPG to believe that the target is incapable of giving a breath sample, or that it would be impracticable to obtain a breath sample, the officer may require that blood samples be provided instead, *provided that* the samples be taken by or under the direction of a qualified medical practitioner who is satisfied that the taking of such samples will not endanger the target.	
Seizure of blood (impaired driving causing injury or death) s. 256	Justice of the Peace	A blood sample may be seized, as soon as practicable, from target for analysis of the concentration of drugs or alcohol in the blood if reasonable grounds to believe:	
	Peace officer (sample to be taken by or under the direction of a medical practitioner)	i) the target has, within the previous four hours, committed an offence under s. 253 and was involved in an accident that resulted in death to any other person, or bodily harm to any person, including the target;	
		ii) a qualified medical practitioner is of the opinion that (a) the target is (as a result of consumption of the intoxicant or effects relating to the accident) physically or mentally incapable of consenting to the taking of a blood sample; and (b) taking the sample would not endanger the life of the target — (*provided that* the warrant may only be executed so long as the physician remains satisfied of these two conditions).	
		May be obtained by telewarrant (s. 487.1(1)).	
		If a sample is taken, a copy of the warrant must be provided to the target.	

12 See s. 254(1).
13 A failure on a roadside breath test (under s. 254(2)), along with other indicia of impairment, may constitute reasonable and probable grounds for the purpose of a s. 254(3) demand: see *R. v. Bernshaw* (1994), 95 C.C.C. (3d) 193 (S.C.C.).

Statutory Power	Judicial Officer Person to be Authorized	Criteria for Issuance	Limitations/Incidental Powers

Warrant to seize DNA for investigative purposes *Criminal Code* s. 487.05	Provincial Court Judge s. 487.05(1) Peace officer or person under the direction of a peace officer s. 487.06 and Form 5.06	Reasonable grounds to believe:
		• a designated offence, as set out in s. 487.04, has been committed;[14]
		• a bodily substance had been found at any of these places:
		  – where the offence was committed
		  – on or within the body of the victim of that offence
		  – on anything worn or carried by the victim when the offence was committed
		  – on or within the body of any person or thing at a place associated with the offence;[15]
		• that the person targeted for DNA seizure is a party to the offence;[16]
		• that forensic DNA analysis[17] will provide evidence as to whether the bodily substance seized in relation to the offence belongs to the person targeted for seizure.[18]
		• that issuing the warrant is in the best interest of the administration of justice;[19]
		• the judge must also consider *all relevant matters*, including:
		  – the availability of peace officer with the ability because of training or experience to take the sample;
		  – the availability of another person, who by virtue of training or experience is able to take the sample under the direction of a peace officer.[20]
			The judge may impose such terms and conditions as considered advisable to ensure the taking of samples is reasonable in the circumstances.[21]
			Only available for offences designated under s. 487.04 (serious criminal offences).
			Execution procedure: according to s. 487.06 (hair-plucking, blood sample, or buccal swab of cheek, lips, or tongue).[22]
			Respect for privacy: The person taking the samples must ensure privacy is respected while the samples are taken, in a manner reasonable in the circumstances.[23] This includes ensuring, in most cases, that a person is not required to expose body parts not ordinarily exposed to view.[24]
			See notice and detention provisions s. 487.07.
			Report to judge to be filed.[25]
			Use of samples and results:
			• Substances collected may only be used for forensic DNA analysis[26] for the investigation of the designated offence.[27]
			• Contravention of either these requirements is an offence.[28]
			• Substances collected from the target, and test results, must be destroyed, without delay:
			  a) If the samples do not match;[29]

Appendix 6: Seizures of Bodily Substances and Impressions • 355

Statutory Power	Judicial Officer Person to be Authorized	Criteria for Issuance	Limitations/Incidental Powers
Warrant to seize DNA for investigative purposes *Criminal Code* s. 487.05 con't			b) If the target is acquitted of the designated offence and any other offence in respect of the same transaction;[30] Following the expiration of one year after discharge following a preliminary hearing; withdrawal or dismissal of charges or stay of proceedings[31] relating to the designated offence;[32] • A provincial court judge may order the non-destruction of samples and results for any appropriate period, if the judge is satisfied they might be reasonably required in: i) an investigation or prosecution of the same person for another designated offence; or ii) another person for the original designated.[33] Even substances obtained on consent of the target (as opposed to by warrant) are subject to destruction protections.[34]

14 *Criminal Code*, s. 487.05(1)(a).
15 *Ibid.*, s. 487.05(1)(b)(i–iv).
16 *Ibid.*, s. 487.05(1)(c).
17 As defined in s. 487.04.
18 *Criminal Code*, s. 487.05(1)(d).
19 *Ibid.*, s. 487.05(1).
20 *Ibid.*, s. 487.05(2)(a) and (b)(i)(ii).
21 *Ibid.*, s. 487.06(2).
22 *Ibid.*, s. 487.06(1). No requirement to use the least intrusive of these procedures: all are deemed to be minimally intrusive. *R. v. S.A.B.* (2001), 157 C.C.C. (3d) 510 (Alta. C.A.).
23 *Criminal Code*, s. 487.07(3).
24 *R. v. S.A.B.*, 2003 SCC 60 [*S.A.B.*] at para.45; *R. v. Briggs* (2001), 157 C.C.C. (3d) 38 (Ont. C.A.) [*Briggs*] at para. 35.
25 Section 487.057.
26 As defined in the *Criminal Code*, s. 487.04.
27 *Criminal Code*, s. 487.08(1) and (2); incidental testing will likely only be permitted to the extent required to match the samples in the investigation in question: *S.A.B.*, above note 24 at para. 13.
28 *Criminal Code*, s. 487.08(3).
29 *Ibid.*, s. 487.09(1)(a).
30 *Ibid.*, s. 487.09(1)(b).
31 As under ss. 579, 572, or 795.
32 Unless there is a recommencement of proceeding or a new information is laid or indictment preferred within that year in respect of the same transaction. *Criminal Code*, s. 487.09(1)(c)(i–iii).
33 *Ibid.*, s. 487.09(2).
34 *Ibid.*, s. 487.05(1).

Statutory Power	Judicial Officer Person to be Authorized	Criteria for Issuance	Limitations/Incidental Powers
Notice to target of seizure Detention of targets to effect seizure *Criminal Code* s. 487.07	Peace Officer or person taking the sample must give the required notice	Applicable to all seizure of all bodily substances under ss. 487.051, 487.052, 487.055, and 487.091.	Before the sample is taken, the peace officer must inform the target of the seizure of: a) the contents of the warrant; b) the nature of the procedures that will be used to take the sample; c) the purpose of taking the samples; d) the authority of the person taking the sample to use necessary force to take the sample; e) that the results of analysing the bodily samples may be used in evidence. **Young persons:** must have notice that the person has the right to (1) a reasonable opportunity to consult counsel; and (2) have the warrant to be executed in the presence of a parent or other appropriate adult chosen by the young person. Any waiver of rights must be recorded as per s. 487.07(5). **Detention:** The target of the seizure may be detained pending the taking of the sample, and may be required to accompany the peace officer to have the sample taken.[35]
Report of peace officer *Criminal Code* s. 487.057	Report to be filed with judge who issued the warrant or authorization or a judge of that court Peace officer authorized to take or cause to take the sample must file the report	Following seizures of samples under ss. 487.05, 487.051, 487.052, 487.055, or 487.091. Report to be filed in Form 5.07 as soon as feasible after samples have been taken. Report to include time and date of taking of sample, and description of the bodily substances taken.[36]	

35 *Criminal Code*, s. 487.07(2).   36 *Ibid.*, s. 487.057(1)(2).

Statutory Power	Judicial Officer / Person to be Authorized	Criteria for Issuance	Limitations/Incidental Powers
DNA Databank seizure order Offences committed after coming into effect of DNA Identification Act (post 30 June 2000). Criminal Code s. 487.051	Court that convicts or discharges an offender under s. 730 or finds a youth guilty under the Young Offenders Act or under the Youth Criminal Justice Act of a designated offence. Peace officer or person acting under the direction of peace officer.[37]	**Dispositions Eligible for Order:** Offender must be convicted, discharged or found guilty under the Young Offenders Act or under the Youth Criminal Justice Act of a designated offence. If the disposition is for a *primary offence*[38] the court is *required* to authorize seizure of the DNA[39] unless the person demonstrates that taking a sample will have a *grossly* disproportionate impact on the person's privacy or security as compared to the public interest in the early detection, arrest and conviction of offenders.[40] If the person is convicted of a *secondary offence*, the court is **not** *required* to order the taking of a sample, but *may* order it if satisfied it is in the best interests of the administration of justice to do so.[41] For secondary offences, the court must consider the offender's criminal record, the nature and circumstances of the offence, and the impact on the person's privacy and security.	Judge must give reasons for its decision for issuing an order in relation to commission of a secondary offence.[42] **Execution procedure:** according to s. 487.06 (hair-plucking, blood sample, or buccal swab of cheek, lips, or tongue).[43] No requirement to use the least intrusive of these procedures: all are deemed to be minimally intrusive.[44] No order to issue if prosecutor advises databank already has the profile of the offence.[45] Samples to be taken at the time the person is convicted, discharged or found guilty, or as soon as feasible afterward, even if an appeal is taken s. 487.056(1). The results of the forensic DNA analysis of the bodily samples collected shall be transmitted to the Commissioner of the RCMP for entry in the convicted offenders index of the national DNA data bank established under the DNA *Identification Act*.[46]

37 Form 5.03; s. 487.056(3).
38 *Criminal Code*, s. 487.04.
39 *Ibid.*, s. 487.051(1)(a).
40 *Ibid.*, s. 487.051(2).
41 *Ibid.*, s. 487.051(1)(b).
42 Section 487.051(3).
43 *Criminal Code*, s. 487.06(1).
44 S.A.B., above note 24.
45 Section 487.053.
46 DNA *Identification Act.*, s. 487.071(1).

Appendix 6: Seizures of Bodily Substances and Impressions • 359

Statutory Power	Judicial Officer / Person to be Authorized	Criteria for Issuance	Limitations/Incidental Powers
DNA databank seizure order Offences committed before coming into effect of DNA Identification Act (pre 30 June 2000), if offender still before the court with jurisdiction over his or her trial. *Criminal Code* s. 487.052	Court that convicts or discharges an offender under s. 730 or finds a youth guilty under the *Young Offenders Act* or under the *Youth Criminal Justice Act* of a designated offence. Peace officer or person acting under the direction of peace officer[48]	Order must be in Form 5.04 The person must be convicted, discharged under s.730 or found guilty under the *Young Offenders Act* or under the *Youth Criminal Justice Act* of *any* s. 487.04 designated offence. The court is *not required* to order the taking of a sample, but *may* order it if satisfied it is in the best interests of the administration of justice to do so.[49]	Any unused portions of the bodily substances shall be forwarded to the Commissioner of the RCMP for the purposes of the *DNA Identification Act* (s. 487.071(2)). Right of Appeal: s. 487.054.[47] **Execution procedure:** according to s. 487.06 (hair plucking, blood sample, or buccal swab of cheek, lips, or tongue).[50] No requirement to use the least intrusive of these procedures: all are deemed to be minimally intrusive.[51] Section 487.052 applies regardless of when the conviction or sentencing occurs, provided that the trial court has not become *functus* and the offender is still before that court on or after June 30, 2000.[52] No order to issue if prosecutor advises databank already has the profile of the offender.[53]

47 Although the section does not specify, it is understood that the appeal lies to the provincial court of appeal if the order was made in a proceeding involving an indictable offence, and to the "appeal court" as defined in ss. 812 and 829 of the *Criminal Code*, where the order is made at a proceeding involving a summary conviction offence. *R. v. Hendry* (2001), 161 C.C.C. (3d) 275 (Ont. C.A.) [*Hendry*] at para. 5. Also, the standard of review on the appeal of an order is one of *deference* to the issuing judge, given that the order is discretionary: *Hendry* at para. 8. However, a more stringent standard applies when the error committed is a legal error, such as failing to provide reasons as required by ss. 487.051(3), 487.052(2), and 487.055 (3.1). In such cases, the standard of review is one of *correctness*. *R. v. North* (2002), 165 C.C.C. (3d) 393 (Alta. C.A.) [*North*] at para. 34.
48 Form 5.04; s. 487.056(3).
49 *Criminal Code*, s. 487.052(1).
50 *Ibid.*, s. 487.06(1).
51 S.A.B., above note 24.
52 *Hendry*, above note 47 at para. 16.
53 Section 487.053.

Statutory Power	Judicial Officer / Person to be Authorized	Criteria for Issuance	Limitations/Incidental Powers
DNA Databank seizure order con't			Samples to be taken at the time the person is convicted, discharged or found guilty, or as soon as feasible afterward, even if an appeal is taken. s. 487.056(1).
			The results of the forensic DNA analysis of the bodily samples collected shall be transmitted to the Commissioner of the RCMP for entry in the convicted offenders index of the national DNA data bank established under the *DNA Identification Act* (s. 487.071(1)).
			Any unused portions of the bodily substances shall be forwarded to the Commissioner of the RCMP for the purposes of the *DNA Identification Act*.[54]
			Right of appeal: s. 487.054.[55]
DNA databank seizure order	Provincial Court Judge Peace officer or person acting under the direction of peace officer[56]	*Ex parte* application[55b]	If the offender is on conditional release, a summons shall be served on the offender in accordance with s. 487.055(4)–(7).

54 *DNA Identification Act*, s. 487.071(2).
55 Although the section does not specify, it is understood that the appeal lies to the provincial court of appeal if the order was made in a proceeding involving an indictable offence, and to the "appeal court" as defined in ss. 812 and 829 of the *Criminal Code*, where the order is made at a proceeding involving a summary conviction offence. *Hendry*, above note 47 at para. 5. Also, the standard of review on the appeal of an order is one of *deference* to the issuing judge, given that the order is discretionary: *Hendry*, above note 47 at para. 8. However, a more stringent standard applies when the error committed is a *legal* error, such as failing to provide reasons as required by ss. 487.051(3), 487.052(2), and 487.055 (3.1). In such cases, the standard of review is one of *correctness*. *North*, above note 47 at para. 3.
55b However, see chapter 3, "DNA Databank Services" and *R. v. Rodgers*, [2004] O.J. No. 1073 (C.A.), where the court held that the crown must justify applying on an *ex parte* basis or else serve notice on the offender.
56 Form 5.05; s. 487.056(3).

Statutory Power	Judicial Officer Person to be Authorized	Criteria for Issuance	Limitations/Incidental Powers
DNA databank seizure order con't. Offences for offenders sentenced prior to coming into effect of *DNA Identification Act* (pre 30 June 2000). *Criminal Code* 487.055		Offender must have been: a) declared a dangerous offender;[57] Or has been: b) convicted of more than one murder committed at different times,[58] or c) convicted of more than one sexual offence (as defined under s. 487.055(3)): provided that the person is still serving a sentence of imprisonment of at least two years for one or more of those offences or has been declared a dangerous offender Application must be accompanied by a 667(1)(a) certificate establishing the offender fits in the criteria listed above, without notice under 667(4).[59] The making of an order is discretionary, and may issue if it is in the best interests of the administration of justice. The judge must consider the offender's criminal record, the nature of the offence, the circumstances surrounding its commission and the impact of the order on the offender's privacy and security of the person.[60]	A warrant may issue if the offender does not attend for the taking of the sample.[61] Samples are to be taken as soon as feasible s. 487.056(2).

57 Section 481.055(1)(a)(b)(c).
58 See *R. v. Samra*, [2003] O.J. No. 3289 (Sup. Ct.) [*Samra*] for the definition of "multiple murders." In *Samra*, McCombs J. held that the definition of "multiple murders" under s. 487.055 does not include those that form part of a single transaction. McCombs J. considered the cases of two offenders: Maljkovich murdered his wife and daughter, attempted to murder his daughter's boyfriend, all in rapid succession in essentially a single incident in the same house; Samra entered a courtroom at Osgoode Hall during a civil motion and fired a handgun multiple times, killing two people and wounding another. Justice McCombs found that, in the circumstances of these cases, the incidents in formed single transactions rather than "multiple murders," and as such fell outside the ambit of s. 487.055.
59 Section 487.055(2).
60 Section 487.055(1) and (3.1), considered to be constitutionally reasonable in *R. v. Engum* (2002), 163 C.C.C. (3d) 198 (B.C.S.C.).
61 Section 487.055(8)–(10).

Statutory Power	Judicial Officer / Person to be Authorized	Criteria for Issuance	Limitations/Incidental Powers
Authorization to obtain additional samples if DNA profile could not be derived from the samples seized. *Criminal Code* s. 487.091	Provincial Court Judge / Peace officer or person acting under the direction of peace officer[62]	Judge may make an *ex parte* order if: • an order or authorization issued under ss. 487.051, 487.052, or 487.055; and • a DNA profile could not be derived from the samples taken pursuant to those orders. Provided the application is within a reasonable time after it is determined that no profile could be derived. Application must state the reasons why the profile could not be derived from the samples taken s. 487.091(2).	Any number of additional samples may be taken as required for the purpose of deriving the profile s. 487.091(1). Section 487.055(4–10) provisions for issuance of summons and warrant apply for persons on conditional release s. 487.091(3).
Collection and storage of DNA information from convicted offenders *DNA Identification Act*		Following sample collection, DNA profiles are created, and stored in the DNA databank under the "convicted offenders index" s. 487.071.[63] The profile contains only "non-coding" or "junk DNA" attributes that allows only for identification of the sample without revealing other personal biological information.[64] This offender profile information can then be compared against information in the "crime scene index," which contains DNA profiles from bodily substances left behind at unsolved crime scenes throughout Canada.[65]	The fact of the match is not evidence for the purpose of criminal proceedings; rather, the match can form all or part of the reasonable grounds for a new DNA seizure warrant (which will itself become evidence in a criminal proceeding).[67] It is an offence to use the DNA information in ways other than provided for under the *DNA Identification Act*.

62 Form 5.08; s. 487.056(3).
63 *Briggs*, above note 24 at para. 11.
64 *Ibid.* at para. 14; *S.A.B.*, above note 24 at para. 49. The samples themselves are also retained at the databank but do not form part of the indices, see *Briggs, ibid.* at para. 14.
65 *Briggs, ibid.*; s. 487.071; *DNA Identification Act*, ss. 6 and 7.
66 *Briggs, ibid.* at para. 16; *DNA Identification Act*, s. 6.

Statutory Power	Judicial Officer / Person to be Authorized	Criteria for Issuance	Limitations/Incidental Powers
Collection and storage of DNA information con't.		If the databank finds a match, the police force investigating the crime is notified only that a match has occurred between their crime scene sample and a convicted offender, and is not given the profile or the sample.[67]	**Destruction of samples:** Samples and profiles taken from convicted offenders must be destroyed in the following circumstances: • When a conviction is quashed and a final acquittal entered;[68] • One year after an absolute discharge;[69] • Three years after a conditional discharge;[70] • For young offenders, whenever the last part of a record is required to be destroyed under ss. 45(2), 45.02(3) or 45.03(3) of the *Young Offenders Act*.[71]

67 *Briggs, ibid.* at para. 16.
68 *DNA Identification Act*, s. 9(2)(a) and s. 10(7)(a).
69 Unless the person is convicted of another offence in the meantime; *DNA Identification Act*, s. 9(2)(b)(i) and s. 10(7)(b)(i).
70 Unless the person is convicted of another offence in the meantime; *DNA Identification Act*, s. 9(2)(b)(ii) and s. 10(7)(b)(ii).
71 *DNA Identification Act*, s. 9.1(1) and s. 10.1. The statute has not yet been amended to include the *Youth Criminal Justice Act*.

ANNOTATIONS

Application of Factors Affecting Discretion to Issue DNA Seizure Orders

Exercise of Discretion: s. 487.051 (primary designated offences committed after 30 June 2002)

DNA seizure orders are essentially mandatory following findings of guilt for *primary designated offences* committed after June 30, 2002, unless the offender can demonstrate that the balance between the public interest and proper administration of justice in early detection, arrest, and conviction, is grossly disproportionate to the effect on the offender's privacy and security of the person.[72] Cases where the offender will be able to demonstrate such an imbalance will be rare.[73] In *R. v. Jordan*, the Nova Scotia Court of Appeal recommended that courts consider the following factors — nature of the offence, nature of the intrusion, and circumstances of the individual — as well as the factors listed in s. 487.051(3) and s. 487.052(2), as a starting point to determine whether in a particular case whether the impact of the taking of DNA samples on the offender's privacy and security of the person would be grossly disproportionate to the state's law enforcement objectives if an order were to issue under s. 487.051. The Court held that the offender *would* meet the threshold of establishing a disproportionate impact if the following factors were present:

1) If the circumstances of the particular offender or of the offence or of the risk of breach of privacy or security of the person vary markedly from the sort of cases which Parliament may be presumed to have had in mind in devising the legislative scheme, the impact of the order may be found to be grossly disproportionate.

2) The second factor relates to the court's power to impose conditions in the authorizing order. The authorizing order should only be refused if the exercise of discretion to impose terms and conditions in the authorizing order cannot adequately restore the appropriate balance. As s. 487.051 makes clear, the burden of establishing that the order should not be made is on an offender who has been convicted of a primary designated offence.[74]

---

72 *R. v. Jordan* (2002), 162 C.C.C. (3d) 385 (N.S.C.A.) [*Jordan*] at para. 28.
73 *Ibid.* at para. 78.
74 *Ibid.* at para. 59.

Exercise of Discretion: s. 487.051(3) (secondary designated offences committed post 30 June 2002) and s. 487.052 (any designated offences committed before 30 June 2002 where offender still before the court)

The factors the court must consider in exercising its discretion to issue an order under s. 487.051(3) and s. 487.052 are identical. The best interests of the administration of justice involves a balancing of the state's interests (which lie in deterrence, detection, solving cold crimes, streamlining investigations, and exculpating the innocent) against the offender's criminal record, the nature of the offence, the circumstances surrounding its commission, and the impact on the offender's privacy and security of the person. See *R. v. Briggs*, above.

There are two lines of cases instructing courts how to resolve the balancing of interests. The Ontario Court of Appeal has held that while the judge has discretion as to whether to make an order under s. 487.052, in light of the minimal intrusion into the security of the person in the ordinary case and the important interests served by the DNA data bank, it will usually be in the best interests of the administration of justice to do so.[75] By contrast, the Alberta Court of Appeal in *R. v. North*[76] found that the Ontario Court of Appeal's approach was inconsistent with the legislative distinction drawn between primary and secondary offences. The Court held that while in many cases the public interest would prevail, if evidence is adduced that the offender's privacy and security interests would be unusually affected, the nature and degree of state interests may be subordinate.[77]

Consideration of Specific Factors under s. 487.051(3) and s. 487.051(4): Criminal Record of the Offender

The offender's criminal record is relevant as it may indicate the likelihood of recidivism; the more likely it is that an individual will commit other crimes, the more likely it is that the person's sample will help identify that person as the perpetrator of another crime.[78]

The record need not show a *pattern* of conduct or general disposition towards committing serious offences or a likelihood of re-offence;[79] the presence of such entries is sufficient to justify the issuance of an order.[80]

---

75 *Hendry*, above note 47 at para. 1.
76 *North*, above note 47.
77 *Ibid.* at para. 53.
78 *Jordan*, above note 72 at 64; *North*, above note 47 at para. 50.
79 *North*, above note 47 at para. 50.
80 *Hendry*, above note 47 at paras. 3 and 42.

The more serious the offender's criminal record, the less discretion the court has to decline the order, especially if that record includes *any* convictions for primary designated offences.[81] In such cases, it would be exceptional not to issue the order.[82]

A serious criminal record is also relevant in the balancing exercise as it may indicate a degree of dangerousness to society which makes the interference with the offender's privacy and security of the person more readily justifiable than it would be, for example, in the case of an offender with a record of only non-violent offences.[83]

If an offender has no prior record and has committed a secondary designated offence with relatively non-serious circumstances, the court may be justified in refusing to make the order.[84]

An authorizing judge is entitled to consider the *whole* of the offender's criminal record, including non-designated offences, and offences committed after the offence attached to the application.[85] DNA orders are not sentences and ought not to receive the same safeguards that apply to sentencing (such as consideration only of *prior* offences).[86]

The Nature of the Offence
This factor refers to the categories of offences designated by the *Code*, which the Court in *Briggs* summarized as: (1) offences related to violence or the threat of violence to the person; (2) other offences against the person; (3) sexual offences mostly relating to children not included as primary designated offences; (4) offences relating to public safety; and (5) property offences.[87]

In *R. v. Jordan*,[88] the N.S.C.A. held that the seriousness of the offence might be mitigated by the particular circumstances, if those circumstances are not typical of the general nature of the offence or demonstrate a low risk of recidivism.[89] The Court recognized however that a low risk of recidivism is not determinative of whether to issue an order. Parliament did not include the likelihood to re-offend as a prerequisite to obtaining a sample,

---

81 *Ibid.* at paras. 24 and 35.
82 *Ibid.* at para. 24.
83 *Jordan*, above note 72 at para. 67.
84 *Hendry*, above note 47 at para. 24.
85 *Briggs*, above note 24 at para. 71.
86 *Ibid.*
87 *Ibid.* at para. 72.
88 *Jordan*, above note 72.
89 *Ibid.* at 68.

and therefore a low risk of recidivism would likely have little weight in the overall assessment.[90]

Whether DNA evidence was found at the scene of the offence, or whether it is the type of offence in which DNA evidence may be expected to be a useful investigative tool is a relevant consideration, though not determinative. The courts have recognized that advances in technology have improved our ability to detect and analyse even minute amounts of bodily substances left at a crime scene, including substances such as dandruff, sweat and saliva that may not relate to the nature of the offence in question, but will identify the offender.[91] Further, the obtaining of a DNA sample may still be in the best interests of justice, as the data bank has purposes that extend beyond conviction of repeat offenders, such as deterrence and public safety.[92]

Circumstances of the Offence

In assessing the circumstances of the offence, the court will examine the severity of the conduct and any aggravating features present in the commission of the specific crime, such as gratuitous or serious violence,[93] or a breach of trust.[94]

A judge may decline to make the order if the behaviour constituting the offence was relatively minor misconduct in the circumstances.[95] For example, assaulting a police officer (a secondary designated offence) that involved merely pushing a police officer acting in the execution of his or her duties might be a fairly trivial instance of an otherwise serious offence.[96]

Aggravating or serious circumstances may tip the balance in favour of ordering DNA seizure, even if the offence was not premeditated, or if the offender has no prior record, or if there was a small risk of re-offending.[97]

The fact that an offender's prior record is for violence or for an offence against a spouse (or another specific person) is *not* a circumstance that militates against the issuance of an order to take a DNA sample for reasons of "already knowing the identity of the offender". Such an argument was

---

90   *Ibid.* at paras. 71 and 75.
91   *North*, above note 47 at para. 51; *Briggs*, above note 24 at para. 76; *Jordan*, above note 72 at para. 70.
92   *North*, *ibid.* at para. 51.
93   *R. v. Ku* (2002), 169 C.C.C. (3d) 535 (B.C.C.A.) [*Ku*] at para. 45.
94   *Hendry*, above note 47 at paras. 29 and 39; *Briggs*, above note 24 at para. 77.
95   *Hendry*, *ibid.* at para. 23.
96   *Ibid.*
97   *Ku*, above note 93 at paras. 44–45.

advanced in *R. v. Hendry*,[98] the accused argued that an offender who only assaults one victim, when the victim knows the assailant's identity, ought not to be subject to DNA sampling. As Rosenberg J.A. explained in *Hendry*, such reasoning is fatally flawed:

> The reasoning of the trial judge would seem to be premised on the fact that because the respondent only assaults his spouse, identity will never be in issue and therefore DNA evidence will be unnecessary. This ignores several painful lessons from the history of spousal abuse. Regrettably, these types of offences can escalate in seriousness to the point where the victim may not be available to identify the offender. Second, on occasion the victim may be so intimidated by the perpetrator that she is unable or unwilling to identify him in court. DNA evidence may indeed be crucial. Third, as was indicated in Bates, this type of offender will not necessarily limit his criminal conduct to the victim, but may assault other persons he believes are close to the victim. Again, DNA evidence may be important to the prosecution's case. The violent offences committed by the respondent are the very kind that would likely result in DNA evidence being available.[99]

It is also appropriate for the court to link the circumstances of the offence to other factors such as the offender's criminal record. In *Briggs*, the court considered as relevant to making the DNA order the offender's prior criminal record for weapons offences, even though in the predicate offence it was the offender's co-accused, and not Briggs himself, who brandished the knife.[100]

A lack of insight into the gravity of the conduct will also influence a court to make the order, as it suggests that the offender is at an increased risk of committing future offences.[101]

The Impact on the Person's Security and Privacy

For "the impact on the person's security and privacy" to affect the court's decision whether to authorize the taking of a sample, the offender may have to demonstrate that the methods for taking the sample would negatively impact the offender *disproportionately to the general population*, given the Supreme Court's acceptance that the procedures for taking the sample are essentially non-intrusive,[102] and that the "informational content" (for infor-

---

98 *Hendry*, above note 47.
99 *Ibid.* at para. 51.
100 *Briggs*, above note 24 at para. 77.
101 *Hendry*, above note 47 at paras. 29 and 40.
102 *S.A.B.*, above note 24; *Briggs*, above note 24 at paras. 78–79.

mation beyond mere identity) of the sample is not available to law enforcement personnel.

Evidence of a specific risk of misuse of the sample, or particular dangers to the health of the offender if the sample were to be taken would tend to show such a disproportionate impact.[103]

The offender's argument against seizure will be further weakened if he or she is sentenced to a custodial term, as the offender will be subject to intrusions of privacy on a routine basis as a result of being incarcerated, that would far outweigh the minimally intrusive short-duration DNA collection procedures.[104] Moreover, the effect on the offender's privacy and security interests is also diminished if the person is a "mature offender" who has previously been sentenced to terms of incarceration.[105]

---

103 *Jordan*, above note 72 at paras. 72–73.
104 *Briggs*, above note 24 at para. 80; *Hendry*, above note 47 at para. 42.
105 *Hendry*, *ibid.* at para. 37.

APPENDIX 7: Related Statutes: Search and Seizure Powers

1) Statutory Power 2) Scope	Judicial Officer Person to be Authorized	Special Requirements
1) *Competition Act* s. 11 Order for oral examination, production, or written return[1] 2) Orders for production of evidence relevant to an inquiry under s. 10 *Competition Act*	Judge of a Superior or county court or of the Federal Court N/A	If there is: 1) an *ex parte* application of the commissioner or authorized rep of the commissioner, on oath 2) an outstanding inquiry under s. 10 of the *Competition Act*; and 3) a person has or is likely to have information relevant to the inquiry, the judge may order the person to: a) attend before a "presiding officer" (s. 13) named in the order, and be examined on oath on matters relevant to the inquiry b) produce a record or other thing specified in the order to the commissioner within a specified time c) make and deliver to the commissioner in a specified time and to a specified place a written return, in the detail specified by the order • a corporation's affiliates can be ordered to produce records if the corporation is the person subject to the inquiry and if the affiliate is in Canada (s. 11(2)) • persons ordered to give testimony are protected from use of the evidence at a subsequent criminal proceeding (other than perjury offences), and may not refuse to participate on grounds of self-incrimination (s. 11(3)) • effective throughout Canada (s. 11(4)) • all persons summoned to attend to give evidence under oath are competent and compellable (s. 12(1)), entitled to witness fees (s. 11(2)), and may be represented by counsel (s. 12(3)) • the person subject to the inquiry may attend all witness examinations, unless the commissioner establishes the person's presence would be prejudicial to the conduct of the examination or inquiry or result in disclosure of confidential information related to the business of the person being examined (s. 12(4)) • the person from whom the items were seized is entitled to inspect the items at any reasonable time and on any reasonable conditions imposed by the commissioner (s. 18(2)) • procedure for seizure when a claim of solicitor–client privilege is made is set out in s. 19

1 See *Thomson Newspapers Ltd. v. Canada (Director of Investigation & Research, Restrictive Trade Practices Commission)* (1990), 54 C.C.C. (3d) 417 (S.C.C.) regarding the constitutionality of the predecessor section; see also *Stelco Inc. v. Canada (Attorney General)* (1990), 55 C.C.C. (3d) 227 (S.C.C.).

Appendix 7: Related Statutes: Search and Seizure Powers • 371

1) Statutory Power 2) Scope	Judicial Officer Person to be Authorized	Special Requirements

1) *Competition Act* s. 15 Warrant for entry into premises
 	
2) Authorizes search and seizure of evidence related to *Competition Act* offences and orders
	Superior or county court or Federal Court judge
	
	Commissioner or any other person named in the warrant
		A warrant authorizing the entry into a premises, and the search and seizure (or copying) of items listed in b) below, in the following circumstances:
		• on the *ex parte* application of the Commissioner or authorized rep., containing information *on oath* setting out:
		  a) reasonable grounds to believe:
		    i) a person has contravened or failed to comply with an order under *Competition Act* ss. 32, 33, 33.1, 34 or Part VIII
		    ii) grounds exist for a Part VIII order
		    iii) a Part VI or VII offence has been or is about to be committed; and
		  b) reasonable grounds to believe there is any record or thing that will afford evidence with respect to the circumstances listed in (a) above.
		• warrant must identify:
		  – the matter in respect of which the warrant is issued
		  – the premises to be searched
		  – the records, things or class of records or things to be searched for (s. 15(2))
		• the warrant must be executed between 6:00 and 21:00 unless the judge specifically authorizes otherwise (s. 15(3))
		• may be executed anywhere in Canada (s. 15(4))
		• if access to a premises is refused initially, the judge may authorize a peace officer to take the steps the judge considers necessary to authorize access (s. 15(5)(6))
		• the person conducting the search may access computer systems on the premises and reproduce the data from the computer (s. 16)
		• the judge who issued the warrant may order may make a specific order naming the individuals who may operate the computer systems, the times they may do, and any other conditions (on application of either the commissioner or person subject to the search), on 24 hours notice of the application to the other party (or such shorter time as the judge orders) (s. 16)

1) Statutory Power 2) Scope	Judicial Officer Person to be Authorized	Special Requirements

1) *Competition Act* s. 15 con't.
 	
2) Authorizes search and seizure of evidence con't.
		In order to properly retain items seized following seizure:
		
		1) The commissioner (or rep) must present the seized items or a report to the judge who issued the warrant as soon as practicable after seizure (s. 17(1))
		— A report under s. 17(1) must detail:
		  a) the statutory power that authorized the seizure of the item
		  b) a description of the premises searched
		  c) a description of the thing seized
		  d) the location of detention (s. 17(2));
		2) Then, obtain authorization from that judge to retain the items. The judge may authorize retention if the judge is satisfied that the item is required for an inquiry or other proceeding under the *Competition Act*. (s. 17(3)).[2]
		
		• the person from whom the items were seized is entitled to inspect the items at any reasonable time and on any reasonable conditions imposed by the commissioner (s. 18(2))
		• procedure for seizure when a claim of solicitor–client privilege is made is set out in s. 19

1) *Competition Act* s. 15(7) Power of warrantless entry in exigent circumstances 2) Same as above	N/A	• warrantless powers of search available if the grounds listed above exist, but exigent circumstances render the obtaining of a warrant impracticable. Exigent circumstances include the destruction or loss of evidence that would occur through the delay necessary to obtain a warrant. (s. 15(7)) The retention hearing under this section can likely proceed *ex parte*, see, e.g., *Cottrell Transport Inc. v. Director of Investigation & Research* (1987), 19 C.P.R. (3d) 117 (Ont. H. C. J.), aff'd 26 O.A.C. 378 (C.A.), however notice to the person from whom the thing seized *may* be given in the discretion of the judge, see *Re Competition Act, s. 17(3)* (1990), 3 F.T.R. 237 (T.D.). However, see *Re Norvinca Inc.* (1987), 16 C.P.R. (3d) 187 (T.D.), re necessity to involve person from whom thing was seized.

2 The retention hearing under this section can likely proceed *ex parte*, see, e.g., *Cottrell Transport Inc. v. Director of Investigation & Research* (1987), 19 C.P.R. (3d) 117 (Ont. H. C. J.), aff'd 26 O.A.C. 378 (C.A.), however notice to the person from whom the thing seized *may* be given in the discretion of the judge, see *Re Competition Act, s. 17(3)* (1990), 3 F.T.R. 237 (T.D.). However, see *Re Norvinca Inc.* (1987), 16 C.P.R. (3d) 187 (T.D.), re necessity to involve person from whom thing was seized.

1) Statutory Power 2) Scope	Judicial Officer Person to be Authorized	Special Requirements
1) *Corrections and Conditional Release Act (CCRA)* s. 47 Routine non-intrusive searches of inmates 2) Non-intrusive searches of: a) the clothed body by technical means, in prescribed manner b) searches of personal possessions carried by a person and any coat or jacket the inmate was asked to remove (s. 46)	No prior authorization Staff member or person providing prescribed class of services to the Service if: a) conducting such searches is provided for in the contract; b) the searches are reasonably related to the person's principal services under the contract; and c) the person has received the prescribed training for conducting such searches	No individualized suspicion required Regulations prescribe the various circumstances under which such searches can be conducted (although the prescribed circumstances must be limited to reasonable security)
1) *CCRA* s. 48 Routine strip searches of inmates 2) Strip search means: a) visual inspection of the naked body, in the prescribed manner b) searches of all clothing, things in the clothing, and other personal possessions that the person may be carrying (s. 46)	No prior authorization Staff member of the same sex as the inmate	Strip searches may be conducted: 1) as prescribed in the regulations; however, the regulations must be limited to situations where the inmate has been in a place where there was likely access to contraband that is capable of being hidden on in the body; or 2) when an inmate is entering or leaving a segregated area No individualized suspicion required
1) *CCRA* s. 49(1) Frisk search of inmate Offence-related strip searches of inmate s. 49(3) 2) Frisk search means: a) a manual search, or search by technical means, of the *clothed* body in the prescribed manner b) a search of personal possessions, including clothing that the person may be carrying and	No prior authorization for frisk search. Authorization by institutional head for strip searches (unless exigent circumstances) Staff member or person providing prescribed class of services to the Service (for frisk searches only) if: a) conducting such searches is provided for in the contract;	Frisk search: reasonable grounds to *suspect* an inmate is carrying contraband or evidence relating to a disciplinary or criminal offence. Strip search: if staff member has reasonable grounds to believe that an inmate is carrying contraband or evidence related to a criminal or disciplinary offence, and that a strip search is necessary to find the evidence

Appendix 7: Related Statutes: Search and Seizure Powers • 373

1) Statutory Power 2) Scope	Judicial Officer Person to be Authorized	Special Requirements
including any coat or jacket the person has been requested to remove See also regulations in accordance with 96(1) (s. 46) Strip search as defined above	b) the searches are reasonably related to the person's principal services under the contract; and c) the person has received the prescribed training for conducting such searches	• if the staff member satisfies the institutional head of those grounds • must be a staff member of the same sex executing a strip search Exigent circumstances • if the staff member believes on *reasonable grounds* that the delay necessary to comply with requirement for same sex strip search or prior authorization from institutional head would result in *danger to human life or safety or the loss of destruction of evidence*, then compliance with those provisions is not required (s. 49(4))

1) CCRA s. 51
X-rays and "dry cell"
 	
2) Use of X-rays (on consent of the inmate) and detention of inmate in a cell without plumbing fixture to detect contraband
	Institutional head
	
	Qualified medical practitioner or X-ray technician
		Where satisfied on reasonable grounds that an inmate has ingested or is carrying contraband in a body cavity, the institutional head may authorize *in writing*:
		a) use of an X-ray machine by a qualified X-ray technician to find the contraband if:
		  i) the inmate consents
		  ii) a qualified medical practitioner consents and/or;
		b) the detention of the inmate in a cell without plumbing fixtures, if
		  i) notice is given to the penitentiary's medical staff
		  ii) it is expected that the contraband will be expelled

1) CCRA s. 52 Body cavity search 2) Physical probing of a body cavity in the prescribed manner (s. 46) on consent of the inmate.	Institutional head Qualified medical practitioner	Available where institutional head is satisfied on grounds: • that an inmate is carrying contraband in a body cavity; and • that a body cavity search is necessary to find or seize the contraband. Authorization to qualified medical practitioner must be *in writing*. Authorization may only be given if *inmate has consented*. • staff members are not permitted to seize or attempt to seize contraband in a body cavity; rather they must inform the institutional head (s.50)

Appendix 7: Related Statutes: Search and Seizure Powers • 375

1) Statutory Power 2) Scope	Judicial Officer Person to be Authorized	Special Requirements

1) CCRA s. 53
Frisk and strip searches in exceptional circumstances
 	
2) Exceptional circumstances to perform frisk and strip searches as defined above
	Institutional head
	
	Staff member of the same sex as the inmate
		Exceptional circumstances exist if:
		• the institutional head is satisfied on reasonable grounds that:
		  a) the contraband is creating a clear and substantial danger to human life or safety, or the security of the penitentiary; and
		  b) a frisk search or strip search is necessary to avert the danger and seize the contraband.
		• no other statutory limitations on the search power

1) CCRA s. 54
Urinalysis demand for inmates
 	
2) Taking of urine sample
	Institutional head (offence related only)
	
	Staff member
		Staff member may demand an inmate's submission to urinalysis:
		a) where staff member believes on reasonable grounds:
		  i) that inmate has committed or is committing offence under s. 40(k) (taking intoxicant) and,
		  ii) that a urine sample is necessary to provide evidence of that offence and where the institutional head has provided prior authorization
		b) as part of a prescribed random selection urinalysis program, without individualized grounds, on a periodic basis, and in accordance with the Commissioner's Directives[3]
		c) where urinalysis is a prescribed requirement for participation in:
		  i) a prescribed program or activity involving community contact; or
		  ii) a prescribed substances abused treatment program.
		• for demands under a), the inmate shall be given an opportunity to make representations to the institutional head before submitting the sample (s. 57(1))

3 Random urinalyses constitutionally valid per *Fieldhouse v. Kent Institution* (1995). 98 C.C.C. (3d) 207 (B.C.C.A.).

1) Statutory Power 2) Scope	Judicial Officer Person to be Authorized	Special Requirements
CCRA s. 55 Urinalysis demand for offenders 2) Urinalysis demand from an offender who is allowed to leave the prison	No prior authorization Staff member or other person authorized by the Service	Staff member or other authorized person may demand submission to urinalysis from offender (inmate or person who is on a form of parole or absence from institution (see s. 2)): a) immediately if reasonable suspicion of breach of any condition of temporary absence, work release, parole, or statutory release that requires abstention from alcohol or drugs; or b) at regular intervals, in order to monitor compliance with a condition of a temporary absence, work release, parole, or statutory release that requires abstention from alcohol or drugs • for a demand under b), the inmate shall be given a reasonable opportunity to make representations to the prescribed official in relation to the length of the intervals (s. 57(2))
CCRA s. 57 Searches of cells[3b] 2) Searches of inmate cells for security purposes	No prior authorization Staff member	Regulations prescribe circumstances in which these searches may be conducted, but which are limited to what is reasonably required for security purposes
CCRA s. 59 Routine searches of visitors 2) Non-intrusive searches of: a) the clothed body by technical means, in prescribed manner b) searches of personal possessions carried by a person and any coat or jacket the inmate was asked to remove (s. 46) Frisk Search means: a) a manual search, or search by technical means, of the *clothed* body in the prescribed manner b) a search of personal possessions, including clothing that the person may be carrying and including any coat or jacket the person has been requested to remove	No prior authorization Staff member	No individualized suspicion Regulations prescribe circumstances for conducting such circumstances, which are limited to searches for security purposes

[3b] See *R. v. Major*, [2004] O.J. No. 2651 (C.A.), where the court finds that a "cell" includes a private family visit trailer on institutional property.

1) Statutory Power 2) Scope	Judicial Officer Person to be Authorized	Special Requirements
1) CCRA s. 60 Visitors: frisk search and strip search 2) Frisk searches as described above Strip search means: a) visual inspection of the naked body, in the pre-scribed manner b) searches of all clothing, things in the clothing, and other personal possessions that the person may be carrying (s. 46)	No prior authorization for frisk searches Institutional head for strip searches Staff member of same sex as visitor	1) Frisk searches: staff member must have reasonable grounds to believe the visitor is carrying contraband or other evidence relating to a s. 45 offence. 2) Strip searches may be conducted on suspicion alone: • if the staff member suspects on reasonable grounds the visitor is carrying contraband or evidence relating to a s. 45 offence; • if the institutional head is satisfied of (a), and that a strip search is necessary to find the contraband or evidence; and • if the visitor is given the option of voluntarily leaving the penitentiary forthwith 3) If the staff member believes on reasonable grounds that the visitor is carrying contraband or evidence of a s. 45 offence, • the visitor may be detained pending authorization from the institutional head to conduct the strip search or to obtain the services of the police • if the institutional head is satisfied on reasonable grounds the visitor is carrying contraband or evidence, the institutional head may authorize the strip search • the visitor must be informed of the reasons for detention, and informed of the right to and given an opportunity to retain and instruct counsel without delay (s. 61(4)) See s. 62 requirement to post warning about searches at entry and visitor control points
1) CCRA s. 61 Vehicle searches 2) Search of vehicles at a penitentiary, on routine and offence related bases	Institutional head (for offence-based searches) Staff member	Routine searches of vehicles at penitentiary: • require no individualized suspicion • must be conducted in prescribed circumstances, which are limited to security searches If a staff member believes on reasonable grounds that contraband is in a vehicle, the institutional head may authorize the search of the vehicle (s. 61(2)). A staff member may proceed *without prior authorization* if necessary to preserve human life or safety or prevent the loss or destruction of the contraband. (s. 61(3)). See s. 62 requirement to post warning about searches at entry and visitor control points

1) Statutory Power 2) Scope	Judicial Officer Person to be Authorized	Special Requirements
1) CCRA s. 63 Routine searches of staff members 2) Non-intrusive searches of: a) the clothed body by technical means, in prescribed manner b) searches of personal possessions carried by a person and any coat or jacket the inmate was asked to remove (s. 46) Frisk search means: a) a manual search, or search by technical means, of the *clothed* body in the prescribed manner b) a search of personal possessions, including clothing that the person may be carrying and including any coat or jacket the person has been requested to remove	No prior authorization Staff member	No individualized suspicion In prescribed circumstances related to security
1) CCRA s. 54 Frisk and strip searches of staff member 2) Frisk search as described above Strip search means: a) visual inspection of the naked body, in the prescribed manner b) searches of all clothing, things in the clothing, and other personal possessions that the person may be carrying (s. 46)	Institutional head Staff member of same sex as other staff member	Staff member must satisfy the institutional head that there are reasonable grounds to believe that another staff member is carrying contraband, or other evidence relating to a criminal offence, and that a frisk or strip search is necessary to find the evidence The staff member may be detained to secure the authorization to search from the institutional head or the services of the police Staff member must be informed promptly of the reasons for detention and informed of the right to and given an opportunity to retain and instruct counsel without delay (s. 64(2))
1) CCRA s. 65 Power to seize contraband and evidence	Authorization as per search power	

1) Statutory Power 2) Scope	Judicial Officer Person to be Authorized	Special Requirements
2) Items found in the course of a search conducted pursuant to ss. 47–64.	Staff member (for ss. 47–64 searches, except for body cavity and X-rays/dry-cell searches) Medical practitioner (if conducting body cavity search or X-ray/dry-cell search) Other person conducting a search pursuant to s. 47(2) or s. 49(2) may seize contraband	
1) CCRA s. 66 Frisk and room searches in community-based residential facilities 2) Frisk searches and searches of rooms in "community-based residential facilities," facilities that provide accommodation to offenders on parole, statutory release or temporary absence (s. 66(3)) Frisk search means: a) a manual search, or search by technical means, of the clothed body in the prescribed manner b) a search of personal possessions, including clothing that the person may be carrying and including any coat or jacket the person has been requested to remove	Employee of community-based residential facility	Such searches may be conducted if: • the employee *suspects* on reasonable grounds[4] that the offender is violating or has violated a condition of release • the search is necessary to confirm the suspected violation The employee may seize any evidence of a violation of the offender's conditions of release found during the search (s. 66(2))

---

4 Suspects on reasonable grounds is a higher threshold than mere suspicion, but lower than belief on reasonable grounds: *R. v. Cahill* (1992), 13 C.R. (4th) 327 (B.C.C.A.).

1) Statutory Power 2) Scope	Judicial Officer Person to be Authorized	Special Requirements
1) *Customs Act* s. 98 Search of the person[5] 2) Searches of the person[6]	Officer (see s. 2, generally, customs officers and RCMP members) of the same sex as the person being searched (s. 98(4)) If no officer of the same sex is present, any suitable person of the same sex may be authorized by an officer to conduct the search (s. 98(4))	The following people are subject to search: • any person who has arrived in Canada, within a reasonable time of arrival; • any person about to leave Canada, at any time prior to departure; • any person who has had access to an area designated for use by persons about to leave Canada, and who leaves the area but does not leave Canada, within a reasonable time of leaving the area Provided that an officer *suspects* on reasonable grounds that the person has secreted on or about his person: • anything in respect of which the *Customs Act* has been or might be contravened • anything that would afford evidence regarding a contravention of the *Customs Act* • any goods the importation or exportation of which is prohibited, controlled or regulated under this or any other Act of Parliament (s. 98(1)) • threshold of "suspicion" constitutionally valid: *R. v. Oluwa* (1996), 107 C.C.C. (3d) 236 (B.C.C.A.) Review of decision to search: • the officer must bring the person about to be searched to a senior officer prior to conducting the search, if the person so requests (s. 98(2)) • the senior officer must discharge the person if not satisfied that reasonable grounds exist to conduct the search (s. 98(3))

5 See also chapter 3, "Reasonable Expectation of Privacy Is Necessary to Challenge a Search" and "At the Border."
6 Searches of the person may include bedpan vigils; see *R. v. Monney* (1999), 133 C.C.C. (3d) 129 (S.C.C.); the section may also authorize X-rays and the administration of laxatives, but requires higher levels of protection against the search, see *R. v. Carpenter* (2001), 151 C.C.C. (3d) 205 (B.C.C.A.), leave to appeal refused 159 C.C.C. (3d) vi (S.C.C.).

1) Statutory Power 2) Scope	Judicial Officer Person to be Authorized	Special Requirements
Customs Act s. 99 Examination of import/export goods	Officer (s. 2)	Examination of goods powers: • prior to the goods release, by the opening of any package or container of imported goods, or examination of any goods, and taking samples of goods in reasonable amounts • prior to its release, examine imported mail prior to release, or open mail, if the officer suspect on reasonable grounds that the mail contains any goods in the *Customs Tariff* or any goods the importation of which is illegal or prohibited, controlled or regulated under an Act of Parliament, and take such reasonable samples of the items in the mail • up to the time of exportation, examine goods reported under s. 95, and open packages and take samples • up to the time of exportation, examine and take samples of mail and anything contained in the mail if the officer suspects on reasonable grounds that the mail contains goods that are prohibited, controlled or regulated under an Act of Parliament • examine and take samples of goods where the officer suspects on reasonable grounds there has been an error in the tariff classification, or where a refund or drawback is request • examine and take samples of goods where the officer suspects on reasonable grounds there was an error made with respect to the origin claimed for goods accounted for under s. 32 • examine any goods and open any package with respect to which the officer suspects on reasonable grounds that any Act of Parliament enforced by the officer was contravened • stop, board and search the conveyance or any goods thereon, open any packages or containers, with respect to which the officer suspects on reasonable grounds that any Act of Parliament or regulations enforced by the officer were contravened (can include searches of cars *R. v. Jacques*, [1996] 3 S.C.R. 312) These powers do not apply to mail that weighs 30 grams or less unless the intended receiver consents or the sender has completed and attached to the mail a label under article RE 601 of the *Letter Post Regulations* (s. 99(2)): • s. 99(1) permits the search and seizure of baggage accompanying a person on an international flight, even if the baggage is "in-transit," if the flight stops in Canada: *R. v. Oluwa* (1996), 107 C.C.C. (3d) 236 (B.C.C.A.) • threshold of "suspicion" constitutionally valid: *R. v. Collymore* (1999), 138 C.C.C. (3d) 306 (Ont. C.A.); *R. v. Oluwa* (1996), 107 C.C.C. (3d) 236 (B.C.C.A.)

1) Statutory Power 2) Scope	Judicial Officer Person to be Authorized	Special Requirements
1) *Customs Act* s. 99.1 Power to stop person 2) Questioning and examination of person's goods if reasonable suspicion that person has not presented him or herself in accordance with 11(1)	No prior authorization Officer (s. 2)	• must occur within a reasonable time after entry into Canada • permits questioning of the person • permits inspection of goods imported by the person, and the taking of samples of those goods
1) *Customs Act* s. 99.2 Search of person after leaving customs controlled area 2) Search of the person for evidence of contravention of the *Customs Act* or regulations or illegal goods	No prior authorization (senior officer if requested by person) Officer (s. 2) of the same sex as person to be searched (or if no officer of the same sex, any suitable person authorized by the officer of the same sex s. 99.2(5))	• can occur after person leaves a customs controlled area • officer needs reasonable suspicion that person has secreted on or about the person anything affording evidence of a contravention of *Customs Act* or regulations or any goods that are prohibited or controlled or regulated by Acts of Parliament • regulations permit the search of other person in prescribed circumstances • the person about to be searched may request to be brought before a senior officer, who may discharge the person if not satisfied that reasonable suspicion exists (s. 99.3(3)(4))
1) *Customs Act* s. 99.3 Non-intrusive examination of goods 2) Examination of goods in custody or possession of person leaving a customs controlled area	No prior authorization Officer (s. 2)	• may search any goods in the custody of a person leaving the controlled area in accordance with the regulations, without individualized suspicion, or • if reasonable suspicion that an Act of Parliament administered or enforced by the officer has been or may have been contravened in respect of the goods
1) *Customs Act* s. 101 Detention of controlled goods imported/exported 2) Detention of goods about to be imported or about to be exported until officer satisfied that goods properly dealt with according to the *Customs Act* or any Act of Parliament dealing with import/export of goods	Officer (s. 2)	No suspicion required

1) Statutory Power 2) Scope	Judicial Officer Person to be Authorized	Special Requirements
1) *Customs Act* s. 102 Disposition of illegally imported goods 2) Goods detained under s. 101		• if goods imported in contravention of an Act, then goods to be disposed of in accordance with Act • if no provision for disposition of the goods, then importer may abandon the goods to Her Majesty or export them • goods may be kept in safekeeping (s.37) until disposed of, and ss. 37–39 apply to their detention in safekeeping
Customs Act s. 103 1) Custody of goods subject to seizure 2) Allows for custody of goods to remain with person from whom goods would have been seized but available for re-seizure at any time.	No prior authorization Officer (s. 2)	• goods may be left in custody of person • notice to be given to the person that goods "deemed" to be seized on the day notice is given • person must then hold goods in safe-keeping, without charge to the Crown, until a final decision is made regarding forfeiture • an officer may take custody of the goods of anytime, and shall take custody where forfeiture or conveyance is final • limitation period for seizure or sending of notice of forfeiture of 6 years following the contravention or use in respect of which seizure is made or notice is sent
1) *Customs Act* s. 110 Seizure of goods or conveyances for contravention of *Customs Act* 2) Seizure of goods, in respect of which the *Customs Act* or regulations have been contravened, or any conveyance made use of in respect of the goods, as forfeit	No prior authorization Officer (s. 2)	• must have reasonable grounds to believe the *Customs Act* or Regulations have been contravened in respect of the goods • may seize as forfeit a conveyance if the officer believes on reasonable grounds that the *Customs Act* or regulations have been contravened in respect of a conveyance or persons transported by a conveyance • officer may seize anything that will on reasonable grounds afford evidence in respect of the contravention • officer must give notice of seizure to person entitled to make a s. 138 application • limitation period for seizure of 6 years following the contravention or use in respect of which seizure is made or notice is sent

1) Statutory Power 2) Scope	Judicial Officer Person to be Authorized	Special Requirements

1) *Customs Act* s. 111
Customs Act search warrant
 	
Warrantless searches in exigent circumstances s. 111(6)
 	
2) Search of building, receptacle or place for seizure of evidence in respect of contravention of *Customs Act* or regulations
	Justice of the peace
	
	Officer (s. 2)[7]
		Justice must be satisfied on information *on oath* in Form 1 of the *Criminal Code* of reasonable grounds to believe that there in a building, receptacle or place:
		a) any goods or conveyance in respect of which this Act or the regulations have been contravened or are suspected of having been contravened,
		b) any conveyance that has been made use of in respect of such goods, whether at or after the time of the contravention, or
		c) anything that there are reasonable grounds to believe will afford evidence in respect of a contravention of this Act or the regulations
		• must be executed by day unless specifically authorized otherwise (s.111(4))
		• may be endorsed by justice of the peace of another territorial jurisdiction
		• officer may also seize, in addition to items listed in the warrant:
		  a) any goods or conveyance in respect of which the officer believes on reasonable grounds that this Act or the regulations have been contravened;
		  b) any conveyance that the officer believes on reasonable grounds was made use of in respect of such goods, whether at or after the time of the contravention; or
		  c) anything that the officer believes on reasonable grounds will afford evidence in respect of a contravention of this Act or the regulations
		• officer may exercise any of the powers in s. 111(1) if the preconditions exist to obtain a warrant but exigent circumstances would render the obtaining of a warrant impracticable (s.111(6))
		• exigent circumstances include circumstances where the delay necessary to obtain a warrant would result in danger to human life or safety, or the loss or destruction of anything liable to seizure (s. 111(7))
		• an officer may, with such assistance as he deems necessary, break open any door, window, lock, fastener, floor, wall, ceiling, compartment, plumbing fixture, box, container or any other thing (s. 112)
		• limitation period for seizure of 6 years following the contravention or use in respect of which seizure is made or notice is sent

7   It is not necessary that any specific officer be named, see *R. v. Keifer* (1990), 4 T.T.R. 317 (Ont. Ct. Gen. Div.).

Appendix 7: Related Statutes: Search and Seizure Powers • 385

1) Statutory Power 2) Scope	Judicial Officer Person to be Authorized	Special Requirements
1) *Customs Act* s. 114 Custody of things seized 2) Duty to retain custody and file a report in relation to anything seized under the *Customs Act*	Officer seizing items under the *Customs Act*	• anything seized under the *Customs Act* shall forthwith be placed in the custody of an officer • the officer must forthwith report the circumstances of the seizure to the Commissioner upon following the seizure of items as evidence • anything seized under the *Customs Act* as evidence alone (that is, not contraband or regulated goods) shall be returned forthwith on completion of all proceedings in which the thing seized may be required
1) *Customs Act* s. 115 Detention of records seized 2) Records examined or seized under the *Customs Act*	Justice of the peace (for further detention past 3 months) Officer (s. 2)	• all records examined or seized under the *Customs Act*, may be copied by the minister, or the officer by whom it is examined or seized, and a copy purporting to be certified by the minister or a person authorized by the minister is admissible in evidence and has the same probative force as the original would have if it had been proved in the ordinary way Records seized as evidence may not be detained for longer than 3 months unless, before the 3 months elapses: a) the person from whom it was seized agrees to its further detention for a specified period; b) a justice of the peace is satisfied on application that, having regard to the circumstances, its further detention for a specified period is warranted and he or she so orders; or c) judicial proceedings are instituted in which the seized record may be required
1) *DNA Identification Act* s. 3 Purpose 2) Statement of purpose		The purpose of this Act is to establish a national DNA data bank to help law enforcement agencies identify persons alleged to have committed designated offences, including those committed before the coming into force of this Act
1) *DNA Identification Act* s. 4 Purpose 2) Principles of the Act		The Act recognizes and declares that: a) the protection of society and the administration of justice are well served by the early detection, arrest and conviction of offenders, which can be facilitated by the use of DNA profiles; b) the DNA profiles, as well as samples of bodily substances from which the profiles are derived, may be used only for law enforcement purposes in accordance with this Act, and not for any unauthorized purpose; and c) to protect the privacy of individuals with respect to personal information about themselves, safeguards must be placed on:

1) Statutory Power 2) Scope	Judicial Officer Person to be Authorized	Special Requirements
1) *DNA Identification Act* s. 4 con't.		i) the use and communication of, and access to, DNA profiles and other information contained in the national DNA data bank, and ii) the use of, and access to, bodily substances that are transmitted to the Commissioner for the purposes of this Act.
1) *DNA Identification Act* s. 5 National DNA databank 2) Establishes national DNA databank and sets out what databank shall house.	Solicitor general to establish a national DNA databank Commissioner of the RCMP, or person authorized by the commissioner, designated to maintain the databank	Section provides that databank must store in a "crime scene index" DNA profiles derived from bodily substances (essentially unknown profiles) that are found a) at any place where a designated offence was committed; b) on or within the body of the victim of a designated offence; c) on anything worn or carried by the victim at the time when a designated offence was committed; or d) on or within the body of any person or thing or at any place associated with the commission of a designated offence The databank is required to keep a second index "the convicted offenders index," which must contain DNA profiles derived from bodily substances described in subs. 487.071(1) of the *Criminal Code*, and subs. 196.22(1) of the *National Defence Act* The DNA databank must also store, in relation to each of the profiles on file, information from which can be established: a) in the case of a profile in the crime scene index, the case number of the investigation associated with the bodily substance from which the profile was derived; and b) in the case of a profile in the convicted offenders index, the identity of the person from whose bodily substance the profile was derived
1) *DNA Identification Act* s. 5 Comparison of stored results, communication of the information 2) Mandates comparison of DNA profiles received for inclusion in convicted offenders index with DNA profiles	Commissioner	The following may be entitled to information contained in the databank: 1) Any Canadian law enforcement agencies or laboratories that the Commissioner considers appropriate may receive: a) information whether the sample is already at the data bank, and b) any information, other than the profile itself, that is contained in the data bank in relation to the profile (s. 6(1))

Appendix 7: Related Statutes: Search and Seizure Powers • 387

1) Statutory Power 2) Scope	Judicial Officer Person to be Authorized	Special Requirements
in the crime scene profiles Authorizes communications of results in designated manner		2) Authorized users of automated criminal conviction records retrieval system (RCMP maintained) may receive information as to whether a person's DNA profile is in the convicted offenders index (s. 6(2)) 3) Foreign governments, international organizations, or foreign government institutions, may receive the information contemplated under 1 and 2 above if Canada has entered into an arrangement with those entities in accordance with the *Privacy Act* to share information for purpose of criminal investigations and prosecution (s. 6(2)(3)(4)(5)) No other use or communication of information is permitted (s. 6(6)(7)) No further disclosure of information permitted by recipients except for purposes
1) *DNA Identification Act* s. 7 Other access to information 2) Maintenance and operation of data bank, training purposes	Commissioner Any person or class of person deemed appropriate by the Commissioner	Permits access to information in the data bank for operational, maintenance and training purposes. No further disclosure of information permitted by the recipients (s. 8)
1) *DNA Identification Act* s. 8.1 Permanent removal of information in crime scene index 2) Regulates circumstances for removal of information in crime scene index		Permanent removal from crime scene index if the profile is of the victim of the offence that was the object of the investigation, or a person who was eliminated as a suspect in the relevant investigation
1) *DNA Identification Act* s. 9 Retention of information in the convicted offenders index Removal of young offender information s. 9.1 2) Information in the convicted offenders		Exceptions to the indefinite retention rule, if information relates to a person: • whose conviction was quashed and a final acquittal entered • who was discharged under s. 730 of the *Criminal Code* of a designated offence, if one year has past since an absolute discharge was granted, or if 3 years has passed since the granting of a conditional discharge and no further convictions have been entered against the person in those years If the person was a young offender at the time of the finding of guilt on the designated

1) Statutory Power 2) Scope	Judicial Officer Person to be Authorized	Special Requirements
index to be kept indefinitely, unless one of the exceptions applies		offence, the information must be removed when the last part of the record is destroyed under ss. 45(2), 45.02(3) or 45.03(3) of the *Young Offenders Act* (YOA). However, s. 9 applies to information in the index to which ss. 45.01 or 45.02(2) of the YOA applies. (The *DNA Identification Act* has not yet been updated to include the *Youth Criminal Justice Act* (YCJA).)
1) *DNA Identification Act* s. 10 Storage and destruction of stored bodily substances 2) Regulates storage of samples received by the databank	Commissioner	• samples must be safely and securely stored for the purpose of forensic DNA analysis without delay • remaining portions to be destroyed • further analysis may be done on stored samples if technological changes make analysis appropriate (s. 10(2)) • DNA profiles obtained from stored samples must be transmitted to Commissioner for inclusion in convicted offender index (s. 10(3)) • access to substances may be granted to any appropriate person to preserve the samples (s. 10(4)) • substances may be destroyed if no longer required for analysis (s. 10(6)) • substances must be destroyed without delay in circumstances set out in s. 9 (s. 10(7)) • substances of a person granted a Pardon must be kept separate from other substances and may not be used for analysis and its existence may not be communicated to anyone.
DNA Identification Act s. 10.1 Destruction of young offenders' bodily substances	Commissioner	• substances of young offender must be destroyed in the circumstances described in s. 9.1(1) • ss. 10(6) and (7) apply to destruction of samples of a young offender relating to a record to which ss. 45.01 or 45.02(2) YOA applies. (The Act has not been updated to include the YCJA)
1) *Income Tax Act* (ITA) s. 231.1 Audit power[8] 2) Power of inspection, audit and examination of books, records, property for the	No prior authorization (unless dwelling house, in which case, Judge of the Superior or Federal Court)	• audit powers may be enforced at any reasonable times (s. 231.1(1)) • person may enter into any premises other than dwelling house where business is carried on or books or records are or should be kept (s. 231.1(1)(c)) • person may require the owner or manager or any person on the premises to give the person *all reasonable assistance and answer all proper questions* relating to ITA enforcement and administration

8 See chapter 4, "Pursuit of Penal Liability and the Predominant Purpose Test: *R. v. Jarvis*," for further discussion on constraints on ability to use this power.

1) Statutory Power 2) Scope	Judicial Officer Person to be Authorized	Special Requirements
purpose of enforcing compliance with the *ITA*	An "authorized person" (s. 231, a person authorized by the Minister)	• person may require the owner or manager to attend at the premises to be inspected, audited, or examined • if the records are in a dwelling house, unless the occupant consents, the person must be authorized by warrant to enter under ss. 231.1(2)(3) • warrant under s. 231.1(3) may be granted if the judge is satisfied by information *on oath* in an *ex parte* application that: a) there are reasonable grounds to believe the dwelling house is a place where business is carried on or book and records are/should be kept; b) entry into the dwelling-house is necessary to enforce or administer the *ITA*; c) entry has been refused or reasonable grounds to believe entry will be refused • judge issuing warrant may also order occupant to provide reasonable access to necessary documents or property in the house (s. 231.1(3)(d)) • judge may order any other order appropriate for carrying out administration/enforcement if access refused/expected to be refused (s. 231.1(3)(e))
1) *Income Tax Act* s. 231.2 Demand for documents[9] 2) Power to give notice by personal service or mail to require *any person* to provide any information or additional information, any returns or documents relating to administration or enforcement of the *ITA*, including demands for amounts owing	No prior authorization (except for demands to third parties regarding unnamed persons, where a judge of the Superior or Federal Court must give prior authorization) Minister	• reasonable time to provide the information must be stipulated in the notice • if demand is made to a third party for information regarding unnamed persons, a judge may issue a warrant on appropriate conditions, if satisfied on information *on oath* following an *ex parte* application that: a) the person or group is ascertainable; and b) the requirement is made to verify *ITA* compliance by the person(s) • the third party may apply for review within 15 days to the same judge or other judge of same court if unavailable; authorization may be cancelled if above conditions not complied with (s. 231.1(5)(6)) • grounds for making the demand: see *James Richardsons & Sons Ltd. v. M.N.R.* (1984), 9 D.L.R. (4th) 1 (S.C.C.): the demand may only be made in relation to an ongoing and serious inquiry into a specific person's tax liability; the section does not authorize fishing expeditions or random inquiries

9   See *ibid*.

1) Statutory Power 2) Scope	Judicial Officer Person to be Authorized	Special Requirements

1) *Income Tax Act* s. 231.3 Search warrant for *ITA* offences
 	
2) Authorizes search for and seize documents or things that afford evidence of an offence under the *ITA*
	Judge of the Superior or Federal Court
	
	Any person named in the warrant
		• *ex parte* application *on oath*
		• must be reasonable grounds to believe:
		  a) an offence under *ITA* was committed;
		  b) a document or thing that may afford evidence of the offence above is likely to be found; and
		  c) the place named is likely to contain the evidence specified (s. 231.3(3))
		• face of warrant must state the related offence, identify the place to be searched, the person alleged to have committed the offence, and reasonably specify what is to be searched for and seized (s. 231.3(4))
		• additional seizure power: the person executing warrant may seize anything reasonably believed to afford evidence of the commission of an *ITA* offence or any offence under an Act of Parliament
		• a report must be filed with the issuing judge (or the items may be filed), as soon as practicable, detailing the items seized (s. 231.3(5))
		• the judge may then order the items to be retained by the Minister, or order the items returned if not required for the investigation or proceedings or was not seized in accordance with the warrant or the section, either on the judge's own motion or on application of an interested person (s. 231.3(6)(7))
		• the person from whom the items were seized retains a reasonable right of inspection and copying (s. 231.3(8))

1) *Income Tax Act* s. 231.6 Demand for foreign-based information 2) Similar to power under s. 231.2, but permits requests for information or documents relevant to *ITA* administration or enforcement which are available or located outside Canada	No prior authorization Minister	• notice must set out a reasonable period of time for production (not less than 90 days), a description of the information/documents sought, and consequences non-production under (8) [essentially disallowance of relying on the documents in a subsequent civil proceeding (s. 231.6(3))] • person receiving notice may, within 90 days of receive notice, apply to a judge for review, who may either confirm, vary or set aside the requirement (if unreasonable) (s. 231.6(4)(5))

Appendix 7: Related Statutes: Search and Seizure Powers • 391

1) Statutory Power 2) Scope	Judicial Officer Person to be Authorized	Special Requirements
1) *Income Tax Act* s. 231.7 Compliance order 2) Permits judge to order person to comply with any prior requests under ss. 231.1 or 232.2 if the person did not comply with the request and the information is not protected by solicitor–client privilege	Judge of the Superior or Federal Court Minister	• 5 clear days notice of application to person affected • judge may impose any appropriate conditions • person liable to finding of contempt of court for non-compliance • appellate review to the level of court responsible for reviewing the issuing judge's decisions. Appellate review does not suspend the effect of an order.
1) *Income Tax Act* s. 231.7 Compliance Order hearing for determining solicitor–client privilege Section 232 seizure of documents where solicitor–client privilege claimed 2) Sets out procedure for obtaining access to documents over which solicitor–client privilege is claimed	Judge of the Superior or Federal Court	• the constitutional soundness of these provisions suspect in light of *Lavallee, Rackel, & Heintz v. Canada* • the common law rules for obtaining a warrant and determining claims of privilege set out in that case ought to be followed
1) *Mutual Legal Assistance in Criminal Matters Act* s. 10 Application of *Criminal Code* 2) Mandates application of *Criminal Code* to issues of search and seizure under this Act, except to the extent the *Code* is inconsistent with this Act		
1) *Mutual Legal Assistance in Criminal Matters Act* s. 11 Approvals and application for warrants 2) Requires Minister to provide the "competent authority" (s. 2: Attorney General of Canada, or of the province) with the documents necessary to apply for a warrant, once assistance is approved by the minister (11(1)) Requires the competent authority to apply *ex parte* for the warrant to a judge (s. 2) of the province where the evidence is believed to be (11(2))		

1) Statutory Power 2) Scope	Judicial Officer Person to be Authorized	Special Requirements
1) *Mutual Legal Assistance in Criminal Matters Act* s. 12 Issuance of search warrants s. 13 Power to seize additional items s. 13.1 Issuance of other warrants	"Judge" of the province to whom application made under s. 11(2) (generally, Superior Court of criminal jurisdiction judges) Peace officer named in the warrant	Judge to be satisfied by statement under oath that there are reasonable grounds to believe: a) an "offence" has been committed (s. 2: offence set out in the relevant treaty, convention or international agreement to which Canada is a party and that contains a provision for mutual legal assistance in criminal matters); b) evidence of the commission of the offence or information that may reveal the whereabouts of a person who is suspected of having committed the offence will be found in a building, receptacle or place in the province; and c) it would not, in the circumstances, be appropriate to make an order under 18(1) [evidence gathering order] (s. 12(1)) – judge may impose any desirable conditions on execution of warrant – judge who issues a warrant shall also fix a hearing to consider the execution of the warrant and a report of the peace officer concerning execution (s. 12(3)) Warrant must on its face: a) set out the time and place for the hearing under s. 12(3) b) state that, at that hearing, a "sending order" will be sought with respect to anything seized; and c) state that every person from whom a record or thing is seized in execution of the warrant and any person who claims to have an interest in a record or thing so seized has the right to make representations at the hearing before any order is made concerning the record or thing. (s. 12(4)) – peace officer must give a copy of the warrant to the person present and who appears to be in charge of the premises before executing it (s. 12(5)) – if no person is present, the peace must affix a copy of the warrant to a prominent place within the place (s. 12(6)) • peace officer required to send a notice to the minister at least 5 days prior to the hearing regarding the warrant, and send the minister a copy of the report forthwith (s. 14) • peace officer executing the warrant may seize additional items, other than those listed in the warrant, if believed on reasonable grounds the items will afford evidence of, has been used in or intended for use in, the commission of an offence against an Act of Parliament, and ss. 489.1–492 *Criminal Code* apply for seizures under this section (s. 13)

1) Statutory Power 2) Scope	Judicial Officer Person to be Authorized	Special Requirements
		• judge may also issue other any other warrant in the manner provided for the *Criminal Code*, to be obtained, issued and executed as prescribed by the *Code*, except to the extent that the provisions are inconsistent with ss. 12(3)(4), 14, 16 of this Act (s. 13.1)
1) *Mutual Legal Assistance in Criminal Matters Act* s. 15 Hearing to send evidence abroad 2) Provides for hearing to review the execution of a s. 12 warrant Permits return of items or sending of items abroad	Judge who issued the warrant presides over hearing or a judge of the same court	• judge to consider the submissions of the minister, the competent authority, the person from whom the items were seized, and any other person with an interest in the items • judge may *order the items returned* to the person from whom it was seized if a lawful possessor or otherwise to the lawful owner, *if not satisfied that warrant executed according terms and conditions or where judge satisfied that an order should not be made*[10] • judge may order the items sent to the requesting state, on whatever terms are desirable • Minister may not send the items abroad until satisfied that the state or entity will comply with conditions imposed in the sending order
1) *Mutual Legal Assistance in Criminal Matters Act* s. 17 Approval for evidence-gathering order 2)1) Requires minister to provide competent authority (s. 2) with documents/information necessary to apply for an evidence gathering order upon approval of request by state or entitle 2) Requires competent authority to apply *ex parte* for an order gathering evidence to a judge (s. 2) of the province where evidence is to be found		

10 See *R. v. Gladwin* (1997), 116 C.C.C. (3d) 471 (Ont. C.A.): the review hearing requires the judge to be satisfied of two matters: (1) warrant was executed according to its terms; and 2) there is no reason why the order should not be made. *R. v. Budd* (2000), 150 C.C.C. (3d) 108 (Ont. C.A.) re conduct of a hearing under this section, and judge's duties to consider conduct of Canadian authorities and the need to foster international investigative cooperation.

1) Statutory Power 2) Scope	Judicial Officer Person to be Authorized	Special Requirements
1) *Mutual Legal Assistance in Criminal Matters Act* s. 18 Evidence-gathering orders 2) Judicial orders for a variety of evidence gathering powers, including: a) orders for examinations under oath or otherwise and the equivalent of *subpoena duces tecum*; b) production order for records or copies and accompanying affidavits; c) designation of persons before whom examinations are to occur or to whom documents are to be produced under a) and b); d) order for a person to answer questions and produce records or things to the person described in c) in accordance with the laws of evidence and procedure in the requesting state (s. 18(2))	Judge (s. 2) Competent authority (s. 2)	• judge must be satisfied that there are reasonable grounds to believe: a) an offence has been committed, and b) that evidence of the commission of the offence or information revealing the whereabouts of a person suspected to have committed the offence will be found in Canada (s. 18(1)) • judge may designate him or herself or any other person to receive the evidence or documents (s. 18(3)) • order may be executed anywhere in Canada (s. 18(4)) • order may be on such terms as judge considers desirable (s. 18(5)) • issuing judge or judge of the same court may vary the order's terms and conditions (s. 18(6)) A person so ordered may refuse to answer questions on grounds of a) privilege (or non-disclosable) under Canadian law; b) breach of privilege in the requesting state; or c) compliance constituting a criminal offence in the requesting state (s. 18(7)) • if the person designated to receive the information is a judge, the person may immediately deal with any compliance objections within his or her jurisdiction (s. 18(8)) • otherwise, if a person refuses to comply for grounds under s. 18, the person must provide a detailed statement in writing to the person designated, explaining the basis for refusal (s. 18(9)) • person under order is entitled to witness fees and living expenses as if the person were a witness before the judge who made the order (s. 18(10)) • designated person required to file a report to the judge, accompanied by all transcripts of examinations, a general description of everything produced under the order, and a copy of statement detailing reasons for objection (s. 19(1))

1) Statutory Power 2) Scope	Judicial Officer Person to be Authorized	Special Requirements
1) *Mutual Legal Assistance in Criminal Matters Act* s. 20 Sending order 2) Order to send abroad evidence and reports obtained under s. 18	Judge (s. 2)	Judge may order the s. 19 report, the items produced, a copy of the order, the any statements filed under s. 18(9) and reasons on the determination of the objections to the requesting state or entity The order may be on such terms and conditions as the judge considers desirable, including terms to preserve the items, to give effect to the request and to protect third parties, after considering submissions of the minister, competent authority, the person who produced items, and the person who claims interest in items • a s. 18 evidence gathering order may continue if the minister is advised that a court of the requesting state (or designate) determines that the reasons are not well-founded • once such a determination is made by the requesting state, the person subject to the order must comply unless specifically excused by the issuing judge or a judge of the same court • no items may be send under s. 20 until the minister is satisfied that the state or entity has agreed to comply with the terms or conditions of sending imposed under s. 20 (s. 21)
1) *Controlled Drugs and Substances Act* (CDSA) s. 11 Search Warrant Warrantless search and seizure in exigent circumstances s. 11(7) 2) Warrant or warrantless search power authorizing search and seizure of anything affording evidence of a *CDSA* offence, including controlled substances and their containers, offence-	Justice (s. 2 *Criminal Code*) Peace officer	• *ex parte* application, supported by information *on oath* • requires reasonable grounds to believe anything affording evidence of a *CDSA* offence, including controlled substances and their containers, offence-related property (s. 2) (11(1)) • no time restrictions (s. 11(1)): see *R. v. Saunders* (2003), 81 C.C.C. (3d) 268 (Nfld. C.A.) • s. 487.1 *Criminal Code* telewarrant provisions available with necessary modifications (s. 11(2)) • may be executed in another province if endorsed by a judge of the other province (s. 11(4)) • peace officers executing the warrant may search "found-ins" if reasonable grounds exist to believe the person has in their possession any controlled substance, precursor, property or thing set out in the warrant (s. 11(5)) • additional seizure power: aside from things listed in warrant, officer may seize any controlled substances/precursors and their containers, offence-related property and anything else affording evidence of an offence under this Act (s. 11(6)), or any other Act (s. 11(8)) • warrantless searches and seizure permitted if the preconditions for obtaining a warrant are present, but exigent circumstances make obtaining a warrant impracticable" (s. 11(7))

11 See chapter 4, "Preservation of Evidence: Post-Enactment of Sections 11(7) *CDSA* and 487.11 *Criminal Code*" for a full explanation of the limitations and application of this exception.

1) Statutory Power 2) Scope	Judicial Officer Person to be Authorized	Special Requirements
related property (s. 2)		• peace officers exercising powers under s. 11 may enlist whatever assistance deemed necessary and use as much force as necessary in the circumstances (s. 12)[12]
1) *Controlled Drugs and Substances Act* s. 13 Report to Justice 2) Property seized under CDSA or common law search powers Makes applicable ss. 489.1 and 490 *Criminal Code* provisions with certain exceptions	Issuing justice or another justice of same territorial division (for reports under this section) Peace officer who seizes a substance	• separate reports required for controlled substances, and only CDSA applicable to treatment of such substances • if any offence-related property seized under this Act is ordered returned under s. 490(9), the judge may require the person enter into a recognizance (s. 13(6))
1) *Proceeds of Crime (Money Laundering) and Terrorist Financing Act* s. 15 Search of the person 2) Search of persons for amounts of money in amounts greater than those prescribed by s. 12 and the regulations, if not reported under s. 12	No prior authorization; or the senior officer, if person detained requests Officer (s. 2 *Customs Act*), of same sex as person detained; if no such officer, then any suitable person of same sex as detainee as authorized by the officer (s. 15(4))	• reasonable suspicion that person has secreted on his or her person an amount of money exceeding that set out in s. 12/regs, and not reported in accordance with s. 12 • person must have just arrived in Canada (within a reasonable time of arrival), be about to leave Canada, or had access to an area for persons about to leave Canada, but who did not leave Canada (s. 15(1)) • a senior officer may discharge the person detained if not satisfied that reasonable suspicion exists (s. 15(3))
1) *Proceeds of Crime (Money Laundering) and Terrorist Financing Act* s. 16 Search of conveyance or baggage 2) Search of any conveyance or baggage for amounts of money in amounts greater than those prescribed by s. 12 and the regulations, if not reported under s. 12	No prior authorization Officer (s. 2 *Customs Act*)	• reasonable suspicion that money or currency in an amount exceeding that set out in s. 12/regs, and not reported in accordance with s. 12, is in the conveyance or baggage

12 See chapter 7, "Who Can Execute and Assist in Executing the Warrant" and "Use of Force," for discussions on the enlisting of assistance and use of force.

1) Statutory Power 2) Scope	Judicial Officer Person to be Authorized	Special Requirements
1) *Proceeds of Crime (Money Laundering) and Terrorist Financing Act* s. 17 Examination and opening of mail 2) Examination of any imported/exported mail and opening of mail if reasonable suspicion that it contains amounts of money in amounts greater than those prescribed by s. 12 and the regulations	No prior authorization Officer (s. 2 *Customs Act*)	No opening of mail weighing 30 grams or less unless the person to whom it is addressed consents or the person who sent it consents or has completed and attached to the mail a label in accordance with article 116 of the Detailed Regulations of the Universal Postal Convention (s. 17(2)) The officer may cause the mail weighing 30 grams or less to be opened in the officer's presence by the person to whom it is addressed (s. 17(3))
1) *Proceeds of Crime (Money Laundering) and Terrorist Financing Act* s. 18 Seizure as forfeit 2) Currency or monetary instruments in contravention of s. 12	No prior authorization Officer (s. 2 *Customs Act*)	• officer must have belief on reasonable grounds that s. 12 contravened • may be returned to the person on payment of prescribed penalty unless the officer suspects on reasonable grounds that the currency or monetary instruments are proceeds of crime within the meaning of subs. 462.3(1) of the *Criminal Code* or funds for use in the financing of terrorist activities • written notice of seizure and right to review or appeal to be provided to person from whom items were seized • if mail seized, notice (and right to appeal) to be given to the person from whom it was seized; if import/export mail, notice goes to the exporter • officer to record in writing reasons for seizure (s. 19.1) and detail circumstances to commissioner and to the centre (s. 2) (20)

☙

Table of Cases

143471 Canada Inc. v. Quebec (Attorney General), [1994] 2 S.C.R. 339 ....118, 121

Alabama v. White, 110 S. Ct. 2412 at 2416 (1990) 94
Attorney-General of Quebec v. Canadian Broadcasting Corp., [1991]
   3 S.C.R. 421, 67 C.C.C. (3d) 517..99, 130, 131–32, 327

Baron v. Canada, [1993] 1 S.C.R. 416, 99 D.L.R. (4th) 350,
   78 C.C.C. (3d) 510 ....94, 119, 145, 147
Bisaillon v. Keable, [1983] 2 S.C.R. 60, 2 D.L.R. (4th) 193,
   7 C.C.C. (3d) 385 ....162, 164, 166, 170
Blouin v. Canada, [1991] F.C.J. No. 1171, 51 F.T.R. 194 (T.D.)............................5, 291
British Columbia Securities Commission v. Branch, [1995] 2 S.C.R. 3, 123
   D.L.R. (4th) 462, 97 C.C.C. (3d) 505 ....60, 85, 99, 116, 117, 118, 119–20, 124
Brown v. Durham Regional Police Force (1998), 43 O.R. (3d) 223,
   167 D.L.R. (4th) 672 (C.A.) 246

California v. Greenwood, 486 U.S. 35, 100 L.Ed.2d 30 (1988) 81, 82
Canada (Attorney General) v. Several Clients and Several Solicitors (2000),
   189 N.S.R. (2d) 313, 2002 NSCA 44..182, 183
Canada Post Corp. v. Canada (Attorney General), [1995] O.J. No. 126,
   95 C.C.C. (3d) 568 (Gen. Div.) 194
Canadian Broadcasting Corp. v. Attorney-General for New Brunswick et al.,
   [1991] 3 S.C.R. 459, 85 D.L.R. (4th) 57, 67 C.C.C. (3d) 544 130

CanadianOxy Chemicals Ltd. v. Canada, [1999] 1 S.C.R. 743, (1998),
   171 D.L.R. (4th) 733, 133 C.C.C. (3d) 426 91
CBC v. Dagenais, [1994] 3 S.C.R. 835, 120 D.L.R. (4th) 12 166
Chartier v. The Attorney-General of Quebec, [1979] 2 S.C.R. 474,
   104 D.L.R. (3d) 321, 48 C.C.C. (2d) 34 142
Cloutier v. Langlois, [1990] 1 S.C.R. 158, 53 C.C.C. (3d) 257 .... 99, 199, 233, 234,
   .... 235, 236, 237, 250
Codd v. Cabe (1876), 1 Ex. D. 352, 45 L.J. M.C. 101 198
Colet v. The Queen, [1981] 1 S.C.R. 2, 119 D.L.R. (3d) 521, 57 C.C.C. (2d) 105 95
Comité paritaire de l'industrie de la chemise v. Potash; R. v. Potash,
   [1994] 2 S.C.R. 406, 115 D.L.R. (4th) 702, 91 C.C.C. (3d) 371 .... 118, 121, 286
Cottrell Transport Inc. v. Director of Investigation & Research (1987),
   19 C.P.R. (3d) 117 (Ont. H.C.J.), aff'd (1988), 26 O.A.C. 378 372
Cuddy Chicks Ltd. v. Ontario (Labour Relations Board) (1991),
   81 D.L.R. (4th) 121, [1991] 2 S.C.R. 5, 50 Admin. L.R. 44 265

Dalglish v. Jarvie (1850), 2 Mac. & G. 231, 42 E.R. 89 .... 207, 312
Descôteaux v. Mierzwinski, [1982] 1 S.C.R. 860, 141 D.L.R. (3d) 590 .... 178, 180, 181
Dow Chemical Co. v. United States, 476 U.S. 227, 106 S. Ct. 1819 (1986) 70
Dubois v. The Queen, [1986] 1 S.C.R. 366, 26 D.L.R. (4th) 481,
   25 C.C.C. (3d) 221 298

Eccles v. Bourque, [1975] 2 S.C.R. 739, (1974) 50 D.L.R. (3d) 753,
   19 C.C.C. (2d) 129 .... 95, 195, 285
Eddy v. Moore, 5 Wash. App. 334 (1971) 56
Eldridge v. British Columbia (Attorney General), [1997] 3 S.C.R. 624,
   151 D.L.R. (4th) 577 18
Entick v. Carrington, (1765), 19 State Tr. 1029 .... 2, 90, 102

Festing v. Canada (Attorney General) (2003), 172 C.C.C. (3d) 321 (B.C.C.A.),
   (2001) 206 D.L.R. (4th) 98, (2000) 31 C.R. (5th) 203
   (B.C.S.C.) 182, 183, 185, 186, 187, 188
Fieldhouse v. Kent Institution (1995), 98 C.C.C. (3d) (B.C.C.A.) 375
Franks v. Delaware, 438 U.S. 154 (1978) 213

Gallaird v. Laxton (1862), 2 B. & S. 363, 31 L.J. M.C. 123, 9 Cox C.C. 127,
   121 E.R. 1109 198
Hunter et al. v. Southam Inc., [1984] 2 S.C.R. 145, 14 C.C.C. (3d) 97,
   11 D.L.R. (4th) 641 .... 2, 6, 16, 26, 27, 37, 84, 89, 95, 96, 98, 99, 119,
   .... 121, 126, 143, 144, 145, 189, 220, 233, 286

Illinois v. Rodriguez, 110 S. Ct. 2793 (1990) 221, 232

Illnicki v. MacLeod, [2003] A.J. No. 605, 2003 ABQB 465 290

James Richardsons & Sons Ltd. v. M.N.R. (1984), 9 D.L.R. (4th) 1 (S.C.C.) 389
Jones v. United States, 362 U.S. 257 (1960) 27

Kligman v. Canada, [2003] F.C.J. No. 70 (T.D.) 292
Knowlton v. The Queen, [1974] S.C.R. 443, (1973) 33 D.L.R. (3d) 755,
　10 C.C.C. (2d) 377 92
Kruger Inc. v. Kruco Inc., [1988] R.J.Q. 2323 (C.A.) 178
Kyllo v. United States (2001), 121 S. Ct. 2038, [2001] SCT-QL 121 .... 71, 75

Lavallee, Rackel & Heintz v. Canada (Attorney General); White, Ottenheim &
　Baker v. Canada (Attorney General); R. v. Fink, [2002] 3 S.C.R. 209,
　2002 SCC 61, 167 C.C.C. (3d) 1, aff'g (2000) 143 C.C.C. (3d) 187
　(Alta. C.A.), 146 C.C.C. (3d) 28 (Nfld. C.A.), 149 C.C.C. (3d) 321
　(Ont. C.A.) 61, 100, 177, 182, 183, 184, 185, 186, 326
Long v. Michigan, 463 U.S. 1032, 103 S. Ct. 3469, 77 L. Ed. 2d 1201
　(1983) 251, 252

Maranda v. Richer, [2003] 3 S.C.R. 193, 232 D.L.R. (4th) 14,
　2003 SCC 67 .... 177, 178, 179, 181, 184, 185
Marks v. Beyfus (1890), 25 Q.B.D. 494 .... 164, 168
Mezzo v. The Queen, [1986] 1 S.C.R. 802, 30 D.L.R. (4th) 161,
　27 C.C.C. (3d) 97 144
Michaud v. Quebec (Attorney-General), [1996] 3 S.C.R. 3, 138 D.L.R.
　(4th) 423, 109 C.C.C. (3d) 289 .... 172, 173
Mitton v. British Columbia (Securities Commission) (1999),
　123 B.C.A.C. 263, 1999 BCCA 186 .... 210, 211
Mitton v. British Columbia (Securities Commission), [2001] B.C.J. 665,
　2001 BCSC 499 .... 119, 120
Monteleone v. The Queen, [1987] 2 S.C.R. 154, 41 D.L.R. (4th) 746,
　35 C.C.C. (3d) 193 144
Mooring v. National Parole Board, [1996] 1 S.C.R. 75,
　132 D.L.R. (4th) 56 .... 265, 266, 269, 270

National Post v. Canada, [2004] O.J. 178 (S.C.J.) 99, 132–35
Nova Scotia (Worker's Compensation Board) v. Martin (2003),
　231 D.L.R. (4th) 385, 2003 SCC 54 .... 266, 267
Nurse v. Canada, [1997] F.C.J. No. 713, 132 F.T.R. 131 (T.D.) 5, 290–94

Pars Oriental Rug (c.o.b. Oriental Rug Bazaar) v. Canada (Attorney General),
　[1988] B.C.J. No. 3055 (S.C.) 200, 201

Prime Realty Ltd. v. British Columbia (Superintendent of Real Estate),
  [1994] B.C.J. No. 561, 42 B.C.A.C. 71 (C.A.) 298

Quebec (Attorney General) v. Laroche, [2002] 3 S.C.R. 708, 169 C.C.C.
  (3d) 97, 2002 SCC 72 .... 14–16, 21, 125, 205, 206, 207, 333, 337

R. v. 4-12 Electronics Corporation (1996), 108 Man.R. (2d) 32, 47 C.R.
  (4th) 20 (Q.B.) 166
R. v. 974649 Ontario Inc., [2001] 3 S.C.R. 575, 206 D.L.R. (4th) 444,
  2001 SCC 81 265
R. v. A.B., [2003] O.J. No. 2010, [2003] O.T.C. 453 (S.C.J.) 41
R. v. A.M., [2004] O.J. No. 2716 (C.J.) 77, 80
R. v. Adams, [2001] O.J. 3240, 203 D.L.R. (4th) 290, 148 O.A.C. 253
  (C.A.) 230, 231
R. v. Agensys International Inc., [1999] O.J. No. 781 (Gen. Div.) 217
R. v. Agostinelli, [2002] O.J. No. 5008 (S.C.J.) 5
R. v. Allain (1998), 205 N.B.R. (2d) 201 (C.A.) 209, 210
R. v. Anderson (1999), 175 N.S.R. (2d) 362 (C.A.) 237
R. v. Araujo, [2000] 2 S.C.R. 992, 149 C.C.C. (3d) 449, 193 D.L.R. (4th) 440,
  2000 SCC 65 .... 89, 153, 204, 205, 208, 209, 210, 211, 212, 213, 312
R. v. Arp, [1998] 3 S.C.R. 339, 166 D.L.R. (4th) 296, 129 C.C.C.
  (3d) 321 .... 11, 33, 226, 227
R. v. Askov, [1987] O.J. No. 1626, 60 C.R. (3d) 261 (C.A.) 254, 258
R. v. Aukton and Koszulap (June 29, 1994), Vancouver Registry
  No. CC921461 (B.C.S.C.) 85
R. v. B.(J.E.) (1989), 94 N.S.R. (2d) 312, 52 C.C.C. (3d) 224
  (S.C.) 191, 193, 199, 328
R. v. Babes (2000), 146 C.C.C. (3d) 465 (Ont. C.A.) 167, 170
R. v. Bedard (1998), 109 O.A.C. 151, 125 C.C.C. (3d) 348 (C.A.) 109, 237, 238
R. v. Belliveau and Losier (1986), 75 N.B.R. (2d) 18, 30 C.C.C. (3d) 163,
  54 C.R. (3d) 144 (C.A.) 253
R. v. Belnavis (1996), 91 O.A.C. 3, 107 C.C.C. (3d) 195 (Ont. C.A.), aff'd
  [1997] 3 S.C.R. 341, 188 C.C.C. (3d) 405 .... 28, 34, 36, 64, 83, 84, 88, 103,
  .... 150, 236, 282, 283, 285, 286, 288, 289
R. v. Benham (2003), 175 C.C.C. (3d) 231, 2003 BCCA 341 .... 85, 86
R. v. Bernshaw, [1995] 1 S.C.R. 254, (1994) 95 C.C.C. (3d) 193 .... 145, 354
R. v. Big M Drug Mart Ltd., [1985] 1 S.C.R. 295, 18 D.L.R. (4th) 321,
  18 C.C.C. (3d) 385 94
R. v. Bisson, [1994] 3 S.C.R. 1097, 94 C.C.C. (3d) 94 .... 205, 208
R. v. Black, [1989] 2 S.C.R. 138, 50 C.C.C. (3d) 1 278
R. v. Bohn (2000), 145 C.C.C. (3d) 320, 2000 BCCA 239 .... 198, 199

R. v. Bordage (2000), 146 C.C.C. (3d) 549 (Que. C.A.) 318
R. v. Borden, [1994] 3 S.C.R. 145, 119 D.L.R. (4th) 74, 92 C.C.C.
    (3d) 404 ....11, 33, 45, 221, 224, 230, 231, 289
R. v. Bourque (2001), 50 W.C.B. (2d) 344, 2001 BCSC 621,
    [2001] B.C.J. No. 1298 ....85, 86
R. v. Branton (2001), 53 O.R. (3d) 737, 199 D.L.R. (4th) 321,
    154 C.C.C. (3d) 139 (C.A.) 207, 297, 298
R. v. Brass (June 29, 1994), Vancouver Registry No. CC921461 (B.C.S.C.) 85
R. v. Breckner (September 10, 1993), Parksville Registry No. 292599 (B.C.S.C.) ..85
R. v. Briggs (2001), 55 O.R. (3d) 417, 149 O.A.C. 244, 157 C.C.C. (3d) 38
    (C.A.) 48, 50, 53, 58, 143, 356, 362, 363, 366, 367, 368, 369
R. v. Brighteyes, [1997] A.J. No. 362, [1998] 3 W.W.R. 276 (Q.B.) 40
R. v. Brown, [1999] O.J. No. 4870 (S.C.J.) 163, 171
R. v. Brown, [2002] 2 S.C.R. 185, 210 D.L.R. (4th) 341, 162 C.C.C.
    (3d) 257 ....169, 170
R. v. Brown, [2003] B.C.J. No.506, 2003 BCCA 141..109
R. v. Brownridge, [2000] B.C.J. 1549, 2000 BCSC 795..160
R. v. Broyles, [1991] 3 S.C.R. 595, 68 C.C.C. (3d) 308..18, 19
R. v. Brunelle (1990), 55 C.C.C. (3d) 347 (B.C.S.C.)..315
R. v. Budd et al., [2000] O.J. No. 4649, 150 C.C.C. (3d) 108
    (C.A.)...204, 209, 210, 393
R. v. Buhay (2003), 174 C.C.C. (3d) 97, 10 C.R. (6th) 205,
    2003 SCC 30 .... 4, 18, 20, 21, 35, 211, 233, 255, 275, 277, 282, 284,
    ....286, 288, 289, 290, 292
R. v. Burke, [1997] N.J. No. 187, 118 C.C.C. (3d) 59 (C.A.)......................................244
R. v. Burlingham, [1995] 2 S.C.R. 206, 124 D.L.R. (4th) 7,
    97 C.C.C. (3d) 385 ....277, 278, 287
R. v. Bushman, [1968] 4 C.C.C. 17, 4 C.R.N.S. 13, 63 W.W.R. 346 (B.C.C.A.) 65
R. v. C.B.C. et al. (2001), 52 O.R. (3d) 757, 142 O.A.C. 1 (C.A.) 299
R. v. Cahill (1992), 13 C.R. (4th) 327 (B.C.C.A.) 378
R. v. Caissie (1999), 214 N.B.R. (2d) 360, 138 C.C.C. (3d) 205 (C.A.) 113
R. v. Cantin (2001), 82 C.R.R. (2d) 161 (Que. C.A.) 200
R. v. Carpenter (2002), 165 C.C.C. (3d) 159, 4 C.R. (6th) 115, 2002 BCCA 301,
    leave to appeal refused 159 C.C.C. (3d) vi (S.C.C.) 5, 44, 295, 296
R. v. Casey (2000), 128 O.A.C. 184, 141 C.C.C. (3d) 506 (C.A.) 270
R. v. Caslake, [1998] 1 S.C.R. 51, 155 D.L.R. (4th) 19,
    121 C.C.C. (3d) 97 ....151, 152, 235, 236, 237, 239
R. v. Chabot (1993), 126 N.S.R. (2d) 355, 86 C.C.C. (3d) 309 (S.C.C.A.) 244, 293
R. v. Chambers (1985), 9 O.A.C. 228, 20 C.C.C. (3d) 440 (C.A.) 170
R. v. Chang (2003), 173 C.C.C. (3d) 397, [2003] O.J. No. 1076 (C.A.) 218, 219
R. v. Chang, [2003] A.J. 1281, 2003 ABCA 293..20, 21

R. v. Charles (1987), 61 Sask.R. 166, 36 C.C.C. (3d) 286 (C.A.) 5, 293
R. v. Cheung (1997), 97 B.C.A.C. 161, 119 C.C.C. (3d) 507 (C.A.) 218
R. v. Chiarantano, [1990] O.J. No. 2603, [1991] 1 S.C.R. 906 169
R. v. Church of Scientology and the Queen (No. 4) (1985), 17 C.C.C.
 (3d) 499 (Ont. H.C.J.) 213
R. v. Church of Scientology and the Queen (No. 6) (sub nom R. v. Walsh),
 (1987), 18 O.A.C. 321, 31 C.C.C. (3d) 449 (C.A.) 60, 205, 207, 213, 297, 313
R. v. Clarke, [2003] O.J. 3884 (Sup. Ct.) 152
R. v. Clauson (1986), 47 Alta. L.R. (2d) 398, 31 C.C.C. (3d) 286 (C.A.) 263
R. v. Cochrane, 2003 PESCTD 47..152
R. v. Colarusso, [1994] 1 S.C.R. 20, 110 D.L.R. (4th) 297, 87 C.C.C.
 (3d) 193...12, 13–14, 17, 33, 35, 90, 278
R. v. Colbourne (2001), 149 O.A.C. 132, 157 C.C.C. (3d) 273 (C.A.) 208, 210
R. v. Collins, [1987] 1 S.C.R. 265, 38 D.L.R. (4th) 508,
 33 C.C.C. (3d) 1 ....89, 138, 233, 275, 282, 285, 286, 287, 288, 291, 296
R. v. Collins, [1999] N.J. No. 44, 133 C.C.C. (3d) 8, 22 C.R. (5th) 269 (C.A.) 5
R. v. Collymore (1999), 138 C.C.C. (3d) 306 (Ont. C.A.)...381
R. v. Cook, [1998] 2 S.C.R. 597, 164 D.L.R. (4th) 1 23
R. v. Cote (1992), 54 O.A.C. 281, 70 C.C.C. (3d) 280 (C.A.)....................................352
R. v. Coulter, [2000] O.J. No. 3452 (Ct. J.), appeal dismissed [2001]
 O.J. No. 5608 (S.C.J.)...5
R. v. Cover, [1988] O.J. No. 1615, 44 C.C.C. (3d) 34 (H.C.J.) 217
R. v. Currie (1871), 31 U.C.Q.B. 582 297
R. v. D.(I.D.) (1987), 60 Sask.R. 72, 38 C.C.C. (3d) 289 (C.A.) 102
R. v. Daley (2001), 156 C.C.C. (3d) 225, 2001 ABCA 155 78
R. v. Davies, [1982] O.J. No.146, 1 C.C.C. (3d) 299 (C.A.) 170
R. v. Dawson (1998), 39 O.R. (3d) 436, 123 C.C.C. (3d) 385
 (C.A.) 215, 216, 217, 269
R. v. Day, [1998] O.J. No. 4461 (C.A.) 38, 155
R. v. Debot, [1989] 2 S.C.R. 1140, 52 C.C.C. (3d) 193, (1986) 30 C.C.C.
 (3d) 207 ....139, 142, 143, 144, 145, 148, 152, 153, 154, 155, 156, 238, 239
R. v. Dedman, [1985] 2 S.C.R. 2, 20 D.L.R. (4th) 321, 20 C.C.C. (3d) 97..........92, 93
R. v. Dellapenna, [1995] B.C.J. No. 1526 (C.A.) 208, 209
R. v. Dennison (1990), 109 N.B.R. (2d) 388, 60 C.C.C. (3d) 342 (C.A.)...............293
R. v. Dersch, [1993] 3 S.C.R. 768, 85 C.C.C. (3d) 1 ....6, 35
R. v. Dewald, [1994] S.C.C.A. No. 434, 92 C.C.C. (3d) 160 352
R. v. Dial Drugs (2003), 63 O.R. (3d) 529 (S.C.J.)...122
R. v. Dore, [2002] O.J. No. 2845, 162 O.A.C. 56, 166 C.C.C. (3d) 225
 (C.A.) 55, 56–58
R. v. Dorfer (1996), 69 B.C.A.C. 197, 104 C.C.C. (3d) 528 (C.A.).....................38, 82
R. v. Dreysko (1990), 110 A.R. 317, [1990] A.J. No. 982 (C.A.)..............................66

R. v. Duarte, [1990] 1 S.C.R. 30, 65 D.L.R. (4th) 240, 53 C.C.C. (3d) 1....6, 8, 61, 62, ...72, 232, 285, 317
R. v. Duguay, [1989] 1 S.C.R. 93, 56 D.L.R. (4th) 46, 46 C.C.C. (3d) 1, (1985), 18 C.C.C. (3d) 289 ....4, 289
R. v. Duong, [2002] S.C.C.A. No. 112, 162 C.C.C. (3d) 242 ....100, 104–6, 160
R. v. Dupuis (1994), 162 A.R. 197, [1994] A.J. No. 1011 (C.A.) 244
R. v. Durette (1992), 72 C.C.C. (3d) 421, 88 C.C.C. (3d) 1, (Ont. C.A.) 216, 319
R. v. Dyment, [1988] 2 S.C.R. 417, 55 D.L.R. (4th) 503, 45 C.C.C. (3d) 244...6, 11, 28, 35, 37–8, 90, 220, 285, 287
R. v. Eagle, [1996] O.J. No. 2867 (Gen. Div.)...162
R. v. Edwards, [1996] 1 S.C.R. 128, 132 D.L.R. (4th) 31, 104 C.C.C. (3d) 136.. 16, 27, 28, 29–30, 34, 218, 230
R. v. Elzein (1993), 82 C.C.C. (3d) 455, 55 Q.A.C. 99 (Que. C.A.) 64
R. v. Engum (2002), 163 C.C.C. (3d) 198, 2002 BCSC 156 ....53–4, 361
R. v. Eton Construction Co. (1996), 89 O.A.C. 298, 106 C.C.C. (3d) 21 (C.A.) 268, 300
R. v. Evans, [1996] 1 S.C.R. 8, 131 D.L.R. (4th) 654, 104 C.C.C. (3d) 23 ....7, 8, 26, ...32–33, 64, 65, 237, 255
R. v. F.(D.M.) (1999), 179 D.L.R. (4th) 492, 139 C.C.C. (3d) 144, 1999 ABCA 267 ....59, 66
R. v. F.(S.), [2000] O.J. No. 60, 182 D.L.R. (4th) 336, 141 C.C.C. (3d) 225 (C.A.) 46, 54, 99, 292
R. v. Fawthrop (2002), 161 O.A.C. 350, 166 C.C.C. (3d) 97 (C.A.) 253, 255, 256, 259, 260
R. v. Feegan (1990) 80 C.C.C. (3d) 356 (Ont. C.A.) 316
R. v. Feeney, [1997] 2 S.C.R. 13, 146 D.L.R. (4th) 609, 115 C.C.C. (3d) 129.......................55, 100, 102, 111, 112, 125, 139, 150, 152, 195, 198, 199, ...231, 278, 279, 280, 281, 282, 286, 322
R. v. Fekete (1985), 7 O.A.C. 152, 17 C.C.C. (3d) 188 (C.A.) 192, 193
R. v. Ferris (1998), 108 B.C.A.C. 244, 162 D.L.R. (4th) 87, 126 C.C.C. (3d) 298 (C.A.) 92, 149, 242, 244, 246, 247, 248, 250, 251
R. v. Finlay and Grellette (1985), 11 O.A.C. 279, 23 D.L.R. (4th) 532, 23 C.C.C. (3d) 48 (C.A.)...62, 312
R. v. Fitt (1996), 103 C.C.C. (3d) 224, (1995) 139 N.S.R. (2d) 186, 96 C.C.C. (3d) 341 (S.C.C.)..66, 255, 258
R. v. Fitzpatrick, [1995] 4 S.C.R. 154, 129 D.L.R. (4th) 129 ....118, 119, 121
R. v. Flintoff (1998), 111 O.A.C. 305, 126 C.C.C. (3d) 321 (C.A.) 292, 293
R. v. Francis (unreported judgment of Festeryga J., Ont. Sup. Ct., 3 October 2003) 270
R. v. Fry (1999), 183 Nfld. & P.E.I.R. 346, 142 C.C.C. (3d) 166 (Nfld. C.A.) 78
R. v. G.(C.M.) (1996), 113 Man. R. (2d) 76, [1996] M.J. No. 428 (C.A.) 244

R. v. Galbraith (1989), 49 C.C.C. (3d) 178 (Alta. C.A.) 316
R. v. Garofoli, [1990] 2 S.C.R. 1421, 60 C.C.C. (3d) 161..............90, 94, 153, 154, 155, 164, 167, 168, 170, 204, 207, 208, 211, 212, 214, 215, 216, 217, 268, 313, 315, 318
R. v. Genest, [1989] 1 S.C.R. 59, [1989] S.C.J. No. 5, 45 C.C.C. (3d) 385 ....1, 139, 190, 195, 196, 197, 283, 287
R. v. George (1991), 5 O.R. (3d) 144, 69 C.C.C. (3d) 148 (C.A.) 269
R. v. Gettins, [2003] O.J. No. 4758, 180 O.A.C. 324 (C.A.) 17, 18
R. v. Gladwin, [1997] O.J. No. 2479, 101 O.A.C. 116, 116 C.C.C. (3d) 471 (C.A.) 64, 392
R. v. Glykis (1995), 84 O.A.C. 140, 100 C.C.C. (3d) 97, 41 C.R. (4th) 310 (Ont. C.A.) 5, 293, 294, 295
R. v. Godoy, [1999] 1 S.C.R. 311, (1998)168 D.L.R. (4th) 257, 131 C.C.C. (3d) 129 ....92, 100, 107, 108
R. v. Golden, [2001] 3 S.C.R. 679, 207 D.L.R (4th) 18, 159 C.C.C. (3d) 449 .... 40, 42, 59, 89, 95, 138, 220, 233, 234, 240, 241
R. v. Goldhardt, [1996] 2 S.C.R. 463, 136 D.L.R. (4th) 502, 107 C.C.C. (3d) 481 ....271, 272, 273
R. v. Goldman, [1980] 1 S.C.R. 976, (1979) 108 D.L.R. (3d) 17, 51 C.C.C. (2d) 1 222
R. v. Golub, [1997] S.C.C.A. No. 571, 117 C.C.C. (3d) 193 ....100, 106–7, 146
R. v. Grabowski (1985), 22 C.C.C. (3d) 449 (S.C.C.) 314, 316
R. v. Grant, [1993] 3 S.C.R. 223, 84 C.C.C. (3d) 173 ....66, 68, 95, 100, 101, ...103, 208, 210, 288, 289, 322
R. v. Greffe, [1990] 1 S.C.R. 755, 55 C.C.C. (3d) 161, 75 C.R. (3d) 257 ......39, 154, 289
R. v. Gregson, [1985] O.J. No. 1474 (C.A.) 228
R. v. Grenier (1991), 51 Q.A.C. 283, 65 C.C.C. (3d) 76 (Que. C.A.)......................259
R. v. Haglof (2000), 149 C.C.C. (3d) 248, 2000 BCCA 604 ....100, 112–13
R. v. Hall (1995), 22 O.R. (3d) 289, 79 O.A.C. 24 (C.A.) 152
R. v. Harrer, [1995] 3 S.C.R. 562, 101 C.C.C. (3d) 193, 42 C.R. (4th) 269 ....5, 23, 273, 274, 275, 291
R. v. Harris and Lighthouse Video Centres Ltd. (1987), 20 O.A.C. 26, 35 C.C.C. (3d) 1..285
R. v. Heikel and MacKay (1984), 57 A.R. 221 (C.A.) 192
R. v. Hendry (2001), 57 O.R. (3d) 475, 153 O.A.C. 167, 161 C.C.C. (3d) 275 (C.A.) 49, 359, 365, 366, 367, 368, 369
R. v. Hern (1994), 149 A.R. 75, [1994] A.J. No. 83 (C.A.) 66
R. v. Hewitt and Davis (1992), 95 Cr. App. R. 81 (C.A.) 175
R. v. Hewlin (2001), 190 N.S.R. (2d) 283, 2001 NSCA 16..........................244, 252
R. v. Hiscock; R. v. Sauvé, [1992] R.J.Q. 895, 72 C.C.C. (3d) 303 (Que. C.A.) 204, 205
R. v. Hosie (1996), 91 O.A.C. 281, 107 C.C.C. (3d) 385 (C.A.) 207, 284
R. v. Hufsky, [1998] 1 S.C.R. 621, 40 C.C.C. (3d) 398 ....7, 84, 87, 121

R. v. Hunter (1987), 59 O.R. (2d) 364, 34 C.C.C. (3d) 14 (C.A.) 162, 167
R. v. Hurrell (2002), 161 O.A.C. 248, 216 D.L.R. (4th) 160, 166 C.C.C.
    (3d) 343 (Ont. C.A.) 96, 107
R. v. Hutchings (1996), 111 C.C.C. (3d) 215 (B.C.C.A.), leave to appeal
    refused [1997] S.C.C.A. No. 21 ....68, 73, 75
R. v. Hyatt (2003), 171 C.C.C. (3d) 409, 2003 BCCA 27 ....24, 273, 275
R. v. Hynes, [2001] 3 S.C.R. 623, 206 D.L.R. (4th) 483,
    159 C.C.C. (3d) 359 ....265, 266, 267, 269
R. v. Inco Ltd. (2001), 146 O.A.C. 66, 155 C.C.C. (3d) 383 (Ont. C.A.)....................90
R. v. J.O., [1996] O.J. No. 4799 (Gen. Div.) 137, 138
R. v. Jacoy, [1988], 2 S.C.R. 548, 45 C.C.C. (3d) 296................................275, 283, 285
R. v. Jacques, [1996] 3 S.C.R. 312, 139 D.L.R. (4th) 223,
    110 C.C.C. (3d) 1..145, 149, 150, 245–46
R. v. Jamieson (2002), 166 C.C.C. (3d) 501, 2003 BCCA 411 109
R. v. Janda, [2003] O.J. No. 326 (S.C.J.)...297
R. v. Jarvis (2002), 219 D.L.R. (4th) 233, 169 C.C.C. (3d) 1,
    2002 SCC 73 ....16, 31, 84, 117, 118, 119, 120, 121–24,
R. v. Johnson (2000), 32 C.R. (5th) 236, 2000 BCCA 204 248
R. v. Jordan (2002), 162 C.C.C. (3d) 385, 2002 NSCA 11 ....58, 361, 362,
    ....363, 364, 366
R. v. Joubert (1992), 7 B.C.A.C. 31, 69 C.C.C. (3d) 553 (C.A.) 178
R. v. Joyal (1995), 43 C.R. (4th) 317 (Que. C.A.) 67
R. v. Kanak, [2003] A.J. 886, 178 C.C.C. (3d) 129 (Prov. Ct.)................................270
R. v. Keifer (1990), 4 T.T.R. 317 (Ont. Ct. Gen. Div.) 380
R. v. Kelly, [1999] N.B.J. No. 98, 169 D.L.R. (4th) 720 (C.A.) 8, 67, 68, 73
R. v. Kennedy, [1996] O.J. No. 4401, 95 O.A.C. 321 (C.A.) 80
R. v. Kenneth Johnson (1989), 88 Cr. App. R. 131 (C.A.)..175
R. v. Kensington Income Tax Commissioners, [1917] 1 K.B. 486 ....207, 312
R. v. Kesselring (2000), 132 O.A.C. 41, 145 C.C.C. (3d) 119 (C.A.) 209
R. v. Khuc, [2000] B.C.J. No. 50, 2000 BCCA 20 34
R. v. Kitaitchik (2002), 161 O.A.C. 169, 166 C.C.C. (3d) 14 (C.A.) 288
R. v. Kokesch, [1990] 3 S.C.R. 3, 61 C.C.C. (3d) 207...................64, 66, 68, 88, 272,
    ....282, 283, 285, 286, 287, 288
R. v. Krall [2003] A.J. No. 1161, 2003 ABPC 171 158
R. v. Krist (1995), 62 B.C.A.C. 133, 100 C.C.C. (3d) 58 (C.A.) 80, 81
R. v. Krist (1998), 113 B.C.A.C. 176, 130 C.C.C. (3d) 347 (C.A.) 210
R. v. Ku (2002), 169 C.C.C. (3d) 535, 2002 BCCA 559 ....50, 367
R. v. Kutynec (1992), 52 O.A.C. 59, 70 C.C.C. (3d) 289 (C.A.)....................263, 264
R. v. Lake, [1996] S.J. No. 886, 113 C.C.C. (3d) 208, [1997]
    5 W.W.R. 526 (C.A.)..244
R. v. Lam (2000), 148 C.C.C. (3d) 379, 2000 BCCA 545 ....167, 174, 175, 176

R. v. Lam, [2003] A.J. 811, 2003 ABCA 201 ....8, 68, 73, 74–77
R. v. Lau (2003), 175 C.C.C. (3d) 273, 2003 BCCA 337 ....138, 283, 284
R. v. Lau, [2003] B.C.J. No. 1929, 2003 BCPC 294 ....5, 139, 196, 197
R. v. Lauda (1998), 106 O.A.C. 161, 122 C.C.C. (3d) 74, 129 C.C.C. (3d) 225
    (Ont. C.A.) 67
R. v. Laudincina (1999), 53 C.C.C. (3d) 281 (Ont. H.C.) 315
R. v. Laurin (1997), 98 O.A.C. 50, 113 C.C.C. (3d) 519 (Ont. C.A.) 67, 283, 285
R. v. Law, [2002] 1 S.C.R. 227, 160 C.C.C. (3d) 449, 48 C.R.
    (5th) 199 ....6, 33, 35, 82, 90
R. v. Law, 2002 BCCA 594, (2002), 171 C.C.C. (3d) 219..............144, 227, 253, 256,
    ....257, 258, 289
R. v. Le, 2001 BCCA 658 200
R. v. Leipert (1997), 112 C.C.C. (3d) 385, [1997] 1 S.C.R. 281 ....161, 162, 163, 164,
    ....165, 166, 167, 168, 169, 170, 171
R. v. Lewis (1998), 38 O.R. (3d) 540, 107 O.A.C. 46, 122 C.C.C. (3d) 481
    (C.A.) 78, 155, 156, 222, 232
R. v. Lind, [2000] S.J. No. 757 (Prov. Ct.)..87
R. v. Linder, [1924] 2 W.W.R. 646, 42 C.C.C. 289, [1924] 3 D.L.R. 505
    (Alta. C.A.) 198
R. v. Loveman (1992), 52 O.A.C. 94, 71 C.C.C. (3d) 123 (C.A.) 264
R. v. M. (M.R.), [1998] 3 S.C.R. 393, 166 D.L.R. (4th) 261, 129 C.C.C.
    (3d) 361 ....18, 19, 35, 78–79, 286
R. v. MacGillivray, [1971] 3 O.R. 452, 4 C.C.C. (2d) 244 (Dist. Ct.) 352
R. v. MacIsaac, [2001] O.J. No 2966 (S.C.J.) 200
R. v. Macooh, [1993] 2 S.C.R. 802, 105 D.L.R. (4th) 96,
    82 C.C.C. (3d) 481 ....100, 111, 112
R. v. MacPherson, [1995] N.B.J. No. 277, 100 C.C.C. (3d) 216 (C.A.) 5, 293
R. v. Major, [2004]O.J. No. 2651 (C.A.) 30, 375
R. v. Mann, 2004 SCC 52, rev'g (2002), 169 C.C.C. (3d) 272
    (Man. C.A.) 92, 149, 240, 241, 242, 243, 244, 245, 246, 248, 250, 253
R. v. Marin, [1994] O.J. No. 1280 (Gen. Div.) 149
R. v. Mason (2000), 112 A. Crim. R. 266...163
R. v. Matthiesen, [1999] S.C.C.A. No. 110, 133 C.C.C. (3d) 93, 1999 ABCA 31 78
R. v. McAllister, [2000] B.C.J. 963 (S.C.)...139, 195, 196
R. v. McAuley (1998), 126 Man. R. (2d) 202, 124 C.C.C. (3d) 117
    (C.A.) 244, 248, 250
R. v. McClure, [2001] 1 S.C.R. 445, 195 D.L.R. (4th) 513,
    151 C.C.C. (3d) 321 ....169, 177
R. v. McCormack (2000), 143 C.C.C. (3d) 260, 2000 BCCA 57 ....100, 104
R. v. McKinlay Transport Ltd., [1990] 1 S.C.R. 627, 68 D.L.R. (4th) 568,
    55 C.C.C. (3d) 530 ....8, 11–12, 85, 99, 116, 121

R. v. Mellenthin, [1992] 3 S.C.R. 615, 76 C.C.C. (3d) 481 ....8, 9, 10, 231, 248
R. v. Mentuck, [2001] 3 S.C.R. 442, 205 D.L.R. (4th) 512 166
R. v. Mercer, [2004] A.J. No. 634 (Prov. Ct.)..8, 76, 78
R. v. Mercer; R. v. Kenny (1992), 7 O.R. (3d) 9, 52 O.A.C. 70,
   70 C.C.C. (3d) 180 (C.A.) 228, 233
R. v. Meuckon, [1990] B.C.J. No. 1552, 57 C.C.C. (3d) 193 (C.A.) 173
R. v. Meyers (1987), 52 Alta. L.R. (2d) 156, [1987] A.J. No. 328 (Q.B.) 228, 230
R. v. Middleton (2000), 150 C.C.C. (3d) 556, 2000 BCCA 660 260
R. v. Milanovic, [2002] O.J. No. 3786 (C.A.) 232
R. v. Mills, [1986] 1 S.C.R. 863, 29 D.L.R. (4th) 161,
   26 C.C.C. (3d) 481 ....263, 264, 265, 267, 268, 269, 297, 298
R. v. Mills, [1999] 3 S.C.R. 668, 180 D.L.R. (4th) 1........16, 60, 99, 125, 126, 128–30
R. v. Monney, [1999] 1 S.C.R. 652, 171 D.L.R. (4th) 1,
   133 C.C.C. (3d) 129..42, 43, 44, 115, 143, 148, 149, 241, 380
R. v. Montoute (1991), 113 A.R. 95, 62 C.C.C (3d) 481 (C.A.)..................................218
R. v. Moore; R. v. Bogdanich (1993), 81 C.C.C. (3d) 161 (B.C.C.A.) 314
R. v. Morris (1998), 173 N.S.R. (2d) 1, 134 C.C.C. (3d) 539
   (C.A.) 208, 209, 210, 212, 213
R. v. Mulligan (2000), 128 O.A.C. 224, 142 C.C.C. (3d) 14 (Ont. C.A.) 65, 66
R. v. Multani, [1999] O.J. No. 3487 (Gen. Div.) 215
R. v. Murray, [1999] J.Q. No. 1037, 136 C.C.C. (3d) 197 (C.A.) 249
R. v. Murrins (2002), 162 C.C.C. (3d) 412, 2002 NSCA 12 50
R. v. N.D.K., [2001] B.C.J. 1831 2001 BCPC 204 270
R. v. Neilsen, [1988] S.J. No. 415, 43 C.C.C. (3d) 548 (C.A.) 221, 258
R. v. Neubert, [2001] B.C.J. No. 393, 2001 BCCA 88 211
R. v. Nguyen (2002), 57 O.R. (3d) 589, 154 O.A.C. 108, 161 C.C.C. (3d) 433
   (C.A.)...59
R. v. Nguyen, [2001] B.C.J. No. 2002 (Prov. Ct.) 193
R. v. Nicholls (1999), 125 O.A.C. 77, 139 C.C.C. (3d) 253 (C.A.) 109
R. v. Nicolosi (1998), 40 O.R. (3d) 417, 110 O.A.C. 189, 127 C.C.C. (3d) 176,
   (C.A.) 239
R. v. North (2002), 165 C.C.C. (3d) 393, 2002 ABCA 134 ....359, 365, 367
R. v. O'Connor, [1995] 4 S.C.R. 411, 130 D.L.R. (4th) 235, 103 C.C.C. (3d) 1......137, 292
R. v. Oickle, [2000] 2 S.C.R. 3, 190 D.L.R. (4th) 257, 2000 SCC 38.................4, 275
R. v. Oluwa (1996), 107 C.C.C. (3d) 236 (B.C.C.A.) 380, 381
R. v. Omelusik, [2003] B.C.J. 1237, 2003 BCCA 319 ....159, 160
R. v. Osmond, [2000] O.J. No. 4267 (S.C.J.)...58
R. v. P.K., [1999] O.J. No. 2447 (Ct.J.)...160
R. v. Palmer (unreported decision of Durno. J., Ont. Sup. Ct.,
   13 November 2003) 270
R. v. Pangman, [2000] M.J. No. 222 (Q.B.)...164, 316

R. v. Parmar (1987), 61 O.R. (2d) 132, 37 C.C.C. (3d) 300
(H.C.J.) 213, 214, 263, 264
R. v. Pasaluko, [1992] B.C.J. No. 2432, 77 C.C.C. (3d) 190 (B.C.S.C.)....................216
R. v. Pastro (1988), 42 C.C.C. (3d) 488 (Sask. C.A.) 316
R. v. Patterson, [1970] S.C.R. 409, 9 D.L.R. (3d) 398 269
R. v. Peck, [2001] O.J. No. 4581 (S.C.J.) 285
R. v. Peet and Ward [1990] B.C.J. No. 607 (Prov. Ct.) 194, 195
R. v. Pheasant, [2000] O.J. No. 4237 (S.C.J.) 31
R. v. Pigeon (1993), 59 Q.A.C. 103, [1993] R.J.Q. 2774 (C.A.) 244
R. v. Plant, [1993] 3 S.C.R. 281, 84 C.C.C. (3d) 203...................21, 36, 60, 66, 68, 85,
....155, 156, 213, 272, 285
R. v. Pleich (1980), 55 C.C.C. (2d) 13 (Ont. C.A.) 314
R. v. Poitras, [1998] O.J. No. 5628 (Gen. Div.) 80
R. v. Polashek (1999), 45 O.R. (3d) 434, 172 D.L.R. (4th) 350, 134 C.C.C.
(3d) 187 (C.A.) 158, 159
R. v. Pratas, [2000] O.J. No. 2286, 133 O.A.C. 350 (C.A.)
R. v. Pringle, [2003] A.J. No. 118, 2003 ABPC 7 5
R. v. Prussic, [2000] O.J. No. 3224 (Ct.J.) 158
R. v. Pugliese (1992), 52 O.A.C. 280, 71 C.C.C. (3d) 295 (Ont. C.A.) 27, 67
R. v. Puskas (1997), 104 O.A.C. 310, 120 C.C.C. (3d) 548
(C.A.) 67, 157, 286, 288
R. v. Quist (1981), 11 Sask.R. 28, 61 C.C.C. (2d) 207 (C.A.) 353
R. v. Rahey, [1987] 1 S.C.R. 588, 39 D.L.R. (4th) 481, 33 C.C.C. (3d) 289 ....267, 268
R. v. Rankine, [1986] 2 All E.R. 566 (C.A.) 175
R. v. Rao (1984), 9 D.L.R. (4th) 542, 4 O.A.C. 162, 12 C.C.C. (3d) 97 (C.A.) 255
R. v. Rendon, [1999] R.J.Q. 2281, 140 C.C.C (3d) 12 (C.A.) 219
R. v. Richards (1997), 34 O.R. (3d) 244, 115 C.C.C. (3d) 377 (C.A.)..........172, 173, 174
R. v. Richardson (2001), 153 C.C.C. (3d) 449, 2001 BCCA 260 160
R. v. Richfield, [2003] O.J. No. 3230, 175 O.A.C. 54 (C.A.) 276, 277
R. v. Rodgers, [2004] O.J. No. 1073 (C.A.)..47, 51–52, 360
R. v. Ross, [1989] 1 S.C.R. 3 238
R. v. Rothman, [1981] 1 S.C.R. 640, 121 D.L.R. (3d) 578..................................4, 275
R. v. Rutherford Ltd. et al., [1995] B.C.J. No. 1953, 101 C.C.C. (3d) 260 (S.C.)......192
R. v. S.(R.J.), [1995] 1 S.C.R. 451, 121 D.L.R. (4th) 589, 96 C.C.C. (3d) 1.............124
R. v. S.A.B., [2003] 2 S.C.R. 678, 2003 SCC 60, aff'g R. v. B. (S.A.)
(2001) 157 C.C.C. (3d) 510 (Alta. C.A.) 46–47, 48, 54, 99, 124–26, 127,
....130, 139, 276, 356, 358, 359, 368
R. v. S.F., [2003] O.J. No. 92, 102 C.R.R. (2d) 288 (S.C.J.) 5, 41, 42, 43
R. v. Samra, [2003] O.J. No. 3289, 178 C.C.C. (3d) 264 (S.C.J.) 360
R. v. Sanderson, [2003] O.J. No. 1481, 170 O.A.C. 285(C.A.).............................110–11

R. v. Sandhu (1993), 28 B.C.A.C. 203, 82 C.C.C. (3d) 236, 22 C.R.
(4th) 300, 47 W.A.C. 203 30
R. v. Sanelli, Fasciano (1987), 61 O.R. (2d) 385, 22 O.A.C. 307 (C.A.) 228
R. v. Saunders (2003), 181 C.C.C. (3d) 268, 2003 NLCA 63 ....144, 395
R. v. Schedel (2003), 175 C.C.C. (3d) 193, 2003 BCCA 364 ....138, 196, 197
R. v. Scott, [1990] 3 S.C.R. 979, 61 C.C.C. (3d) 300 ....162, 163, 168, 170, 171
R. v. Seaboyer, [1991] 2 S.C.R. 577, 83 D.L.R. (4th) 193, 66 C.C.C. (3d) 321 269
R. v. Serendip, [2003] O.J. No. 2407, 227 D.L.R. (4th) 520, 175 C.C.C.
(3d) 474 (S.C.J.) rev'd [2004] O.J. No. 4653 (C.A.).......................130, 136, 137–38
R. v. Sewell (2003), 175 C.C.C. (3d) 242, 2003 SKCA 52 ....222, 223, 224, 237
R. v. Shalalah, [2000] N.B.J. No. 14 (C.A.) 209
R. v. Shayesteh (1996), 31 O.R. (3d) 161, 111 C.C.C. (3d) 225 (C.A.).......................218
R. v. Shearing, [2002] 3 S.C.R. 33, 214 D.L.R. (4th) 215, 165 C.C.C. (3d) 225........129
R. v. Sieben, [1987] 1 S.C.R. 295, 38 D.L.R. (4th) 427, 32 C.C.C. (3d) 574
(C.A.)..285
R. v. Silveira, [1995] 2 S.C.R. 297, 124 D.L.R. (4th) 193,
97 C.C.C. (3d) 450 ....64, 66, 100, 101, 282, 285, 286, 289, 322
R. v. Silvini (1997), 96 O.A.C. 310 (C.A.) 215
R. v. Simmons, [1988] 2 S.C.R. 495, 45 C.C.C. (3d) 296,
55 D.L.R. (4th) 673 ....38, 39, 42, 44, 98, 99, 113, 114–15,
....140, 143, 148, 238, 237, 281, 286
R. v. Simpson (1993), 12 O.R. (3d) 182, 60 O.A.C. 327,
79 C.C.C. (3d) 482 (C.A.) 9, 10, 92, 93, 149, 243, 244, 245, 246, 247
R. v. Sismey, [1990] B.C.J. No. 757, 55 C.C.C. (3d) 281 (C.A.) 208, 209
R. v. Smith (1998), 161 D.L.R. (4th) 331, 126 C.C.C. (3d) 62,
1998 ABCA 418 ....32, 158, 253, 260
R. v. Spindloe, [2001] S.J. No. 266, 154 C.C.C. (3d) 8,
2001 SKCA 58 ....253, 256, 257, 258, 259
R. v. Starr, [1998] M.J. No. 80, 123 C.C.C. (3d) 145 (C.A.) 170
R. v. Stenning, [1970] S.C.R. 631, 10 D.L.R. (3d) 224, [1970] 3 C.C.C. 145..............92
R. v. Stillman, [1997] 1 S.C.R. 607, 144 D.L.R. (4th) 193, 113 C.C.C. (3d) 321 ....8, 37,
44, 45, 54, 58, 59, 80, 82, 83, 88, 126, 144, 235, 240, 275, 276–77, 278, 279, 285
R. v. Stinchcombe, [1991] 3 S.C.R. 326, 68 C.C.C. (3d) 1 168
R. v. Storrey, [1990] 1 S.C.R. 241..144, 150
R. v. Strachan, [1988] 2 S.C.R. 980, 56 D.L.R. (4th) 673,
46 C.C.C. (3d) 479 ....192, 193, 194, 271, 272, 282, 291
R. v. Tang, 2001 BCCA 165...222
R. v. Terry, [1996] 2 S.C.R. 207, 135 D.L.R. (4th) 214 ....22, 23
R. v. Tessling, 2004 SCC 67, [2004] S.C.J. No. 63, rev'g [2003] O.J. No. 186,
168 O.A.C. 124, 171 C.C.C. (3d) 361 (C.A.) 68–73, 82

R. v. Therens, [1985] 1 S.C.R. 613, 18 D.L.R. (4th) 655, 18 C.C.C.
(3d) 481 ....271, 282, 286, 291
R. v. Thomas, [1998] O.J. No. 1400, 59 O.T.C. 81, 124 C.C.C. (3d) 178
(Gen.Div.) 163, 175
R. v. Thompson, [1990] 2 S.C.R. 1111, 73 D.L.R. (4th) 596,
59 C.C.C. (3d) 225 ....31, 139, 200, 314, 315, 316
R. v. Trang (2001), 46 C.R. (5th) 274, 2001 ABQB 825 167
R. v. Tricker (1995), 96 C.C.C. (3d) 198, 8 M.V.R. (3d) 47,
21 O.R. (3d) 575 (C.A.) 65
R. v. Truong (2002), 168 C.C.C. (3d) 132, 2002 BCCA 315 ....77, 78
R. v. Turpin, [1989] 1 S.C.R. 1296, 48 C.C.C. (3d) 8..............................221, 228
R. v. Vanweenan and Chesson (1988), 43 C.C.C. (3d) 353 (S.C.C.) 313, 315
R. v. Walker, [1999] O.J. No. 653 (Gen. Div.)........................166, 167, 214, 217
R. v. Waterfield, [1963] 3 All E.R. 659, [1964] 1 Q.B. 164..........92, 94, 108, 243, 244
R. v. West (1997), 100 B.C.A.C. 36, 122 C.C.C. (3d) 218 (B.C.C.A.) 64, 193
R. v. White, [1999] 2 S.C.R. 417, 174 D.L.R. (4th) 111 ....48, 291, 292
R. v. Wholesale Travel, [1991] 3 S.C.R. 154, 84 D.L.R. (4th) 161,
67 C.C.C. (3d) 193 ....84, 117
R. v. Wijesinha, [1995] 3 S.C.R. 422, 127 D.L.R. (4th) 242, 100 C.C.C. (3d) 410 28
R. v. Wiley, [1993] 3 S.C.R. 263, 84 C.C.C. (3d) 161...66, 68
R. v. Williams (a.k.a. Buckshot) (2003), 180 O.A.C. 171, 181 C.C.C. (3d) 414
(C.A.) 215
R. v. Willis (2003), 174 C.C.C. (3d) 406, [2003] S.C.C.A. No. 281........246, 248, 249
R. v. Wills (1992), 7 O.R. (3d) 337, 52 O.A.C. 321, 70 C.C.C. (3d) 529
(C.A.)...149, 221, 222, 225, 226, 227, 228, 230, 231–32
R. v. Wilson, [1983] 2 S.C.R. 594, 4 D.L.R. (4th) 577, 9 C.C.C. (3d) 97 90
R. v. Wilson, [1990] 1 S.C.R. 1291, 56 C.C.C. (3d) 142 ....244, 268
R. v. Wise, [1992] 1 S.C.R. 527, 70 C.C.C. (3d) 193...6
R. v. Wismayer (1997), 99 O.A.C. 161, 115 C.C.C. (3d) 18 (C.A.)..........................270
R. v. Wong, [1990] 3 S.C.R. 36, 60 C.C.C. (3d) 460.......................................63, 72
R. v. Wong, 2003 BCCA 188 160
R. v. Woodall, [1991] O.J. 3558 (Gen. Div.) 201
R. v. Woodall, [1993] O.J. No. 4001 (C.A.) 201, 202
R. v. Wray, [1971] S.C.R. 272, [1970] 4 C.C.C. 1, 11 D.L.R. (3d) 673.................4
R. v. Yanover et al. (1982), 68 C.C.C. (2d) 151 (Prov. Ct.) 203
R. v. Yorke (1992), 77 C.C.C. (3d) 528 (N.S.C.A.) 316
R. v. Young (1984), 3 O.A.C. 254, 13 C.C.C. (3d) 1 (Ont. C.A.) 5
R. v. Young (1997), 34 O.R. (3d) 177, 101 O.A.C. 81, 116 C.C.C. (3d) 350
(C.A.) 10, 11, 232
R. v. Zammit (1993), 13 O.R. (3d) 76, 62 O.A.C. 272, 81 C.C.C. (3d) 112 (C.A.) 157
Rakas v. Illinois, 99 S.Ct. 421 (1978) 28

Re Andre Corbeil & The Queen (1986), 13 O.A.C. 382, 27 C.C.C. (3d) 245
 (C.A.) 297–98
Re Dagenais et al. v. C.B.C. et al., [1994] 3 S.C.R. 835..299
Re Forsythe and The Queen, [1980] 2 S.C.R. 268, 112 D.L.R. (3d) 385,
 53 C.C.C (2d) 225 298
Re Mayo County, 14 Ir. C.L. Rep 392..297
Re Norvinca Inc. (1987), 16 C.P.R. (3d) 187 (T.D.) 372
Re Ontario (Commission on Proceedings involving Guy Paul Morin) (1997),
 97 O.A.C 59, 143 D.L.R. (4th) 54, 113 C.C.C. (3d) 31 (C.A.) 166
Re Rideout and The Queen (1986), 31 C.C.C. (3d) 211, 61 Nfld. & P.E.I.R. 160
 (Nfld. S.C.) 168
Re Vancouver Sun (Air India), [2003] B.C.J. 1992, 2003 BCSC 1330....................166
Re Zevallos and the Queen (1987), 22 O.A.C. 76, 37 C.C.C. (3d) 79
 (C.A.) 268, 298
Reference re an Application for an Authorization, [1984] 2 S.C.R. 697,
 14 D.L.R. (4th) 546, 15 C.C.C. (3d) 466 ....94, 313
Reiger v. Burgess, [1989] S.J. No.240 (Q.B.) 178
Richards. v. Wisconsin 520 U.S. 385 (1997) 195
Robson v. Hallett, [1967] 2 All E.R. 407, [1967] 2 Q.B. 939 65
Rotman v. Commissioner of Police for the Metropolis, [2002] 2 A.C. 692 237

Schreiber v. Canada (Attorney General), [1998] 1 S.C.R. 841, 158 D.L.R.
 (4th) 577 ....21, 291
Semayne's Case (1604), 5 Co. Rep. 91 a, 77 E.R. 194 (K.B.) 285
Smith v. Canada, [2001] 3 S.C.R. 902, 210 D.L.R. (4th) 289 121
Solosky v. The Queen, [1980] 1 S.C.R. 821..177, 178
State v. Garcia, 618 A.2d 326 (N.J. 1993)...176
State v. Zenquis, 618 A.2d 335 (N.J. 1993)...176
Stelco Inc. v. Canada (Attorney General) (1990), 55 C.C.C. (3d) 227 (S.C.C.) 370
Stevens v. Canada (Prime Minister), [1998] 4 F.C. 89, 161 D.L.R. (4th) 85
 (C.A.) 178, 179

Terry v. Ohio, 392 U.S. 1 (1968) 242, 244, 238
Tétreault-Gadoury v. Canada (Employment and Immigration Commission)
 (1991), 81 D.L.R. (4th) 358, [1991] 2 S.C.R. 22, 50 Admin. L.R. 1 265
Texas v. Brown (1983), 75 L. Ed. 2d 502 253
Thomson Newspapers Ltd. v. Canada (Director of Investigation and Research,
 and Restrictive Trade Practices Commission), [1990] 1 S.C.R. 425,
 67 D.L.R. (4th) 161, 54 C.C.C. (3d) 417 ....11, 60, 84, 95, 96, 99, 116–17, 118,
 ....119, 121, 286. 370
Tipene v. Apperley [1978] 1 N.Z.L.R. 761 163

U.S. v. Banks 124 S. Ct. 521, 157 L. Ed. 2d 343, 72 U.S.L.W. 4005 (2003) 195
U.S. v. Kalish, 271 F. Supp. 968 (D.P.R. 1967)...56
U.S.A. v. Friedland, [1996] O.J. No. 4399 (Gen. Div.)....................................207, 313
United States of America v. Sheppard, [1977] 2 S.C.R. 1067,
 (1976) 70 D.L.R. (3d) 136, 30 C.C.C. (2d) 424 144
United States v. Cortez, 449 U.S. 411 (1981) 244
United States v. Cortez, 449 U.S. 411, 101 S. Ct. 690 (1981) 94
United States v. Matlock, 94 S. Ct. 988 (1974) 228, 229

Weatherall v. Canada (Attorney General); Conway v. Canada, [1993] 2 S.C.R. 872,
 105 D.L.R. (4th) 210, 83 C.C.C. (3d) 1 58
Weber v. Ontario Hydro (1995), 125 D.L.R. (4th) 583, [1995] 2 S.C.R. 929, 30
 Admin. L.R. (2d) 1 265

Index

Abandoned property, 80–83, *See also* Medical waste
Acts outside of Canada. *See* Extraterritorial search
Additional DNA seizures. *See* DNA Databank seizures, Unsuccessful attempts
Advanced technology, *See* Technology
Agent of the state, 18–21, 22–25, 125, 192
ALERT test. *See* Roadside breath test
Amplification, 205, 211–13
Anticipatory search, 310
Apartment building common areas. *See* Common areas (multiple unit dwellings)
Areas open to public, *See* Business establishment, privacy in
Aerial surveillance, 8, 67, 73–74
Articulable cause, 9, 10, 149–50, 244–45
Assistance order, 194, 326
Assistance, voluntary, 191–93, 328
Automobile. *See* Motor vehicle

Backing of authorization, 325
Backyard, 67, 74
Bad faith. *See* Illegal police conduct
Banks. *See* Financial institutions, seizures at
Bawdy-house, search of, 321
Forfeiture, *in rem*, 321
Bedpan vigil, 43–45
Active and passive bedpan vigils distinguished, 44
Betting-house, search of, 321
Forfeiture, *in rem*, 321
Bill of Rights, United States. *See* Fourth Amendment
Blood sample, 12–14, 17–18, 45, 46, 90, 191, 226–27
Bodily impressions, 353. *See also* Fingerprints
Bodily substances. *See* ALERT test, Blood sample, Breath sample, Breathalyzer test, Buccal swab, Hair sample
Body cavity search, 38–40, 115, 240–41, 374, 380

415

Border search, 38, 41–43, 77–78, 114–116, 149. See also Customs Act
Breath sample. See ALERT test, Breathalyzer test, and Bodily samples
Breathalyzer test, 191, 226, 354
Buccal swab, 355–56
Business establishment, privacy in, 66, 256, 258–59

Canada Evidence Act, 167–68, 174
Canine searches, 74–78
Charter of Rights and Freedoms
  s. 10, 22, 39, 139–42, 240, 243, 278, 279, 295
  s. 11, 274
  s. 24, 4–5, 29, 36, 71, 87, 88, 100, 160, 226, 228, 262–99
  s. 32, 18
  s. 7, 19, 24, 25, 48–51, 125–28, 139, 174, 270
  s. 9, 9, 223, 285
  s. 2, 100, 130–35, 298–99, 327
Children. See Minor children
Cock pit, seizure of cocks, 323
Common areas (multiple unit dwellings), 67, 230–32
Common law, search and seizure at, 2–4, 45, 65, 90, 92–94, 101–2, 106–10, 167, 192–97, 203, 219–59, 260–61, 271–75
Competition Act,
  Entry to premises, 371–72
  Exigent circumstances, 372
  Orders for oral examination, 370
  Production order, 370
  Report to Justice, 372
  Written returns order, 370
Confidential relationships. See Informer privilege, Journalistic privilege, Solicitor-client privilege, and Therapeutic records
Conscriptive evidence, 277, 282
Consent to search. See Waiver of privacy
Constitution Act, 1982, s. 52(1), 3

Contraventions Act, 56, 362
Controlled Drugs and Substances Act, 101, 103–6, 202, 283, 395–96
  Assistance, 396
  Telewarrant, 395
  Warrant, 395–96
Conveyance. See Motor vehicle
Coroner's Act, 12
Corrections and Conditional Release Act, 373, 379
  Bodily searches, 373–79
  Body cavity search, 374
  Cell searches, 376
  Community-based residential facilities, 379
  Dry cell, 374
  Exceptional circumstances, 374, 375
  Frisk searches, 373–79
  Staff, 378
  Security searches, 373–76
  Seizure of contraband, 378–79
  Seizure of evidence, 378–79
  Urinalysis, 375–76
  Visitors, 377
  Vehicles, 377
  X-rays, 374
Counterfeit money, tools and tokens, seizure of, 323
Court of competent jurisdiction, defined, 264–70
Covert entry, 314, 326
Criminal organization. See Interception of communications — Criminal organizations
Custodial searches, 41–43, 58–60, 79. See also Corrections and Conditional Release Act
  Short-term detention and incarceration distinguished, 60
Customs Act, 38, 41–43, 114–16, 140, 149, 380–84. See also Border search
  Bedpan vigils, 380
  Body searches, 380

Custody of seized property, 383, 385
Conveyance seizure, 383
Detention of person, 380, 382
Detention of goods, 383–85
Examination of import/export goods, 381
Exigent circumstances, 384
Forfeiture of property, 381
Inspection of goods, 382
Questioning, 382
Report to Commissioner, 385
Search warrants, 384
Customs search. *See* Border search

Dangerous offender. *See* DNA Databank — Historic offences
Derivative evidence, defined, 277–78
Designated offences, DNA databank, 45, 46, 48, 355
Detention of property, 329–30
Dialed number recorder (DNR), 99, 148, 312
Discarded bodily substance, 58–59, 83
Disclosure, duty of Crown, 306, 313
DNA databank, 45, 48–54, 358–64, 364–69. *See also* DNA Identification Act
 Collection, 358–69
 Destruction, 363
 Historic offences, 51–54, 366
 Impact on offender's privacy and security, 357, 369–70
 Multiple murders, 51–54, 361
 Pre-June 30, 2000 offences, 361, 365–68
 Primary designated offences, 358
 Post-June 30, 2000 offences, 358, 364
 Storage, 25, 251
 Secondary designated offences, 358
 Unsuccessful attempts, 362
DNA Identification Act, 385–88
 Access to results, 386–87
 Comparison of results, 386

Convicted Offenders Index, 386–87
Crime Scene Index, 386–87
Destruction of results, 387–88
Destruction of samples, 387–88
Disclosure of results, 386–87
Purpose of Act, 385
Storage, 386, 388
DNA Investigative warrant, 45–48, 355–57. *See also* Bodily substances, Notice of application, Detention, Report to Justice
DNA sample, 44, 45–54, 125–29, 137, 191, 228, 240, 355–62. *See also* Discarded bodily substance
DNA warrant. *See* DNA Investigative warrant
Dog, drug-detection. *See* Canine searches
Domestic baggage, 78
Driver's license. *See* Motor-vehicle documents
Due-diligence defence, rebuttal of, 306
Dwelling house, 8, 63, 64–71, 77, 85, 88, 102, 104, 106–15, 196, 231, 237, 286

Electricity records. *See* Utility records
Epithelial cells, seizure of, 46, 355, 358
Ex parte application, 47, 52, 132–35
Exclusion of evidence, 4, 5, 84, 262–92
Exigent circumstances, 100–113, 146–47, 196, 198–99, 237, 286, 307
Explosives, seizure of, 328
Extraprovincial search. *See* Backing of authorization
Extraterritorial search, 22–25

Facial validity of warrant, 305–6
Factual innocence. *See* Innocence at stake
Fairness of trial. *See* Trial fairness
Financial institutions, seizures at, 327
 Inspection of documents, 327
Fingerprints, 54–58, 352
 Retention, 55–58

Mandatory Destruction, 56–58
Firearms, 87–88, 106–7, 146, 334
Force, use of, 196–97, 396
Foreign acts. *See* Extraterritorial search
Forfeiture. *See* Seized property, forfeiture and Forfeiture, *in rem*. *See also* Proceeds of Crime
Forfeiture, *in rem*, 321, 329–51
Forward-looking infrared (FLIR). *See* Heat Emissions
Found-ins, 199, 321, 395
Fourth Amendment, 4, 71, 81–82
Freezing premises, 66
Frisk search, 114, 200, 235–36, 250, 252, 373, 355–80, 382

Gaming-house, search of, 322
   Forfeiture, *in rem*, 322
Garbage. *See* Abandoned property
Gemstones, Precious metals, 323
General warrant, 310–11

Hair sample, 45, 46, 226, 355, 359
Halfway House. *See* Corrections and Conditional Release Act — Community-based residential facilities
Hate propaganda, 322–23
   Forfeiture, *in rem*, 322
   Internet — Shutting down website, 322
Health records. *See* Therapeutic records
Hearsay, as grounds for authorization, 153
Heat emissions, 68–73
Home, *See* Dwelling house
Hot pursuit, 102–3, 111–13
Hotel room, 63, 109, 229–33

Identification of Criminals Act, 54–58, 363. *See also* Fingerprints
Illegal police conduct, 4, 94, 207–11, 284, 289
Implied license to knock, 7–8, 32–33, 65, 69–70, 227, 255
Income Tax Act, 97, 120, 123–25, 388–91

Audit, 388–89
Compliance order, 391
Demand for documents, 389
Demand for foreign information, 390
Inspection, 388–89
Search warrants, 390
Solicitor-client privilege, 391
Informants. *See* Tips, Informer privilege
Informer privilege, 161–72, 174, 177, 203, 221
Infrared. *See* Heat Emissions
Inherent jurisdiction, 297
Innocence at stake, 168–72
Inter partes hearing. *See* Ex parte application
Interception of communications, 8, 47, 61–64, 191, 202–219, 232, 263, 313–20
   Duty not to disclose, 320
   Consent of one party, 317–18
   Covert entry, 313
   Criminal organizations, 316
   Exigent circumstances, 316–17, 319
   Ex parte application, 313
   Investigative necessity, 313
   Known persons, 314–15
   Notice of interception, 320
   Prevention of bodily harm, 319
   Renewals of authorization, 314
   Requirements for authorization, 313–16
   Terrorism316
Internet
   Shutting down website. *See* Hate propaganda
Investigative detention, 149, 220, 241–53
Investigative necessity, 47, 61, 182, 184, 313

Jailhouse search. *See* Custodial search
Journalistic privilege
Judicial discretion, 97

Justice, definition of. *See also* Justice of the Peace, definition of
Justice of the Peace, defintion of, 301

Knock and announce, 138, 195–97, 199, 283, 326
Knock-on search. *See* Implied license to knock

Law Office. *See* Solicitor-client privilege
Lumber, search for, 322

Media. *See* News media and *see* Journalistic privilege
Medical waste, privacy in, 83
Minerals, valuable, search for. *See* Gemstones, Precious metals
Minor children, 79
Motor vehicle, 148, 83–84, 237, 239
Motor-vehicle documents, 7, 83–84, 88
Mutual Legal Assistance Act, 391–95
    Evidence gathering order, 393–94
    Ministerial Approval, 391
    Seizure of items, 391–92
    Sending hearing, 395
    Warrants, 391

Narcotic Control Act, 101, 192, 196
News media, 64, 125, 130–35, 299. *See also* Journalistic privilege
Night, execution of warrant at. *See* Time of execution of warrant
No-knock entry. *See* Knock and announce
Non-conscriptive evidence, defined, 276
Notice of application. *See* Ex parte application

Obscene publications, search, 322
    Child pornography, 322
    Crime-comic, 322
    Forfeiture, *in rem*, 322
Observation post-privilege, 174–76. *See also* Public interest privilege, Informer privilege

Odour of contraband, 32, 76–77, 104, 158–60, 260–61
Offence, statement of. *See* Facial validity of warrant
Offence-related property, definition, 309
Open field, privacy in, 66

Parole board, 269–270
Pat-down. *See* Frisk search
Peace officer, definition of, 190, 305
Perimeter search, 66, 68, 272
Personal Information Protection and Electronic Documents Act, 86
Plain smell doctrine, 158, 260–61
Plain view, 67, 219, 253–60, 328
Preliminary hearing, 172, 173, 217, 269, 268
Prerogative relief, 298–300
Proceeds of crime, 14, 337–51. *See also* Proceeds of Crime (Money Laundering) and Terrorist Financing Act
    Absconding accused, 345–47
    Costs or Damages, 337
    Death of accused, 345–47
    Disclosure, CRA documents, 341–43
    Forfeiture, 343–48
    Management order, 340
    Restoration, 341–42
    Restraint order, 339–40
    Special search warrants, 337–38
    Variation of order, 341–42, 347
Proceeds of Crime (Money Laundering) and Terrorist Financing Act, 396–97
    Baggage, search of, 396
    Conveyance, search of, 396
    Mail, search of, 397
    Money, seizure of, 397
Property rights, 3, 15–16, 27–28, 84–86, 285
Public interest privilege, 172–76

Racial bias, 284–85
Real evidence, 4, 279
Reasonable doubt, 144

Reasonable expectation of privacy, 3, 6–7, 26–88, 217–19, 227, 285
Obligation to provide evidentiary basis, 34
"Totality of the circumstances", 28
Subjective and objective components, 34
Reasonable grounds, 10, 39–40, 41, 46, 61, 80, 96, 123, 143, 60, 244, 256, 285
Defined, 143–48, 150–52
Reasonable suspicion, 42, 150–52
Rectal search, *See* Body cavity search
Regulatory searches, 84–85, 87–88, 99, 116–25
Remedies for unlawful search or seizure, 4–5, 262–99
Report to Justice, 329–30, 335–36
Restraint order, proceeds of crime, 14–16, 204–5
Return of property. *See* Seized property, return to lawful owner
Risk analysis, 62–63
Roadside breath test, 225

School, search in a, 19, 79–80, 220
Sealed packet. *See* Wiretap packet
Search incident to arrest, 41, 106, 107, 146, 199–200, 220, 233–41
Search warrant (*Note*: selected references only), 1, 145–47, 189–219, 254–55, 297
Search, definition of, 6–11
Securities Act (British Columbia), 119–121
Security guards, 20–21
Seize and Freeze. *See* Freezing premises
Seized property, detention of, Report to justice, 329–30, 335–36
Seized property, forfeiture, 329–35
Seized property, return to lawful owner, 218–30
Seized property, voidable transfer, 332

Seizure, definition of, 11–18
Self-incrimination principle against, 48, 127–30, 179, 281, 292. *See also Charter of Rights and Freedoms*, s. 7 and *see also* Trial fairness
Simpson-stop. *See* Investigative detention
Smell. *See* Odour of Contraband, Plain smell doctrine, Canine searches
Solicitor-client privilege, 61, 100, 125, 130, 135, 137, 169, 177–88
Special warrant of search and seizure, proceeds of crime, 14–15, 204–7, 337–38
Standing to challenge a search or seizure, 28, 218, 219–21
State agent. *See* Agent of the State
Statutory interpretation, 92, 101–2
Stolen property, rightful owner's privacy in, 82–83, 227, 256
Stop-and-frisk. *See* Investigative detention
Strip search, 39, 40–43, 59–60, 115, 240–41

Technology, 63, 68–77
Telephone records, production of, 402
Telewarrant, 307–10, 325
Terrorism. *See* Interception of communications — terrorism. *See also Proceeds of Crime (Money Laundering) and Terrorist Financing Act*, Terrorist property
Terrorist property, seizure, 324
Management orders, 324
Restraint, 324
Terry-stop. *See* Investigative detention
Therapeutic records, 60, 128–30, 135–38, 269
Third-party privacy, 30–31, 108, 128–30, 135–38, 318–19, 269
Time of execution of warrant, 200–2, 305

Tips, 153–59, 175. *See also* Informer privilege
Tracking device, 311
Trash. *See* Abandoned property
Trespass, 2–3, 65, 101
Trial fairness, 5, 274–75, 276–82, 287, 262

Utility records, 36, 69, 77, 84–87, 156

Vehicle. *See* Motor vehicle
Vehicle stop, random, 8
Video surveillance, 63–64, 310–11
Videotaping. *See* Video surveillance
Voidable transfer. *See* Seized property, voidable transfer

Waiver of privacy, 31–33, 62–63, 90, 141–42, 164, 221–33, 227
Warrant, duty to carry and produce, 325
Warrantless search, 30, 64, 79–80, 95, 100–14
Website. *See* Hate propaganda
Wiretap. *See* Interception of communications
Wiretap packet, 202–3, 217, 268, 319

ය

About the Authors

Susanne Boucher, LL.B. 1996, LL.M. 2002 (Osgoode), was called to the Bar of Ontario in 1998 and is Counsel for the Department of Justice Canada, Ontario Regional Office. She is a trial and appellate lawyer, prosecuting criminal cases primarily under the *Criminal Code, Controlled Drugs and Substances Act, Copyright Act, Radiocommunication Act*, and *Income Tax Act*. She has written several articles on criminal law and prosecution topics, and has lectured at prosecutors' seminars and training seminars for investigative agencies.

Kenneth David Landa, B.A. 1997 (McGill University), LL.B. 2000 (Osgoode) was called to the Bar of Ontario in 2002 and is currently pursuing his Master of Laws at the University of Toronto. His primary area of study is solicitor–client privilege and the regulation of the legal profession. Prior to entering graduate study, he practised corporate law in Toronto.

Pierre Elliott Trudeau Public School

"Blazing New Trails"

Our First JK-Grade 8 Cohort

Erika Armstrong
Christopher Ballantyne
Kennedy Bacher
Jacob Bachewich
Nicholas Benson
Cassidy Cooke
Amanda Goehring
Spencer Harrison
Victoria Kinghorn
Sydney Livingstone

Connor MacLeod
Ryann McQueen
Gaelan Moffat
Joshua Nancekivell
Troy Richard
Maggie Scott
Chelsea Smith
Kristen Werry
Kadie Wilde

Choir

Kennedy Bacher
Michelle Chung
Zoe Cotter
Rebecca Hubbell
Holly Jaeger
Meghan Killingsworth

Victoria Kinghorn
Amanda Nagy
Megan Nicholson
Shailene Panylo
Margaret Scott
Chelsea Smith
Kadie Wilde

Band

Bailey Boudreau
Amy Cornish
Taylor Dale
Joshua Jealouse
Nick Kapanaiko
Aaron Kenyon
Amber Kitchen

Nicholas Linnen
Sarah Mulrooney
Greg McArton
Quentin McIntyne
Mykelti Page
Jakob Savard
Shania Sewell

Many thanks to the Grade 7 parents who generously donated items and volunteered their time to make this evening a success for our Graduates.

GRADUATION CEREMONY

CLASS OF 2011

Pierre Elliott Trudeau Public School
Grade 8 Graduation
June 27, 2011

Please rise while Graduates enter and remain standing for O'Canada

Welcoming Remarks: .... B. Hardy

Greetings from the Board: .... DDSB Chair, L. Jacula

Greetings from the SCC: .... SCC Chair, S. Procunier

Graduation Certificates: .... J. Skelly, L. Lynch, D. Keeler

Honour Medals: .... J. Legree

Message to Graduating Class: .... T. Worsley

First Cohort Presentation: .... T. Worsley

Special Presentation: .... Sidney Livingstone, Erika Armstrong

Individual Awards: *Presenter:*

Fanny Hislop Award: .... M. Salvati

English Award: .... K. Davies

History Award: .... L. Nicholson

Geography Award: .... L. Lynch

Science/Technology Award: .... J. Skelly

French Award: .... M. Wight

Math Award: .... J. Skelly

Instrumental Music Award: .... L. Lynch

Art Award: .... D. Keeler

Drama/Dance: .... J. Plath

Top Athletic Female: .... D. Campbell

Top Athletic Male: .... Q. Maechtel

Outstanding Student Award: .... D. Keeler

Kiwanis Citizenship Award: .... C. Hoyle

IODE: .... J. Plath

Trailblazer Award: .... T. Worsley

Principal's Award: .... B. Hardy

Valedictorians: .... B. Hardy

Closing Remarks: .... M. Salvati

Passport To The Future

🍁 Graduates

- 🍁 Erika Armstrong
- Parker Ayliffe
- Kennedy Bacher
- 🍁 Jacob Bachewich
- 🍁 Mitchell Badgley
- Christopher Ballantyne
- Nick Benson
- Mitchell Bizjak
- Blake Burnside
- Israel Chavez-Aliaga
- Michelle Chung
- Brayden Claener
- Natalya Companion
- Cassidy Cooke
- Chad Cooper
- Zoe Cotter
- Keron Dacres
- Erin Demille
- Aidan Dinham
- Kyla Evans
- Christopher Fransicso
- Jake Galea
- Derek Glaspell
- 🍁 Amanda Goehring
- Justin Gomme
- Jennifer Greier
- Spencer Harrison
- Daniel Hill
- Jessica Horky
- 🍁 Amreen Hossain
- Rebecca Hubbell
- Keirsten Jackson
- 🍁 Holly Jaeger
- Tricia Katradis
- Meghan Killingsworth
- 🍁 Victoria Kinghorn
- 🍁 Ariel Lazurko
- 🍁 Sydney Livingstone
- 🍁 Hunter MacLean
- 🍁 Connor MacLeod
- Anton Mauti
- Ashley McArtney
- Ryann McQueen
- 🍁 Gaelan Moffat
- Amanda Nagy
- Jane Nagy
- Joshua Nancekivell
- Tyler Nankishore
- 🍁 Joshua Nelson
- 🍁 Megan Nicholson
- 🍁 Shailene Panylo
- Jeremy Parsons
- Alicia Pettifer
- 🍁 Troy Richard
- Ben Routledge
- Billy Routledge
- Margaret Scott
- Matthew Skinner
- 🍁 Chelsea Smith
- Gage Smith
- William Spence
- Maegan St. Aubin
- Caitlin Sturge
- Kimberley Sullivan
- Nicholas Thebeau
- 🍁 Alexander Tsai
- Kristen Werry
- Kadie Wilde

🍁 Honours Achievement

*Thank you to the
Pierre Elliott Trudeau
School Community Council
for its financial support of this year's Grade
Eight Graduation.*

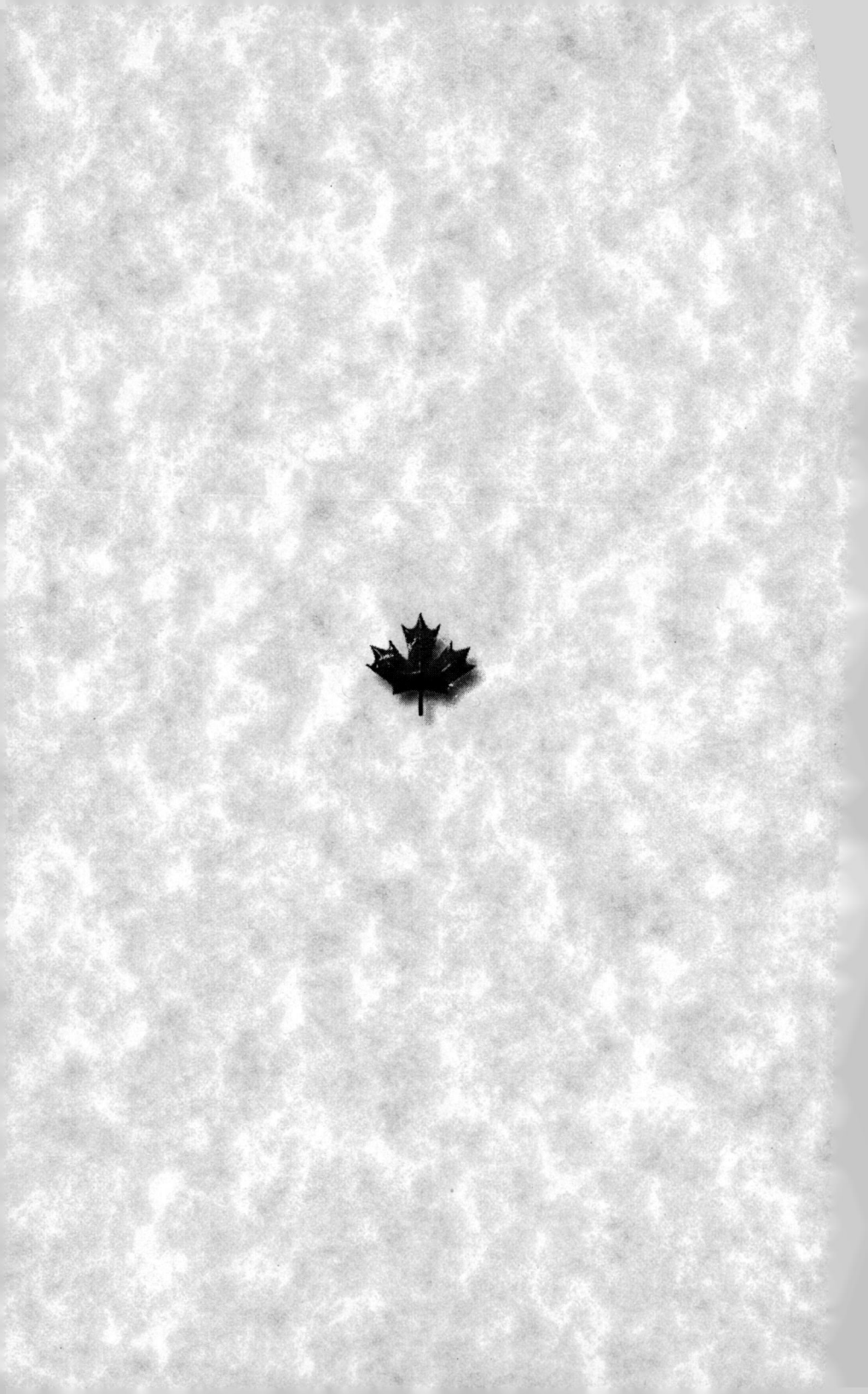